DATE DUE

AG 1 '05			
AG 16 '05			
SE 20 '05			
OC 12 '05			
NO 12 '05			
OE 31 '05			
JA 18 '06			
AP 0 6 '10			

Demco No. 62-0549

BY LARRY MCMURTRY

The Colonel and Little Missie
Loop Group
Folly and Glory
By Sorrow's River
The Wandering Hill
Sin Killer
Sacajawea's Nickname: Essays on the American West
Paradise
Boone's Lick
Roads
Still Wild: A Collection of Western Stories
Walter Benjamin at the Dairy Queen
Duane's Depressed
Crazy Horse
Comanche Moon
Dead Man's Walk
The Late Child
Streets of Laredo
The Evening Star
Buffalo Girls
Some Can Whistle
Anything for Billy
Film Flam: Essays on Hollywood
Texasville
Lonesome Dove
The Desert Rose
Cadillac Jack
Somebody's Darling
Terms of Endearment
All My Friends Are Going to Be Strangers
Moving On
The Last Picture Show
In a Narrow Grave: Essays on Texas
Leaving Cheyenne
Horseman, Pass By

BY LARRY MCMURTRY
AND DIANA OSSANA

Pretty Boy Floyd

Zeke and Ned

Larry McMurtry

~

The Colonel and Little Missie

Buffalo Bill, Annie Oakley, and the Beginnings of Superstardom in America

SIMON & SCHUSTER

NEW YORK   LONDON   TORONTO   SYDNEY

SIMON & SCHUSTER
Rockefeller Center
1230 Avenue of the Americas
New York, NY 10020

SIMON & SCHUSTER and colophon are registered trademarks of Simon & Schuster, Inc.

For information about special discounts for bulk purchases,
please contact Simon & Schuster Special Sales at
1-800-456-6798 or business@simonandschuster.com.

Designed by Karolina Harris
Photography consultant: Kevin Kwan

Manufactured in the United States of America

10   9   8   7   6   5   4   3   2   1

Library of Congress Cataloging-in-Publication Data
McMurtry, Larry.
The colonel and Little Missie : Buffalo Bill, Annie Oakley, and the beginnings of superstardom in
America / Larry McMurtry.
    p. cm.
Includes bibliographical references and index.
1. Buffalo Bill, 1846–1917. 2. Oakley, Annie, 1860–1926. 3. Entertainers—United States—Biogra-
phy. 4. Shooters of firearms—United States—Biography. 5. Scouts and scouting—West (U.S.)—
Biography. 6. Buffalo Bill's Wild West Company. 7. Wild West shows. I. Title.

GV1821.B8M38 2005
978.02'092'2—dc22
[B]   2005042515
ISBN 0-7432-7171-8

Photo credits will be found on page 245.

Contents

The Colonel
and
Little Missie

Superstardom

1

KINGS and potentates, and their queens and lovers, someday die and have to be entombed, interred, or consumed on splendid pyres.

So too with performers—even the greatest among them, the true superstars. Elvis died, and Garbo, and Marilyn Monroe, and Frank Sinatra. Elvis at least left us Graceland, his Taj on Old Man River; of the others we have merely records and movies, recorded performances that allow us at least distant glimpses of their gaiety, their beauty, their gifts. Show business imposes its own strict temporality: no matter how many CDs or DVDs we own, it would still have been better to have been there, to have seen the living performers in the richness of their being and to have participated, however briefly, in the glory of their performance.

When I was eight years old, I was sitting in a hot pickup near Silverton, Texas, bored stiff, waiting for my father and two of my uncles, Charlie and Roy McMurtry, to conclude a cattle deal. I was reading a book called *Last of the Great Scouts*, by Helen Cody Wetmore, Buffalo Bill Cody's sister. At the time I was more interested in the Lone Ranger than in Buffalo Bill Cody, but when my father and my uncles finally returned to the pickup, my Uncle Roy noticed the book and reminded Uncle Charlie that they had once seen Cody. This had occurred in Oklahoma, near the end of Cody's life, when he had briefly

3

merged his Wild West with the Miller Brothers' 101 Ranch show. Both agreed that Cody, an old man at this time, hadn't actually done much; mainly he just rode around the arena on his white horse, Isham, waving to the crowd.

Still, there was Buffalo Bill Cody, one of the most famous men in the world, and they had seen him with their own eyes.

Sixty years have passed since that hot afternoon in Silverton. I mainly remember the heat in the pickup—but it was true that two of my uncles, not men to veer much from the strict path of commerce, did perk up a bit when they remembered that they had actually seen Buffalo Bill Cody ride his white horse around an arena in Oklahoma. And like millions of others, they had made a trip precisely for that purpose, such was Cody's fame.

2

BUFFALO BILL and Annie Oakley were, in my opinion, the first American superstars—in the 1880s and 1890s, at the height of their fame, their images were recognized the world over. Buffalo Bill was probably the most famous American of his day; he was easily more famous than any president, more famous even than Theodore Roosevelt.

Annie Oakley, in the days just before the movies took off, was as popular as any actress. One thing she and Cody had in common was that they had both killed game and sold the meat in order to support their families. Little Phoebe Ann Moses—Annie's real name—used a heavy, muzzle-loading gun to shoot rabbits and quail, which found their way through a middleman to restaurants in Cincinnati. She became Annie Oakley, Oakley being a district of Cincinnati.

For most of her sixteen seasons with Buffalo Bill's Wild West, she was probably the most celebrated female performer in the world. The short, slight, young-and-then-not-so-young country girl from Darke County, Ohio, equably took the measure of such folks as Queen Victoria; her son Edward, Prince of Wales; his wife, Princess Alexandra; the Austrian emperor Franz Josef; Bismarck; Kaiser Wilhelm II; and of course, the difficult Hunkpapa leader Sitting Bull, who adored her and even adopted her, sort of.

William Frederick Cody's first fame came as a hunter, of course; the slightest of his kills probably outweighed all Annie's rabbits and quail. In his season as a hunter for the Union (later Kansas) Pacific

5

Railroad, Cody probably killed around three thousand buffalo. His wife, Louisa (usually shortened to Lulu), estimated that her husband, who with his crews of butchers usually took only the choice parts of the buffalo, may have left as much as 3 million pounds of buffalo meat to go to waste. He was not—as we shall see—either the first or the last hunter to be called Buffalo Bill, but he was easily the most famous.

From the early 1880s to the end of his life, in 1917, Buffalo Bill Cody was about as famous as anyone could be. He was the hero of no less than seventeen hundred dime novels, many of them written by the wildly prolific pulper Colonel Prentiss Ingraham.

And in Cody's case, the fame didn't exactly die with the man—at the end of the twentieth century, Buffalo Bill's Wild West was still pulling in crowds at Euro Disney, in France, a country where Americans are not thought to be popular. Few showmen have managed to project their acts over more than a century.

3

I<small>N</small> show business, superstardom of the sort achieved by Buffalo Bill and Annie Oakley needs certain preconditions to be met; in America those conditions didn't coalesce until the fourth quarter of the nineteenth century. Rapid and reliable rail transport was one such precondition. At the height of its popularity Buffalo Bill's Wild West employed more than five hundred people, and transported hundreds of animals as well. The 1885 tour, the first to be really profitable, played in more than forty cities—later the show made as many as 130 stops in a year. Without good railroads the troupers could not have made these dates; similarly, without ocean liners, they could not have become such a great international success.

But the making of superstars requires more than trains that run on time to lots of cities. Management and publicity are necessary elements too, as the career in our own day of Madonna illustrates. It was always obvious that Madonna was going to go to the top, and then over the top, but she could not have got there so quickly and lucratively but for the efforts of Freddie DeMann, her manager, and Liz Rosenberg, her publicist.

Fortunately, from the early 1880s on, Buffalo Bill's Wild West profited from the services of an extraordinary manager, Nate Salsbury, and a gifted press agent, Major John M. Burke, both of whom the Colonel and Little Missie often frustrated.

Nate Salsbury, a stage star himself, was an unimposing-looking man who did not particularly like performers and resented having to

7

give them individual billing. Nonetheless, he happened to be sitting around the big arena in Louisville, Kentucky, one day in 1885 when a young female sharpshooter (Annie Oakley) and her husband-manager, Frank Butler, happened to be rehearsing their act. At this time shooting acts abounded—Cody had already turned the Butlers down once; sixteen female sharpshooters were even then blasting their way around America. Annie Oakley and Frank Butler had been performing with vaudeville, and with the Sells Circus, and generally wherever they could get a booking. It was with some reluctance that they had even been offered an audition, but before the rehearsal was even well begun, the hard-to-impress Nate Salsbury suddenly came alive. He rushed over to the young couple and urged them to let him send them downtown to have some up-to-date tintypes made. He also immediately ordered $7,000 worth of posters featuring the young sharpshooter, Annie Oakley. Later, Salsbury told Cody that Annie was a "daisy" who could easily put their retiring sharpshooter, Captain Adam H. Bogardus, in the shade.

When the critical moment came, Annie Oakley walked out in Louisville before seventeen thousand people and began the brilliant career that would more than justify Nate Salsbury's surprising expenditure.

For the next fifteen years, with both Buffalo Bill and Annie Oakley huge superstars, Cody and Salsbury's Wild West had many glorious runs, both in America and in Europe.

The show's success was not accidental, however. Both Cody and Annie understood costume and appearance; both were consummate performers, though Cody's performances consisted mostly of showing off his own good looks and excellent horsemanship. Nate Salsbury organized the tours and hired the performers, while John M. Burke, usually known as Major Burke, hustled the press and got out the crowds. But the show had a big payroll—some runs were profitable and some weren't. As the nineteenth century gave way to the twentieth, competition was rampant, and things began to slow down. Nate Salsbury, who had been in increasingly poor health for some years, died in 1902; he was deeply mourned by Annie Oakley, Buffalo Bill, and many of the performers. Salsbury had been the Great Organizer; Cody had seldom organized anything more complicated than a buffalo hunt. As a businessman he had been almost as bad as his fiscally suicidal contemporaries Mark Twain and Ulysses S. Grant. Like them he invested wildly in mines, irrigation schemes, hotels (usually in places tourists had no interest in going), and even products such as White Beaver's Laugh Cream, the Great Lung Healer, an herbal remedy that reached drugstores roughly a century too soon.

With Salsbury dead, everyone expected Buffalo Bill's Wild West to quickly collapse, but it didn't. Cody never liked working at a desk or dealing with day-to-day business details, but he *could* do it when he had to, and he did do it until he was able to hire another highly competent manager, James Bailey, the less-well-known half of Barnum and Bailey, who, if anything, was more competent than Salsbury. Under his management the troupe had several good runs, but times were changing—there were as many as two dozen troupes wandering around America, flooding the market to such an extent that the public grew weary of so much Wild West. Some companies failed outright, while others merged, but Wild West shows seemed, for a time, to be everywhere.

Young Will Rogers, who would become a superstar himself, was mightily impressed by the rope tricks of Vincente Orapeza while visiting the big Chicago Exposition in 1893. Will went home to Oklahoma and began to practice rope tricks himself. Not long afterward he went to South Africa on a cattle boat and was soon doing rope tricks for audiences that included Mohandas Gandhi himself, then a young lawyer in Johannesburg. The Wild West, in its theatrical form, seemed to be everywhere. When Henry Adams and his friend the artist John LaFarge made their somewhat libidinous trip to Polynesia, they traveled with a Wild West troupe bound for Australia.

Buffalo Bill Cody continued to be much the biggest name in the business—by this time Annie Oakley had retired, though she reemerged from time to time to compete in shooting contests, nearly all of which she won.

Cody liked Indians, and from the beginning hired far more of them than any other impresario, though this involved frequent difficulties with the Department of the Interior and the commissioner of Indian Affairs, whose wards the Indians were. Eventually Cody sup-

plemented his Indian performers with horsemen of many types—
Cossacks, Arabs, and so on—whom he called his Congress of Rough
Riders of the World, a nomenclature Theodore Roosevelt would
eventually appropriate.

Cody and Annie Oakley traveled together for sixteen seasons,
and were always respectful of one another, if not exactly close. She
always addressed him as Colonel, the rank he had more or less
adopted for himself, and he always called her Missie, though she was
a married woman for more than forty years. Annie Oakley liked her
privacy, and Cody, as we'll see, never knew quite what to make of any
woman, Annie Oakley included. It may be that these courtesy titles
helped the two performers get along.

4

I T seems to me that the best way to characterize these two linked but very different human beings—Bill Cody and Annie Oakley—is to start with a brief description of their funerals, which were absolutely in character. Buffalo Bill lost control of his own death, just as he had, by this time, lost control of large patches of his life. He was not even buried until five months after his death, and then wasn't buried either in the place or in the manner of his choosing.

By contrast Annie Oakley died as precisely as she shot, even going to the trouble to secure a female undertaker to embalm her. As her hour approached she picked out an apricot dress and told the undertaker, Louise Stocker—the only lady undertaker in that part of Ohio—exactly what to do. Louise Stocker did as instructed, though, since Annie had suffered from anemia and was very pale, she did take it upon herself to add a little color to her cheeks.

In our day we have come to expect superstars, particularly female superstars, to behave badly, at least to the help. Martha Stewart and Courtney Love spring to mind. But this was not always so. Both Buffalo Bill and Annie Oakley were deeply loved, not least by their help. Here is a comment by the American artist Dan Muller, whom Bill and Lulu Cody took in as a fatherless boy and helped raise at Scout's Rest, their big place near North Platte, Nebraska:

> Buffalo Bill was one of the world's great men. I don't mean wise, but I do mean great. His heart was as big as his

11

show tent, and as warm as a ranchhouse cookstove. Around his supple body there was an aura that people loved to share, whether they were Edward, the King of England, or the lonely tyke of a penniless widow [Muller himself]. We who loved him—we who didn't depend on his largesse—suffered as weakness gradually caught up with that warm, magnificent man.

And here is Annie Oakley, when she learned of Cody's death:

> I traveled with him for seventeen years. There were thousands of men in the outfit during this time, Comanches, cowboys, Cossacks, Arabs and every kind of person. And the whole time we were one great family loyal to one man. His words were better than most contracts. Personally I never had a contract with the show once I started. It would have been superfluous.

There Little Missie exaggerated a bit. She had contracts, meticulously negotiated by her husband, Frank Butler, and she herself probably read every line of the small print. But the sentiment was true: Cody inspired extraordinary love and loyalty. Even sometimes bitter rivals, such as Gordon Lillie (Pawnee Bill), knowing that Cody had no head for business, tolerated much foolishness while remaining fond. Many were happy to cheat him, and did, but there were more who loved him.

Perhaps Black Elk, the Ogalala sage, who went to England with Cody in 1887, got lost, was found again and sent home by Cody—he recognized how homesick the young man was—said it most simply: "Pawhuska [Cody] had a strong heart."

Buffalo Bill Cody was outgoing, generous, gushing, in a hurry, incautious, often drunk, and almost always optimistic; in manner Annie Oakley was his polar opposite: she was reserved, modest to the point of requiring a female embalmer, so frugal that many of the troupers believed that she lived off the lemonade that Cody and Salsbury served free to all workers, Quakerish, quiet. But she, like Cody, was a showperson through and through. Even after a bad car wreck, rather late in her life, she once got onstage and danced a jig in her leg brace.

Annie Oakley was also about as competitive as it is possible to be. No sooner had they got to England for Queen Victoria's Jubilee than a vexing diplomatic problem arose. Grand Duke Michael of Russia, a confident wing shot, proposed a shooting match with Little Missie. Cody and Major Burke, the publicist, were horrified. Of course you mustn't beat him, they urged. He's a grand duke!

Nate Salsbury, made of sterner stuff, favored a real contest. Frank Butler kept very quiet—he knew better than to suggest to his wife that she throw a match, any match. In fact, on her first English tour, Annie Oakley *was* occasionally beaten, but only because she had too heavy a gun or used shot too light for the gusty English shooting conditions. In the contest with Grand Duke Michael she missed three birds out of fifty; the grand duke missed fourteen, but evidently there were no hard feelings and a good time was had by all.

So far as I can determine, Annie Oakley never *let* anyone beat her. Her first biographer, Courtney Ryley Cooper, put a question to the young Texas sharpshooter Johnny Baker, whom Annie loved, mothering him and helping him in many ways. Although technically a rival, she even helped him improve his act. (She was later to be just as fond of his daughters.)

"Johnny," I asked, "tell me something. When you used to shoot against Annie Oakley, and she always won, was it because you weren't trying, or because she was a better shot than you? . . ."

"There was never a day when I didn't try to beat her," he said. "But it just couldn't be done. You know, the ordinary person has nerves. They'll bob up on him in spite of everything; he'll notice some little thing that distracts his attention, or get fussed by the way a ball travels through the air. Or a bit of light will get on the sights—or seem to get there, and throw him off. I wasn't any different from the average person, but Annie was. The minute she picked up a rifle or a shotgun, it seemed that she made a machine of herself—every action went like clockwork. And how was a fellow to beat anybody like that? To tell the truth . . . it would have made a better show if I could have beat her every few performances. But it couldn't be done."

When Annie retired, Johnny Baker, who had long been like a son to her, became the principal shooting act for Buffalo Bill's Wild West.

Annie Oakley cloaked her competitiveness under her modest demeanor, but plenty of people who worked with her knew it was there. She made no secret of her dislike for Lillian Smith, the chubby California teenage sharpshooter whom Cody brought into the show. Technically several of the sharpshooters Annie performed with should have been able to beat her—but they rarely managed to. Like Johnny Baker said, she could become a shooting machine and the others couldn't.

Competitive or not, Annie Oakley, like William F. Cody, was faithfully and deeply loved, both by her audiences and by her friends. Near the end of her life, when she was at home in Dayton, Ohio, still plagued by her leg brace and suffering from anemia as well, a man who was by then a great superstar himself, Will Rogers, who had been playing Dayton, took notice and paid her a visit. At the time he wrote a daily newspaper column called "The Worst Story I've Heard Today," which ran in more than two hundred newspapers and reached some 35 million readers; soon he would go on to become the highest-paid performer at 20th Century-Fox. Here is his tribute:

> This is not the worst story. It is a good story about a little woman that all the older generation remember. She was the reigning sensation of America and Europe during the heyday of Buffalo Bill's Wild West show. She was their star. Her picture was on more billboards than a modern Gloria Swanson. It was Annie Oakley, the greatest rifle shot the world has ever produced. Nobody took her place. There was only one.

Then—it being an innocent age—he actually gives his 35 million readers Annie Oakley's address, so her old fans can write to her. Then he adds:

> She is a greater character than a rifle shot . . . Annie

14

Oakley's name, her lovable traits, her thoughtful consideration of others will live as a mark for others to shoot at.

She died on November 3, 1926—the story immediately went out to the world over the AP wire. The story said, among other things, that she was the friend of monarchs and the confidante of her old boss, Buffalo Bill.

Her husband, Frank, ill himself, had gone to Michigan to recuperate. When news reached him of Annie's death he stopped eating; eighteen days later he died, just in time to be placed in the grave beside her—here's Shirl Kasper's report:

> . . . on Thanksgiving day, November 25, Annie Oakley made her last trip past the old Public Square where she had sold her quail and rabbits to G. Anthony and Charles Katzenberger so long ago. The old home folks carried her remains up north, past Ansonia and Versailles and the fields and forests that were so familiar to Annie Oakley. Just south of the village of Brock, they turned off Highway 127 into a little cemetery hemmed in on all sides by fields and trees . . .
>
> Up North Star way, just five miles distant, the rabbits scampered over the field and the quail darted from their covey, just as they had done years before when the girl Annie Moses sat on a moss-covered log with Jacob Moses's old Kentucky muzzle-loader across her knees. The forests weren't so thick anymore, but still this quiet farmland was home to Annie Oakley. They buried her under a plain headstone that bore a simple inscription:

> *Annie Oakley*
> *At Rest*
> *1926*

5

IN contrast to Little Missie's modest burial the big farewell to Buffalo Bill Cody, on top of Lookout Mountain, near Denver, in June of 1917, was, in its way, his final Wild West show. Cody had actually died in January, but could not be buried until June because Lookout Mountain was, after all, a mountain. It could not be reached by motorcade until after the spring thaw, which meant June at the earliest.

Cody himself had planned to be buried on top of Cedar Mountain, near the town of Cody, Wyoming, a community in which he had sunk and lost millions but which he loved—and was loved by—anyway. His last years, like the last years of many showmen, were rich mainly in humiliation. He fell in debt to many people, some of them honorable like Pawnee Bill, but also to others who were merely exploiters, like the Denver newspaper magnate Harry Tammen and his sometime partner Frederick Bonfils, who worked Cody to a frazzle in this show and that circus until the old man was near to dropping. But even in shabby settings that Cody would not have so much as sniffed at in his heyday, he never quite lost his commanding presence. He hated Tammen and sometimes reflected that he ought just to kill him—surely a tempting thought, since Tammen had once sold all Cody's assets, including his horse Isham, at a sheriff's sale. Tammen held Cody in contempt, but that didn't stop him milking the old showman for all he was worth.

When Johnny Baker, performing in New York, heard that Cody was dying he got on the first train but arrived at the bedside of his

16

idol just a little too late. At a few minutes past noon on the tenth of January 1917, Buffalo Bill Cody died. At once the news went out over a special open telegraph line to all the world—and much of the world mourned. President Woodrow Wilson at once sent condolences to Lulu, and the king of England soon followed suit.

Harry Tammen, who had exploited Cody so ruthlessly while he was alive, saw no reason to stop just because the man was dead. Somehow or other, either with bribes or with flattery, Tammen persuaded the grieving widow that burying Cody in a remote village in Wyoming would really be a loss to the nation. Few would journey to distant Cody to see the great man's grave, but many—indeed millions—might come if the grave was in easy reach of Denver, where, of course, they would be free to do some shopping and perhaps buy a copy of Tammen's newspaper. One way or another, Lulu was persuaded, and when the snows thawed in June a lengthy procession made its way, with much grinding of gears, up to the rocky grave site.

Gene Fowler, the excellent, too little remembered newspaperman who gave us a fine portrait of John Barrymore in *Good Night, Sweet Prince*, and a moving one of W. C. Fields in *Minutes of the Last Meeting*, happened to be working in Denver at the time—for Harry Tammen, in fact. He went to the funeral and left this wonderful report:

> Six of the Colonel's old sweethearts—now obese and sagging with memories—sat on camp chairs by the grave hewed out of granite. The bronze casket lay in the bright western sun. The glass over the Colonel's handsome face began to steam over after a while, on account of the frosted pane . . . one of the old Camilles rose from her camp chair, with a manner so gracious as to command respect. Then, as if she were utterly alone with *her* dead, this grand old lady walked to the casket and held her antique but dainty parasol over the glass. She stood there throughout the service, a fantastic, superb figure. It was the gesture of a queen.

One thing Buffalo Bill always had was a robust sense of humor. If he could have been at his own funeral, perhaps sitting by the devoted Johnny Baker, he would, undoubtedly, have laughed long and hard.

6

SOME celebrities—sports heroes particularly—can be seen to earn their fame; they acquire authenticity as they go along, doing what they do. Others just seem to drift into fame, without paying much attention to its arrival. When Buffalo Bill first began to work as an actor in simple Western melodramas, he could rarely remember his lines, few and simple though they were. His friend Wild Bill Hickok was even more tongue-tied; he rarely said anything while onstage. Once in a while Cody and the scout Texas Jack Omohundro might reminisce a bit about some hunt they had been on—when even this commentary dried up, Ned Buntline, who got the two scouts into the acting business, might finish the evening with a temperance lecture. At first the crowds didn't seem to mind these laconic proceedings—at least they got to look at authentic frontiersmen and, in Hickok's case, a real gunfighter, whom *malchance* would soon lead to draw that dead man's hand in the illegal town of Deadwood— illegal because it was on Sioux land. Aces and eights was the dead man's hand. Before Hickok was killed he had managed to organize a buffalo hunt near Niagara Falls.

The wind that blew ill for Hickok blew fair for Cody, who did more shows, and yet more shows, until finally he was confident enough to start his own show. But he knew that part of his draw as an actor was that for much of the year he was still a prairie scout— as late as 1876, when he had been on the stage several years, he managed to get back to the West and get into an Indian fight, a famous one, which he was still reprising in his shows until nearly the end of his life. Cody's clouded record as an Indian killer, rather than as a tracker of Indians, we will look at later—but the fact that he was still often out west where the wild men were added much to his box office appeal. Also, he was very good-looking and he soon mastered certain aspects of showmanship—people were coming to see him in increasing numbers; by the late seventies Bill Cody had a fairly well advanced career on the stage.

Annie Oakley's stardom was different. Cody had really survived thrilling adventures that could be dramatized and were dramatized. Annie Oakley had mainly her sense of occasion, and her consummate skill with the gun. She did develop an act of sorts, pouting if she missed and giving a charming little back kick if she shot well; but the act was at the service of her shooting. Much later she too appeared on the stage, in a melodrama called *The Western Girl*, which had a successful run.

In real life she was not a Western girl at all. She loved the cool forests of Ohio, where she had first hunted. Though she traveled west with the show she never actually lived farther west than Cincinnati. The "authentic" part of Annie's performances was that her bullets almost always hit their targets. She had a long, quiet marriage, and mostly kept to herself while she was performing, though she did like to give tea and cookies to whatever children wandered up. She traveled to Europe more than once and conquered several of the reigning monarchs of the day, of which more later. Her fame did not lessen when she began to limit her performances, mainly to shooting contests. There have been at least eight biographies and a famous musical, *Annie Get Your Gun*. Many of her biographers eventually find themselves running out of much of anything to say. She shot, she went to her tent, she shook hands with whatever local dignitaries might be assembled; then, the next day, in a different city, she did it again.

Buffalo Bill's numerous biographers—of which none are recent—have more or less the opposite problem: there was always more to say about Buffalo Bill Cody than could be got between the covers of a single book—though much of it had to be extracted and expanded (or reduced) *from* a single book, that being the autobiography Cody published in 1879. He probably wrote at least part of it. Sometimes he freely gave chapters of it to other writers on the West. There were many reissues, several plagiarized variants, and for the bibliographer, an unholy mess. Two of his sisters published books about him and so did Lulu, his much-put-upon wife.

The autobiography itself deals with Cody's life as a plainsman; it stops a couple of years before his career as a serious impresario begins. It contains many of the set pieces—tropes drawn from Cody's life—which we'll look at soon. These tropes are repeated over and over again in the many knockoffs of the autobiography; there are seven or eight at least, some of which awkwardly merge chapters from Cody with newspaper or magazine accounts of his various exploits. These crudely written accounts are tediously repetitive, but they kept appearing, year after year—as did the estimated seventeen hundred dime novels in which he appears.

About a decade after Cody's death Charles Lindbergh, the Lone Eagle, made his famous flight and became an instant superstar because of it. Lindbergh's enduring fame resulted from a single act, but Cody's fame did not develop that quickly, nor did his celebrity really depend on the solid facts of his life. It didn't depend on his having made the third-longest Pony Express ride in history, or whether he actually killed Tall Bull in 1870 or Yellow Hair in 1876.

Cody's fame depended, instead, on his truly smashing appearance, which only seemed to get better once his hair began to turn white. He was also a superb horseman. People just seemed to like to watch Buffalo Bill Cody even if all he was doing was riding around an arena waving his hat.

Tim McCoy, the sometime cowboy and star of many silent Westerns, thought Buffalo Bill was the most impressive man he had ever seen; plenty of others thought the same. He couldn't have moved his Wild West from town to town without good trains, and he couldn't have become the star he became without the camera. The camera loved him, and it loved Annie Oakley too. They both had the absolute good luck to be photogenic. Cody and Annie were photographed thousands of times. There are many scores of pictures of Buffalo Bill in the midst of his huge troupe—the eye naturally and easily singles him out.

Several times, in writing about the West, I've mentioned the big point that was perhaps best elucidated by the William Goetzmanns, father and son, in their seminal study *The West of the Imagination*. The point is that in the Eastern settled parts of America there was an immediate and an insatiable hunger for images of and information about the West. The hundreds of dime novels featuring Buffalo Bill are a case in point; but the visual artists, in this case, got there before the writers. Artists began to flock into the high West as soon as there was steamboat travel on the Missouri River—that is, in the 1830s. George Catlin, Karl Bodmer, and Alfred Jacob Miller were the most prominent of the first generation of artists to penetrate the inner West. Plenty of others followed in their tracks or made tracks of their own. As the technical means for reproducing works of art—the works of art in the age of mechanical reproduction that the critic Walter Benjamin wrote about—improved, images of the West soon filled the magazines or hung, as prints, on walls in the East.

Those distant, romantic figures—the mountain men—may have been the first targets of Eastern fantasy. By the 1840s there were already proto–dime novels—short prose novelettes—featuring Kit Carson, Jim Bridger, and other mountain trappers. Kit Carson, the man, was once trying to rescue a white captive, Mrs. James White, from some Apaches; he caught up with the group that had Mrs. White and might have saved her had his commanding officer not refused to let him charge. The officer thought the Apaches might want to parley; they didn't. Here is Kit Carson's description of what happened next:

> There was only one Indian in camp, he running into the river hard by was shot. In about two hundred yards the body of Mrs White was found, perfectly warm, had not been killed more than five minutes, shot through the heart with an arrow . . .
>
> In the camp was found a book, the first of the kind that I had ever seen, in which I was made a great hero, slaying Indians by the hundreds and I have often thought

that Mrs White would read the same and knowing that I lived near, she would pray for my appearance and that she might be saved. I did come but I had not the power to convince those that were in command over me to pursue my plan for her rescue.

It was a moment when Western reality and Western fantasy smacked together with a force that Kit Carson would never forget. Except for his wife, Josefa, Mrs. James White is the only woman mentioned in the short autobiography he dictated near the end of his life.

Bill Cody got to Fort Laramie—then the center of social life on the plains—in time to meet Carson, Bridger, and others of the mountain men, the first white explorers of the inner spaces of the American West. He so admired the meticulous Carson that he named his only son Kit Carson Cody.

7

TIMING counts for much in the development of public careers, including careers in show business. Most of Buffalo Bill's actual Indian fighting was a matter of small-scale skirmishes which took place in the 1860s and 1870s. Cody actually won the Congressional Medal of Honor for a skirmish that involved eleven Indians, though it should be noted that Indians seldom traveled in large groups and eleven Indians could be plenty deadly. (In 1916 the honor was rescinded because Cody was not a member of the army at the time of the fight—he was often only a member of the army in a loose, informal way.)

Considering that he was well on his way to becoming a showman, what these skirmishes with Indians brought him was excellent publicity. Whether Cody actually killed Tall Bull or Yellow Hair is a matter we will discuss later. Indeed, a little farther along in his career, by hiring Indians, paying them adequately, and getting them off their unhealthy reservations, he not only helped but probably saved far more Indians than he was supposed to have killed. It is likely that real Indian killers, such as George Armstrong Custer, never took Cody seriously as a fighter; some of the Indians he is supposed to have fought probably felt the same way.

What Custer actually thought about Cody is not easy to determine. In 1866 and 1867 Cody worked mainly as a guide, in which capacity he was respected and trusted by a number of military men. In 1867 Cody did once guide Custer on a fairly short (sixty-five-mile) trip from Fort Hays to Fort Larned in Kansas. Custer was at first annoyed that Cody chose to ride a mule rather than a horse, but the mule soon proved his mettle. Cody said that Custer offered him employment anytime, but for whatever reason, the offer was never taken up and Cody is not mentioned in Custer's autobiography.

The two were thrown together at least one other time, at the big buffalo hunt which Cody organized for Grand Duke Alexis of Russia. Cody did not scout for Custer at the Battle of the Washita (1868), though he was nearby and the battle occurred in country he knew well. Probably Custer just considered Cody a fop. After Custer's death, at the Little Bighorn, Cody was on friendly terms with Custer's lively widow, Libbie, who was his guest at some of Cody's more hifalutin, or at least more metropolitan, Wild West shows.

As I mentioned at the beginning of this chapter, timing is important in any career, and Bill Cody's timing was almost perfect. He first dipped his toe in show business in 1872, while still keeping a firm footing in his career as a scout and guide. From about that time on his scouting gradually decreased—he shifted a little and began to organize hunts for rich men, little safaris which gave them at least a taste of the Wild West.

But for big occasions, such as the search for Custer's killers in 1876, Cody was immediately back in the West and part of the hunt. It was then that the famous "duel" with Yellow Hair (in Cheyenne Wey-o-hei) occurred. This duel became one of the central tropes of Cody's career, endlessly reprised in the Wild West shows and, finally, even in a movie. This trope will be examined in more detail later.

Whether Cody killed Yellow Hair or not, he *did* scalp him and at once sent the scalp, plus Yellow Hair's warbonnet and weapons, to Lulu, then living in Buffalo. Cody was hoping she could get a local department store to display them—good publicity for a play he was about to put on in that same city. Somewhat to Cody's surprise, Lulu was not pleased by these grisly trophies.

Cody's encounter with Yellow Hair (often mistranslated, even by Cody, as Yellow Hand) took place only three weeks after Custer and the Seventh Cavalry were wiped out at the Little Bighorn. Cody, in scalping Yellow Hair, claimed the "first scalp for Custer," which got him huge publicity. (It may not have been quite the only scalp for Custer, but it was one of few—the warriors who fought at the Little Bighorn immediately melted away.)

In the publicity story after the duel with Yellow Hair, Cody was briefly a national hero—it was at this favorable moment that he moved definitively into show business.

Cody was no fool. He knew that where the Plains Indians were concerned, hostilities were nearly over. Sitting Bull had gone to Canada. Crazy Horse held out until May of 1877 and there were a few other resisters, but the Plains Indian wars were all but finished. If he wanted to remain an Indian fighter his best option would have been to accompany General George Crook—the Gray Fox—to the Southwest, where he might have helped the general try to catch Geronimo.

This prospect hardly enticed. Custer was bloodthirsty, Cody was not. In later days, when asked how many Indians he had killed, Cody always said that he never killed any Indians unless he felt that his life was in immediate jeopardy. As it happened, the year of the Little Bighorn turned out to be a terribly unhappy year for Cody anyway— it was the year his beloved son, Kit Carson Cody, died of scarlet fever. Cody could not even be there at the end—he was performing in the East at the time. Cody grieved over this loss for the rest of his life. When the sharpshooter Johnny Baker came along, Cody more or less adopted him, but it did not make up for the loss of his son.

8

C ODY first trod the boards in a somber melodrama called *The Prairie Scout,* directed—if one could call it that—by Ned Buntline, whose real name was Edward Zane Carroll Judson. Cody's fellow scout Texas Jack Omohundro also appeared with him. Realism was not increased by the use of red flannel scalps. The run—after many interruptions—eventually ended in Port Jervis, New York, and earned Cody a mere $6,000. He considered it very measly pay. At first he felt that Buntline and Omohundro had conspired to cheat him. Indeed, he felt so strongly about the matter that he never performed with Buntline again, though he was soon back on good terms with Texas Jack. Cody and Buntline eventually repaired their friendship but stayed clear of one another professionally.

Before turning in detail to Cody's career as actor and impresario, I should mention the brief period when he served as a kind of white hunter, taking rich and important people on carefully managed buffalo hunts. The one held for Grand Duke Alexis got the most publicity, but an earlier hunt organized for General Phil Sheridan and some of his cronies was, if anything, done on a more lavish scale. I mention this here because it illustrates an essential aspect of Cody's celebrity: he was always presentable, and rich people immediately felt comfortable with him. General Henry E. Davies was on the Sheridan hunt and had this to say about Bill Cody:

At the camp we were introduced to the far-famed Buffalo

26

Bill . . . we had all heard of him as destined to be our guide. William Cody, Esq. . . . was a mild, agreeable, well-mannered man, quiet and retiring in disposition though well-informed and always ready to talk well and earnestly on any subject of interest . . .

Tall and somewhat slight in figure, though possessed of great strength and iron endurance; straight and erect as an arrow, and with strikingly handsome features, he at once attracted to him all with whom he became acquainted and the better knowledge gained of him during the days he spent with our party increased the good impression he made upon his introduction.

General Davies was so impressed with Cody that he could hardly contain himself. Here is his description of Cody's (well-studied) entrance into camp—an entrance that would in time be repeated in hundreds of arenas around the world:

The most striking feature of the whole was the figure of our friend Buffalo Bill Cody riding down from the fort to our camp, mounted on a snowy white horse. Dressed in a suit of light buckskin, trimmed along the seams with fringes of the same leather, his costume lighted by the crimson shirt worn under his open coat, a broad sombrero on his head and carrying his rifle lightly in his hand as his horse came forward toward us on an easy gallop, he realized to perfection the bold hunter and gallant sportsman of the plains.

Cody, from the beginning, was capable of making what we now call a fashion statement; here is his reflection on the same occasion:

I rose fresh and eager for the trip, and as it was a nobby and high-toned outfit which I was to accompany, I determined to put on a little style myself.

There we have the birth of the fringed jacket so popular with

27

the lawyer Gerry Spence and others—many hundreds of such jackets can be seen in Western films, including some quite recent ones.

Cody liked General Davies's description of him so much that he copied it into his autobiography as if it were his own. The point, though, was that "nobby and high-toned" people nearly always liked Bill Cody and felt immediately at ease in his company. From this point on he dressed with an eye to his entrance. He had even had a number of promotional photographs of himself in scout's garb made—the photographer he used was Matthew Brady, famous for his photographs of Lincoln and of the Civil War. Once Cody decided that show business was to be his vocation, he left as little as possible to chance. Like most professional show people, he trained, and he improved.

9

AROUND 1880, with the Plains Indians finally subdued, it began to be clear to Cody that *Prairie Scout*–like melodramas had about had their day. Audiences would not come forever just to see stiff performers in buckskins. The notion of something rather more outdoorsy in the way of spectacle was in the air—something that might possibly involve a roper or two, or a little sharpshooting. If a few cowboys and some buffalo could be included, so much the better. Notions of this sort began to percolate in Cody's mind, and in the minds of other protoimpresarios as well. The sharpshooter Doc Carver, whom Cody mostly feuded with but at one point attempted to partner with, had similar ideas. Perhaps they had heard of old P. T. Barnum and the herd of skinny buffalo that he used to have chased around Staten Island, mainly to promote the ferry business, of which he had a cut—this had occurred in 1843.

It was around this time that Cody met the man who was to help make his fortune, not once but many times: the actor and manager Nate Salsbury. It would be a few years, however, before the two men formally joined forces.

In one of Cody and Carver's early team efforts an event was created in which skilled cowboys roped a buffalo, threw it, and then rode it. (It may be that this strange, short-lived event was the precursor of the now popular bull-riding events.) Most of the cowboys who worked this show were not exactly eager to apply their riding skills to buffalo, but they gave it their best, excepting only one huge buffalo named Monarch that no cowboy cared to attempt. A team of ropers did manage to catch and throw Monarch, but none of these gallants had any desire to try and ride the huge beast.

With a crowd to please, Cody, always confident of his riding skills, decided to ride Monarch himself. Buffalomanship, however, proved to be a much rougher sport than merely riding broncs. Cody made what in today's terms would probably be a qualifying eight-second ride—but when Monarch finally threw him, Cody was so badly hurt that he had to be hospitalized for two weeks. Gordon Lillie, who, as Pawnee Bill, was later to be Cody's rival before the two became partners, observed this dustup and learned from it. Neither man ever attempted to ride a buffalo again—the act was modified, the riding omitted. Pawnee Bill said later that the only time he saw Cody dead sober in his life was when he emerged from the hospital after having attempted to ride Monarch, the champion bucking buffalo.

I've mentioned earlier that many people loved Cody; what should be added is that almost everyone who met him, with the exception of a few professional rivals like Doc Carver, really liked him. He was not loath to promote himself, but he was not obsessive about it, either; many commentators remarked that he didn't seem to take himself all that seriously. All agreed that he was generous to a fault. Even his wife, Lulu, who battled with him for four decades, admitted that he was probably the most generous man alive, and also, in her view, a great man. When Lulu went up to join him at the big Chicago Exposition in 1893 she arrived at their hotel only to find that a Mr. and Mrs. Cody were already registered—the other Mrs. Cody turned out to be the actress Katherine Clemmons, with whom Cody had a long and financially disastrous affair. It was Katherine Clemmons he was referring to when he said he had rather manage a million Indians than one soubrette.

The outraged Lulu, not unexpectedly, threw a considerable fit that day in Chicago—she was to throw many in the course of forty years with and without Bill Cody. But she didn't go home unrewarded. Her generous husband, in hopes of making amends, presented her with the finest house in North Platte, Nebraska.

BOOK ONE

The Tropes

1

I T is not my intention in this book to attempt a straight birth-to-death biography of William F. Cody—or Annie Oakley—though some attention to their family histories is desirable, even though it doesn't really explain how the two became world celebrities.

For Cody particularly a fresher approach would be to proceed through his career with reference mainly to what might be called the highlighted events—episodes or adventures that Cody retold or reenacted so many times that they took on the nature of tropes. The killing of Cody's first Indian, at age eleven, is one such trope; the duel with Yellow Hair in 1876 is another example. These and perhaps a dozen other famous episodes from Cody's life found their way over and over into dime novels, into melodramas, into his autobiography, into promotional materials, into general histories, and finally, into minidramas that were acted out in the Wild West performances. These episodes have become not so much history as folklore, and some of them are still being performed even now at Euro Disney.

A brilliant beginning in this approach to Cody's career has been made by Joy S. Kasson, in her stimulating *Buffalo Bill's Wild West: Celebrity, Memory, and Popular History* (2000), in which these same tropes are studied iconographically, through their evolution in visual forms: dime novel covers, book illustrations, and poster art. The Wild West shows needed hundreds of posters, reproduced in thousands of copies, to be put up ahead of the performance in order to bring out the crowds and prepare them for the glorious spectacle which awaited them. Some of the posters are brilliant works themselves, the originals of which are now much sought after by collectors.

It was Joy Kasson's provocative book that first got me thinking about the Colonel and Little Missie; but in this study I would like to drive my wagon in the opposite direction: to proceed from the folklore and its pictorial underpinnings back to the historical event—when there is one—that underlies the folklore.

Some of the later tropes—Cody's conquest of the English royal family, for example—have been, if anything, overdocumented. From the time Cody and his big troop disembarked at Gravesend (not far from where Pocahontas is buried) the press was out in force. Princess Alexandra liked the show so much that she once snuck into the press box incognito. (In the farcical divorce proceedings which Cody initiated against Lulu in 1905, both Princess Alexandra and her mother-in-law, Queen Victoria, were named by Lulu as women who had paid her husband very improper attentions, though it is well documented that the queen's eye, at least, lingered longest on the handsome Ogalala Red Shirt, who is more than once mentioned in the royal diaries. To Cody himself the queen was merely polite.)

For the earliest and most complex tropes—what we might call the prairie tropes—there were at first no media reports at all, there being, as yet, no media in the areas where the events took place. Cody claimed to be eleven when he killed his first Indian, which would have put the event in 1857. Young Cody was a cowboy, or teamster, at the time, helping to move a herd of cattle across the plains. The first newspaper in Leavenworth, Kansas, was started about that time, but it seems unlikely that Cody would have been released from his duties to report the death of one Indian to a fledgling newspaper.

Much research has been expended on this elusive first kill, all of it inconclusive. Most commentators, like Cody's reputable if perhaps mildly credulous biographer Don Russell, give Cody the benefit of the doubt, on the grounds that he was an essentially truthful man. Even if his accounts of the events do not tally, point by point, with what historical evidence exists, Don Russell and other students of Cody's career like to think that their hero wasn't just a big liar. In their view, when Cody recounts an incident in his early life, something of the sort had probably occurred.

I am less confident of Cody's accuracy as a historian of himself, and as we go through the episodes, I'll make my doubts known. One reason I'm skeptical is that in later times, when there *were* witnesses to some of these events, Cody's version rarely tallies with what others report. When you examine the accounts carefully Cody soon begins to seem like a spinner of colorful yarns, many of which reflect well on his behavior. This, among autobiographers, is common, of course; many people who report on themselves scatter a few seeds of truth in the rich soil of exaggeration. Buffalo Bill was hardly alone in this regard. Even the mostly scrupulous Annie Oakley was not above lopping six years off her official age when Cody suddenly presented her with a teenage rival, the sharpshooter Lillian Smith.

2

WILLIAM FREDERICK CODY was born in Iowa in 1846, but his parents—Isaac Cody and Mary Ann Laycock Cody—moved to Kansas as soon as it became a territory, settling in the Salt Creek Valley, near Fort Leavenworth.

It should be mentioned here that for at least ten years *before* the Civil War, and another ten years *after* it, Kansas and Missouri were probably the most dangerous places in America—places where neighbor often fought neighbor and brother brother. The trouble was slavery: it was in Kansas and Missouri that passions over slaveholding were the most intense; they didn't call it "Bleeding Kansas" for nothing. Guerrilla activity, vigilantism, and homegrown militias flourished and fought. In these parts the Civil War lasted something like twenty years, rather than four. As late as 1875 the outlaw Jesse James—who was a warrior from early youth—was complaining that fewer and fewer people seemed to be in the mood to fight Yankees anymore.

My own grandparents William Jefferson and Louisa Francis McMurtry were farming in western Missouri when the Civil War ended—for a few more years they nourished the hope that the violence would finally abate, but it didn't. In the 1870s, not willing to raise their children amid such risks, they moved to Texas. Theirs was a common story.

Isaac Cody, Bill's father, was not an abolitionist—he was willing to let those who had slaves keep their slaves—only his preference was that no settlers would bring slaves to Kansas, which he hoped to see remain all white. In the eyes of his neighbors this wasn't enough: they saw it as just abolitionism watered down.

In 1854, when young Bill was eight, Isaac Cody was swept, much against his will, into a heated political rally and forced to declare himself, which he was attempting to do when an enraged proslavery neighbor rushed forward and stabbed him. The assailant's name was Charlie Dunn; he worked at the time for Cody's brother Elijah. He was not arrested, though he did lose his job.

Isaac Cody recovered from his wound and, for three more years, led what would seem to have been a fairly active life. He cleared fields, he surveyed, and he was a very hardworking member of the first territorial legislature. Nonetheless, when he died in 1857, the family attributed his demise to the stab wound he had received from Charlie Dunn.

Alive, Isaac Cody managed to make a pretty good living for his family; but his death brought them close to destitution. Fortunately Mary Cody had friends in Leavenworth, and Bill Cody, then eleven, was a vigorous, able, appealing young man, who soon, with his mother's help, found work as a mounted messenger for the freighting firm of Majors and Russell (later Russell, Majors, and Waddell), the firm that—only three years later—would create one of the most glamorous of Western enterprises, the Pony Express.

Bill Cody in time became much the most famous of Pony Express riders; he kept a Pony Express act in his Wild West shows for more than thirty years, the only act to last anywhere near that long, but his first job was considerably more mundane. Mounted on a mule, he carried messages from the freight yard to the telegraph offices in Leavenworth, a distance of about three miles. So efficient was young Billy at hustling these messages back and forth that his superiors finally warned him that the messages were not so urgent that he needed to wear out his mule.

It was from these three-mile deliveries that young Bill Cody rose, in a natural sequence, to being a drover, cowboy, herdsman, teamster, helping to move livestock or freight from one location to another—

this mostly meant delivering beef on the hoof to sometimes distant army posts. He was eleven at the time.

Before I proceed to the vexed question of the first Indian killed, I should call attention to the fact that in the 1850s and 1860s it was perfectly normal for rural youths to be expected to do a man's work at the age of eleven or twelve. All my eight rancher uncles were gone from home and self-supporting at that age. My father, the stay-at-home, had just turned twelve when he was sent off with a small herd of cattle to a market about twenty-five miles away, where he was to sell the cattle and hurry home with the money. He did this without giving it much thought—in the context of the times it was a perfectly normal task. *Not* to have accomplished it smoothly would have resulted in diminished prospects.

In fact, even at the ages of seven or eight Cody and his sisters were frequently sent considerable distances—fifteen miles, say—to bring home livestock that had strayed from the immediate premises.

At the age of ten, I myself was once set the task of bringing in the milk cows to the headquarters of a large ranch in New Mexico of which my uncle was foreman. The milk cows, as it happened, were plainly visible on the vast, distant plain—at least they were visible to everyone except my myopic self. I rode more than half an hour in the direction of these invisible milk cows but I just couldn't see them. My uncle concluded that I must be going blind—he impatiently loped past me and brought in the cows.

From such humiliations I concluded that I probably would not have lasted long in frontier life.

3

Now let's look at the killing of William Frederick Cody's first Indian, which occurred—if it occurred at all—during a cattle drive along the South Platte River in 1857. The cattle belonged to Majors and Russell, and the drive was supervised by Frank and Bill McCarthy. At noon one day Indians—but which Indians?—managed to stampede the herd and kill three cowboys (although cowboys were not yet called that). The McCarthy brothers rallied their men and took cover in a slough which wound its way to the South Platte. They didn't stop the herd when night fell; what cattle the Indians hadn't run off in daylight they might attempt to run off at night. Fortunately the high banks of the river, when they reached it, gave good cover. Young Bill Cody was at the rear of the drive, in charge of the slower cattle (later, they would be called drags). Here is the story in Cody's own words:

> I, being the youngest and smallest of the party, became somewhat tired, and without noticing it I had fallen behind the others quite some little distance. It was about ten o'clock and we were keeping very quiet and hugging close to the bank when I happened to look up to the moonlight sky and saw the plumed head of an Indian peeping over the bank. Instead of hurrying ahead and alarming the men in a quiet way, I instantly aimed my gun at his head and fired. The report rang out sharp and loud in the night air;

and was immediately followed by an Indian whoop; the next moment about six feet of dead Indian came tumbling down into the river. I was not only overcome with astonishment, but was badly scared, as I could hardly realize what I had done. I expected to see the whole force of Indians come down upon us. While I was standing there thus bewildered, the men who had heard the shot and the war whoop and had seen the Indian take a tumble, came rushing back.

"Who fired that shot?" cried Frank McCarthy.

"I did," replied I rather proudly, as my confidence returned and I saw the men coming up.

"Yes, and little Billy has killed an Indian stone dead—too dead to skin," said one of the men.

Cody later claimed that when he got back to Leavenworth, he was interviewed by a reporter, probably from the *Leavenworth Times*, and found his name in print as "the youngest Indian slayer on the plains."

Though many have looked, no such report has been found, in that paper or any other, but then a feature of many of Cody's stories is that they have no very exact time line. Such a claim could have shown up in some small newspaper a year earlier or a year later, maybe. But his best biographer, Don Russell, looked and looked and failed to find it. He admits that the evidence is inconclusive but decides to take Cody's word for it on the ground that he was broadly truthful.

In some respects Cody *was* a truthful man; he makes no effort, for example, to whitewash his disreputable jayhawking activities during the first years of the Civil War. He was an out-and-out horse thief, whose political motivation was slight at best. But by the 1870s, when the autobiography appeared, Cody's fortune had come to depend on his ability to romanticize his career as a scout and Indian fighter. It is perhaps foolish, considering the loose journalistic standards of the times, to apply very severe critical methods to what in the main is promotional, ghostwritten autobiography; but one has to start somewhere.

The passage quoted is accompanied in the book by a dark,

grainy illustration in which a frontiersman who looks much older than eleven stands in shallow water and fires upward at a startled Indian who wears a bit of a headdress and also a necklace of claws. The illustrator was True Williams, a prolific artist who also illustrated *Tom Sawyer* and *Roughing It*. The Indian looks as if he could be Mohawk, or Huron, or Every Indian. One of the things that bothers me about the passage is the generic nature of the term "Indian" which Cody uses in this passage and throughout the autobiography generally.

Mountain men, plainsmen, trappers, miners, soldiers, surveyors—indeed everyone who concerned himself with the developing West—usually were very tribe-specific when describing their adventures with Indians. Kit Carson knew he was chasing Apaches when he tried to rescue Mrs. White. He knew he was fighting Navahos when, later in his career, he drove the Navaho out of their homelands and sent them on the Long Walk.

Later in his own career Cody was certainly tribe-specific about the Indians he fought, or those he employed. He knew Sitting Bull was Sioux; he knew Yellow Hair was Cheyenne. But in the autobiography Indians are often just Indians, which is troubling. Surely it would have been a concern of the McCarthy brothers, who were responsible for both men and cattle. Were they being attacked by Osage, Southern Cheyenne, Pawnee, Kickapoo? Someone in the party would have known—after all, the Indians had killed three of them.

This Indian, though killed, managed to emit a whoop—then "about six feet of dead Indian came tumbling down into the river." This startled boy somehow had time to calculate the man's height, in a river and by moonlight. More doubt.

Then Frank McCarthy and some of the men come rushing back and Cody's confidence rises.

"Yes, and little Billy has killed an Indian stone dead—too dead to skin," said one of the men.

By "skin" one assumes he meant "scalp," another puzzler. Most Indians dead enough to allow themselves to be scalped would presumably be stone dead. What if this Indian was just playing possum? At night, and in the water, how sound was the helpful drover's examination? Why wouldn't they have scalped him?

This passage has been reprinted innumerable times, with only minor embellishments. Many scholars doubt it ever happened, regarding it as a yarn that somehow got embedded in our national folklore, neither provable nor disprovable. It's not likely, now, that we'll ever know one way or the other, and Cody's coyness about the episode in later life hardly strengthens a tendency to believe him. When asked about his first Indian kill he would usually laugh and say something like, "That Indian's tied to me like a tin can to a dog's tail." He never quite suggested that it was untrue, and why would he? It was the creation myth of the legend of Buffalo Bill, Indian fighter.

4

BEFORE I address the second major trope—Cody's prominence as a rider with the Pony Express—it might be well to consider the curious turn he made in his career: from Indian killer to the Indian's friend. In his years as a showman he probably employed more Indians than all the other shows put together. He paid a healthy price in the form of bonds, too. Sometimes a bond of $10,000 got him one hundred Indians, while at other times it only got him thirty. He continued to hire Indians over the protests of the Department of the Interior and the commissioner of Indian Affairs, who didn't at all like the fact that Indians were becoming show business stars—as Sitting Bull, Red Shirt, and a few others did. Moreover, the Indians he employed liked him and let it be known that he treated them well. When the first Indian protective agencies were formed, Cody was more than once accused of mistreating Indians on his European tours, but the Indians themselves hurried to refute these charges. Two or three Indians had died en route, but the Indians pointed out that they had been sick before they left and would have died anyway. Cody took ninety-seven Indians to Queen Victoria's Jubilee and got home with most of them, though not, in all cases, immediately. Black Elk, the sage-to-be, somehow got stranded in Manchester, made it to Paris, lived with a French family, and was sent home by Cody when the show played Paris a year later.

Sitting Bull, despite his strong admiration for Annie Oakley, left the Wild West after one season but it was not because he disliked

Cody. What he didn't like was the hustle and chatter and noise of the white people's cities—that and their strange lack of concern for the poor. It is not likely that Cody or anyone else was really sorry to see Sitting Bull go. Cody described him as "peevish," one of the great showman's few understatements.

Yet a twist occurred, and a big one, in Cody's career. In showbiz he was first promoted as an Indian killer, and he garnered huge publicity for having killed, or claimed that he killed, two particular Indians, the Sioux Tall Bull and the Cheyenne Yellow Hair, though it is far from certain that he killed either one.

Whatever the true body count—it's never likely to be established—Cody was never an Indian hater, as so many of his contemporaries were. He was not moved to kill Indians, but merely to avoid being killed by them. In his young years as a plainsman—from 1857 to well after the Civil War—he worked in places where there were plenty of Indians, and at this time they were far from being a conquered people. Various biographers estimate that Cody was in fifteen or sixteen skirmishes with Indians in his life, and one or two real campaigns, the longest of them culminating in the Battle of Summit Springs, in which Tall Bull was killed. Cody was an able plainsman and a good—though not an exceptional—rifle shot. Fighting as often as he did, it might be wrong to claim that he had never killed an Indian, but the kills, if there were any, are very hard to pin down—and Cody himself was no help because he was always vague about dates and other facts of his own history. It's probable that he shot an Indian or two but it's unlikely that he killed many. His own word is unreliable, but we know from various sources much about his character and it doesn't seem that he was violent in any of his relations. It is not evident that any of the old combatants who worked in his Wild West shows had ever considered Cody a serious opponent, in the sense that Custer was a serious opponent, or Crazy Horse. Many of the Indians he had hired had had ample opportunity to size up warriors—few seem to have considered Cody to be much of one.

Once the necessary promotional work had been done and William F. Cody established as the star of stars, he rarely bragged about his Indian killing, and if he did talk about it, it was usually to repeat once again the particulars of the "duel" with Yellow Hair. This set piece was reenacted in many forms, including a movie. The duel with Yellow Hair was, with the Pony Express, the most enduring of all Cody's tropes—it was what would now be called a signature scene.

But showbiz apart, there is every evidence that Bill Cody liked Indians. At the very end, once he essentially belonged to Harry Tammen, he may have liked them better than he liked white people.

5

I HAVE already written that rich people, even royals, just seemed to like Bill Cody. The same might be said of bad people—even the notoriously violent Joseph "Alf" Slade, Cody's boss when he rode for the Pony Express, just seemed to like the kid. Here's Cody's account of their first meeting, when Cody showed up looking for a job:

Among the first persons I saw after dismounting from my horse was Slade. I walked up to him and presented Mr. Russell's letter, which he hastily opened and read. With a sweeping glance of his eye he took my measure from head to foot and then said:

"My boy, you are far too young for a pony express rider. It takes men for that business."

"I rode two months last year on Bill Trotter's division, sir, and filled the bill then; and I think I am better able to ride now."

"What! Are you the boy that was riding there and was called the youngest rider on the road?"

"I am the same boy," I replied, confident now that everything was all right for me.

"I have heard of you before. You are a year or two older now, and I think you can stand it. I'll give you a trial anyhow, and if you weaken you can come back to Horse-shoe Station and tend to stock."

That ended our first interview. The next day he assigned me duty on the road from Red Buttes on the North Platte to the Three Crossings on the Sweetwater, a distance of 76 miles, and I began riding at once. It was a long piece of road, but I was equal to the undertaking; and soon after had an opportunity to exhibit my power of endurance as a pony express rider.

One day I galloped into Three Crossings, my home station. I found that the rider who had expected to take the trip on my arrival, had got into a drunken row the night before and been killed; and that there was no one to fill his place. I did not hesitate for a moment to undertake an extra ride of 85 miles to Rocky Ridge, and I arrived at the latter place on time. I then turned and rode back to Red Buttes, my starting place, accomplishing on the round trip a distance of 322 miles.

Slade heard of this feat of mine and one day as he was passing on a coach sang out to me: "My boy, you're a brick and no mistake."

Slade, though rough at times and always a dangerous character—having killed many a man—was always kind to me. During the two years I worked for him as pony express rider and stage driver, he never spoke an angry word to me.

This passage, like the killing of the first Indian, is central to the rapidly swelling legend of Buffalo Bill.

Alf Slade, who never said an unkind word to Cody, seems to have poured hot lead into everybody else. To say that his temper was capricious was akin to saying that Sitting Bull was peevish. Alf Slade is thought to have killed about twenty-six men. If particularly incensed, as he was in at least one case, he might take the trouble to remove his victim's ears, one of which he used as a watch fob. Slade was finally hung by vigilantes in Silver City, Montana—yet he happily sang out a commendation to young Cody.

* * *

Holding that exceptional piece of luck on Cody's part in mind, I should take a moment to consider the brief day of the Pony Express itself. Cody's biographer Don Russell correctly remarks that some sort of mounted delivery system was an old, not a new, thing. If we are to believe Marco Polo, Kublai Khan had some sort of pony express.

Nor was the Pony Express, founded by the firm of Russell, Majors, and Waddell, unique in America in Cody's youth. John Butterfield, whose firm is still in business, pioneered a kind of Big Bend route that nearly touched the Mexican border before curling through the Arizona desert to San Diego. With good luck a letter might be delivered to the West Coast within three or four weeks. However, there were many splendid opportunities for bad luck to happen, in which case the mail never arrived.

Russell, Majors, and Waddell initiated their Pony Express runs in April of 1860—the run started in St. Joseph, Missouri, and edged across country to Sacramento, California. To say that it was hazardous would be to understate. When in full operation the route consisted of 190 stations, five hundred horses, and about eighty riders.

Did Russell, Majors, and Waddell seriously expect to make a profit from this curious venture? Probably not. They were successful freight haulers, transporting freight to various forts or anywhere else, depending on the whim of the client. No doubt they were looking to expand—in particular, to lock up some juicy government contracts. The Pony Express might be effective advertising—at least it might if things went well for a few months. The number of forts in the West was ever increasing—or at least they were until 1868, when Red Cloud and his allies forced the evacuation of three Wyoming forts, all of which had been unwisely situated in the Sioux holy lands.

Russell, Majors, and Waddell probably hoped that the Pony Express—a romantic endeavor if there ever was one—would be excellent advertising, but this seemed to have been a misjudgment on their part. The Pony Express went largely unnoticed at the time. Their young and essentially minor employee Bill Cody in later years reaped many times more publicity from his tour with the Pony Express than did the enterprise itself. He used it as an emblematic element in his shows for over three decades, keeping alive the memory of this short-lived venture for millions who had never heard of it while it was actually in operation.

To this day we lack a fully adequate history of this famous venture—and again, Cody indirectly profited from this lack; many of the details of his Pony Express career can neither be refuted nor confirmed, because of poor documentation.

There are plenty of skeptics who don't believe that Bill Cody rode with the Pony Express at all. One argument against him is the condition that Alf Slade mentioned: Cody's youth. He was only fourteen when the Pony Express runs were initiated, and not quite sixteen when they ended.

Had Cody showed up cold and asked for a job with a company where no one knew him, the age factor might indeed have been decisive. But such was not the case: Cody had already been riding for Russell, Majors, and Waddell for three years; he was known to be an able hand and had already undertaken several cattle-driving expeditions for the firm which were only marginally less dangerous than the Pony Express. In 1860 he was a proven, reliable plainsman whose horsemanship no one doubted.

Still, absolute proof that Cody rode with the Pony Express is elusive. Don Russell manages to find a snatch of testimony that convinces him, though it doesn't convince me. It's a comment from the wealthy Chicago contractor Edward Ayer, the man who formed the wonderful Native American collection now at the Newberry Library in Chicago:

> About six or seven years ago I attended a reception and dinner party given by all the diplomats of Paris to Buffalo Bill. I said it wasn't necessary to introduce me to Bill Cody; that I had crossed the plains in 1860, and he was riding by our train about a month, and would give us the news in a loud voice as he rushed by, so that we became much attached to him. At the reception Bill wouldn't let me get out of his sight, thereby disarranging the seating plan at the banquet.

That snatch is from Edward Ayer's privately printed journal. It seems a very curious passage, to me. Where was the train going, that a Pony Express rider could rush along beside it for about a month? Pony Express runs were not straight runs beside a train track. Why would Cody, isolated as he was in remote places, have "news" that a Chicago businessman wouldn't have? And how would Cody become so familiar with Ayer, whom he had only glimpsed through a train window, that he could recognize him at a banquet in Paris two and a half decades later?

I don't think Ayer's comment proves anything at all about Buffalo Bill and the Pony Express, but I *am* inclined to think he did ride with it, since that would merely have been a more or less natural extension of a job he already had.

The first rider out of St. Joseph may have been Bob Haslam, whom Cody would later employ in his Wild West shows—in fact he went on to employ a surprising number of prairie characters he had known in his years on the plains.

On literary grounds, too, I'm inclined to think that Cody's Pony Express work was real, if possibly exaggerated. The passages about Pony Express work are much less theatrically written than the passages about Indian fights or Indian killing. There's less conflation, more of a feel that Cody might have written this part himself.

The 322-mile ride he claimed—that's about the distance from Los Angeles to Phoenix—is thought to be the third-longest made during the brief, eighteen-month life of the Pony Express. The longest ride, 384 miles, was made by Bob Haslam, who lived to re-create it in many arenas. The second-longest, 330 miles, was made by one Howard Egan. Cody, at 322 miles, comes in third. He seems to have once thought he made a 384-mile ride, and one of his sisters clings to that figure, but it resulted from a clear miscalculation of his routes. Arithmetic was never one of the great scout's strong suits.

The Pony Express per se was in business from April of 1860 until November of 1861. The owners knew they were racing the telegraph, and the telegraph soon beat them: The two coasts were linked in November of 1860—the singing wires, as the Indians called them, had come to stay.

Buffalo Bill's 322-mile ride took twenty-two hours and was accomplished with the help of twenty-one horses, which suggests that he got about an hour's hard work out of each horse.

Most writing about the Pony Express emphasizes how hard the work was on the riders, but little has been written about the horses that made the enterprise possible. Initially the stations had been twenty-five miles apart, but it was soon lowered to about half that distance—too few horses were able to go hard for twenty-five miles. (Some Indians were said to be able to get fifty to seventy-five miles out of a horse, after which, probably, they ate the exhausted animal—this too is probably an exaggeration.)

Cody often mentions his mounts, a few of whose names have come down to us. When some Indians jumped him near Horse Creek on one ride he mentions that he was mounted on "a roan California horse, the fleetest steed I had." Agnes Wright Spring has produced a pamphlet about Cody's horses, the most famous of which was his buffalo-shooting horse Brigham. Two other horses from his scouting days were Buckskin Joe and Charlie. Buckskin Joe eventually went blind, presumably from having to carry Cody nearly two hundred miles on one ride. Isham was the most famous of the show horses. Harry Tammen callously sold Isham at the sheriff's sale, along with the rest of Cody's livestock, but some friends bought the old horse back and presented him to the old rider.

I mention the horses because, clearly, Cody's horsemanship, and his judgment about the speed and staying power of his mounts, was essential to his survival.

The otherwise vicious and homicidal Alf Slade took such a shine to young Cody that he decided to keep him at his own station and only use him as a kind of supernumerary rider—a curious word to come out of the mouth of such a rough old sort, but that's the word Cody reports.

Life at Horseshoe Station being comparatively easy, Cody one day decides to venture out on a bear hunt—or as he puts it:

> One day, when I had nothing else to do, I saddled up an
> extra Pony Express horse, and arming myself with a good
> rifle and a pair of revolvers, struck out for the foothills of
> Laramie Peak for a bear hunt. Riding carelessly along, and

breathing the cool and bracing autumn air which came down from the mountains, I felt as only a man can feel who is roaming over the prairies of the far West, well armed and mounted on a fleet and gallant steed. The perfect freedom he enjoys is in itself a refreshing stimulant to the mind as well as the body. Such indeed were my feelings on this beautiful day, as I rode up the valley of the Horseshoe.

The day continues beautiful and eventually turns into night without Cody having stirred up any bears. What he locates, instead, is a meadow with fifteen or twenty horses grazing in it. Prudence might have suggested to the young man that he turn and skedaddle, but he chooses to investigate and soon finds himself in a den of horse thieves, encamped in a kind of cave. Some of the men he recognizes as having been discharged from a freighting company he is familiar with. Cody soon realizes he is in a tight spot; he has left his horse some distance away and offers to leave his rifle with the men while he recovers the animal. The ruffians are happy to take the rifle but have no intention of leaving Cody any chance to escape. Two men go with him to fetch the horse, one in front of him and one behind. The men had not bothered to search him and do not know about the two pistols. As they are leading his horse up to the meadow Cody manages to drop a sage hen he had killed earlier in the day. When the man behind him stops to pick it up Cody whacks him hard with the pistol and turns just in time to shoot the man ahead of him, killing him dead. Then he flees into some rocky foothill country—his horse has to be abandoned but he makes good his escape.

Now, Cody had many narrow escapes in his career on the prairies. Even as early as nine he was forced to flee a group of thugs calling themselves the Border Ruffians, a primitive, violently proslavery vigilante group who wanted to do violence to young Billy because he was the son of a man they considered to be an abolitionist.

Always, though, young Cody just escapes—almost as the hero might do at the end of a movie serial. The Border Ruffians he manages to outrun until he reaches the home of friends, leaving his pursuers to retreat empty-handed.

All of Cody's pursuers, whether white or Indian, from the mid-fifties on to the late seventies, are forced to retreat empty-handed. Cody always has a better horse, or knows the country better; he keeps a cool head and manages to escape.

He admitted to being scared when he shot the first Indian, and he was no doubt not happy to have stumbled into the cave of the horse thieves—if he did—but the evidence suggests that Cody really did keep an uncommonly cool head, and this despite the fact that he was frequently drunk. Cody's drinking I'll discuss a little later, but his ability to either outrun or else hide from people who were pursuing him with deadly intent manifests itself often in his book. In most cases the reader is not inclined to doubt him. Plenty of people traveling those prairies did get chased in those times; working as Cody did, where and when he did, meant that rapid flight was more or less part of his job skills.

The den-of-thieves incident reads very dime-novel-like, but its main significance, if it happened, is that it marked the only time in his life when Cody claims to have killed a white man.

As if suspecting that some readers might want to verify such a claim, he goes on to mention that Alf Slade and a well-armed group followed him back to the site—the horses and the horse thieves were gone but there was a fresh grave in the meadow, presumably the final resting place of the man Cody shot.

In the autobiography, only a page or two earlier, there is an amusing illustration of Alf Slade summarily gunning down a stagecoach driver who had managed to offend him. Alf Slade always felt free to dispense his own justice, as did the vigilantes in Montana when they hung him.

Apart from the fact that his job with the Pony Express required Cody to ride farther and faster than he would normally have done, it didn't really change the customary pattern of his life very much. He would likely have been somewhere on the central plains of the West, riding horses, scouting, hunting, delivering messages for some military man—maybe General Carr or General Sheridan—or some hauling company.

One of his more ballsy efforts was his successful attempt to get the Sioux chief Spotted Tail (uncle of Crazy Horse) to come south and put on a little show—sham fighting, real killing of buffalo from horseback with bow and arrow, some dancing—as entertainment for the grand duke Alexis on his much-publicized visit. Though Spotted Tail himself was friendly to whites, plenty of his young warriors were much less so and would have been glad to take Cody's scalp had they run into him on his way north. Yet Cody got away with his rather daring infiltration and the Sioux came and did their bit to entertain a nobleman from a country they had never heard of.

Cody was active, he was able, he was trusted by both the army and the freight companies, and he accepted several courier jobs in country dangerous enough that most men might have declined the assignment. All through his youth and young manhood he worked mostly alone, breathing the cool free air of the prairies.

It was when first youth had passed, and the plains life became less and less free, that Cody, like many another plainsman, trapper, or meat hunter of his generation, came to realize that he would soon have to find another way to make a living. What Bill Cody recognized, more acutely than most of his contemporaries, was that all most Americans would know of the great adventure of the American West was whatever he could bring to them in his Wild West shows; he also figured out that a nearly ideal place to start would be the Pony Express—after all, what would be more appealing than the sight of the racing riders of the Pony Express? As a business, it hadn't worked out, but as a spectacle it thrilled audiences everywhere.

1

William F. Cody in young manhood.

Cody at the height of his fame.

2

Cody reenacting the taking of the first scalp for Custer, his Indian War Pictures, 1913.

Cody on a mock buffalo hunt.

4

BUFFALO BILL'S WILD WEST

AND

Congress of Rough Riders of the World.

Personal Courtesy.   ADMIT ONE.

Compliments of

Chicago, 1893.

B. B. W. W.

5

Personal Courtesy.

ADMIT ONE.

GRAND STAND.

JOHN M. BURKE,
Gen'l Manager.

*A ticket to Buffalo
Bill's Wild West.*

*Annie Oakley
promotional
photograph.*

6

Annie Oakley in a stage pose about 1880.

Annie Oakley giving a shooting lesson.

Louisa Cody about the time of her marriage.

9

The Codys in their sixties.

10

Ned Buntline, Buffalo Bill, the peerless
Morlacchi, and Texas Jack Omohundro
as they appeared on stage.

James Butler
(Wild Bill) Hickok.

13

Major John Burke, Cody's loyal press agent.

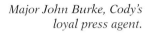

Red Cloud and Major Burke.

14

Nate Salsbury, the formidable manager of the Wild West.

15

Top row: Julius Meyer, Red Cloud.
Bottom row: Sitting Bull, Swift Bear,
Spotted Tail.

17

Black Elk, the Ogalala sage.

16

6

Two things young Bill Cody had very little use for were practical soldiering and politics. His father, Isaac, had been quite political, with a good attendance record in the fledgling territorial legislature, but it is hard to find anything in Cody's autobiography or his various interviews that could be considered a political statement. He soldiered, usually rather listlessly and in a ragtag way, with the Seventh Kansas and, somewhat later, with the Fifth Cavalry and one or two other units. Real military fervor, of the sort Sherman had, or Custer, was simply absent from Cody's makeup. In 1889 he was made a brigadier general—this was when he was invited by General Miles to take a hand in the Ghost Dance troubles, an invitation that, perhaps foolishly, was reversed before Cody ever reached Sitting Bull's camp; but he preferred the title of Colonel, a rank he never officially held. It seems he simply awarded it to himself when he realized that his pay equaled a colonel's pay: so why couldn't he have the rank?

The terrible Civil War, a war that was ripping the nation apart, didn't seem to much excite Cody, one way or another. His prejudices and his loyalties were essentially local. He had promised his mother that he wouldn't enlist while she was alive, and he kept his promise, though he did some irregular scouting during the early years of the war. Mary Laycock Cody died in 1863.

Among Cody's strong and specific prejudices was a dislike of Missourians, whom he blamed for the death of his father. Becoming a Jayhawker—Kansans of a rough nature who stole horses from

Confederates and sometimes sold them to the Unionists and other times just sold them. Rougher even than the Jayhawkers were the Red Legged Scouts, so called because their leggings were made from a red sheepskin popular with shoemakers in those days. The Red Legged Scouts were mainly just thieves and murderers, as young Bill Cody soon realized. He blamed his involvement on drunkenness, which he was much given to in those days. James Butler (later Wild Bill) Hickok became friendly with Cody around this time and even stayed as a guest in the hotel the Cody family was attempting to run in the Salt Creek Valley. Cody and Hickok were to remain buddies throughout the Civil War and afterward. Hickok eventually became a Union spy but at first he was, like Cody, not much excited by the war.

It may be that Cody and Hickok's rather lackadaisical attitude toward the war was due to their lack of proximity to the real action. Near the end of the war, in 1864, Cody occasionally did get drawn into some fairly sharp action near Independence, Missouri. Later in life, when in a tale-telling mood, he claimed to have been in a scouting party that captured Major General John Sappington Marmaduke near the Marais des Cygnes River, the so-called Swamp of the Swans, where the great tundra swans come, an area beloved by birdwatchers today. According to Cody he and General Marmaduke shared lunch and a bottle of whiskey.

Cody served a little more than a year and a half with the Seventh Kansas. On mustering out he was still a private. There is no evidence that he ever acquired much interest in military protocol, and he seems to have had even less interest in military training. What he had to offer the army—any army—was his knowledge of the country; he knew how to get from here to there, and could usually do so even if hostilities were in progress.

Though he liked to brag a little about his lunch with General Marmaduke, Cody was not vainglorious about his soldiering—and the same could be said for his Indian fighting. Frequently he would remark of a particular skirmish or chase that, really, it didn't amount to much—in these instances he was truthful. Many short engagements didn't amount to much.

Cody, who could be quite specific about details if he chose to be, could never quite remember actually enlisting in the Seventh Kansas. In Leavenworth, after his mother's death, he

> entered upon a dissolute and reckless life—to my shame, be it said—and associated with gamblers, drunkards, and bad characters generally. I continued my dissipation about two months and was become a very hard case—I met quite a number of my old comrades and neighbors, who tried to enduce me to enlist and go south with them. I had no intention of doing anything of the kind; but one day, after having been under the influence of bad whiskey, I awoke to find myself a soldier in the Seventh Kansas.

He enlisted in February of 1864, which was rather late in the war. But for the bad whiskey he might never have enlisted at all.

7

BECAUSE Bill Cody, by the standards of our time, started work so young, and because the highlighted episodes—what I have called the tropes—so much dominate the story of his fame, it's easy to forget that the narrative of his life is one story and the narrative of his fame another.

When Cody obliviously enlisted in the Seventh Kansas he was only eighteen. He had quit the Pony Express in 1861 and was for a time at loose ends, rather in the manner of teenagers everywhere. Cody just happened to be a good deal more experienced than most teenagers would have been. When he was thirteen his mother actually got him to go to school for two months, the longest period of instruction he ever suffered.

This brief educational interlude ended when the Colorado gold rush caused gold fever to flare up across the nation. It was Pikes Peak or bust for many an American youth. Cody rushed off west with some friends, none of whom knew the slightest thing about mining. Very soon they were bust. Fortunately Cody ran into a wagon master he had worked for previously; once again he found himself a teamster, working his way home.

It was about this time that Mrs. Cody turned the Cody home into a hotel, a short-lived effort. The few guests she could lure in were mostly just her son's friends, Wild Bill Hickok among them.

Mining having failed, young Cody next turned to trapping, partnering with Dave Harrington, who had briefly been one of his lively sister Julia's suitors. This was in 1859, just before his Pony Express job. The beaver boom had ended some decades previously, mainly because the beaver themselves were more or less ended—though there were still a few rich pockets of these valuable rodents. Probably there was a good deal of nostalgia in the Cody-Harrington expedition—yearning of a sort that sometimes seizes thirteen-year-olds. It gave the boys a chance to feel that they were actually of the mountain man generation, which they may have fantasized about much as young cowboys will still fantasize about having been trail drivers. Cody idolized Kit Carson and was probably seeking at least a taste of Carson's experience.

At any rate Cody and Harrington were soon trapping the Republican River, in Colorado. Though they had an ox team and abundant supplies, luck did not attend their efforts. One ox slipped on some ice, dislocated a hip, and had to be shot. Then a bear attacked the other ox. Cody managed to shoot the bear, but then he too slipped on the ice and broke his leg. Harrington set the leg but winter was upon them. They made a fairly snug dugout in the side of a hill, after which it was decided that Harrington should leave Cody and go for help. They reckoned that he could probably make the necessary round trip in about three weeks, but bad weather intervened and it was twenty-nine days before Cody saw Dave Harrington again.

Cody had abundant supplies—at least he did for a while—and weathered the interval well enough but for one close call, a visit by a party of Sioux who were on the prowl. Probably they would have made short work of this boy had it not been for the fortunate intervention of a Sioux elder Cody had happened to meet at Fort Laramie during one of his hauls.

The Sioux elder was old Rain in the Face, who—at least as the trope has it—intervened and persuaded the hostile warriors to spare the young man's life. The warriors submitted grudgingly. They took Cody's guns and the lion's share of his provisions, but they didn't kill him.

Dime-novelish as this story sounds, it was more than likely true. The young trappers were in a country thick with Sioux, and a leader, or at least an elder, named Rain in the Face did exist. His son, young Rain in the Face, fought in the Battle of the Little Bighorn and, for a time, claimed to have fired the shot that killed Custer. This claim is no longer given much credit. Sitting Bull pointed out that everyone was shooting at Custer (though his body bore only two bullet wounds).

In his book Cody expresses considerable annoyance at the Indians for making free with his possessions, though they could readily have made just as free with his life. Being saved by old Rain in the Face made a good tableau in the Wild West shows, but the incident, assuming it happened, was actually one of Cody's narrowest escapes—if the old Sioux hadn't remembered him, or if he had just chosen to stay in his lodge that day, it is doubtful that there would have been many legends of Buffalo Bill.

8

THERE was one significant aspect of his life that Buffalo Bill Cody could never convert into a trope or reduce to a playlet in his Wild West shows, and that was his long, mostly turbulent marriage to Louisa Frederici, a comely St. Louis girl of French descent. In her youth Lulu was both very attractive and very spirited.

The two were introduced by Lulu's cousins in a somewhat awkward way. Cody and the cousin walked in, found Lulu dozing over a book, and promptly jerked the chair out from under her—Cody never quite determined the right way to approach women. Louisa, meaning to slap her cousin, slapped Cody instead. Since Louisa had a date that evening with a gentleman she didn't really want to see, she persuaded Cody to stick around and help her pretend that she and Cody were engaged.

According to Louisa, this auspicious meeting occurred in May 1865.

Forty years later, when he was trying unsuccessfully to divorce Lulu, Cody had this to say about the mock engagement: "Boylike, I thought it very smart to be engaged. I asked her to marry me, or asked her if she would marry me if I would come back after the war was over. And jokingly she said yes."

If the engagement really began in May of 1865, then of course the war *was* over, though Cody, who had never been much interested in the war, may not have taken in this fact. Cody was on the move, as usual, and claimed to be a little surprised when he got home to Leavenworth and found several letters from Lulu, asking him to keep his word. Perhaps surprisingly, he *did* keep his word. In the divorce proceedings in 1905 he tried to pretend he was tricked into a marriage he never wanted, but a passage in the autobiography was there to trip him up: "I returned to St. Louis, having made up my mind to capture the heart of Miss Frederici, whom I adored above any young lady I had ever seen."

Louisa's heart *was* captured, and the two were very soon married, but it was not long before Louisa had an inkling that the ruse of their engagement may have chased off the wrong suitor. Just as the boat was pulling out, to take the honeymooners upriver to Leavenworth, a gang of ruffians rushed at them. Someone had recognized Cody from his jayhawking days and proposed to hang him then and there, an impulse Louisa soon came to sympathize with. Accustomed from birth to the amenities of the old French Quarter in St. Louis, she was unprepared for the amenityless village that Leavenworth then was. She was also unprepared for Bill's rough acquaintances, some sixty of whom were at the dock with a brass band when their boat pulled in, eager to perform a kind of prairie charivari, a practice that probably came as a big shock to the gently bred Louisa.

This is not to say that Louisa Cody lacked the fighting spirit; where Bill Cody was concerned she could more than take up for herself—when she could catch him, that is. But Bill, true to his nature, was usually on the move. At one point he guided General Sherman, then commander of the Division of the Mississippi, from Fort Riley to Fort Kearny—much later Sherman thanked him by giving him a blurb for his Wild West show. It's a safe guess that Cody's thoughts turned none too often to the young bride he had left at home in Leavenworth.

Louisa had nothing of the pioneer in her. She missed city pleasures and city ways. And she missed her husband. If Bill Cody had at least stayed home to fight with her she might have stuck it out in Leavenworth, but with him gone most of the time and their first child coming, she, sensibly, took herself back to St. Louis. Bill Cody accepted this move as nonchalantly as he had accepted the end of the Civil War. He liked St. Louis himself—the prairie just happened to be the place where he made his living.

Children came, riches came, mistresses came—some of them very expensive mistresses, such as the actress Katherine Clemmons, whose meager talent Cody spent some $80,000 promoting—but Louisa was still his wife, housed at first in tents and barracks, then later in grand houses in North Platte, Nebraska, or Rochester, New York, but not very happy in any of the above. The boy they took in, Dan Muller, loved Louisa and wrote poignantly of the sadness he felt when she informed him that she could no longer live with Uncle Bill. Yet the union, despite Bill's strange attempt to end it in its fortieth year (when Louisa revealed her jealousy of Queen Victoria), remained somehow a marriage.

In writing about two other classically difficult marriages—those of the Carlyles and the Tolstoys—the critic V. S. Pritchett spoke of these tightly bound yet eternally warring couples as "the professionals of marriage." But the Carlyles and the Tolstoys faced their difficulties in lockstep, under the same roof, whereas Louisa's principal difficulty was in keeping Bill home for any length of time. When old Count Tolstoy finally wandered off from Yasnaya Polyana, he left a venerable, long-established country seat. Bill Cody had no such seat, although he built several great piles that might have served as one had he been a settled person. But he had grown up as a virtual nomad on the wild free prairies and it was a liking for the nomad's life, rather than a dislike of his wife, that kept him on the move. For most of his life he made his living through nomadic pursuits, and this didn't really change when he became an impresario. The shows still had to move. And Cody had to move. It is doubtful that he could have stayed put for a whole year even if there was a big stipend to be earned.

Louisa soon learned to be practical in her abandonment. As soon as Cody had money he began to buy property; at least he would if he could close a deal before he squandered the money. When she saw this pattern emerging Louisa soon developed a rather good head for business, which, in this case, meant seeing that all of the property was put in her name, a fact Cody didn't notice until he ran into financial difficulties in the eighties and nineties.

Bill and Louisa's fights were on a par with the Tolstoys'—many were as ridiculous as any farce ever staged, but like most marital fights, they were only funny if one happened to be a spectator, not a player. Bill Cody was never really indifferent to Lulu; their children came and there were times when he recovered his early affection for her, but it didn't keep him from being gone a lot, leaving a restless woman stuck on the lonely plains.

In their fifty-one years of marriage it is doubtful that Cody was home even for six months at a stretch. He missed births—he even missed deaths. They were together so irregularly that they never fully got used to one another—every time Bill came home there would have to be an awkward period of readjustment to their domestic state. At the very end, after all the fights, all the mistresses, all the long estrangements, were the war-worn Codys glad that they had one another still?

The question is hard to answer because no biographer with much psychological acuteness has troubled to look hard at the Cody marriage. The complexities of Bill's career really overshadowed it. In 1920, three years after Cody's death, Lulu wrote a little memoir with the help of Courtney Ryley Cooper, Annie Oakley's first biographer. It's a readable effort, though with some massive gaps and a good deal of vagueness and imprecision. Lulu Cody had lived in North Platte, Nebraska, for some thirty-five years and yet seemed to believe that the town and also Bill's ranch were close to the Wyoming line. They weren't.

The source most likely to tell the reader what Lulu Cody's life was like is a book by the diminutive (four foot eight) but vigorous Nebraska historian Nellie Snyder Yost. Her book is called *Buffalo Bill: His Family, Friends, Fame, Failures, and Fortunes*—it's not as good on Cody himself as the books by Don Russell and Joy Kasson, but it's much better than either of those on the Codys' home life, to the extent that they had one.

Nellie Snyder Yost had the advantage of living on the spot— North Platte, Nebraska—where much of the Codys' domestic life took place. She knew several Codys, and of course heard many tales. To this day Buffalo Bill is a huge presence in North Platte—in a way he's the only presence, even now. Nellie Yost has done her best to separate truth from rumor, something that becomes harder and harder to do as the years pass. I doubt that she's one hundred percent successful—no biographer is—but she comes a good deal closer than either Bill or Lulu has done. Somehow she gets the feel of what the prairie scout and his often left at home wife really felt about one another.

Lulu Cody's book, *Memories of Buffalo Bill by His Wife,* is interesting in part because of what it leaves out. Annie Oakley is never mentioned and neither is Katherine Clemmons or any of the six old girlfriends who showed up at Cody's funeral. On the page, at least, Lulu finally had Bill Cody to herself.

9

FROM 1857, when he began to work for Russell, Majors, and Waddell, William F. Cody could fairly be described as an able all-round plainsman. He could drive teams, he could cowboy, he was a sought-after courier, he was a more than competent hunter as well as an organizer of hunts. He could fight Indians if required, although he clearly preferred to live and let live where the Indians were concerned. But when the Civil War ended he was still a youth, essentially unestablished, just one more mustered-out private.

Then along came the dime novelist Ned Buntline, who sensed a different potential for Bill Cody. It was Buntline who first nudged Cody toward what would become a brilliant career as a showman, a career that would occupy him during the second half of his life.

His fame as Buffalo Bill, however, was forged on the plains, during the half decade between 1866 and 1871, when Cody, without exactly pushing himself, managed to receive major publicity for what looks now to have been a very minor role in the almost constant Indian wars that were fought on the great plains during these critical years.

A word of background may be helpful.

When the Civil War finally ended America was a war-weary nation. A few years of peace would not have been amiss, and yet, only in the industrial Northeast was there much peace. The South was soon engulfed in the struggles of Reconstruction, and in the West there were a goodly number of very warlike tribes who were by this time awake to the fact that their way of life was under serious threat.

A few privileged Indian leaders—Red Cloud, Spotted Tail, Sitting Bull, and others—thanks to the government's shrewd policy of bringing such leaders east, to show them the majesty of Washington and New York, with perhaps a visit to the president thrown in, knew that what lay ahead for their people was more in the nature of a promise than a threat: but a deadly promise it was, as Red Cloud recognized. Late in his life he remarked that the whites had made many promises, more than he could remember, but they had only kept one. They said they would take the Indians' land, and they took it.

Sitting Bull, after coming to Washington and meeting with President Cleveland, recognized immediately that there was really no hope. The Indians would have to do what the white men wanted them to do, and live where they wanted them to live, or the Indians would die.

Even if every Indian killed a white man with every step he took, Sitting Bull said, it would change nothing. The whites were too many, the Indians too few; besides which, the whites had better weapons.

Still, no matter how clear their insight, or how grave their doubts about the future, the Plains Indians were warrior societies, and they were defending homelands and long-held traditions which they loved. So they were going to fight. They were warriors, it was their country, they knew it better than even the best white scouts; for a time there would be wholesale war.

The white soldier with perhaps the clearest strategic vision where the Indians were concerned was General William Tecumseh Sherman, who shortly after the Civil War ended was made commander of the Department of the Mississippi. Sherman's way of fighting impressed itself on the nation in his great, deadly march to the sea. War was hell; the more brutal it could be made, the quicker it would be over.

In the settled South there was no escape, if one happened to be in Sherman's path.

But the West was not the settled South. The Indians were skilled mobile fighting units; they didn't have plantations or small farms that could be torched—though when an American commander did happen to hit a well-supplied village, as Crook did in Montana in 1875, the soldiers did burn everything, including food-stuffs that they themselves would later come to need.

Sherman may have been the first to realize that the advance of the railroads would very shortly doom the Indians. Most of them, with the buffalo they depended on, would be caught between the Union Pacific and the Northern Pacific. If one hunter, Buffalo Bill Cody, could kill three thousand buffalo in a short space of time, what chance did the buffalo have when whole trainloads of professional hunters could come right to the herds by rail? No chance, of course; the buffalo would vanish and the soon-to-be-starving Indians would have to do as they were told.

Sherman's theory was flawless—the only difficulty was politi-cal. The tracks of the two railroads were rapidly getting laid, but would-be settlers, thousands of them, were making tracks of their own at an even more rapid rate. Westering became a national com-pulsion; there was no stopping the tide of immigrants along the Platte, across the Santa Fe Trail, or any way that seemed convenient at the moment.

Ahead of these immigrants lay many dangers, but no danger greater than the aroused fury of the Plains Indians. The U.S. Army, tired and depleted though it may have been in the first postwar decade, was very soon being asked to make a safe way for all the white folks seeking land.

Sherman had no tolerance for Indians who wouldn't behave. His policy was clearly exterminationist; it may be that he best ex-pressed it in a letter he sent to General Phil Sheridan as the great battle for the plains was about to be joined:

> As brave men and as the soldiers of a government which
> has exhausted the peace efforts, we, in the performance of
> a most unpleasant duty, accept the war begun by our ene-
> mies, and hereby resolve to make its end final. If it results
> in the utter annihilation of these Indians it is but the re-
> sult of what they have been warned against again and
> again, and for which they seem fully prepared. I will do
> nothing to restrain our troops from doing what they deem

proper on the spot, and will allow no mere vague general charges of cruelty and inhumanity to tie their hands, but will use all the powers confided in me to the end that these Indians, the enemies of our race and our civilization, shall not again be able to begin and carry on their barbarous warfare on any kind of pretense that they may choose to allege . . . You may now go ahead in your own way and I will back you with my whole authority, and stand between you and any efforts that may be attempted in your rear to restrain your purpose or check your troops.

Sherman may have been referring to the Peace Party, those Congressmen or politicians who felt there should be an effort to find a middle ground with the Indian tribes. For this movement, which was not wholly ineffective, Sherman had nothing but contempt. He is one of three individuals to whom the bluntest of all policy statements—that the only good Indian is a dead Indian—has been attributed. The first to say it was probably the Montana congressman James Cavanaugh; then Sheridan picked it up, and finally Sherman, who (according to Mencken) said it to an Indian who was panhandling at a railway station as Sherman was disembarking. "Me good Indian," the old man said, to which Sherman replied, "So far as I know the only good Indian is a dead Indian." It is doubtful that the old panhandler received a cent.

The harshness of Sherman's policy where Indians were concerned accounts for the fact that George Armstrong Custer, despite a court-martial or two and many callous infringements of military rules, kept being called back to command in the West. The fact that he abandoned Major Joel Elliott and eighteen men at the time of the Washita battle was not forgotten by either the officers or the rank and file, but Custer shrugged it off. He was by no means as able a commander as Sherman but his willingness to fight was evident to all. In a sense he lived to fight. He was harsh to and hated by his men, as well as by most of his fellow officers, but he was, nonetheless, the kind of man Sherman was looking for: one to whom fighting came first.

When President Lincoln, sorely beset at the outset of the Civil

War by dithering generals, began to receive reports of victory after victory secured by the nearly unknown Ulysses S. Grant, he said, in admiration: "He fights."

Exactly the same could be said for Custer, although Grant was reliable and Custer wildly erratic: he might simply ride off from his command to go have a romantic tryst with his wife—he did this in Kansas—but fighting was what he liked to do best, and he always returned to it once his critical superiors had been appeased. Sheridan moved mountains to get Custer out of his various scrapes; he wanted him back in the West. Yet Custer's achievements in the West, once you boil them down, amount to very little.

His one victory was the Battle of the Washita, and how wise a victory was that? He succeeded in killing Black Kettle, the most famous peace Indian of his time. A few warriors were killed but most of the dead were women and children. His reconnaissance, as usual, was feeble; it was only after he wrapped up Black Kettle's village that Custer realized that the part of the plains where he was seemed to be swarming with Indians. He at once hustled back to a less exposed position, having achieved his one and only victory in the Plains Indian wars—and achieved it against the one Indian who didn't want to fight.

Black Kettle's tough wife was also killed in this battle, though their two bodies were not immediately identified. During the terrible massacre at Sand Creek, Black Kettle's wife had received no less than nine wounds, but Black Kettle somehow managed to carry her the forty miles to Fort Lyon, where the doctors saved her.

It would be almost eight years before George Armstrong Custer led his gallant Seventh Cavalry against another Indian village. This was on a Montana plain in June of 1876, and when it was over, "Long Hair comes no more," the Indian women sang.

10

THAT General Sherman was philosophically willing to totally exterminate the Plains Indians was clear enough from the letter
quoted, and from numerous other statements. He would have been
glad to mow them down and plow them under, but when he actually
began to put armies in the field in 1866–1867, it soon became obvious that he didn't have the muscle to accomplish any such genocidal
program.

The Confederate soldiers against whom Sherman had made his
reputation as a fighting general mainly stood and fought, dying if
necessary. But the Sioux, the Cheyenne, the Pawnee, the Comanche,
the Kiowa, the Arapaho, the Apache, and so forth much preferred to
fight and run. When sent to retaliate for some raid or other, the U.S.
Army could rarely catch the Indians they were after. They were not
particularly well provisioned, and in any case, were temperamentally
unsuited to long pursuits. The chases were frustrating, so much so
that the soldiers usually fell back on punishing any Indians they happened to run into. Since their high command was on record as believing that the only good Indian was a dead Indian, why
discriminate?

In time, though, there would appear officers of the highest cal-
iber, such as General George Crook, who *did* discriminate. General
Crook, on his tours of duty in Arizona, spent a lot of time sorting out
the Apache situation. There were nine branches of the Apache peoples; Crook's distinction was that he took care not to punish the

71

wrong tribes. He was fair, the Apaches realized it, and Crook came to be treated with respect. And the northern Indians, too, mostly respected Crook, particularly after they spent a whole day whipping up on him at the Battle of the Rosebud in 1876.

As for the fire-breathing William Tecumseh Sherman, irony soon overtook his effort to secure the northern plains. It soon became apparent that he didn't have the manpower, which forced him into tedious negotiations and slow diplomacy, tasks for which he was not well suited. Sherman probably sat through more peace powwows than any other general. His principal opponent in these debates, the Ogalala Red Cloud, was noted for his long-winded oratory. He might talk half the day—on the other hand, he might not bother to show up at all. If some buffalo crossed his path while he was on the way to a powwow he might decide to hunt first and negotiate later.

When he did arrive Red Cloud made it clear that if the whites wanted peace they needed to stop building forts in the Sioux lands. Three such forts—Fort Reno, Fort Phil Kearny, and Fort C. F. Smith—had foolishly been built right in the Sioux holy lands. There had been a gold strike in Montana—the three forts were supposed to protect immigrants along the Bozeman Trail. But the forts' defenses were so weak that the army was forced to abandon them in 1868—although many warriors owing no allegiance to Red Cloud were involved in harassing the forts, the victory was attributed to Red Cloud and the episode became known as Red Cloud's War.

The victory, of course, was pyrrhic—the slackening on the part of the U.S. military was only temporary. Within a decade of the closing of those forts, Custer was dead, Spotted Tail was dead, Crazy Horse was dead, Sitting Bull was in Canada, Buffalo Bill had had his famous "duel" with Yellow Hair, and except for a few stubborn Apaches in the rocks of Arizona and New Mexico, the contest for the Western lands was over. A decade after Custer lost his last command, Geronimo and his eighteen warriors came in. The great contest was over, though paranoia about Indian intentions and capabilities was not quick to subside. Out of just such paranoia came the more or less meaningless flare-up in 1890, at Wounded Knee. Again for reasons of paranoia—administrative this time—the by then world-famous Buffalo Bill Cody was prevented from meeting his old star, Sitting Bull, soon to be killed by native policemen.

Much later Cody made a movie about Wounded Knee, but few came to see it.

11

HELEN CODY WETMORE, Cody's younger sister, titled her rose-colored biography of her brother *The Last of the Great Scouts*. Was Cody a great scout, and if so, what does that mean?

Again, a little background might help. One of the most ineffectual military campaigns mounted in the post–Civil War West was that under the command of General Winfield Scott Hancock, which lumbered off into the central plains in 1867, spinning off, as it went, many smaller commands, some of which promptly got lost. Skeptics might argue that General Hancock himself was lost for much of this campaign. He was, however, the overall commander. Wherever he happened to find himself became true north, in a sense.

Why this large, unwieldy force thought it could catch up with and punish small, highly mobile groups of Native American horsemen is one of those military mysteries that can never be explained. Sherman, realist in military matters, can hardly have placed much faith in this expedition. Sheridan, a major participant, was often vexed by the difficulty of engaging the enemy in numbers that might have made the whole thing cost effective. General Hancock and many of his semidetached commands mostly floundered around to no purpose, trying to sift through the ever-shifting mass of rumor in hopes of locating a grain or two of usable intelligence that might eventually lead them to an Indian.

Here, for example, is an indication of the use Sheridan was able to make of Cody, upon receiving the unwelcome news that the Comanches and the Kiowa were on the warpath, information that needed to be conveyed to central command, or at least *some* command, as quickly as possible:

> This intelligence required that certain orders should be carried to Fort Dodge, ninety-five miles south of Hays. This too being a particularly dangerous route—several couriers having been killed on it—it was impossible to get one of the various "Petes," "Jacks," or "Jims" hanging around Hays City to take any communication. Cody learning of the strait I was in, manfully came to the rescue and proposed to make the trip to Dodge, though he had just finished his long and perilous ride from Larned. I gratefully accepted his offer, and after four or five hours rest he mounted a fresh horse and hastened on his journey, halting but once to rest on the way, and then only for an hour, the stop being made at Coon Creek, where he got another mount from a troop of cavalry. At Dodge he took six hours sleep and then continued on to his own post—Fort Larned—with more dispatches. After resting for twelve hours at Larned, he was again in the saddle with tidings for me at Fort Hays, General Hazen sending him this time, with word that the villagers had fled to the south of the Arkansas. Thus, in all, Cody rode about 350 miles in less than sixty hours, and such an exhibition of endurance and courage was more than enough to convince me that his services would be extremely valuable in the campaign, so I retained him at Fort Hays until the battalion of the Fifth Cavalry arrived and then made him chief of scouts of that regiment.

Don Russell, a careful map reader, corrected General Sheridan's arithmetic, concluding that Cody only rode 290 miles on this particular circuit, not 350, but it still works out to an average of 116 miles a day, no mean pace, and a pace maintained through country where he might have encountered hostile Indians at any time.

General Eugene Carr was also impressed with Cody's daring,

and with his ability to cover country. He called Cody the "best white
trailer" he had ever worked with. General Carr took over the Fifth
Cavalry during this campaign and used Cody often.

Of course Cody, as courier, was merely doing the job he had
been doing since the age of eleven. He had by this time had plenty of
training, and was thoroughly familiar with the country he was crossing. He seems to have had an excellent inner compass and was apparently never lost, a characteristic he shared with the great Texas
cattleman Charles Goodnight, a plainsman also noted for his ability
to chew up ground. And yet General Sheridan was surely right to applaud Cody, for he *was* taking very substantial risks. At least five
times in the autobiography he finds himself in a race for his life,
races that, as I have said, he only narrowly won. Some Kiowa under
the important chief Satanta were once after him nip and tuck, one
Kiowa coming so close that Cody was forced to shoot the horse out
from under him.

One of the "authentic" aspects of Cody's life as a scout was his
often repeated decision to aim for the horse rather than the rider—
the horse obviously made a considerably bigger target. Indeed, students who don't think Cody actually killed Yellow Hair agree that he
did shoot his horse out from under him, making him much more
killable.

Cody, as a performer, often loped around one arena or another,
shooting glass balls with a smoothbore rifle whose cartridges were
filled with birdshot, an easy enough thing for a seasoned marksman to
do. As a hunter Cody killed many buffalo from horseback, but in most
cases he was within a few feet of his victim—he merely had to point
and pull the trigger. When questioned about his Indian fighting he was
frank and modest about the problems of shooting from horseback
while traveling fast. When racing horsemen shot at one another, he admitted, the normal result was that nobody hit anything.

Don Russell and others have pointed out that during the wasteful
1867–1868 plains campaign scouts were hired to *find* Indians, not
fight them—the army's one purpose was to fight them. Sometimes
Cody could locate Indians but he readily acknowledged that Native

American scouts were far better trackers than he ever became. It was the Pawnee scouts working with Major Frank North who found Tall Bull's camp, in the Battle of Summit Springs.

In general, all across the West and Southwest, Native American scouts were usually called in when there was serious tracking to do—in some cases they did serious fighting, too. General Crook's Crow and Shoshoni scouts fought heroically at the Battle of the Rosebud. These scouts, witnesses thought, kept that battle a narrow defeat for Crook, rather than an absolute rout. In the Southwest particularly the Apache scouts were invaluable. Without them Geronimo might still be out.

Strategically the 1867–1868 campaign amounted to very little. General Hancock finally turned his immense command around and lumbered home. Custer's attack on the Washita was the one major battle of the campaign, and it was ill-directed.

I will look a little later at the Battle of Summit Springs, which was not really a major engagement. It's of interest here because it was the first occasion when Cody claimed a kill he probably hadn't made—the same was to occur, under equally debatable circumstances, in the conflict with Yellow Hair.

Sheridan and Carr were, however, right to praise Cody for his willingness to take big risks in order to move (dubious) intelligence from one fort to another. He deserved their praise and earned his $100 bonus. Being a scout and courier happened to be the only military work Cody could perform creditably. As a courier, however dangerous the country, he was once again on his own, enjoying the real if dangerous freedom of the plainsman. He was not afraid to stake his life on his horsemanship, either.

In national terms he may not really have been a *great* scout. He could not claim to have traveled the great reach of territory that Kit Carson, Jedediah Smith (dead before Cody was born), or the Delaware scout Black Beaver all mastered. But he was a better horseman than any of the above—it is entirely fitting that in the poster art created for his shows he is nearly always on horseback. It was on horseback that he looked most like himself—as I have said elsewhere, it is hard to overestimate how far a man can go in America if he looks good on a horse.

77

He seems never to have lost his skill with horses. Near the end of his life a show horse reared and fell over backwards with him. This is a much dreaded occurrence that has killed many cowboys and not a few rodeo hands. (Such a death occurs in the second volume of my *Lonesome Dove* tetralogy.) But Cody eluded the falling horse, at the cost of a slight injury to his leg. He was still quick enough and horse-savvy enough to mostly get out of the way.

It might be argued, against Helen Cody Wetmore, that her brother William was not quite the last of the great scouts—in that running one would have to at least mention Lonesome Charley Reynolds, the scout Custer sent ninety miles through *very* hostile country to announce that the general had discovered gold in the Black Hills—a place neither general nor scout was supposed to be. Though his horse died and his tongue swelled so from thirst that he couldn't close his mouth, Lonesome Charley made it through to Fort Laramie.

It was General Custer's message about the Black Hills gold that once more, and for the last time, set the high plains ablaze.

12

For at least a decade after the Civil War it seemed that every military man west of the Mississippi was either actively pursuing Indians with the intent to kill them or else sitting under a tent painfully hacking out treaties with them, most of which would be broken within weeks, if not sooner.

The writer Alex Shoumatoff has estimated that the U.S. government has broken something like 474 treaties with the native peoples, plenty of which were made and broken during the sixties and seventies of the nineteenth century.

These powwows and treaty-making sessions seem to have frustrated everyone who took part in them, one reason being the language difficulties involved. (Exactly the same difficulties are plaguing coalition soldiers right now in Iraq. Reliable translators from Arabic are proving hard to find.) Few Native American leaders spoke much English, and even fewer of the military negotiators spoke more than a few words of any native language, the consequence being that after a powwow both sides went home without really understanding what they had agreed to. And in any case the government abided by these treaties only to the extent that was convenient.

One especially inconvenient treaty was the one made at the end of the 1860s, giving the Sioux peoples their holy Black Hills in perpetuity, with no whites allowed to be within the sacred area.

General Custer's discovery of gold in these same Black Hills caused one of the most abrupt about-faces in the shameful history of our treaty making and breaking. Perpetuity turned out to be less than five years, after which the greedy Americans tried to buy the land they had so recently surrendered.

General Crook, no fool, advised the Indians to take the money, since nothing could be more obvious than that the whites would anyway soon be taking the land.

The most dramatic years of plains warfare were from 1867 to 1877, that is, from the launching of the Hancock expedition to the surrender of Crazy Horse in May of 1877. Many treaties were made during this decade, mainly because the army did not yet have the manpower to simply overrun the Indians.

Buffalo Bill Cody was in the neighborhood of some of these powwows but the solemnities of oratory and negotiation seem to have held little appeal for him, though later he would do a fair amount of powwowing when he began to hire Indians for his Wild West shows.

Without anyone at first exactly being aware of it, show business began to slyly extend itself out into prairie life. In the beginning this took the form of scouts with colorful monikers, names that might look good on posters or marquees. Besides the guide-turned-showman Texas Jack Omohundro, there were at least two other Texas Jacks, one of whom was hung in Oklahoma for a variety of crimes. There was also a multiplicity of California Joes and, of course, a veritable plethora of Buffalo Bills.

In 1911 or thereabouts Cody was taken to task by a retired hunter named William Mathewson, who insisted that he was the first to be called Buffalo Bill, and that Cody knew it. Cody probably didn't know it but he cheerfully agreed that he had not been the first hunter to be called Buffalo Bill. Later he met Mathewson, saw that he was down on his luck, helped him recover a cherished rifle he had been forced to sell, and quietly settled some of his debts. He and Will Mathewson became good friends.

This was the Cody people loved—many similar stories exist.

One of the first organized showbiz buffalo hunts seems to have occurred somewhere east of Sheridan, Kansas. The hunt featured two Buffalo Bills, Cody and a part-Cheyenne hunter named William

Comstock, who occasionally found himself on the wrong side of the law.

Some doubt that this first show hunt ever took place; the best evidence seems to be archaeological, in the form of a dump containing many beer and champagne bottles. The biographer Courtney Ryley Cooper had a poster advertising the contest, but its authenticity is questionable. A special train holding one hundred spectators chugged out from St. Louis to watch the shooting. Cody claimed to have shot sixty-nine buffalo that day, to Comstock's forty-six. As an additional nicety, which anticipated the showman that he soon would be, Cody managed to kill the final buffalo of the day right in front of the ladies, some of whom may have fainted. Louisa Cody says that the hunt did happen.

Soon after this event or nonevent Cody was part of a group sent to round up deserters from General Hancock's big force. Some of the deserters may simply have been soldiers who got hopelessly lost. Theodore David, a reporter for *Harper's Weekly*, happened to be along on this strange excursion, and it was Wild Bill Hickok, not Buffalo Bill Cody, whose dandyism most stirred the reporter's ire:

> . . . in his usual array Wild Bill could have gained unquestioned admittance to the floor of most fancy dress balls of metropolitan cities. When we ordinary mortals were hustling for a clean pair of socks, as prospective limit of change in wearing apparel, I have seen Wild Bill appear in an immaculate boiled shirt, with collar and cuffs to match—a sleeveless Zouave jacket of startling scarlet, slashed with black velvet . . . the French calfskin . . . boots fitted admirably and were polished as if the individual wearing them had recently vacated an Italian's throne on a sidestreet near Broadway . . . the long wavey hair that fell in masses from a convenient sombrero, was glossy from a recent anointment of some heavily perfumed mixture.

Bill Cody probably read that description of his old friend and learned from it. As much as Hickok he wanted to impress and usually managed to display a casual elegance that, on closer inspection, may not have been so casual—but he never quite slipped over to full dandyism, in the manner of his friend. The reason he didn't was because he had still to sell himself as a workingman of the West, a humble scout, a man who might have to take a hand and drive a stagecoach at any time.

Wild Bill Hickok may have learned from Cody too. One of his bolder experiments, before he made that fatal trip to Deadwood, was to organize that buffalo shoot at Niagara Falls.

13

BEFORE plunging into the dense ambiguities of Cody's two most controversial Indian fights—the Battle of Summit Springs and the "duel" with Yellow Hair—it might be well to finish with the white-hunter phase of Buffalo Bill Cody's career. There is also one lesser Indian fight that is worth mentioning because of the strong element of the theatrical that is apt to be present in any anecdote in which Bill Cody actually claims to have killed an Indian.

In this case, while in pursuit of horse thieves, Cody claims to have killed two Indians with one shot—not impossible, since the two were fleeing on the same horse. This action occurred near the North Platte. Cody then claims that he took the two Indians' warbonnets and gave them to the daughters of General Augur. Warbonnets on men, so surprised that they had to flee on the same horse? Warbonnets, when the Indians were merely out to steal horses? Of course, assuming they had their warbonnets with them, Cody *could* have scavenged them from the raiders' camp.

I raise the question because this is by no means the last time warbonnets occur in Cody's narrative. From here on out virtually every Indian he pursues or claims to have killed is equipped with a warbonnet—though it is usually thought that warbonnets, expensive to produce, might mostly be reserved for formal or ceremonial occasions, such as powwows or ritual dances.

We will keep our eye on warbonnets as we proceed through the final years of Cody's career as a scout.

83

Later, it seems, there was disagreement as to which general should reap the glory for this chase with horse thieves. What comes clear in the debate is that some military had become acutely jealous of William F. Cody, who was now widely thought of as Sheridan's pet.

With the exception of the grand duke Alexis, most of the hunt organizing Cody did was for rich and influential men who happened to be cronies of Phil Sheridan. James Gordon Bennett of the *New York Herald* was among them, as well as at least two members of the prominent Jerome family, the family which produced the famous Jenny Jerome, Winston Churchill's mother. Bennett was almost as quick as Buntline to recognize Cody's high marketability—it was not long before Cody was summoned to New York, where he was feted by the famous editor and others.

Meanwhile more than one train carload of bankers, financiers, and magnates of various stripes came to Kansas to be stimulated for a day or two while eating buffalo ribs, drinking a lot of champagne, and occasionally shooting off guns.

It might be noted that these mostly half-assed American sportsmen had been preceded on the teeming hunting grounds of the West by several serious hunters from Europe—in particular, from England. The Scotsman William Drummond Stewart hoped to start a large game park in Scotland filled with Western animals. Even before Stewart, Prince Maximilian zu Wied-Neuwied had been up the Missouri, hunting for science rather than for sport. Drummond Stewart took the artist Alfred Jacob Miller with him; the prince of Wied had taken Karl Bodmer; and the enterprising George Catlin took himself: he headed upriver in 1832 on the first steamboat that went. It's because of Miller that we know what the mountain men looked like, while both Catlin and Bodmer left us vivid portraits of many members of the Missouri River tribes in their years of glory, before smallpox and other white man's diseases began to decimate them.

The earl of Dunraven always wanted to establish a large game park, but his was to be in America, not England. He acquired some sixty thousand acres of Colorado, in the Estes Park region, for this purpose, but before the game could be protected the Indians had to agree to stop eating it—the earl's diplomacy was not equal to this task.

Cody himself guided Sir John Watts Garland, an Englishman who liked hunting so much that he established a line of hunting camps, complete with dogs and keepers, to which he returned every year to refresh himself with a little shooting. Sir John seemed less interested in buffalo than in elk, an animal that took some careful stalking.

Some of the English were the opposite of conservationists: they came for slaughter and more slaughter. A fittingly named Englishman, St. George Gore, is said to have killed at least twenty-five hundred buffalo, to the disgust of Jim Bridger and others.

Cody also briefly guided the famous pioneering paleontologist Othniel Charles Marsh, who ventured out often from his citadel at Yale.

The duck hunt recently enjoyed by Vice President Cheney and Supreme Court Justice Antonin Scalia is exactly the sort of well-planned excursion that Cody was good at managing. Shouldn't busy and prominent men be allowed to shoot guns and drink whiskey in their own company now and then?

As Don Russell points out, royals of any stamp were rare in America in the nineteenth century. When one promised to show up—even if the royal was only a third son, as was the case with the grand duke Alexis, not exactly the sharpest knife in the Romanov drawer—big attention needed to be paid, and America was eager to pay it. The Russian royal fleet took a long time getting across the pond, but eventually, in the fall of 1871, it showed up.

Cody was at this time still chief of scouts of the Fifth Cavalry, which was about to depart for Arizona to deal with the elusive and troublesome Apaches; but a letter from General Sheridan arrived just in time to keep Cody from leaving. He was to find buffalo for the grand duke—a promising hunting site some forty miles west of Fort McPherson was soon selected, and what came to be called Camp Alexis was hastily constructed.

Cody was probably pleased with being awarded this plum, but

he may have been less pleased when he found out that Alexis was particularly eager to see some wild Indians while he was on this hunt.

The royal hunt was to take place early in 1872, a time when it would not have been hard to find plenty of wild Indians—the catch was that they might just want to behave like what they were, *wild* Indians. The war for the great plains was still very much a going thing: Fetterman and his eighty men had been wiped out only a few years before the grand duke's visit, and one of the duke's hunting partners, George Armstrong Custer, would be wiped out a few years after their hunt. Every army officer knew that if invited to do a war dance, the young braves might forget that they were actors and do some fine scalping while they had the chance.

Since nobody wanted to say no to a grand duke, a chief had to be chosen and asked if he and some of his warriors would mind providing some entertainment for this important person from across the seas.

The military powers decided on Spotted Tail, the more or less cooperative leader of the Brulé Sioux. Spotted Tail had been to Washington and was well aware of how the cookie was likely to crumble, where his people were concerned. He was at the time hunting buffalo on the Republican River, where Cody, traveling alone, found him and persuaded him to oblige General Sheridan, if it wouldn't be too much trouble.

It wasn't too much trouble. Spotted Tail (who was eventually killed by one of his own people) showed up right on time and put on a splendid show—very probably it was this event that convinced Cody it would not be impossible to use Indians in the Wild West shows. The war dance was most effective and a particularly skilled hunter named Two Lances much pleased the grand duke by shooting an arrow completely through a running buffalo.

General Custer, as was his wont, flirted with one of Spotted Tail's comely daughters, neither the first nor the last flirtation Custer pursued with good-looking native women.

Matthew Brady, pioneering photojournalist, showed up and took everybody's picture.

The grand duke Alexis, a rather stolid youth, had a passionate interest in firearms but an almost total absence of skill when it came to using them. Alexis had visited the Smith & Wesson factory on his way west—he was eager to drop a buffalo with one of his new pistols and proceeded to empty two six-shooters at a buffalo standing some twenty feet away; the twelve bullets went somewhere, but the buffalo was unfazed.

Reluctantly the grand duke gave up the revolver but allowed Cody to loan him his famous buffalo rifle, Lucretia Borgia (a breech-loading Springfield), as well as his best buffalo horse, Buckskin Joe, which swiftly carried the grand duke to within a yard or two of a buffalo. Lucretia Borgia spoke and the buffalo fell over, much to the relief of everyone involved. Champagne flowed, as it was to do later in the day when the grand duke brought down a buffalo cow. On the way back to camp Cody treated the grand duke to a stagecoach ride, another proto-act which later proved popular in London, where Cody once got four kings into the Deadwood stage.

The grand duke gave Cody a fur coat and some cuff links—but the main thing he gave him was something to think about. The hunt was just one more rich man's frolic, but the fact that the Indians had agreed to provide entertainment, and *had* provided entertainment, was, at the time, a singular thing. Cody may not have immediately connected it with his own future, but he didn't forget it, either. Within a decade's time some of the Indians who had entertained the grand duke Alexis found that they had nothing better to do than to let Pahaska put them in a show.

Cody himself, once the grand duke departed, found that his management of this tame hunt reaped a huge amount of publicity, all of it favorable to himself. With the Fifth Cavalry gone west there was not much for him to do, so he accepted James Gordon Bennett's invitation and went to New York, after which visit—though he continued to go back to the plains—his life was never to be quite the same.

14

I T is perhaps best to step back a year from these high-profile hunts to the somewhat inconclusive prairie campaigns of 1869–1870, spin-offs to General Hancock's expensive but largely futile expedition. Cody was still chief of scouts of the Fifth Cavalry, but at the reduced pay of $75 a month; he was briefly stationed at Fort Lyon in eastern Colorado. It was to Fort Lyon that Black Kettle carried his wounded wife after the Sand Creek Massacre. There were plenty of Indians to fight—during one brief skirmish Cody received one of his very rare wounds: his hat was shot off and his scalp creased, producing a heavy blood flow. Cody kept on fighting, a fact that impressed General Carr so much that he awarded him a bonus of $100.

The so-called Battle of Summit Springs, in which the Cheyenne leader Tall Bull and a number of his dog soldiers were apparently killed, was perhaps the most confusing of Cody's many confusing fracasses. As many as twenty versions of this conflict exist, half of those emanating, over a period of some sixty years, from one informant—Luther North, brother of Major Frank North, who may or may not have killed Tall Bull himself. At the time of the battle Frank North was the organizer and leader of a group of Pawnee scouts. (Later Frank North was to partner with Cody, both in the cattle business and the Wild West shows.)

The confusions produced by this battle result from the fact that the trail along which the cavalry was pursuing the main band of Cheyenne split at some point. Cody and some of the troop proceeded along what seemed to be the main trail and eventually arrived at the

Cheyennes' main camp, while Frank North, his brother, and some of the Pawnee scouts followed a smaller trail and eventually encountered a small force of Indians in a ravine. One of these Indians may have been Tall Bull. Frank North tricked this Indian into showing his head, at which moment he shot him. Only later, after talking with the Pawnee scouts, did he conclude that the dead Indian was Tall Bull.

Cody's version, appearing in various editions of his autobiography, is at first glance simpler. As battle raged in the large village Cody saw an Indian on a magnificent bay horse; he promptly shot the Indian and claimed the horse, which later proved the swiftest in all Nebraska, winning Cody many races. In Luther North's version, or one of them, this splendid horse is cream-colored; in even later versions the horse becomes a gray. One version mentions that the horse had received a stab wound.

Then, in the Cody version, the dead Indian's wife begins to wail and he learns that he has killed her husband, Tall Bull. In the course of the battle this same woman had herself dispatched one of the two white captives the troop had been hoping to rescue. The victim was a Mrs. Alderdice, brained with a tomahawk and buried at the scene. The other captive, a Mrs. Weichel, though wounded, survived the battle and married the hospital orderly who tended her at Fort Sedgwick.

Cody's mandate, on this adventure, was to find the Indians, and with the help of the able Pawnee scouts, he did find them. Whether he had any idea who Tall Bull was is not clear: he shot an Indian because he wanted his horse—for the time being the matter of Tall Bull did not interest him.

Luther North, however, continued to be mildly obsessed with the killing of Tall Bull until at least 1929, when he issued the last of his nearly innumerable versions. He became obsessed with the need to correct the record and establish that his own brother, Frank North, had killed this important chief.

At first Frank North himself was no more invested than Cody in the killing of Tall Bull. He had tricked an Indian who was hiding in a ravine. The Indian fell dead. North, like Cody, may not have considered Tall Bull to be particularly important.

When asked by his importunate brother Luther why he didn't correct the record, Frank North merely pointed out that Cody was in show business whereas he wasn't.

Much later, perhaps because his brother wouldn't let the matter fade, Frank North did develop a bias against Cody over the matter of Tall Bull. George Bird Grinnell, author of *The Fighting Cheyenne*, accepted Luther North's version, or one of them, and included it in his book. But Frank North's annoyance was temporary—for the rest of his life he worked with Cody amiably enough.

In Cody's many versions of the conflict, the battle itself tends to slide around. At first Cody claimed he shot Tall Bull off the handsome bay from a distance of about thirty feet; this grew, in time, to "fully four hundred yards," and again, a warbonnet finds its way into the story. It seems that in Cody's memory of the old West the major Indians were as clothes conscious as he was himself. They all seemed to wear their warbonnets at all times, even at breakfast.*

The Tall Bull business became even more confusing when one of the many reprints of Cody's book was in press. The copy the printer was working from proved to be missing several pages—unfortunately the pages had to do with the Battle of Summit Springs. Cody was in England when this problem was discovered. All the printer had to go on was an illustration from an earlier edition of the book. The illustration was called *The Killing of Tall Bull*. On his own initiative the printer scribbled in his version of what the Battle of Summit Springs must have been like. In his version the body count rises from fifty-two (itself probably an exaggeration) to six hundred. The book this version appears in is called *The Story of the Wild West*. Cody had little interest in reading about these old battles and was probably unaware of the vastly inflated body count. Whether he killed Tall Bull or not never greatly interested him. His primary job had been to find the Indians, and he found them, acquiring, as a bonus, an excellent racehorse (bay, cream-colored, or gray as it may be). Also he had helped free one of the two female captives. Most scholars agree that Tall Bull was killed that day, but who killed him will probably remain in dispute.

* The artist Charles Schreyvogel has a painting called *The Summit Spring's Rescue 1869* in which Cody is shown shooting an Indian warrior who killed Mrs. Alderdice. Paul Andrew Hutton, in his excellent study *Phil Sheridan and His Army*, says that Cody took no part in the rescue of the captives but believes that he did kill Tall Bull.

15

BILL CODY'S interests were eclectic. He was able to appreciate many things, among them the city of New York, about which he was soon as enthusiastic as he had been about the cool air and large freedoms of the prairies. He was a handsome addition to the great metropolitan scene—in no time he was receiving so many invitations that he got mixed up and missed an important dinner hosted by James Gordon Bennett.

One person he got little help from on this visit was Ned Buntline, who had troubles of his own, chief among them bigamy. Buntline was living with a fourth wife, while remaining imperfectly divorced from the first three, a costly situation in more ways than one.

The only thing Buffalo Bill didn't like on this visit to New York was his own performance in *Buffalo Bill: King of the Border Men*, a role he found so terrifying that the few words he managed to mumble could not even be heard by the orchestra leader, a few feet away. Fortunately General Sheridan soon interrupted this period of internal stage fright; Cody was summoned back to Fort McPherson so abruptly that he forgot his trunk and was forced to plunge right into an Indian fight while still in evening dress—in my view an unlikely story, since there were not a few haberdasheries between New York City and Fort McPherson, in Nebraska.

According to Cody the reason the general wanted him back in such a hurry was an outbreak of horse thieves. Cody claims that he rode right up beside an Indian on a stolen horse and shot him in the head, a big deviation from his usual practice of aiming for the horse and not the man.

Not much that Cody said about this particular period, when he was trying to learn to lead a double life, now on the plains and now on the stage, can be taken literally. Much telescoping and probably much invention was involved. Cody thought the skirmish in which he shot the Indian in the head to be of little account, but, bizarrely, he got the Congressional Medal of Honor for it anyway, although the award was rescinded in 1916 since Cody had apparently been a civilian at the time of this fight.

Meanwhile, back in North Platte, Lulu was delivered of Orra Maude, their third child. The earl of Dunraven asked Cody to guide him on a hunt but Cody turned this attractive chore over to Texas Jack Omohundro, with whom he often worked.

Cody then ran for the state legislature and was elected, but charges of hanky-panky were raised and he never took his disputed seat. Instead, once Texas Jack was free the two of them went to Chicago and were soon on the stage. Cody even began to lose his stage fright—for the next ten years Cody would be back and forth between prairie and stage. Ned Buntline escaped all four of his wives and showed up in Chicago, where he first distinguished himself by taking part in an anti-German riot. Though he scribbled off many terrible plays both Cody and Omohundro kept him at arm's length. Wild Bill Hickok tried the stage with Cody a few times but the stage lighting bothered his weak eyes; the same poor eyesight caused him to fire his blank bullets too close to the bare legs of the stage Indians, resulting in painful powder burns. It seems to me, contra Evan Connell, that Hickok, rather than Cody, was the real mixture of thespian and assassin. Hickok's myopia suggests that in real fights his victims must have stood very close to hand. This was clearly the case in his famous fight with the McCandles brothers. One thing Cody and Hickok had in common was that their public images soon eclipsed anything resembling reality. They became legends in their own time, which was lucky in the case of the rising young showman Bill Cody, but was not so lucky in the case of James Butler Hickok.

16

T H E death, in June of 1876, of General George Armstrong Custer and some 250 men of the famed Seventh Cavalry was a shock to the nation comparable in some ways to Pearl Harbor or 9/11. The scale may have been much smaller but the shock was still tremendous; like 9/11 the massacre at the Little Bighorn was completely unexpected. In fact, in his report for 1875, the commissioner for Indian Affairs stated that it was no longer probable that even five hundred belligerent warriors could ever again be mustered for a fight.

Obviously military intelligence was as imperfect in 1875 as it is today, since the very next summer an estimated ten thousand Indians assembled near the Little Bighorn, and, as Custer was shortly to discover, they were quite belligerent.

Once the shock had been absorbed by a confused nation, there arose, as was inevitable, a cry for punishment, but punishment was never to be conclusively administered because the ten thousand hostile tribespeople simply melted away into the prairies and the hills. The figure mentioned by the commissioner in his 1875 Report—five hundred—would now, indeed, have been hard to locate.

Cody had been fulfilling theatrical obligations in the East; he continued to fulfill them even though griefstricken by the death of his son, Kit Carson Cody. He ended his run with a benefit performance in Wilmington, Delaware, about two weeks before the Custer massacre and was already on his way west when the massacre occurred. Apparently the army intended to send Cody to scout for General George Crook, who was about to fight the taxing battle of the Rosebud, a week before the Little Bighorn.

Cody didn't immediately make it to the Rosebud, although Crook could certainly have used him. Instead Cody joined his old company, the Fifth Cavalry, then commanded by General Merritt— the Fifth was generally charged with keeping peace at the populous Red Cloud agency, the one place where five hundred ready-and-willing warriors might have been found. The Red Cloud agency was northeast of Fort Laramie, across the Platte from Fort Robinson, where Crazy Horse would eventually be killed. By the time Cody reached his company it was the middle of July, about two weeks after the massacre.

Frightened, fearful of reprisals, lots of Indians did leave the Red Cloud agency during this confusing period, and neither General Merritt nor anyone else knew quite what to do about them.

On the night of July 16, the Fifth Cavalry camped near Hat Creek, sometimes called Warbonnet Creek, just northwest of the Red Cloud agency. On the morning of the seventeenth, Cody was out at dawn and he soon noted signs of restlessness in the big Cheyenne camp nearby. He approached a young signalman, Chris Madsen, and told him to signal General Merritt that the Cheyenne seemed to be preparing to move.

In fact a portion of the big Cheyenne party split off, in the hopes of intercepting two military messengers who were coming toward General Merritt's camp, unaware of how much trouble they were about to find themselves in. Cody and a number of cavalrymen hurried to cut off the Cheyenne who were trying to cut off the messengers. Cody seems to have been dressed in a black velvet suit at the time, though upon reaching the bivouac he had been wearing immaculate white buckskins.

Here is Cody's version—many times repeated and reenacted but not really embellished—of his "duel" with Wey-o-hei, or Yellow Hair (called Yellow Hand by Cody and almost everyone else):

We were about half a mile from General Merritt, and the Indians whom we were chasing suddenly turned on us, and another lively skirmish took place. One of the Indians, who was handsomely decorated with all the ornaments usually worn by a war chief when engaged in a fight, sang out to me in his own tongue: I know you, Pa-he-haska; if you want to fight come ahead and fight me.

The chief was riding his horse back and forth in front of his men, as if to banter me, and I concluded to accept the challenge. I galloped toward him for about fifty yards and he advanced to me about fifty yards, the same distance, both of us riding at full speed, and when we were only about thirty yards apart, I raised my rifle and fired; his horse fell to the ground, having been killed by my bullet.

At almost the same instant my own horse went down, he having stepped into a hole. The fall did not hurt me much and I instantly sprang to my feet. The Indian had also recovered himself, and we were both on foot, not twenty yards apart. We fired at each other simultaneously. My usual luck did not desert me, for his bullet missed me while mine struck him in the breast. He reeled and fell, but before he had fairly touched the ground I was upon him, knife in hand, and had driven the keen-edged weapon to the hilt in his heart. Jerking his warbonnet off, I scientifically scalped him in about five seconds . . .

The whole affair from beginning to end occupied but very little time.

As the soldiers came up I swung the Indian chieftain's top knot and bonnet into the air and shouted: the first scalp for Custer!

Some of the other Cheyenne, seeing that Cody was alone, charged down at him, but the quick-thinking General Merritt already had reinforcements on the way, and anyhow, Cody had some cavalry with him when he set out to cut off the Cheyenne.

The novelist, mountaineer, military man, and longtime friend of Henry Adams, Clarence King, happened to be with the Fifth Cavalry that morning and was deeply impressed—intoxicated, even—with the glamour of the fighting Cheyenne. He may also have been liter-

ally intoxicated, which could have caused his enthusiasm for native
color to rise to a fever pitch:

> Savage warfare was never more beautiful than in you. On
> you come, your swift, agile ponies swinging down the
> winding ravine, the rising sun shining on your trailing
> warbonnets, on silver armlets, necklace, gorget; on bril-
> liant painted shield and beaded leggin; on naked body and
> fearless face, stained most vivid vermilion. On you come,
> lance and rifle, pennon and feather glistening in the rare
> morning light, swaying in the wild grace of your peerless
> horsemanship; nearer, till I mark the very ornament on
> your leader's shield.

Signalman Madsen probably had the best view of the Cody and
Wey-o-hei fight, a view rather less Knights of the Round Table than
Cody's own:

> Cody was riding a little in advance of his party and one of
> the Indians was preceding his group. I was standing on
> the butte where I had been stationed. It was some distance
> from the place where they met but I had an unobstructed
> view of all that happened. Through the powerful telescope
> furnished by the Signal Department the men did not ap-
> pear to be more than 50 feet from me. From the manner
> in which both parties acted it was certain that both were
> surprised. Cody and the leading Indians appeared to be
> the only ones who did not become excited. The instant
> they were face to face their guns fired. It seemed almost
> like one shot. There was no conversation, no preliminary
> agreement as has been stated in some novels written by
> romantic scribes.
>
> They met by accident and fired the minute they faced
> each other. Cody's bullet went through the Indian's leg and
> killed his pinto pony. The Indian's bullet went wild. Cody's
> horse stepped in a prairie dog hole and stumbled but was
> up in a moment. Cody jumped clear of his mount. Kneel-

ing, he took deliberate aim and fired the second shot. An instant before Cody fired the Indian fired at him but missed. Cody's bullet went through the Indian's head and ended the battle. Cody went over to the fallen warrior Indian and neatly removed his scalp while the other soldiers gave chase to the Indian's companions. There is no doubt about it, Buffalo Bill scalped this Indian who, it turned out, was a Cheyenne sub-chief called Yellow Hair.

Signalman Madsen, unlike Cody and everybody else, actually got Yellow Hair's name right. The confident Madsen later took the trouble to poke no less than twenty-eight holes in Clarence King's account of the skirmish. Yet another signalman, Sergeant John Powers, who was riding with a small wagon train at the time, further deromanticized Cody's "duel" with Yellow Hair in a report which appeared in the *Ellis County Star,* a paper which thoroughly scooped both the *New York Herald* and the *Chicago Times* on this occasion. Here is Sergeant Powers's version:

> Three or four Indians started out on a run to cut off the dispatch bearers. They had not seen the command and were not aware that we were in the vicinity; but Bill Cody and his scouts were watching them . . . He then got around the Indians and when he felt sure of the couriers Cody raised up behind a little hill and shot the pony of one of the redskins. Then starting after his victim he soon had him killed and his scalp off . . .
> The Indian killed by Buffalo Bill proved to be Yellow Hand, sub–war chief of the Southern Cheyenne.

The *New York Herald* asked Cody for a report on the incident and Cody persuaded King to file one—it was this account that Signalman Madsen poked twenty-eight holes in. When Clarence King was shown the clipping some fifty years later he disclaimed it.

Cody himself wrote Lulu the day after the fight, enclosing Yellow Hair's scalp, warbonnet, whip, and guns. The Codys were then living in Buffalo, and Cody wanted these spoils of war exhibited in a local department store, to help advertise a Western melodrama he was committed to. These have long since migrated to the Cody museum in Cody, Wyoming. The "duel" aspects of the encounter have since grown in the telling, chiefly through elaborations in Cody's sister's books.

As the years passed several people challenged Cody's claim to have killed Yellow Hair. One claim that has at least vague plausibility was made by the ubiquitous scout Baptiste "Little Bat" Garnier, a well-traveled plainsman who at one time was a friend of Crazy Horse. Little Bat was present that day but didn't claim the kill himself; it was claimed for him by his son, Johnny Bat, who said that Cody had actually been challenged to a knife fight by Yellow Hair and was prepared to take up the challenge. Little Bat, being of the opinion that Cody would swiftly be cut to ribbons, got off his horse and shot the Indian.

A grislier variant of this claim surfaced in 1927—indeed, several of the wilder accounts did not appear until the late twenties, probably because by this time Cody had made a movie about his duel with Yellow Hair—it was called *Indian Wars*. The grisly version is that Little Bat had actually killed Yellow Hair a couple of days before at a buffalo wallow and had simply let him lie. Later, hearing that Cody wanted a scalp, Little Bat led Cody to the buffalo wallow and Cody then took the somewhat fragrant trophy—this strikes me as unlikely.

In 1929 Herbert Cody Blake, who sounds like a disgruntled relative, published an anti-Cody pamphlet called *Blake's Western Stories*, in which five soldiers claiming to be present that day all testify that Cody did *not* kill Yellow Hair. Blake's is a debunking polemic and the testimony came fifty-two years after the event.

Around this time (the twenties) several common soldiers showed up, all insisting that they had killed Yellow Hair. Most of these belated claimants do not appear in army registers; they seem to have just convinced themselves, after much brooding, that they probably killed the famous Indian.

Another report from the twenties mentions that Yellow Hair's wife showed up at headquarters and cut off a finger, to show her distress.

In fact Yellow Hair had *not* been a famous Indian—he became famous with his death. Both Madsen and Powers identify him as a subchief. He seems merely to have been an alert lookout who quickly saw a chance to cut off the two messengers.

The composer and diarist Ned Rorem remarks somewhere that all life is really *Rashomon*—a matter, that is, of individual point of view. Most of Bill Cody's encounters with Indians demonstrate this quality. Cody wrote his autobiography, three years after his "duel," to energize his theatrical career. Naturally he and his ghostwriter splashed in as much color as possible.

By his own account he and Yellow Hair were more than one hundred yards apart when the Cheyenne "sang out" his challenge. He would have had to sing it pretty loud for Cody to hear it—Cody, of course, did not speak Cheyenne nor Yellow Hair English. Besides, Yellow Hair knew that there was a large company of soldiers near at hand. It is extremely unlikely that he would have put himself in jeopardy to enjoy some kind of duel with Bill Cody, whom he may not even have recognized, despite the latter's velvet suit.

I see no reason to doubt the sober testimony of the two signalmen, Madsen and Powers; both had a good view and neither had any axe to grind. Some discrepancies usually pop up in battle reports. Cody shot Yellow Hair in the leg yet the bullet hit his horse in the head, killing him. Some say both men's first shot missed. The claim that Cody took advantage of a hill or rise to conceal himself makes sense. Cody had always been prudent. Yellow Hair may have slipped, for a time, into a shallow ravine. Each would have naturally used whatever topographical advantage they could find. That Cody, once unhorsed, went down on one knee and took deliberate aim is convincing—he often complained about the difficulty of making precise shots from moving horses. It was characteristic of him to shoot the horse first—he did this some half a dozen times. Certainly he was not fool enough to allow himself to be drawn into a knife fight, and of course he was aware that Yellow Hair had massive reinforcements at hand: the charging Cheyenne Clarence King was so impressed with.

Neither signalman mentions Cody stabbing the Indian—merely scalping him.

General Merritt was on top of the situation and sent Cody rapid backup.

Much later, when the regimental history was compiled, here's the summing up: "William F. Cody, the favorite scout of the regiment, was conspicuous in the affair of the morning, having killed in hand-to-hand conflict Yellow Hand, a prominent Cheyenne chief."

Cody informed Lulu that he had killed the Cheyenne in single-hand fight and mentioned that he would forward the warbonnet and the rest as soon as he reached Fort Laramie. He also said she would be reading about it in the papers.

The eight hundred Cheyenne, whatever they thought of the hand-to-hand conflict, allowed themselves to be conducted back to the Red Cloud agency, where they washed off their war paint and put away their warbonnets. Don Russell remarks that the Cheyenne were pretty impressed with Cody—probably because of the suit rather than the fight. Cody too was friendly. It was no doubt in the back of his mind that he might need some of these Indians someday.

The exploit made the *New York Herald* on July 23, 1876. It was perhaps the most newsworthy report to come out of the West for the duration of the rambling, rumbling military effort to punish the northern tribes for Custer's spectacular defeat.

An odd consequence of it was that Cody's sister Josephine married Big Bat Pourriere—he was called Big Bat to distinguish him from Little Bat Garnier.

On August 2 this death-filled summer claimed one more well-known star: Wild Bill Hickok was murdered in Deadwood while playing cards.

17

THE Fifth Cavalry did finally join up with General George Crook—the Gray Fox, to the Indians—and Cody became chief of scouts with the Bighorn and Yellowstone expeditions. Crook, notoriously, was a no-frills general. His cooking equipment consisted of a cup and a stick. In the cup he boiled his coffee; on the stick he cooked his bacon. His attire was of the plainest. The contrast with General Terry's large, beautifully equipped company became evident a little later, once the two armies joined up. Cody, no opponent of luxury, was nonetheless made a little uneasy by the cumbersome nature of Terry's equipage. It seemed unlikely they would catch the fleet Sioux or the equally fleet Cheyenne while traveling so heavy. General Crook probably thought the same, but he was polite to Terry, by all accounts a genial and likable man.

This top-heavy command was soon made even more top-heavy by the arrival of General Nelson A. Miles. Exactly what this massive force supposed it was doing is not entirely clear, although there is a huge literature that follows the various generals on an almost day-to-day basis. Mainly it was supposed to prevent the Indians who were responsible for the massacre from getting away, although it was of course clear to even the dullest military man that they had already gotten away.

Cody, as chief of scouts, loped around hither and thither but found no Indians. The conflict with Yellow Hair had occurred in the middle of July—by the middle of August Cody was tired of this aim-

101

less proceeding. In late August he resigned and headed downriver on the steamer *Yellowstone,* but he soon ran into his old partner Texas Jack Omohundro, who was headed upriver with dispatches for various and sundry. Since Cody was not particularly eager to get home to Lulu and the children, he decided to hang around with Texas Jack.

Then General Whistler and General Terry convinced themselves that the woods near the Yellowstone River were crawling with savages—this was mostly paranoia, but it meant that Cody's skills as a courier were once more, and for the last time, in demand. He made several dangerous rides, carrying various dispatches. Once, dozing in a ravine, he was nearly overrun by some thirty Indians who were chasing buffalo. They made several kills and butchered the animals on the spot, but did not discover Cody, who hid until nightfall and then made a wide swing around them.

For this last flurry of scouting Cody was paid $200, much the largest sum he had ever earned as a scout. Once he resigned for a second time, he took the steamer *Far West* as far as Bismarck, and then went home to Rochester by train.

Had he so chosen, Cody could have hung on one more year as a scout. In the winter of 1877 Ranald Mackenzie relentlessly pursued Dull Knife and his Cheyenne. Both Sitting Bull and Crazy Horse were still out; General Miles pursued them in a generally futile winter campaign. The Indians thought the whites must have gone crazy—no one with any sense fought in winter. Sitting Bull soon took his Hunkpapas to Canada. In May of 1877 Crazy Horse came in, with nine hundred people and two thousand horses. Not long afterward the Nez Perce fled Idaho and made their own race for Canada—they were stopped by General Miles just forty miles short of their goal. Chief Joseph vowed to fight no more forever and in fact was not given the chance. Except for the aberrant breakout at Pine Ridge in 1890, the Plains Indian wars were over.

The only remaining problem was Geronimo and a few of his Apache allies. General Crook tried a second time to straighten out Apache affairs. Crook seemed to like Cody, who was always deferential to generals, and probably would have hired him to locate the renegade Apaches, but Cody expressed no interest. Although he would eventually go to Arizona and build a big hotel at Mountain View, he did not want to follow the Gray Fox into the snakes and boulders of the distant, dusty Apacheria.

When the last of the great scouts stepped off that steamer in Bismarck and transferred to the rails, he had—whether he was aware of it or not—ended a phase of his life. He was thirty years old and had been a scout for fully half that time. The adventures he had had would provide colorful fodder for hundreds of tableaux, playlets, dime novels, and Wild West shows. Cody had an excellent memory for landscape but a poor memory for almost everything else. He became confused about much that he had done, getting dates and distances mixed up and sometimes claiming a deeper involvement than he may actually have had in various little skirmishes. He nevertheless *was* Buffalo Bill Cody, a figure who had held a colorful place on the American frontier. He *had* done a lot, he was bona fide; he didn't get lost and danger didn't deter him.

Though he would never be employed as a scout again, something of what he had done remained part of him to the end. He was a fine horseman—just the way he carried himself on a horse mesmerized audiences.

The former scout who boarded the train to Rochester had forty years to live. Though he bought a ranch, invested in this and that, tried various forms of entrepreneurship, he was essentially in showbiz for the rest of his life.

BOOK TWO

The Troupes

1

THE American theater in the last quarter of the nineteenth century, when Bill Cody turned to it for his livelihood, was a very catch-as-catch-can institution. Actors had begun to realize that they could not book their shows, direct their shows, write their shows, find costumes for their shows—not if they were expected to have energy left to *act* in their shows, though acting was for them the whole point.

Those shadowy figures—advance man, booking agent, and publicist—were clearly needed but had not yet cleanly separated themselves from the actors. Ned Buntline was an all-purpose showman. He performed all the above-mentioned functions—advance man, booking agent, publicist—but he didn't perform any of them very well.

Amateurishness abounded, but Cody and Omohundro and Buntline all realized that some sort of administrative system had to develop if they were to make any kind of consistent money. They could not just flounder helplessly from melodrama to melodrama, hoping things would somehow work out. Audiences were now past the point where they would pay just to see a bunch of tall yokels in buckskins walking around onstage with guns.

Cody had installed his family in Rochester. He returned to them in September of 1876, about two months after he had killed Yellow Hair—an experience which he at once converted into actionable material. The agile Prentiss Ingraham rushed out a dime novel called

The Right Red Hand: Or Buffalo Bill's First Scalp for Custer. This brash effort was quickly converted into a five-act play, a dramatic vehicle which Cody modestly described as being "without head or tail . . . it made no difference which act we commenced the performances . . . It afforded us, however, ample opportunity to give a noisy, rattling gunpowder entertainment and to present a succession of scenes in the great Indian war." The play was first staged in the Rochester Opera House but soon moved on to the Grand Opera in New York City, where Cody tried for a time to exhibit Yellow Hair's scalp and warbonnet to perk the crowd's interest. When the play toured New England he had problems with the clergy and had to withdraw the scalp from the showcase, but he still kept it handy and offered lots of people a look at it. This did not hurt the gate receipts.

Cody's use of Yellow Hair's scalp did not stop there—he showed it to the press at almost every show, a fact which gives a measure of credibility to Little Bat Garnier's assertion that Cody—knowing his time as a scout was nearly over—was really looking to acquire a scalp. His encounter with Yellow Hair was probably a surprise to both men—but Cody was very capable of thinking ahead to a day when a scalp and a warbonnet might come in handy, publicity-wise, particularly if the scalp happened to be the "first scalp for Custer."

There is no evidence that Cody scalped Tall Bull, if it was Tall Bull he killed, or any other of the various Indians who may have fallen to his gun.

In the 1870s what we would now call troupes or even repertory companies were mostly called "combinations." These combinations would need to have a male lead, a female lead, some villains, stooges, maybe an Indian or two, maybe a juggler, and so forth. When Cody returned to the East it seemed that his old friend Texas Jack Omohundro, whom he had recently seen in the Yellowstone country, had got the jump on him when it came to putting together a crowd-pleasing combination.

For one thing Texas Jack, with whom Cody always had amiable relations, had taken the prudent step of marrying his beautiful costar, Giuseppina Morlacchi, always referred to as the "peerless

Morlacchi," a dancer who was also a professional actress, able to handle many roles. She was a very beautiful young woman, one of her claims to fame being that she had introduced the cancan to America. Texas Jack also employed the man who would later become Cody's lifelong press agent, John M. Burke, then an actor known as Arizona John, whose role seemed to have required him to empty his pistol rapidly at every performance.

Cody always had too much raw star power for Texas Jack to compete with, but when it came to organizing a modern theatrical troupe, Texas Jack for a time pulled ahead. He had, for one thing, his charming wife, described by one Chicago critic as "a beautiful Indian maiden with an Italian accent and a weakness for scouts."

Unfortunately, in 1880, just three years after he and Cody had resumed their friendly rivalry, Texas Jack Omohundro suddenly died while performing in Leadville, Colorado. He can be seen in many photographs, in most of which he is standing beside his lovely, diminutive wife and his tall friend Buffalo Bill.

2

As a performer, Bill Cody dealt in broad strokes, one reason his shows turned out to work best in arenas or sports palaces. But even on a small stage, he got better notices than Ned Buntline, whom one harsh critic described as being "simply maundering imbecility. Ludicrous beyond description is Ned Buntline's temperance address in the forest."

Recognizing perhaps that the finer points of acting were, and might always be, beyond him, Cody, at the very beginning of his performing career, immediately announced a farewell tour—the first of many such:

> This will be the last season that Buffalo Bill (W. F. Cody) will travel as a theatrical star. The company he now has is engaged for fifteen months, one of which is to be passed on vacation. The troupe, about the middle of June, will arrive in Omaha, and then they will be transported at the manager's expense to his ranch on the North Platte, where they will be at liberty to do as they please. Toward the end of June they will start for San Francisco and play there for four weeks. Thence through California, Oregon, Nevada, and Utah, back to Omaha, where they will disband, Buffalo Bill going to his ranch, to remain there the rest of his life as a cattle dealer and gentleman farmer. He now has 4,500 head of cattle and hopes to have 10,000 by the close

of next year. He will, therefore, retire from the stage with ample competence.

The farewell tour was in fact an inaugural tour, led by a young actor of thirty-one years, who had no competence to speak of, if by competence he meant money. This same Buffalo Bill Cody would continue to perform for almost exactly forty more years, many times in what he called farewell performances. The final performance, in Chicago in 1916, was more of a rodeo than a Wild West show, leaning heavily on cowboy contests.

What Cody recognized at the outset of his career was that "farewells" always play—many a spectator's eye, over these forty years, would go misty at the thought that they might never see Buffalo Bill again. Cody, like many another impresario, milked farewells for whatever they were worth. His theatrical instincts may have been crude, but they were mainly sound.

It was this instinct which led him, against all advice, to launch a West Coast tour. It was suggested to him that people who actually lived in the West were not likely to respond to these absurd Western melodramas; but Cody's instinct was sharper. He recognized that the westering experience was a source of powerful myth, and that many people who lived in the West might prefer, for an hour or two, the fantasy rather than the reality. Theater, like the movies which followed, wasn't about reason or good sense; it was an *escape* from reason, common sense, and the daily grind. Cody realized this early on; what he offered was a pageant of the past, colorful if not necessarily realistic. The people lapped it up.

Lulu Cody, who stayed for a while in Denver, where Cody's sisters lived, actually accompanied him on much of the West Coast tour, an experience she would not repeat. Probably she went in order to keep an eye on her husband, which meant remaining constantly on the alert. When the troupe finally disbanded in Omaha, all the actresses in the troupe insisted on kissing their Papa Bill good-bye. Cody remembers that the girls were all having a glass or two of beer, so he had a glass or two with them, to be convivial. Cody seldom turned down drink, and had no objection to kissing pretty women.

Lulu, however, had loud objections: she had a fit, bawled him out, and rarely traveled with him after that. As to the kissing, Cody could not understand what Lulu thought could possibly be wrong with it.

> I do not think that most wives would have felt a little angry to know and hear her husband in an adjoining room on Sunday morning, drinking beer and kissing the theatrical girls of his company. I think they would have been rather proud of a husband who had six or seven months work with a party of people who were in his employ, to know and feel that they were on a kindly people footing . . . Not one of them got up and kissed papa goodbye, but all four of them rushed up and kissed papa, their old manager, goodbye . . . Actresses are not narrow-minded people . . . I was just 31 then, just the right age.

I don't know if Lulu Cody saw this long statement, but if she did it no doubt confirmed her worst fears: actresses were not narrow-minded people and her husband was just the right age; besides that he was to stay the right age for most of the rest of his life and was to encounter several actresses, among them Katherine Clemmons, who were even less narrow-minded than the girls of that first troupe.

House receipts for the California tour were very encouraging—one night in San Francisco they pulled in $1,400. Lulu went home to North Platte and saw to the erection of the big house they called Scout's Rest. Cody had proven that Western plays, if anything, did better in the West than in the East. Not long after that, convinced that a few real Indians were essential if he was to keep his productions exciting, he journeyed to the Red Cloud agency and secured the services of a few, a move that was not welcome in Washington—the government considered Indians wards of the state, and preferred them to stay put. Cody then visited both Carl Schurz, the secretary of the interior, and E. A. Hyat, commissioner of Indian Affairs, to point out that the employment he was offering could benefit both the Indians and the republic. Cody was required to post a bond for the use of the Indians. Sometimes $10,000 got him one hundred Indians, but sometimes the same amount only got him thirty. Cody's personal diplomacy worked—for many years he hired Indians—but the U.S. government was never entirely happy with the situation. Where Indians were concerned, the U.S. government wanted full control, a fact Cody realized to his sorrow many years later at the time of Sitting Bull's death. Probably Sherman's only-good-Indian-is-a-dead-Indian policy was still the dominant view.

3

T H O S E who knew Buffalo Bill Cody well must have been a little shocked, if they were privy to the announcement of this first farewell tour, to discover that he intended to live out his days as a rancher and a gentleman farmer. Up to this point in time Cody had never exhibited the slightest interest in farming, gentlemanly or otherwise—and, if possible, had showed even less interest in ranching. His few statements about cowboy life in the autobiography are less than glowing, although by the time the book came out (1879) Cody *was* a rancher, if not a very enthusiastic one.

In fact, he went into the cattle business with Major Frank North, whose brother Luther so long and vehemently disputed Cody's never-too-insistent claim to have killed Tall Bull.

In 1877 neither Bill Cody nor Frank North owned a ranch, at least not in the accepted sense of the word. The large concerns, mostly British or Scottish, which began to acquire ranches in Wyoming and Montana operated on a very vast scale—though seldom profitably. Most of these enterprises were syndicates—they lost money steadily until they gave up; like plenty of high plains ranchers, many were ruined by the terrible winter of 1885–1886.

The notion that Cody would be a "gentleman farmer" will appear, to anyone who has spent time in North Platte, Nebraska, to be about as ludicrous as some of Ned Buntline's temperance speeches. In 1877 much of Nebraska was open range, owned merely by the U.S. government. Land agents had begun to appear—the writer Mari

114

Sandoz's famous father, Old Jules, was one of them—but naturally, the land agents were trying to sell the most appealing land, perhaps land watered by a spring or creek. Certainly at this time no one was trying to sell the Nebraska sand hills, or much rather bleak land north of the North Platte. Only a cracked land agent would have tried to sell the sand hills first.

In 1877 Cody and North went to Ogallala and purchased about fifteen hundred head of cattle, which they duly branded and drove north, to a promisingly grassy piece of acreage on the South Fork of the Dismal River. I have often thought that the Dismal River must be one of the most aptly named streams in our land; by horse it was about a day's ride north of North Platte—by car it can be reached from that city in about an hour.

Cody may, for a while, have attempted to convince himself that he liked cowboying, but in fact he and Frank North had hardly got the herd settled in up along the South Fork when Cody took himself off to the Red Cloud agency to recruit more show Indians for his next tour.

Why *would* he have liked ranch life in northern Nebraska, where there was a scarcity of female company and even saloons were few and far between? Also, it was already fairly obvious that the great American open range was about to become a thing of the past. The government might allow each family 160 acres, but 160 acres along the Dismal River would hardly support fifteen hundred head of cattle, much less the ten thousand that Cody had bragged about. Fortunately Cody and North managed to cash out just in time, selling the operation in 1882 for something like $75,000.

Bill Cody, the showman, was not entirely wasting his time with all those bovines. He noticed that cowboys were always competing with one another in roping contests or bronco-riding contests. Cody quickly concluded that if these ranch competitions could be organized, people might pay to see them. If such competitions could be linked to some patriotic theme or occasion, then *lots* of people might pay to see them. His own dislike of cowboying did not keep him from appreciating the skill of these young riders and ropers.

Probably Cody's central insight as an impresario was that it was always a good idea to link patriotism to performance. The Wild West, as it evolved under his leadership, was always, however

115

crudely, a pageant of American life—and particularly that part of it that had involved the settling of the American West.

Cody's notion—even as he and Frank North were selling their cattle business—was to organize and promote a big cowboy competition in North Platte to celebrate the Fourth of July.

Where Wild West shows were concerned, Cody eventually had the best that were ever staged, but it's not clear that he had the first. Many troupes had, for some time, been wandering around America, most of them half circus and half Wild West show. Cody perfected the show and made it internationally viable as a form of entertainment, but several people were fumbling with the idea of converting the Wild West into entertainment.

Rodeo is a different matter. There had been informal ranch contests as long as there had been ranches, but few of these attracted more than local attention. Cody at once organized a rodeo that set the standard for what would become a very popular sport.

His rodeo was called the Old Glory Blow Out and was held in North Platte on the Fourth of July 1882. Cody had hoped to get as many as one hundred entrants in the contests; but as the time approached, he soon found that he had closer to one thousand. So popular was this first event that for a few days the great central plains became virtually depopulated: everybody seemed to be rushing to North Platte.

One reason this first rodeo was held in North Platte was because the city boasted a racetrack with a sturdy fence around it. Had Cody lacked a fenced arena, a good many spectators could easily have been trampled.

Rodeo caught on quickly. The very next year the town of Pecos, Texas, had a Fourth of July rodeo—Prescott, Arizona, and many other communities soon followed suit. Nowadays there is hardly a town in the West, large or small, that doesn't attempt to stage an annual rodeo. As a boy of nine I rode in the first rodeo in my hometown of Archer City, Texas—the community's sixtieth rodeo has just taken place, and all this because Buffalo Bill Cody, long ago in Nebraska, recognized that cowboys and the skills they practiced were an interesting part of the American experience. Ever since, rodeo has brought a bit of color to small-town life.

It was far from being one of Bill Cody's worst ideas.

4

I'VE said earlier that Buffalo Bill, in his mellow moods, while not exactly making light of his own achievements, didn't normally exaggerate them either—not unless he was lending himself to a promotion. He was as relaxed about his not very impressive career as an actor as he had been about those various skirmishes with Indians that, in his view, just didn't amount to much. He knew that the prairie-and-campfire melodramas he starred in with Texas Jack Omohundro and his wife, the "peerless Morlacchi," didn't amount to much, where theater was concerned.

But his Wild West shows, once hammered into workable form, *did* amount to something—they were the source of Cody's extraordinary celebrity, which, in his day, was not exceeded by anyone in the world. Celebrity did amount to much—Cody was one of the first performers to truly acquire superstardom.

Even in the innocence of the late nineteenth century celebrity seldom happened unless some effort was made. Queen Victoria was a celebrity because she was a queen; her fellow monarch Franz Josef was a celebrity not so much because he ruled an empire but because he had married—not happily—the most beautiful woman in Europe, the empress Elizabeth.

But Cody was not a royal; his origins were humble. He was an extraordinary horseman and, from his youth, a very handsome man. Looks and horsemanship combined to give him his start. Early on, as we have seen, even when he was doing fairly mundane work as a scout or hunter, he had a sense of image. When he had his first promotional photograph made, Matthew Brady took it—and was to take many, many more. In this first promotional photograph Cody is in scout's buckskins and is leaning on a rifle, probably his buffalo gun Lucretia Borgia. Joy Kasson's fine book shows how careful Cody was about his own iconography—he realized at once that his fortune depended on his looking the part of a Western frontiersman. He and his colleagues then evolved a complex outdoor operation in which national memory and popular history combined to form a visually and emotionally satisfying panorama. Photographs, posters, and book illustrations all had their job to do—before Cody was done, in 1917, many thousands of images of him had been seen by audiences in America and Western Europe. They are still being seen at Euro Disney.

The first of Buffalo Bill's Wild West shows from which at least some continuity can be traced was held in Omaha in 1883; the last, as I have mentioned, was in Chicago in 1916, which means that for about thirty years the onetime scout William F. Cody was engaged in putting on shows: indoor shows when a sports palace was available, outdoor shows when necessary. Many performers had their hour and departed. Annie Oakley performed with Cody for sixteen seasons but afterward exercised her talents in other forums.

In this thirty years of organizing large groups of people into workable teams and troupes, many managers, part managers, owners, half owners, banks, lawyers, accountants, and press agents devoted much energy to making sense of Bill Cody's tangled affairs. Most failed. His assets were threatened with seizure more than once, but since buffalo and Indians were among the assets, seizing them usually turned out to be more trouble than it was worth. Cody and Doc Carver once flipped a coin to determine who got what when they ended their brief, contentious partnership. Cody got the Deadwood stage.

It is not my intention in this book to chart the comings and goings of the many financial players involved. Sarah Blackstone has published two fine books on the business life of Buffalo Bill Cody. Her *Buckskins, Bullets, and Business* cannot be bettered as a study of the purely financial history of the Wild West shows.

Nor do I intend to plod through Cody's thirty-two seasons as a showman, describing the splendors and miseries of each.

What might be useful, though, is an annotated listing of the major characters who were involved with Cody and the shows. Many were once famous, and Cody and Annie Oakley are still famous; but most of these gifted or not so gifted folks are now just forgotten players from a bygone era. Giuseppina Morlacchi was a very beautiful woman who perhaps did bring the cancan to America, but the only book about herself and her husband, Texas Jack Omohundro, was published fifty years ago. One will find little trace of her today. The same can be said for Doc Carver, Pawnee Bill, and many others.

Buffalo Bill did manage to get his shows off the ground at the right time, just when outdoor spectacles became popular. The Ringling Brothers started their circus only a year later—at one time the Ringlings were part owners of Cody's show.

It should be emphasized that Cody did not advertise his spectacle as a "show." It was Buffalo Bill's Wild West, which meant that in his mind it was history—our history—and not just a collection of sharpshooters, trick riders, and the like. It was not, in his mind, a circus, although it contained many elements taken from the circus. What Cody wanted were tropes such as the attack on the Deadwood stage, or a battle between settlers and Indians, or himself taking the first scalp for Custer.

Cody's vision prevailed and is prevailing still, somewhere or other. When my county attained its centennial year, in 1980, the pageant put on every night for two weeks in our small rodeo arena was pure Cody.

All serious commentators on Cody's career agree on one thing: his shows succeeded—as, for example, did the TV miniseries of my own novel *Lonesome Dove* (125 million viewers)—because of the immense, worldwide appetite for anything pretending to portray life in the old West. In our time a Frenchman named George Fronval has published at least six hundred Western novelettes, and even in distant Norway there's a writer, named Kjell Halbing, who has produced more than sixty.

The thing to remember about this appetite for Westerns and the West is that the millions who possess it are *entirely* uncritical. They'll take anything in buckskins, literally. The Karl May cult in Germany has not even begun to slow down, although May died in 1912 and was himself never west of Buffalo. Indeed, as I discovered with *Lonesome Dove*, it is really impossible to get people to look at the West critically—they just refuse. The director John Ford is said to have decreed that if you have to choose between the truth and the legend, print the legend. From my experience I'd say that there's really no choice: for most readers and viewers it's the legend or nothing.

It seems that Bill Cody figured this out instinctively at the very beginning of his career. The Old Glory Blow Out in North Platte, plus the success of his various melodramas, which he knew to be terrible, combined to give him the necessary clue.

So, banking on his good looks and his horsemanship, he made it happen.

In the next few chapters I'll look at some of the people who either helped him make it happen or else got in his way.

5

ONE aspect of late-nineteenth-century performance that has long since gone the way of the passenger pigeon was the endurance shoot, in which contestants fired thousands of bullets or pellets at a variety of targets, including live pigeons. Some blame these shoots for the extinction of the passenger pigeons; the popularity of squab at high-end restaurants was another factor in the passenger pigeon's fade, along with habitat destruction, mass hunts, and the like. (The term "stool pigeon" derives from these stupendous all-day shoots. The stool pigeon was a decoy bird tethered to a stool or fence post.)

By the time of Buffalo Bill's Wild West the endurance shooters mainly shot at glass balls, trap-thrown, or wooden blocks. Captain Adam Bogardus, who shot with Cody's show on some occasions, had a hand in the invention of the skeet trap; he also may have been the first marathon shooter to use the Ligowsky clay pigeons, an invention which in time regularized skeet shooting, a sport that once enjoyed a much greater popularity than it does today. Annie Oakley and her husband, Frank Butler, ran a high-end skeet club after they had left Cody's show.

These endurance shoots were popular everywhere. Doc Carver did particularly well in the Hoboken area, where there were many German shooting clubs. It was not a sport for those with little stamina. In Brooklyn on one occasion Doc Carver broke 5,500 glass balls out of 6,211 thrown. Doc Carver and his opponents, of course, had loaders. Annie Oakley, on one occasion and perhaps one occasion only, shot 5,000 clay pigeons in a day, loading her own guns. She broke 4,772 or thereabouts.

The real problem in these endurance shoots, as Doc Carver testified, was eyestrain, the result of so much squinting. After the 6,000-ball shoot in Brooklyn, Carver had to go to bed with a cloth over his eyes for two days. Although he did more than anyone else to popularize these shoots, he was not, as he often claimed, the absolute top marathon shooter of his day—the title probably belonged to one Adolph Topperwein, who committed only nine misses out of 72,500 balls thrown.

On the other hand, Doc Carver made his living as a competitive shooter for almost half a century, taking on all comers in advertised shoots in America, Europe, and Australia. He probably shot more shots, most of which hit their targets, than any competitive shooter of his day.

W. F. Carver and W. F. Cody had been rivals to some degree since their buffalo-hunting days. They ran into one another in New Haven in 1883 and immediately decided to put on a Wild West show together. Carver claimed that he already had a Wild West show and merely invited Cody to come in as an act of generosity. The reader should be warned that absolutely everything that Cody and Carver said about one another, in the course of a rivalry that lasted at least four decades, should be taken with a large grain of salt. When speaking of one another, neither is to be believed.

What is true is that the first show operated by Cody and Carver was the same show that opened in Omaha in May of 1883. It boasted a title that many would consider cumbersome: "The Wild West, W. F. Cody and W. F. Carver's Rocky Mountain and Prairie Exhibition." Carver wanted to get in the phrase "Golden West," a locution he was fond of and later used in his independent productions.

Like many first efforts the show did not go off seamlessly. A number of Omaha dignitaries, including the mayor, were invited to ride in the Deadwood stage while it came under mock attack from a party of Pawnees. The Pawnees had been recruited by Frank North. As soon as the Indians started whooping and hollering, the mules panicked and made several bouncy circuits of the arena before they could be stopped. This indignity so angered the mayor of Omaha that he had to be restrained from attacking Cody physically.

Doc Carver was six years older than Bill Cody, but outlived him by a decade, perhaps because he didn't drink as heavily—which is not to imply that he was actually reluctant to bend the elbow. He was born in Illinois and, like Cody, was on his own at an early age. He was a teamster for a time, did some scouting, fought in several skirmishes with Indians, and like Cody, was a professional buffalo hunter. He was probably a better overall marksman than Cody; when shooting competitions began to be popular he soon figured out that shooting at glass balls or tossed coins was a lot easier than the demanding life of the frontier.

Carver was not as good-looking as Cody, nor was he as immediately acceptable to rich people—though, in time, he acquired polish and was not far behind Cody when it came to seducing, socially, the rich and the royal. He was practically the only one of Cody's close rivals who developed a real animus against him, the basis for which may have been mostly financial. From the time of that first show in Omaha the two could never agree about how much one partner owed the other. Carver claimed that Cody originally agreed to put in $27,000 but instead stayed drunk most of the summer and never put in a cent. Cody's bankers, though not denying that Cody had a tendency to go on what he called "toots," claimed that the financial situation was the other way around. They insisted that Carver didn't put in a cent, either—yet somehow the show got mounted, and expensively, too. For the next several years the two showmen made various legal lunges at one another, most of them inconclusive. Cody may have offered to flip a coin to settle the matter, but Carver was not charmed by the gamble. Coins were flipped, perhaps, and Cody did surrender $10,000 at one point, while keeping possession of the Deadwood stage.

Doc Carver billed himself as the "Spirit Gun of the West," whatever that means, but many who worked with him called him the "Evil Spirit of the West." Though never quite as famous as Cody, he was famous enough and industrious enough to eventually get bookings on three continents. His temper, to say the least, was uncertain. Once, at Coney Island, he broke his rifle over his horse's head; similar flare-ups were frequent. Still, most of his performers seemed to like him, and tolerate his outbursts, but the idealized fame that Cody won eluded the Spirit Gun—even though he won hundreds of shooting competitions. Cody won none.

Among Carver's partners was Cody's friend the poet-scout Jack Crawford (the father, perhaps, of cowboy poetry). Carver was awarded almost as many medals and prizes as Cody—he ended up with a wagonload of fancy guns. He bragged about these trophies but they didn't soothe his restless spirit much. He married and acquired a ranch in California but that didn't soothe his restless spirit either. Within weeks he would be back to mounting shows. When Cody took his troupe to Europe in 1887 Carver was not far behind. Occasionally, to the annoyance of both, they would show up in the same European city at the same time. This happened in Hamburg in 1890. Since the two troupes hated, or professed to hate, one another, the citizenry of that stout German city were, for a time, terrified, at least in the opinion of a reporter for the *New York World:* "Hamburg is filled with a howling mob of Indians and cowboys who are awaiting the chance to scalp one another. As soon as Cody's bills are posted, Carver's assistants come along and tear them down."

It may be that, in the long run, Carver did better in Europe than Cody because he traveled with a smaller, more manageable troupe. Cody took ninety-seven Indians and lots of white performers, not to mention an extensive crew, when he first went to England, in 1887. Carver got by with twenty Indians and a few other acts. His ace in the hole was his own shooting. It always seemed to please crowds, though not as much as Annie Oakley's shooting pleased crowds.

Carver took his troupe to places such as St. Petersburg and Australia, where Cody had never worked up to going. Russia was not easy to get into but Carver applied to Ulysses S. Grant himself; Grant got the players in under a kind of blanket visa.

Despite his fits and frequent surliness, Carver was a man of considerable principle. When he reached Australia he was appalled to discover that beautiful parrots and ibises were being destroyed in planned shoots; he loudly spoke against the practice. In San Francisco he attacked the local merchants for their too frequent use of wooden Indians, which he considered an insult to the real Indians, members of a noble race, that he himself had just brought around the world.

Doc Carver survived and kept shooting. He outlived another sharpshooter, Annie Oakley, by a year. He remained to the end his own man, although to continue to compete in the cutthroat world of road shows he had to constantly scramble to develop new acts.

Toward the end Doc Carver's acts became more like boardwalk attractions. He invested in some diving horses and even a diving elk. A female daredevil rode the horses off a forty-foot platform into a fourteen-foot tank, which certainly took guts on the part of the daredevils.

The elk, so far as I can discover, dove alone.

6

JOHN Y. NELSON, whose Sioux name was Cha Sha Sha Opo-geo, was one of the few plainsmen to stay on good terms with Wild Bill Hickok, Doc Carver, and Buffalo Bill Cody (a moody triumvirate), though John Y. Nelson himself was a man of uncertain temperament. He sometimes sustained deadly feuds for decades. His status among the Sioux was especially high because he was married to Red Cloud's daughter, who eventually bore him a vast brood, which he insisted on traveling with despite various impresarios' reluctance. His most conspicuous physical attribute was a magnificent full beard. Perhaps it was the beard that attracted photographers—John Y. Nelson appears in many photos.

Nelson worked for both Carver and Cody but the appearance that contributed most to his fame occurred in London. On the night that four kings rode in the Deadwood stage, John Y. Nelson, with his bushy beard and his inscrutable manner, rode shotgun. There is a famous photograph of the four not unapprehensive kings sitting in the stagecoach and of John Y. Nelson, equipped with shotgun, inscrutably observing it all. The kings were of Austria, Denmark, Saxony, and Greece. What John Y. Nelson may have been inscrutably considering was whether the Deadwood stage—a vehicle that had careened around too many arenas, chased by too many Indians, for too long—would fall apart, with all those nobs inside it. The kings themselves did not impress him.

The show's manager, Nate Salsbury, who firmly held the line on

126

expenses, had failed either to purchase a new stagecoach or to have the existing one repaired.

But Cody, taking no chances, drove the stage himself. Judging from other photographs, Cody seems pretty tense. Perhaps he was remembering the runaway in Omaha, and his near fistfight with the outraged mayor. Still, having four kings in the stagecoach plus the Prince of Wales, who sat on the driver's seat with Cody and John Y. Nelson, was thumping good publicity. Major Burke, the press agent, was of course ecstatic.

John Y. Nelson stayed with Cody through many tours and many vicissitudes. In group pictures of the troupe he is usually seen in the front row, seated with his wife and many lively children. Without his beard he would have closely resembled the Italian peasant whose shack is nearly shaken to pieces by the close passage of trains, in Sergio Leone's *For a Few Dollars More*.

7

WHEN Cody and Carver and their soon-to-be rival Gordon Lillie (Pawnee Bill) began to drift into the performing life at the beginning of the 1880s, it was in part because, behind them to the west, the frontier as they had known it was closing. They were vigorous men with an abundance of frontier skills which were rapidly becoming obsolete. Railroads girdled the continent; and the telegraph, the singing wires, carried messages a lot quicker than anything Russell, Majors, and Waddell could have devised. In distant Arizona the Apache wars continued but otherwise the native warriors of the plains and forests were no longer a threat.

Cody, Carver, and Lillie all had wives, but none of them could be described as well domesticated. They were vagabonds and soldiers of fortune. What did they do now? What would their model be?

When Bill Cody set out on his "farewell tour" to California he described himself as a theatrical star—perhaps it was Major Burke who supplied the term. At this point in time what we now call the star system—mainly just a method of financing shows of one kind or another—was not well advanced. But in Cody's case the description was not unfair. If any retired scout and part-time actor could be called a star, it was he. Thanks to the dime novels and more or less constant press coverage he was much better known than any of the other frontierless frontiersmen.

The one true superstar in the theatrical world in this time was Sarah Bernhardt (Henriette-Rosine Bernard), who, from her base at the Théâtre Français, made frequent appearances both in England

and in New York. Even losing a leg didn't stop the Divine Sarah—she continued to work and outlived Cody by six years.

When, in 1883, Nate Salsbury signed a partnership contract with Bill Cody and the then-reigning sharpshooter, Captain Adam Bogardus, to form an entity called "Buffalo Bill's Wild West—America's National Entertainment," it is doubtful that he expected Cody's fame to so completely eclipse his own (and Bogardus's too, of course). In the theatrical world of that time there was a fair sprinkling of stars, one of whom was Nate Salsbury himself. General William Tecumseh Sherman remembered the young Nate Salsbury, aged perhaps sixteen, delivering an uplifting version of "Oh! Susanna," at an impromptu entertainment during the difficult Georgia campaign. Nate survived a period at the dreadful Andersonville prison and briefly pursued the study of law before devoting himself permanently to the theater.

Nate Salsbury was not ungifted, either as actor or playwright. He rose to be leading man at a theater in Chicago, but soon left to form his own troupe, which he called the Troubadours, a troupe he kept together for about a dozen years. Like Doc Carver he even took his actors to Australia. His specialty was light farces, one of which, *Patchwork*, achieved an eighteen-month run. Another, called *The Brook*, played successfully for about five years.

Thus, when he made his contract with Cody, it was star joining star; and as a longtime man of the theater, Salsbury's skills were much sharper and his experience much broader than Cody's. Also, when necessary, he could write. Cody, despite the flamboyance of his autobiography, really couldn't.

In our day we have many superstars to choose from, but in Cody's day they were thin on the ground and at first no one—certainly not Nate Salsbury—was willing to consider Cody a superstar. He was not the Divine Sarah.

Major Burke, whom Salsbury regarded as a necessary evil—somebody had to hustle up publicity in order to get out the crowds—might call Cody a star but to Salsbury, at first, the man remained a tall, frequently drunk, former scout. Gordon Lillie, who became the manager of the show at one point, did like Major Burke, or at least approved of the job he did.

The more complicated question is whether Salsbury really *liked*

Cody, or whether one star's envy of another star's immense success colored their relationship almost from the first. It quickly became apparent to Salsbury and everyone else that the tall former scout was going to be a very big star indeed.

Nate Salsbury wrote a memoir, but in his lifetime made no attempt to publish it. Some of it saw magazine publication many years after all the principals were dead. It was a jaundiced memoir, though rarely really mean. Salsbury may have been the first to see that Cody was becoming dependent on the adulation of the very people who were bleeding him financially; he also made a real effort to get control of Cody's drinking, which was heavy. When Salsbury finally got Cody to agree to limit his intake to one drink a day Cody foiled him by securing a tankard that held at least a quart of whiskey. Cody, from his jayhawking days on, made no secret of his fondness for drink. Once, in apologizing to the poet-scout Jack Crawford for being so slow to answer an inquiry, he excused himself thusly: "I was on a hell of a toot and I seldom attend to anything except hoof her up when I am that way."

Others dispute the stories of Cody's excessive drinking. It was obvious that he enjoyed his liquor but he usually managed to show up sober when the occasion was serious enough to demand it.

Nate Salsbury possessed excellent managerial skills, and he, of course, had a stake in the success of the Wild West too. At first he applied his skills to the task of keeping the company solvent, until Cody's extraordinary charisma kicked in, first nationwide and, eventually, worldwide.

The reader will remember that it was Salsbury who, in only a few minutes that day in Louisville, recognized Annie Oakley's star quality and ordered all those posters. He was thus midwife to the birth of our first huge superstars, Buffalo Bill and Annie Oakley. Salsbury was probably as surprised as anybody at how broad their celebrity became.

Nate Salsbury probably had enough of a performer's ego to be a little sour when Cody put him so wholly in the shade; he couldn't resist sniping at Cody a bit, but whatever jealousy he felt did not destroy his judgment or his showmanship. Though his name appeared as proprietor on all programs, he was not required to merge his troupe with Cody's or to be with the Wild West for every performance. In fact he was performing in Denver when the first of many calamities overtook the Wild West. The troupe was on a steamboat headed down the Mississippi to New Orleans when the boat hit another steamer and sank. The crew, the troupe, and most of the horses survived, but the elk and the buffalo, Captain Bogardus's guns, and many props went to the bottom. Salsbury was about to step onto a stage in Denver when he received a succinct telegram from Cody: "Outfit at bottom of river, what do you advise?"

According to Don Russell the coolheaded Nate Salsbury merely asked the conductor to repeat the overture while he scribbled a telegram to Cody saying, "Go to New Orleans, reorganize, and open on your date."

Cody did manage to reorganize and to open on his date, but otherwise, their run at the New Orleans Exposition was one of the low points of Cody's career. It rained for forty-four days, during which the Wild West doggedly performed, but to very poor turnouts. The shipwreck, the rain, and other difficulties left the Wild West $60,000 in the red; there were other difficulties too. Frank North, Cody's old friend, was seriously injured when a girth broke; he died in the spring, by which time it is unlikely either North or Cody really knew or really cared which of them killed Tall Bull.

The Sells Circus was in New Orleans at the same time as the Wild West—occasionally the bored performers would visit back and forth, one of them a small woman from Ohio who called herself Annie Oakley. Not long afterward, she had her famous audition in Louisville.

Cody left New Orleans vowing to go on a drunk that would really be a drunk. Probably he kept this vow, but when and where and with whom is not recorded.

8

WE are not through with Nate Salsbury and the management of the Wild West, a long involvement with a few breaks in it. Like some presidents, Cody was a man of overflowing, at times overpowering, energies. He quickly wore people down, his wife, Louisa, among them. Much as she complained about her Billy's absences, when he did show up he was likely to have a mob with him, a mob that would likely have taxed the patience of any wife.

Salsbury too probably had periods of Cody fatigue. Sometimes he needed a breather, and went his own way for a while. Still, he had a clear mandate to manage everything: salaries, personnel, transport. It was he who set the order in which performers appeared. But when Cody was around it became impossible to maintain a clear separation of powers. Cody regarded it as *his* show; he could not resist meddling in everything: particularly personnel. To the end of his days, almost, he insisted on employing numerous former scouts or old army men whom he had known in frontier times: Frank North, Bob Haslam, John Y. Nelson were among this group but there were many others. Cody's incessant meddling no doubt irritated Salsbury and led to his occasional disappearances—though he took care never to be out of reach of the telegraph. Nowadays he would have bristled with cell phones. His instant response to the sinking of the steamboat is indicative of his capacity to maintain some measure of oversight.

Even though the first two seasons lost money it was clear that the show would draw plenty of customers once certain operational problems had been dealt with. By the third season, 1885, Buffalo Bill's Wild West made a profit. This was the year that Annie Oakley joined the troupe.

Another benefit Salsbury derived from his little absences was that he would not have to be irked by the fulsome behavior of the press agent, Major Burke. Veterans with long memories recalled that Burke himself had once been a performer who called himself Arizona John. One reason Salsbury came to dislike Burke was because the press agent absolutely worshiped Cody. He was puppylike in his need for Cody's approval, which, mostly, he had. With the troupe in America Burke mostly stayed on top of his tasks, which mainly involved tooting Cody's horn to a lot of editors, journalists, and advertising men.

Once the troupe began to travel about Europe, however, opportunities for mismanagement were sharply increased. Sometimes Burke lost his interpreter, the result being that the Wild West ship might dock, or train arrive, with no one there to help them unload.

One such arrival occurred in Naples. Burke was nowhere to be seen, there was no one there to help load, and the bemused Italians merely gaped at them. When Burke did show up, drenched in sweat and very anxious, Cody promptly fired him, and fired him in the thunderous tones he summoned when he lost his temper.

Salsbury was enjoying a vacation in London when this telegram reached him, its author being Major Burke: "My scalp hangs in the tepee of Pahaska at the foot of Mount Vesuvius. Please send me money to take me back to the Land of the Free and the Home of the Brave."

Before Salsbury could even figure out what the ruckus was about, Cody's fit passed, and as Louisa Cody says in her book, "the god and his admirer were arm in arm once more."

The god and his admirer? Louisa was not exaggerating when she labels Burke's feeling for Cody as being little short of idolatry; her book, *Memories of Buffalo Bill*, contains the most generous appraisal we have of the gregarious Major Burke.

Lulu Cody's book is an odd but not unreadable production. She mentions very few of the troupers: mainly just Cody, Burke, and the young sharpshooter Johnny Baker. Nate Salsbury—she spells it "Salisbury"—comes in for a few cautious mentions. Probably Lulu suspected that Salsbury didn't worship Cody—a sin in her book—although she herself was far from worshipful where Bill Cody was concerned.

Virtually the only woman mentioned in *Memories of Buffalo Bill* was Mlle. Morlacchi, the premiere danseuse and wife of Texas Jack Omohundro. The reason Mlle. Morlacchi came in for so much mention was that Major Burke had a mad but hopeless crush on her. Lulu Cody happens to have been the person Major Burke chose to confide in, while in the grip of this hopeless passion. The position of confidante appealed to Lulu, as it does to most women; she and Major Burke spent a good deal of time together, talking about nothing else. In fact the premiere danseuse and the tall scout were happily married, leaving Major Burke to nurse his longing in vain.

An odd aspect of Lulu Cody's memoir is that it is a free-flowing time line, with very few dates given. Now we're in Leavenworth, or Hays City, or Rochester, or North Platte; it's hard to say on a given page whether the Codys had been married two years or twenty. Lulu definitely remembers opening the box and finding Yellow Hair's smelly scalp in it. When Bill comes home and regales the girls with a colorful account of his famous "duel," which, in this telling, was a knife fight pure and simple, Lulu displays no doubt.

In *Memories of Buffalo Bill* Lulu Cody comes across as a spunky woman who is going to have her say, and precisely her say. She blandly leaves out all discord, admits only once or twice to loneliness, and generally paints as admiring a picture of her husband as even Major Burke could have produced. No mention of other women sullies her pages; even Little Missie is not allowed to appear. Then, with no warning, we're at the end:

> Many a year followed that, many a year of wandering, while Will went from country to country, from nation to nation, from state to state. There were fat times and there were lean times, there were times when storms gathered, and there were times when the sun shone; but always in cloud or sunshine, there was ever a shadow just behind

him [Cody], following him with a wistful love that few men can ever display, Major John M. Burke. And when the time came for that Will and I said goodbye forever, another man loosed his hold on the world. Throughout every newspaper office in the country, where John Burke had sat by the hour, never mentioning a word about himself, but telling always of the progress of his "god" there flashed the news that Major John M. Burke, the former representative of William Frederick Cody, had become dangerously ill. And six weeks later the faithful old hands were folded, the lips that had spoken hardly anything but praise of Buffalo Bill for half a century, were still. Major Burke had died when Cody died, only his body lingered on for those six weeks, at last to loose its hold on the loving, faithful old spirit it bound and allow it to follow its master over the Great Divide.

The death of Cody himself is recorded less grandiloquently; then, a few pages on, it's Lulu's turn.

Yes, my life is lived, and out here in the West, where every evening brings a more wonderful, more beautiful blending at sunset, I watch the glorious colorings and feel a sense of satisfaction that it will not be long now before I see the fading of the sunset of my own little world, until the time shall come when I am with the children I loved and the man I loved . . . on the Trail Beyond.

Lulu had indeed outlived her children and Bill Cody. She outlived Texas Jack Omohundro by forty years, and his lovely wife, the peerless Morlacchi, by thirty-four. Texas Jack Omohundro died of pneumonia in Leadville, Colorado, in 1880, and his wife, the premiere danseuse so admired by Major Burke, succumbed to cancer in Lowell, Massachusetts, in 1886. Nate Salsbury went in 1902, Cody in 1917, Lulu in 1920. But three of the best rifle shots ever, Johnny Baker, Doc Carver, and Annie Oakley, were still going strong.

9

O N E thing we've learned in the celebrity-rich last century is superstars cleave to other superstars. Rock stars hang out with other rock stars, movie stars with other movie stars, Michael Jordan with Larry Bird, and so on.

By 1886, when Cody and Salsbury brought the Wild West to the Erastina resort on Staten Island for an extended stay, Cody had become such a huge star that he had no peer to hang out with. Fortunately he had an entourage, and Annie Oakley's star was rising rapidly. At some time during this season Sitting Bull went home, but not before Cody presented him with a gray horse and a fine sombrero; in later years the difficult Hunkpapa was very particular about this hat. When one of his relatives decided to try it on, Sitting Bull was not pleased: "My friend Long Hair gave me this hat. I value it very highly, for the hand that placed it on my head had a friendly feeling for me."

Before departing Sitting Bull made his "Little Sure Shot," Annie Oakley, a member of the Hunkpapa tribe.*

After the sinking of the steamboat and the huge losses they incurred in their first two seasons, Cody and Salsbury had to give seri-

---

* Sitting Bull had first seen Annie shoot in a theater in St. Paul in 1884. He sent $65 to her room in hopes of getting a photograph. She sent the money back but went to see him the next day. Adoption into the tribe, she later noted, would have secured her "five ponies, a wigwam, and no end of cattle."

ous consideration to profits, which could best be achieved, it seemed to them, by settling in for an extended run in a big population center such as New York. This might produce not only famous spectators but also repeat spectators. Staten Island, where P. T. Barnum had first chased his buffalo, proved to be nearly ideal.

Soon enough celebrities began to attend the Wild West, and they were not sparing of endorsements. General Sherman attended the first show and uttered some fairly cryptic praise. P. T. Barnum himself was more direct. "They do not need spangles to make it a real show," he said. Libbie Custer proclaimed the Wild West "the most realistic and faithful representation of a western life that has ceased to be, with advancing civilization."

Mark Twain was even more fulsome, claiming that the Wild West

> brought back to me the breezy, wild life of the Rocky Mountains and stirred me like a war song. Down to its smallest detail the show is genuine—cowboys, vaqueros, Indians, stagecoach, costumes and all; it is wholly free from sham and insincerity and the effect produced on me by its spectacles were identical with those wrought upon me a long time ago by the same spectacles on the frontier . . . it is often said on the other side of the water that none of the exhibitions which we send to England are purely and distinctively American. If you will take the Wild West show over there you can remove that reproach.

Twain's enthusiasm for the Wild West never waned; he even went so far as to write a short story from the point of view of Cody's horse.

Long before the troupe did depart for England, in 1887, Cody had collected a bale of highly complimentary letters from virtually every prominent American military leader: Sherman, Sheridan, Crook, Merritt, and Bankhead, just to name the generals who wrote glowingly about Cody's splendid behavior. At least a score of colonels also weighed in.

The odd thing about these testimonials is that they all praise the show's realism, opinions contradicted—to my mind at least—by the many thousands of photographs of these same performances. What was realistic about Annie Oakley shooting glass balls? The only thing Western about her act was her costumes—she wore boots, which few Western women did at the time. The *events* that were most realistic, such as King of the Cowboys Buck Taylor's bronc riding, were closer to rodeo than to Indian fights and buffalo chases. The same could be said of the roping act of the champion vaquero Antonio Esquivel.

Somehow Cody succeeded in taking a very few elements of Western life—Indians, buffalo, stagecoach, and his own superbly mounted self—and creating an illusion that successfully stood for a reality that had been almost wholly different. Even hardened journalists such as Brick Pomeroy took fairly crude stagecraft for realism:

> It is not a show. It is a resurrection, or rather an importation of the honest features of wild Western life and pioneer incidents to the East, that men, women, and children may see, realize, understand, and forever remember what the Western pioneers met, encountered, and overcame. It is in secular life what Christ and the apostles proposed to be in religious life, except that in this case there are no counterfeits but actual, living, powerful, very much alive and in earnest delegates from the West, all of whom have most effectively participated in what they here reproduce as a most absorbing educational realism.

The *Montreal Gazette* was no less convinced of the show's fidelity to the life that had been:

> The whole thing is real. There is not a bit of claptrap about it. It is the picture of frontier life painted in intense realism, each scene standing forth in bold relief—painted, did I say? No, not painted, but acted as it is being acted along the entire frontier line that stretches from the Gulf of Mexico to the Great Slave Lake. It is a place and a scene

to visit, therefore, not for mere amusement, but for the sake of studying in a school where all lessons are objective and in which have been gathered materials for observation and instruction which, in the nature of things, are perishable and soon destined to vanish.

Both these reports to a large degree affirm to the success of Cody's instinctive decision not to call the show a *show*. It was, in his mind, and in the minds of most of the spectators, history, not fiction—easy to understand fiction that allowed the audience to participate vicariously in the great and glorious adventure that had been the settling of the West, an enterprise not yet wholly concluded even in 1886.

According to the now famous Professor Frederick Jackson Turner, the American frontier finally closed in 1893, seven years after Cody and Salsbury brought their troupe to Staten Island. A fair number of performers in the Wild West had been frontiersmen, many of them old friends of Cody; all of the Indians were, of course, Indians. And yet the claim that the skits were wonderfully realistic still startles—though, by the low standards of the day, perhaps they were: Cody, after all, had begun his career as an actor in Western melodramas so crudely staged that red flannel was used for scalps.

On the prop level, at least, Buffalo Bill's Wild West did considerably better than that, despite which wholly unrealistic elements frequently crept in. In the real West, contra Mark Twain, few marksmen felt confident enough to shoot *behind* themselves, with the help of a mirror, as Annie Oakley did. The Deadwood stage, which Cody won in a coin flip, was real enough, but Cody's obsession with warbonnets wasn't. The Indians in the show were much more gloriously feathered than they could have afforded to be back at the Red Cloud agency, or even in pre-Custer times. There is a famous photograph in Carolyn Thomas Foreman's book about Indians abroad in which a relaxed crowd is watching two Indians playing Ping-Pong, all the while trailing full-length warbonnets and wearing white buckskins.

Realistic or not, Buffalo Bill's Wild West drew enormous crowds during its long Staten Island run. On a single sunny week in July nearly two hundred thousand spectators took the ferry and saw the show. For the portion of the crowd that had never been west of the Hudson, the skits and playlets probably did seem like the real thing—after all, it was pretty close to what they had been told the West was like in all those dime novels Ned Buntline and Prentiss Ingraham had been providing them with.

Mark Twain's credulity seems a bit harder to fathom. He was more or less in the publishing business by then—perhaps he thought a little adroit flattery might encourage the wildly popular Cody to become one of his authors. Or he could have been drunk. We must hope he was drunk when he penned "A Horse's Tale," the short story written from the point of view of Cody's show horse.

The turnout for the Staten Island run was extremely cheering to Cody and Salsbury: a show that had fumbled through two seasons, losing both money and personnel, found its footing in 1885 and solidified it with the long Staten Island run. It finally looked like a viable proposition, one that could make the two principals a lot of money. Perhaps it was Twain's remark about the low quality of our theatrical exports that got the two men to thinking about England.

But before we shepherd our ever-expanding troupe aboard the good ship *State of Nebraska* it is time to consider in more depth the blossoming career of Little Missie, the small but formidable woman whom few ever managed to outshoot.

Annie

1

BUFFALO BILL CODY wore his heart on his sleeve—all his life he was a soft touch, a partygoer and party giver who was never reluctant to pick up the tab. His kindness to the old buffalo hunter William Mathewson, perhaps the first hunter to be called Buffalo Bill, has already been noted. If he came across a homeless or impoverished youth he would sometimes keep him with the troupe as an errand boy, as he himself had once been. Both Dan Muller, the artist, and Johnny Baker, the sharpshooter, attracted Cody's sympathies—both were allowed to earn their pay. Cody at least provided a roof over their heads, and a little schooling.

Annie Oakley was as tightfisted as Cody was openhanded. Among the troupers she was thought to be as tight as Hetty Green, the so-called Witch of Wall Street. Some thought that Annie subsisted entirely on the free lemonade that Cody and Salsbury made available to everyone in the troupe. Most of her fellow performers forgave her this and loved her anyway. It was mainly her rivals who used her frugality as a point of attack. At the height of her fame she softened a bit, sometimes serving tea and cookies to whatever youngsters wandered up. But tea and cookies were about the limit of her largesse.

Annie was not Cody—she never wore her heart on her sleeve. She was interviewed often but she rarely exposed much of herself. What she felt as she became one of the most famous women on earth we don't really know. She did have a heart, as well as a more or less normal allotment of performer's ego. She made no secret of her disdain for female rivals such as Lillian Smith. The women of the troupe were not a sisterhood; had there been an effort to form one, it is unlikely that Annie Oakley would have been much help.

She was married to Frank Butler for about four decades; he was one of the few people Annie seemed genuinely comfortable with, and yet it is possible to wonder if she allowed even her husband to know her real feelings. She always dressed modestly—she never performed in pants. She was only five feet tall and, for most of her life, weighed only a little more than one hundred pounds, and yet she had made a profound impact on crowds. She was attractive, but not a raving beauty. As a performer she was animated, skipping into the arena and launching rapidly into her various shooting acts. Once she had become famous her appearances rarely lasted more than ten minutes, a fact she reflected on when she was introduced to the old Austrian emperor Franz Josef in 1890:

> I really felt sorry when I looked into the face of the Emperor of Austria . . . his face looked both tired and troubled. I then and there decided that being just plain Annie Oakley, with ten minutes work once or twice a day, was good enough for me, for I had, or at least I thought I had, my freedom.

Franz Josef was to plug on for twenty-five more years, doing his lonely and vexatious job; Annie was wise to note that his was not a role to be envied. She was often dead on the mark when assessing European royalty.

Cody always called Annie "Missie" and she was usually described in promotional materials as a "little girl" from the West who just happened to be an unparalleled rifle and wing shot. Her purity was always part of the sell, but so was her attractiveness, her seductiveness, even. The one visible sign of sex was her long lustrous hair. Occasionally she allowed herself to be photographed with it hanging loose, which certainly made a womanly appeal.

Where the real Annie was in all of this is impossible to tell and was always impossible to tell. Her husband, Frank Butler, the man who knew her best, published a few sporting articles about guns or fishing but, except for one or two husbandly jibes about her hatred of housekeeping, Frank Butler kept mum.

The Butlers were childless, which doesn't mean that the marriage was sexless. Annie wanted no male hand to touch her once she was dead, but what she may have wanted in the way of touching while she was alive cannot now be determined. She did, however, dote on her dogs, and she also exhibited maternal concern for young Johnny Baker, once he joined the show; she also took an interest in his children when they came along.

There is much about Annie Oakley that we will never know—in her own lifetime very few would claim to know her well.

So far as her life as a performer went, the mystery was surely part of the potency.

2

THE roots of Oakley's frugality are not hard to account for: in her girlhood she had known great poverty. She was born in Darke County, Ohio, in 1860, though she unabashedly changed her birth date to 1866 when the fifteen-year-old sharpshooter Lillian Smith joined Cody's show.* To the end of her life she casually lied about her age, though her lopping off of the six years did not go entirely unnoticed in the papers. The change is one more indication of her steely will. What she didn't accept, she altered, and then ignored the alteration, pretending that it had always been thus.

In any case, Charles Dickens had nothing on Annie Oakley when it came to a bad childhood. Annie's parents, Susan and Jacob Moses (or Mozee), were very poor; the situation then became desperate when Jacob Moses froze to death while attempting to bring supplies home through a blizzard. Susan Moses was destitute. One of Annie's sisters was given away to a family who offered to raise her. Though Annie killed her first bird at six and her first squirrel at eight, she was as yet too small to support her family by hunting.

At ten Annie was sent to the county poor farm, a place called the Infirmary. She was soon more or less leased out to a farmer who

* There were normally three shooting acts per show: Annie's, Lillian Smith's, and Johnny Baker's. Captain Adam Bogardus had been Cody's first sharpshooter. His decision to go on his own prompted Annie's famous audition in Louisville. "She's a daisy!" Salsbury reportedly said. "She'll easily put Bogardus in the shade."

needed help with his milking. Annie never identified this farmer, or his wife—she referred to them merely as the "wolves," and it was with the "wolves" that she spent the darkest hours of her childhood. She was overworked, starved, and beaten; once the wife put her out in a storm to freeze, but the husband, who had no intention of losing his slave, arrived in time to save her. She continued to be overworked and physically abused until she turned twelve, at which point she ran away and walked back to the poor farm, a distance of some forty miles. By this time, fortunately, the Infirmary was run by a nice couple named the Edingtons, who soon put Annie in charge of their sizable dairy. They even paid her a wage, most of which Annie saved, as she was to do throughout her life. Nancy Edington taught her to embroider—needlework soon became a passion, one she was to pursue throughout all her touring years. It was what she did in her tent, when she wasn't practicing her act.

The Edingtons also put Annie in school, where she proved a quick learner. At about age fifteen she went back to her mother, who had remarried. Very soon Annie worked out a deal with the grocers Samson and Katzenberger, who had a flourishing grocery in Greenville, Ohio. They had known Annie from before and liked her. They soon agreed to buy whatever small game she cleaned and shipped to town. One thing the grocers noticed right away was that the quail, rabbit, or grouse Annie sent was not shot or torn up. She either caught the game in snares or shot them through the head, so the meat would be prime. The grocers liked her so much that they presented her with a new shotgun. She was then only in her midteens, but from that time on, one way or another, Annie Oakley made her living with her gun.

3

WHY human beings like what they like or, to put it more strongly, obsess over what they're obsessed with, remains—despite much psychological commentary—a mystery. There's just no accounting for taste, and no way to know why Annie Oakley liked guns so much and mastered them so easily.

But like them she did. *Her* creation myth, to be put beside Cody's first Indian, involved a squirrel that lingered on the family fence too long, until Annie managed to pull down her father's big muzzle-loading rifle, propped it on the windowsill, and shot the squirrel right through the head. She always claimed that it was one of the better shots she ever made.

There is a somewhat less romantic version of Annie Oakley's first shot—in this version her brother hands her a shotgun, hoping the kick will discourage her and stop her from pestering him about guns. The kick breaks her nose but of course she brings down the bird.

The old muzzle-loading gun was much too heavy for Annie, but she did her best, often depending on snares and traps of various kinds to help her secure rabbits and quail. From the first she seems to have had absolute confidence in her shooting; she kept this confidence all her life. Ted Williams and Joe DiMaggio were said to be the exceptional hitters that they were because their eyesight was so keen that they could see the seams of the baseball as it came toward them. Perhaps Annie Oakley too had better eyesight than most. She gave many shooting clinics once she left Cody's tour; she taught her students correct posture and the importance of an easy swing; her teachings made it all sound simple—indeed, almost Zenlike: "You must have your mind, your nerve, and everything in harmony. Don't look at your gun, simply follow the object with the end of it, as if the tip of your barrel was the point of your finger."

She herself never seemed so clearly in a state of harmony as when she was shooting her gun. Many opponents observed this. Somehow she remained supremely ladylike when firing a rifle or shotgun, weapons which had largely been the domain of the male until she came along. During her first English tour she had her worst day of shooting ever, trying to hit a swift variety of pigeons called blue rocks. The shoot was held at a gentlemen's shooting club. Annie, shooting a gun that was too heavy, with shot too light for the windy weather, only managed to hit five pigeons out of twenty, a deep embarrassment for her. But the gentleman who managed the club, who had not been impressed with Lillian Smith, *was* impressed with Annie. He told her that she was much less of a shot than he expected, but much more of a lady.

A fine English gunsmith named Charles Lancaster was there that day, and at once figured out what was wrong. He persuaded Annie to let him make her a lighter gun, a twelve-gauge that only weighed six pounds. Before she left England she tried the blue rocks several more times, eventually managing to bring down forty-one out of fifty.

But this is to get far ahead of the story. The shotgun the Greenville grocers gave Annie was a Parker sixteen-gauge, as good a shotgun as could be had in America at that time. They also gave her a tin of high-grade gunpowder, a gift so unexpected that it was some weeks before she could bring herself to open the can. These gifts changed Annie from being merely a somewhat bohemian wood sprite into a shooter with a future. She repaid their kindness by shipping them game that had been meticulously cleaned and packed—soon they were relaying some of it to high-end restaurants in Cincinnati. With the grocer's encouragement, she soon began to enter shooting matches. She entered and she won.

In the late 1870s such matches abounded. Sharpshooters traveled from town to town and hamlet to hamlet, rather as pool sharks were later to do, eager to take on the local champion and perhaps win a few dollars. The shoots were advertised in the local papers and were commonly well attended, there being little else to be enjoyed in the way of entertainment in the Ohio woods in those days.

Frank Butler was an Irishman with a good deal of confidence in his shooting, but on this occasion, the fact that his opponent was a mere slip of a girl, dressed in knickerbockers, seems to have unnerved him. Annie beat him, hitting twenty-three pigeons to his twenty-one—other accounts say that she only beat him by one bird.

She not only beat him, she won him. The romantic progress of little Phoebe Moses and the dapper Frank Butler is somewhat clouded, but one way or another, there *was* a courtship, followed by a marriage that was to last a lifetime. Exactly when and where they married is disputed. Frank Butler was in the process of getting a divorce—it may be that legal complications caused Annie and Frank to fudge matters a little. They were married in 1882, when Annie was twenty-two; the newlyweds then traveled the variety circuit for some three years, shooting wherever they could find a match, or a weekend's engagement. They were, for a while, a shooting team, but Frank soon dropped into a managerial role, securing bookings and trying to establish his wife in what was a very crowded field. Trick shots and sharpshooters of all stamps were thick on the ground. The young couple stayed in theatrical boardinghouses and traveled as cheaply as possible. They were young, of course, and resilient, but Annie's years as a slave to the "wolves" were not forgotten: to the end of her life it bothered her to turn down work; probably she never fully believed that she could afford to turn down work. Long after her retirement from Cody's show she appeared more than once in Tony Pastor's Opera House, headlining a bill that included Samson, the Strongest Man on Earth, as well as the Ossified Man, whose torso gave back a stony sound when struck with a hammer; beside these attractions there was the Elastic Skin Lady, contortionist extraordinary, a one-armed juggler, and a troop of musicians. It was, in other words, a freak show, but, just to be on the safe side, Annie did the show and banked the money. She had already starred in *The*

Western Girl, a stage melodrama not much better than some of those Bill Cody had once starred in.

By this time, with the glories of Europe behind them and thousands of shows under their belt, Frank Butler might have been inclined to give a real and final farewell performance—a farewell performance that took, unlike Colonel Cody's.

Annie had no very strong objection to Frank's desire for more time to fish and hunt, but her strongest instinct was never to turn down work. Even after her car wreck in 1922 she was not entirely ready to put a period to her career.

4

IN her long life as a performer Annie Oakley is said to have missed only five performances due to illness. Four of these missed shows occurred early in the troupe's stand on Staten Island, after a bug crawled into her ear while she was asleep. Various doctors thought they had flushed the bug, but all failed. For a few days, just as the troupe was girding up for the big opening day parade in Manhattan, Annie Oakley, instead of getting better, got worse. Oils, leeches, everything was tried, but nothing worked—for a time it seemed as if her rival, Lillian Smith, would be in the parade, but not her. Annie had already lopped six years off her age because of this troublesome teenager: the thought that Lillian Smith might upstage her before all New York was too much.

The train carrying most of the troupe had already left, but Annie ordered her horse saddled, changed clothes while this was happening, and raced off to catch the train, which she did. The parade was a long one, but at least she was in it. By the time it ended she was too weak to dismount. Salsbury ordered the best doctors and the ear was finally lanced, but the verdict was blood poisoning. For the next four days, while Buffalo Bill's Wild West packed the ferries and the trains, Annie Oakley lay close to death. But on the fifth day, she showed signs of life and by showtime was ready to perform, although with a heavily bandaged ear.

The long stay on Staten Island left Annie plenty of time in which to develop new acts. Her immediate ambition was fueled by her intense desire to outdo Lillian Smith, the young California sharpshooter whose mere presence on the lot irritated Annie to an extreme. Whatever nice things she said about Cody later, it's not clear that she ever forgave him for bringing Lillian Smith into the troupe.

Lillian Smith was billed as a rapid-fire shooter; she broke innumerable glass balls or plates in quick succession. Insofar as there was a division of labor in this early stage of the show's evolution, Lillian Smith was the rifle shot, Annie Oakley the genius of the shotgun. Annie, who could shoot either weapon proficiently, decided to up the ante by developing acts in which she herself was in motion. She shot while riding a bicycle, and then moved on to horses. Frank was skeptical and Salsbury fearful but Annie soon became an excellent horsewoman. She shot lying full-length on her horse's back, and even learned to shoot standing up on her mount. The fact that she was shooting birdshot out of a smoothbore gun helped a lot when it came to breaking glass balls; but even the great Cody used a smoothbore gun when he shot his glass balls. (Cody and Doc Carver did at first use bullets but the result was too many broken windows from houses several blocks away.)

During this relatively settled period on Staten Island, Cody, Salsbury, and Major Burke had time to give some thought to what lay ahead. They had already committed themselves to go to England and perform at Queen Victoria's Golden Jubilee; they were in the midst of their most successful season ever, and yet Cody already felt the need for more. There were too many shows in the field. Pawnee Bill would soon have a good one up and running, and old Barnum himself was not finished.

Cody's insight, at this juncture, was that mere "combinations," however star-studded, weren't going to satisfy audiences much longer. It was fine to have Annie Oakley and a couple of other sharpshooters; fine to have buffalo, Indians, cowboys, trick ropers, a brass band, and so on. Some of the skits from his own frontier experience—the Pony Express, the attack on the settler's cabin, or the Deadwood stage—were fine skits; they provided the audience with at least a whiff of the Wild West. But Cody wanted more narrative—he always wanted more narrative, even though it would be narrative in its broadest, crudest form.

What he didn't want was a show that was merely an advanced form of rodeo, with the safest acts (like the grand entry) first and the more dangerous acts, like bronc busting, later.

What Cody wanted was a theme; and since he was about to go international, the broader the theme, the better. The concept he came up with, after much brainstorming with Salsbury and Burke, was the broadest theme possible: civilization itself.

At first blush this sounds ridiculous. How could a bunch of poorly educated scouts and actors pretend to enact the drama of the advance of civilization—and yet that is exactly what they proceeded to attempt.

Already, too, Cody was looking to the day when more and more performances would be held indoors, in vast sports palaces, which would protect them from debacles such as the forty-four days of rain in New Orleans. As it happened, a promising venue lay just across the way: Madison Square Garden, where Salsbury had already arranged a short run just before the troupe departed for England.

Already Major Burke's press books were growing longer and more elaborate—the one for the great Chicago Exposition of 1893 would be sixty-four pages long. Buffalo Bill's Wild West was publishing its own history, even as it made it.

By the time the show ended its successful run on Staten Island and prepared to move into town, the new concept under which they all were to labor had been finalized. Buffalo Bill's Wild West would be presenting nothing less ambitious than the Drama of Civilization, beginning deep in the primeval forest and bouncing forward in great leaps.

Where the Drama of Civilization was concerned, Annie Oakley kept her thoughts to herself. Her part in the drama, in any case, was just to keep breaking glass balls. The worst time she had in Manhattan was when the company's pet moose, Jerry, who had been trained to pull a cart, could not resist the smell of a big pile of nice juicy apples on a vendor's stand. The vendor was not pleased to have his stock ravished by a moose—Little Missie had to fork over $5 in order to make peace with the man.

Grandmother England

1

BUFFALO BILL'S Wild West went to England in Queen Victoria's Jubilee year ostensibly to add a little flavor to a big American trade fair, which was already open in Earl's Court, though receiving little attention. It never did garner much attention. The big troupe of wild Westerners soon sucked away what few visitors the trade show had managed to attract. The tail immediately began to wag the dog: the American Exposition was a big flop, and Buffalo Bill's Wild West an enormous success, playing to some two and a half million people before moving on to shorter runs in Manchester and Birmingham. The enormous turnout was still just enough to save Cody and Salsbury's financial bacon due to the expense of the huge troupe they brought over, a full count of which is hard to come by. There were 97 Indians, 160 horses, 16 buffalo, a couple of bears, elk, deer, and of course, scores of performers and stagehands.

Among the Indians making the trip, besides Black Elk and the popular Red Shirt, were Mr. and Mrs. Walking Buffalo, Mr. and Mrs. Eagle Horse, Moccasin Tom, Blue Rainbow, Iron Good Voice, Mr. and Mrs. Cut Meat, and Double Wound, to give only a very abbreviated list. Were this not enough, the bushy-bearded John Y. Nelson managed with his wife to produce a fine papoose along the way, a little boy much appreciated by the royal family. There was also a thirty-six-piece band.

In general the Indians trusted Pahaska (sometimes Pawhaska) Cody, but were nonetheless apprehensive about crossing the Big

Water; going behind the sunrise, as they saw it, could not be a good idea. It was a rough crossing, too; some thought they were doomed—more than one death song floated up from the underdeck. Almost everyone got seasick, though Annie Oakley didn't. There was much rejoicing when the *State of Nebraska* finally reached the Albert Dock. Major Burke, of course, was there ahead of them, doing the same things that press agents do now: securing advertising, setting up interviews, and so forth.

Annie Oakley was soon secure in her snug, nicely carpeted tent—she quickly found that she liked English ways and said more than once that if it had not been for the need to see her old and ailing mother, she would have been well content to make England her home.

Because it was Grandmother England's—the Indians' name for Queen Victoria—Jubilee year, much of the world's royalty (to which, in many cases, she was literally the grandmother) stayed in or at least passed through London while the Wild West was performing. The future Kaiser Wilhelm II was there, as well as Crown Prince Rudolf of Austria, who was soon to die by his own hand in the tragic suicide at Mayerling. Almost everyone loved the show, although there were a few sourpusses, one of them being the poet James Russell Lowell, who had recently been our minister to the Court of St. James. Lowell was much too high-minded for such populist entertainment, attributing the show's immense success to "the dullness of the average English mind."

One night there were no fewer than twenty royals crammed into the royal box, among whom were the four kings who would soon find themselves careering around the arena in the Deadwood stage.

The one person who liked the wildly successful Wild West even less than James Russell Lowell was George Sanger, head of the largest and best-established English circus company, from whom Cody drained spectators as easily as he had from the big trade fair. Indeed, throughout the whole six-month run there was hardly a day when Cody's name did not appear in the London newspapers, where he was usually referred to as the Honorable William F. Cody. Aware that the English might be picky about titles, Cody had come prepared with a sheaf of testimonials from many military men; he had even persuaded the governor of Nebraska to make him a colonel, though exactly what unit he was supposed to be colonel of was not easy to say.

George Sanger was so annoyed at constantly seeing Cody referred to as "the Honorable" that he summarily added an "Honorable" to his own name.

Very fortunately for Mr. Sanger, Queen Victoria, upon being informed of George Sanger's aggressive act, decided in this instance to be amused.

2

FROM the viewpoint of the Honorable George Sanger, the circumstance that most added insult to injury where Cody was concerned, was the fact the one person who did the most to siphon customers to Buffalo Bill's Wild West was his own sovereign, Queen Victoria. Major John Burke could have labored in the English pressrooms for years without securing as much good publicity for the show as the queen did merely by agreeing to attend.

Queen Victoria's appearance at their London show was the greatest stroke of luck Cody and Salsbury were to have on any of their European outings. Grandmother England to the Indians, she was, as I have said, literally grandmother to most of the sitting royalty of Europe. Both the soon-to-be Kaiser Wilhelm II of Germany and the soon-enough-to-be Tsar Nicholas II of Russia were her grandsons, and there were many more grandchildren scattered through lesser duchies and states.

What made Victoria's appearance at a command performance in Earl's Court so extraordinary was that she had remained in mourning for twenty-six of her fifty years as queen—in mourning for her beloved husband, Albert. Until Cody and the Wild West came along, if the queen wanted to see a play or a revue, the players came to her, usually at Windsor Castle, where they performed in her own theater.

And in fact, she would have had the Wild West perform at Windsor had she not been persuaded that it would be physically impossible to have so many animals running around the castle. The buffalo might abscond, as they once had from P. T. Barnum on Staten Island.

What probably whetted the queen's curiosity to an intolerable pitch was gossip that floated back to her from the two command performances that preceded hers, one ordered by Prime Minister Gladstone and the other by her own son, the often disappointing Albert Edward, Prince of Wales, by whom she was very seldom amused though frequently annoyed because of the prince's gambling or philandering activities that were sure, sooner or later, to embarrass the throne. No one would ever defend more seriously the dignity of that particular throne than the small plump lady who sat on it from 1837 until her death, in 1901.

The first command performance, for the prime minister, went off rockingly, after which Cody, Annie Oakley, Red Shirt, Lillian Smith, and others came up to be presented to the Prince of Wales and his shy, gentle wife, the long-suffering Princess Alexandra. When it became Annie Oakley's turn to shake, or at least touch, hands with the royal couple, Annie boldly dispensed with protocol and shook the princess's hand first. "I'm sorry," she said to the startled prince, whose hand she then shook. "I'm an American and in America ladies come first."

Annie Oakley's shooting act was wildly successful in London, so successful that no one much wanted to comment on this gaffe. Although a mature woman of twenty-seven at the time, she still looked like a slip of a girl. No one wanted to be harsh, so the slip was put down to girlish naivete, when in fact it was probably the one purely feminist act of Annie Oakley's life. Annie knew—because everyone knew—that the Prince of Wales was a shameless and, indeed, a serial philanderer. The gentle Alexandra was much beloved, and not least because of the grace with which she ignored, to the extent that was possible, the prince's terrible behavior. Annie Oakley did what she did in order to show support for a sister of a sort. Whether Princess Alexandra understood this is unclear, but she did love the Wild West and, as I mentioned earlier, once slipped incognito into the press box in order to watch it without herself being quite so onstage.

* * *

Buffalo Bill Cody got along splendidly with the Prince of Wales, with whom he shared many faults. Cody saw the prince as a man he could happily drink with, carouse with, shoot with, club with. Throughout the show's run the prince frequently invited Cody here and there, and Cody usually went. One or two aristos may have snubbed Cody, or at least have maintained a stiff formality; but Cody, as usual, was too affable and too presentable to be kept out.

When Queen Victoria showed up for her command performance, or later, when she summoned the troupe to Windsor for tea and a visit, she was not rude to Cody but she also made no effort to single him out for attention. She told Annie Oakley that she was "a very clever little girl" and she definitely admired Red Shirt's good looks. It may be that she saw in Cody a man whose habits were too much like her eldest son's.

3

THERE are numerous printed accounts of Queen Victoria's visit to Buffalo Bill's Wild West—she herself twice recorded her admiration for Red Shirt and her surprise that the Indians, mainly Sioux, were so good-looking. The visit was mentioned in many memoirs and picked up by so many newspapers that Louisa Cody heard about it and concluded that both Queen Victoria and Princess Alexandra had paid improper attentions to her husband. Bitterness over the queen's visit surfaced eighteen years after the fact, in the ill-conceived and unsuccessful divorce attempt that Cody pressed in 1905.

Of the many accounts of the earth-shattering visit of the queen, who had been absent from the public eye for twenty-six years, the most poetic and most charming by far is that of Nicholas Black Elk, the young Ogalala who had been coaxed into coming on the trip because he was the best dancer the Sioux could boast.

In Black Elk's account, "Grandmother England" arrived in "a big shining wagon with soldiers on both sides."

Black Elk and his friends proceeded to dance themselves silly:

We stood right in front of Grandmother England. She was little but fat, and we liked her because she was good to us. After we danced she spoke to us. She said "I am sixty-seven years old . . . I have seen all kinds of people; but today I have seen the best looking people I know. If you belonged to me, I would not let them take you around in a show like this."

We all shook hands with her. Her hand was very little and soft. We gave a big cheer for her and then the shining wagons came in and she got into one of them and they all went away.

Then, Windsor:

. . . in about half a moon we went to see Grandmother. They put us into some of those shining wagons and took us . . . to a very big house with sharp pointed towers on it. There were many seats built high in a circle, and these were just full of Wasichus [whites] who were all pounding their heels and yelling: Jubilee! Jubilee! Jubilee! I never heard what this meant.

Then we saw Grandmother England again . . . Her dress was all shining and her hat was all shining and her wagon was all shining and so were the horses. She looked like a fire coming . . .

We sent up a great cry and our women made the tremolo . . . when it was quiet we sang a song to the Grandmother . . .

We liked Grandmother because we could see that she was a good woman, and she was good to us. Maybe if she had been our grandmother it would have been better for our people.

4

WHEN the long run at Earl's Court ended, the troupe loaded up and played Birmingham and then Manchester, after which they sailed for home, with young Nicholas Black Elk not among them. Always curious, and habituated to running on his own notion of time, rather than the playbill's, he somehow failed to make the disembarkment and was wandering around Manchester when he bumped into some other Indians who were similarly stranded. Fortunately they were all to some extent show people now; they soon managed to get on with an impresario named Mexican Joe whose troupe was then performing in London. Mexican Joe didn't have many Indians; he was glad to take them on at a wage of $1 a day.

When Mexican Joe moved on to Paris he took the Indians with him. Black Elk was particularly wary of the Metro—he didn't like the sight of people disappearing into the ground.

Black Elk got very sick in Paris. The Indians who were with him decided he was a goner and went out to make a coffin; but Black Elk recovered and was taken in by his French girlfriend for the rest of his stay. While lying near death in her Paris apartment, Black Elk had one of his greatest visions: the vision of the cloud that came to take him home.

Then I was alone on the cloud, and it was going fast, I clung to it hard because I was afraid I might fall off. Far down below I could see houses and towns and green land and streams, and it all looked flat.

Then I was right over the big water. I was not afraid any more, because, by now, I knew I was going home. It was dark and then it was light again, and I could see a big town below me, and I knew it was the one where we first got on the big fireboat, and that I was in my own country again. The cloud and I kept going very fast, and I could see streams and towns and green lands. Then I began to recognize the country below me. I saw the Missouri River. Then I saw far off the Black Hills and the center of the world where the spirits had taken me in my great vision.

Then I was right over Pine Ridge, and the cloud stopped and I looked down and could not understand what I saw, because it seemed that nearly all my people were gathered together there in a big camp. I saw my father and mother's teepee. They were outside and she was cooking. I wanted to jump off the cloud and be with them, but I was afraid it would kill me. While I was looking down my mother looked up, and I felt sure she saw me. But just then the cloud started going back, very fast . . . I was very sad, but I could not get off . . . soon the cloud and I were going right back over the big town again, then there was only water underneath me, and the night came without stars; and I was all alone in a black world and I was crying. But after a while some light began to peep in far ahead of me. Then I saw earth beneath me and towns and green land and houses, all flying backward. Soon the cloud stopped over a big town, and a house began to come up toward me, turning round as it came. When it touched the cloud it caught me and began to drop down, turning round and round with me.

It touched the ground and I heard the girl's voice.

Soon after Black Elk recovered, Cody arrived in Paris on his first continental tour. Black Elk soon found his way to him. Cody offered him a job, but he soon saw that Black Elk was too homesick to be much use. With his usual generosity Cody got him a berth home and gave him $90 to see him through to Dakota. It was because of this kind act that Black Elk said Cody had a strong heart.

Cody's European tour of 1889 will be dealt with later. Both he and Black Elk were to be in Dakota again. Cody was blocked in his final attempt to see and possibly soothe Sitting Bull, and Black Elk lived to deliver the saddest statement about the unnecessary tragedy of Wounded Knee.

Before we get to that sad day I would like to finish the account of the triumphs of the Colonel and Little Missie in London—the home of Grandmother England.

5

ALTHOUGH Annie Oakley was outshot a couple of times on her first acquaintance with English shooting, in the main she went, as always, from triumph to triumph and garnered as much good publicity as anyone except Cody himself. Both of them were constantly in the news, with Cody being feted by the biggest wigs in the land. At one point he returned the favor and held a buffalo roast, which greatly pleased all who were invited. The Indians cooked the buffalo and ate their part with their hands—a tiny but vivid illustration of the drama of civilization, which most spectators felt free to ignore. What they liked was the riding and the whooping.

On one shoot at least Annie, boasting the new light gun that Charles Lancaster had crafted for her, scored a triumph over both her archrival, Lillian Smith, and her boss, Bill Cody. This was held at the famous Wimbledon sporting club, which featured a mechanical deer which raced along on a track.

In this era most shooting clubs were, of course, all-male institutions. In many cases Annie Oakley was the first female to set foot in them, and famous though she was, her presence in this rigidly male precinct did not please all members. There were many snubs, both in America and England, and the snubs continued throughout her long career. Annie did her best to ignore them. She stood on her considerable dignity and her even more considerable abilities with the gun.

Lillian Smith also got invitations to shoot and accepted some of them. Probably the reason she didn't accept more was because it was painfully clear that even though she might win the shooting, Annie would inevitably win the crowd.

By the time of the Wimbledon shoot Lillian Smith was under attack in the press; a skeptical English journalist named Carter studied her act through binoculars and accused her of cheating. Most trick shooters cut a corner here and there. Sights that were supposedly covered might not in fact *be* covered. The matter of Lillian Smith's cheating filled the shooting papers for some time, inconclusively. What hurt her more than these accusations was her racy dress. When she arrived at the Wimbledon sporting club she wore a dress that sported a vivid yellow sash, and a plug hat the likes of which had never been seen in this august club before.

The sash and the hat might have been overlooked had Lillian shot well, but she didn't. She twice missed the running deer outright, and then only managed to hit it in the haunch, which, in English eyes, was worse than missing. Members who hit the haunch were in fact fined, since a haunch hit meant a wounded deer.

Lillian Smith tried to make light of the matter, claiming she had brought too heavy a rifle—she agreed to come back, more effectively equipped, and she readily agreed to pay the fine.

In fact, she did neither, annoying the directors of the Wimbledon sporting club no end.

Even more annoying to them was the fact that Buffalo Bill Cody never showed up to shoot at all. Annie was very popular, but Cody was still the headliner and one of the most popular men on earth. Though he may have gone on a few toots while in London, he never neglected his appearance, and his fame was as high as it was possible for fame to be. Why he never showed up to shoot at the mechanical deer has never been explained; probably he was just too busy. It seems unlikely that he doubted his shooting; in real life he had hit more than one running deer.

Cody didn't come, but Annie did. She hit the deer readily, and not in the haunch, either. It was perhaps her most conspicuous triumph over Lillian Smith.

Shortly after this well-publicized shoot there was an attack on Annie, a critique published somewhat remotely, in a California journal called *Breeder and Stockman*. Remote as this calumny seemed to be—some thought it had been commissioned by Lillian Smith—Nate Salsbury and Frank Butler took it very seriously—any threat to Annie's credibility as a markswoman must be taken seriously by those running the show. Salsbury knew how much the show needed Annie Oakley—her ability to draw crowds was exceeded only by Cody's. (In France, as we shall see, she was *more* of a draw than Cody, at least at first.)

Frank Butler wrote a long rebuttal to the piece in the *Breeder and Stockman*. Most thought that he had successfully defended his wife's reputation.

Then, just as the troupe was ready to pack up and head for Birmingham, Annie Oakley and Frank Butler made a decision that rocked Nate Salsbury, even though he may have seen it coming. The couple quietly quit the show and made their way back to New York.

6

EXACTLY why Annie Oakley and her manager-husband decided to take herself out of Buffalo Bill's Wild West at this juncture will probably never be known—at least not in full. There had always been rumblings and occasional disagreements with Cody, but no more serious rumblings than could be expected of any star performer amid the pressures of an extended run.

What Annie claimed, in her little eulogy to Cody on the occasion of his death—that she had never had a contract with him—was as big a lie as her instinctive lie about her age. She had many contracts with Cody's Wild West, all of them meticulously negotiated by Frank Butler. In these contracts it was clearly stated that Annie had the right to do considerable shooting on her own. She could give exhibitions and enter shooting competitions; she did both and made good money at it, sometimes as much as $750 a week, big money indeed for that day and time.

At one point she received an excellent offer to compete in Germany, and she meant to accept, but Salsbury seems to have blocked it by insisting that he couldn't do without his star for that long. Or Cody may have grumbled. At this point Annie and Frank had been with the Wild West a little more than three years, during which time Annie's fame had steadily risen. She wanted to shoot in Germany and eventually did.

I doubt, myself, that Cody was jealous of the attention Annie got in the London papers. The attention brought in more customers, and in any case, he got more publicity and was still the bigger star.

I don't think there's any need to claim that the Butlers' break with the show posited some huge falling-out between themselves and management—that is, Cody and Salsbury. Nowhere in the numerous biographies is there much indication that the Butlers and Cody were really close friends. They were star performers, working together in a show—possibly there were tiffs, but when aren't there tiffs? Cody was gregarious and outgoing; he liked to drink and carouse and had an abundance of opportunities to do so in the great world capital where he found himself.

Annie Oakley, by contrast, was very private. Her spirits during this run seemed to have been high, but that didn't mean she was out with the boys, slugging them down. She stayed in her tent and did her needlework. Frank may have slipped his lead now and then, but not very seriously. As far as dissipation went Annie might occasionally allow herself a glass of beer, particularly if someone else was paying.

Annie's intense dislike of Lillian Smith may have been a big part of the reason she and Frank left the Wild West at this time. Or it could merely have been that the Butlers felt they could do better financially on their own.

Cody, for his part, may have reasoned that the Wild West was now so well established that even the loss of a big star would not really affect the box office that much.

The shift to independence seemed to have proved, for the Butlers, mildly disappointing. They easily got bookings, but much travel was involved and $750 weeks were few and far between. They more than held their own but freelancing soon proved to be quite a bit harder than working for Cody.

When the likable Gordon Lillie (Pawnee Bill) offered to hire them for a short tour they readily accepted and the tour did well, a fact that Cody and Salsbury, back in New York by then, certainly noticed. The Wild West was preparing for a big tour of Europe in 1889 and both men realized that after all, they still needed Annie Oakley. She was a bigger star than anyone except Cody himself.

For their part, it probably didn't take the Butlers long to figure out that they functioned better as part of an established troupe. Cody and Salsbury offered the best environment; with them, Annie—shooting maybe twenty minutes a day—could remain a major superstar. The transportation would be arranged for them, and they didn't have to carry their own instruments, as it were. Besides that, Annie could profit from the energetic talents of Major Burke, a man Annie came to like, although she was not as deeply fond of him as Louisa Cody seemed to be.

In any case the Butlers soon sat down with Salsbury and ironed out whatever differences there may have been. Annie Oakley happily came back to Buffalo Bill's Wild West. Not until the traumatic train wreck in 1903 would she leave it again.

When Annie returned, Lillian Smith resigned. The two sharpshooters would rarely cross paths again.

7

THE tour of Europe which Cody and Salsbury plunged into in 1889 was as ambitious as any season they would ever mount. In Paris, where they had a seven-month run, the importance of having Annie Oakley in the troupe was quickly demonstrated. The first show came very close to being a flop, the French remaining true to their reputation of being hard to get. The crowd seemed glacially indifferent to Cody, cowboys, buffalos, broncos, Indians, ropers, and the thirty-six-piece band. It was clearly the wrong place to speak of the Drama of Civilization, since the French *were* civilization, at least in their eyes.

At first they were wholly reluctant to clap for anything they were seeing.

Sensing disaster, Salsbury rushed Annie into the arena and she immediately saved the day, riding and shooting so brilliantly that the crowd leapt to its feet and in the end called her back for six encores. Once the show got established the French quickly acquired a strong yen for Indian souvenirs: moccasins, baskets, and bows sold in great numbers.

The Wild West eventually went on to Barcelona, Naples, Rome, Florence, Bologna, Milan, and Venice, where Indians in full warbonnets were photographed on the Grand Canal. They then played Vienna, took a little trip on the Danube, and went into winter quarters in Benfield. It was in Naples that Major Burke was briefly fired.

For this second tour over the waters Cody and Salsbury took

seventy-two Indians from Pine Ridge, five of whom died during the tour. Two men, Lone Wolf and Star, are buried in Brompton Cemetery, London.

These deaths, which the Indians said were to be expected, were nonetheless noted by the authorities at home. In Berlin two U.S. consuls came and inspected conditions; both reported that they had never seen Indians looking so well-fed and so healthy.

Still, there were complaints from America, both from within the government and out, a problem Cody and Salsbury took very seriously. If they were denied Indians the whole tour would be compromised. Salsbury stayed in Europe to keep things in good order, and Cody went home, taking some of the Indians with him.

8

B ILL C O D Y ' S oblique and frustrating near involvement with the Ghost Dance crisis on the Dakota reservations in December of 1890 is perhaps the oddest thing that happened to him during his long career, as first a fighter of, and then an employer of, Indians.

For the now essentially captive Sioux, the decade of the 1880s had been one long disappointment. With the exceptions of Sitting Bull and Red Cloud their major leaders were dead. More and more white settlers poured into the northern plains, the result being that the Sioux had to watch their reservations being constantly whittled down. They were repeatedly asked to make do with less; the buffalo were gone, they were dependent on agency beef, they had no work and were in an increasingly dismal situation.

Sitting Bull was at the Standing Rock reservation, living quietly and occasionally riding the show horse that Buffalo Bill had given him. The fine sombrero he kept mainly for ceremonial occasions.

Sitting Bull, when possible, avoided conflict with Agent James McLaughlin, who administered the Pine Ridge agency. Throughout the reservation system complaints about the slow and puny food allotments were constant. The beeves that the Indians depended on were usually slow in arriving, and were usually too few in number.

Indeed, the Pine Ridge and Standing Rock reservations were wretched places to be, as they still are. With the buffalo gone, an old and established life way was destroyed. The general wretchedness and drunkenness made it easy for Cody to get Indians to sign up for his shows. It was better than staying home and being depressed.

Agent McLaughlin and other honest administrators knew that the Indians were miserable. They worried that somehow there might yet be an outbreak and they overreacted to the slightest sign of independence among the bands. Their response to the Ghost Dance was just such an overreaction. Though it must have been obvious that the Sioux lacked the arms and the leadership necessary to any sort of sustained revolt, the arrival of the Ghost Dance somehow tipped the balance. Worry became paranoia.

Native American millenarianism was hardly a new thing—Native American prophets began to preach against the whites as early as the sixteenth century; they predicted that the whites would vanish, the dead return, and the world be restored to the condition it had been in before the whites arrived.

Many prophets preached some version of a Return story, in which the Native American world would regain its old fullness. In the late nineteenth century these prophets mostly emerged from the desert places. In 1881 an Apache preacher named Noch-ay-del-klinne was killed, with a number of his followers, on Cibicue Creek, in Arizona. He too preached of the Return, a powerful idea that gave hope to an essentially powerless people.

The prophet most associated with the flourishing of the Ghost Dance was a short fat Paiute named Wovoka, whose white name was Jack Wilson. He lived mostly with a white family in Nevada. When Indian leaders from far away—Kansas, Oklahoma—wanted to learn about the Ghost Dance they came to Jack Wilson for instruction. He left a few instructional texts—Messiah letters, these were called—about how to perform the dance and what to expect. There was no call to violence in the letters or in his preaching. The Ghost Dance was a long dance that brought the dancers to a state of spiritual purification. Jack Wilson goes out of his way to warn the dancers to leave the whites alone. The dancers were merely to dance for a long time, then bathe in the creek and stay with their families.

Nonetheless, thanks to the long history of plains warfare, the white administrators were simply unable to take a calm view of sizable groups of Indians assembling for any purpose at all. The whole reservation system had been designed to separate tribe from tribe and lessen the risks that they associated with large assemblies.

Agent McLaughlin was unhappy when the Ghost Dance arrived at Pine Ridge, but for a time at least, he tried to maintain perspective. In several dispatches he mentions that the Sioux were behaving well. Above all, he hoped to keep the army out; the army had a way of making things worse.

McLaughlin's relationship with Sitting Bull had been touchy, but so far not catastrophic. At one point he went to visit the old Hunkpapa to express his concern about the Ghost Dance, his fear being that the young warriors would get so stirred up by the dancing that they might go back to killing whites. Sitting Bull seems to have genuinely tried to mollify McLaughlin. It is just some people dancing, he said—it was nothing to be alarmed about. Then he made McLaughlin an unusual offer, so some authorities say. He himself didn't put much stock in preachers or Messiahs, but if McLaughlin was so worried about this man Wovoka, perhaps the two of them ought to pay him a visit. If they found him and he was indeed a Messiah then they could determine what his disposition was. But if Wovoka failed to convince, then Sitting Bull could tell his people that the Ghost Dance was all hooey. It wasn't going to bring the buffalo back, or cause a new earth to rise, or raise the dead, or drive the whites away.

If this offer was made Agent McLaughlin would have done well to take it, but he didn't. No doubt he feared to leave his agency at such a nervous time.

Meanwhile, in New York, Buffalo Bill Cody, indignant about the charges that he had mistreated Indians, was prepared to go to Washington with a number of Indians to refute these charges. Of course, with several troupes in Europe, all of them employing Indians, some abuse may have occurred, but most of the complaints usually boiled down to seasickness. None of the Indians enjoyed crossing the great water.

Before Cody could get his group on the train to Washington, he received a bolt from the blue, in the form of a succinct telegram from General Nelson A. Miles, whom he had known for some time. It read:

> Col. Cody,
> You are authorized to secure the person of Sitting Bull and . . . deliver him to the nearest com'g officer of US troops, taking a receipt and reporting your action.
>
> Nelson A. Miles

On the back Miles had scribbled a note assuring Cody that the army would offer him all the assistance he needed.

Cody had just returned from a long stay in Europe. Whether he knew of the Ghost Dance excitement I'm not sure, but to receive an order from a major general asking him to proceed to the very heart of Sioux country and summarily arrest their leader in the midst of his people could only have come as a major shock.

It was no less a shock to Agent McLaughlin, when he received a copy. For Cody or anybody else to ride into Standing Rock and arrest Sitting Bull would very likely mean bloodshed and probably provoke the revolt McLaughlin was trying so hard to prevent.

Agent McLaughlin immediately got on the singing wires, telegraphing everyone he could think of to assure them that the situation was peaceful at Standing Rock. He insisted that there was no immediate threat—if it eventually seemed necessary to arrest Sitting Bull, then native policemen could probably handle the arrest without bloodshed.

Buffalo Bill Cody McLaughlin distinctly did *not* need—but the man was already on the way. The military and the administrators had got their wires crossed. General Miles continued to insist that Cody was their best bet, but by the time Cody actually reached South Dakota various official barricades had been thrown up. Cody saw General Miles but never got close to Sitting Bull—in hindsight it's hard not to think that McLaughlin used bad judgment here. Sitting Bull knew that Cody had friendly feelings for him—if Cody had been permitted to see his old star it is not likely that he would have tried to arrest him, but it might have defused the tense situation.

Cody had come a long way for nothing and was more than a little annoyed. He went down to his home in North Platte, though not before he secured a few fresh Indians from Pine Ridge for his show.

A few days before Sitting Bull's death, legend has it, he was taking a walk and minding his own business when a cheeky meadowlark, speaking in Sioux, informed him that he would soon be killed by his own people. Sitting Bull probably wished the meadowlark, too, had minded his own business; but the prophecy soon came true. McLaughlin sent a troop of native policemen to ask Sitting Bull to come to the agency, a request he usually complied with, though with much grumbling. The native policemen arrived early, hoping to get Sitting Bull out before the camp was well awake. They were early, but not early enough. Sitting Bull started to submit, but changed his mind when he saw that quite a few Ghost Dancers had lined up to support him. A scuffle ensued: two native policemen, Bull Head and Red Tomahawk, both shot Sitting Bull, who died on the spot, along with one of his sons and several others. Had the army not thoughtfully provided a sizable backup force all the native policemen would very likely have been killed.

Cody was out of the way well before this happened. He would have seen nothing wrong about visiting his old friend Sitting Bull; the two might have had a good powwow, but it is unlikely he would have said anything about turning him over to the army. His show depended in good measure on the goodwill of the Sioux, which he would have quickly lost if he had tried to arrest Sitting Bull. General Miles's simple hope seems to have been that Cody could lure him away from the reservation with the promise of medals or something, after which the army could have taken over.

It may be that, once he was in striking distance, some officer told him that Sitting Bull was already on his way to Pine Ridge, using a different road. Cody was relaxing in North Platte when he learned of Sitting Bull's death.

The death of their toughest chief threw all the northern Sioux into confusion. They expected big trouble to result, and big trouble did result, although not immediately. Sitting Bull was killed on the fifteenth of December 1889. Because six native policemen had died in the struggle to arrest him, the Sioux expected reprisals—many fled to the hills, while others made their way to the comparative safety of the Pine Ridge agency.

Among the groups headed for Pine Ridge were the people led by Chief Big Foot, who was ill with pneumonia at the time. Indeed, he was so ill that the officer who took charge of this group immediately ordered him a doctor and a heated tent as well. This occurred near Wounded Knee Creek, not far east of Pine Ridge.

The next morning, with a large contingent of the Seventh Cavalry standing by, an attempt was made to disarm the Indians in Big Foot's camp. The attempt was hurried and rough. The exact sequence of events which led to the massacre has been debated ever since; but at some point the soldiers began to shoot the Indians and the Indians fought back with knives, hatchets, and small arms. A massacre occurred, Big Foot was immediately killed, as were a total of 146 Sioux, many of them women and children. So desperately did the Sioux fight that twenty-five soldiers also died; nearly forty more were hurt.

Nicholas Black Elk, looking over the carnage of this battle, left the most elegant statement that we have about the tragedy of Wounded Knee:

And so it was all over.

I did not know then how much was ended. When I look back from this high hill of my old age, I can still see the butchered women and the children lying heaped and scattered all along the crooked gulch as plain as when I saw them with eyes still young. And I can see that something else died there in the bloody mud, and was buried in the blizzard. A people's dream died there. It was a beautiful dream.

And I, to whom so great a vision was given in my youth, you see me now a pitiful old man who has done nothing, for the nation's hoop is broken and scattered. There is no center anymore, and the sacred tree is dead.

181

Buffalo Bill was so annoyed by the poor use the army had made of him that he billed them some $500 for expenses on his unnecessary trip.

Though the Sioux were essentially finished, a brief revolt did flare up. It lasted about two weeks. Cody left North Platte and became a kind of roving liaison man, his main task being to persuade terrified Nebraskans that they need not flee south. Some fled anyway. By the sixteenth of January the last miscreants had given up and the last Sioux outbreak was over. Eleven thousand soldiers were there to assure the surrender.

By this time Major Burke was in Pine Ridge himself—he was escorting some fifty of the Indians who had been in the show back to the place he was supposed to return them.

What Cody really thought about this sad debacle is not easy to say. The film he later made about it no longer exists, of which more later. Perhaps Cody unburdened himself to Major Burke, or Salsbury, or even his wife, but he said nothing disrespectful about the military to any of the reporters who pursued him.

From this distance in time it seems that both General Miles and Agent McLaughlin lost their heads. McLaughlin had visited Sitting Bull only two weeks earlier; the old man may have grumbled, but there was no violence, no threat. Cody was a friend; he might have helped, but the left hand ignored the right hand and the blood of another two hundred people stained the much-stained northern plains.

There was to be one more irony: when the Sioux surrendered in January 1890, they allowed the whites to take nineteen hostages. For their part in the last Sioux revolt they were consigned, by way of punishment, to Buffalo Bill Cody, who had been cleared of all charges relating to abuse.

A short time later the nineteen Sioux were performing in Europe.

The sharpshooter Johnny Baker, whom Annie Oakley mothered and Cody helped raise.

Lillian Smith, Annie Oakley's great rival.

Will Rogers.

Ned Buntline, dime novelist and impresario. 21

Doc Carver, Cody's persistent rival. 22

Gordon Lillie, Pawnee Bill.

Buffalo Bill with his sometime partner Pawnee Bill.

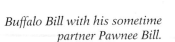

Katherine Clemmons, the actress who was Cody's most expensive mistake.

John Y. Nelson who rode shotgun on the Deadwood stage when it held four kings and a crown prince.

Queen Victoria, who came out of mourning to take in the Wild West.

Red Shirt, Ogalala much admired by Queen Victoria.

The Grand Duke Alexis of Russia, an exceptionally poor shot.

Spotted Tail, leader of the Brule Sioux and (probably) Crazy Horse's uncle.

The Deadwood stage. On top is John Y. Nelson with two of his children.

One of the railroad cars that carried the Wild West into as many as 130 cities a year.

32

9

THERE is debate about the origins of the term "Rough Rider." On big ranches half-broken horses were referred to as the "rough string," and the cowboys whose job it was to improve their behavior might have been called "rough riders." It seems clear that Cody and Salsbury used it before Theodore Roosevelt appropriated it for his Cuban campaign. By 1893 Cody's show was grandly called Buffalo Bill's Wild West and Congress of Rough Riders of the World—by this time Salsbury had added gauchos, Cossacks, vaqueros, and Arabs to the mix.

Salsbury was in Europe while Cody was in the Dakotas. Though the abuse accusations were easily settled, Salsbury, looking far ahead, decided that it would be wise to slowly shift the emphasis of the show from historical skits to horsemanship. Cody could never have been weaned entirely from his beloved skits, but he was an exceptional horseman himself and would never object to more riders.

The 1891 tour through northern Europe involved ten stops in Germany alone, with only occasional mishaps or alarums. One occurred while Annie Oakley was giving shooting lessons to a Bavarian prince—a horse broke loose and came charging their way, forcing Annie to wrestle the startled prince to the ground.

Kaiser Wilhelm saw her shoot a cigarette out of her husband's mouth and demanded that she try it with him, which she did, though she didn't like the Kaiser and later remarked that he was just the sort of man who would start a war. After he had, she informed him that if they ever tried the trick again she could not guarantee the results.

Needless to say, they never tried the trick again. Her appraisal of the Kaiser shows how quickly and accurately the young woman from Darke County, Ohio, could size up people—particularly the great and famous. Bismarck, she remarked, looked like a mastiff. Throughout their travels together she exhibited far less tolerance than Cody for the company of stuffed shirts—though she did give shooting lessons to a good many of them, and to their children as well.

The 1891 tour boasted the show's most swollen roster, with 640 "eating members"—and eating members ate three full meals a day, an arrangement that the Indians found very satisfactory.

Grandmother England came to the Wild West again and was particularly pleased that Cody had added Cossacks to the roster. Cody was again presented to the queen. He was on the wagon that summer, under strict orders from Salsbury to indulge in no more toots. When offered drinks by the queen's equerry Cody staunchly refused; Salsbury merely accepted a glass of wine. Cody's abstinence drew favorable notices from the Salvation Army and the temperance societies.

In an unusual ceremony in Manchester, the nineteen survivors of the Charge of the Light Brigade were honored. Not mentioned, but also present, were nineteen survivors of the Battle of Wounded Knee.

10

B Y 1893 Buffalo Bill's Wild West had put behind them a number of successful runs, with the show on Staten Island and their appearance at the Golden Jubilee being among the best. Millions saw the show on its European runs, and more millions saw it in America. But nothing Cody or Salsbury had done or would ever do surpassed their success at the World's Columbian Exposition in Chicago in 1893.

Salsbury, unable to get adequate space inside the exposition grounds, wisely rented two large lots right across from the main entrance to the fair itself. So vast was the scale of this exposition, one of the most successful in history, that many people probably wandered into the Wild West thinking they were seeing the fair itself: many of them spent all their money with Cody and Salsbury and never caught the real fair across the street.

The great Chicago Columbian Exposition was open from May until the end of October, and some 27,500,000 people poured through the gates; an amazing 716,000 paid admission on one day, October 9. Major Burke saw to it that Cody was constantly in the papers. Cody was the only private citizen to join two thousand legislators and watch President Grover Cleveland push a button and turn on the lights to get the exposition going.

With time to spare, Major Burke outdid himself, producing a lavishly illustrated sixty-four-page booklet which didn't stint in its praise, calling the show:

The biggest outdoor animated amusement exploit extant or known either ancient or modern. Life, action, skill, daring, danger defied; one thousand animated pictures in two hours given by flesh and blood; creation's greatest handiwork, nature's noblest mechanism too natural and colossal for canvas or building. The greensward our carpet, heaven's blue canopy our covering . . . an affair of magnitude, second to none in novel entertainment enjoyment, instruction, interest and educative merit.

Cody had insisted on one major change in the standard program: for the ever-popular Attack on the Settler's Cabin he substituted the even more popular Battle of the Little Bighorn, which became the show's finale. Once again Cody was acutely exploiting—as he had with the scalping of Yellow Hair—the tragic fate of the erratic general whom he had, so long ago, guided across the plains.

Annie Oakley's wildly popular shooting act came second on the program, right after the Grand Entry of the Rough Riders of the World. She too was feted in Chicago, but not as much as Cody.

Since the big exposition attracted scores of celebrities, Major Burke devised foolproof techniques for getting them over to the Wild West to have their pictures taken. Among those so snatched was the maharajah of Kapurthala and Frédéric Bartholdi, the sculptor of the Statue of Liberty.

In Chicago Burke and Salsbury saw a way to get the Wild West favorable publicity by organizing the occasional charity performance. Cody liked children—at least he liked them in short stretches—and was often photographed beaming on several in a grandfatherly way. Soon his hair would begin to turn and he would have to consent to wigs, but in Chicago he was a fine-looking man of forty-seven. Someone had the idea of having a "poor children's day" at the exposition, a good idea vetoed by the fair's manager, Harlow Higinbotham, who feared the sight of ten thousand grubby waifs might put off paying customers.

Cody, Salsbury, and Burke at once leapt into this breach, readily paying for a picnic, a parade, and a day at Buffalo Bill's Wild West for poor children from no less than seven orphanages and homes. The publicity that resulted was music to Major Burke's ears:

> Colonel Cody is a true philanthropist. He does not distrib-
> ute tracts, but sandwiches; he does not inculcate any high
> moral lessons, but he smooths the rugged pathway of the
> children of the streets for at least one day by taking them
> away from their squalid surroundings. So, too, shall
> Colonel Cody's trail toward the happy hunting grounds be
> made easy and fringed with prairie flowers because he has
> done this much to lighten the lives of others.

From Chicago a great lesson was learned; after that, charity days for poor children were to be a regular feature of Buffalo Bill's Wild West.

The one event that didn't quite work out as planned was the thousand-mile horse race from Chadron, Nebraska, to Chicago. Cody, having himself ridden a 322-mile Pony Express run, initially saw nothing wrong with a thousand-mile horse race; but very soon, every form of animal protection society then extant was on his back. Major Burke was forced to issue a number of exculpatory leaflets, pointing out that Buffalo Bill was a charter member of the Humane Society and that he had also been among the first to lobby for the use of clay pigeons rather than live birds in pigeon shoots.

Nonetheless, five horses finished and a rancher from Chadron took home the big first prize.

So far as Rough Riders went, Cody pulled out all stops for the Chicago run. Besides the Cossacks, gauchos, and vaqueros, he added Syrian and Arabian horsemen. He also hired the great trick roper Vincente Orapeza, who became the teacher of Will Rogers.

Also, the Indians were resplendent. John Y. Nelson was still on hand, with his many half-Sioux children. Two tiny survivors of Wounded Knee were there, one of whom, Little No Neck, Major Burke commendably adopted. The very respected Sioux leader Young Man Afraid of His Horses was there, and Red Cloud's son Jack.

It may be that the Chicago run in 1893 was the high-water mark for Buffalo Bill's Wild West. The success was due partly to location and partly to advertising. Swollen as the troupe was, this stand made money—estimates are that Cody and Salsbury cleared close to a million dollars.

Encouraged by this great box office, and concluding, perhaps, that their longer runs were their most successful, they decided to go back to New York, add a few attractions, and hope the crowds would come.

This time they chose south Brooklyn, where there was ample space. Salsbury no longer wanted to be vulnerable to the vagaries of the weather, so a covered grandstand was built. Major Burke kicked up as much publicity as he could and the shows ran twice a day, admission fifty cents.

But to the shock of the owners and promoters, customers declined to come. Chicago had been a new, bursting-at-the-scenes city on the rise. Not only was the exposition a big draw, but the whole of the Midwest looked to Chicago as the likeliest place to find entertainment. So in they flowed.

The same could not be said for south Brooklyn. New Yorkers, then as now, always have too much entertainment to choose from. Cody was no longer a novelty and there were troupes of many sorts to lure the crowds.

The failure was sharp and painful. Within six months of his greatest financial triumph Cody was forced to borrow $5,000 from Salsbury. In south Brooklyn it cost nearly that much a day just to feed the performers and mount the show.

To make matters worse, it was just at this troubled point that Nate Salsbury's health began to fail. Cody himself was occasionally under the weather, probably because he was drinking heavily again.

But the big troupe of riders and performers had been laboriously acquired and neither of the half-sick showmen wanted to let them go. A few performers peeled off and went to Pawnee Bill but most stayed put and tucked in their three meals a day while the bosses did some serious thinking.

The thinking soon yielded a solution that promised profits: they hired the mostly unsung junior partner of P. T. Barnum, the man who, more than any other, had mastered the logistics of moving large companies of performers around America in the cheapest and most efficient way.

His name was James Bailey. South Brooklyn was soon abandoned and Buffalo Bill's Wild West, grown yet larger by the addition of some colorful Zouaves, set out on the road. Annie Oakley and Frank Butler had their own railroad car, one of the eighty-two that it took to transport this vast company from place to place. At one point the Wild West performed in as many as 130 towns a year, many of them so small that they had never expected anything as exciting as Buffalo Bill's Wild West to show up in their neighborhood. Bailey added sideshows, making the Wild West more circuslike. At one point Salsbury, not content, decided that minstrel shows were the coming thing; he soon had three hundred black performers going from town to town across the South. But the black Wild West did not succeed.

11

WHAT might be called saturation touring became the pattern
for Buffalo Bill's Wild West as the nineteenth century moved
toward its close. James Bailey knew his business well. He seemed to
have a map of the nation's rail system in his head, and an up-to-date
timetable as well. He had thoroughly mastered the complex economics of touring companies and kept the show profitable, though with
only a minuscule margin of error. Cody and Annie Oakley remained
the headliners, becoming, with such broad exposure, even greater
superstars than they had been. Johnny Baker's star was also rising.

However, as any touring actor or musician knows, touring takes
its toll. Annie and Frank adapted to it better than Cody, whose tendency to burn the candle at both ends left him often irritable.

When the Spanish-American War broke out in 1898, Cody, who
had been running his Congress of Rough Riders for some years, was
naturally expected to volunteer. How could America have a war
without Buffalo Bill? His old friend General Miles, who seemed to
turn to Cody in every military emergency, naturally urged him to
take a command. Cody was probably in no mood for war at this
time, but he grandly offered to provide forty-five scouts and four
hundred horses, though his troupe owned only about 450 at this
time. Nothing more was heard of this offer—Buffalo Bill did not
fight in the Spanish-American War. Theodore Roosevelt soon recruited his own Rough Riders; it is unlikely that T.R. would have
wanted to share the stage with Cody anyway. General Miles himself

made only a modest contribution to the conflict, just as it was winding down.

The Wild West continued to tour, always running just a step or two ahead of financial disaster. Don Russell pointed out that Cody was trapped by his own ambition. He couldn't afford either to quit or not to quit. He was still making good money, so much that he couldn't afford to turn it down, and yet, if he had stopped touring, he would have been broke within two months.

12

W H E N the nineteenth century ended William F. Cody was undoubtedly one of the most famous people on earth. Most of
the seventeen hundred dime novels that featured him had already
been published. Tens of thousands of photographs of him had been
taken; tens of thousands of posters showing him on a horse had been
distributed. James Bailey had concluded that 130 shows a year
might be pushing it, but the Wild West still did at least one hundred,
and the troupe still employed nearly five hundred people. Virtually
every celebrity to pass through America since 1883 had seen at least
one performance, including Sarah Bernhardt. Cody had met every
president and was an icon looked up to by millions of American children.

Cody was only fifty-four when the century ended—they had
been very active years but he had not lost his looks and, for that matter, never would. Nobody in America looked better on a horse, an
asset he exploited until the end of his life, in 1917. He was an unusu-
ally buoyant, optimistic man. Had he been a worrier he might well
have worried himself into the grave years earlier, but despite myriad
troubles he had the ability to relax and recharge. In show business
he had, essentially, no way to go but down; the same comment could
be made for almost anyone of a certain age in show business; and
yet, as he partnered with various people and plunged into venture
after venture, he frequently managed to rise again, to find pockets of
profitability that no one else could have found.

There is no doubt, though, that for the last fifteen years of his life he was in a long footrace with his creditors. The footrace, from time to time, left him feeling very worn out. Various of his competitors were always counting him out, only to have him bob up again. As late as 1905, after Annie Oakley had left the show, Cody had one of his most profitable runs ever, in Paris. A year later, in Marseilles, he had such a spectacular opening week that he decided he could afford to donate $5,000 to victims of the eruption of Mount Vesuvius; but these bright moments were soon shadowed by the death of James Bailey, who had so brilliantly managed the enterprise for some twelve years. Salsbury had died in 1902. The 1907 season was the first ever in which Buffalo Bill Cody was sole manager of his own show. From its incorporation in 1883 either Nate Salsbury or James Bailey had done most of the organizational work.

But a big show was planned for Madison Square Garden and there was no one to run it but Cody himself. Many expected him to falter, or throw up his hands, but he didn't, nor did he during the next two years of touring. According to his own testimony he was in his office by eight-thirty every morning and he worked all day, though, as he frankly admitted, such desk work was not his forte.

By this point Cody only owned one-third of his own show. The Bailey estate had bought out Salsbury's interest; they owned two-thirds. A $13,000 note turned up in the Bailey documents. Cody said he had paid it but the Baileys weren't so sure. Cody certainly did his best to manage the show well and protect the Baileys' interest. The $13,000 note is worth mentioning only because squabbles over credit were to be a feature of the rest of Cody's life.

Cody had carried on a fairly polite rivalry with Gordon Lillie (Pawnee Bill) for many years. Cody irritated Lillie by lording it over him, but eventually it became clear to both men that they ought to team up, so Buffalo Bill's Wild West with Pawnee Bill's Wild East did good business for a while. The Wild East featured musical elephants, camel caravans, boomerang throwers, fakirs, and the like. When Annie Oakley considered coming out of retirement in 1909, Cody and Lillie tried to hire her, but she went instead with a new show, called Young Buffalo's Wild West, for a few years, and then left show business again.

Eventually Gordon Lillie bought out the Baileys' two-thirds interest in the Wild West. He had already acquired Cody's third. Finally, as sole owner of the world's most famous troupe, Lillie got to lord it over Cody a bit. He was usually generous with Cody—for one thing he saw to the cancellation of the $13,000 note; this was part of his deal with the Baileys. Buffalo Bill and Pawnee Bill could neither live with nor live without one another—wranglings over who owed how much to whom continued until the end of Cody's life.

13

LATE in October 1901, Buffalo Bill's Wild West was traveling deep into the night, bound for Danville, Virginia, where they would play their last engagement of the year. All the performers were probably looking forward to being home, if they had homes apart from the show itself. Annie Oakley and Frank Butler were asleep in their private car.

At three in the morning a railroad engineer named Lynch, perhaps not realizing that the show train consisted of two sections, pulled a switch at the wrong time, so that the show train plowed into a freight train loaded with fertilizer. Brakemen on both trains realized that calamity was inevitable but managed to slow the trains to a speed of about eight miles an hour when they collided.

Even so the carnage was horrifying, with the cars carrying livestock being the worst hit. Five cars full of horses were almost wholly lost; hundreds of horses either died outright or had to be killed. Cody and Johnny Baker estimated the loss as between $50,000 and $60,000—a worse calamity even than the sinking of the steamboat.

Fortunately the show's personnel were traveling in the rear cars—no employee was much more than shaken up by the collision. Frank Butler told reporters that his watch got smashed—Annie Oakley had wrenched her back. Both Butlers walked away from the wreck readily enough—news stories focused on the loss of the horses and other livestock.

The fact is, however, that Annie Oakley never fired another shot as a member of Buffalo Bill's Wild West. She retired, and maintained that her retirement was necessary because of the dreadful internal injuries that she suffered in the train wreck. Frank Butler, who at the time said everything was fine, later maintained that his wife had sustained a terrible injury to her hip.

Most of the early biographers, including the usually hard to fool Walter Havighurst, accepted the "dreadful injury" theory of Annie's retirement; but recently Shirl Kasper has given all this the lie. Less than two months after the wreck, Kasper points out, Annie competed in a shoot near Lake Denmark, New Jersey, and hit twenty-three of twenty-five live pigeons. A reporter for *American Field* praised her shooting highly and mentions that she was quite recovered from the shaking up she had received in the train wreck. Not only did she appear to be in her usual good health, but her long hair was evidently still lustrous and brown, as it had been during all her years as a performer. Had it mysteriously changed color, as women's hair sometimes does, someone at this well-attended shoot would no doubt have commented on the change.

The competition at Lake Denmark occurred on the seventeenth of December 1901. Only a month later, the sixteenth of January 1902, Annie competed at another shoot, this one on Long Island. She shot well and appeared to be in fine health, but except for a strand here and there, her hair had turned snow white.

What happened?

Frank Butler, who lost nothing but a watch in the train wreck, maintained that the shock of the collision was so great that his wife's hair had, within about eighteen hours, turned white. It hadn't, of course, or someone would have noticed it at Lake Denmark, or even sooner, given the publicity the big train wreck received.

Shirl Kasper's dogged sleuthing turned up two clippings in a scrapbook Annie Oakley kept, both blaming the hair color change on an inattentive attendant at a spa in Arkansas, very likely the famous Hot Springs, which Annie liked and often visited. She was left too long in a bath too hot and her hair turned. It may be that Annie gave this explanation to a friend, never supposing it would surface in a newspaper. Kasper thinks that Annie's obsessive modesty made her reluctant to admit that she had been scantily clad, even for thera-peutic purposes.

As to leaving the show, perhaps she was merely tired of touring. She may have been emboldened to retire because Frank had just se-cured a lucrative job as the representative of an ammunition com-pany. The Butlers no doubt felt that Frank's new salary, plus what Annie could earn in shooting competitions, would keep them nicely—and it did.

It is perhaps worth mentioning that Frank Butler's job with the cartridge company relied on what is now called product placement—the conspicuous use of brand-name products in shows and exhibi-tions was going strong in Cody's day. Buffalo Bill was advertised as using only Winchester ammunition. Annie Oakley only shot Stevens shotguns, while Johnny Baker had an exclusive commitment to the Parker arms company.

In 1903, a couple of years after Annie's hair turned white, an incident occurred that shocked her so that her hair might well have turned white had it not already been white. A story appeared in Hearst's Chicago papers, the *Examiner* and the *American*, with this headline:

ANNIE OAKLEY ASKS COURT FOR MERCY!

The reporter, somewhat incredibly even for Hearst, informed the public that Annie Oakley was in jail for stealing the trousers of a black man, meaning to sell them and buy cocaine. Given Annie's ex-treme modesty, the notion that she would touch the trousers of any man except her husband, and then only to launder them, must have sent her reeling. The story, written by a reporter named Ernest Stout, went out over the Publishers Press wire and was picked up by many newspapers all over the country. Astonished friends, who knew the story couldn't be true, clipped the stories and sent them to Nutley, New Jersey, where the Butlers were then living. The more Annie read, the angrier she became.

The fact that the story could be easily disproved didn't really as-suage the hurt and fury. It was easy enough to establish that she had not been in Chicago for more than a year, but what may have hurt most in the absurd story was the suggestion that she was poor. In her youth she *had* been poor—she knew its terrors and shame too well.

That Hearst ran this story, which he knew would be picked up by many newspapers, suggests how uncritical the world of yellow journalism really was. It was tabloid journalism, pitched well beyond the boundaries of believability. Nowadays such a story might claim that Hillary Clinton had sex with aliens, or something of the sort. Nonetheless, the effect on Annie Oakley was real.

For the next five years Annie went about the tiresome, expensive business of clearing her name. Her whole life had been devoted to building her reputation as a lady, and a lady of firm character as well. She was not about to see it lost. The libel process was tricky, as it is now, but she pursued her nemesis with the same determination that she had once applied to her shooting.

According to Shirl Kasper, the first twenty newspapers she sued paid her sizable libel fees. Hearst, in an effort to sully her if he could, sent a reporter to Greenville, where the Butlers had moved; but the locals were so outraged that someone was trying to dig up dirt on their beloved Annie that the town refused the detective a room for the night.

When the trials began, Annie was often sharp-spoken in her own defense. She denied having ever turned somersaults in her act; she denied having worn leggings, or having allowed her skirts to fall. When asked about education she said it was a very good thing in a person with common sense but a very bad thing in the hands of a cheap lawyer.

In time she sued fifty-five newspapers, collecting from all but one. Many of the awards were merely tokens but Hearst had to cough up $27,000 at least. Frank Butler claimed that every cent earned above their legal expenses went to charity, but that may not have been strictly true. The Butlers didn't live lavishly—Annie was too frugal for that—but they did live well.

Competitive shooting remained a very popular sport. In 1916 the *New York Times* claimed that 36 million clay pigeons had been broken in that one year alone. Annie Oakley—although she chose her shoots carefully—probably broke several thousand of that total.

She still, though, encountered the occasional snub from patrons of the all-male clubs. She was thus very pleased when, in 1913, a rich woman in Wilmington, Delaware, opened the first shooting club for women only.

Frank began to tour a little with his company's shooting team; sometimes Annie went with him. In a big shoot in Kansas City in 1902 she encountered her old rival, Lillian Smith, who had since been adopted into the Sioux tribe, shooting under the name of Wenona. Essentially, Lillian was in vaudeville. Whether the two met, or what they had to say to one another, is not recorded.

The elite trapshooting circles in those days attracted wealthy men who were usually very good shots. Someone not wealthy would not have been able to afford the travel, or the ammunition. For much of his life Frank Butler shot as well as his wife—he won his share of competitions—but he accepted the fact that Annie was the star; living in her shadow did not seem to bother him. Annie may have had a little more grit and a little more stamina. In 1906 she hit 1,016 brass discs without a miss. She was competitive, she enjoyed winning, and to the end, she was reluctant to pass up money.

14

WHY, when she decided to return to touring in 1911, Annie chose the fledgling Young Buffalo's Wild West, is something of a mystery. She did visit Cody and Gordon Lillie first; she had worked for both of them and liked them. Perhaps she merely wanted a higher salary than that beleaguered pair could readily afford. Perhaps the maintenance upkeep on a major star was more than they felt they could undertake. Annie may have had no desire to upstage Johnny Baker, who was the big shooting attraction at the time. Perhaps she liked it that Young Buffalo's show was a little more circus-like, with six elephants and some very talented clowns.

When she quit Young Buffalo in 1913 she was through with touring forever, though not entirely through with show business. The movies were beckoning. She had been persuaded to take a primitive screen test, though not much came of overtures from this new medium. She was fifty-three at the time. A little later she had her last encounter with Cody, an old man by then and already sadly in the grip of the financier Harry Tammen. Cody and Gordon Lillie had been operating a kind of half circus called the Two Bills Show. Although Cody only owned half the show he unwisely made a note to Tammen that failed to secure Lillie's half for Lillie. When the note came due Tammen sold the livestock and equipment at a sheriff's auction. Though Gordon Lillie was financially well off, he probably—and with justice—never forgave Cody for this last betrayal. Cody may not have forgiven himself either—he knew that what he had done was disgraceful, but by then he was leading a slipping-down life and could not arrest the slippage.

15

OVER the years, whenever Cody fancied himself somewhat ahead in the financial game, he formed the habit of sending sizable sums of money home to Lulu, back in North Platte, with the instruction to buy real estate. Lulu had always been nothing if not practical. She was well capable of securing a good piece of land, or a well-constructed house, if one came on the market.

Cody, of course, thought he was building himself a secure financial position by this method. If the show failed he always had his holdings in North Platte. He could ranch if necessary. He could sell some of that cheaply acquired property.

Imagine his shock, when he found himself in a financial crisis in the 1880s, to discover that this financial haven did not exist. Lulu had been buying real estate all right, and buying it as shrewdly as he had expected, but the catch was that she had put every plank and acre in her own name. Except for his interest in Scout's Rest, where Lulu would no longer consent to live, he owned nothing much in Nebraska that could be turned into ready cash. The cushion he had been counting on simply did not exist.

No doubt Cody laid heavy siege to Lulu at this time—after all, she was still his wife. He knew he hadn't been a perfect husband, but neither had he been a total scoundrel—at least not in his opinion. Hadn't he provided for her handsomely? Hadn't he left her more or less unrestricted?

In Lulu's mind he had left her far too unrestricted—in her mind that meant loneliness and abandonment. She quarreled frequently with his sisters—she thought brother Bill was far too generous with them.

Nor could she reconcile herself to his girlfriends. This came out in court depositions in 1905, when Cody was trying to divorce her. Not only was Lulu jealous of Queen Victoria and Princess Alexandra, there were other less distant women to provoke her jealousies, the actress Katherine Clemmons being one. But there were a number of others, and when Lulu's temper was up, the mere mention of any of them was enough to put her into a glass-breaking mood. At one point, hearing a female voice in her husband's room in New York, she proceeded to destroy her own well-appointed room. This fit, which must have been spectacular, cost Cody more than $300.

Though the Cody marriage constantly veered from melodrama to farce, there were elements in it which were genuinely heartbreaking. Lulu had married for love, but her husband moved her to an ugly prairie town and left her. She spent much of her life feeling abandoned. Cody was never any particular help with the children. He provided well financially—Lulu was never impoverished—but he didn't provide well emotionally. Clearly Lulu would rather have had less money and more time with Bill—that is, she would have until she grew hardened.

Cody never entirely lost his affection for his wife—it was just that his affection was fitful. He made one of his brothers-in-law, Al Goodman, general manager of the Nebraska properties, with instructions to try not to mind Lulu. Here, from a letter he wrote Goodman: "I often feel very sorry for her. She is a strange woman, but don't mind her—remember she is my wife—and let it go at that. If she gets cranky just laugh at it, she can't help it."

But the kettle of the Cody marriage continued to seethe, seething and seething for more than forty years. Cody's actress-kissing tendencies were always likely to surface. At one point Lulu strongly suspected that he had bestowed a kiss or two on his press agent, Bessie Isbell, after her visit to North Platte.

An odd, sad grievance surfaced in the divorce proceedings in 1905. One of the reasons he wanted out, Cody claimed, was that Lulu had tried to poison him on a Christmas visit in 1900. The artist Dan Muller was witness to this strange incident and confirms that

Cody collapsed and was temporarily deprived of speech, while having some sort of drink with his wife. Dan Muller loved Lulu, and knew she was not a poisoner, but something had happened to bring the Colonel low that night.

The "something" turned out to be a love potion that Lulu, in her desperation, had purchased from a Gypsy. It was called Dragon's Blood. What it contained nobody knows, but its purpose, of course, was to enable Lulu to recapture Bill Cody's affections. After thirty years, she was still trying.

Lulu's attorney suggested that it was probably not the first time that Colonel Cody had been falling-down drunk—but the fact of the Dragon's Blood was soon revealed.

16

DESPITE his looks, fame, and willingness to kiss girls, Buffalo Bill Cody was not a notable success with women. The first one, after Lulu, to bedevil him was the American actress Katherine Clemmons, whom Cody met during his first London show. She was good-looking, but no Bernhardt or Duse, as Cody fondly supposed her to be. He financed one play in England and another in America, the latter a spectacular flop that cost Cody many thousands.

Katherine Clemmons was an energetic opportunist. She had had a frontier background and was more than able to keep up with Cody when it came to drinking. How much she ever cared for Bill Cody is at this distance hard to say, but he was far from being the only suitor to enjoy her favors. She was tempestuous and could match Lulu fit for fit if need be. Perhaps the fits were what prompted Cody to say that he had rather manage a million Indians than one soubrette.

Still, the two carried on for a few years, until Katherine Clemmons concluded, accurately, that Cody didn't really have much money and would be more than likely to lose most of what he had. She was looking for bigger bucks and secured them—or supposed she had—by marrying the son of the fabulously wealthy Jay Gould. Howard Gould was as eligible a bachelor as anyone could hope for, but by 1907 he divorced Katherine, citing infidelity with several men, one of them Buffalo Bill Cody.

The end of this sordid story does Cody great credit. During the divorce proceedings the Goulds offered Cody a goodly sum—$50,000—if he would testify against Katherine. Cody, though desperate for money at the time, threw the gentlemen out of the room.

Lulu wasn't always on the attack. During the divorce proceedings, which failed, she remarked to one reporter that "Will was the kindest and most generous of men."

Cody proved to be a terrible witness for himself. Aside from the ridiculous matter of the poisoning he couldn't come up with any convincing reason as to why the judge should grant him a divorce. He could not remember dates or incidents, and was constantly tripped up in his testimony, not only by Lulu's lawyers but by his own.

Divorce was no snap in 1905. The judge believed every word Lulu uttered, but believed few words of Cody's. He rejected the petition, leaving the Codys to struggle on with one another for another dozen years.

17

Except for his misguided attempt to ride the brute buffalo known as Monarch, Buffalo Bill, as a showman, did well with his namesake animal, the buffalo. Horses were another matter. He lost nearly five hundred in the big train wreck near Danville in 1901, and disaster was to strike his horse herd a second time, in Europe in 1906, when the show horses were stricken with glanders, reducing their numbers by two-thirds.

Cody's was hardly the only touring company to find itself at the mercy of events. The Miller Brothers' famous 101 Ranch troupe toured with some success in the years before World War I—the Millers sported the amazing black bulldogger Bill Pickett. Will Rogers sometimes practiced his rope tricks at the 101 Ranch, and movie star Tom Mix had worked there as a cowboy.

Nonetheless it fell to the Millers to launch the worst-timed Wild West tour of all time: they set out to play Europe in the early fall of 1914. Not long before sailing for England one of the Millers had purchased a lot of half-broken Mexican horses, figuring to tame them as they went along, but they had scarcely disembarked in London when their entire herd was requisitioned for the British war effort. A lot of these unruly Mexican steeds soon saw service on the Western front—very likely most of them were eaten. This tour, or rather nontour, became a nightmare for the Millers. They had already loaned out some Indians to a German circus before the guns began to roar. Getting these Indians back to the States was not easy, but most finally managed to return through Scandinavia.

Cody's reputation as a lackadaisical figurehead who left all administrative work to Salsbury or Bailey was a little unfair. He was always prone to jaunts—the freedom to enjoy the Western plains and mountains never lost its appeal to Cody. A jaunt or a hunting trip rarely failed to restore his spirits. One of Katherine Clemmons's big issues with Cody was his tendency to leave on short notice, or no notice. If a bear hunt was offered just as one of Katherine's ponderous plays was opening, Cody more often than not chose the bear hunt.

He could, though, work when he had to. Not long after Nate Salsbury's death he penned this complaint:

> . . . with the death of my partner I have all the more to do . . . & more responsibility . . . every day, year in and year out, is a rush day for me. I cannot even get one hour to myself to quiet my nerves. Someone wants my time all the time. I have to attend to my own business—and receive company at the same time—to say nothing of the letters I am compelled to write.

It was plain that a company employing over five hundred people and at least that many animals could not be run from a Western campfire, between attempts to locate bears. Cody grew up on the plains; half his life had been spent under the great skies of the West. Yet for most of the second half of his life he was an urban man, a traveler amid the capitals of Europe. Doubtless he enjoyed many of his urban possibilities—actresses, for example; but undoubtedly there were times when he would have liked to chuck it all and go back to North Platte, a choice now rendered impossible because of Lulu's stubborn refusal to allow him any access to the money she had saved.

In fact, Cody was never—financially—in a position to chuck it all. Despite his endless financial crises and defeats, he remained eternally optimistic about the future. Many propositions came his way: mining ventures, hotels in scenic spots, irrigation schemes to make the desert flower, and of course, inventions and patent medicines on the order of White Beaver's Laugh Cream.

Cody may have made a little money here and there—he invested in so many schemes that one or two of them probably paid off—but the bottom line, always, was that his main asset was himself. People would come in sizable numbers just to see him ride his horse and shoot glass balls. It was as a showman, showing mainly himself, that Cody got the money to pay his bills. Sometimes he even got a little ahead.

The administrative skill that it took to organize large touring companies is uncommon in any time; Cody was lucky to find, first, Salsbury and then Bailey. Salsbury, observing James Bailey while he still worked with Barnum, left a short description of that well-known modern figure, the workaholic:

> Bailey's capacity for work is enormous, or at least it seems so to me, for I never hear of him devoting any time to anything but work. He told me himself that he cared for nothing but to make a success of his business at any cost. I never heard of him taking any sort of social pleasure. I do not believe he ever attended a theatre or any other form of amusement for the sake of the amusement.

But Salsbury only lasted until 1902, and Bailey to 1906, after which the crème de la crème of big-show managers were no longer available, which is why Bill Cody hitched up his belt and sat down at his desk every morning at eight-thirty. But as he said, desk work was not his forte; and it was the clear need for administrative help, as well as solid financing, that caused him to turn in 1908 to his old rival Gordon Lillie, or Pawnee Bill.

Lillie and Cody had known one another a long time. Cody was fifteen years older than Lillie; the latter was at first, and in some way remained, a good deal starstruck. Lillie had taught for a while at the Pawnee agency; he served as interpreter when Cody and Doc Carver were trying to recruit a few Pawnees for their first show. Lillie was there the day Monarch put Cody in the hospital. Cody may have lorded it over the younger man too much, and he certainly was wrong to blithely imperil Lillie's half of the Two Bills show, but through it all, Lillie remained clear about one thing: Buffalo Bill was still the biggest name, and the most solid asset, in the touring world of that time. If you had Buffalo Bill, the seats would not be empty. It was because of this certainty that Lillie persuaded the Bailey family to forgive the $13,000 note. He wanted to give Buffalo Bill's Wild West with Pawnee Bill's Wild East a chance. (What to us seem cumbersome titles did not discourage the crowds of the time. When Bill Cody worked briefly for the Miller Brothers the show was called "The Military Preparedness, Buffalo Bill [Himself] Combined with the 101 Ranch Show." The show was a combination rodeo and military review, and didn't last long.)

Pawnee Bill took a natural, if short-lived, satisfaction in finally becoming the boss of his old hero. He tolerated Cody's weaknesses and kept things on a fairly even keel.

When Cody died Lillie was deeply moved. "I was a friend of Buffalo Bill's until he died," he said. "He was just an irresponsible boy."

Many would have agreed with Gordon Lillie, but most would have agreed, too, that Cody's irresponsibility wasn't the whole story.

18

BEFORE Buffalo Bill and Gordon Lillie finally split, they took one more big step in unison: they made a movie together. Neither feared innovation and both saw that moving pictures were the coming thing. Cody had started lighting his arenas with Edison's electric lights as early as 1893. He was always buying generators and dynamos, hanging more lights, acquiring the latest gadgets. Several pioneering cameramen filmed scenes from the Wild West shows. Cody was caught by the kinetoscope many times as he made his grand entry. There were movie booths in the St. Louis Exposition of 1904—the first of many movies about Cody's idol Kit Carson appeared in that year.

By the turn of the century cameramen were ubiquitous. Annie Oakley was screen-tested more than once; there may still exist somewhere a few faded frames of her performing at shooting contests, breaking clay pigeon after clay pigeon. We have fairly full reports of the making of many films in the first decade of the twentieth century, but precious little of this early footage survives.

Cody had survived as a showman since 1872 by repeating, over and over in simple skits, the story of the Plains Indian wars. He saw no reason not to continue repeating it in this new and potentially thrilling medium—neither did Pawnee Bill. And where better to begin than with the story of Cody's life. *The Life of Buffalo Bill* was a one-reeler filmed in 1912 by the Buffalo Bill and Pawnee Bill film company.

In the opening sequence Cody plays himself, an old scout making a lonely camp on a lonely trail. The old scout has a dream in which an actor playing Cody relives Cody's much-relived life. Indians dash about, chasing stagecoaches; then, as the centerpiece to a well-planned dream, there's the duel with Yellow Hair. The story, as well as the characters, move at a furious pace.

The partners were proud of this maiden work, but by 1912 they were by no means the only showmen around who were making Westerns. According to Joy Kasson, Biograph, by 1912, had already made seventy Westerns, some of them directed by D. W. Griffith. One of the most famous of these was the Mary Pickford version of *Ramona*.

Pawnee Bill seemed to find filmmaking even messier and more chaotic than putting on arena shows; he was not wrong. The strain soon wore him down; he retired to his ranch in the far West and lived until 1942.

Cody, however, saw a chance to do something really ambitious, something that could preserve for future generations of Americans the grand story of the settling of the West. It might also, if it worked, restore both his fortunes and his self-respect.

What he proposed, and mostly completed, was a work called *Indian War Pictures* (though, at various times, this sequence of films used many more titles, *Buffalo Bill's War Pictures* being one of the more ordinary). This was not to be one film but several, which would, of course, touch many of the old bases: Killing of Tall Bull, First Scalp for Custer, and so forth. Cody managed to get his old friend General Miles interested—movies were such a big attraction in those years that a man of Cody's fame had not too much difficulty in securing financing. Before he was through he even secured some from Harry Tammen, although he surely knew by this time how unscrupulous Tammen was.

When Cody set out to restore his name by making motion pictures, he decided that their hallmark would be authenticity, an elusive element in any art at any time. He always tried to make his arena shows as realistic as possible by using real props (the Deadwood stage) and, in many cases, real Westerners such as John Y. Nelson and, of course, the many Indians. Cody managed, throughout his long career, to think of himself as mainly a kind of pictorial historian. He tried, to the best of his abilities, to show Western life as it had been. And he also managed to sustain a forty-year career playing only one character, himself.

Some of the old tropes from his arena shows worked fairly well as short films. The Battle of Summit Springs (Tall Bull) and the First Scalp for Custer (Yellow Hair) presented no huge problems to the filmmakers—after all, only a couple of years later D. W. Griffith would mass thousands of extras for his great film *Intolerance*. There were people of experience who could direct Westerns competently. Joy Kasson's estimate is that Westerns comprised about twenty percent of American film production by then. The early Western star Bronco Billy (Anderson) had already made some 150.

At first things went swimmingly for *Indian War Pictures*, but Cody had never been good at quitting while he was ahead. In this instance his miscalculation was his decision to finish the Indian Wars sequence with a reenactment of Wounded Knee, the horror that had taken place only twenty-three years earlier.

Cody had been blocked from visiting Sitting Bull before he was killed, and had not himself witnessed the carnage on the battlefield. Black Elk had not yet made his famous statement about the broken hoop, the sacred tree, and the death of his people's dream. What Cody failed to realize was that, for the Sioux people, Wounded Knee was a scar that had not healed and would never heal. They were not ready to go back to that place where so many warriors, women, and children had died. Though they knew the difference between real life and playacting—Cody himself had employed many of them—they may not have believed that General Miles and his six hundred soldiers were arriving just to make a show.

Perhaps the guns were loaded with blanks, but not every Sioux was convinced of that. The Sioux women in particular were very disturbed; some, it is reported, began to sing their death songs.

Cody had not reckoned with the swelling up of pain and anger that this particular reenactment produced, not all of it on the Indians' side. There was a rift between Cody and Miles, because the latter insisted that the eleven thousand soldiers that had assembled at Pine

Ridge to accept the Sioux surrender on January 16, 1890, be faithfully represented.

Cody was for authenticity, but not authenticity on quite such an expensive scale. So the six hundred soldiers had to be marched around and around in front of the cameras. Though General Miles didn't know it, most of the cameras contained no film.

The shoot at Wounded Knee took thirty-four days in the fall of 1913 and produced some thirty thousand feet of film. It was released in various formats (five, six, and eight reels), all of which failed. It appeared under a variety of titles, but changing the title didn't help. Both Tammen and the ever-loyal John Burke tried to promote it but nothing worked. Cody even rode his famous horse Isham onstage in Denver. He got a cheer, of course, but that did nothing for the show in Chicago. Cody's reputation didn't suffer from this failure, but his fortune was not recouped.

The negative for this film is lost, and the copy in the Cody museum has deteriorated beyond repair. Nothing now remains of Cody's ambitious effort except a few faded fragments and a set of remarkable still photos, which show Cody, gaunt and old now, scalping Yellow Hair yet one more time. A version called *The Adventures of Buffalo Bill*, released in 1917 to take advantage of Cody's death, also failed.

In trying to redo the massacre of Wounded Knee, Cody had taken matters too far, and pleased no one. The military hated the picture because it made them look like the killers they had been. The public avoided it because it slammed home the uncomfortable fact that the destruction of the Indians and their tribal lifeways had been a brutal tragedy.

What Cody felt is hard to know. He knew that he had spent much of his life recycling his own early experience—he was now an old man. The way of life he had loved best, the scout's free life in the good air of the West, was as gone now as the buffalo that had helped make his fame. The West was settled, the frontier was closed. Most of the friends of his youth—Texas Jack Omohundro, Wild Bill Hickok—were dead. His most ambitious effort to show what it had been like in the old West—the *Indian War Pictures*—had failed in part *because* of its authenticity. He had spent much of his life peddling illusions about the West and the illusions succeeded where the reality failed. He had been right at the beginning, correctly perceiving that it was illusion that the people wanted. The reality, whether they had lived it or not, just wasn't as appealing.

Reality might not sell, but the man himself, Buffalo Bill, was still wanted, still a great draw. Even as late as 1914 a variety show in London offered him $2,500 a week just to appear; Cody turned them down—he thought he was worth twice as much.

One of the things he fancied might save him was the dude ranch. Had he not just spent forty years watching young Eastern women go nuts over cowboys? Wouldn't well-heeled Easterners pay to spend a month or two on a "ranch" in the West, riding horses, punching cattle in a light way, and singing corny songs around campfires under the great Western sky?

Again, Cody was right. They would pay. It could be argued that the survival of ranching in Montana and Wyoming is the result of the fact that so many Eastern girls came west and married cowboys, bringing their money and their taste with them. Sheridan, Wyoming, where the queen of England comes occasionally to buy racehorses, probably has the best small-town public library in America. Visitors to Sheridan may even be entertained in one of Cody's houses. In that part of the West his influence is still very much felt.

19

ANNIE OAKLEY never lost her great appeal to crowds. On
in a while she performed at big fairs, and the magic was s
there. In the main her retirement was pleasant. She and Frank w
particularly fond of a resort hotel called the Carolina, in Pinehu
North Carolina. They stayed there often, enjoying plantation q
shooting, and now and then a duck hunt.

Both Butlers still occasionally competed in shooting mat
but Annie more and more preferred to sponsor shooting cl
mostly for women. She claimed to have taught some fifteen
sand women how to shoot. When World War I broke out the
found it difficult, for a time, to get either revolvers or ammu
Several times Annie remembered how much she had disli
Kaiser—after all, millions might not have lost their lives if
just shot the Kaiser rather than his cigarette.

However comfortable Annie may have been with Fra
as a husband—it is doubtful that her eye ever roved—cor
mesticity was something that had never really suited
himself, though he doted on Annie, was bold enough tc
out:

> Her shooting record is much better than her house
> mark . . . Riding, shooting and dancing come nat
> her but she is a rotten housekeeper . . . her recor
> department is seven cooks in five days.

215

Indeed, Annie admitted to being extremely picky. Details mattered to her. All too often closets were positioned wrong, or sinks would be too high, lights were too bright or else not bright enough. Without the spur of competition to drain off her energies her pickiness was sure to intensify. She did like dancing, though, and once won a prize at the Carolina Hotel at a dance in which she came dressed as an Indian woman, with feathers in her hair.

Despite the comforts of the Carolina Hotel, or of the various nice houses the Butlers occupied for varying lengths of time, the Butlers were more or less rolling stones. Annie readily agreed with her husband that she was not meant for homemaking—she was still in some ways the bohemian wood sprite who liked to go out amid the trees and the critters with her gun.

"You can't cage a Gypsy," she admitted once. "I went all to pieces under the care of a house."

The Butlers kept on the move, but they were leisurely moves—they always took their guns and their dogs, and sometimes their boat. Annie was asked to do many charity shoots and usually accepted. She had been a poor child and her memory was long. She often contributed to poor farms and orphanages. When she toured with Young Buffalo she followed the example set by Cody and Salsbury in Chicago—free tickets went to orphans, particularly the poor orphans of Darke County, Ohio, where she had grown up.

Annie Oakley had traveled the world, shooting and winning. She was a high achiever, as Type A as anyone could be. She felt, and said, that—except for heavy lifting—she was the equal of any man at anything. But she resisted feminism per se and was ambivalent about giving women the vote. Cody was all for suffrage and argued with her about it. Working outside the home and earning a salary seemed better to him than staying home with the cat.

Annie wasn't so sure. She thought she might be for suffrage if only the good women would vote. But she was never particularly indulgent about her sex and worried about what might happen if too many bad women voted.

Part of her objection to feminism seemed to be an aesthetic ob-

jection to bloomers. She hated them and, so far as is known, never wore them. In her day all real ladies wore skirts, and that was that. She was, after all, a mainly Victorian lady, although she certainly expanded the bounds of that role when she took up show business.

On the other hand she was adamant in her belief that women deserved to be, and should be, armed. Modesty and fear of abuse played a part in this belief. Whatever happened to her in the two years she was with the "wolves" was not discussed, but she openly considered rape a threat most women should take seriously. She several times made it clear that she would have no qualms about shooting any man who threatened her honor. "If accosted I could easily fire," she insisted. She thought that every school ought to have a rifle range and that both boys and girls should receive adequate instruction about how to use a firearm.

When World War I broke out Annie even toyed with the idea of organizing and leading a women's regiment, even though it might mean relaxing her role on pants for women. She once broached this idea to Theodore Roosevelt, who immediately told her to forget it.

Unable to load up and attack the Hun directly, Annie did the next best thing, which was to visit army camps and inspire the soldiers with her shooting. She later said that her shooting exhibitions in the camps were more inspiring to her than even her best successes with the Wild West shows.

Annie and Frank were at Pinehurst the day the Great War ended—there was a big victory parade and she capped the festivities by giving an impromptu shooting exhibition.

From then until the end of her life she did more and more charity work. Two of her sisters had died of tuberculosis, so she always contributed to efforts to defeat that disease. At one point she melted down her medals and contributed the money to a sanatorium.

In 1922 she did a much-reported shoot on Long Island for wounded soldiers. This seems to have been the last time she attempted her full act, skipping if she hit and pouting if she missed, as it had been in days of yore, with her patented crowd-pleasing little back kick at the end, the same kick that won her so much applause with the Wild West. And as in days of yore, the crowd absolutely loved her. A film clip survives of this high-profile shoot, with a few frames of Annie coming through a door. It may be that her old friend Fred Stone, a prolific moviemaker, was there with his camera, trying to persuade her to go before the cameras in *The Western Girl* or some other suitable melodrama.

Annie was certainly aware by this time that she was indeed a Gypsy—she was never going to settle down. She had told herself, and the world, many times that she was through with show business. These announcements were her version of Buffalo Bill's countless farewell tours. She probably thought she would be done with show business, but in practice being done with it wasn't that easy. She kept trying to quit, perhaps thinking each time that she *would* quit, but in reality she never did quit—not until her health finally failed her. Once a performer, always a performer; and for a performer who had been a very big star, the business was just not that easy to give up. The attention and the need for competition kept bringing Annie Oakley back.

To a reporter who interviewed her just after a shoot at a big fair in Brockton, Massachusetts, she admitted that the rush of celebrity and the hurly-burly of showbiz still had its seductiveness for her. She also frankly pointed out that she had made $700 for twenty minutes' work. She and Frank Butler never lost sight of the financial picture—how else, other than by shooting, could a sixty-two-year-old woman make $700 in less than half an hour?

Very shortly after the lucrative shoot in Brockton, a car wreck—that increasingly common American disaster—interrupted any plans Annie and Frank might have been nursing in regard to a return to the tour. In early November 1922, the Butlers were in Florida vacationing when their car flipped over, pinning Annie underneath it. Frank was uninjured, but Annie suffered both a broken hip and a broken ankle.

Her injuries were not life-threatening, but they of course had an effect on Annie's morale. Though she didn't know it immediately, she would need to wear a brace on one leg for the rest of her life. She was two months in the hospital, receiving thousands of sympathy cards during her stay.

Still, the next spring, she shot at the Philadelphia Phillies training camp, hitting tossed pennies as readily as ever.

She shot, now and then, at various gatherings, though seldom with quite her old enthusiasm. Once or twice she did summon the old spirit; she even once danced a jig despite her brace.

Then, little by little, she finally began to let show business go. By then she took a certain amount of looking after. Frank, though docile enough, could not be bothered with domestic chores, though he did, now and then, cut a pile of firewood for Annie's little stove. Fortunately the Butlers moved to Ohio, to Darke County in fact, where Annie had four nieces who saw that their famous aunt was well looked after.

When the Butlers made their will, Frank left a little something to his first wife, Elizabeth, and their daughter, Kattie. It makes one wonder where these two had been for forty years. Annie was many things, but she was not a sharer. The other ex-wife and the grown child were never mentioned.

The end of Annie Oakley's story I gave at the beginning of this book. She had anemia, and it worsened; Frank Butler was rapidly fading too. The nieces saw that what could be done was done. Frank, in Michigan, was well taken care of.

Then one day the lady undertaker, Louise Stocker, did her duty. Soon Annie went home up North Star way.

Will Rogers, who loved her, sent this comment: "Whenever I think of Annie Oakley I stop and say to myself: it's what you are, not what you are in, that makes you."

The address on his letter was Beverly Hills, California.

20

WILLIAM F. CODY never lost his looks, though he did lose his hair. As early as the nineties Burke and Salsbury convinced him he would have to make do with hairpieces, and he did so for some twenty years. Occasionally he embarrassed himself by lifting his hairpiece when he lifted his hat. These occasions put him out of temper; he was not without vanity. Also he knew that a legend had to behave like a legend. His appearance, to a large extent, was still his meal ticket.

Despite the many vexations that come with aging, Cody remained a remarkably resilient man. He suffered many lows, but he also rose above many humiliations, the worst of which was the failure of the Two Bills show and the subsequent sale of its assets—mainly livestock—at a sheriff's auction in 1913. After this sad event Cody said of Tammen: "He was the man who had my show sold at a sheriff's sale, which broke my heart." It also broke his relationship with Gordon Lillie, who owned half the show. Some friends, feeling sorry for Cody, bought his show horse Isham at the auction and gave him back to Cody.

Gordon Lillie was not slow in realizing that Tammen got Cody on the ropes financially and set a clever trap: what he wanted and what he got was de facto control of Cody, still in Tammen's eye a very valuable asset. The movie stars were coming. Chaplin, Douglas Fairbanks, Mary Pickford, and others would soon achieve a fame that even Cody's couldn't equal. But for a time there was still plenty of money to be made off Buffalo Bill.

Tammen was right—Cody was still world-famous. It was at this time that the big offer came in from the variety show in England. Though Cody rejected the offer, the mere fact that it had been made convinced him that he could make yet another comeback. Tammen still had him working in the Sells-Floto Circus, but what working meant in this context was mainly just that Cody showed up and made a few trips around the arena, sometimes on Isham, sometimes just in a phaeton. He had stopped breaking glass balls on any regular basis, though sometimes he would break a few as a flourish. He seemed spent, he seemed blocked, and yet it was at about this point that he flung himself into moviemaking, even using some of Tammen's money. Movies were clearly there to stay; Tammen, like many another tycoon in the decades to follow, wanted to get in on the show, meet the stars, bask in the glamour. Harry Tammen would soon learn the bitter lesson that many a tycoon has since learned: movies can lose a lot of money; just swallow it up, as a dry lake swallows water. How could a movie about Buffalo Bill and the Indians lose money? he probably asked himself. He soon found out exactly how, which is not to say that his gamble was a bad one going in.

What defeated the *Indian War Pictures* was Cody's desire for authenticity—this was General Miles's desire too, and in fact, the simpler parts of the *Indian War* skits probably *did* work. Custer's defeat, the attack on the settler's cabin, Cody's scalping of Yellow Hair were effective. What sunk them was the attempt to do Wounded Knee, a huge, tragic event where simplification was not possible. Included in the thirty thousand feet of footage were some scenes of the Ghost Dance as well as the death of Sitting Bull; these, taken alone, might have been effective. But marching the six hundred soldiers around and around the empty camera was just silly.

Besides, the newsreel had been born by this time. In 1915 American audiences were transfixed by the sight of a much more deadly, unfictionalized slaughter—the slaughter that was happening day by day on the Western front in World War I.

When *Indian War Pictures* was finally withdrawn from the movie screens, the greatest showman of his time had only a year or two in which to wander in the shadows of old age. He continued to make occasional appearances, and now and then he would get excited about some new scheme—a mine that couldn't possibly fail, a resort that would soon fill up with Eastern nobs—but these notions were feebly pursued because Cody had no money with which to pursue them. He found himself in the same position as another great hero of the West, the explorer John Charles Frémont, who had once himself had millions but was at the end dependent on what his resourceful wife, Jessie Benton Frémont, could earn with her journalism. On the whole Cody held up better than Frémont, who, in the last photographs, looks very, very distinguished but also very, very sad.

As Cody's finances failed, so did his health. Fortunately, as the end approached, he had his sisters. He had always been extremely generous to his sisters, who were all, of course, convinced that Lulu had neglected him terribly—it had actually been the other way around.

But by this time Lulu too was glad to help—wasn't he still her husband? All his family gathered around and tried to buoy him up.

As he was dying Cody apparently said, "Let my show go on!" and efforts were made to see that he got his last wish. The sharpshooter Johnny Baker, griefstricken at the death of the man who had raised him and given him his calling, managed to bring in the Miller Brothers (they had bought most of the livestock at the Two Bills auction) and a few other old performers, many of them veterans of Cody's shows, and worked up one last tour. This was Cody's true farewell tour, which the boss himself had to miss. Some Indians came. They realized that in losing Pahaska they had lost a friend.

But this short tour was mounted in 1917, while World War I, the Great War, still raged. Buffalo Bill's name was on the marquee one last time but it was the wrong year in which to expect people to be interested in Wild West shows. The farewell tour folded in Nebraska, which was fitting, since the first show had been mounted in Omaha.

21

BUFFALO BILL'S death made big headlines. The Cambridge-
born poet E. E. Cummings, then twenty-one years old, read the
headlines and scribbled a note or two in his journal.

Some years later, pondering his notes and remembering the
man who had inspired the headlines, E. E. Cummings, who had by
this time decided to pitch his poetical tent in the lower case alpha-
bet, wrote this poem:

> Buffalo Bill's
> defunct
> > who used to
> > ride a watersmooth-silver
> > > > > stallion
> and break onetwothreefourfive pigeonsjustlikethat
> > > > > > > > Jesus
>
> he was a handsome man
> > > > > and what i want to know is
> how do you like your blueeyed boy
> Mister Death

The most recent and most comprehensive edition of E. E. Cummings's *Complete Poems* is more than eleven hundred pages long.
The Buffalo Bill poem is the most famous lyric in this long book,
though, of course, we still don't know what Mr. Death thought about
his blue-eyed boy.

22

NONE of those who knew Cody well were surprised that he was impoverished at the end. Annie Oakley didn't go to his funeral, but she gave several interviews about him, all of which mentioned his generosity. Once, she remembered, Frank Butler, herself, and Cody came out of a stage door in Manhattan to see a ragged group of bums huddled miserably on a freezing night. Cody at once asked the Butlers how much cash they could scrape up. The three of them managed to dig out $25—Cody insisted on giving $23 of it to the men, ordering them to use it to get a meal and a bunk out of the cold. He and the Butlers, left with $2, dined, as Annie put it, "on simple fare." (She herself had developed such a taste for fare that was not simple that she once reportedly bloomed up to 138 pounds. But she soon got it off and was slim again at the end.)

Everyone who knew Cody mentioned that his weakness was that he could never deny assistance—usually financial—to anyone who asked him. This is not the worst failing a man could have. He may have ended up broke, but he also ended up famous and widely, almost universally, beloved. He was so famous that within a few hours of his death both the president of the United States (Woodrow Wilson) and the king of England (George V) had cabled in condolences and regrets.

The boy who grew up half wild in the Salt River Valley had undoubtedly come a long way. He lived long enough into the movie era to see what huge stars the movies could produce. He may have been bemused by the soaring fame of Chaplin, Mary Pickford, the Gish sisters, William S. Hart. Bemused, but probably not seriously envious. They were wonderful players, but in his time, he had been a big player too—indeed, probably the biggest player, the best-known star. William F. Cody was one of the people who have a fair claim to having invented the star system, for better or for worse.

The man who helped him do it, the faithful press agent John M. Burke, outlived his master and idol by only thirteen weeks.

23

I N the dining room of the Onion Creek Grill, a café in my hometown, Archer City, Texas, there is a Cody poster that I sometimes
study if I happen to land in the right booth. It's not really an old
poster, but it's old enough to have got smoked up a little—there are
suggestions of grease along the lower edge. It's one of thousands of
Cody artifacts, but it happened to be hanging in the right place to
start me thinking about the man.

Though it is not a very large poster, a great deal of potent im-
agery has been crammed into it.

In the center of the poster Cody reclines in an oval, his hair
long and loose, his manner benign. Behind him stretch the great
prairies of the West. Animals—a little indistinct—graze in the far distance. Cody has a rifle but he is not hunting. The drawing is Flax-
man-like. Cody looks about himself with a noble gaze—he might be
the Zeus of the West.

Surrounding the central oval is a frieze of the usual high spots
from Cody's career. There he is driving a stage, riding with the Over-
land Mail, trapping beaver. The frieze is complex and runs all the
way around the poster. Of course there is the Taking of the First
Scalp for Custer—but then there is also the Challenge Buffalo Hunt,
the one some biographers even doubt took place. And finally there
is General Sheridan, making Cody chief of scouts before all the
troops on the parade ground of a fort. It seems unlikely that Sheridan would have ordered up such a show for the scout who had al-

226

ready been doing the work anyway; but there it is, lower left.

The poster, with Cody resting Zeuslike at the center, is emblematic; it attempts to encompass the whole destiny of the American frontier where Cody had lived and acted. Nothing very significant to the long effort of settlement has been left out. There are Indians, plains, buffalo, hunters, soldiers, settlers, even beaver. To my mind the beaver is a particularly important touch. Cody himself trapped beaver for only a few weeks, but beaver provided the first wealth to come out of the West, and they belong in the story. It was the beaver who brought the mountain men, the mountain men who brought the settlers; then the Indians fought the settlers and the soldiers came to fight the Indians. Buffalo Bill, in the frieze, is punching cattle, driving a stagecoach, riding on the Pony Express, scouting for General Sheridan and being honored for it, after which he gets to the right place at the right time and takes the first scalp for Custer.

When it came to cramming the history of the settling of the American West onto one poster, Buffalo Bill Cody knew exactly what to do.

24

SUPERSTARS cannot exactly create themselves, no matter how skilled—the public can be manipulated vis-à-vis superstars only up to a point. The public must, at some point, develop a genuine love for the performer—a love that grows and grows as long as the performer lasts. When great stars die, thousands mourn and mourn genuinely. Exactly how this chemistry works no one quite understands—but some deep identification is made or superstardom doesn't happen.

Examples abound. Robert Duvall is a brilliant actor, one of the finest of his generation. He's never short of work, but he's not a superstar.

As an actor John Wayne was not really in Duvall's class, but as a performer he was in a higher class: the class of superstars. Why John Wayne and not Robert Duvall? Who knows? John Ford, who, with Howard Hawks, made John Wayne a superstar, is supposed to have said, "The son of a bitch just looks like a man." Wayne, of course, was a competent but seldom an inspired actor; his famous, slightly tilted walk was endlessly rehearsed. Was it the walk that made him a superstar? Or was it something closer to what made Cody a superstar: the sense that this guy just belongs in the West. From *Stagecoach* on Wayne was, in a way, the new Buffalo Bill.

Cody rehearsed his moves too, just as Annie Oakley rehearsed her shooting tricks and her mannerisms. Without Cody to showcase her Annie Oakley might have been a celebrated shot, but she would not likely have become the international star that she became.

And yet, the prominence of Cody's venues doesn't explain her superstardom, either. Perhaps what won the crowd was the little pout when she missed, or her jaunty little back kick when she was pleased—of such tiny but well-rehearsed bits of business are great superstars made. Think of Chaplin—think of Jackie Gleason.

Annie Oakley's stardom was real, just as was Bill Cody's. People liked to see Cody ride his horse fast and pop a few glass balls. He wanted to embody history—the history he had been a part of—and to an extent he did. In this matter he and his audiences were one in that, somehow, they wanted the West, the gloriously dangerous West, the mythic romantic West, the cowboy-and-Indian-filled West, and Cody came closer to giving it to them than anyone else because he had it in *himself* and audiences could see that. He invented rodeo, sponsored cowboys, supported and promoted Indians, many Indians. He drew forth those seventeen hundred dime novels. Thanks to his shows millions of people came to know, or to think they knew, at least a little of what westering, in the broadest sense, had been like.

Whatever his flaws, and there were many, Cody's life work was no mean achievement.

Let Annie Oakley, his greatest star, speaking elegiacally, in terms appropriate to the times, speak the final words:

Goodbye, old friend. The sun setting over the mountain will pay its tribute to the resting place of the last of the great builders of the West, all of which you loved, and part of which you are.

Western Heroes, Heroines, and Villains

HOW LONG THEY LASTED

Meriwether Lewis	1809
Sacagawea	1812
Manuel Lisa	1820
Jedediah Smith	1831
William Clark	1838
Kit Carson	1868
George Catlin	1872
Captain Jack	1873
Alfred Jacob Miller	1874
George Armstrong Custer	1876
James Butler Hickok	1876
Crazy Horse	1877
Texas Jack Omohundro	1880
Billy the Kid	1881
Jim Bridger	1881
Doc Holliday	1887
Phil Sheridan	1888
Ranald S. Mackenzie	1889
Sitting Bull	1889
George Crook	1890
John Charles Frémont	1890
W. T. Sherman	1891

John Wesley Hardin	1895
Calamity Jane	1903
Chief Joseph	1904
Red Cloud	1909
Geronimo	1909
F. Remington	1909
Quanah Parker	1911
William F. Cody	1917
Theodore Roosevelt	1919
Annie Oakley	1926
Charles Russell	1926
Doc Carver	1927
Charles Goodnight	1929
Wyatt Earp	1929
Bill Pickett	1932
Libbie Custer	1933
Will Rogers	1935
Gordon Lillie	1942
Nicholas Black Elk	1950

Bibliography

Black Elk, Nicholas. *Black Elk Speaks.* As told through John G. Nei-
hardt (Flaming Rainbow). University of Nebraska, 1979.

Blackstone, Sarah. *The Business of Being Buffalo Bill: Selected Letters
of William F. Cody.* New York, 1988.

———. *Buckskins, Bullets, and Business.* New York, 1986.

Blake, Hubert Cody. *Blake's Western Stories.* Brooklyn, 1929.

Bruce, Robert. *The Fighting Norths and Pawnee Scouts.* Lincoln,
1932.

Burke, J. M. *"Buffalo Bill" from Prairie to Palace.* Chicago, 1893.

Burke, John. *Buffalo Bill: The Noblest Whiteskin.* New York, 1973.

Cody, Louisa Frederici. *Memories of Buffalo Bill.* With Courtney
Ryley Cooper. New York, 1919.

Cody, Wm. F. *The Life of Hon. William F. Cody, Known as Buffalo Bill,
the Famous Hunter Scout and Guide. An Autobiography.* Foreword by Don Russell. University of Nebraska, 1973.

———. *Life and Adventures of Buffalo Bill.* New York, 1927.

———. *Letters from Buffalo Bill.* Billings, 1948.

Cooper, Courtney Ryley. *Annie Oakley.* Hurst and Blackett, n.d.

Foreman, Carolyn Thomas. *Indians Abroad.* University of Oklahoma,
1943.

Havighurst, Walter. *Annie Oakley of the Wild West.* Introduction by
Christine Bold. University of Nebraska, 1954. Reprint, 1992.

Hedren, Paul. *First Scalp for Custer: The Skirmish at Warbonnet
Creek.* University of Nebraska, 1980.

Hutton, Paul Andrew. *Phil Sheridan and His Army*. University of Nebraska, 1985.

Kasper, Shirl. *Annie Oakley*. University of Oklahoma, 1992.

Kasson, Joy S. *Buffalo Bill's Wild West: Celebrity, Memory, and Popular History*. New York, 2000.

Lamar, Howard R., ed. *The New Encyclopedia of the American West*. New Haven, 1998.

Leonard, Elizabeth Jane, and Julia Cody Goodman. *Buffalo Bill, King of the Old West*. Kissimmee, Florida, 1995.

Logan, Herschel. *Buckskin and Satin: The True Drama of Texas Jack (Omohundro) of the Old West and His Celebrated Wife, Mlle. Morlacchi, Premiere Danseuse, Originator of the Can-can in America*. Harrisburg, Pennsylvania, 1954.

Moses, L. G. *Wild West Shows and the Images of American Indians 1883–1933*. University of New Mexico, 1996.

Muller, Dan. *My Life with Buffalo Bill*. Chicago, 1948.

Riley, Glenda. *The Life and Legacy of Annie Oakley*. University of Oklahoma, 1994.

Rosa, Joseph G., and May Robin. *Buffalo Bill and His Wild West: A Pictorial Biography*. University of Kansas, 1989.

Russell, Don. *The Life and Legends of Buffalo Bill*. University of Oklahoma Press, 1960.

Slotkin, Richard. *Gunfighter Nation*. New York, 1992.

Swartwout, Annie Fern. *Missie: The Life and Times of Annie Oakley*. Blanchester, Ohio, 1947.

Wetmore, Helen Cody. *Last of the Great Scouts*. Harrisburg, Pennsylvania, n.d.

Yost, Nellie Snyder. *Buffalo Bill: His Family, Friends, Fame, Failures, and Fortunes*. Chicago, 1979.

Index

Photo Credits

The Boundaries of

Freedom of Expression & Order

in American Democracy

The Boundaries of Freedom of Expression & Order in American Democracy

EDITED BY

THOMAS R. HENSLEY

THE KENT STATE UNIVERSITY PRESS

KENT, OHIO, & LONDON

© 2001 by The Kent State University Press, Kent, Ohio 44242

ALL RIGHTS RESERVED

Library of Congress Catalog Card Number 00-010682

ISBN 0-87338-692-2

Manufactured in the United States of America

06 05 04 03 02 01   5 4 3 2 1

Library of Congress Cataloging-in-Publication Data

The boundaries of freedom of expression and order in American democracy /
edited by Thomas R. Hensley.

p.   cm.

Includes bibliographical references and index.

ISBN 0-87338-692-2 (alk. paper)

1. Freedom of speech—United States.   I. Hensley, Thomas R.   II. Title.

KF4772 .B68 2001

342.73'0853—dc21   00-010682

British Library Cataloging-in-Publication data are available.

Contents

Preface

Shortly after noon on May 4, 1970, the sound of gunfire erupted on the campus of Kent State University. Members of the Ohio National Guard fired sixty-one shots into a crowd of students, some of whom had gathered at noon to protest the recent escalation of the Vietnam War as well as the presence of the National Guard on the Kent State campus. Four students—Allison Krause, Jeffrey Miller, Sandra Scheuer, and William Schroeder—were killed, and nine students were wounded: Alan Canfora, John Cleary, Thomas Grace, Dean Kahler, Joseph Lewis, Donald MacKenzie, James Russell, Robert Stamps, and Douglas Wrentmore.

The shocking events on the Kent State campus had immediate and dramatic repercussions throughout American society. In the direct aftermath of the shootings, the first nationwide student strike in American history resulted in hundreds of American colleges and universities shutting down. President Richard Nixon appointed a Commission on Campus Unrest to study the causes of the student protest movement and to recommend policies regarding the turmoil on the nation's campuses. The commission issued special reports on Kent State and Jackson State, where two African Americans, James Green and Phillip Gibbs, had been killed by local police on May 14, 1970. Numerous additional governmental and nongovernmental investigations occurred in the aftermath of the shootings. Criminal and civil court proceedings were initiated at both the state and federal levels; nonetheless, when the various litigative activities finally came to a conclusion nearly ten years after the shootings, not a single person had been found legally responsible for any of the events of May 4, 1970.

Just as debate still exists over responsibility for the tragedy at Kent State, so too does disagreement exist regarding the historic significance of May 4, 1970. Some argue that the tragedy served to shorten the war in Vietnam. In contrast, others maintain that the shootings weakened dramatically the student antiwar movement. Yet other analysts reject any type of direct effect of May 4, 1970, on American society, arguing instead that the shootings at Kent State have had the primary effect of serving as a symbol of one of America's most turbulent historical periods, the Vietnam War era.

Whatever the effect of the May 4 shootings on American society, the impact of the event on the Kent State campus was truly profound. The campus was closed immediately after the shootings, with faculty and students being forced into ad hoc arrangements to finish the last half of the spring quarter. The campus was not opened for students to attend classes for almost two months. When classes began in fall quarter of 1970, the atmosphere was tense and uncertain. The burgeoning enrollments of the sixties had ended, and the bright promises of growth and distinction had turned into concern for institutional survival. Kent State University, a beautiful residential campus with a proud tradition of excellent teaching and a growing reputation as a major research institution, was now known worldwide for one primary reason—the place where college students had been wounded and killed.

Perhaps not surprisingly, successive administrations at Kent State University struggled to find an appropriate manner in which to respond to the tragedy. Several important and meaningful responses were quickly initiated, including the creation of the Center for Peaceful Change and a May 4th Room at the Library. Many critics argued, however, that the leadership of the University was not sufficiently sensitive and responsive to the tragedy. This frustration led to the forming in the mid-seventies of the May 4th Task Force, a student-based organization committed to year-round educational programs as well as planning an annual commemoration program each May 4.

Student reaction against perceived insensitivity of the university administration to May 4, 1970, reached a boiling point in 1977, when officials announced plans to build an annex to the University's gymnasium on portions of the land where Guardsmen and students had confronted each other on May 4, 1970. Student activists formed the May 4th Coalition and pitched tents on the proposed construction site. The University administration eventually prevailed, but not until the coalition had involved the state courts, the Ohio legislature, the governor's office, federal courts, members of Congress, and the White House. Kent State's public image and reputation had taken another major hit, and distrust between the University's administration and student activists had widened even farther.

An uneasy and distrustful atmosphere surrounded May 4 during the eighties, and even the dedicated efforts of a new president, Michael Schwartz, to establish a memorial met with considerable conflict and controversy. Schwartz's work resulted in the dedication in 1990 on the twentieth anniversary of the shootings of a sizable granite memorial near the site of the shootings, and the guest speaker, former governor Richard Celeste, issued a formal apology for the shootings. Even these developments were not without controversy, however. Some student activists argued that the memorial was an inadequate, token representation, because it cost only $100,000 rather than the million dollars that had been mentioned earlier. From the other side of the political spectrum, Governor Celeste received substantial public criticism for his statement, which was perceived by some as condoning student rioting and as not reflecting the view of the majority of Ohioans.

Carol Cartwright became president of Kent State University shortly after the twentieth anniversary of May 4, 1970. During the nineties, the University experienced a relatively quiet period regarding May 4–related activities, but uncertainty and ambivalence continued to characterize the University's position on the tragedy. As the thirtieth anniversary approached, however, Cartwright launched the University in new directions. Drawing upon advice from a variety of sources, she made the decision to have the university come to grips with May 4 not only by recognizing the past but also by embracing the future, through using May 4 as a platform for examining the challenges of living in a democratic society.

Several developments in the 1999–2000 academic year symbolized this new commitment. In the fall semester, the University dedicated four permanent markers in the Prentice Hall parking lot, where the four students had been fatally shot. The families of each of the students participated in the moving ceremonies dedicating the markers. In the middle of the academic year, the University's logo was altered in a symbolically important manner, when "Kent" in capital letters was replaced with "Kent State" in capital letters. The third major development involved the decision to begin an annual national scholarly symposium during the week of May 4 with a focus on the great issues of American democracy. This book is the product of the first symposium. The topic selected for the symposium, like the title of this book, was "The Boundaries of Freedom of Expression and Order in American Democracy."

This topic is certainly an important and enduring issue in a democratic society. Freedom of expression and order are both important values that are deeply cherished in the United States. They are values embedded into our constitutional structure, and they are absolutely essential to a stable and free society. These two values are ideally compatible and even mutually supportive. Freedom of expression allows those with criticisms and complaints against the government to voice those concerns peacefully and perhaps to be effective in producing change. In turn, an orderly society ideally provides the sense of security and stability in which heated discussion and debate will be tolerated. But freedom of expression and order can come into conflict, especially when expression threatens violence, clashes with contemporary moral standards, and even challenges the very tenets of democracy. Under such conditions, when freedom of expression presents serious challenges to social order, where are the boundaries at which government can legitimately interfere with freedom of expression?

This question is one with which Americans have struggled for centuries, and no absolute answers exist. The contributions in this book do not claim to have the answers, but they do represent an impressive range of thoughtful analyses by some of the nation's leading First Amendment scholars about many of the most important and difficult issues involving freedom of expression in the United States.

A strong link exists between the symposium and book theme of the boundaries of freedom of expression and order, on one hand, and the events of May 4, 1970, at Kent State University, on the other. When demonstrating students gathered on the Commons—a large, grassy area in the center of campus—to protest the Vietnam War and the presence of the Ohio National Guard on campus, many demonstrators felt they were engaged in expressing their First Amendment rights of freedom of speech and assembly. In direct contrast, Ohio National Guard troops operated under the assumption that all assemblies had been banned because of serious disturbances on three previous days, and they were under instructions to preserve order by dispersing all rallies. The confrontation between two groups supporting two fundamental but clashing societal values ended tragically with the deaths of four Kent State students and the wounding of nine other students. The contributions of this book and the symposium upon which it is based are an effort to learn from the terrible tragedy and to ensure that it never happens again.

Turning now to the process associated with the creation and development of the symposium on which this book is based, in July of 1999 a 30th May 4 Commemoration Coordinating Committee, composed of approximately forty faculty, staff, students, and Kent residents, was created and held its first meeting. The charge to the Coordinating Committee was to create a structure through which the University could not only continue to remember the past but also contribute to a forward-looking consideration of the democratic values that are the foundation of American society. Several subcommittees were formed to handle various facets of the thirtieth anniversary, and the decision was made to create a Symposium Subcommittee to begin an annual scholarly conference each week of May 4 focusing upon the enduring issues of American democracy. The initial topic selected was "The Boundaries of Freedom of Expression and Order in American Democracy."

The subcommittee members quickly made several major decisions. They agreed that a two-day symposium should be held, with the symposium to begin the evening of May 1 and continue through May 2. A top priority was the recruitment of one or more keynote speakers with national reputations, thus assuring a high-quality event by drawing a group of accomplished scholars and attracting national attention. The decision was also made to have from six to ten major papers presented, with discussants from Kent State as well as from other colleges and universities present-ing critiques of each paper, and to allow the authors of the papers to respond to the discussants.

Although it took a few months, the search for major keynote speakers was an unqualified success. The Symposium Subcommittee had hoped to attract one key-note speaker. Instead, three truly distinguished First Amendment experts agreed to participate: Kathleen Sullivan, dean of Stanford Law School as well as the Rich-ard E. Long Professor of Law and the Stanley Morrison Professor of Law; Anthony Lewis, two-time Pulitzer Prize–winning columnist of the *New York Times* and the author of two major First Amendment books, *Gideon's Trumpet* and *Make No Law: The Sullivan Case and the First Amendment*; and Cass Sunstein, the Karl N. Llewellyn Professor of Jurisprudence at the University of Chicago Law School. Sullivan was asked to present the opening keynote address on the evening of May 1, focusing on the past and present of freedom of expression in American society; Lewis agreed to present a noon luncheon address on May 2; and Sunstein accepted an invitation to give the closing keynote speech, analyzing the future issues of freedom of expres-sion.

Once the keynote speakers had been secured, a nationwide call for papers was issued. We hoped that three strong stimuli would attract a substantial number of paper proposals: the participation of the three distinguished keynote speakers, the chance to participate in the inauguration of a leading scholarly symposium associ-ated with a major event in the history of American higher education, and an hono-rarium. The incentives worked. One hundred ten proposals were received from scholars across the country representing numerous disciplines.

The decision was made to select a total of nine papers, allowing three one-and-one-half-hour sessions on Tuesday, May 2, with three papers being read concur-rently at each session. Because only one of every twelve proposals could be accepted, an extensive set of criteria was utilized to guide the subcommittee in accepting pro-posals. These criteria included the following seven questions: Does the proposal fit with the theme of the symposium? Does the proposal deal with an interesting, im-portant topic? Can the paper be completed by April 1, 2000? Does the proposal fit well with the other accepted proposals? Do the proposals make a coherent edited book? What is the record and reputation of the author? Do the authors represent a variety of disciplines? The nine scholars—along with their disciplines, institutions, and topics—who were selected include:

Saul Cornell, history, Ohio State University, "A Right to Kill Bears or Bear Quills? A Critical Commentary on the Linkage of the First and Second Amendments in Recent Constitutional Theory"

David M. Estlund, philosophy, Brown University, "Deliberation Down and Dirty: Must Political Expression Be Civil?"

Katheryn D. Katz, law, Albany Law School of Union University, "Student Academic Freedom: An Oxymoron?"

Susan B. Kretchmer, communications, Johns Hopkins University, and Rod Carveth, communications, Southern Connecticut State University, "Challenging Boundaries for a Boundless Medium: Information Access, Libraries, and Freedom of Expression in a Democratic Society"

Daniel Perlstein, education, University of California at Berkeley, "Unspoken Dangers: The Curtailment of Free Expression and the Endangerment of Youth"

Gerald N. Rosenberg, law and political science, University of Chicago, "The Sorrow and the Pity: Kent State, Political Dissent, and the Misguided Worship of the First Amendment"

Ellen W. Schrecker, history, Yeshiva University, "Free Speech on Campus: Academic Freedom and the Corporations"

J. David Slocum, communications, New York University, "Violent Expressions of Freedom: Negotiating Narratives of Social Order and Disorder in Contemporary U.S. Media"

James Weinstein, law, Arizona State University, "Hate Speech, Viewpoint Neutrality, and the American Concept of Democracy"

Two discussants for each paper were also selected and offered honoraria to participate. For each paper, one discussant was selected from Kent State University, and one from another college or university. Discussants were selected from the group of 110 paper proposals, and the selection of discussants was based upon the quality of their original proposals, their prior teaching and research on freedom of expression, and their fits in terms of disciplinary affiliation. Each discussant was to receive the paper by April 1, 2000, and was to provide a five-page reaction to the other members of the panel by the end of April. The Kent State discussants were Michael Byron, philosophy; Florence W. Dore, English; Norman Fischer, philosophy; Paul M. Haridakis, communications; Donald M. Hassler, English; Mary Anne Higgins, communications; Eric D. Miller, psychology; Timothy D. Smith, journalism; and Don A. Wicks, library and information science. The nine discussants from other colleges and universities included Nancy C. Cornwell, communications, Western Michigan University; Juliet Dee, communications, University of Delaware; Susan Newhart Elliott, law, University of Dayton; Jonathon L. Entin, law, Case Western Reserve University; Leslie Friedman Goldstein, political science, University of Delaware; Mark A. Graber, political science, University of Maryland; David E. Kyvig, history, Northern Illinois University; Ladelle McWhorter, philosophy, University of Richmond; and Robert M. O'Neil, law, University of Virginia.

A large number of people deserve to be recognized for their contributions to the symposium and the subsequent book. First and foremost, it is important to recognize the talented and dedicated members of the Symposium Subcommittee who gave countless hours of their valuable time to make the event and the book a success: Pamela Anderson, Gail Beveridge, Richard Bredemeier, David Brenner, Laura Davis, Paul Haridakis, Carole Harwood, Elaine Huskins, John Jameson, Jerry M. Lewis, Sarah Northcraft, Gayle Ormiston, Jacqueline Parsons, and Timothy Smith. It was truly a pleasure to work with this wonderful committee of people, who constituted the most impressive, capable group with whom I have ever worked in my thirty-one years at Kent State University.

Another important group of people who made significant contributions to the symposium were the individuals who served as moderators of the nine panels. These individuals were Larry Andrews, dean of the Honors College, Kent State University; Richard Aynes, dean of the College of Law, University of Akron; Joseph Danks, dean of the College of Arts and Sciences, Kent State University; James P. Louis, Associate Provost, Kent State University; Joanne Schwartz, dean of the College of Education, Kent State University; Steven H. Steinglass, dean of the Cleveland-Marshall College of Law, Cleveland State University; George Stevens, dean of the College of Business Administration and Graduate School of Management, Kent State University; Scott Sullivan, dean of the College of Fine and Professional Arts, Kent State University; and Mark W. Weber, interim dean of University Libraries and Media Services, Kent State University.

Many other individuals also deserve special recognition. The president of Kent State University, Carol Cartwright, developed the original idea to have Kent State sponsor an annual May 4 symposium series focusing on the challenges of living in a democratic society, and her strong, unqualified support of the symposium was instrumental in the success of the event. John Hubbell and Joanna Craig of The Kent State University Press were wonderfully supportive of the book project. John provided encouragement and then a firm commitment to the book project at an early stage, and Joanna provided remarkably quick editorial feedback to the authors of each contribution. Two Kent State undergraduate students made important contributions to the book: Natalie Martin worked diligently in preparing the initial draft of the bibliography, and Sarah Northcraft prepared the index of cases, in addition to serving on the Symposium Subcommittee. Special recognition must be extended to Elaine Huskins, who has served efficiently and cheerfully for the past year as the secretary for the Symposium Subcommittee and who did most of the technical work in combining the contributions of thirty scholars into a cohesive manuscript.

All royalties from this book will be donated to the May 4 Memorial Fund. This fund is dedicated to paying for the expenses incurred when Kent State University constructed and dedicated in the fall of 1999 the four permanent markers where Allison Krause, Jeffrey Miller, Sandra Scheuer, and William Schroeder were fatally wounded on May 4, 1970.

This book is dedicated to the memories of Allison, Jeffrey, Sandra, and William. Nothing can replace the tragic loss of their lives, but the annual symposia series and resulting books on the enduring issues of American democracy will, we hope, create a lasting legacy that respectfully honors the memory of these four Kent State University students.

Thomas R. Hensley
Department of Political Science
Kent State University

Foreword

As All Life Is an Experiment

ANTHONY LEWIS

Columnist, New York Times

To participate in this symposium is a painful honor for me. I say painful because of the memories of what happened at Kent State thirty years ago. Before turning to the First Amendment, I must say a word about that moment in history.

Everyone involved in the symposium knows that four Kent State students were killed by National Guard bullets on May 4, 1970. But many today are too young to have a real idea of what led up to those killings. The American war in Vietnam, the full-scale war, was five years old by then. Richard Nixon had campaigned for president in 1968 on a promise to get this country out of the war. But on April 30, 1970, he widened the war by sending American soldiers on an invasion of Cambodia. I was in London at the time. I wrote a column about Cambodia that I am going to quote now. It is a bit unusual to quote oneself, but I think it indicates the feelings of that time.

"'This is not an invasion of Cambodia,' President Nixon said." "If the young judge those who run American society by the standard of truth in that statement," I wrote, "should anyone be surprised at cynicism or unbearable frustration on the campuses of the United States?

"It has been hard for most of us middle-class, middle-aged Americans of liberal instinct to accept the apocalyptic vision of many students. We believed in reason.

"But the President's course in Cambodia would make the most optimistic rationalist despair for his country. . . . By this action President Nixon has calculatedly chosen to widen the division among the American people, to inflame instead of heal."

I believed what I wrote then. I believe it now. I think the men who planned the invasion of Cambodia will always carry a terrible responsibility: Richard Nixon, Henry Kissinger, and the rest. What they did led to deaths here and at Jackson State

College in Mississippi. Cambodia divided the country then, and in a serious way the division persists. Our country has not yet recovered the internal trust, the common faith it lost in Vietnam and Cambodia. Kent State is a powerful, tragic symbol of what we lost.

This symposium is in a sense a reminder of what went wrong here on May 4, 1970—not just politically but constitutionally. It was for expressing their views that four students died. Those who gave the orders to fire, like the leaders in Washington, had forgotten, in their zeal and paranoia, that this country is for people of fundamentally different views—and that government must tolerate those differences. Indeed, "tolerate" is the wrong word. It sounds grudging. Our system welcomes differences of opinion. Out of that nettle danger we pick the flower safety.

The papers prepared for this symposium seem to me an extraordinary collection of scholarly work, both learned and fascinating. My task is not a scholar's. It is, as Professor Hensley explains it, simply to pay tribute to the importance of the First Amendment. That is a pleasant assignment. But the tribute does not belong only to James Madison and the others who drafted and ratified the constitutional command, "Congress shall make no law . . . abridging the freedom of speech, or of the press." It belongs as much to those who, over a long history, have given meaning to those words.

To indicate what I mean, imagine the following scenario. Go back a year, to the war over Kosovo. U.S. aircraft are bombing targets in Serbia. One day a group of Americans opposed to the war drops anonymous pamphlets from the tops of buildings in New York City. The pamphlets denounce the president's policy and say we should leave Serbia alone to deal with Kosovo as it wishes. Half a dozen people who wrote and dropped the pamphlets are arrested, charged with sedition, tried, convicted, and sentenced to prison—twenty years in prison. They take their case to the Supreme Court, where their lawyers argue that their criticism of government policy was speech protected by the First Amendment. But the Court rejects the argument.

I asked you to imagine that scenario, but it is hard to do so. Twenty years in prison for disagreeing with a war policy—disagreeing peacefully, in a pamphlet? The idea is quite unthinkable in the America we know. But it happened, exactly like that, eighty years earlier.

In 1919, a group of radicals were sent to prison for twenty years for throwing from rooftops pamphlets that criticized President Woodrow Wilson's dispatch of American troops to Russia after the Bolshevik Revolution. And the Supreme Court affirmed the convictions for sedition, rejecting the claim that the First Amendment protected that political speech.

The words of the First Amendment have not changed since 1919. But you can be sure that if Congress passed a sedition act today and prosecutors used it to try Americans who peacefully criticized a war, the Supreme Court would find any conviction unconstitutional. It would do so, I am confident, unanimously.

So something has happened in the last eighty years to the perceived meaning of the First Amendment's words—to the understanding of the place of free speech in our constitutional universe. In fact, there has been a dramatic historical process, which began in the very 1919 sedition case I have just mentioned. When the Supreme Court upheld those convictions and savage sentences, Justice Oliver Wendell Holmes, Jr., joined by Justice Louis D. Brandeis, dissented. Holmes's opinion was the first ever in the Supreme Court that expounded freedom of speech as a fundamental value of the Constitution. I know I risk sounding the familiar, but I must quote a few of Holmes's words.[1] "Persecution for the expression of opinions," Holmes said, "seems to me perfectly logical. If you have no doubt of your premises or your power, you naturally express your wishes in law and sweep away all opposition. . . . But when men have come to realize that time has upset many fighting faiths, they may come to believe even more than the foundations of their own conduct that the ultimate good desired is better reached by free trade in ideas—that the best test of truth is the power of the thought to get itself accepted in the competition of the market. . . . That at any rate is the theory of our Constitution. It is an experiment, as all life is an experiment. . . . While that experiment is part of our system I think that we should be eternally vigilant against attempts to check the expression of opinion that we loathe and believe to be fraught with death."

Over the next ten years Holmes and Brandeis dissented again and again when the Court upheld the convictions of speakers whose words offended authority. Gradually those dissents persuaded the country—and the Court. Beginning in the 1930s, the Court for the first time reversed some of those convictions. One notable case, in 1937, was that of Angelo Herndon, a black Communist Party organizer in Georgia. (Professor Herbert Wechsler, the greatest lawyer I ever met, worked on the Herndon case as a young man. I mention that as a gesture of respect to Professor Wechsler, who died April 26 at the age of ninety.)

The strands of free speech theory were woven together, finally, in 1964, to give us the extremely broad interpretation of the First Amendment that we now enjoy. The case was *New York Times v. Sullivan*;[2] it was briefed and argued for the *Times* by Professor Wechsler. I think it is worth taking a moment to sketch the strategy he developed, because it shows how counsel as well as courts shape the meaning of our Constitution over time.

As most of you know, the Sullivan case concerned an advertisement in the *Times* that criticized the brutal treatment of Dr. Martin Luther King, Jr., and other civil rights leaders by southern officials. The ad named no officials; it referred to them collectively as "southern violators of the Constitution." But a commissioner of the city of Montgomery, Alabama, L. B. Sullivan, claimed that some of the charges of abuse would be read as applying to him. He brought an action for libel, and an all-white jury awarded him half a million dollars—at that point the largest libel judgment in Alabama history.

In presenting the case to the Supreme Court, Wechsler faced a daunting challenge. Libel had always been treated as outside the protection of the First Amendment. No libel judgment, however outlandish, had ever been found to violate the federal Constitution. Libel was a matter of state law.

Wechsler dealt with that daunting history by arguing that libel was only a cover here for an attempt to suppress unwelcome speech. He analogized it to a prosecution for sedition. And he countered the history on the other side with history of his own: the story of the Sedition Act of 1798, when a Congress dominated by the Federalist Party sought to keep down Jeffersonian editors before the election of 1800 by making it a crime to criticize President John Adams. In electing Thomas Jefferson, Wechsler said, the American people had delivered a judgment against that kind of suppression.

When the case was decided, Justice William J. Brennan, Jr., for the Court, adopted the Wechsler argument. "Although the Sedition Act was never tested in this Court," he said, "the attack upon its validity has carried the day in the court of history." The Supreme Court thus, in effect, retrospectively held unconstitutional a statute that had expired 163 years before. "The central meaning of the First Amendment," Justice Brennan said, is "the right to criticize government and public officials." Our system requires "robust, uninhibited and wide-open" debate on public issues.

What is especially interesting about the Sullivan case is how the broad free speech doctrine adopted by the Supreme Court worked in the real world. Dr. King had based his campaign on the belief that Americans, if they saw the brutality of southern racism, would oppose it. That required that the national press and broadcasters tell the story. As a result of the Sullivan decision, they were able to—and public opinion led to effective civil rights and voting legislation.

In 1969, five years after the Sullivan decision, the Supreme Court completed its turn away from the suppressive doctrine against which Justice Holmes had protested in 1919. The case, *Brandenburg v. Ohio*,[3] looks modest in the Supreme Court reports: a rather brief *per curiam*, unsigned opinion. But it had large implications. Brandenburg, a Ku Klux Klan leader, had addressed a public meeting in language derogatory to blacks and Jews. He had been convicted of violent speech under the Ohio Criminal Syndicalism Act, fined, and imprisoned for one to ten years. The Court reversed his conviction, holding that speech advocating lawlessness or violence could not be punished unless it was designed to incite "imminent lawless action" and was "likely to incite or produce such action." That is an extremely stringent test. Only an impassioned speech to a mob seething with hate and ready for violence is likely to be punishable.

So in fifty years our law went from allowing condign punishment for pamphlets criticizing a president's policy to forbidding punishment for hateful speech except in the most extreme circumstances. Of course there were many other signposts along the way, for speakers and for my profession, the press. But it is the role of judges that I wanted to bring home to you today.

Years ago I was at a conference of lawyers, journalists, and judges. It was one of those role-playing affairs constructed by the late Fred Friendly, where people had to examine their own professional urges. Justice Potter Stewart of the Supreme Court had agreed to attend, but only on condition that he not be asked to say anything. Well, something about the discussion brought out the extreme in some of my journalist colleagues. They angrily denounced the courts for occasionally deciding cases against the press. The First Amendment rights of the press were absolute, they said, and judges who did not agree were derelict in their duty. Finally Justice Stewart could stand it no longer. Despite his vow of silence, he intervened. "Where do you suppose all these rights that you talk about came from?" he asked. "The stork didn't bring them. The judges gave them to you: those terrible judges you're talking about."

Needless to say, judges can go wrong. Judicial interpretation of the First Amendment is not a one-way street to freedom and glory. I need only mention the Supreme Court's misbegotten 1951 decision in the Dennis case, finding that leaders of the American Communist Party—by then a tattered remnant, heavily infiltrated by the FBI—could be punished because they presented a clear and present danger of something. The Court's other decisions in the Joseph McCarthy period were not always models of liberty or courage either.

But I think it is fair to say that today we are as free to say and print what we want in this country as we have ever been, and freer than any other people on earth. I mean free in the special sense that the courts will protect us. Americans have always been outspoken. Thomas Jefferson had to endure attacks about as rancid as anything thrown at his current successor, and as biased. After he had been president for six years, he wrote to a friend: "Nothing can now be believed which is seen in a newspaper. Truth itself becomes suspicious by being put into that polluted vehicle."[4] But when forces of repression sought to silence particular views, the First Amendment was not an effective shield until quite recently. In the two years before the election of the year 1800, many of the leading Jeffersonian editors and proprietors were convicted and imprisoned under the Sedition Act, notwithstanding Madison's protests that the act violated the First Amendment.

In recent years there has been one striking change of attitude toward the First Amendment. Through most of our history the forces of repression came from the Right: the Federalists who imprisoned Jeffersonian editors, the federal prosecutors who imprisoned protestors in World War I and swept up alien socialists after the war, the state prosecutors who went after syndicalists, Joe McCarthy, and so on. But now conservatives have become converts to the protection of free speech. Senator

Mitch McConnell is ready to die on the barricades for his version of free speech: the right to spend without limit in political campaigns—or, I should say, the Supreme Court's version in *Buckley v. Valeo*.[5] I agreed with Paul Freund's comment on that decision: "They say that money talks. I thought that was the problem, not the solution." But conservative acceptance of free speech as a constitutional necessity goes far beyond the self-interested campaign spending issue.

Perhaps because nature abhors a vacuum, we now have attacks on the First Amendment from another quarter—an unexpected one, at least by me—that is, from some voices on the Left. You are all so familiar with the phenomenon that I need not expound it. Free speech is fine—so long as it does not denigrate this group or that. An even broader attack from the Left sees the First Amendment as a handmaiden of privilege. Years ago I heard Professor Richard Delgado of the University of Colorado Law School speak about what he called, sarcastically, "the mighty First Amendment." Freedom of speech, he said, "advantages only the dominant" in society. "You find that your words are not free if you attack the wealthy or powerful."[6]

Think back to the case of Angelo Herndon, one of the first to find a majority of the Supreme Court on the side of free speech. Herndon was a black Communist Party organizer in Georgia in 1937. Can you imagine anyone less privileged, less powerful than that?

Most of the Supreme Court decisions protecting speech or publication under the First Amendment have been on behalf of beleaguered, unpopular minorities: pacifists, radicals of all kinds, Jehovah's Witnesses, Ku Klux Klan speakers. Others, if not radicals, were those who sought to change society by overthrowing the forces of power. The *New York Times* was not the only winner in the Sullivan case. Sullivan had also sued four black Alabama ministers whose names had been used in the *Times* advertisement without their knowledge. They and all the other leaders of the civil rights movement were the real winners of the Sullivan case—for the decision freed the national press from the threat of crippling libel actions if it continued to cover the movement and to tell the country about the brutal realities of racism in the American South.

Freedom of expression is so woven into our culture today that we take it for granted. We do not think about why it matters. But that is evident to Americans—and not just those who discuss the First Amendment at conferences—when we look at other countries.

In societies ruled by tyranny, expression is always repressed. The apartheid system in the old South Africa developed exquisite methods of political repression. Opponents of the regime were served with banning orders, which forbade them to visit a university or a newspaper or meet more than one other person at a time; it was a crime to quote their words or publish their pictures. Expressions of discontent could be punished as "terrorism."

In Zimbabwe today, Robert Mugabe sends thugs to intimidate the political opposition. In Yugoslavia, Slobodan Milosevic seizes broadcast stations that tell the truth.

Those methods are not simply cruel to individuals. They lower the quality of public decision making. A government that is not open to meaningful criticism will make mistakes and persist in them. That is so even of governments that are not tyrannical but merely closed. A good example is Britain, a country like ours in many respects but at least until lately much more restrictive of speech. I lived there for nine years and was stunned, over and over, by the tradition of secrecy in government: a secrecy enforced by common-law doctrine and criminal statutes. I became convinced that secrecy was one reason for the poor performance of British governments over many years.

The First Amendment, Learned Hand said, "presupposes that right conclusions are more likely to be gathered out of a multitude of tongues than through any kind of authoritative selection. To many this is, and always will be, folly," he added, "but we have staked upon it our all."[7]

Staked upon it and won, I would say. Not in the sense that unfettered speech has produced perfection—I am painfully aware of how far short we fall of a just society. This huge, populous, unruly country has always been difficult to govern wisely. But its unruliness is its saving grace.

The freedom to think as we will and to speak as we think is the great gift we have been given by the framers of the First Amendment—and by the judges who have, finally, given its words their true meaning. Just fourteen words—"Congress shall make no law . . . abridging the freedom of speech, or of the press"—have liberated poets and preachers and all of us to express what is in our hearts, and liberated the country to govern itself.

NOTES

1. *Abrams v. United States*, 250 U.S. 616, 621, 627–31 (1919).
2. *New York Times Co. v. Sullivan*, 376 U.S. 254 (1964).
3. *Brandenburg v. Ohio*, 395 U.S. 444 (1969).
4. See Saul Padover, *Thomas Jefferson on Democracy* (New York: Mentor, 1939), 92.
5. *Buckley v. Valeo*, 424 U.S. 1 (1976).
6. Notes made by the author.
7. *United States v. Associated Press*, 52 F. Supp. 362, 372 (D.C. S.D.N.Y. 1943).

1

Freedom of Expression in the United States

Past and Present

KATHLEEN SULLIVAN

Law, Stanford University

Americans tend to think of free expression and democratic social order as mutually reinforcing. On the one hand, we have freedom of expression because we have social order. The free speech guarantee has been read to forbid a heckler's veto of unpopular speech.[1] Speakers prevail over hecklers because freedom of speech has been read implicitly to require publicly financed police protection for unpopular speakers when their ideas stir listeners to anger and unrest.[2] Armed guards have enabled parading in public streets by marchers from civil rights demonstrators[3] to neo-Nazis[4] seeking to express written, spoken, or symbolic messages eliciting local hostility. Indeed, in the contemporary United States, we largely take for granted that such police protection for dissidents will be forthcoming no matter how unpopular their views.

The assumption of stable police protection likewise permits speakers freer rein. Even hateful views gain airing, because in turn we trust government to prevent physical violence against those targeted by hate. Jewish residents of the village of Skokie, Illinois, for example, can be confident that the police will keep them safe from harm if goose-stepping neo-Nazi brownshirts march through their neighborhoods bearing swastikas. It is not equally clear even in the year 2000 that British troops can reliably do likewise to protect residents of Catholic settlements in Belfast when members of the Orange Order carry out triumphalist marches to commemorate the victory of the Protestant William of Orange in the 1690 Battle of the Boyne.

In short, freedom of speech depends on material preconditions, and first among them is the availability of strong police protection. If unpopular speakers are protected from hostile audiences, then the views of majorities may be publicly challenged. If the government is prepared to deploy legitimate force to provide genuinely equal protection of the law, then expression of views that are hostile to subparts of the population pose no ultimate physical menace. Trust in constitutionally bounded force prevents both listeners from vetoing speakers and speakers from inciting angry mobs.

On the other hand, we often suppose that we enjoy social order precisely because we have freedom of expression. There is no need for sabotage or revolution when peaceful expression of dissent is possible.[5] Spoken disagreement prevents entrenchment of any regime and keeps clear the channels of political change. Similarly, freedom of speech and press ensures a free flow of information about what the government is doing.[6] There is no need to overthrow a government that is accountable through transparency, no need for subtly subversive or underground speech when open protest is allowed.

Against the backdrop of this contemporary conventional wisdom, the shootings of student antiwar demonstrators by National Guardsmen at Kent State on May 4, 1970, appear anomalous: freedom of expression understood not as an aspect of public order but rather as a threat to public order, and enough of a threat to warrant the use of martial force. The tolerance and even approval expressed by many at the time contrasts sharply with the widespread horror expressed more recently, for example, at the carnage wrought by Chinese troops firing upon prodemocracy demonstrators in Tiananmen Square on June 4, 1989.[7] Was the use of martial force in response to protest in the Kent State shootings simply an aberration in our free speech tradition, difficult to contemplate after the passage of thirty years without similar incident?

Not entirely—violent repression of protestors seeking to exercise free speech rights is not a new feature of American political life. There are numerous precedents in our history for government-backed suppression of public demonstrations of affiliation or protest, especially in times of perceived crises of national or state security.

To take an early example, consider the attack the First Amendment came under only seven years after it was ratified. In July 1798, the nation faced a deteriorating relationship with postrevolutionary France. At the urging of the Federalist Party, led by Alexander Hamilton, Congress passed the Alien and Sedition Acts, which authorized the president to expel aliens perceived as dangerous and to punish the publication of writings perceived as malicious toward the U.S. government.[8] The acts were never reviewed for constitutionality[9] before their expiration in 1801 after American victories at sea over the French calmed fears of invasion. But during their pendency, they permitted the Federalist-led repression of Republican political opponents charged with French sympathies, including Hamilton's personal use of force, in his capacity as commander of the army.

As a second example, recall the pronounced restriction of civil liberties during the Civil War and Reconstruction. President Abraham Lincoln suspended the writ of habeas corpus on three occasions and used the suspension to suppress the views of Southern sympathizers. Federal marshals and other law enforcement officials were authorized to arrest and imprison those who discouraged enlistment or other disloyalty to the Union cause.[10] Lincoln made clear that expressions of protest deserved no immunity simply because they were speech; as he wrote in a June 12, 1863, letter to Erastus Corning, "Must I shoot a simple-minded soldier boy who deserts, while I must not touch a hair of a wily agitator who induces him to desert? . . . I think that in such a case, to silence the agitator, and save the boy, is not only constitutional, but, withal, a great mercy."[11]

If these first two examples focus more on the use of such formal state sanctions as arrest and imprisonment, however curtailed their procedural protections, examples from a third period in American history exemplify the use of spontaneous and lethal force at public gatherings in ways more reminiscent of the events at Kent State. In the period between Reconstruction and World War I, mass labor demonstrations became increasingly prominent vehicles for expression of worker unrest.[12] The rise of mechanized large-scale industry, coupled with economic volatility in the employment cycle, spurred labor mobilization, which depended on speech and expressive association in the form of strikes, pickets, newsletters, pamphlets, marches, placards, and songs. Government did much to stifle union organizing, through the use of injunctions, police harassment, prosecutions for restraint of trade, and enforcement of anti-union contracts. But law enforcement officials also engaged on occasion in arrests, beatings, and killings of labor demonstrators.[13]

For example, the railway strike of 1877, an initially nonviolent protest that began in New York, eventually spread nationwide and posed a serious threat to business. Police killed twelve striking workers in New York, and thereafter President Rutherford B. Hayes called up federal troops to quell a near insurrection.[14] Nearly a decade later, the notorious Haymarket Affair of 1886 involved mass arrests of workers on strike at a McCormick reaper factory. In 1891, Pennsylvania state militia members fired upon striking coke workers fleeing after a protest, killing ten and wounding fifty.[15] In 1897, again in Pennsylvania, local law enforcement officials fired on unarmed striking miners, killing twenty and wounding forty. In the early years of the twentieth century, as the Industrial Workers of the World (the "Wobblies") launched a free speech movement that pioneered the use of the streets and parks as public forums, government frequently responded by arresting demonstrators for offenses such as obstructing sidewalks, blocking traffic, vagrancy, and unlawful assembly.[16] Suppression was often violent even when a strike or protest was initially not, and the escalating labor-government violence in turn was used as a basis to pass laws further limiting labor speech and organization.

To take a fourth example, anticommunist suppression from the aftermath of the Russian Revolutions to the McCarthyism of the Cold War period involved a variety of uses of official force. The Espionage and Sedition Acts of 1917 to 1918 enabled arrest and imprisonment of pacifists, socialists, and anarchists.[17] The Smith Act of 1940 allowed widespread punishment of communist sympathizers for advocating the overthrow of the federal government.[18] While much of the contest between government and dissidents in these periods concerned leaflets, speeches, and organizing conferences, it also sometimes involved violent street clashes, such as the 1950 fight between New York police and some two thousand communist-affiliated demonstrators protesting the Korean conflict. That violence in turn spurred Congress to pass the Internal Security Act and other legislation designed to combat the perceived risk of communist influence.[19]

As a fifth example, consider the history of the civil rights movement, which eventually desegregated the South. Free speech controversies in this struggle during the 1950s and early 1960s revolved largely around the violent suppression of peaceful demonstrations, whether by law enforcement officials or by private citizens insufficiently checked by government restraint. Peaceful protests through marches and boycotts against segregated restaurants, buses, and stores frequently culminated in beatings, firebombings, and the use of violent techniques of dispersal.[20] Perhaps the most notorious example occurred in Birmingham, Alabama, in May 1963, when Sheriff "Bull" Connor loosed police on a peaceful meeting of a thousand or so African Americans, including many children, assembled at the Sixteenth Street Baptist Church. Prominent news coverage of the event displayed officers swinging nightsticks into skulls, and attack dogs spreading panic among the crowd.[21]

Finally, recall the Vietnam War protests, in which the events at Kent State on May 4, 1970, played the most lethal part. As with anticommunist suppression, the federal government under both Presidents Lyndon B. Johnson and Richard M. Nixon undertook a host of measures of surveillance and intimidation of antiwar activists, short of violent clashes on the street.[22] But as with labor protest at the end of the nineteenth century and the civil rights movement in the twentieth, protest against the war increasingly took the form of public demonstrations, especially on university campuses, and suppression of such protest increasingly took the form of official force in response. Arrests on university campuses for political violence totaled more than four thousand in 1968–69 alone, rising to 7,200 the following year. After the May 4 events at Kent State, over 430 colleges were forced to shut down at least once in response to protests that became violent, and the National Guard was called out several dozen more times, nationwide.[23]

How might these incidents—this undercurrent of free speech antihistory—be reconciled with our canonical tradition that the First Amendment confers the highest protection upon dissident political expression? The repression of public protest for the sake of social order is usually explained by two kinds of exception to the

First Amendment. The first rests upon the well-worn distinction between speech and conduct. Under this distinction, speech normally functions as the medium for peaceful disagreement and dissent, and as the vehicle for demanding accountability from, and influencing the behavior of, the government. But speech interests attenuate, the distinction holds, when speech becomes the stimulus to sympathetic violent action (incitement)[24] or responsive violent action (fighting words).[25] A distinction between speech and conduct similarly explains why the Supreme Court has held that criminal sentencing may be enhanced for racially motivated assault but not for the deployment of symbols likely to arouse racial hostility or unrest.[26]

It is widely agreed that meaningful enforcement of the First Amendment depends upon some such expression/action or speech/conduct distinction; the core debates in First Amendment law in the twentieth century revolved around the point at which the dividing line has been crossed. Judicial review of convictions for anarchism, syndicalism, and aiding and abetting the enemy during World War I, the Red Scare, and the McCarthy era was relatively toothless, permitting government to suppress words with a bad tendency to bring about revolutionary sympathies in listeners and readers, and thus to nip any ultimate lawlessness in the bud without awaiting imminent disturbance of public order.[27]

Half a century of case law later, the Supreme Court eventually came around to the view of the dissenting justices in these early cases, notably Justices Oliver Wendell Holmes and Louis D. Brandeis, that the First Amendment ought to put government to much stricter requirements of probability, imminence, and causation in its assessment of material danger before it suppresses speech. In its 1969 decision in *Brandenburg v. Ohio*,[28] the Court held that laws against incitement might legitimately punish only imminent and intentional triggers of violent action—the mob on the barricades, not the organizing convention in the downtown hotel. Specifically, *Brandenburg* invalidated a criminal-syndicalism conviction of a Ku Klux Klan leader who had, with a string of bigoted epithets toward African Americans and Jews, preached to a straggling band of followers in an Ohio wood about potential "revengeance" in the name of white supremacy. Government might punish incitement to lynching, the Court implied, but not the mere ideological promotion of attitudes that might someday lead a racist to use the noose. It might punish the shouted command to street protestors, armed with rocks and bottles, to advance upon public guardians but not the cry of "Kill the Pigs" if shouted, even in anger, by unarmed street demonstrators as pointed political hyperbole.

In short, the Court has read the First Amendment to require that punishable incitement to violence be narrowly defined, with advocacy of ideas protected, however subversive they might be in their ultimate logic. This approach rests on a philosophical dualism, a distinction that separates ideas from action ontologically, much as theories of identity might separate body and mind. It also reflects a liberal political theory that sees government as justified in intervening in the exercise of individual liberty only when material harm is posed, and sees speech as presumptively incapable of doing material harm. In the Court's view, government may regulate the clash of bodies but not the stirring of hearts and minds. On this view, the government's suppression through force of labor organizers, communists, civil rights marchers, and demonstrators against the war in Vietnam reflected the judgment that they threatened to bring about the clash of bodies.

The history of violent suppression of dissident speech might alternatively be explained by a second conventional exception to the strong protection of free speech: the notion that public-emergency justifications might sometimes be sufficiently compelling to justify limiting pure speech even if it has not crossed some ontological line into the realm of conduct. Such a justification has long been accepted as a ground for embargoing truthful factual information—for example, the revelation of the identity of spies or the whereabouts of troops in combat. Such security justifications have been deemed powerful enough to permit prior restraint of speech, normally one of the cardinal sins of First Amendment law.[29] Times of war and other public emergency may be thought to demand unity of purpose and attention to collective security that trump individual rights of expression.

Against this background in modern First Amendment law and its exceptions, how should we view the government's use of lethal martial force against Kent State students on May 4, 1970? Were the students the mob on the barricade, posing a danger to the guardsmen or bystanders that justified the use of tear gas and guns to disperse massed protest? If so, then the issue at stake was the probability of violence. Were the students instead mere advocates of an ideology that deserved constitutional protection even if it was capable, if it caught on widely enough, of bringing about a reversal of government policy or even a change of regime? If so, then the issue was the possibility of persuasion. Or were they the bearded, tie-dyed, and sandal-footed emblems of opposition to the dominant social order, and the shootings an enraged response to upturned middle fingers rather than to either the content of conscientious objection or the upturned barrel of a gun? If so, then the issue was social nonconformity or social deviance.

Under the first of these three interpretations, the only issue at stake was whether the students' antiwar protest posed any genuine threat of erupting into violence—into material physical harm. Was there a danger that speakers and demonstrators would become rebels, injuring guardsmen and bystanders and university property, even if their projectiles were more likely to be rocks than bullets or tear gas canisters? As outlined earlier, speech may be curtailed to prevent the clear and present danger of materially harmful consequences; thus, intervention was plainly constitutionally permissible at some point, and the only issue was the accuracy of empirical prediction. How probable and imminent was the escalation of words and chants into violence? Were the guardsmen ever at risk of physical harm? Even if they were, did the guardsmen overreact prematurely when they might have availed themselves of nonviolent alternatives, such as retreating or regrouping? Whose point of view should govern—the sober assessment of an objective observer after the fact, or the subjective perspective of a young, skittish, undertrained guardsman, stifling and blurry-eyed in a gas mask?

The interpretation most sympathetic to the guardsmen would see the responsive force by the government as the students' own fault. They had left the quiet protest of the senior thesis or letter to the editor, in favor of mass and potentially violent assembly on a grassy field in sight of the still-smoking embers of the former ROTC outpost. In so doing, they had assumed grave risk. That was President Nixon's reading of the events of May 4, 1970; the next day, he sought to arouse the nation's anger against the students, not the guards, stating, "When dissent turns to violence it invites tragedy."[30]

The free speech tradition as it had emerged through the 1950s and '60s, with the decline of McCarthyism and the rise of judicial protection of the civil liberties of civil rights protestors, would normally have condemned such an assessment as a capitulation to exaggerated fear. The strong protection of speech and assembly reflected in such decisions as *Brandenburg* picked up where the dissents and concurrences of Justices Holmes and Brandeis had left off decades earlier. As Justice Brandeis famously wrote, concurring reluctantly in a conviction for attending a Communist Labor Party convention in *Whitney v. California*,[31] "Fear of serious injury cannot alone justify suppression of free speech and assembly. Men feared witches and burned women. It is the function of speech to free men from the bondage of irrational fears."

Similarly, Justice Holmes, famously dissenting in *Abrams v. United States*,[32] protested the conviction of Bolshevik sympathizers for distributing leaflets that supposedly impeded the war effort against Germany in World War I, in violation of federal espionage laws. While conceding that government constitutionally may punish speech threatening clear and imminent danger, he wrote, "Now nobody can suppose that the surreptitious publishing of a silly leaflet by an unknown man, without more, would present any immediate danger that its opinions would hinder the success of the government arms or have any appreciable tendency to do so." He further noted that he could find nothing additional in the record to warrant fear of the "poor and puny anonymities" who had authored the leaflets.

Finally, dissenting from the Court's affirmation of a set of Smith Act convictions in *Dennis v. United States*,[33] Justice William O. Douglas ridiculed the majority's deference to legislative assessments of the communist menace: "In America [communists] are miserable merchants of unwanted ideas; their wares remain unsold." He argued against regulating speech and association based on "senseless fear." The opinions of Holmes, Brandeis, and Douglas call for a sensibility of genteel bravado in the face of popular paranoia. To be sure, their bravado turned upon their empirical assessments that the "poor and puny anonymities" who were being suppressed were hardly likely to be effective in touching off revolution. But had these three justices been channeled onto the scene at Kent State on May 4, 1970, they are unlikely to have seen the motley collection of students assembled there as any greater a threat to peaceful public order.

The robust Holmes-Brandeis-Douglas approach might also criticize government for poorly matching means and ends if its attempt at suppressing speech and assembly for the sake of public order is ineffective. Suppression often has unintended consequences, which become all the more likely the broader the publicity it is given through the mass media. Consider the outrage and sympathy for the protesters aroused by news photos of Bull Connor's police dogs and by the tanks rolling into Tiananmen Square. It was no surprise the riveting and prize-winning magazine-cover photograph of a protestor grieving over a slain body at Kent State had similar effects upon some strands of American public opinion.[34] Similarly, official violence might well beget further violence; recall that in the aftermath of the Kent State shootings, an average of one hundred demonstrations per day occurred on college campuses and that, as noted above, 430 colleges were shut down and the National Guard was called in on numerous occasions.

Under an approach that assesses the probability that speech will eventuate in violence, everything turns on context. Extravagant tolerance for anti-Semitic speech might be one thing in Skokie, Illinois, another thing in postwar Germany. Speech espousing racial bigotry might be one thing in contemporary New York City, another thing in postapartheid South Africa or a modern Austria facing a rising tide of xenophobia toward an influx of foreign refugees. Attacks on the Middle East peace process might be one thing outside embassies in Washington, D.C., another thing in Israel in the midst of intense criticism of public leaders.[35] The default rule of the modern American free speech tradition, however, is to defer government intervention to prevent speech-related violence until the last possible, inescapable moment.

Under the second interpretation of the provocation for the shootings, the problem with the students was not so much their proximity to violence as their ideas. In this view, the danger was that the protesting students would be persuasive to the body politic through the exercise of critical rationality, exposing the war to argument and undermining government arguments through logic and debate. In this view, what was to be extinguished was the ideas themselves, regardless of the means by which they were expressed.

This is at least a plausible hypothesis of government motivation. Recall from the historical examples mentioned earlier that the suppression of public demonstration has often been embedded in a much broader pattern of suppression of ideas. For example, Lincoln's Union government suppressed newspapers with Southern sympathies, and it roughed up inciters to draft resistance. State and federal authorities suppressed labor organizers by a variety of civil means as well as exercises of official force, and they used violent clashes between labor and law enforcement as justifications for further antilabor legislation. Anticommunism was enforced not just by force but through such means as loyalty oaths and the destruction of the employment opportunities and reputations of suspected sympathizers.

However, under the modern free speech tradition that dominates contemporary First Amendment jurisprudence, any such government suppression of speech for reason of its ideas would have been flatly impermissible; viewpoint discrimination by the government is the cardinal First Amendment sin, all the more so when it is directed against political dissent.[36] Because the government's motivation rather than its method is the problem, the presumptive ban on ideologically driven suppression of speech applies just as much to street protestors as to allegedly seditious newspaper advertisements.[37] Under this approach, one may express any idea one wants as long as it remains on the idea side of the mind/body line, no matter how unpatriotic and no matter how far beyond the pale it might seem in civilized society.

In this respect, contemporary First Amendment law differs notably from the approach to oppositional speech taken in other cultures. A number of nations whose orientations to civil rights and liberties otherwise resemble that of the United States do hold some ideas to be beyond the pale on the ground of their antisocial content. For example, consider the International Covenant on Civil and Political Rights, a document adopted by the United Nations General Assembly in 1966 as the outgrowth of a process that began with adoption of the Universal Declaration of Human Rights in 1948.[38] Article 20 provides, "Any propaganda for war shall be prohibited by law," and "Any advocacy of national, racial or religious hatred that constitutes incitement to discrimination, hostility or violence shall be prohibited by law." The experience of the Holocaust was thought sufficient by most signatories to put discriminatory speech off limits. However, because Article 20 would limit hate speech and protest to a greater extent than First Amendment understandings would permit, the United States ratified the covenant only with express reservations.[39]

In a similar vein, Article 11 of France's Declaration of the Rights of Man and Citizen proclaims "free communication of thoughts and opinions" a basic right, but at the same time it cautions that free speech may be curtailed "for abuse of that liberty as determined by law"—an abuse that might sometimes, in times of crisis, be found to consist of departure from the general will so as to reveal divisions in the national consensus.[40] Likewise, the German *Grundgesetz*, or Basic Law, provides in

Article 5 for a guarantee of free expression, but it is subject to the limitation, set forth in Article 18, that "whoever abuses freedom of expression, in particular freedom of the press, freedom of teaching, freedom of assembly [or] freedom of association . . . in order to combat the free democratic basic order, shall forfeit these basic rights."[41] Accordingly, Article 131 of the German Penal Code, entitled "Protection of the Public Peace," prohibits any writing or broadcast that incites racial hatred or describes inhumane acts of violence in a way that glorifies or minimizes them, and it elsewhere enforces strict bans on the use of Nazi propaganda, salutes, and symbols.[42] As a final example, the Constitution of Ireland provides for freedom of speech but provides that it "shall not be used to undermine public order or morality or the authority of the State; the publication of blasphemous, seditious or indecent matter is an offence."[43]

Whatever the tendency in other democracies to permit the suppression of speech for reason of its antigovernment or antisocial content, American constitutional law draws a canonical distinction between words as triggers to action and words as vehicles for ideas. Thus the government could not constitutionally have conceded an ideological motivation for the use of force at Kent State on May 4, 1970. The structure of First Amendment law drove President Nixon inevitably in the direction of defending the government's action as, instead, a preemptive response to imminent violence.

Nonetheless, however canonical it might be in our tradition, the distinction between words as regulable triggers to action and words as protected vehicles for ideas fails to take account of crucial understandings of the world now commonplace, after the end of the twentieth century. At a minimum, the mind/body distinction is not a clean one. Modern neuroscience suggests that our very affect, emotions, and feelings are patterned in our limbic systems.[44] Modern theories of cognitive psychology and organizational behavior posit that we exercise a variety of irrational choices. Postmodern cultural theories suppose that speech does not emanate from a rationally self-determining mind but rather participates in complex social constructions that condition our actions and make us who we are.

In short, in contemporary views of social life, speech and conduct are not distinct but continuous; ideas construct reality and reflect it back. Thus, a society with violent entertainment might well be more violent than it would otherwise be; the use of women's images in advertising and pornography might well help to construct and reinforce male dominance in politics and markets. We are not only what we eat; we are what we read, what fashion tells us to be, and what we see on television, whether a gospel station or MTV.

A running subtheme within the modern free speech tradition has long captured this complexity, even while affirming as a practical matter that government should never regulate speech for its ideas and that it should regulate speech for its material dangers only when they are serious and nearly nigh. For example, Justice Holmes, dissenting when the Court sustained a criminal anarchy conviction, wrote that "[e]very idea is an incitement. It offers itself for belief and if believed it is acted on unless some other belief outweighs it or some failure of energy stifles the movement at its birth."[45] Justice Brandeis wrote similarly, "Every denunciation of existing law tends in some measure to increase the probability that there will be violation of it."[46]

If these two examples seem too steeped in a model of rational persuasion for the post-twentieth-century mind, consider the words of U.S. Circuit Judge Frank Easterbrook, affirming the invalidation of an ordinance permitting sanctions against pornography, defined as speech that subordinates women. He conceded that pornography has a socializing effect: "People often act in accordance with the images and patterns they find around them. . . .Words and images act at the level of the subconscious before they persuade at the level of the conscious." He thus accepted the empirical premises of this legislation but denied its constitutionality:

> Depictions of subordination tend to perpetuate subordination. . . . Yet this simply demonstrates the power of pornography as speech. . . . If pornography is what pornography does, so is other speech. Hitler's orations affected how some Germans saw Jews. Communism is a world view, not simply a Manifesto by Marx and Engels or a set of speeches. . . . Racial bigotry, anti-semitism, violence on television, reporters' biases [all] influence the culture and shape our socialization. . . . Yet all is [sic] protected as speech, however insidious. Any other answer leaves the government in control of all of the institutions of culture, the great censor and director of which thoughts are good for us.[47]

Observing the breakdown of the speech/conduct distinction in contemporary social theory leads to the third possible reading of the Kent State events of May 4, 1970. In this third view, the shootings were not just about a misestimation of the danger of violence, or about the suppression of cogent, rationally articulable political ideas. Instead they served to suppress a form of social deviance. In this view, public protest in defiance of government authority was perceived as being in itself a threat to the public order, irrespective of its particular political content. In this view, the shootings responded to symbolic disorder, to the subtle undermining of trust in government that comes from the refusal to conform to norms of authority. Here the danger was not so much violence or a change of political regime under the old rules of political engagement; it was, rather, a reconstruction of the social order itself. In this view, the problem with the student protests was not their possible consequences but the very construction of social relationships they embodied. The students symbolized a loss of the structures that condition citizens to respect authority—the authority of the president, of the military, of local police, deference to political leadership in general. The disobedience itself connoted subversion, whatever the demonstrators might have been arguing in specific terms about the U.S. military's incursion into Cambodia.

Turning back to the historical examples discussed earlier, the same interpretation might be given to the forcible suppression of laborers challenging the supremacy of capital, or of civil rights protestors stepping out of their places in a legislated hierarchy of racial supremacy. What was being punished was not the signified ideas so much as the rupture of conventional hierarchy and power.

This interpretation resonates with Vice President Spiro Agnew's comments about campus antiwar demonstrations. Agnew characterized antiwar activists as "home front snipers" and "the glib, activist element who would tell us our values are lies."[48] One month before Kent State, in April 1970, he offered in a speech a "modest" suggestion that campus protestors should be treated as though they were wearing brown shirts or white sheets. For Agnew, it was not the ideology that mattered—hippies, Klansmen, and Nazis were all fungible. What mattered was that they represented a kind of hooliganism, or social rupture.

This third possibility is much harder than the first two to classify in traditional First Amendment terms. As suggested earlier, it defies the canonical distinctions between speech and conduct, advocacy and incitement, expression and action. It starts from the contrary assumption that speech and action interpenetrate, that ideas determine and are determined by the material structures in which we live.

But protecting speech and symbolic conduct that ruptures social convention is at heart of a broader tradition in American constitutional law: one that views civil rights and civil liberties as supporting social fluidity rather than entrenchment in fixed groups. The underlying assumption of much of the law of freedom of association, as well as of laws against discrimination on the basis of race, is that we should not be stuck in group identities that are ascribed to us—through, for example, the operation of prejudice or selective disregard or indifference. Instead, we should be able to join or exit our interest-group memberships and our expressive and intimate associations relatively easily. Taken together, protections in favor of voluntary group affiliation and against disadvantage based on ascribed identity create myriad overlapping identities, no one of which envelops or structures an individual's life entirely. Identity, in this view, is forged and remade through endlessly shifting recreations of self. One may experience these shifting involvements as more or less permanent, but even the degree of permanence any of them creates is itself largely a matter of choice.

We are in this respect different from places like Kosovo, where tribal, religious, ethnic, or national identity that was forged in ancient conflict is passed down across generations, inheritable and nondisclaimable, etched in surnames, accents, and dress codes like a brand. In such a nationalist or tribal conception of social groups, one's fate—one's craft and marriage prospects, one's cultural repertoire, the very footpaths one deems safe to travel through town—is indelibly tied to one's ancestry. In contrast, American constitutional traditions reject a totalizing conception of social groups in which a particular social identity regulates most or nearly all of an individual's social relationships. In addition to freedoms of association and guarantees of equal protection, federalism promotes such fluid (rather than fixed) group identities, through guarantees of interstate mobility, and the religion clauses do likewise, by precluding any national sectarian orthodoxy.

Public speech, association, and symbolic protest that defy a social orthodoxy serve this function. They remind us that in a constitutional democracy, fidelity to authority must be based not on duty coercively imposed but on commitment willingly offered. In a decision upholding the right of young Jehovah's Witness children not to be compelled to salute the American flag at public school, Justice Robert Jackson, in a famous paean against government imposition of orthodoxy, wrote that "[s]truggles to coerce uniformity of sentiment" have always resulted in "ultimate futility"; he suggested that "[t]o believe that patriotism will not flourish if patriotic ceremonies are voluntary and spontaneous instead of a compulsory routine is to make an unflattering estimate of the appeal of our institutions to free minds." In the spirit of genteel bravado exemplified by the Holmes, Brandeis, and Douglas opinions discussed earlier, he offered reassurance that "freedom to be intellectually and spiritually diverse or even contrary" would not "disintegrate the social organization," and he concluded that "rich cultural diversit[y] flourishes only at the price of occasional eccentricity and abnormal attitudes." Unlike Holmes and Brandeis, however, he suggested that the "freedom to differ" is required not only for poor and puny anonymities, or "for things that do not matter much," but also "as to things that go to the heart of the existing order."[49]

On this understanding of American constitutional tradition, the rupture with convention and authority itself serves a useful purpose, independent of its contribution of particular, articulate ideas to the debate. It reminds us that social orders in our democratic society are to be constructed from the bottom up by the people, not from the top down by the state.

For this reason, there is much to be thankful for in remembering the students killed at Kent State on May 4, 1970—Allison Krause, Jeffrey Miller, Sandra Scheuer, and William Schroeder—as well as the shooting victims who survived—Alan Canfora, John Cleary, Thomas Grace, Dean Kahler, Joseph Lewis, Donald MacKenzie, James Russell, Robert Stamps, and Douglas Wrentmore. They gave us a lesson not only about freedom of expression but about freedom, pure and simple.

1. See *Terminiello v. Chicago*, 337 U.S. 1 (1949), which reversed a breach-of-the-peace conviction of an abrasive public speaker who had insulted a hostile crowd, reasoning that one of the functions of free speech is to invite dispute and even anger.

2. See *Forsyth County v. Nationalist Movement*, 505 U.S. 123 (1992), which invalidated a variable fee to cover extraordinary costs of preserving public order during demonstrations on public property.

3. See *Edwards v. South Carolina*, 372 U.S. 229 (1963); *Cox v. Louisiana*, 379 U.S. 536 (1965); *Gregory v. Chicago*, 394 U.S. 111 (1969).

4. See *Collin v. Smith*, 578 F.2d 1197 (7th Cir. 1978), *cert. denied*, 439 U.S. 916 (1978).

5. See *Whitney v. California*, 274 U.S. 357 (1927) (Brandeis, J., concurring): "Those who won our independence [knew] that fear breeds repression; that repression breeds hate; that hate menaces stable government [and] that the path of safety lies in the opportunity to discuss freely supposed grievances and proposed remedies."

6. See *New York Times Co. v. United States*, 403 U.S. 713 (1971) (Stewart, J., concurring): "The only effective restraint upon executive policy and power in the areas of national defense and international affairs may lie in an enlightened citizenry [and] it is perhaps here that a press that is alert, aware, and free most vitally serves the basic purpose of the First Amendment."

7. See Nicholas D. Kristof and Sheryl WuDunn, *China Wakes: The Struggle for the Soul of a Rising Power* (New York: Times Books, 1994), 90, noting that estimates of the number of protestors killed varied widely.

8. See Craig R. Smith, "The Hamiltonian Federalists," in *Silencing the Opposition: Government Strategies of Suppression*, ed. Craig R. Smith (Albany: State University of New York Press, 1996), 5–9.

9. But see *New York Times Co. v. Sullivan*, 376 U.S. 254 (1964), in which Justice Brennan, writing for the Court, noted that the view that the acts were unconstitutional has "carried the day in the court of history."

10. See Craig R. Smith and Stephanie Makela, "Lincoln and Habeas Corpus," in Smith, ed., *Silencing the Opposition*.

11. Ibid., 26.

12. See Andrew Sachs, "Silencing the Union Movement," in Smith, ed., *Silencing the Opposition*, 125–32.

13. See Patrick Garry, *An American Paradox: Censorship in a Nation of Free Speech* (Westport, Conn.: Praeger, 1993), 19; Daniel M. Rohrer, *Freedom of Speech and Human Rights: An International Perspective* (Dubuque, Iowa: Kendall Hunt, 1979), 2.

14. See Sachs, "Silencing the Union Movement," 134.

15. See ibid.

16. See David M. Rabban, *Free Speech in Its Forgotten Years* (Cambridge: Cambridge University Press, 1997), 77–128.

17. See *Abrams v. United States*, 250 U.S. 616 (1919).

18. See *Dennis v. United States*, 341 U.S. 494 (1951).

19. See Craig R. Smith, "The McCarthy Era," in Smith, ed., *Silencing the Opposition*, 151.

20. See generally Robert Weisbrot, *Freedom Bound: A History of America's Civil Rights Movement* (New York: Norton, 1990); David J. Garrow, ed., *We Shall Overcome: The Civil Rights Movement in the United States in the 1950s and 1960s* (Brooklyn, New York: Carlson, 1989); Anna Kosof, *The Civil Rights Movement and Its Legacy* (New York: Watts, 1989).

21. See Weisbrot, *Freedom Bound*, 68–73.

22. See Gerald N. Rosenberg, "The Sorrow and the Pity: Kent State, Political Dissent, and the Misguided Worship of the First Amendment," in this volume.

23. See Sharon Downey and Karen Rasmussen, "Vietnam: Press, Protest, and the Presidency," in Smith, ed., *Silencing the Opposition.*

24. See *Brandenburg v. Ohio*, 395 U.S. 444 (1969).

25. See *Chaplinsky v. New Hampshire*, 315 U.S. 568 (1942).

26. Compare *R.A.V. v. City of St. Paul*, 505 U.S. 377 (1992) with *Wisconsin v. Mitchell*, 508 U.S. 476 (1993). See James Weinstein, "Hate Speech, Viewpoint Neutrality, and the American Concept of Democracy," in this volume.

27. See *Gitlow v. New York*, 268 U.S. 652 (1925).

28. 395 U.S. 444 (1969).

29. See *Near v. Minnesota*, 283 U.S. 697 (1931). "The protection even as to previous restraint is not absolutely unlimited. But the limitation has been recognized only in exceptional cases. . . . No one would question but that a government might prevent actual obstruction to its recruiting service or the publication of the sailing dates of transports or the number and location of troops."

30. Robert B. Semple, Jr., "Nixon Says Violence Invites Tragedy." *New York Times*, May 5, 1970, 17.

31. 274 U.S. 357 (1927).

32. 250 U.S. 616 (1919).

33. 341 U.S. 494 (1951).

34. Contrary to Professor Rosenberg's provocative thesis that such sympathy, and hence willingness to endorse free speech, depends upon substantive agreement with the message expressed, such sympathy might just as well flow from repugnance, government's excessive response to the peaceful conveyance of a message one substantively condemns.

35. See Ruth Gavison, "Incitement and the Limits of Law," in *Censorship and Silencing: Practices of Cultural Regulation*, ed. Robert C. Post (Los Angeles: Getty Research Institute, 1998), 46, describing how prior to Prime Minster Itzhak Rabin's assassination on November 4, 1995, demonstrators massed near his residence and called out insults and made it difficult for him to speak in public gatherings, and how law enforcement efforts against incendiary speech increased in the wake of the assassination.

36. See *Texas v. Johnson*, 491 U.S. 397 (1989), and *United States v. Eichman*, 496 U.S. 310 (1990), which struck down, respectively, a state and a federal law directed at flag burning as a form of symbolic protest.

37. See *New York Times Co. v. Sullivan*, 376 U.S. 254 (1964), which invalidated a punitive-damages judgment for libel of a public official.

38. See generally Marc J. Bossuyt, *Guide to the "Travaux preparatoires" of the International Covenant on Civil and Political Rights* (Boston: Klower Academic, 1987).

39. See David P. Stewart, "U.S. Ratification of the Covenant on Civil and Political Rights: the Significance of the Reservations, Understandings and Declarations," *Human Rights Law Journal* 14 (1993): 77. The United States also found troubling the elasticity of Article 19(3), which provides that the right of free speech is subject to restriction where necessary "for respect of the rights or reputations of others," or "for the protection or national security or of public order, or of public health or morals."

40. See Jean-Marie Guehenno, "Legal and Constitutional Protections of Freedom of Speech in France," in *Liberty of Expression*, ed. Philip S. Cook (Washington D.C.: Wilson Center, 1990), 65.

41. See Sabine Michalowski and Lorna Woods, *German Constitutional Law: The Protection of Civil Liberties* (Aldershot, Hunts. England: Ashgate, 1999), 199.

42. See John F. McGuire, "When Speech Is Heard around the World: Internet Content Regulation in the United States and Germany," *New York University Law Review* 74 (1990): 750.

43. Constitution of Ireland, Article 40, quoted in Michael Forde, *Constitutional Law of Ireland* (Cork: Morcier, 1987), 455; see ibid., 464–79 (outlining a series of acts implemented under authority of this article).

44. See, e.g., Thomas Lewis, Fari Amini, and Richard Lannon, *A General Theory of Love* (New York: Random House, 2000).

45. *Gitlow v. New York,* 268 U.S. 652 (1925) (Holmes, J., dissenting).

46. *Whitney v. California,* 274 U.S. 357 (1927) (Brandeis, J., concurring).

47. *American Booksellers Association v. Hudnut,* 771 F.2d 323 (7th Cir. 1985); *aff'd mem.,* 475 U.S. 1001 (1986).

48. Quoted in Charles Goodell, *Political Prisoners in America* (New York: Random House, 1973), 169.

49. *West Virginia State Board of Education v. Barnette,* 319 U.S. 624 (1943).

2

The Sorrow and the Pity

Kent State, Political Dissent, and the Misguided Worship of the First Amendment

GERALD N. ROSENBERG

Law and Political Science, University of Chicago

INTRODUCTION

On May 4, 1970, Ohio National Guard troops patrolling the campus of Kent State University opened fire on students protesting U.S. involvement in the war in Vietnam. When the shooting stopped, four students were dead, and nine had been wounded. The tragedy was met with anger and disbelief in some parts of the country, and by sad resolve in other parts that protest must be stopped no matter how high the price. How could students, exercising the celebrated American right of political protest, be gunned down by government troops? What patterns of beliefs could lead to such a tragedy?

In this essay I explore this question by putting the events of thirty years ago in historical perspective. In looking at historical practice and carefully exploring public-opinion research available in the second half of the twentieth century, I will examine the tension between abstract commitment to free speech and substantive opposition to particular viewpoints. I will argue that while the American public is deeply committed to free speech as an abstract category, it is also quite willing to repress speech with which it does not agree. Despite the majestic language of the First Amendment and the existence of courts with the power of judicial review, when it comes to political dissent in practice, the boundaries of freedom of expression in the United States have been more narrowly drawn than in any other major Western democracy. Practice in the United States has been repressive. I will argue, then, that the historical record suggests that the events at Kent State are widely seen as tragic not because the right of political protest is well supported but primarily because the public and elites were divided over the war in Vietnam, stretching the boundaries of freedom of expression wider than they had been in the past.

At the end of the paper I will build on this historical analysis to suggest that the First Amendment as text has a paradoxical relationship to the level of protection afforded to speech. On the one hand, to borrow from the title of the symposium, the "Boundaries of Freedom of Expression and Order in a [this] Democratic Society" have more to do with entrenched political and economic power than they do with the constitutional guarantee. On the other hand, the existence of the constitutional text has resulted in the "legalization" of free speech discourse. Substantive questions about the appropriate limits of freedom of expression in a democratic society are shunted aside in favor of abstract conceptions and formalistic legal debates about bright lines, tests, and distinctions. Substantive policy decisions become hidden under the shibboleth of "free speech." To put the point succinctly, the current legalistic understandings of freedom of speech in the United States make democratic deliberation about the appropriate limits of freedom of expression in a democratic society difficult to sustain. They may also fail to serve underlying democratic interests. If my history is persuasive, the sorrow and the pity lie in the fact that they seldom have.

KENT STATE, THE WAR IN VIETNAM, AND POLITICAL DISSENT

The immediate reactions to the killings at Kent State were to deplore them as a tragedy and then point the finger at various causes. Those opposed to the war in Vietnam put the blame on political leaders, while supporters of the war effort blamed the students. Correlated with these responses were differing views on the acceptability of political protest.

In reaction to the killings, President Richard M. Nixon issued a statement, through presidential press secretary Ronald L. Zeigler, that the shootings "should remind us all once again that when dissent turns to violence it invites tragedy."[1] In a speech delivered by Vice President Spiro Agnew to the American Retail Federation the night of the killings, the vice president said that antiwar demonstrators had engaged in "a calculated, consistent and well publicized barrage of cynicism against the principles of this nation."[2] This was nothing new for the vice president, whose attacks on all who disagreed with the administration were legendary. For example, he had referred to opponents of the war as "home front snipers."[3] He had even been criticized in the pages of the *Wall Street Journal* for describing colleges as "circus tents or psychiatric centers for over-privileged, under-disciplined irresponsible children."[4] Similarly, the Friday before the shootings President Nixon had described student antiwar demonstrators as "bums" in off-the-cuff remarks at the Pentagon that were widely noted.[5] Part of the message from the president and vice president was that the protestors got what they deserved.

The *Wall Street Journal*, although labeling the events a tragedy, took the attitude that political dissent inevitably leads to violence. This "we told you so" hostility to political dissent is illustrated by the May 6 editorial: "This ghastliness must be confronted especially by those of us who have repeatedly warned that appealing political decisions to the streets is a risky tactic that will inevitably lead to grief. . . . Somehow the trends of our times have made a tragedy like this one inevitable at some point or another."[6] The *Journal's* view was that political decisions should be made in reflective legislative chambers, without the influence of political protest. Reacting to protests against the expansion of the war into Cambodia that had led to the killings at Kent State, the *Journal* editorialized, "Just when judgments about Cambodia ought to be withheld, the protests force them."[7] Reacting to an antiwar demonstration on Wall Street, the editors confessed that when "the shouts and obscenities float up from the crowd at Broad and Wall, the blood starts to surge."[8]

There was also a widely shared view, noted in the *Wall Street Journal*, that political dissent inevitably leads to violence. This equation of dissent with violence appears as both a product of the hostility to dissent and a cause of it. So when "hard hat" construction workers attacked an antiwar protest on the Friday after Kent State, the *Journal* editorialized: "We share the revulsion of most Americans to the brutal violence of some of the construction workers Friday, but we wish more of those who support anti-war actions would recognize that many of their countrymen react with exactly the same emotions, and with the same justice, when the violence is done by students."[9]

If administration officials and the conservative press put the blame for the killings on political dissenters, opponents of the war and the liberal press put it squarely on the former's hostility to political protest. Commenting on the president's reaction to Kent State, the *New York Times* editorialized: "The deploringly unfeeling statement by the President of the United States—through an intermediary—certainly does not provide either any answer or any comfort—nor does it show any compassion or even understanding. Mr. Nixon says that the needless deaths 'should remind us all once again that when dissent turns to violence it invites tragedy,' which of course is true but turns this tragedy upside down by placing the blame on the victims instead of the killers."[10]

In an editorial on May 8, the *Times* noted the resignation of Anthony Moffett as liaison between the government and American youth and his declaration that "he could no longer serve an Administration bent on discrediting nonviolent protest."[11] Similarly, the *Washington Post*, quoting President Nixon's comments about violence, editorialized that "it is not enough now to brush this incident aside as the President did Monday night, with [his] comment. The administration must . . . sympathize with at least the right to dissent."[12]

As these comments suggest, political dissent during the Vietnam War was met with considerable hostility. The reaction to the killings at Kent State is but one illustration of the hostile reception antiwar protestors and other political dissenters received. In the 1960s and 1970s, government at all levels took steps to harass civil rights and antiwar activists. It is now well known, for example, that the FBI had Dr. Martin Luther King, Jr., under surveillance.[13] The Black Panthers were also watched and harassed, with numerous arrests, although few convictions.[14] The antiwar movement suffered the same governmental attacks on fundamental freedoms. For example, in early 1968 a group of antiwar leaders, including Dr. Benjamin Spock and the Rev. William Sloane Coffin, was indicted for conspiracy to counsel, aid, and abet draft resistance. Convicted at trial, it took an appeal to preserve these individuals' right to criticize government actions.[15] It was also the case that the federal government engaged in massive surveillance of the lawful political actions of countless Americans, action that was upheld by the Supreme Court in 1972 in *Laird v. Tatum*.[16] Senator Charles Goodell, a Republican critic of the war, discovered that his phone had been tapped.[17] During the 1972 Democratic primaries, H. R. Haldeman, the president's White House chief of staff, went on national television to charge that the Democratic contenders' criticism of the Nixon war policy was "consciously aiding and abetting the enemy," which, Senator Goodell noted, "is the constitutional definition of treason."[18] The FBI even kept a "confidential file on the United States Supreme Court"; wiretapped or monitored conversations involving Chief Justice Earl Warren and Associate Justices William O. Douglas, Abe Fortas, and Potter Stewart; and used selected Court employees to report information heard throughout the Court building and to keep tabs on who came and went.[19] Those who publicly dissented against the war in Vietnam—and even some who did not, such as parents, relatives, and friends of protesters—ran the risk of government surveillance and harassment.

In the press area, in 1971 the U.S. government made a major attempt to censor the press when it sued to prevent the *New York Times* and the *Washington Post* from publishing the *Pentagon Papers*.[20] A temporary restraining order against the *Times* was issued in the Southern District of New York, while the Washington, D.C., District Court denied the government's motion for injunctive relief. Ten days later the Supreme Court agreed to hear the cases, holding oral argument the next day and announcing its decision (*per curiam*)[21] allowing publication four days later.

Turning to the less-established press, there was a good deal of governmental harassment. This is particularly true of the 1960s and early 1970s, when the antiwar and counterculture movements spawned an "underground" press comprising, at its height, approximately 450 papers with a total circulation of about five million.[22] Irreverent and often virulently antigovernment, these publications were often treated with hostility by local authorities. There are documented instances of government harassment of underground papers in many cities, including (but not limited to) Washington, D.C., Los Angeles, San Diego, Dallas, Jackson (Mississippi), New Orleans, and Buffalo.[23] In Washington, D.C., alone, Olga and Edwin Hoyt found that in the late 1960s and early 1970s two underground papers were "subject to some 300 incidents of harassment by the District of Columbia police."[24] Army surveillance of antiwar activists during the Nixon era that came to light in *Laird v. Tatum* affected at least fifty-eight underground papers in 1969 and 1970.[25] Incidents such as these led the Twentieth Century Fund to conclude in a 1971 study that "there has been a double standard of treatment, one for the underground and one for the established press—a double standard that is inconsistent with the First Amendment's guarantee of freedom for all the press."[26]

Where did this opposition to dissent come from? Was it an aberration, a temporary repudiation of American beliefs, traditions, and rights? In the next section I explore this question, by examining governmental responses to dissent throughout U.S. history. The findings show that far from being an aberration, the repression of dissent is the norm. The Vietnam era was exceptional not for the repression of dissent but for the leniency with which it was treated.

POLITICAL DISSENT IN U.S. HISTORY

Pre–Cold War

The *Washington Post*'s plea that the administration "sympathize with at least the right to dissent" finds little resonance in American history. Until the later part of the twentieth century, the U.S. record in protecting the rights of political dissidents was not good. From the Alien and Sedition Acts to the Civil War, to the repression of the First World War, and the subsequent decades of the silencing of labor and left-wing activists, the First Amendment provided little protection for political dissent.[27] Governments at all levels repeatedly and consistently silenced speech critical of their actions. The great free speech opinions of Justices Oliver Wendell Holmes and Louis D. Brandeis, for example, in cases like *Abrams v. U.S.*,[28] *Gitlow v. New York*,[29] and *Whitney v. California*,[30] were either concurrences with or dissents from rulings upholding convictions for speeches critical of the government. As David M. Rabban points out, these and similar decisions in "selective Draft Law and Espionage Act prosecutions during and immediately after World War One were neither a temporary aberration from a libertarian tradition nor the consequence of an initial encounter with the First Amendment. The wartime and postwar decisions were depressingly similar to their prewar antecedents. They continued an existing tradition of hostility to free speech claims."[31] It was not until 1965 that the U.S. Supreme Court invalidated a congressional act on First Amendment free speech grounds.[32] Of course, the First Amendment was entirely useless in protecting the speech rights of African Americans.[33]

This pervasive hostility to political dissent meant that the First Amendment and the courts with the power to enforce it provided little protection to political dissidents. In examining the history of judicial reaction to governmental repression of political dissent prior to World War I, Rabban notes that the "overwhelming majority of prewar decisions in all jurisdictions rejected free speech claims, often by ignoring their existence."[34] His study finds a "pervasive hostility"[35] to political dissent, even a "tradition of judicial hostility to free speech."[36] Finding that "No court was more unsympathetic to freedom of expression than the Supreme Court,"[37] he also discovered that state court decisions were mostly "as unresponsive to First Amendment values as their Supreme Court counterparts."[38] Consider, for example, the conviction of Upton Sinclair for "leading a peaceful demonstration in front of the Standard Oil Company building to protest John D. Rockefeller's alleged responsibility for killing women and children during labor unrest in Colorado."[39] The point is simple: despite the First Amendment and an independent judiciary with the power of judicial review, historically, political dissent in the United States has been repressed.

The Cold War

This point is well illustrated by the treatment of political dissent during the Cold War. In 1940 Congress enacted the Alien Registration Act, also known as the Smith Act. Passed overwhelmingly, with only four negative votes cast in the House, the new law made it a criminal act to advocate the forcible overthrow of the U.S. government or to organize a group, or be a member of a group, that advocated such action.[40] In July 1948, the national leadership of the American Communist Party (CPUSA) was indicted under the act. Its members' convictions for conspiracy to organize and advocate in violation of the act were upheld by the U.S. Supreme Court in 1951, in the *Dennis* case.[41] After *Dennis,* the government indicted nearly 150 secondary CPUSA leaders, convicting more than a hundred.[42] Party leaders who served their terms and were released from prison were then rearrested and charged with violation of the "membership" clause of the act. The use of this clause was upheld by the Court in 1961.[43]

This attack on political dissent also can be seen in a host of other bills. For example, Section 9(h) of the Taft-Hartley Act of 1947[44] denied the protection of the National Labor Relations Act to any union unless the union's officers filed affidavits swearing that they did not believe in, and were not members of any organization that believed in, the forcible overthrow of the U.S. government. The Supreme

Court upheld the legislation in 1950,[45] and the National Labor Relations Board estimated that in the years 1947–57 there were "at least 1,500,000 individual affidavits filed."[46] There were also, of course, the famous legislative investigations of the House Un-American Activities Committee. Relying on the spotlight of exposure and supported by the contempt powers of the Congress, the committee probed into the political beliefs of Americans, their colleagues, and friends. Its practices were repeatedly challenged under the First Amendment, but the challenges were unsuccessful.[47]

Efforts were also made at all levels of government to purge political dissidents from employment and to prevent their hiring.[48] On the federal level, executive orders and congressional legislation required an investigation into the loyalty of every person seeking or holding employment in the U.S. government. Basic procedural safeguards, including the rights to see all charges against one and to be informed of, or cross-examine, witnesses, were not guaranteed. By 1955, at least nine million Americans were covered by federal programs, and about half the states required them for their own employees, including teachers.[49] By the end of 1956, approximately 11,500 Americans had lost their jobs under loyalty-security programs.[50]

The states also entered the act. By 1958, for example, thirty-five states had enacted statutes prohibiting parties or persons advocating the violent overthrow of the government from running for office.[51] As late as 1968, Minnesota denied the Communist Party a place on the ballot,[52] and it was not until 1974 that Indiana's exclusion of the Communist Party from the ballot was invalidated by the courts.[53] Other state governmental action prevented dissidents from "becoming lawyers, jurors, or accountants and (in Indiana) from obtaining licenses as professional boxers."[54]

Professional organizations also stifled dissent. Led by the American Bar Association, which voted in 1951 to expel from its ranks any member of the Communist Party or anyone who "advocates Marxism-Leninism,"[55] many states inquired into lawyers' and bar candidates' political beliefs and disbarred or denied bar admission to those thought subversive. On the whole, the Supreme Court upheld such exclusions.[56] The motion picture industry acted in similar fashion. The Hollywood blacklist and similar purges serve witness to the extent to which dissent was stifled.

To summarize, in the Cold War years both the federal government and many state governments acted to silence left-wing critics of government. While most Americans retained the right to participate in political debate, that right was protected only so long as they communicated "acceptable" ideas. When they did not, the First Amendment and the courts did not protect their rights. This repressive practice, however, was not new. It was simply a continuation of hostility to political dissent that had marked U.S. history. If history serves as a guide, the killings at Kent State were part of a historical pattern of hostility to political dissent.

This point is strengthened by a brief comparison of the treatment accorded political dissidents by the United Kingdom, France, and Australia during the Cold War. Perhaps the "communist threat" was of such a magnitude that no democracy was safe. In comparison to the United States, none of the three countries had a full-fledged First Amendment, and neither the United Kingdom nor France had a tradition of judicial review whereby courts could invalidate the acts of the other branches of government. Further, both Britain and France were "weaker militarily and economically" than the United States, and in terms of "proximity," both were closer to the Soviet Union.[57] While the United States had suffered from a certain amount of espionage, the "English had their Fuchs, their Pontecorvo, their Burgess and MacLean, and still others."[58] The French Communist Party garnered roughly 20 percent of the vote in Cold War elections. In the United States, in contrast, Shapiro has noted the "whole pitifully ineffective record of the Communist movement"[59] and pointed out that despite massive FBI work, the best case the government could bring against American communists was for "conspiracy to advocate," not for any actual espionage or violent actions.[60]

What makes these differences so surprising is that both Britain and France did a substantially better job in protecting political dissent than did the United States. While there were dismissals from government employment for security reasons in Britain, for example, they were minimal. Employees charged as security risks were provided with many due-process rights and, where charges were upheld, were allowed transfers to nonsensitive posts where possible.[61] No action was taken against unions, teachers, or other professionals. France acted much the way Britain did. On the whole, the French Assembly did not enact antidissent laws as did its American counterpart. In Australia, which lacks a bill of rights, Parliament did pass a bill in 1950 outlawing the Communist Party; however, it was invalidated by the Australian High Court in a March 1951 decision.[62] The fate of the Communist Party was then put to the voters in a special constitutional referendum on September 22, 1951. In a close vote, Australians (despite the absence of even a bill of rights!) rejected the attempt to stifle dissent.

This brief comparison shows that in protecting the right of political dissidents during the Cold War, the British, although lacking formal constitutional obligation, did an excellent job, while the French, with some constitutional provision, did well too. In Australia, the people themselves protected the right of dissent. The United States, with the strongest constitutional protection, did the least well. Indeed, the U.S. treatment of political dissent in the Cold War years stands out among Western democratic nations, being characterized by Robert A. Dahl as a "deviant case"[63] and by Shapiro, more bluntly, as "pathological."[64] What can explain the record of repression in the United States?

Constitutions are interpreted and enforced within given political cultures. Many students of the United States see in its political culture rigid pressures for conformity alongside important beliefs in freedom. Most famously, Alexis de Tocqueville worried about the uniformity of American culture and the "tyranny of the majority." What he found "most repulsive" about America was the "shortage of guarantees against tyranny." Once the majority makes up its mind, "everyone is silent, and friends and enemies alike seem to make for its bandwagon." The price for dissenting, Tocqueville wrote, in language that is chillingly prophetic of the blacklists of the 1950s, was to be cast out of the social fabric: "When you approach your fellows, they will shun you as an impure being, and even those who believe in your innocence will abandon you too, lest they in turn be shunned."[65] As Mark Twain put it, "It is by the goodness of God that in our country we have those three unspeakably precious things: freedom of speech, freedom of conscience, and the prudence never to practice either of them."[66]

This suggests that the level of protection afforded dissent will be governed less by written documents than by general notions of acceptable behavior. Tocqueville, as well as others, "insisted that America was held together not by its political institutions but by its widely shared values and *moeurs*."[67] It is these beliefs that form the contours of human rights protection and provide the framework in which political institutions operate and legal documents are interpreted. Survey research sheds some light on these beliefs.

Pollsters have asked Americans their views of fundamental democratic freedoms and political dissent for the last fifty years or so. Overall, responses quite clearly shows that Americans are both deeply committed to free speech in the abstract *and* strongly opposed to free speech for unpopular groups. For example, national samples were asked in both 1938 and 1940, "Do you believe in freedom of speech?" Ninety-six and 97 percent, respectively, responded affirmatively.[68] In 1958, when the question was worded in a more testing way, a full 89 percent of respondents agreed.[69]

At the same time that Americans were overwhelmingly supporting free speech in the abstract, they were denying it to specific groups. In the 1938 poll cited above in which 96 percent of respondents professed a belief in freedom of speech, only 38 percent of the free speech supporters would extend that right to "allowing radicals to hold meetings and express their views in this community." Similarly, in the 1940 Gallup poll above in which 97 percent of respondents supported free speech, only 22 percent of them were willing to support it for "Fascists and Communists."[70] In the summer of 1954, Samuel Stouffer employed 537 interviewers to interview a cross-section of 4,900 Americans and 1,500 selected community leaders about civil liberties. Stouffer found that 91 percent of the cross-section supported firing a communist high school teacher and 89 percent a communist professor. Sixty-eight percent of the national cross-section supported the firing of a communist store clerk,[71] while 77 percent would take away a communist's American citizenship.[72] In no surveys from 1953 to 1964 did more than 20 percent of respondents say that communists should be allowed to speak on the radio.[73]

These responses were not based on fear of communist espionage and sabotage. When asked what aspects of communism were most troubling, only 8 percent mentioned sabotage or espionage, while more than a quarter (28 percent) mentioned "the danger of Americans today becoming converts to Communism or Communist ideas."[74] The results were even more striking among community leaders, with 5 percent mentioning sabotage, 6 percent espionage, and a full 36 percent citing conversion or the spreading of ideas.[75] In Stouffer's words, "substantial proportions of the American population are intolerant *in spite of the fact* that they perceive relatively little internal Communist threat."[76]

HAS THE UNITED STATES GROWN MORE TOLERANT?

The events at Kent State, however, happened in 1970, decades after the Cold War repression I have described, and more than a century after the earlier episodes of governmental repression. Could it be that despite the country's historical repression of political dissent, opinion had changed by 1970? If so, the events at Kent State truly were an aberration.

At first blush, there are data that suggest such change has occurred. Nunn and colleagues, relying on survey data from 1973, followed up on Stouffer's work and concluded that Americans had indeed become more tolerant of communists. For example, they found an increase of thirty-eight points in the proportion of the general public willing to protect the innocent even if it meant not finding some communists (32 percent to 70 percent), a twenty-point increase in tolerance for a socialist's right to teach (33 percent to 53 percent), a thirty-two-point increase in willingness to let an "admitted Communist" store clerk keep his or her job (25 percent to 57 percent), and a twenty-six-point increase in willingness to let an "admitted Communist" speak in one's community (27 percent to 53 percent). Further, they found an increase of twenty-four points in the proportion of the general sample that was "More Tolerant," on an overall tolerance scale (31 percent to 55 percent).[77] Is this not good evidence that the historical support for suppression of political dissent has dissipated?

The answer, it turns out, is no. Americans remain deeply hostile to protecting political dissenters whom they do not like. What has changed is that they no longer care very much about communists. In surveys in 1976 and 1978, Sullivan et al. asked respondents what groups they most disliked and then asked them a series of questions about those groups. In a 1978 National Opinion Research Center survey they commissioned, they found, for example, that only 16 percent would *not* ban a member of the group they most disliked from being president, only 19 percent would allow a member to teach in public schools, and only 29 percent would *not* outlaw the group.[78] In other words, they argued, "the mass public is still generally intolerant today."[79] All that had changed was that the salience of communists as the focus of intolerance had waned, in favor of other groups.[80] The U.S. public, they concluded, now displayed "pluralistic intolerance" instead of a monolithic anticommunism. Thus, despite the increase in tolerance for the dissenting views of communists, Americans appear as supportive as ever of silencing those whose views they do not like.

One of the reasons that Americans may be willing to give up so readily the rights to speech, press, and protest is that they are not interested in them. As Mueller reminds us, "most people never say anything that anyone else—even the most paranoid of dictators—would want to suppress."[81] But another reason is that they appear unaware that the First Amendment guarantees free speech. In December 1979, Gallup asked respondents the following question: "Do you happen to know what the First Amendment to the U.S. Constitution is, or what it deals with?" Only 24 percent were able to identify correctly any part of the amendment, while 76 percent either gave an incorrect answer or said they did not know. Only a third of those in the highest income bracket gave a correct answer, and only 42 percent of college graduates.[82] Similarly, surveys done in 1997 and 1999 for the Freedom Forum found that fewer than half of respondents named "freedom of speech" as one of "the specific rights that are guaranteed by the First Amendment," and barely 10 percent named freedom of the press.[83] While it could be the case that Americans know that they have a constitutional right to free speech, just not what particular provision contains it, other results bolster the view that they simply do not care very much about political dissent.

This combination of lack of interest in, and hostility to, political dissent has been captured in many other surveys. For example, in both 1997 and 1999 Freedom Forum surveys asked respondents, "Are there any particular rights or freedoms that you feel are most important to American society?" While 50 percent did name freedom of speech in both years, only 6 percent (1999) and 5 percent (1997) named freedom of the press. Even more striking, the "right to protest" was chosen by only 1 percent in 1999, placing it in a tie for thirteenth place; in 1997, no one chose it at all.[84] The forty-nine-point difference between the categories "freedom of speech" and "right to protest" suggests that the freedom of speech that respondents find important does not include political dissent.[85]

The contrast between supporting free speech in the abstract but opposing it for groups one dislikes is also illustrated in the Freedom Forum surveys. For example, while 86 percent (1999) and 90 percent (1997) "strongly agree" or "mildly agree" that "People should be allowed to express unpopular opinions,"[86] only 44 percent agree that "militia groups, white supremacists, skinheads or Nazis be allowed to protest in a community like yours."[87] Once the group is named, support for the right of free speech drops a whopping forty-two points (86 percent to 44 percent). Similarly, while 62 percent (1999) and 72 percent (1997) "strongly agree" or "mildly agree" that "Any group that wants should be allowed to hold a rally for a cause or issue even if it may be offensive to others in the community," only 44 percent remain supportive when the group turns out to be "militia groups, white supremacists, skinheads or Nazis."[88] Again, once the groups are named, there is a drop of eighteen points (1999) and twenty-eight points (1997) in support for free speech.

These views hostile to political dissent carry over to opposition to press criticism of the government. In the spring of 1970, 55 percent of respondents to a poll done by CBS News for the television show *60 Minutes* "felt that newspapers and other media should *not* enjoy an absolute right to publish articles that the government felt might be harmful to the national interest, even in time of peace."[89] Despite generally supportive views of the press, when asked by Gallup in 1979 to address the issue of whether "present curbs placed on the press are too strict—or not strict enough?" more than twice as many respondents said the restrictions were not strict enough than said they were too strict (37 percent to 17 percent).[90] This represents considerable erosion in support for the press, since a comparable 1958 question found that 21 percent would approve of placing greater restrictions on the press and that 58 percent would disapprove.[91]

In delving behind the aggregate numbers, Gallup discovered that one of three main reasons respondents gave for wanting stricter curbs placed on the press was that newspapers publish information "that should not be made public because it is not in the best interests of the nation." As Gallup summarized these results, it noted a "lack of knowledge about the right to a free press as guaranteed in the Constitution."[92] Similarly, a recent survey undertaken for the American Bar Association found that 46 percent of respondents believed that Congress should ban the press from reporting on any national security issue without prior governmental approval.[93] A 1992 survey of American attitudes toward free speech issues conducted by the American Society of Newspaper Editors concluded that "free expression is in very deep trouble."[94] The point these data support is that the historical opposition to political dissent in the United States remains alive and well.

"AMERICA, LOVE IT OR LEAVE IT"

This historical hostility to political protest greeted anti–Vietnam War protestors. From the ever-present bumper sticker "America, Love It or Leave It" to constant verbal and physical abuse of antiwar demonstrators, to the killings at Kent State, Americans demonstrated their hostility to political dissent. Survey data illustrate these feelings. In reaction to what was subsequently labeled a "police riot" at the 1968 Democratic Convention in Chicago, a majority of Americans (56 percent) told Gallup that they approved of the "way the Chicago police dealt with the young people who were registering their protest against the Vietnam war at the time of the Democratic convention" (fewer than one-third disapproved).[95] In four of the years 1968–74, the National Election Study asked respondents whether they would "approve" of "taking part in protest meetings or marches that are permitted by local authorities." In no year did more than 19.5 percent of respondents approve.[96] When asked in November 1969 about "reactions to the current anti-war demonstrations," Gallup found that "unfavorable comments outweigh favorable ones by the ratio of 3 to 1. Those who disapprove of the demonstrations frequently raise the following objections: (1) They accomplish nothing; (2) We should support our country; (3) Demonstrations demoralize our troops; (4) They prolong the war—show the enemy we are divided; (5) Demonstrations hurt our image abroad; (6) They are Communist-inspired."[97] In a 1970 poll done by CBS News for *60 Minutes*, "more than 76 percent of 1100 adults sampled believed that, even in the absence of a 'clear danger of violence,' not all groups should be allowed to organize protests against the government."[98] When asked by Gallup in May 1969 "What is your biggest gripe about young people today?" 30 percent of respondents, the largest response by nearly two to one, chose "Undisciplined behavior, campus protests."[99] Indeed, in late May 1970 82 percent of respondents told Gallup that they disagreed with "college students going on strike as a way to protest the way things are run in this country" (15 percent agreed).[100] In that same poll, "Campus unrest" was chosen as the "most important problem facing this country today," ahead of the "Vietnam war (including Cambodia)."[101] Students and others protesting against the war in Vietnam were seen as troublemakers.

Given this aversion to political dissent, how then were so many Americans able to dissent during the Vietnam War? Why were there not more Kent States?[102] The answer, I believe, is that the country was divided over the war, with sizable minority opposition that grew as the war dragged on. In 1964, for example, 60 percent of respondents to a University of Michigan Survey Research Center (SRC) poll thought the United States had done the right thing getting involved in Vietnam. Just four years later, in 1968, the approval figure had dropped to 36 percent.[103] Gallup polls reported similar results in response to the question of whether the United States had "made a mistake sending troops to fight in Vietnam."[104] By 1970 the SRC was reporting that more respondents (38 percent) supported an immediate pullout of U.S. troops than supported the United States taking a stronger stand (26 percent).[105] "In both 1968 and 1970 opinion was very much divided with no alternative coming close to even a simple majority."[106] In addition, a sizable minority of political leaders opposed the war, including elected officials from around the country. In today's political climate it may seem bizarre, but senators from both parties and from states like Idaho (Frank Church), Indiana (Birch Bayh), South Dakota (George McGovern), and Kentucky (John Sherman Cooper) opposed the war and lent their names to bills to stop it. This created a political space for protestors.

The existence of sizable elite and public opposition to the war made suppression of dissent costly. In examining political repression in the Western world, Dahl suggests that suppression is most likely when the costs of doing so are small.[107] It is easier to ban small, ineffective parties than larger, stronger ones. In the United States during the Cold War, one might have thought that given the anemic state of the CPUSA and the tradition of free speech symbolized by the First Amendment, the physical costs of repression would have been slight and the philosophical and legal costs very high. But given the historical repression of dissent in the United States and the unpopularity of the CPUSA, repression was virtually cost-free. As the *Fort Worth Star-Telegram's* editorial reaction to the *Dennis* case (upholding the jailing of the leadership of the CPUSA for its speeches) put it: "We cannot feel that the Supreme Court's decision endangers any of the fundamental American rights."[108] During the Vietnam War, however, the size of the opposition raised the cost of repression. Harassment of, and attacks on, protesters and dissenters failed to silence them and indeed may have generated further dissent. When prominent elected officials and media organizations like the *New York Times* and the *Washington Post* take up the cause of political dissent, it is likely to be better protected than when such elite support is missing.

In the foregoing analysis I argued that political dissent has seldom been protected in the United States. Historically, the courts have not acted to stem the tide of intolerance. Throughout American history, "none of our most serious periods of repression was influenced significantly by judicial enforcement of the first amendment."[109] In the "two most significant periods of national pathology in this century, the Red Scare and the McCarthy Era, the courts did very little to stem the tide of intolerance."[110] Indeed, as Dan Gordon puts it, the actions of the Supreme Court in the 1950s "showed the impotence, indeed the emptiness, of the words of the first amendment in the face of public determination to limit some people's speech."[111] In the Vietnam era, public and elite opposition to the war created a political space that allowed political dissent to exist, albeit in a state of uneasy tension with the underlying public hostility to it. The great surprise is not that there was deathly violence at Kent State but that there was relatively little of it.

If this language is too strong, it is not so by very much. The First Amendment does have importance, if only as a symbol. Such political and cultural battles as are fought over the meaning of free speech and a free press can be fought in the framework of constitutional aspiration for protection of dissent. That is the good news. At the very heart of democratic society is the freedom to engage in political discussion and to dissent. If the First Amendment can contribute to that freedom, even imperfectly, it does have importance.

But there is also bad news, and it is this: to the extent that the battle over the appropriate boundaries of speech is put in legal terms, the result is likely to be the "legalization" of free speech discourse, in which substantive questions about the appropriate limits of freedom of expression in a democratic society are shunted aside in favor of abstract conceptions and formalistic legal debates about bright lines, tests, and distinctions. Substantive policy decisions become hidden behind the shibboleth of "free speech." In practice, this means that the winners in free speech adjudication are likely to be those with political, economic, and cultural power. The losers are the rest of us, and particularly the democratic process itself.

An example of the legalization of speech discourse that disserves democratic society is the set of barriers the Supreme Court has put in the way of campaign-finance reform. The United States, virtually alone among Western democracies,[112] allows corporations and the wealthy to spend without limit, distorting the political process.[113] Rather than asking whether campaign finance legislation furthers the democratic deliberation essential to democracy, First Amendment jurisprudence focuses on the abstract principle of the free market and the rights of individuals, including artificial ones, such as corporations. The legalization of free speech discourse turns the focus away from the actual workings of the democratic political system to the abstract notion of political communication as a "free market" of ideas. This free market understanding mistakenly sees virtually any government regulation as interference with constitutional rights. But campaign finance reform is not a conflict between an unregulated market and government interference with that market and with individual rights. Rather, it is a question of which regulations, the current ones or those contained in reform legislation, better further the constitutional goal of deliberative democracy.[114] Thus, the legalization of free speech discourse distorts the substantive policy question, replacing it with an abstraction that serves the interests of the wealthy.

Another example is the treatment of hate speech—speech aimed at individuals' immutable characteristics and spoken in hateful and hurtful ways. When rights are defined as individual, as they are understood to be in the Constitution, it becomes easy to ignore the fact that individuals live and act in a broader society. So the First Amendment "right" of an individual to spew forth hateful and hurtful words about minorities and the relatively disadvantaged is protected, and efforts to limit that speech are seen as an illegitimate attempts to curtail the speakers' rights. There can be no inquiry into the broader harm that may be done, or even the harm to the individual target of the speech.

Similarly, pornography is protected, and arguments that it may harm women are derided as "thought control"[115] because they interfere with the rights of an individual to produce pornography. The individual "right" of the pornographer is protected, while any "harm" his actions might cause to other individuals is brushed aside as irrelevant. In contrast, other Western democracies, like Canada, that highly value freedom of expression treat many of these issues differently.

The broader point is that rights-based talk, which is part and parcel of First Amendment jurisprudence, can turn public debate away from concerns with justice and fairness toward a more limited focus on abstract rights.[116] While Ronald Dworkin is surely right in stressing the importance of individual rights in any just society,[117] no person is an island. For example, allowing competing political visions to be heard may mean limiting the access of some to the media. Creating a civil society that respects all may mean denying individuals the right to discriminate. The First Amendment focus on individual rights effectively precludes policy debates in which various factors could be weighed, in favor of a clash of abstract rights wherein such factors are seen as unprincipled and irrelevant.[118]

CONCLUSION—THE CONSTITUTION AS CULTURE

A "constitution can truly shape a community's politics only if it expresses the community's culture—that is, its most fundamental ideas and practices."[119] As I have argued, American culture contains strands highly supportive of fundamental political freedoms in the abstract *and* highly antagonistic to them when they are asserted in opposition to publicly shared beliefs. First Amendment interpretations and protection, then, vary with the strength of political currents. The late Phil Kurland saw this, understanding changes in the judicial protection of free speech as determined by the political support of the parties seeking it. Thus Kurland wrote that the "communist conspiracy" will produce a repressive First Amendment, while the civil rights movement, whose members were "the beneficiaries of the Court's own 1954 Emancipation Proclamation," will produce an expansive, protective one.[120] The First Amendment matters only because it provides the forum for substantive political battles, not because it provides substantive content. When dissent has elite and popular support, the boundaries of freedom of expression stretch to protect it. When dissent lacks such support, the boundaries are drawn tighter.

The paradox of the First Amendment is that while it holds out the promise of protecting political dissent, it has seldom done so. At the same time, the current legalistic understandings of freedom of speech in the United States make democratic deliberation about the appropriate limits of freedom of expression in a democratic society difficult to sustain. They may also fail to serve underlying democratic interests. If my history is accurate, they seldom do—and that is the sorrow and the pity.

The upshot of this discussion is that the innumerable, often sophisticated, and sometimes brilliant arguments that fill law reviews and law libraries about how to strengthen First Amendment doctrine will not do very much to guarantee more protection for political dissent in the United States. What will strengthen freedom is understanding that its extent is determined by the political and cultural support it has and by expending energy to build such support. Legal and constitutional arguments, however cogent, will be overpowered by other, *more constitutive* claims. Writing in 1951, Elliot L. Richardson understood this well: "The great battles for free expression will be won, if they are won, not in courts but in committee rooms and protest-meetings, by editorials and letters to Congress, and through the courage of citizens everywhere. The proper function of courts is narrow. The rest is our responsibility."[121]

NOTES

1. Robert B. Semple, Jr., "Nixon Says Violence Invites Tragedy," *New York Times*, May 5, 1970, 17.
2. Ibid.
3. Quoted in Charles Goodell, *Political Prisoners in America* (New York: Random House, 1973), 169.
4. Alan L. Otten, "Cambodia: Escalation on the Home Front," *Wall Street Journal*, May 7, 1970, 12.
5. Semple, "Nixon Says"; also noted in "Campus Crisis," *Wall Street Journal*, May 6, 1970.
6. "Tragedy at Kent State," *Wall Street Journal*, May 6, 1970, 18.
7. "Review and Outlook: Forced to Choose?" *Wall Street Journal*, May 8, 1970, 8.
8. Ibid.
9. "Review and Outlook: Toward Conciliation," *Wall Street Journal*, May 11, 1979, 14.
10. "Death on the Campus," *New York Times*, May 6, 1970.
11. "Youth's Faith . . . ," *New York Times*, May 8, 1970, 30.
12. "The Aftermath of Kent State," *Washington Post*, May 6, 1970, A24.
13. David J. Garrow, *The FBI and Martin Luther King, Jr.* (New York: Penguin, 1981).
14. For a brief summary of harassment of the Black Panthers written by a former U.S. senator, see Goodell, *Political Prisoners*, 110–25.
15. *United States v. Spock*, 416 F.2d 165 (1st Cir. 1969). For a brief discussion of other conspiracy indictments for anti–Vietnam War activities, see Goodell, *Political Prisoners*, chap. 9.

16. 408 U.S. 1 (1972). On the extent of government surveillance, see Note, "The National Security Interest and Civil Liberties, *Harvard Law Review* 85 (1972): 1130.

17. Goodell, *Political Prisoners*, 261.

18. Ibid., 171.

19. "F.B.I. Kept Secret Files on the Supreme Court," *New York Times*, National Edition, Aug. 21, 1988, sec. 1, 13.

20. *New York Times Co. v. United States*, 403 U.S. 713 (1971).

21. Chief Justice Warren Burger and Justices John Harlan and Harry Blackmun dissented.

22. Robert Justin Goldstein, *Political Repression in Modern America from 1870 to the Present* (Cambridge, Mass.: Shenkman, 1978), 430.

23. *Press Freedoms under Pressure: A Twentieth Century Fund Task Force Report on the Government and the Press* (New York: Twentieth Century Fund, 1971), 22–23; Goldstein, *Political Repression*, 518; Olga G. and Edwin P. Hoyt, *Freedom of the News Media* (New York: Seabury Press, 1970), 79–84.

24. Hoyt, *Freedom*, 79.

25. Goldstein, *Political Repression*, 480.

26. *Twentieth Century Fund*, 23.

27. There is a literature that records this history. Often-cited material includes Goldstein, *Political Repression*, 480; Paul L. Murphy, *World War I and the Origins of Civil Liberties in the United States* (New York: W. W. Norton, 1979); Russel B. Nye, *Fettered Freedom* (East Lansing: Michigan State Univ. Press, 1963) (on the 1830–60 period); William Preston, Jr., *Aliens and Dissenters* (New York: Harper & Row, 1963) (on the 1903–33 period); David M. Rabban, "The First Amendment in Its Forgotten Years," *Yale Law Journal* 90 (1981): 514; Leon Whipple, *The Story of Civil Liberty in the United States* (New York: Vanguard, 1927).

28. 250 U.S. 616 (1919).

29. 268 U.S. 45 (1925).

30. 274 U.S. 357 (1927).

31. Rabban, "Forgotten Years," 558. See also David M. Rabban, *Free Speech in Its Forgotten Years* (New York: Cambridge Univ. Press, 1997).

32. *Lamont v. Postmaster General*, 381 U.S. 301 (1965).

33. *Herndon v. Lowry*, 301 U.S. 242 (1937) to the contrary, notwithstanding.

34. Rabban, "Forgotten Years," 523.

35. Ibid.

36. Ibid., 589.

37. Ibid., 523.

38. Ibid., 543.

39. Ibid., 547, citing *People v. Sinclair*, 86 Misc. 426, 149 N.Y.S. 54 (Ct. Gen. Sess. 1914).

40. 54 Stat. 670 (1940).

41. *Dennis v. United States*, 341 U.S. 494 (1951). Only Justices Hugo Black and William Douglas dissented.

42. Jack W. Peltason, "Constitutional Liberty and the Communist Problem," in *Foundations of Freedom in the American Constitution*, ed. Alfred H. Kelly (New York: Harpers, 1954, 1958), 119; Robert Mollan, "Smith Act Prosecutions: The Effect of the *Dennis* and *Yates* Decisions," *University of Pittsburgh Law Review* 26 (1965): 705, 708–10. In *Yates v. United States*, 354 U.S. 298 (1957), the Supreme Court reversed the convictions of five defendants (and remanded nine for new trials).

43. *Scales v. United States*, 367 U.S. 203 (1961).

44. 61 Stat. 136 (1947).

45. *American Communications Association v. Douds*, 339 U.S. 382 (1950).

46. Cited in Norman Dorsen, Paul Bender, and Burt Neuborne, *Emerson, Haber, and Dorsen's Politi-*

cal and Civil Rights in the United States, vol. 1, 4th ed., law school ed. (Boston: Little, Brown, 1976), 110.

47. See, for example, Barenblatt v. United States, 360 U.S. 109 (1959), and Uphaus v. Wyman, 360 U.S. 72 (1959).

48. In general, see Eleanor Bontecou, The Federal Loyalty-Security Program (Ithaca, N.Y.: Cornell Univ. Press, 1953); Ralph S. Brown, Jr., Loyalty & Security: Employment Tests in the United States (New Haven, Conn.: Yale Univ. Press, 1958); Earl Latham, The Communist Controversy in Washington (Cambridge, Mass.: Harvard Univ. Press, 1966); Report of the Special Committee on the Federal Loyalty-Security Program of the Association of the Bar of the City of New York (New York: Dodd, Mead, 1956). For a brief history with special emphasis on court cases, see Dorsen et al., Political and Civil Rights, 131–53.

49. Herbert H. Hyman, "England and America: Climates of Tolerance and Intolerance," in The Radical Right, ed. Daniel Bell (Garden City, N.Y.: Anchor, 1964), 289n. 35, 290. New York City, for example, even required a loyalty oath for subway conductors (upheld by the U.S. Supreme Court in Lerner v. Casey, 357 U.S. 468 [1958]).

50. Alan F. Westin, "Constitutional Liberty and Loyalty Programs," in Kelly, Foundations, 211; Brown, Loyalty-Security Program, appendix A, 487–88.

51. Kathleen Barber, "The Legal Status of the American Communist Party: 1965," Journal of Public Law 15 (1966): 94, 103 n.92.

52. Dorsen et al., Political and Civil Rights, 89.

53. Communist Party of Indiana v. Whitcomb, 414 U.S. 441 (1974).

54. Daniel C. Kramer, Comparative Civil Rights and Liberties (Lanham, Md.: University Press of America, 1982), 49.

55. American Bar Association Journal 37 (1951): 312–13.

56. See, e.g., Konigsberg v. California, 366 U.S. 36 (1961); In re Anastaplo, 366 U.S. 82 (1961); Law Students Civil Rights Research Council v. Wadmond, 401 U.S. 154 (1971). In general, see Dorsen et al., Political and Civil Rights, 114–31; Jerold Auerbach, Unequal Justice (New York: Oxford Univ. Press, 1976), chap. 8.

57. Hyman in Bell, The Radical Right, 274. Hyman was writing about Britain, but his statements fit France as well.

58. Ibid., 276.

59. Martin Shapiro, Freedom of Speech: The Supreme Court and Judicial Review (Englewood Cliffs, N.J.: Prentice Hall, 1966), 134.

60. Ibid., 125.

61. Mark R. Joelson, "The Dismissal of Civil Servants in the Interests of National Security," Public Law 51 (1963): 54–56; Hyman in Bell, The Radical Right, 48.

62. Australian Communist Party v. Commonwealth (1950) 83 CLR 1.

63. Robert A. Dahl, "Epilogue," in Political Oppositions in Western Democracies, ed. Robert A. Dahl (New Haven, Conn.: Yale Univ. Press, 1966), 391.

64. Shapiro, Freedom of Speech, 109.

65. Alexis de Tocqueville, Democracy in America, ed. J. P. Mayer (Garden City, N.Y.: Anchor, 1969), 252, 254, 256.

66. Quoted in Lee C. Bollinger, The Tolerant Society (New York: Oxford Univ. Press, 1986), 7.

67. John Patrick Diggins, "Class, Classical, and Consensus Views of the Constitution," University of Chicago Law Review 55 (1988): 570.

68. OPR and Gallup polls, cited in Hazel Erskine, "The Polls: Freedom of Speech," Public Opinion Quarterly 34 (1970): 483, 485, 486.

69. Herbert McClosky and John Zaller, The American Ethos: Public Attitudes toward Capitalism and Democracy (Cambridge, Mass.: Harvard Univ. Press, 1984), 17.

70. Cited in Erskine, "The Polls," 489.

71. In contrast, in Britain, after the John Lewis department stores began in 1949 to require signed statements from employees as to their political beliefs, a nationwide poll found that 78 percent of respondents disapproved of requiring employees to sign such a statement as a condition of employment. BIPO Poll of May 18, 1949, cited in H. H. Wilson and Harvey Glickman, *The Problem of Internal Security in Great Britain 1948–1953* (Garden City, N.Y.: Doubleday, 1954), 66.

72. Samuel A. Stouffer, *Communism, Conformity, and Civil Liberties: A Cross-Section of the Nation Speaks Its Mind* (Gloucester, Mass.: Peter Smith, 1963), 40, 43.

73. Cited in Erskine, "The Polls," 488.

74. Stouffer, *Communism*, 158, 160.

75. Ibid., 158.

76. Ibid., 208.

77. Clyde Z. Nunn, Harry J. Crockett, Jr., and J. Allen Williams, Jr., *Tolerance for Nonconformity* (San Francisco: Jossey-Bass, 1978), 37, 39, 43, 51.

78. John L. Sullivan, James Pierson, and Gregory E. Marcus, "An Alternate Conceptualization of Political Tolerance: Illusory Increases 1950s–1970s," *American Political Science Review* 73 (1979): 781, 787.

79. Sullivan et al., "An Alternate Conceptualization," 789.

80. In the Sullivan et al. survey, those groups included the Ku Klux Klan, the Symbionese Liberation Army, and the Black Panthers.

81. John Mueller, "Trends in Political Tolerance," *Public Opinion Quarterly* 52 (1988): 1, 22.

82. "First Amendment and the Press," *Gallup Opinion Index Report* no. 174, Jan. 1980, 25.

83. "State of the First Amendment 1999" (Nashville: First Amendment Center, 1999), Question 2, 14 [hereafter "Freedom Forum"]. See "State of the First Amendment: A Survey of Public Attitudes,"1999 Questionnaire, "Freedom Forum," on the World Wide Web at http://www.freedomforum.org/first/sofa/1999/questionnaire.asp.

84. "Freedom Forum," Question 1, 13.

85. It is possible, however, that respondents assumed that the right of political protest and dissent was included in the right of free speech.

86. "Freedom Forum," Question 16, 18.

87. Ibid., Question 24, 20.

88. Ibid., Question 38, 24; Question 24, 20.

89. CBS survey of 1,100 adults broadcast on April 14, 1970, cited in Jonathan D. Casper, *The Politics of Civil Liberties* (New York: Harper & Row, 1972), 2.

90. "First Amendment and the Press," *Gallup Opinion Index Report* no. 174, Jan. 1980, 24.

91. Ibid., 23.

92. Ibid.

93. "ABA Survey Reveals Americans Don't Know Their Rights," 1992 *Bar Report* (Washington: D.C. Bar Association, Dec.–Jan. 1992), 5.

94. Quoted in "ABA Survey," 5.

95. George H. Gallup, *The Gallup Poll: Public Opinion 1935–1971*, vol. 3 (New York: Random House, 1972), 2160.

96. The data were compiled from the National Election Study and can be found online at http://csa.Berkeley.edu:7502/.

97. "The Gallup Poll," 2225.

98. CBS survey of 1,100 adults broadcast on April 14, 1970, cited in Casper, *Civil Liberties*, 1–2.

99. "The Gallup Poll," 2195.

100. Ibid., 2250.

101. Ibid., 2252.

102. Readers should recall that on May 14, 1970, less than two weeks later, Mississippi Highway

Patrolmen and Jackson City police opened fire on demonstrators at Jackson State University, killing two students and wounding twelve others. See *The Report of the President's Commission on Campus Unrest* (Washington, D.C.: 1970), 411–59.

103. Cited in Richard E. Dawson, *Public Opinion and Contemporary Disarray* (New York: Harper & Row, 1973), 35.

104. Cited in Dawson, *Public Opinion*, 36.

105. Ibid., 7.

106. Ibid., 37–38.

107. Robert A. Dahl, "Epilogue," xii, 390.

108. Quoted in John Lofton, *The Press as Guardians of the First Amendment* (Columbia: Univ. of South Carolina Press, 1980), 241.

109. Robert E. Nagel, "How Useful Is Judicial Review in Free Speech Cases?" *Cornell Law Review* 69 (1984): 302, 316.

110. Vincent Blasi, "The Pathological Perspective and the First Amendment," *Columbia Law Review* 85 (1985): 449, 508.

111. Dan Gordon, "Limits on Extremist Political Parties: A Comparison of Israeli Jurisprudence with That of the United States and West Germany," *Hastings International and Comparative Law Review* 10 (1987): 347, 366.

112. For example, fully democratic political systems such as those of Austria, Denmark, France, Israel, Japan, the Netherlands, Norway, Sweden, and the United Kingdom do not allow paid political advertising during election campaigns. Ireland allows it but allocates it in proportion to representation in Parliament.

113. *Buckley v. Valeo*, 424 U.S. 1 (1976); *National Bank of Boston v. Bellotti*, 435 U.S. 765 (1978).

114. For an elaboration of this view, see Cass R. Sunstein, *Democracy and the Problem of Free Speech* (New York: Free Press, 1993).

115. *American Booksellers Ass'n v. Hudnut*, 771 F.2d 323 (7th Cir. 1985), *aff'd* without opinion, 475 U.S. 1001 (1986).

116. Mary Ann Glendon, *Rights Talk: The Impoverishment of Political Discourse* (New York: Free Press, 1991).

117. See, Ronald Dworkin, *Taking Rights Seriously* (Cambridge, Mass.: Harvard Univ. Press, 1977).

118. The focus on rights has negative consequences in other areas as well. For example, providing equal opportunity may mean limiting individual choice. Reducing the amount of deadly violence may mean limiting an individual right to own firearms. Debating abortion policy as a clash of rights ignores the many issues involved in abortion policy, including the danger of illegal abortions, battered and abandoned children, the cost of caring for children with horrendous genetic abnormalities, and so forth.

119. J. David Greenstone, "Against Simplicity: The Cultural Dimensions of the Constitution," *University of Chicago Law Review* 55 (1988): 413, 428.

120. Philip B. Kurland, "The Irrelevance of the Constitution: The First Amendment's Freedom of Speech and Freedom of Press Clauses," *Drake Law Review* 29 (1979) 1, 10.

121. Elliott L. Richardson, "Freedom of Expression and the Function of Courts," *Harvard Law Review* 65 (1951): 1, 54.

The Sorrow and the Pity from May 4, 1970
Response to Rosenberg

ERIC D. MILLER

Psychology, Kent State University, East Liverpool Campus

Freedom of expression does not come without a price. Kent State University will forever have as part of its history and legacy the extraordinary events of May 4, 1970. The parents and friends of the four victims will not let us forget. Social activists will not let us forget. Media sources will not let us forget. And neither should Kent State University: in fact, it should embrace the events of May 4, 1970.

However, Rosenberg explains the tragic events of May 4, 1970, by (in essence) arguing that they are not that extraordinary—especially when we consider America's paradoxical relationship with the First Amendment. Rosenberg's central thesis is that "while the American public is deeply committed to free speech as an abstract category, it is also quite willing to repress speech with which it does not agree." Although Rosenberg offers many valid points to buttress his viewpoints, there are several counterpoints that he fails to consider fully. While much of the following commentary will reflect a psychological perspective, it also addresses relevant material from legal and political sources.

Rosenberg provides many pointed and compelling instances and examples of how Americans—those with and without tangible political power—have been intolerant and often rather inhospitable to those who sought to express their (usually unpopular) views. Our country does indeed have a very shocking record of flagrant disrespect for freedom of expression and hostility toward those who do not uphold what seems to be the majority opinion. Some of the more infamous examples include: our legacy of slavery and lynchings; the fact that it took nearly 150 years after the founding of America to allow women the right to vote; extreme distrust and hostility to immigrants and foreigners; and the formation of the House Un-American Activities Committee.

Ultimately, Americans are individuals—individuals who are prone to the foibles and strengths of that which makes us human. As much as we may want or would like all Americans not to make distinctions between freedom of expression in theory and practice, the fact that this often occurs is simply an artifact of human nature.

For instance, Rosenberg points out that the *Wall Street Journal* wrote an editorial two days after the Kent State incident suggesting that the students and their "political decisions" had been the main impetus for the shootings. Many social psychologists[1] have discussed the widespread use of the "just-world" phenomenon, which is a general belief that people deserve what they get and get what they deserve. Clearly, this is an unfair assumption. Should we tell this to a rape victim or a bereaved parent?

Rosenberg also discusses the prevalent "America, Love It or Leave It" mentality, which had particular resonance during the Vietnam War era. Again, it may be tempting to view such a belief as an attack on freedom of expression. However, once more, we see human nature and psychology at work. People tend to view distinctive others in a more extreme fashion.[2] In other words, someone who is a "political protestor" seems like an "exotic other" to an "average" person. Since it is difficult to relate to that person, we grow suspicious of, perhaps even disdainful toward, him or her. Moreover, psychological research has shown that humans have a very strong preference for stability.[3] When a political protest occurs, stability is inherently threatened—so we too may show intolerance toward those protestors.

We should not at all condone attitudes that seek to stifle political or personal expression. We need to understand fully that such attitudes may not be expressions of intolerance but be by-products of human nature. For instance, some may conclude that it is a sad commentary that most Americans would not see the burning of the American flag as a form of political expression (despite the 1989 *Texas v. Johnson*[4] U.S. Supreme Court decision that makes just that point). But of course, the American flag is a defining life-symbol for many Americans, particularly veterans. For many, our visceral, emotional reactions blind cooler, deliberative thinking. This is a tendency that needs to be kept in check; we must remember how Hitler was swept into power largely by unchecked, visceral reactions. The point remains that the fact that Americans do not always seem supportive of those with whom they disagree does not necessarily mean that they *truly* feel that way.

Using polling and survey data, Rosenberg makes a very strong point that Americans fully respect the First Amendment in principle—yet in practice are much less willing to do so if they do not approve of the cause or of the individuals who espouse that cause.

However, there are notable flaws with the survey data that Rosenberg presents; indeed, these are flaws that could plague *any* survey instrument. Specifically, given the nonexperimental nature of this research, it is impossible to make causal assumptions about the data. For instance, Rosenberg cites a 1938 poll that found that only 38 percent of Americans approved of "allowing radicals to hold meetings and express their views in the community." While this could be reflective of intolerance toward political expression, it also could suggest that in a time of horrific economic and political strife people were wary of upheaval in general. It is often argued that under threatening conditions, we tend to become more close minded or conventional in our beliefs.[5] Rosenberg also states that from 1953 to 1964 no more than 20 percent of respondents approved of allowing communists to speak on the radio. People have a general concern for social acceptability when pollsters ask them questions.[6] Given that this poll was conducted at the height of the Cold War era, it is not surprising that individual Americans would not want to appear sympathetic to communists.

Since polling data inherently produces ambiguous causal conclusions, it is simplistic to conclude that Americans are usually against subject-specific speech that contradicts their personal views. Such a perspective assumes that Americans are inherently close minded; when we make such assumptions, we commit the fundamental attribution error.[7] We need to realize that situational factors can greatly influence behavior; in other words, once more, even though Americans may not seem to support certain types of expression, they may not actually feel that way. But what about the view that repressive speech is repressive speech—and that reality is all that matters? Rosenberg's warning about the vagaries of support for freedom of expression (particularly during times of political threat) is well taken. However, if we are to understand truly why speech is often attacked, we must fully appreciate the specific factors that may cause such episodes. While we should try to prevent repression of speech, we will be able to do this only by understanding why it occurs in the first place.

As the Kent State tragedy shows, the public expression of one's attitudes—whether they are political, social, or personal in nature—can have profoundly devastating consequences. Yet "public expressions" occur on a regular basis about a plethora of issues, whether regarding the abortion debate, fostering democratic values in a certain country, or celebrating a winning sports team. Moreover, there have been other "public expressions," in the United States and other countries, in which individuals have been killed or injured.

However, to dissent from Rosenberg's thesis somewhat, there is *something* different about the events of May 4, 1970; very few other tragedies (especially those that began as statements of expression) receive the notoriety that this event does. Why is that? Perhaps the general circumstances of that era were so emotionally charged that they sparked the trauma associated with this event. An even more compelling rationale is rooted in basic social and cognitive psychological research: distinct and unusual events tend to be particularly recalled, because of their very nature.[8] We do not expect young people to die. We certainly don't expect young people to die as a result of a political protest—at the hands of our own military *at a major American university.* Sadly, other colleges and universities can point to instances of acts leading to on-campus violence; however, the specific type of violence, emanating from an act of political expression, is unique to Kent State University—an institution that aims to foster and encourage free expression of ideas.

The end result of the events surrounding May 4, 1970, is indelible. In fact, it is very likely that we will have future tragedies in which individuals die as a result of expressing their views. We must learn to embrace these losses. Although Kent State University signifies so much more than the events of May 4, 1970, this tragedy is part of its identity. When an individual experiences a personal loss, such as the death of a spouse or child, or develops a physical disability, it transforms and changes that individual on many levels.[9] Such is the case with respect to the events of May 4, 1970, and Kent State University; they are inextricably linked—and like a grieving individual, Kent State must embrace its tragic legacy, (in part) *as an expression of hope.*

By understanding the events of May 4, 1970, we truly understand the essence of freedom of expression; it is something that people have died for. We must continue to remember the events of May 4, 1970, in order to remember the courageous four young people who died while trying to express their views. Ultimately, by embracing the events of May 4, 1970, we not only realize the power associated with freedom of expression, but we realize also that traumatic events can often cause us to reevaluate what is (or should be) most cherished in our lives.[10]

We may never truly understand why the deaths of Allison Krause, Jeffrey Miller, Sandra Scheuer, and William Schroeder occurred. But we can embrace what it revealed: the importance of complete, absolute, and peaceful freedom of expression.

NOTES

1. Melvin J. Lerner, *The Belief in a Just World: A Fundamental Delusion* (New York: Plenum, 1980), 2; L. L. Carli and J. B. Leonard, "The Effect of Hindsight on Victim Derogation," *Journal of Social and Clinical Psychology* 8 (1989): 331–43.

2. Ellen J. Langer and L. Imber, "The Role of Mindlessness in the Perception of Deviance," *Journal of Personality and Social Psychology* 39 (1980): 360–67.

3. Fritz Heider, *The Psychology of Interpersonal Relations* (New York: Wiley, 1958).

4. *Texas v. Johnson*, 491 U.S. 397 (1989).

5. M. Rokeach, *The Open and Closed Mind* (New York: Basic Books, 1960).

6. David G. Myers, *Social Psychology,* 5th ed. (New York: McGraw-Hill, 1996).

7. R. E. Nisbett and L. Ross, *Human Inference: Strategies and Shortcomings of Social Judgment* (Englewood Cliffs, N.J.: Prentice Hall, 1980).

8. R. Brown and J. Kulik, "Flashbulb Memories," *Cognition* 5 (1977): 73–99.

9. John H. Harvey, *Embracing Their Memory: Loss and the Social Psychology of Storytelling* (Needham Heights, Mass.: Allyn and Bacon, 1996).

10. Viktor E. Frankl, *Man's Search for Meaning* (New York: Washington Square, 1959), 2; Ronnie Janoff-Bulman, *Shattered Assumptions: Towards a New Psychology of Trauma* (New York: Free Press, 1992).

The Sorrow and the Pity

Response to Rosenberg

ROBERT M. O'NEIL

Law, University of Virginia

While I find myself in substantial agreement with Professor Rosenberg on his central points, a panel on free expression would not be very lively without modest dissonance. My differences are mainly on matters of degree; I tend to be more sanguine than he about the evolution and the current state of free expression in this country—though I fully share his alarm over the extent of repression that marked the period we recall through this commemorative program.

Let me begin by simply noting the irony of Kent State—of all places where such a tragedy might have happened, why here? There were a number of politically volatile college campuses at that time—I taught at Berkeley throughout the 1960s, so I can attest to one of them—but Kent State would not have been put in that category. Indeed, the Friday evening antecedents of Monday's confrontation were about as nonpolitical as one could have imaged. It was basically an old-fashioned early spring, pre-exam blast. Yet it was at Kent that the most visible and violent events occurred, and it is appropriately at Kent that we gather this spring to reflect on those events.

My major exception to Professor Rosenberg's thesis concerns the condition of the First Amendment. Since I have taught and litigated in the field of free speech and press for nearly forty years, I tend to take a fairly long view, which may tend to make it more sanguine than a shorter perspective would be. I fully share Professor Rosenberg's major premises—that political dissent has never fared as well in this country as the text of the Bill of Rights would suggest it should, and that the fortunes of a constitutional guarantee of expression wax and wane with the vagaries of political will and popular tolerance. My difference is only with the larger context in which those conclusions properly belong. Several feature of that context seem to me worth noting.

First, the undoubted insensitivity toward political dissent is less evident in other areas where free expression has been tested. Indeed, protest and demonstration may have fared least well among the major expressive interests. When it comes to such issues as gagging the press by prior restraint, protecting privacy against unwanted publicity, or silencing hateful speakers, this country's record is probably better than that of almost any other. We are about the only nation that steadfastly refuses to imprison virulent anti-Semites, give damages to celebrities photographed in compromising situations, or prevent publication of embarrassing exposés of secure documents. We have also gone farther and faster than others in granting essentially full protection to speech on the Internet. While I am not sure what explains our greater tolerance for the Farmbelt Fuhrer than for the campus radical, the contrast seems to me worth noting.

Second, I view our intolerance of protest as somewhat cyclical. If conditions were as bad today as they were in the sixties, I would have expected much more hostility and reprisal toward the World Trade Organization protestors in Seattle and the anti-IMF and World Bank groups in Washington. I heard no voice in Congress suggesting that the District of Columbia police were too tolerant with the demonstrators, even though the meetings were inconvenienced, if not disrupted. I do not doubt the level of intolerance and repression that marked the sixties may return someday, but they are not with us now to the same degree.

Let me add that I am hardly myopic about how bad things were in the Vietnam era. I served on the Northern California ACLU Board and chaired the Berkeley Academic Senate Committee on Academic Freedom in those years. I also had the chastening experience, closer to this campus, of being laughed out of an Ohio legislative committee hearing just weeks after Kent State; I had come to Columbus to urge tolerance for academic freedom, in my role as general counsel of the American Association of University Professors, but I lost what little credibility I might have brought when I was introduced as a visitor from Berkeley!

My third and most substantial point is that even in the area of protest and dissent, the courts—admittedly slow to respond and sometimes inadequate in doing so—eventually restrained most of the excesses of which Professor Rosenberg is rightly critical. Ironically, the illiberal Court of the late 1930s reversed the convictions of several communist organizers on rather broad First Amendment grounds, and in 1942 it held that a radical labor leader could not be punished for sending to a judge a telegram making threats about a pending case. While those gains were lost—and then some—in the 1940s and early 1950s, the Supreme Court eventually regained perspective. Loyalty oaths died for good in 1967; in my AAUP role I wrote several briefs that eventually helped the courts to give such disclaimers a decent burial. Campus speaker bans had ceased to have much force a couple of years earlier; part of the coup de grace was an extraordinary statement condemning such bans by none other than Barry Goldwater.

Legislative investigations of suspected subversive activity did inflict irreparable harm in the forties and fifties, but they were eventually curbed by the courts on First Amendment grounds. Congressional witch-hunts never really resumed, even after the discovery that—unlike in the McCarthy era—there really were Soviet spies, like Aldrich Ames, in sensitive government posts. In short, it seems to me that eventually—too late and in some ways too little, to be sure—most of the repressive measures that Professor Rosenberg cites and decries, as do I, were put to rest on free speech and free press grounds. So my critique of the courts, and my anxiety about the status of First Amendment liberties, would be somewhat more cautious.

In fact, Kent State itself offers a curious confirmation. Soon after the shootings and the closing of the campus, a Portage County grand jury convened to assess blame and recommend sanctions. Its report, made public in clear violation of Ohio law, castigated a statement issued by twenty-three Kent State faculty members who were conscientiously seeking to calm both campus and community tensions in the aftermath. Some of the cited professors brought suit in federal court, claiming the grand jury had abridged free speech and academic freedom. In a quite remarkable (and unexpected) decision, a federal judge in Cleveland agreed completely with the plaintiffs; he added that he had seen and heard evidence that the report was "dulling classroom discussion and is upsetting the teaching atmosphere," citing specific examples of material that had been removed from, or not taught in, fall classes out of fear of reprisal.

To make sure the whole community got his point, the federal judge ordered that the original copy of the grand jury report be destroyed; it was in fact burned at dawn in the parking lot of the Portage County courthouse. Thus did the events that we recall today—through another of those curious twists of fate—create one of the strongest academic-freedom decisions ever entered by any judge. It is a precedent I have cited often, and with good results—always reflecting on the fact that but for the benighted hostility of good citizens of Portage County, Ohio—and the enlightened objectivity of a strong federal judge—academic freedom and the First Amendment would be much the poorer. This is simply one more of the many ironies that surround the tragic events of May 4, 1970.

Hope and Despair—First Amendment Doctrine, Human Nature, and the Protection of Political Dissent

Response to the Discussants

Gerald N. Rosenberg

In their thoughtful comments, Professors Robert M. O'Neil and Eric M. Miller suggest, respectively, that I have overlooked recent, major changes in judicial interpretations of free speech that are protective of political dissent, and that I have given insufficient attention to the psychological bases of human nature. Professor O'Neil's optimism is contagious, but, I will suggest, unsupportable. In contrast, Professor Miller's emphasis on human nature presents a deeply despairing and pessimistic portrait of the ability to protect political dissent. If he is correct, then the challenges of protecting political dissent are virtually insurmountable.

Professor Miller's central point is that opposition to political dissent is "simply an artifact of human nature." Human beings, he suggests, have a "very strong preference for stability." Opposition to political dissent, then, does not necessarily reflect intolerance. Rather, such attitudes are the "by-products of human nature," which is wary of change. As Professor Miller puts it, "The fact that Americans do not always seem supportive of those with whom they disagree does not necessarily mean that they *truly* feel that way."

I am not trained as a psychologist, and I do not know if Professor Miller is correct. But in regard to the potential of the First Amendment to protect political dissent, I'm not sure it matters whether hostility to political dissent is driven by ideology or human nature. Whatever the cause, repression is the result. Whatever the cause, the First Amendment is unlikely to offer a great deal of protection unless elites are willing to protect dissent. Whether Americans are *truly* hostile to political dissent, time and time again they have acted to repress it. Professor Miller's understanding of the motivations for this behavior does not affect my main point that the First Amendment is unlikely to protect dissent.

Professor Miller's argument becomes even more despairing when he notes that in times of economic trouble and political strife human beings become more close minded in their beliefs. If this is the case, then the protection of political dissent is in even greater trouble. It is precisely under these sorts of conditions that vocifer-ous political dissent is most likely to appear, and most likely to need protection. As a psychological matter, Professor Miller suggests that in these conditions human beings will be most resistant to protecting political dissent.

Again, I do not know if Professor Miller is correct, and again, I'm not sure it matters. The underlying point is that the First Amendment is unlikely to protect dissent in times of strife.

Professor Miller makes two other points that bear a response. First, he warns of the vagaries of surveys and of the danger of making causal inferences from nonexperimental survey data. Professor Miller's caution is well taken. Surveys are sometimes manipulated to produce preferred results, and responses to survey ques-tions are not necessarily indicative of true feelings. That being said, these responses to survey questions have been consistent for half a century, and political practice has mirrored the views expressed in those surveys. At the very least, this suggests that they have tapped something that is real.

Professor Miller's second point is that the events at Kent State are so well re-membered, and commemorated, because they were "unique." If only this were so. As I note, on May 14, 1970, less than two weeks after the Kent State killings, Missis-sippi Highway Patrolmen and Jackson City police opened fire on demonstrators at Jackson State University, killing two students and wounding twelve others. The events at Jackson State are not well remembered; indeed, they are hardly known. Kent State is remembered, I suggest, because the students killed were white and middle class, and because political elites, and to some extent the U.S. population as a whole, were increasingly divided on the war in Vietnam.

In contrast to Professor Miller's pessimism, Professor O'Neil presents an opti-mistic picture. In essence he suggests that while historically the United States has not been protective of political dissent, the bad old days are now gone. His "most substantial point" is that courts "eventually restrained most of the excesses," such as loyalty oaths and legislative investigations. He notes that the United States has one of the best records of protecting the press, and the best record of protecting speech on the Internet. Further, the United States is "about the only nation that steadfastly refuses to imprison virulent anti-Semites." He also points to the lack of hostility and reprisal toward the somewhat violent political protest at the meeting of the World Trade Organization (WTO) in Seattle in the spring in 2000 as evidence of the country's tolerance of political dissent.

I wish I could share Professor O'Neil's optimism. Unfortunately, I cannot, either in its removal of courts from the larger society in which they operate or in its sub-stantive embrace. Substantively, for Professor O'Neil, all speech appears worthy of protection, regardless of content. Thus, he appears to celebrate the protection of the speech of "virulent anti-Semites." Perhaps this is the most morally defensible position (and one that James Weinstein explores elsewhere in this volume). But it is not obvious that it is. As I suggest in my chapter, focus on the First Amendment works to preclude discussion of whether all speech ought to be axiomatically protected or whether a just and democratic society can and ought to limit certain kinds of speech.

Professor O'Neil's analysis credits the courts with more influence than they have. It was the broader society and political system that "eventually restrained most of the excesses" of Cold War repression, not the judicial system. The judicial system played a role, but it was a relatively minor one. For example, the House of Representatives itself closed down its Internal Security Committee (formerly the Un-American Activities Committee), not the courts. When fear of communists no longer seemed politically exploitable by politicians, repression lessened. The courts then followed.

My argument that the level of protection of political dissent depends broadly on the views of the public at large, and specifically on the positions taken by elites, goes a long way toward explaining the anomalies Professor O'Neil presents. The press may be well protected in the United States, for example, because it is a business with powerful and wealthy interests. An attack on one publication is invariably seen as an attack on the press as a whole, and corporate elites rally to the cause of the defendant, providing enormous resources. Compare this situation to the political protestor who lacks such an elite, resource-rich support network. Understanding the protection of political dissent through the lens of public and elite views, not the First Amendment, can explain why the press has historically been better treated than other vehicles of political protest.

Similarly, the lack of reprisal toward the political protest at the 2000 meeting of the WTO in Seattle may reflect the fact that elites are divided on the appropriate role of the WTO, creating a space for protest. Further, the American public is not riled up over the issue. No one's patriotism or love of country is challenged by protest against the WTO.

Finally, Professor O'Neil wonders "what explains our greater tolerance for the Farmbelt Fuhrer than for the campus radical." From the perspective I have offered, the answer appears straightforward. Throughout American history there has been a deep cultural commitment to the Protestant religion and a deep hostility to any form of socialist political organizing. Judges, political elites, and the population at large are all products of this culture, and they react accordingly. In other words, the Farmbelt Fuhrer does not threaten core cultural understandings in the same, visceral way that the campus radical does. The Constitution, and the First Amendment, can only reflect these values.

Overall, then, my concern with Professor O'Neil's analysis is that he reifies courts and removes them from the broader culture in which they operate. Courts have a role to play in protecting political dissent, but it is marginal. If the protection of political dissent is a value we cherish, then we must make the case for why it is good. Arguing that the First Amendment requires it is historically unsupportable, substantively unsatisfying, and, if I am right, dangerous. For if the protection of political dissent depends on a broad cultural consensus and the commitment to it of elites, there is little the courts can or will do when that consensus is lacking and elites urge repression. If we truly wish to commemorate the killings of Allison B. Krause, Jeffrey G. Miller, Sandra L. Scheuer, and William K. Schroeder, and the wounding of Alan Canfora, John Clearly, Thomas Grace, Dean Kahler, Joseph Lewis, Donald MacKenzie, James Russell, Robert Stamps, and Douglas Wrentmore, we must strive to create a cultural understanding that accepts the importance of political dissent. Focusing on the First Amendment will not help.

3

Deliberation Down and Dirty
Must Political Expression Be Civil?

DAVID M. ESTLUND

Philosophy, Brown University

CARVING OUT A QUESTION

The idea of civility can suggest perniciously narrow norms of public behavior.[1] In the context of political expression in particular, calls for civility run the risk of morally tolerating far too little. My hypothesis in this essay is that there are moral standards of civility in political expression but that they can accommodate much vigorous, disruptive, disturbing, embarrassing, and even illegal expressive activity. This approach may seem to defend civility by using the name to refer to something else, something more defensible. Rather, the dispute is framed here as about what the idea of civility really does require. One proposal applies the idea of politeness to the public sphere. I sketch a different view, in which civility's point is different from that of politeness and in which its content is different as a result. Politeness cannot make room for sharp and disruptive behavior, but civility can.[2] Calling this type of behavior "uncivil" would suggest a strong presumption against it. On the view I will defend here, wider boundaries of civility are triggered specifically as remedial responses to certain violations of the conditions needed to foster good democratic deliberation—in particular, power's interference with reason. There is no strong presumption against sharp and disruptive political expression, because there is no general reason for presuming that the conditions in which narrow civility has its place normally obtain.

Many today accept that sharp and disruptive tactics are within the legitimate repertoire of responsible citizens. At the same time, many doubt that sharp political expression of various kinds can be properly accommodated within the increasingly popular idea of "deliberative democracy."[3] One goal in this discussion is to find a basis for the permissibility of sharp political expression in a deliberative conception of political legitimacy. Attention to the ways in which democratic deliberation can improve democratic decisions (its "epistemic value") lends support to the idea that while narrow civility has its place in political expression, in real and imperfect political life wider and more permissive standards are often appropriate. It is not just that narrow standards are unrealistic and often violated in the real world. An emphasis on the value of democratic deliberation gives an important place to political expression that transgresses the narrow standards of civility, but it also supports new standards—more permissive but still not unconstrained—in many cases. Throughout, the question is not the epistemic value of a particular expressive intervention but the epistemic value of publicly recognizing certain wider or narrower standards of civil public expression.

There is some impulse to reject the very idea of "duties of civility" in political expression, on the grounds that they give some classes illegitimate control over others, dampen dissent, and stifle change, even where change is urgently needed. Politics is, among other things, an engagement between the weak and the powerful, between abusers and victims, between the complacent and the desperate, the self-righteous and the disparaged. Calm talk must certainly have its place, but only among a much wider range of less civil modes of expression. Even if the members of a society agreed to be relatively just, political choices would often involve the high stakes of potential injustice, and the interventions of, or on behalf of, potential victims could not be limited to the pages of etiquette manuals or anything like them. The idea of civility is dangerous in this way.[4]

It would be wrong, however, to suppose that the critics of the calm-talk model reject any doctrine of civility. They are not committed to condoning every brutal or dangerous ploy that might be offered up in politics, such as the Willie Horton ads run by the George Bush campaign or radical calls to turn the guns on the ruling class. A wide range of visions of politics can agree on the general idea that there are duties of civility in political expression. The remaining dispute, then, is what shape this duty of civility should have.

The defenses and criticisms I will consider will not endorse or reject the speakers' messages. I do not mean, however, to suggest that the content of the message never has any bearing on whether it is appropriate to express that message; of course, it does. This is, however, a different issue from the one I wish to consider, which is what basis there might be, on a viewpoint-neutral basis, for standards of permissible political expression that are, on the one hand, bounded and, on the other hand, capacious enough to permit sharp political expression under some circumstances.

John Rawls speaks of a "duty of civility," by which he means a duty to conform one's publicly offered justifications for exercises of political power to the political conception of justice one finds most reasonable, and that is believed to be acceptable to all reasonable citizens, including those with divergent and mistaken worldviews. So, for example, a judge may not offer as a political justification for a law the purported fact that it is God's will, since that is not a premise that will be acceptable to all reasonable citizens, such as reasonable atheists. A similarity between civility in this Rawlsian sense and civility as I understand it here is that, as Rawls says, "This duty, like other political rights and duties, is an intrinsically moral duty. . . . [I]t is not a legal duty, for in that case it would be incompatible with freedom of speech."[5]

But even speech that meets this duty sometimes raises clear questions of civility in a more familiar sense. Consider, for example, my exposing, on good evidence, a candidate for office as being a secret homosexual. This is a straightforward factual claim (at least in some cases), and so it does not appeal to any premises or values that are not acceptable to all reasonable citizens. Yet it raises a question of civility. It may in the end be either permissible or not, but that is a question of civility in political expression. It is not a question that is taken up by Rawls's account of the duty of civility, which might better be called a "duty of public reason" and treated as only one part of civility.

TWO TOWN MEETINGS

Alexander Meiklejohn famously discussed the traditional New England town meeting in order to illustrate how certain restrictions on expression are compatible with, "indeed necessary for," a meaningful freedom of speech.[6] He argued that without rules forbidding such things as talking out of turn, disobeying the moderator, speaking far off the appointed topic, etc., the quality of the deliberation at the meeting on the topics at hand would be harmed. He pointed out that even under such restrictions on speech, participants would be free to express their views on the matters at hand, whatever their views might be. There would remain, in short, freedom of speech.

Meiklejohn's point was that some coercively enforced restrictions can be justified without destroying the essence of freedom of speech. Our topic is parallel in certain ways but also importantly different. The question of appropriate standards of civility, as conceived here, involves no question of interference with speech, either legally, by a meeting's sergeant at arms, by social pressure, or any other way. The standards of civility I want to consider are not modes of interference, nor am I assuming that they justify any kind of interference with transgressions. The question is not what laws or positive rules there are or ought to be. Neither is it what a society's morals *are*, because that would still leave open the question of whether the citizen ought to abide by her society's morals. Rather, the standards of civility that are my topic are, in effect, answers to a question that any citizen faces: "What kinds of restraint ought I to exercise in my political expression, and under what conditions might the appropriate standards be more or less permissive?" This is a certain kind of moral question, applying to a person in his or her role or status as a citizen.[7]

There is a danger in emphasizing the town-meeting context. The town meeting is not an accurate microcosm of the broad and diverse universe of public political expression, despite its value for illustrating certain points. It is important to emphasize, then, that by beginning with the town-meeting context I do not mean to suggest that the broader realm of public political expression is usefully conceived as a town meeting writ large. The hope is that lessons about the structure of the duty of civility will be a useful start in understanding the diverse standards of civility that are appropriate in various contexts of political expression. I consider only one extension here, one that begs to be analyzed on the model of a town meeting.

The town meeting is a useful starting point for several reasons. In a town meeting, the rules tend to be exceptionally clear. I do not mean only the rules of procedure, or the rules that will be enforced, but also the rules of good behavior. Different kinds of meetings suggest different specific behavioral standards, and there are many other contexts of political expression that suggest other standards yet. In the context of a town meeting, not only are the normal standards of civil behavior clear, but they coexist with other sets of behavioral rules that are quasi-legal—such publicly known and enforced rules of procedure and order as Robert's Rules of Order. These official rules of a town meeting are distinct from the standards of civility or good meeting behavior. For example, the official rules may permit a recognized speaker to ridicule opponents in a way calculated to disturb the meeting, but that would not settle whether this was within the speaker's duties of civility. So the standards of civility are not simply the same as the official rules of the meeting, and this distinction in a meeting context mimics the structure of a broader political context, where there are laws permitting and regulating expression but also separate standards of civility with no force except that of a citizen's duty.

It will be useful to begin with a contrast between certain narrow standards of civility and a set of behaviors that violate those narrow standards but nevertheless seem to me to be justified. Then the question becomes whether an account can be devised to support this intuitive response.

Imagine a New England town meeting. Suppose that attendance is limited by space and that passes are distributed on a first-come-first-served basis. Opportunities to speak are ample and fairly administered, and the public officials are respectful and responsive to the public. Suppose further that the matter under discussion is whether to pay for high school athletic uniforms with public money. I will call this hypothetical example the "Local Town Meeting." Under these conditions let us suppose that some or all of the following expressive tactics are condemnable by appropriate standards of civility, standards that I will call "narrow."

· Obtaining entrance with counterfeit passes in order to participate uninvited
· Ignoring moderator's rules
· Stepping to the microphone to speak out of turn
· Shouting questions from the floor out of turn
· Disrupting the meeting with chants.

Contrast this with a different meeting, an internationally televised public forum held at a government's request at a location chosen by that government, broadcast exclusively by one global network handpicked by the government, with attendance screened, and with the right to speak granted only to participants screened by the government's handpicked network.[8] Suppose also that the issue to be discussed is not athletic uniforms but whether the United States should drop bombs on Iraq. Suppose further, hypothetically, that this event is held at a state university in Ohio. Our case is not actually hypothetical, of course; it describes the ironically titled "International Town Meeting" held at Ohio State University in February 1998.[9]

The disruptive behaviors listed above were all apparently engaged in by protestors at the International Town Meeting, and the setting puts them in a different light from that of the Local Town Meeting.[10] I find myself agreeing with a protestor at Ohio State who said, "If we had just been sitting there quietly listening, people watching on television would have thought we were supporters of the war, which we certainly were not. Sometimes you've just got to say what you think and make sure that your voice is heard. And, if they won't listen in a polite manner, then you've just got to be rude."[11] The two town meetings, between them, capture the distinction for which I would like to find some plausible normative basis: narrow standards of civility that apply in some conditions, alongside wider, more permissive standards that apply in others.

TOWARD A THEORY: POWER'S INTERFERENCE WITH REASON

The case of the two town meetings could be explained by a view according to which narrow standards of civility are appropriate so long as certain background conditions are met; when these conditions are violated, the narrow standards give way to wider, more permissive standards. On a view of this kind, the permissibility of the Ohio protesters' tactics is not a function merely of the political content or significance of their message (since such tactics would then be appropriate also in the Local Town Meeting, which we are assuming they are not). They are made permissible instead by the fact that the meeting is so set up, or occurs in a context such that the background conditions necessary for the appropriate application of the narrow standards are violated. For example, the fact that the International Town Meeting was so pervasively controlled by one side in the debate while presented as an open forum could be taken to weaken greatly the legitimacy of narrow standards of civility. This approach relies on what we might call "circumstances of civility." As circumstances of narrow civility are less fully met, wider and more permissive standards of civility come into effect, at least for certain participants. But again, these wider standards still depend on meeting certain circumstances, in order to forestall wider standards yet.

Herbert Marcuse offers perhaps the best known defense of sharp and disruptive interventions in political expression, and I believe his theory is usefully interpreted as a breakdown of theory of this kind.[12] We may usefully sketch an interpretation of Marcuse's reasoning, even though his question is not quite the same as ours. His reasoning, or at least a line of reasoning suggested by his essay, fits naturally with an emphasis on the epistemic value of public political deliberation, and so it gives an idea of how such an emphasis might treat behavior on the boundaries of civility. Marcuse wonders when private citizens might permissibly interfere with public political expression, a question he takes up from John Stuart Mill in order to offer a different answer. But since that question is about permissible interference with expression, it is narrower than the general question of civility, which asks what kinds of nonviolent public political expression are morally permissible, consistent with one's responsibilities as a citizen.[13] Still, Marcusean interference with expression is certainly one kind of behavior that would be condemned by narrow standards of civility, as conceived here. Marcuse, in effect, defends a wider conception of civility according to which such interference is indeed permitted.[14]

Marcuse agrees with Mill on a great deal.[15] He agrees with Mill that there are objectively correct answers to many normative political questions.[16] He also evidently agrees with Mill that under favorable conditions the truth will tend to prevail in the course of full and open public deliberation.[17] He agrees with Mill that among the set of conditions that are most favorable to the social discovery of truth is a widespread tolerance. By "tolerance" Marcuse means restraining oneself from interfering with the expression by others of views with which one strongly disagrees. Tolerance is not simply one of the social conditions favorable to the social discovery of truth; that epistemic function is what gives tolerance its point. As Marcuse succinctly says, "The *telos* of tolerance is truth."[18]

Tolerance does not, by itself, promote truth, however. It promotes truth only in conjunction with certain other conditions. This gives rise to questions that Mill said little about: What are the other conditions that join with tolerance to promote truth? What is the effect of tolerance when those other conditions are violated in various ways? What implications does this have for the practical question facing a citizen, "Ought I to be tolerant of this highly disagreeable view?" Marcuse offers a rough account of the circumstances of tolerance and an argument that they are pervasively violated, at least in modern America.

On Marcuse's view, wider standards of civility come into their own when there is a failure in, or breakdown of, the conditions in which tolerance serves its purpose. The circumstances of (narrow) civility could presumably break down in non-political as well as political contexts, possibly warranting wider standards. The importance or urgency of the matters at hand plays a role here, and sometimes political matters have a great urgency. But urgency is by no means limited to politics. Consider a nonpolitical context, a meeting of doctors in which a patient's life is at stake. Decorum and civility have their places, so long as they are parts of an arrangement in which the patient's interests will be best served. But suppose that the meeting is chaired by an appointee of an HMO who shamelessly uses his position to do whatever will minimize company costs even at dire risk to the well-being of patients. Narrow civility no longer has its point in that case. The triggers for wide civility, then, are not uniquely associated with politics. This allows a breakdown account to hold the Local Town Meeting to narrow standards but the International Town Meeting only to wider ones.

Applied to the matter of civility in political expression, the breakdown approach asks: What is the point of narrow civility? If we follow Mill's, Meiklejohn's, and Marcuse's approaches to tolerance of expression, we will answer that an important part of narrow civility's point is as part of an arrangement in which the exchange of ideas tends to promote true or at least objectively better views and social decisions. The *telos* of civility is, in part, truth. Plainly this is not its only point, but it is worth seeing what follows from its having this point.

Consider the International Town Meeting, with these questions in mind. Here is the U.S. government, hoping to mobilize public opinion behind bombing a faraway country. We do not need to decide whether that bombing would be wrong in order to notice important distortions in the Millean truth-seeking function of free public discussion. For one thing, officials in the Clinton administration handed the cable television network CNN exclusive rights to broadcast the event. CNN was free to share the event with competing outlets but refused to do so, presumably in order to reap the ratings and consequent profits for itself.[19] This produced an obvious incentive for CNN to produce the kind of event the administration wanted, in order to attract other exclusive offers in the future. If the event had been a simple broadcast of a presidential speech, this cozy relationship might not have had any important effect on the quality of public discourse. But this was an event that could have gone very well or very badly for the government, depending on how it was structured and handled. ๏

As it happened, David Marcus reports, "The scene became so unruly that at one point audience members could hear a CNN producer frantically telling moderator Bernard Shaw that assistants to Secretary of State Madeleine Albright, Defense Secretary William S. Cohen, and White House National Security Adviser Samuel "Sandy" Berger wanted phone calls from viewers who supported the administration. Shaw angrily shushed the producer during a commercial."[20] CNN clearly had strong incentives to structure the event so as to favor the administration's aims, which included not only mobilizing support for bombing but also displaying public support to the leaders and citizens of other countries, including Iraq.[21]

It would be absurd to suggest that the narrow rules of civility lapse whenever some powerful speaker presents only one side of an argument. It would be silly to think that the International Town Meeting opened the door to the disruptive tactics of the protesters simply by being biased in favor of the probombing point of view. There is a more significant kind of breakdown here stemming from the presentation of the event under the name and in the format of a town meeting. This suggested to viewers worldwide, and gave a legitimate expectation to attendees, that there would be no exercise of control over the viewpoints expressed by those who spoke from the (metaphorical) floor. When this expectation of freedom is violated, obedience to the narrow standards of civility appropriate to a town meeting no longer serve their purpose of providing an orderly method for a variety of points of view to be publicly offered and discussed. Assuming with Marcuse, Mill, and Meiklejohn that the value of that kind of orderly deliberation is that it enhances the truth, or wisdom, or quality of the resulting social decisions, narrow civility no longer promotes truth once the other components of an orderly but free deliberation are missing, and if standards allowing deviations from narrow civility could remedy the epistemic situation. In general, the defective background conditions permit transgression of narrow civility for remedial purposes, but only within the constraints of a wider civility. For convenience, I will refer to this normative structure as one of "constrained transgression."

How do wider standards of civility serve the epistemic goal in these defective conditions? Marcuse's own argument does not discuss the context of a town meeting, but its structure is similar and instructive. He argued that in this era (he wrote in the late sixties, but his argument probably applies to ours now) there is a systematic cluster of interests (especially those associated with owners of productive capital) that have disproportionate control over the course of public, especially political, discussion. As a result, certain favored points of view can be made to attract support on grounds other than their merits, the actual reasons that exist in their favor. Behavior outside of the narrow bounds that would make sense under more ideal conditions is permitted in order to restore partially the truth-promoting value of public discussion.

Marcuse calls for "selective intolerance," acts by private citizens that suppress messages that are so advantaged by power. My topic in this essay is somewhat different, as I have said, placing no special emphasis on behaviors that suppress the expression of others. Plainly, one of the effects of the disruptive tactics at the International Town Meeting was to limit the ability of the administration officials to present their own message. Another important effect, though, and one that is separable from any suppressive effects, was the presentation of a strongly dissenting point of view.

From an epistemic viewpoint, the relevant breakdown consists of *power's interference with reason*.[22] The justification for wider standards of civility in these conditions is that they partially remedy the power imbalance. Marcuse's strategy of selective intolerance through private acts of suppression operates by reducing the power of dominant viewpoints. The wider standard of civil expression operates by increasing the power of nondominant points of view.

The circumstances of narrow civility in political expression, then, include the condition of power's noninterference with reason. It would be absurd to think that this condition could be fully met in any real context of public political expression, but that does not deprive the idea of normative significance. Jürgen Habermas, Marcuse's leading successor in what is known as the "Frankfurt school" of critical social theory, adopts the idea of power's noninterference with truth as the core of his moral and political theory, without supposing that it is a condition that could ever really be met. Roughly, Habermas holds that a legitimate political arrangement is whatever would, hypothetically, be unanimously accepted in a practical discourse involving all affected people and in which power did not interfere with reason. It might seem that since power always *is* actually interfering with reason, this account leaves it entirely to the philosopher, rather than to any public process, to ascertain the conditions of justice or legitimate government. Habermas, however, insists that the philosopher cannot credibly claim to know what such an ideal discourse would produce, absent actual discourse.[23] But actual discourse always falls short of the ideal discourse, and normative conclusions must be drawn by concentrating on these discrepancies. The greater the shortfall, the less the moral legitimacy of the normative conclusion, since this enlarges the biasing role of the philosopher's own particular perspective.

Marcuse's view is often criticized as arrogantly bypassing public discussion and presuming to know the proper conclusions of that discussion.[24] However, Marcuse's view is most charitably read as advocating remedial interventions in the discursive system so as to restore some normative significance to its conclusions. One strategy that is suggested by this approach is not to try to generate conclusions by a solitary application of reason but, as far as possible, to approximate real social conditions in which power does not interfere with reason—or, failing that, in which a remedial feature exists that supports our ability to infer from the imperfect, real discourse some conclusions about what would have been accepted had the discourse been ideal. Such a view admits from the beginning that real discourses are not ideal, but it still gives the idea of ideal discourse—the idea of power not interfering with reason—a central critical role.

The importance of these points for our purposes arises from the sobering fact that the conditions in which narrow civility has its distinctive epistemic point are always violated to a greater or lesser extent. Power is always interfering with reason. When the shortfall is great, the question is whether narrow standards of civility any longer serve the guiding idea of a public discourse in which conclusions are driven as much as possible by reason rather than power. If we stick to the epistemic point of standards of civil political expression, we will arguably be led to a new, more permissive set of standards in which advocates of nondominant views may permissibly press their own viewpoints with an added degree of power. The more permissive standard is defended on the grounds that this might countervail the antirational effect of the initial pollution of the discourse by systemic power that irrationally favors one side.

It may seem that this approach supports an egalitarian distribution of power over political discourse. In that case, the circumstances of narrow civility could be shown to be violated simply by demonstrating that power over public political thinking is unequally distributed. But whether narrow civility is then truly violated would depend on whether every unequal distribution of such power in fact amounts to power's interference with reason. That does not seem to be true as a general matter. The reason is that it is not guaranteed that reason will be more free under every equal distribution of power than it would under any unequal distribution. First, simply as a logical matter, it could be that under the only available equal distribution of power, reason would have hardly any scope at all. Power is not necessarily interfering with reason here.

But power is not the only threat to the exercise of reason; equally distributed poverty might place the public exercise of reason far down the list of individuals' practical priorities. If the only way to remove such poverty and so bring reason more fully into play depended on distributing power less equally, it would be wrong to say that, on balance, this new inequality in power is an instance of power interfering with reason. My point is not to draw any direct political conclusions, since actual power inequalities seem clearly to interfere with the public exercise of reason far more than they enable it. The point here is simply to avoid mistaking the ideal of power's noninterference with reason with an egalitarian principle for distributing power. Its distributive implications are not essentially egalitarian, even though they lead in an egalitarian direction under certain contingent circumstances.[25] The mere fact of unequal distribution of power over public political expression and thought is not enough to establish that the circumstances of narrow civility are not met; to establish that they are not met requires showing that reason is being interfered with, rather than enabled, by the inequality.

On the other hand, when power distributions trigger wider standards of civility, this dispensation is not given to all speakers, whatever their messages. It is only remedial if wider standards are given selectively, and only to those whose viewpoints are being denied their due hearing by an imbalance of power. Still, the view that the wider standards are triggered for the benefit of the disadvantaged view is some distance from an egalitarian principle of distributing power.

The constraints of a wider idea of civility are naturally suggested on this account. Even on a Marcusean analysis, there would be no apparent justification for so extreme suppression of a message that it disappeared from public awareness altogether. The power-imbalance argument provides only a basis for leveling the playing field, in order to recover partly the epistemic virtues of freedom of expression that Mill emphasized.

WIDE CIVILITY IN THE INTERNATIONAL TOWN MEETING

How did the breakdown of orderly discussion at the International Town Meeting harm the epistemic function of public discussion? How did the transgressions of narrow civility provide some remedy? I believe many citizens were struck by the official speakers' inability to answer credibly two challenges raised at the forum. First, was U.S. policy consistent in its use of military might against countries whose governments severely violated human rights? Second, was the enormous peril to innocent Iraqis commensurate with the action's likely benefits? That is, was "sending a message" rather than toppling Saddam Hussein a good enough reason to kill civilians and destroy their infrastructure? An administration that realizes that it cannot be convincing on such matters has reason to doubt its ability to keep public opinion on its side. In this case, press reports repeated and amplified these challenges and emphasized the resulting instability of public opinion. In the end, plans to bomb were aborted, though air strikes had seemed inevitable to many just days before.[26] My point is not to make a causal claim (much less a partisan one) about this particular case but only to illustrate mechanisms by which it would be possible for such transgressive expression to have epistemic value in public deliberation.

Another important question, which I can take up only indirectly, is: What are the new limits at Ohio State? If movement toward wider civility is both remedial and constrained, what new limits does this suggest for the protesters at the International Town Meeting? We should expect it to be difficult to state the specific standards involved in cases like this. In any given contest there is a continuous gradation of wider standards, not a quantum jump from one set to another. Also, contexts of political expression are diverse, and the appropriate standards of civility vary greatly from one to another.

As a start, though, we can list several limits within which the protesters did in fact remain—though we must defer the question of whether they were obligated to do so. The protests were not violent; no one was physically assaulted, and no property was attacked or damaged. There were apparently no violations of the law, or at least only minor ones—for example, perhaps the protesters got in by using counterfeit tickets, which may have been illegal.

Further, the protesters refrained from obscene language. I note this because it seems to have been a conscious decision.[27] One chant, for example, was "One, two, three, four, we do not want your racist war!"—a rewriting of a traditional chant so as to avoid its obscene language. This is noteworthy as a significant concession to narrow standards of civility. It may be a surprising one as well, at least to those of us who are not easily offended by so-called bad language; yet it would be easy to underestimate the significance of this boundary. The use of bad language in this kind of setting tends to signal a broad contempt: for the official speakers being opposed; for the many members of the audience who would be offended by its use in such a setting; even, perhaps, for the general structure of social authority.[28] Obscenity may also be an issue if potential speakers are deterred from participation by fear of attracting such an aggressive response.[29] Still, it would be a worthwhile, if difficult, task to discern whether a morally significant boundary separates the term "fucking war" from the equally inflammatory "racist war."

Fourth, in another concession to narrow civility, one protester, when finally allowed to approach the microphone, began by saying, "I want to apologize for disrupting earlier. The reason I did was I was told by this person I would not be allowed to speak."[30] This reasoning neatly matches the breakdown account, wherein wider standards are warranted when the circumstances of narrow civility are violated. The apology apparently reflected an acknowledgment of the legitimacy of the narrow standards under the proper conditions and signaled a conditional commitment not to interfere further so long as those conditions were respected.

Finally, though the protesters' actions were partly suppressive, they were primarily expressive. While the chanting palpably delayed the speakers' ability to continue their speeches, in no case did it prevent a speaker from finishing. Still, the chanting contained an element of suppression, or at least interference, that went beyond mere refusal to wait until one's turn came, according to the rules, before expressing one's own view. There is no question that such interference transgresses the narrow bounds of civility that would be appropriate in the Local Town Meeting, and no doubt that it requires the special justification of prior violation of the circumstances of narrow civility. But, as suppression or interference go, the chanting, and so on, at the International Town Meeting was not extreme; it remained within limits that could have been transgressed if the protesters had chosen to do so. Without pretending to know the protesters' motives or what else would have been possible for them, we can note the important difference between interfering with the proceedings by intermittent chants and heckling, on one hand, and seeking, on the other hand, a general disruption in which speakers would be unable to continue at all. These observations do not suffice for an account of what the new wider standards should be, but they show how citizens might try to answer that question within a framework of "constrained transgression" structured as a remedy to violations of the circumstances of narrow civility.

BEYOND CIVILITY?

Let us briefly consider the application of this general approach to increasing degrees of disruptive political behavior—political behavior that is essentially expressive but has the remedial aim of adopting wider standards of civility in order to restore to public political expression some missing epistemic dimension. This remedial aim, as I have argued, gives rise to a constrained transgression, but this does not imply that the model could never condone illegal or violent activity. I take for granted that both illegal political action and violence can be justified under the appropriate circumstances. Perhaps surprisingly, the model of constrained and remedial expressive transgression can embrace many such cases. It is not my aim here to provide a complete account of the justifiability and limits of illegal or violent political activity, but only to show how the kind of reasoning we have employed might be relevant to one.

To begin with a few widely agreed cases, few these days deny that civil disobedience is a category of illegal political activity that is justified under the right circumstances. Perhaps the most widely embraced examples are the sit-ins and other nonviolent but illegal demonstrations that aimed at dramatizing the growing demand for civil rights by African Americans in the 1950s and 1960s. The epistemic approach to civility in political expression might seem too narrow to cover these cases, either because such acts as sit-ins and traffic blocking are not in the realm of political expression but are political actions of a different kind, or because illegality, whether justified or not, must be counted as outside the bounds of even widened standards of civility.

However, as a number of theorists of civil disobedience emphasize, while expressive aims may not be necessary for the justification of civil disobedience, they are often its central characteristics and important parts of its justifiability. Civil disobedience is often theorized as a form of expression, and a civil one at that. Rawls, for example, treats it as a last-resort appeal urging the society to remedy deep and persistent injustice within the framework of a legitimate political system. Given its remedial function, it is a form of constrained transgression—transgressing the boundaries of both narrow civility and the law, but accepting further limits imposed by the intent to signal acceptance of the rule of law generally, rather than wholesale rejection of it or a call for rebellion.[31] Without placing too much importance on the terminological question, there is some reason to treat at least some civil disobedience as political expression, within the wider standards of civility triggered by certain violations of the circumstances of narrow civility. Civility, then, does not stop at the boundaries of legality.[32]

This would be harder to maintain in the case of political violence, which any sensible use of language forces us to call uncivil—reflecting the broadly held presumption against the permissibility of political violence. Still, Americans widely accept the permissibility of the Boston Tea Party, even though it was an act of political violence, in its destruction of property (the tea). Clearly, the Boston Tea Party was primarily an act of expression, being insufficient, except through publicity, to make any dent in either the tea trade or in British policy in the colonies. Even if this offense against property cannot be called civil behavior, there is little doubt about its justifiability, or about the justifiability of similar expressive acts constrained by their remedial aims and by the limited degrees of breakdown involved. The expressive nature of an act is important in identifying the relevant form of breakdown.

In particular, resorting to property violence as a form of public political expression would seem to depend partly on failures in the system of political expression, not merely at objectionable policies. As it happens, the Boston Tea Party criticized primarily "taxation without representation," the ability of the British Parliament to levy taxes on the colonies when none of its members had been elected by the colonists themselves. The targeted failure was in the system of expression, broadly conceived: the absence of democratic involvement in the formulation of the laws. Lacking an official voice in the political process, dissidents found an unofficial voice in the publicity that could be gained for their cause by imaginative acts of violence against property. There was evidently no thought of expressing acceptance of the legitimacy of the underlying system as civil disobedience normally does, since Parliament's denial of representation to the colonists placed the political system's very legitimacy in question. Yet this is not an act of unlimited rebellion but a call for the fundamental reform of establishing political representation for the colonies.

Violence against persons is a further escalation of the level of transgression, generally depending for its permissibility on more extreme moral failures in the underlying systems of authority. Still, many would accept that political violence against people is justifiable under certain conditions. Much of this sort of violence (including also lesser transgressions against civility) is simply instrumental without being essentially expressive. For example, many would condone Nat Turner's famous slave rebellion in 1831, but it is not clear that any expressive purpose was important to the actors or to the justifications that people would now be inclined to offer. Certainly, more severe violence requires graver circumstances for its justification, and the account given here of political expression has little to add in a case like that one. Still, much political violence against persons is essentially expressive, with targets chosen less for their intrinsic strategic value than for their ability to dramatize the dissenters' complaints. As Robert Post writes of conduct that communicates a message even though it does not bring the First Amendment into play, "Such conduct ranges from terrorist bombings to written warnings on consumer products."[33]

Since even bombings can have central expressive purposes, the question of their justification must consider what kinds of (presumably catastrophic) breakdown in the underlying expressive system could, along with a very urgent cause, ever justify them. I am not prepared to say when bombing buildings and so risking lives would be justified. It should not be assumed, though, that once bombing is allowed no moral constraints would any longer be in place. Just as there are moral constraints in warfare, there would be moral constraints here. Karl Armstrong's bombing of the Army Math Research Center at the University of Wisconsin in 1970, with its attendant threat to safety (one person was killed), presumably would require a serious breakdown in the expressive system in addition to the urgency of the case against the war. It could be justified more readily, however, than could a campaign of revolution, targeting large numbers of people and aiming to bring down the government.[34] That too, of course, might be justified in the right circumstances, as citizens of democratic societies that themselves originated in violent revolutions will often concede. My only point here is that even political violence can exhibit certain features of civil behavior—for example, as transgressive expression, with a remedial purpose and a constrained compass. Such purpose and constraint would not be enough to count the violence as civil or justified, but they add something to the complex of issues that bear on its justifiability. In particular, its expressive dimension cannot be ignored by a deliberative or epistemic account of political legitimacy.[35]

CONCLUSION

Among the state officials being heckled at Ohio State was Secretary of Defense William Cohen, whose closing comment was this: "If I could just indicate to the audience, this really is a tremendous example of what democracy is all about." This is a familiar response in America to sharp political expression, an affirmation that it too is part of the proud American tradition of freedom of expression. As Cohen made clear, however, what he was proud of was the government, not the demonstrators: he continued, "The people who are here expressing opposition and criticism would not be allowed to do that in a number of countries, including Iraq."[36] The proud American tradition he refers to is the practice, recent and uneven, of permitting nonviolent expressions of political dissent without state interference. It is important to see that praising America's strong legal protection of sharp political expression is not the same as praising exercise of that freedom even when it is disruptive and transgressive of normal standards of civility.

Disruptive political expression cannot be denied an important and noble place in the democratic repertoire. But many noble ideas find their homes only in unfortunate or even desperate conditions. We erect a strong presumption against genuine incivility, and yet we all know that political arrangements are ordinarily far from the ideal conditions in which narrow, polite standards of civility would make the most sense: conditions in which things are already more or less right, or at least in which procedures for change are fair and open to good ideas, whatever their source. There should be no strong presumption, then, against disruptive and impolite political expression, especially when it is legal, nonviolent, and does not suppress the speech of others, and so we ought not to call all such action uncivil. When conditions diverge even more widely from appropriate background conditions of democratic deliberation, illegality and private suppression might also be called for, and these too can be seen as exhibiting the distinctive features of civil behavior, in that they seek to remedy underlying failures without calling the whole system into question. Even violence may ultimately be justified, and here civility runs out. In our politics, deeply flawed but still tenable, the presumption is against violence, even though it too can exhibit something of the structure of broadly civil transgressive political expression, to the extent that it is remedial and constrained.

This moderate view of disruptive expression may be a corrective to certain approaches, but it is hardly unique in rejecting both exaggerated politeness and a facile anarchism. It may give a better idea than some models, though, of how an account of democratic legitimacy that places great weight on properly conducted public political deliberation might avoid charges that it is excessively timid, complacent, or rationalistic. Disruptive political expression has often proven its epistemic value. It is not merely another kind of social power, one that, say, raises the costs of continued oppression—though it can also be that. It has often injected ideas, complaints, and perspectives into public discourse in ways that enable the kind of reasoning to which democratic deliberation aspires. Deliberative democracy certainly has its own unrealistic ideals, as do most normative approaches to politics, but it has much to say in the breach as well.

1. I am grateful for useful comments on an earlier draft from Alon Harel, Tim Sommers, Patrick Durning, and John Tomasi, and for valuable research assistance from Anne Fujimoto.

2. Civility is explicitly presented as politeness in Mark Kingwell, *A Civil Tongue: Justice, Dialogue, and the Politics of Pluralism* (University Park: Pennsylvania State Univ. Press, 1995), and Stephen L. Carter, *Civility: Manners, Morals, and the Etiquette of Democracy* (New York: Basic Books, 1998).

3. See Lynn Sanders, "Against Deliberation," *Political Theory* 25 (June 1997): 247; Iris Young, "Activist Challenges to Deliberative Democracy" (paper presented at a conference on "Deliberating about Deliberative Democracy," University of Texas, Austin, February 3–4, 2000).

4. Benjamin DeMott, "Seduced by Civility," *Nation*, December 9, 1996; Randall Kennedy, "State of the Debate: The Case against Civility?" (review of Carter, *Civility*), *American Prospect* 41 (Nov.–Dec. 1998): 84.

5. John Rawls, "Idea of Public Reason Revisited," *The Law of Peoples* (Cambridge, Mass: Harvard Univ. Press, 1999), 136.

6. Alexander Meiklejohn, *Political Freedom* (New York: Harper, 1960).

7. One's duties as a citizen might, for all I say here, often be outweighed or overruled by other moral considerations, but I will be supposing that citizens, as such, are subject to certain moral constraints, among them civility properly understood. My question is how properly to understand civility.

8. See David Evans, "Heckled in Columbus," *Columbus Free Press*, Feb. 25, 1998.

9. The CNN broadcast was titled, "Showdown with Iraq: An International Town Meeting." Video of complete proceedings can be viewed on the World Wide Web at http://www.cnn.com/WORLD/9802/18/town.meeting.folo/index.html. A complete transcript is available on Nexis, transcript 98021801V54.

What follows is a brief press account of the event, from the *Atlanta Journal and Constitution* of February 19, 1998:

SHOWDOWN OVER IRAQ; Policy pitch meets flak; Civics lesson turns uncivil as protesters at town hall meeting voice their doubts—loudly. Bob Deans; Columbus, Ohio: President Clinton's national security team tried Wednesday to use live, talk show television to tell the American heartland why UNITED STATES warplanes are poised to bomb Iraq, but the message repeatedly was drowned out by boisterous opponents and the forum listed toward disarray. U.S. Secretary of State Madeleine Albright scarcely had opened the program—a 90-minute "town meeting" aired live internationally by CNN—before her voice was overwhelmed by dozens of protesters. "One, two, three, four, we don't want your racist war," they shouted, in a chant that was picked up by scores of sympathizers seated around St. John Arena at Ohio State University. "No blood for oil," one protester shouted as Albright, silenced by catcalls for several minutes, made a tense appeal for quiet. "We came to listen, and we will," she said as university security guards and State Department aides tried to restore order. "But I would appreciate the opportunity of making my statement." Secretary of Defense William Cohen and National Security Adviser Sandy Berger, both of whom followed Albright with attempts to explain the threat Iraq's chemical and biological weapons pose to global security, also were forced to ask for the floor. "Walt Whitman said he heard America singing," Cohen said. "I hope we can hear America singing, and not shouting." But his appeal was met with another chant: "Iraqi children are under attack; what are we doing acting like that?" The most vocal criticism was leveled at Albright, and at one point she responded with a challenge of her own. "I am willing to make a bet with anyone here," she said, "that we care more about the Iraqi people than Saddam Hussein does." Doubters, however, were manifest.

10. David Evan, "Heckled."

11. Trish (no last name given) quoted by David Evans, "Heckled."

12. Herbert Marcuse, "Repressive Tolerance," in *A Critique of Pure Tolerance*, ed. Robert Paul Wolff, Barrington Moore, Jr., and Herbert Marcuse (Boston: Beacon Press, 1969).

13. I limit the definition of civility to nonviolent behavior only because it would be absurd to call violence "civil behavior." Yet uncivil behavior might be justified in some cases, and I discuss this question below.

14. I believe Carter *(Civility)* misses the relevance of Marcuse to the topic of civility, dismissing his critique of pure tolerance with a one-liner: "Its popularity is easy to understand because it allows us to win without actually bothering to argue against those who disagree with us" (214). By failing to engage any of Marcuse's arguments (which Carter does briefly repeat) for private acts of suppression under certain social conditions, Carter unfortunately neglects the power these arguments might have for supporting nonsuppressive political activity of questionable civility. Carter laments (with Marcuse) the dominance of market reasoning, but he never considers the question whether a narrow civility might cement this unfortunate status quo. Carter asserts that Marcuse "simply failed to hit upon religious revival as the solution" (214).

15. John Stuart Mill, *On Liberty* (any edition).

16. Marcuse, "Repressive Tolerance," 89.

17. Marcuse speaks of "freedom of thought and expression as preconditions of finding the way to freedom" (88). While he never clearly says that tolerance would promote truth under proper conditions, the structure of his argument seems to assume this, at least for the sake of argument. He argues that, in any case, the conditions under which pure tolerance might be thought to support truth do not obtain.

18. Marcuse, "Repressive Tolerance," 90.

19. "CNN Reliable Sources," Feb. 21, 1998, broadcast Saturday at 6:30 P.M. Eastern Standard Time, transcript 98022100V50 (available on Nexis).

20. "Many Doubts That Polls Don't Show," *Boston Globe*, Feb. 22, 1998.

21. For an attribution of these motives, see Ann Hodges, "White House Sends Message to Iraq in CNN-Staged Town Meeting," *Houston Chronicle*, Feb. 20, 1998. Indeed, there are signs of a disturbing working relationship between the U.S. government and CNN, including the employment of officers from army psychological operations units at CNN headquarters during the Kosovo war in 1999. See Alexander Cockburn, "CNN and PSYOPS," *Counterpunch*, March 26, 2000.

22. Of course, reason could itself be called a kind of power. A deeper objection would be to claim that reason, as power, is not normatively less objectionable than any other. That sort of critique cannot be considered here.

23. Jürgen Habermas, *Moral Consciousness and Communicative Action* (Cambridge, Mass.: MIT Press, 1990), 67.

24. See Carter (note 14, above) for a clear example of this.

25. I discuss the application of these points to the question of the distribution of political influence in "Political Quality," *Social Philosophy and Policy* 17 (Winter 2000): 127–60.

26. Jon Carroll wrote in the *San Francisco Chronicle* of February 6, 1998, "At the moment, almost every talking head not actually employed by the government of Iraq agrees that the bombing of Iraq is inevitable, that diplomatic solutions are sure to fail, that Saddam Hussein and his 'weapons of mass destruction' must be stopped." (For his own part, Carroll argued against this consensus.) David Cortright holds that protests and other peace activism, especially the Ohio State action, significantly contributed to averting war; see "A Victory for Peace," March 1, 1998, available on the World Wide Web at http://www.webcom.com/peaceact/VictoryForPeace.htm.

27. David Evans, "Heckled."

28. See David Paletz and William Harris, "Four Letter Challenges to Authority," *Journal of Politics* 37 (Nov. 1975): 955–79.

29. Robert Post discusses civility's value for making public discourse possible in ways like this. See his *Constitutional Domains* (Cambridge, Mass.: Harvard Univ. Press, 1995), especially chapter 4. Since disruptive or aggressive actions have such costs, it would be natural to permit wider standards of civility only when they have some reasonable chance of success in remedying the breakdown to some extent. This point cannot be pursued here.

30. "Showdown with Iraq."

31. For discussion of views of civil disobedience as speech, see Clyde Frazier, "Between Obedience and Revolution," *Philosophy and Public Affairs* 1 (Spring 1972): 315–34. For an influential and elaborated example, see John Rawls, *A Theory of Justice* (Cambridge, Mass.: Harvard Belknap Press, 1971), chap. 6.

32. It has sometimes been argued that civil disobedience is protected expression under the First Amendment even though it involves intentional violation of the law. For discussion of one such case see Carl Cohen, "Law, Speech, and Disobedience," in *Nation*, March 28, 1966, 357–62 (reprinted in *Civil Disobedience*, ed. H. Bedau [New York: Pegasus, 1969]). Few who have said that civil disobedience is a form of address or expression have claimed that it is therefore constitutionally protected on freedom-of-expression grounds, and none of my points here depend on this legal issue.

33. Robert Post, "Reconciling Theory and Doctrine in First Amendment Jurisprudence," forthcoming in *California Law Review* 89 (January 2001).

34. Armstrong said later that the motive was to trigger a political trial in which the government could be called to account for its conduct of the war in Vietnam. See this interview with him in Glen Silber and Alexander Brown, *Vietnam: The War at Home,* 1979 (distributed by MPI Home Video beginning in 1986).

35. Ted Honderich argues that political violence can sometimes be a form of address and so "shares an attribute with activity that its integral to the democratic practice." See his "Democratic Violence," *Philosophy and Public Affairs* 2 (Winter 1973): 190–214, esp. 211.

36. CNN, "Showdown with Iraq."

Whose Power? Which Rationality?
Response to Estlund

MICHAEL BYRON

Philosophy, Kent State University

In "Deliberation Down and Dirty," David Estlund seeks a deeper understanding of that most American of political paradoxes: regulated free speech. To that end, he sketches a normative basis for an intuitively appealing idea. The idea is that the boundaries of civility in political expression are proportional to power's interference with reason. That is, the more that power undermines the conditions of free and orderly political expression, the wider the scope of what should count as "civil" expression, perhaps including even violence.

Estlund explicates his account with three important claims. First, democratic deliberation fosters what he calls the "social discovery of truth." The epistemic value of such deliberation is the primary rationale for narrow norms of civility, since sharp political expression would be counterproductive in circumstances of ideal deliberation. Second, when the conditions of democratic deliberation are undermined in specific ways, the scope of civility widens. Estlund calls this a "breakdown" account of civility: when open deliberation breaks down (though this is, Estlund realizes, a matter of degree), formerly uncivil measures become civil. Third, permissible sharp expression aims to restore the conditions of narrow civility. Sharp expression when civil is thus remedial, since it must aim to recreate the circumstances of free and open deliberation. These three claims form the heart of Estlund's account of civil expression, and I would like to explore each of them in turn.

The first claim is that "democratic deliberation can improve democratic decisions," presumably by providing a tolerant forum for the free exchange of ideas and perspectives. Estlund approvingly cites Mill and Marcuse, who agree that widespread tolerance is "among the set of conditions that are most favorable to the social discovery of truth." The point seems to be that where many alternative views contend publicly and freely, people are most likely to take the best decisions. Whatever its other virtues, then, democratic deliberation's salient characteristic seems to be its epistemic value, which is to say its capacity to foster the social discovery of truth.

Estlund probably does not mean that democratic deliberation yields the "truth" about how to live. Liberal political theorists more commonly seek to provide institutions and practices for making decisions in the absence of a widely shared conception of the good. So we should ask him to explain more about the sort of truth democratic deliberation helps society discover. That explanation should take into account some further facts about deliberation. One is that deliberation, strictly so called, is about what promotes ends—either means to ends or what would count as attaining an end. Deliberation in this narrower sense does not choose ends. Political disagreement, however, is often about the ends themselves, and so merely knowing how to attain divergent and incompatible ends—one kind of truth discovered by deliberation—will not in general resolve political disagreements.

Moreover, the sustained dialectical argument that *can* resolve disagreements about ends (in ways that do not involve force or fraud) depends on systematic appeals to some conception of the good. Yet democratic theorists attempt to rule out appeals to comprehensive accounts of the good, on grounds of tolerance and pluralism. In practice, of course, liberal political theory itself embodies a distinctive account of the good, and this account grounds most practical agreements that actually emerge. Hence, in a pluralistic society whose citizens do not share a conception of the good, free and open discussion does not promise to resolve political disagreements except through the covert imposition of liberal political theory's own conception of the good. What remains to be shown is that this means of resolving political disputes is correctly to be described as "the social discovery of truth."

Now consider the second claim: to the extent that political, economic, military, or other institutional power operates in ways that undermine reason as embodied in democratic deliberation, the scope of civility widens—so, at any rate, Estlund seems to suggest with his account of the "International Town Hall." Beyond the commonplace that "power is always interfering with reason"—to some degree or other, but always perniciously—Estlund's rhetoric lines up fiercely against this phenomenon. He writes, "The more permissive standard [of civility] is defended on the grounds that this might countervail the *antirational* effect of the initial *pollution* of the discourse by systemic power that *irrationally* favors one side" (my emphasis). The presupposition throughout seems to be that democratic deliberation, when free from the distorting influences of power, yields a better result than alternative modes of decision making. This empirical claim links the breakdown account of wider civility to the first claim about rational deliberation being a means to discovering truth. Two recent events challenge the empirical claim.

Consider first Algeria, where in 1991 the Islamic Salvation Front (FIS), having dominated local elections the previous year, won the first round of general elections and was poised to create an Islamic state. The military forced the liberal president to resign, discontinued the elections, and suspended the parliament. Here is a clear instance of power interfering with the democratic process: the vast majority of Algerians wanted a conservative, nonliberal Islamic state. Since 1992, the military has reinstituted democratic rule, and a new president was elected in a multiparty election last year. The FIS boycotted the election, which they claimed was rigged, and indeed six of the seven candidates withdrew prior to the election for the same reason. Nonetheless, many liberals might applaud the Algerian military's resistance to the FIS, on the ground that the military at least intended to restore democratic deliberation. That is, power interfered with reason in order to preserve it.

The situation is reminiscent of Rousseau's idea in *The Social Contract* that one could be forced to be free (I, VII). Rousseau, of course, envisions a lone dissenter from the general will who must be forced to be free; the case of Algeria suggests that the outcome of democratic processes need not be democratic or even liberal. The same antiliberal outcome may yet emerge from the recent elections in Austria, where Jörg Haider's Freedom Party won 27 percent of the vote, second only to the Social Democrats' 33 percent. Haider is notorious for his remarks that Hitler had "sound employment policies" and that veterans of the Nazi SS were "men of character"; yet his party has joined the government. Suppose Haider himself had not resigned; suppose that he had quietly joined the government and become more popular; and suppose that the Freedom Party swept the next elections in Austria. I imagine that the liberal international community would call for nothing less than "power interfering with reason," at least in the sense of not allowing a democratically elected Haider to lead Austria.

What is wrong with these Austrians and Algerians? Don't they see that they are aiming their countries away from democratic deliberation? Don't they value the "social discovery of truth?" Liberals tread carefully here, as it won't do to criticize the "values" of other cultures. At the same time, it seems presumptuous to claim that such people have their facts wrong. To what else can democratic deliberators appeal? These cases put liberals in an awkward position, since the outcomes are at once democratic and antiliberal. They foist a dilemma on Estlund in particular: if power's interference with reason is always wrong, then it seems he should support the democratic yet antiliberal outcomes in Algeria and Austria and condemn interference there with the democratic process. On the other hand, if power's interference with reason is not always wrong, then the rationale for widening the scope of civil expression goes by the board, and we have further grounds for doubting that deliberation fosters the discovery of truth.

Finally, I have a brief question about the third claim, that sharp political expression under widened norms of civility must aim to ameliorate the political situation in order that the narrower norms might again apply. The question is simply, why must sharp political expression aim for this goal? Why not for more concrete goals, such as stopping the bombing of Iraq? Or for more abstract goals, such as consciousness raising or increased political participation? Estlund seems to want sharp political expression to be a self-consuming artifact, such that if it succeeds then it will quietly disappear. But beyond the suggestion that narrower norms are more desirable, by virtue of the desirability of the ideal conditions of deliberation under which those norms apply, it is not quite clear why civil yet sharp political expression ought to be remedial in the specified sense.

Estlund's inventive account of the shifting norms of civility strives to accommodate sharp political expression within an orderly democratic society. His view inherits its flaws from the political theory in which it resides: liberal assumptions about the universality of deliberative rationality fare poorly on empirical examination. People reason differently about what to do, and their modes of reasoning are embedded in diverse ways of life and accompanying conceptions of the good. To declare those modes and those conceptions moot for the sake of liberal procedural ideals may amount to "deliberation down and dirty," but doing so can hardly be expected to yield noncontroversially rational political decisions. And in that case, we should perhaps be suspicious of the liberal presumption in favor of narrow norms of civility, together with their promise of the "social discovery of truth."

Civility or Justice?

Response to Estlund

LADELLE MCWHORTER

Philosophy, University of Richmond

Too often, academic discussion of political and moral issues is framed in terms far removed from any questions that ever face individual citizens. We engage students and colleagues in endless debates over the morality of legalized abortion, capital punishment, or certain forms of discrimination, but we seldom ask them—or, I fear, ourselves—what it is that we ought to *do*—that is, how I as an individual citizen ought to conduct myself in light of the fact that abortion is legal in this country or that convicted criminals are executed in my state or that the evidence suggests that banks in my region discriminate against African-American loan applicants. Academics, acting in our professional capacities, rarely frame political and moral questions in terms of "What ought I to do?" By avoiding raising questions in those terms, I suspect that we not only let ourselves off the hook, morally and politically speaking, but also contribute to the conceptual erasure of what some philosophers have called "practical reason"—deliberation that results not in belief (or not merely in belief) but in action.

I want to begin by thanking Professor Estlund for raising his question in individualized, personal terms and for giving us a concrete example of a political action that every person in this room might at some time be in a position to undertake. Professor Estlund's question is: "What kinds of restraint ought I to exercise in my political expression?" He helps us think through this question by considering the kinds of restraint exercised by antiwar protesters at the "International Town Meeting" at Ohio State University in February 1998. This, it seems to me, is a very productive and intellectually honest way to approach a very difficult politico-theoretical and moral issue.

At the conclusion of Professor Estlund's paper, I find myself willing to accept his claim that under certain conditions one remains within the bounds of civility even though one may exceed the bounds of courtesy and perhaps even, in a limited sense, tolerance. I am convinced that the actions of the protesters at Ohio State, for example, were civil and civilly responsible. Nevertheless, despite my appreciation of his approach and my agreement with his conclusion, I am troubled by some aspects of Professor Estlund's analysis.

In order to get at what troubles me, I want to set out Professor's Estlund's argument in outline form. Although he doesn't lay it out this way, I believe his argument runs pretty much like this:

1. The purpose of democratic deliberation is production (or discovery) of truth.
2. Reason is the means by which truth is produced (or discovered).
3. Typically, power interferes with the exercise of reason (and hence with truth production/discovery); so power's presence is best kept to a minimum.
4. When power's influence is at an acceptably low level, civility (narrowly defined) is conducive to production of truth.
5. When power's level of influence is high, however, civility (narrowly defined) is not conducive to production of truth, so the boundaries of civility may be widened. This widening is justified, because it serves the principal purpose of democratic deliberation, namely, producing truth.

I have concerns about several aspects of this argument, but I am going to focus my comments on the first premise, that the purpose of democratic deliberation is the production or discovery of truth.

I take this first premise to be normative rather than descriptive. If descriptive, it is false; some would assert, "No, the purpose of most people's deliberation is personal gain," and indeed they would probably be right. But I think what Professor Estlund means to say is that when we engage in public, political deliberation, our main purpose *ought to be* to help produce or discover truth.

A legitimate question to ask Professor Estlund at this point would be: Why? Why should we aim to help produce truth when we engage in public deliberation? One answer that could be offered is a simple historical account of the practice of democratic deliberation; the practice—including the skills involved, the procedural rules, the legal safeguards that have been put in place—came into existence as a means for producing truth. The purpose of democratic deliberation is truth production, in the same sense that the purpose of hammers is nail pounding. Democratic deliberation is a tool invented to do a job, and that job is the production of truth. Another answer might be that the practice of democratic deliberation does not make sense in some basic way when it is undertaken for a goal other than truth production—as, for example, the practice of weaving thread just makes no sense, in some basic way, when it is undertaken for a goal other than cloth production.

Other answers might also be offered, and I would be interested to hear them. But in the meantime I will venture an alternative suggestion. It seems to me that the goal of democratic deliberation ought *not* to be truth. (Further, I would be willing to add that, historically, truth has not been its goal and that the practice makes perfect sense even when truth is not a goal.) Many philosophers have drawn a distinction between what they call speculative reason, on the one hand, and practical reason, on the other. The goal of speculative reason is knowledge, or justified true belief—in short, the goal of speculative reason is truth.[1] The goal of practical reason, however, is not true belief; it is right action. I believe the proper goal of democratic deliberation, which might be construed as a matter of practical rather than speculative reason, is right action—justice, not truth.

Let us look again at the actions of the Ohio State protesters. Professor Estlund's analysis, which foregrounds truth production, interprets their actions primarily as political *expression*; their aim in disrupting the International Town Meeting was to express their dissenting viewpoint. Not to have expressed their dissenting viewpoint would have created the false belief in the television audience that they, as participants in the meeting, supported the bombing of Iraq and the killing of Iraqi civilians. Therefore they felt compelled to stretch (and Professor Estlund maintains they were morally justified in stretching) the bounds of civility in order to be sure their voices were heard. But were the protesters most interested in making their opinions heard? Were they most interested in making sure that the TV audience formed the true belief that they opposed the war or that the war was wrong? I think not. I think their main concern was stopping the bombing of Iraq. I think their main objective was not to speak truth or avoid bearing false witness but to prevent what they perceived as a horrific injustice—the killing of innocent human beings. They acted in the service of justice. In the process they may have expressed truth— or deployed or exposed truth—but neither expression nor truth was the point; the point was to act to create conditions under which those who were about to perpetrate injustice would refrain from it.

I am suggesting, then, two analytical alterations: that we understand political expression as a species of political action and analyze it as action, and also that we understand the normative goal of public political action, including expressions of opinions and dissemination of information, as the pursuit of justice rather than of truth. To these two suggestions I want to add a third: that we redefine *power* in such a way that we do not see it as necessarily opposed to reason or truth—that we define *power* as action upon action.[2] In other words, to exercise power is to act with the intention of influencing how someone else will act. If we understand power in this way, we can analyze the International Town Meeting not as reason confronting power but as a power struggle, in which all parties were attempting to influence the actions of other parties, with the ultimate goal being to decide the corporate action—the "national" action, namely, that the United States would bomb Iraq, or not. One way—and often a very effective way—of acting upon other people's actions is to express opinions forcefully and bring new information to their attention. In other words, reason and power are not opposed; the exercise of reason is very often—and very fortunately—also an exercise of power.

What does this set of suggestions get us? Well, for one thing, it gets us this entirely new personal ethical question: "How might I exercise power to enact and promote justice?" If this is our question, we do not need to worry about whether we are being civil. Civility, however construed, is not at issue. What is at issue is civic responsibility, just action with regard to all concerned—our fellow citizens, elected officials, and the other people that our collective actions may affect. It seems to me the protesters at Ohio State found a good answer to that question. They acted with as much respect toward their political opponents as possible, while doing what they could to pressure those in control of the bombs to withhold the order to drop them. If instead of worrying about civility we worry about civic responsibility, the Ohio State protesters were exemplary.

NOTES

1. This distinction crops up in the work of many philosophers. For our discussion here it is significant that it comes up in classical liberal and Enlightenment thinkers such as Immanuel Kant and John Locke. Locke mentions the distinction without elaborating on it, presumably because it was a commonplace, in the first book of his *Essay Concerning Human Understanding*. See Book I, chapter 3, paragraph 3.

2. This is not my innovation. It is Michel Foucault's. See for example, the afterword in Hubert Dreyfus and Paul Rabinow, *Michel Foucault: Beyond Structuralism and Hermeneutics,* 2d ed. (Chicago: Univ. of Chicago Press, 1983), 220. There Foucault says, "What defines a relationship of power is that it is a mode of action which does not act directly and immediately on others. Instead it acts upon their actions: an action upon an action, on existing actions or on those which may arise in the present or the future."

Deliberation and Wide Civility
Response to the Discussants

David M. Estlund

The shootings at Kent State have little to do with the First Amendment, but they have everything to do with freedom of expression more broadly conceived.[1] Political repression often begins in disapproval. Dissent always risks disapproval and opposition on substantive grounds, but disruptive and disturbing tactics of dissent only magnify this risk. If sharp and disruptive tactics of political expression are widely thought to be irresponsible and despicable, repression—through social pressure or law or violence—is likely to follow. In "Deliberation Down and Dirty" (in this volume) my topic is not the standard free speech question of when interference with speech is permissible but when sharp and disruptive speech itself is permissible. My hypothesis is that there are moral standards of civility in political expression but that they can accommodate much vigorous, disruptive, disturbing, embarrassing, and even illegal expressive activity. I develop this idea partly by reflecting not on the events at Kent State in 1970 but on another event at an Ohio campus just a few years ago, the inaptly titled "International Town Meeting." I do not address the protests and shootings at Kent State directly, but my aim is partly to see whether a better theory of civility might help prevent the impulse toward repression from finding a foothold in moral disapproval.

Before replying to several of the points raised by the commentators, it is useful to divide my claims into three stages. At the most general level, I propose what I call a "breakdown account" of civility. On a view of this form, more permissive standards of civility would be triggered by the breakdown or failure of certain background conditions, the conditions in which the narrower standards of civility would indeed apply. I call these the "circumstance of (narrow) civility." A breakdown account guards against the temptation to think that the conditions in which narrow civility would be required are typically met under real conditions.

A second stage in my account, then, is to suggest that the conditions in which narrow civility applies (I call these the "circumstances of civility") might be drawn from an account of what the point of narrow civility is. I suggest that at least one of its central points is, broadly speaking, epistemic. Narrow civility makes sense because (and when) it promotes the goal of public political deliberation with some capacity for wisely determining what ought to be done. But this epistemic goal will not be achieved by the practice of narrow civility unless other conditions are met as well. A focus on the epistemic aim directs our attention to the background conditions that would be required in order for narrow civility actually to promote wise decisions, and without which narrow civility loses its point.

In a third stage, I suggest that among the circumstances of narrow civility is a background in which power is not interfering with reason. If power is interfering with reason in certain ways, narrow civility merely cements the epistemic damage this involves, whereas certain wider, more permissive standards of behavior might allow the power imbalance to be partially remediated. Under defective distributions of power, narrow civility loses its point, but civility of a wider kind, with limits of its own, seems the natural replacement.

I divide the account into these stages partly in order to show that the earlier stages do not depend on the later ones. Even if the power/reason account of the circumstances of narrow civility, or the epistemic account of the point of civility, is ultimately inadequate, the general form of a breakdown account might yet be the right direction for an account of civility to take.

Professors Byron and McWhorter both wonder whether a remedial view of disruptive or disturbing expressive tactics places implausible restrictions on political agents. Does a protester's aim have to be the establishment of the circumstances of narrow civility, rather than, say, the promotion of social justice, or even the simple expression of moral outrage? My suggestion is that the wider standards of civility would be supported by the remedial effects of generally accepted wider standards under certain defective conditions. The resulting standards apply to actions, not motives. If narrow civility has an epistemic point, then wide civility gains a natural basis under conditions in which narrow civility harms, or at least no longer serves, that purpose. The wider standards of permissible action, then, have a remedial basis, but the actions they permit need not be remedially motivated.[2]

When Kent State students gathered at noon on May 4, 1970, most of them were behaving civilly in the narrow sense, but after they were ordered to disperse by the National Guard their presence was certainly defiant and possibly illegal.[3] On my view, wide standards of civility might have applied in these circumstances (for example, governmental efforts to repress dissent about the Vietnam War). If so, the students' defiant refusal to disperse (which I regard as primarily expressive) was permitted even by the duty of civility. None of this depends on whether the participants aimed to remedy the imbalance of power with respect to the public debate about the war. The motives of the students seem to have been diverse and partly mysterious: to protest the invasion of Cambodia, to protest the presence of the National Guard on campus, to express contempt for existing authority structures generally, to show solidarity with fellow students who had more primary motives, et cetera.[4] Even though some motives for disruptive expression would be morally wrong,[5] the standards of civility I propose apply to actions rather than motives. Moreover, there would be a variety of permissible motives for engaging in the kinds of behavior that would be permitted under the applicable wide standards of civility, though I make no specific proposal about the limits of permissible motives.

In sum, the view that wide civility is based on its ability to remedy a certain kind of breakdown does not place implausibly restrictive moral constraints on the motives of political actors.

In the short space remaining I can address only briefly some points the commentators have made about my normative approach to democracy. Professor McWhorter questions whether it is useful to think of democratic participation in terms of the use of theoretical or "speculative" reason rather than as a use of power, in accord with practical reason. I agree with her that public reasoning is a species of social power, but that would not yet show that an adequate account of democratic legitimacy could proceed wholly in terms of power. As Professor McWhorter would grant, might does not make right. She proposes that we conceive proper democratic participation as the exertion of power in the interest of justice, something I accept as far as it goes. What this would not yet give us is any account of why the results of such a procedure are normally authoritative over all citizens, even those who doubt the justice of the results. One might try saying that this authority derives from the fairness of a procedure in which each has an equal chance to exert power. But a coin flip is also entirely fair to participants, in giving them all equal shares of power, and yet it is absurd to think a coin flip gives all citizens any significant reason to submit to the law. I doubt, then, that an adequate account of legitimacy will be possible without incorporating some tendency of democratic processes to arrive at good decisions, and I do not see how to do this without bringing in epistemic properties of public reasoning.[6]

Professor Byron doubts the epistemic approach to democracy, on the grounds that democratic choices can be disastrously wrong. He also detects a kind of liberalism in my view that I gather he opposes and thinks to be inconsistent with my epistemic approach to democracy. I will not take up his challenge to a certain kind of political liberalism here, partly because there is already a vast literature on the points he raises, and partly because the main points in my account of civility seem to be separable from such a view.[7] As for the fact that democratic decisions can be seriously wrong and even sharply antiliberal, surely no one denies it. Epistemic approaches to democracy vary as to their response.[8] Some, such as Rousseau, would apparently say that democratic results have no legitimate authority when they are mistaken. Other views, such as the one I have defended elsewhere, and which I call "epistemic proceduralism," hope to ground democratic authority not on the actual correctness of each authoritative decision but on a certain, admittedly very imperfect, epistemic value of the deliberative democratic procedure. On this view, decisions can be legitimate even when mistaken, though some mistakes would be so profound as to lack legitimacy on such special, narrow grounds as violations of certain basic rights. Also, nothing in such a view entails that all or any existing democratic procedures meet the requirements for producing legitimate law. That would be a separate question, and one that is likely to yield sharp criticism of many existing arrangements.

I hope the epistemic approach to sharp and disruptive political expression that I have suggested can be integrated with this broader theory of democratic legitimacy. But I also hope that it has some value, at least at one or another of its three stages, even apart from these broader theoretical commitments.

NOTES

1. I am very grateful to Ladelle McWhorter and Michael Byron for their thoughtful comments, and I regret that I cannot address all of their points in this short space.

2. Rawls argues that civil disobedience ought to be carried out only when there is a reasonable chance of actually fixing the injustice that is the target. This conclusion should depend on whether a reasonable person could accept the permissibility of the practice only under that condition, something I am inclined to doubt. It seems likely to vary from one kind of protest to another. This also seems the way to handle a similar condition on other political expression that goes beyond narrow civility. Often there is no need to ensure that it will make a significant difference, though in some cases and contexts such a requirement may well be appropriate.

3. Peter Davies argues that the gathering was lawful and peaceful until the National Guard intervened and that the guard had no legal authority to order the protesters to disperse. Peter Davies, *The Truth about Kent State* (New York: Farrar Straus Giroux, 1973), 31–32.

4. These leave aside the many students who were apparently simply moving between classes or had been drawn by the spectacle, because students in these latter categories would not be engaging in expression. Perhaps a more important application of the concept of wide civility to the Kent State case would concentrate on events of the previous few days, events that might have fostered an environment of strong disapproval of the student protesters. But these earlier events involved burning the ROTC building and smashing windows of downtown stores, actions that could not be called civil even in a wide sense, though this would not settle whether they were justifiable. The backlash effects of disruptive or illegal expression must always be reckoned in determining their permissibility, and the chance of an unjust repressive state response is often among the possible consequences to consider. I thank Kathy Jenni for raising this point.

5. Suppose some students had sought to provoke the National Guard into shooting so as to help turn public opinion against the state. I have no reason to believe this was the motive of anyone present that day.

6. I discuss these matters at length in "Beyond Fairness and Deliberation: The Epistemic Dimension of Democratic Authority," in *Deliberative Democracy*, ed. James Bohman and William Rehg (Cambridge, Mass.: MIT Press, 1997).

7. For example, Mill does not adhere to the brand of political liberalism I would defend, which derives mainly from Rawls (see, e.g., his *Political Liberalism* [New York: Columbia Univ. Press, 1993]). Yet I do not see how this would block a Millean from accepting anything in my account of civility.

8. I discuss the points in this paragraph at greater length in Estlund, "Beyond Fairness."

4

Violent Expressions of Freedom
Narratives of Social Order and Disorder
in Contemporary U.S. Media

J. David Slocum

Grdauate School of Arts and Sciences, New York University

Popular understandings of violence turn on the context provided by narratives: media narratives that represent social conflicts and anxieties and the resolutions appropriate for them; narratives in media as well as the actual world that give violent incidents their meaning and even legitimation; conflicting cultural narratives that negotiate individual identities and social order and norms; and narratives that give shape to laws and economic practices. Even accounts *of* media—including new media and cyberspace—and their regulation rely on narrative structures; that is, the way that violent content in communications and entertainment media is defined and then limited or constrained emerges largely through narrative framing. In fact, as a symbolic form, narrative promises to continue shaping our organization and understanding of new media technologies and cyberspace and, consequently, our comprehension of violence. The scholarly subfield of legal narratology has increasingly sought to explicate the significance and implications of storytelling forms and patterns in legal and statutory practice.[1] That inquiry is especially relevant today as new technologies and cyberspace develop rapidly, and as efforts to regulate them legally, economically, technologically, and socially continue to evolve.

SYMBOLIC FORMS AND MEDIA REGULATION

The episode of U.S. media regulation best known to the public is almost certainly that of motion pictures in the late 1920s and early 1930s. Coinciding with the arrival of sound cinema technology and the onset of the Great Depression, this episode featured public outcry over the sexual permissiveness of "fallen women" films and Mae West, or over the glorification of criminality in gangster movies. By 1934, the film industry had established means for self-regulation of content through a Motion Picture Production Code, enforced by an office overseen by Will H. Hays. At the time and for decades following, the film industry itself and its chroniclers lent detail to, but mounted no critique of, this recounting of the code's emergence. Only more recently, as film historian Richard Maltby argues, have these "official" accounts been critiqued for following the narrative structure of a Hollywood melodrama, with Will Hays as a crusader fighting the turpitude of filmmakers and finally triumphing in the name of moral decency and popular will.[2] The conclusion is that this earlier account of regulation was itself marketed by Hollywood in order to affirm its concern for prevailing social values and, finally, to protect and consolidate its commercial enterprise.

Accounts of the regulation of radio draw similar conclusions. Radio technology proliferated during the first two decades of the twentieth century and enjoyed an immense range of uses by individuals and groups of various sizes and political inclinations. Following the end of the First World War, public concern over the variety of political expression, coupled with an expansion of governmental regulation, brought increasing attention to radio content and, especially, the communication sector through which it was delivered. Then, in the late 1920s, as Robert McChesney has shown, corporate interests saw the potential for profit in network operation and commercial advertising of radio. A contest erupted between those in favor of commercialization and reformers wanting to preserve open access to airwaves, as well as a range of broadcasting alternatives. The primary result was the passage of the Communications Act of 1934, which established the Federal Communications Commission and authorized it to regulate broadcasting.[3] Having successfully argued that commercial broadcasting was inherently democratic in affording the public an opportunity to respond freely, as consumers, corporate radio operators embraced government regulation as a triumph of American values.

Accounts of radio regulation also speak to the emergence of broadcast television after the Second World War. Both McChesney and Susan Smulyan, writing independently, note that the commercialization of radio as institutionalized in network broadcasting paved the way for corporate interests to develop television as a commercial medium. By the late 1940s, and especially after the FCC's spectrum-allocation plan was adopted in 1952, social and political attention to content were the overriding concerns of regulators.[4] These regulatory efforts, such as those encouraged by Senator Estes Kefauver to address the allegedly harmful effects of programming content on juvenile delinquents, were celebrated for highlighting the industry's sensitivity to popular values and partnership with government.

Accounts of newspaper regulation in the twentieth century are different, of course. While syndicates emerged in the early decades, the significance of corporate consolidation and technological innovation was distinct from that of other media; perhaps most important was the locus of regulation, the "print model" of the First Amendment affording as it does a "hands-off policy" to be enforced by the judiciary rather than a government agency like the FCC. Accounts from the 1970s and 1980s of newspapers and journalism nevertheless contain elements that correspond to the regulation of other media. For example, "objectivity," long a guiding standard of newspapers and the measure by which the ascension of late nineteenth- and twentieth-century reporting could be celebrated, fell under scrutiny.[5] Like the self-propagated moral concerns underlying the Motion Picture Production Code, objectivity and independence served as organizational principles for accounts of newspaper industry self-regulation. Even more, because these principles were linked to the idea of unfettered public discussion—of "a marketplace of ideas"—presupposed by the First Amendment, they implicitly linked that self-regulation to predominant social values.

A number of shared tendencies emerge from these accounts of twentieth-century media regulation. First, all these accounts were produced during the last three decades, a period in which the linguistic (and later, for some, cultural) turn brought great attention to narrative. Scrutiny brought to bear on narrative as a regnant but not inevitable mode of organizing experience raised questions about previous accounts of institutional controversies and of regulatory efforts. James Carey wrote in 1974 of a "Whig history" that had long shaped journalism's sense of its own past and celebrated the evolution of the fourth estate.[6] Specifically, he challenged the traditional narratives at the root of journalism history—of progressive truth seeking, of "objectivity," of unabridged freedom of the press, of bearing the public trust—by piercing their symbolic value and submitting them to close and skeptical examination. At a time when other long-standing cultural and national narratives were called into question, Carey was among the students of media who revisited familiar histories of regulation and recast them as social constructions.

A second tendency of these accounts is the way in which they highlight the complexity of relationships between technology, media institutions, corporations, government, and the public, and then trace their consolidation. Regulation of media in this century has turned less on their content than their technology—especially as those technologies are institutionalized. McChesney's account of radio in the 1920s chronicles the shift from wide-ranging and varied public use of the technology to increasing commercial interest and conflict with public users, to the eventual triumph of corporate broadcasting with the support of the government. That progressive reformers and individual radio users eventually lost out becomes insignificant, however, in the predominant narrative of the media's development. More central is the establishment in 1934 of the Federal Communications Commission and the model of well-regulated commercial broadcasting that continues today.

The partnership between corporate media, which exemplifies the triumph of the free market, and the government, which represents the best interests of the public, serves in these accounts as a basis for media operation and regulation that is, on its face, thoroughly democratic.

A third tendency is recent historians' scrutiny of the institutional relationships underlying media, which corresponds to their close examination of the content of that media and popular culture. As scholars like McChesney *denaturalize* the corporate and governmental forces that continue to shape media systems and messages, they have sought to *demythify* the familiar symbolic forms and narratives that have been so central to the success of mainstream media and popular culture. One aspect of this demythification has involved the place of violence in U.S. society and culture. The Western movie genre, for instance, which constituted fully a quarter of Hollywood film production up to 1970, has accordingly been subject to self-conscious and deconstructive critiques that call attention to the intolerance, destructiveness, brutality, and even genocide integral to the genre's underlying myths of the frontier, heroic individualism, and community building. Even more, the narrative forms featured in films, television, and journalism—structured causally to resolve conflicts and to elucidate and perpetuate communal values—have been shown to rely on violent action and incidents for their very structure and movement. Violence, in short, has become in recent scholarship a fundamental structure and signifier of national culture and the media narratives that shape that culture.

Contrasting such claims by scholars is a fourth shared tendency, which sees public policy makers according priority to certain social and political concerns in the history of these media. As just noted, corporate consolidation and government oversight are important, but everyday accounts of media, especially, dwell on content and the negotiation of cultural values disseminated by the medium. While violence has moved to the center of some scholars' visions of American ideology and media history, in other words, it has typically remained for many others a political concern discrete from institutional conditions. For example, notwithstanding the arrival of sound technology, industry restructuring, and the rapprochement between the government and the studios in early 1930s Hollywood, the emphasis remained on the content of films, especially those featuring gangsters and fallen women. Taking precedence were public discussions about the morality and social effects of motion pictures that helped both to mark the limits of permissible film content and to define how the medium would regulate itself. Put differently, the concern becomes the productions and shape of the ideological superstructure rather than (as Maltby notes, in his analysis of the genesis of the Motion Picture Production Code) any sustained attention to the economic or industrial base.

The use of such Marxian language is not inappropriate. In fact, it is worth being explicit here about the term "regulation." Antonio Gramsci, an Italian writer imprisoned between 1929 and 1935, adapted and complicated Marx's ideas about the relationship between the economy and culture. He was the first to suggest, albeit generally, that there were intervening modes of regulation between economic production and the culture of consumption. The 1970s and 1980s saw the development of economic-regulation theories, by Michel Aglieta among others, asserting that every form of production requires a complementary form of consumption. In turn, and crucially, this complementarity requires a mode of moral and social regulation that is maintained and preserved through state, educational, and media institutions. Moral regulation operates in part to establish certain behaviors, identities, and practices as natural or normal and to mark others as unnatural or deviant. The result is an identifiable correspondence between historically specific regimes of production and consumption *and* the cultural forms and practices that operate within—but also sustain—them.[7]

Moral regulation can also be viewed from another related perspective. Since 1989 and its fervent efforts to comprehend and advance changes in Eastern European societies, the notion of "civil society" has enjoyed a renaissance. Originally developed by John Locke and Adam Ferguson in the late seventeenth century to refer to that realm of institutions and associations beyond the economy or the state, in the mid-nineteenth century the term was pejoratively associated with market capitalism by Marx. Today, following the writing of Jeffrey Alexander, John Keane, and others, the term has taken on new meaning. Civil society is a historically specific complex of institutions, customs, and discourses; it is a subsystem of society that includes media and communications institutions and is charged with the moral regulation of that society. Much of this regulation concerns the ongoing negotiation of boundaries between social order and disorder—that is, between legitimate and illegitimate violence or proper and improper expression.[8]

Theories of economic regulation and civil society are not immediately compatible, though their concerns overlap and recent theorists have sought to examine Gramsci's writings, especially, in the context of contemporary models of civil society.[9] I refer to both here, however, because of their shared focus on the broader dynamics among the state, economy, and culture-building institutions. Again, the precise roles of the state or of noninstitutional or nontraditional realms are subject to debate. Yet it is utterly crucial—for a fuller understanding of media regulation and free expression—to retain a broad view and to acknowledge the many parties and institutions that shape given media practices and inform media regulation. Especially important here is the cultural realm, which is regularly, as in the case of

Hollywood, the subject of public debates and controversies over media content but rarely included in more integrated models of media or its regulation. In fact, to reiterate, the public discourse addressing the morality or values of content in terms of scandal and controversy serves to displace necessarily related attention to economic and governmental concerns.

How does this cultural realm operate? As Jeffrey Alexander writes, "The language that forms the cultural core of civil society can be isolated as a general structure and studied as a relatively autonomous symbolic form."[10] That language constitutes a binary—or, for Alexander, "bifurcating"—discourse, in which elements are opposed in terms of whether they serve democratic or nondemocratic purposes. Pure, autonomous, and rational motivations for individual and social action in this way appear in contrast to the polluted, dependent, and hysterical. It is the contest between putatively democratic and nondemocratic individuals, groups, and behaviors that gives form and shape to civil society; the binary structure marks the boundaries of acceptable expression and positions its constituents vis-à-vis prevailing society and its norms.[11] In the process, language celebrating democracy and demonizing nondemocracy not only inscribes cultural productions and media but establishes social legitimacy and illegitimacy.

This symbolic form illuminates in part the preoccupation with violence in media policy and public debate. While numerous reasons have been adduced for media violence, many are variations on John Fiske's suggestion that it is a cultural response to perceived social pressures.[12] The precise correspondence between media violence and actual behavior is, of course, the nub of the debate. Cast in binary terms, social pressures are polluting and nondemocratic, threats to democracy and prevailing order. Violence in media is perceived as a break from norms of cultural production and, especially, conventional narrative. What makes that language all the more resonant is the widespread cultural connotation of violence as oppositional, nonconformist, and threatening—that is, a violation of rational norms for social association or narrative construction. Violence is an aberration, a break against which legitimate standards might be clarified and oppositional elements confirmed. It is also, nevertheless, a commonplace in cultural practice, precisely because its representation so effectively and familiarly punctuates narratives that convey the negotiation of social values and norms.

Focusing on violence underscores an important conceptual shift in the reformulation of regulation and, more specifically, censorship that has taken place over the last thirty years. No longer is regulation viewed simply as the unidirectional legal suppression of speech by the state; that traditional monopoly of power is now seen as having been dispersed and operating across multiple institutional and everyday practices.[13] Such operation recurs, moreover, throughout our everyday lives, continually marking the boundaries of free expression. In the words of Pierre Bourdieu, the structure of the cultural field itself circumscribes "both access to expression and the form of expression."[14] Regulation becomes productive, constructing knowledge and establishing the practices that help to define us as social subjects. It is no longer an exceptional practice aimed at curbing putatively deviant expression, like containing violence, but a normative one constituting the shape and boundaries of expression. Of course, in legal or political practice, efforts to suppress, rate, block, or establish standards have continued in traditional forms ranging from the film rating system to content advisories on television.[15] Yet it nevertheless remains necessary to acknowledge the broadening appreciation for the process of regulation as not merely descriptive but constitutive.[16]

In the United States in the twentieth century, civil society and, especially, its component media institutions have quite effectively produced and communicated consistent norms for expressions of violence in media. Using Ronald Jacobs's words, "The semiotic code is organized around the sacred signs of rational and controlled motivations, open and trusting relationships, and impersonal, rule-regulated institutions."[17] The predominant symbolic form in which these signs circulate is narrative, which helps individuals and groups to understand their progress in moving toward democratic values and away from those opposed. "The basic plot of civil society," Jacobs writes plainly, "is the story of integration, participation, and citizenship"—and, we might add, the active repudiation of threats to community and individual rights.[18] The regulation of media violence relies on presuppositions of rational law and society underwritten by a discourse of liberty as well as by the continuity of a delimited semiotic code and symbolic forms. Narrative here performs a dual function: it serves as the form of expression through which instances of violence are contextualized and regulated, and it provides the basis for our understanding of those contexts as well as the rationale for social and cultural regulation. The result is a public discourse on media violence that tends to negotiate vociferously the moral norms of media content while avoiding close scrutiny of, or interference in, media practice.[19] Especially lacking is any serious reconciliation of the putatively democratic accountability of media systems with imperatives of the marketplace.[20]

This is not to claim that media systems are monolithic or that the narrative form operating through and around them is static. The specific processes of perpetuating narratives and myths of democracy and the manner of upholding rational and democratic norms change over time. But past accounts of media development have tended not to address fully the links between technological innovation and transformations in civil society, the state, and the economy; this has certainly been the case for models of the regulation of media. Beyond lip service to the novel capabilities of new technologies—especially for economic productivity and ease of communication—little attention is paid to the relationships between these media and our shared values of democratic access, rational public discourse, and freedom of expression. By extension, too little attention is paid to the links between the regulation of media and that of social meanings and norms.[21]

New media technologies have the potential to transform social norms and symbolic forms alike. From multimedia encyclopedias, CD-ROMs, and computer games to the Internet, the Web, and other realms of cyberspace, vast collections of data elements are structured in a particular way for access and organization. Most new media operate through technological architectures that combine a data structure and an algorithm—that is, an interface or sequence of operations that enables a user to order or experience data. These media rely more on fragmentary and open-ended investigations constructed through the active participation of consumers than on linear and self-contained narratives intended for more passive consumption. In his forthcoming *Language of New Media*, Lev Manovich documents the significance of database form in new media: "As a cultural form, database represents the world as a list of items and it refuses to order the list. In contrast, a narrative creates a cause-and-effect trajectory of seemingly unordered items (events)."[22] Narrative becomes only one method for the interactive ordering of data, and it makes exceptional both the linear story that prevailed in earlier media *and* the passivity characterizing its spectators.

Manovich is one of many theorists trying to make sense of the contest being waged today between new media and more traditional narrative-based forms. He claims, for instance, that "new media does not radically break with the past; rather, it distributes weight differently between the categories which hold culture together, foregrounding what was in the background, and vice versa." Janet Murray likewise draws links between characteristics of new and earlier media, but she does so in order to take a longer view, considering possible developments in new media narrative. In *Hamlet on the Holodeck,* she sees precedents of the "multiform story" so well suited to new media in the bardic oral tradition (based in improvisation and the lack of canonical versions) and in folk tales (involving multiple versions of a single core story). Character improvisation has roots for her in the *commedia dell'arte,* and the allure of interactive "agency" in new technologies is analogous to the participatory role of the jazz musician. Perhaps Murray's most important claim is that despite having initially provoked confusion and experimentation, contemporary innovations, like past breakthroughs in media technology, will eventually lead to greater stability and the adoption of storytelling conventions that integrate long-standing narrative tendencies with new ones.[23]

When Murray illuminates the present by reference to the revolutionary eras in which the printing press was invented and cinema was born, she makes the important point that technological innovation inevitably brings with it an initial period of exuberant confusion. Yet in that process she also sees a strong parallel between these media, and she perhaps inadvertently implies that the variety of media in use today is narrower than it actually is. The many media we tend to collapse under the umbrella term "new media" need to be understood as heterogeneous. The World Wide Web and e-mail may accordingly be most familiar to many, but they are hardly the only media with far-reaching cultural importance today. MUDS, MOOS, chat rooms, bulletin boards, computer games, CD-ROMS, and other online and virtual environments must be included despite their varied, shifting, and overlapping nature. Thus, even as we might postulate with Manovich the defining symbolic form of the database, or posit with Murray the gradual narrativizing of that form, it is necessary to remain cognizant of the multiple interactive technologies and media at the base of our discussion.

The status of narrative is crucial here, because of its importance in framing the meaning of violent incidents or spectacles. In older media especially, violent spectacle occurs within a linear story organized through well-honed narrative conventions. While an explosion, shooting, or fistfight may afford a transitory shock or visceral pleasure, in other words, the *meaning* of those events typically accrues from their place within the context and experience of a linear story. Furthermore, because popular media tend to structure stories in binary or bifurcated terms, violence marks, illuminates, and exaggerates the oppositions between terms. Even still images, Leo Bersani and Ulysse Dutoit have argued, contain a narrative dynamism, generated by the tension between their component elements, which conveys the prospect of violent conflict.[24] Briefly put, as narrativizing tendencies continue to alter the shape and storytelling conventions of cyberspace, the presence, perception, and meaning of violence there will likewise be affected.

Enlightenment and Romantic traditions are rife in recent accounts of technological transformation in cyberspace and the actual world: these include espousal of the values of individual expression, social reintegration, spiritual renewal, and liberal and democratic society.[25] Historically, this is predictable. New technologies, especially those that mediate communication and entertainment, have typically elicited responses that employ existing communal values, standards, and practices as benchmarks for celebrating or decrying prospects for the future. In fact, as David Nye has perceptively argued, technological innovations have traditionally been appropriated very quickly in contemporary contests over American identity and self-representation.[26] Also, despite certain challenges from post-Enlightenment or postmodern thinkers today, existing values and the narratives through which they are circulated and reinforced in culture continue to have far-reaching importance in cyberspace. The fundamental bifurcating discourse of civil society embraces democratic codes of participation, integration, and citizenship while repudiating purported threats to communal values and individual rights. This bifurcation and the narratives of opposition produced by it thus cannot but shape our understandings and experiences of our contemporary technologized society.

As far-reaching as are the challenges new media pose to narrative storytelling and the organization of information and experience, they are linked to other contemporary social and cultural transformations that go still farther. Civil society as it has been heretofore theorized is changing. This is true not only because of technological innovation; the more traditional economic and state institutions for which civil society afforded moral and cultural cohesion and regulation are themselves transforming. One of our foremost political economists, Manuel Castells, has written, "Current political systems are still based in organizational forms and political strategies of the industrial era, they have become politically obsolete, and their autonomy is being denied by the flows of information on which they depend. This is a fundamental source of the crisis of democracy in the Information Age."[27] Castells points to the loss of both political and economic sovereignty of the nation-state, the corresponding reconfiguration of global and local governance and communication, and the resulting dissolution of the shared identities afforded by nation, state, and other traditional organizational forms. Put simply, a crisis of legitimacy, of order amidst pluralism, currently besets individuals and societies alike.

Among the changes urged by Castells's characterization of the contemporary world is a better-coordinated approach to regulation, one that transcends the legal or governmental and addresses the increasingly transnational links between legal, social, economic, and technological conditions. This also echoes legal scholar Lawrence Lessig's argument that even as separate modalities of regulation constrain differently, they nevertheless interact. Lessig's four modalities—law, the market, social norms, and technological architecture—differ from Castells's and do not privilege cultural productions. He nevertheless calls for some of the same overarching reforms to the ways in which we address the concept of regulation and, in the process, shape cyberspace.[28] Lessig's valuable work seeks to expand and update existing legal and regulatory structures to accommodate new media; especially in the realm of freedom of expression, such debates have raised important issues about the relationships of these new technologies and practices to legal precedents and have produced fuller appreciation for the distinctiveness of contemporary media and society.

In practice, however, the links between new media and changes in civil society are left underexamined. Media coverage of the tragedy at Columbine demonstrated again the tendency to scapegoat individual media productions and, for the most part, avoid serious debate about contemporary media technologies and practices.

Even more, despite the recurrence of such tragedies, there seems little willingness to challenge traditional notions of a good and morally coherent civil society or to rework them in light of the far-reaching shifts taking place in culture today.[29] Henry Jenkins has insightfully commented that part of this avoidance and unwillingness stems from anxiety about new technologies and how they have altered the world (hence the initial focus at Columbine on the list of Web sites visited by the teenaged perpetrators).[30] This is hardly an unprecedented response; in an overview of reactions to new technological media of the last four centuries, Ithiel de la Sola Pool went so far as to note that regulation can be "seen as a technical necessity when [new] communications technologies emerge."[31]

A related change that induces anxiety in many in the United States is the perceived loss of sovereignty and privilege of the nation-state and the emergence of transnational and global forces. Narratives of nation, rooted in bifurcating discourses that privilege the democratic, rational, deliberative, and ordered, still exert a powerful influence on visions of new media and the new global order. Moreover, these narratives are inflected by myths of American exceptionalism, of individualism, of the democratic free market, and of government of, by, and for the people— myths that, despite being critiqued and deconstructed by scholars, retain enormous power to shape expectations and understandings of the world. These narratives also continue to guide popular thinking, certainly popular media stories. One of the results is that even as violence is proliferating in both media and the actual world, our conceptions of it—especially those operative in the regulatory systems and the norms that presumably enable us to cope—remain bounded by deeply held assumptions and communicated through traditional symbolic forms, that is, narratives of the good society.

CONTEMPORARY NEGOTIATIONS OF MEDIA FORM AND REGULATION

Narrative as a form restores predictability and stability. Both within media productions and in accounts of media development, narrative serves as a familiar basis for understanding technological innovation and cultural change. Not unrelatedly, the law maintains its own reliance on narrative as a mode of organizing information and making it coherent; as a result, narrative has the potential to delimit the ways we comprehend new media technologies and make sense of experiences in and through them.[32] Traditional means for regulating media—the establishment of standards, prohibition of content, prevention of access—are likewise seen as stabilizing.[33] It should not be surprising, then, that like the narrative forms and social contexts surveyed above, contemporary regulatory efforts continue to be rooted in older models. Despite the demonstration in *Turner Broadcasting* that the Supreme

Court would not make decisions about new media simply on the basis of perceived analogies with traditional media, the weight of precedent of broadcast and telephonic media continues to loom large, especially in regulatory responses to cybermedia.[34] A similar cultural burden exists for those wanting an up-to-date vision of contemporary society; the use of terms grounded in industrial-era and nation-based politics to describe shared values and democratic political practices shield or ignore actual practices and conditions today (such as those involving severe inequities of access to new technologies and to the economic opportunities they afford).

Few policy makers have reconceived regulation so as to reflect the nature of new media, much less changes in contemporary society. Especially in the U.S. context, traditional approaches to technological and institutional regulation have persisted. The Telecommunications Act of 1996, which followed the telephone network model by attempting to distinguish basic "telecommunications" from enhanced "information services," betrayed an overall lack of sensitivity to the operation of new technologies.[35] Its provisions for regulating content involved a patchwork of schemes, based in traditional models, without meaningful new media–specific provisions. Title VII of the Telecommunications Act, which became known as the Communications Decency Act, began with a lengthy section on the "Obscene or Harassing Use of Telecommunications Facilities under the Telecommunications Act of 1934," before recounting subsequent efforts to address "obscenity and violence" (such as the scrambling of cable television programming) to protect minors and to empower families.[36] The CDA was overturned by *Reno v. ACLU* in 1997, but a more limited regulation, the Child Online Protection Act (also known as "CDA II"), remaining as of this writing under a restraining order, still seeks to restrict access and impose rules and standards for new media content in the manner, chiefly, of older broadcast media. This reliance on outmoded regulatory models, underscored by the act's separation of commercial service or technological regulation, on the one hand, and content or access regulation on the other, illustrates a continuing unwillingness to confront the very real relationships between the economic, cultural, and social aspects of new media. Such reliance on past schemes also reiterates and extends existing narratives of legal regulation, thereby urging close attention to specific legal and technical constraints while limiting the larger models developed to describe new technologies.

Attempts to regulate content—that is, individual forms of violent expression on the Internet and World Wide Web—have remained narrowly focused and mostly ineffective.[37] Despite raising far-reaching issues about the nature of cyberspace and the relevance or applicability of existing "real world" laws and standards to that realm, recent efforts have done little more than replay familiar controversies about governmental constraints on technology and content. Thus the opportunity to initiate a public discussion about the place and meaning of violence in contemporary media and society is being evaded. Instead of seeking to reconceptualize our understanding of violence and to develop innovative public policy and laws to address it, the president and Congress—and commercial interests—take the easy approach of rather conventional filtering software that aims to control access to the Internet or World Wide Web by establishing ratings for prohibiting certain content of usergroups and Web sites. We are by now familiar with anecdotes illustrating the inadequacy and even absurdity of blocking technologies: the historian of the Holocaust unable to disseminate details of the physical tortures committed by Nazis at Auschwitz, the cancer survivor unable to access a support group's Web site because "breast" is in its title, the students at the University of Kansas blocked from conducting research at their own Archie R. Dykes Medical Library, and so on. Of greater concern are general objections that blocking software arguably justified for protecting children constitutes an unfair infringement of the rights of adults. Perhaps most troubling, though, is the seeming unwillingness of policy and lawmakers to do more than extend conventional strategies for content suppression, rating, and blocking into cyberspace; not only have these strategies proven largely ineffectual in the past, they actively inhibit broader public discussion of media violence.

Current filter and blocking programs follow familiar strategies for restricting access to content and have led some to brand the technology "censorware." The Platform for Internet Content Selection (PICS) has formulated a nomenclature for Web ratings systems, such as SafeSurf and RSACi; it allows site owners to rate content and, in turn, gives users the option to restrict various types of content. Stand-alone blockers like CyberPatrol, SurfWatch, and CYBERSitter prohibit access to prescribed lists of sites or sites containing one or more entries on a list of terms or symbols considered obscene, indecent, or otherwise objectionable—most, it should be emphasized, referring to sexuality and sexual violence rather than violence generally. As Jonathan Weinberg has argued, these systems rely on the formulation and enforcement of rules and standards, which by their very nature are inexact and impose a cost on the freedom of access of users.[38] These are systems that would appear, again, to emerge from models based in older technologies that feature neither the extraordinary variety and nuance nor the volume and changeability of new media. Of course, what is more generally lacking in the development and proliferation of these programs is a broader discussion about the community of shared values presumably operating in cyberspace or the contemporary real world, or about the effect new media technologies may have on that community and values.

The uncertain status of Web sites and other cyberspaces espousing racist, anti-Semitic, homophobic, or xenophobic views betray the failure of public and legal discussions regarding these new technologies to engage complicated issues concerning community standards and freedom of expression. Clearly, legal tests of "hate speech" and "true threats" are at least as difficult in cyberspace as in the real world or other media. Yet as blocking and filtering software come to dominate the social, cultural, and legal focus on new technologies, concerns with pornography and sexual explic-itness exclude attention to other forms of expression, like that depicting or encour-aging graphic violence.[39] The point is not, of course, to deny scrutiny to sexually explicit images and texts; indeed, many pornographic sites combine sexually explicit with graphically violent content. Rather, policy makers should attend to forms of putatively violent expression that have been largely neglected in discussions about new media. The Web sites and newsgroups of so-called "hate groups" that call for race war, deny the Holocaust, threaten the government, and provide instructions on weapon construction and operation are only the most extreme examples. Arguably more insidious and widespread is the individualized problem of "cyber stalking" via bulletin boards, chat rooms, and electronic mail. Here the very interactive and net-worked nature of cyberspace facilitates the emergence of harassing or even threat-ening electronic speech. The cases reveal that current statutes largely fail to address patterns of harassment or annoying conduct, the often indirect transmission of threats and harassment to online bulletin boards and chatrooms, or encouragement by one individual for another to harass or threaten a third party.[40]

Beyond the regulatory struggle to extend statutes against stalking and violent or sexual harassment into cyberspace, even more fundamental issues of identity and social practices in that realm need to be sorted out.[41] Probably the most famous case of violence in new media occurred in late 1993 in LambdaMOO, a MUD, or multiuser dimension, a networked database located on a computer in Palo Alto, California. In articles appearing first in *The Village Voice* and then in *My Tiny Life*, Julian Dibbell detailed the virtual rape and sadomasochistic acts, such as sodomy with a kitchen knife, committed against female members/characters in one of the domain's public spaces. The episode raises issues about the meaning and status of violence in new media and, especially, interactive cyber-environments, where the boundaries between the body and the mind, the real and the symbolic, and real-life and virtual identities are blurred.[42] The account on LambdaMOO also urges consideration of the applica-bility of so-called "real world" legal precedents to incidents in online or virtual envi-ronments. Most of *My Tiny Life* is not about Mr. Bungle's behavior but about the varied efforts of members of LambdaMOO to respond, that is, to decide and to act as a community in the face of his behavior.[43] This matter of considering openly and deliberately how new technologies engage individuals and prospective members of community is precisely what warrants sustained critical, legal, and regulatory atten-tion. It is consideration, furthermore, that deserves to be conducted in concert with efforts to establish regulatory standards or implement structures.

Sherry Turkle has discussed the ramifications for personal identity of interact-ing via constructed online identities.[44] Yet it is also crucial to address the ramifica-tions of cyberspace for explicitly social and community identities. This does not only mean attention to the communal or social characteristics of cyberspaces, or the transnational society of the actual world transformed by these technologies. Rather, the current revision of social narratives and collective myths of community should be understood in the context of a contemporary world in which "real" and cyber-realms commingle.

In the process, "community" has become an expansive and heavily contested notion. Myths and narratives of local, national, global, and virtual communities consequently suffuse writings about cyberspace.[45] Even the most basic terms for defining community are at issue: that is, whether and how it is formed by social aggregations, interpersonal interactions, shared values, consensual governance, the generation of social norms, or economic exchange.[46] Many writings are, as a result, utopian or apocalyptic. Mike Godwin, for instance, writes of the potential of cyberspace to "restore American identity"—a vaguely promising phrase that conveys the open-ended appropriation of traditional (here nationalistic) political discourse in writings about new media technologies that nevertheless fail to address the specific conditions or effects of those technologies specifically.[47] Legal debates have engaged many of these concerns in seeking to establish "community standards" appropriate to cyberspace, models for sovereignty and governance, and paradigms that enable existing "real-world" laws, notably the First Amendment and guarantees of freedom on expression, to apply to cyberspace.[48] Indeed, Lawrence Lessig has noted that legal standards concerning new media and activities in cyberspace have the power to shape these nascent technologies, their resulting roles in society, and whatever sense of community they are accorded.[49]

It is necessary amid this theorizing to retain consideration of the community and society that exist in the actual world, that is, outside cyberspace, and the community or communities that overlap the cyber and actual worlds. An aspect of that consideration should address what Robert McChesney has termed "the ideology of the infallible marketplace in communication and elsewhere [that] has become a virtual civic religion in the United States and globally in the 1990s." Amidst the rush to riches of Microsoft millionaires, an ongoing stream of high-tech IPOs, and unprecedented general economic prosperity, it is perhaps not surprising that the commercial imperatives of new media have mostly gone unquestioned.[50] Yet the entrenchment of this ideology necessarily takes place to the exclusion of other possibilities, such as public interest communications and nonproprietary software. It is, in fact, precisely the predominance of commercialism in the development of new media that invites critique and prompts questions about what forms, practices, and values are being excluded.

Drafting policy, approving regulations, and conceiving models does nothing less than circumscribe the range of opportunities for new media, their place and role in contemporary society, and their regulation. "How courts and legislatures answer these questions will necessarily be both descriptive and constitutive: not only will they describe the cyberspace we currently know, but they will also forge cyberspace's future shape, functions, and meanings."[51] As a result, the aim of legal regulators and paradigm makers should not merely be a more coordinated understanding of new media and contemporary society, but the production of information policy that addresses actual practices and conditions.[52] They might also profitably engage long-standing issues of democracy and community that have particular currency today and consider their relevance or applicability to new media. Cass Sunstein, for example, has spoken of opportunities to resuscitate Madisonian principles by applying them to new technologies; this may be apt, though it might be precisely the public deliberation of these principles and contemporary conditions that constitute the most valuable opportunity.[53] Discussions would do well to begin with an acknowledgment of the traditional values, symbolic forms, and social narratives still very much operative in the production of laws, conceptions of technology, activities in the marketplace—and the construction and meaning of violent media content. Doing so would facilitate attention to essential questions of community and values and how we organize, order, and experience our worlds.[54]

ESTABLISHING THE BOUNDARIES OF NEW MEDIA EXPRESSION: WORKING CONCLUSIONS

It took at least a decade before the consolidation of the classical Hollywood norms with which we are all familiar: multidimensional, psychologically motivated characters; causally driven narrative grounded in conflict and resolution; coherent fictional worlds in which these characters and narratives exist; and spectacles of violence contained and explained by narrative context.[55] A kaleidoscope of social, economic, legal, and cultural forces contributed to the process of regulation that constituted these cinematic norms and practices.[56] Today, negotiations of meaning and legitimacy are currently going on, in and about cyberspace. As noted, Janet Murray suggests that the negotiation taking place between narrativizing tendencies and database form in new media will also, in time, almost inevitably stabilize around a core set of innovative narrative forms and conventions. Less often cited, however, is the contest between traditional narratives of rational democracy and the emerging global network of communities. This exclusion becomes all the more resonant when considering violence, a phenomenon that relies for its definition and meaning on context that has been so consistently provided by narrative forms. To close, I would like to make a few brief recommendations for how we might more fully and productively understand these narrativizing and prospectively stabilizing tendencies.

First, "regulation" should be reconceived in public as well as policy making and legal discourse. Most basically, this requires acknowledgment that so-called *de*-regulation in the form of allowing the commercial marketplace, through putatively open competition, to determine new media technologies, institutions, and practices does not produce a free trade in ideas. (It produces, instead, the commercialization of access and information handling, as well as the corporatization of cyberspace, especially in the form of global alliances and conglomerates.)[57] More ambitiously, however, it is an opportune moment to move beyond perfunctory policies about licensing and fee structures or continued application of traditional public utility and broadcasting standards to commercially driven initiatives. The convergence of new media technologies and practices, especially, urges expansive and imaginative consideration of cyberspace and its increasingly far-reaching role in everyday as well as economic and social lives.

Attention should be paid to symbolic and cultural forms—and, crucially, how they conduce with legal and economic issues to shape media. What, for example, will the merger of AOL and Time Warner mean for the overall media market and, specifically, for the survival of smaller, perhaps alternative forms of content provision? How will it affect or shape the variety and quality of readily accessible content? To quote Robert McChesney once more, "Without a principled critique of the market and the types of censorship it systematically imposes, [the] blanket adoption of the First Amendment can also serve to provide the purely commercial aspirations of corporate America with a constitutional shield from justified public criticism."[58] Yet discussions of regulation should be fuller still and acknowledge that in media today, the commercial, legal, social, technological, and cultural intermix. What is called for in addressing cyberspace is nothing less than an interdisciplinary sociology of new media and their regulation.[59] Among the approaches to be employed, legal narratology could illuminate both new media content and efforts to regulate it.

Second, such a well-rounded conception of regulation would correspond to conceptions of civil society altered in large part by the proliferation of new media. To appreciate fully the new, analysts must survey widely today's complicated media landscape and recognize the changes taking place. These media should be seen as inextricable components of society, culture, and politics; the media, new and old, are not discrete entities but pervade other institutions, providing the social "glue" or "cement" for the contemporary world. Any account of the evolution of media technologies should address the concomitant transformation of the civil society of which they are integral parts.

Necessarily, forthright engagement with changes in contemporary civil society will need to address the phenomenon of globalization. This will require acknowledgment of the commercial and economic forces driving development of cyberspace— often at the cost of alternative, noncommercial, and public service technologies and practices. Long-standing narratives of individualism, of ordered, deliberative, and democratic society, and of capitalist economy should be scrutinized, especially for their contemporary relevance. It will be crucial to recognize the binary discourse shaping conceptions of emerging communities in cyberspace and the actual world, of new manifestations of order and disorder, democracy and nondemocracy. Also necessary is thoroughgoing discussion of the potentially distinctive social interactions and, hence, innovative regulatory practice reflecting the impersonal and increasingly global character of cyberspace. At its broadest, addressing globalization would involve debate over the shifting status of national and international law, sovereignty, and community.

Third, such discussion would provide the opportunity to revise and complicate conventional approaches to violence. It is an opportune moment to confront and move beyond the rationales that regularly inhibit effectual public deliberation and policy debates concerning media violence.[60] Some scholars have advocated a far-reaching reexamination of the status of violence in the law. Kevin Saunders argues for the treatment, in certain circumstances, of violence as "obscenity" and therefore as expression excluded from the First Amendment guarantees.[61] Saunders's specific proposal, especially where it seems to curtail rights, demands close examination. His more general call for increased public concern and debate over violent expression is, however, encouraging: while stopping short of calling for a wide-ranging public discussion, his proposal urges careful consideration of both the notion of "community" and the "standards" traditionally underpinning legal regulations of expression or media content.

Today's constituting of new media technologies and practices affords a rich opportunity for regulators and the public alike to engage in wide-ranging investigations of violence. Yet without a commitment to reconceive regulation and to broaden discussions of community and civil society, responses to the violence that pervades media will continue to be superficial and largely ineffectual. Recent attempts to establish distinctive "cultures of violence," which link rates of violent crime to specific social and economic conditions, may provide one approach. Legal scholar Dov Cohen has argued that white cultures in the southern and northern United States ascribe different meanings to violence and honor and, as a result, may be understood as operating in different systems of cultural meaning.[62] With emergent norms of social interaction in cyberspace and elsewhere due to new technologies, it is worth exploring whether novel cultures of violence exist across media and around the globe and, if so, how they might be conceptualized and regulated.

Instead of using this era of sweeping technological and cultural change to revise public discussion of violence, however, most contemporary regulatory efforts are extending a familiar understanding of violence into cyberspace. Legislators, courts, and policy makers should engage in public discussions that expand our conceptions of violence in cyberspace as well as develop innovative approaches to understanding and coping with its existence. One possibility might be a public service campaign for "violent media literacy" that explores for users both the significance of violence as, inter alia, a storytelling device in conventional media narratives of conflict and resolution, a recurrent feature in defining episodes of U.S. and world history, and a means for legitimating certain individuals, groups, and behaviors while criminalizing others.

Fourth, regulation should be seen as proactive and ensuring the survival of alternative, noncommercial, and public service voices. Thoughtful and specific models already exist. Yochai Benkler, for instance, has proposed "an alternative approach based on assessing the impact of regulatory choices affecting communications infrastructure on social distribution of communicative capacities."[63] More generally, Cass Sunstein has proposed to require public service options in cyberspace: on AOL Web sites, say, an icon might appear that would, if clicked, enable a link to another site or sites offering alternative viewpoints or opinions on given topics.[64] Besides working to ensure the accessibility and exposure to multiple viewpoints, these efforts might endeavor to develop more acute appreciation for the contexts in which violence is expressed. Whatever the specific priorities or forms of required public service options—and they should, and inevitably *would*, be vigorously and publicly debated—the guiding priority should be the enhanced interaction among mainstream, commercial, and alternative voices.

Fifth, a multiplicity of views must be made a special priority in addressing violence. Because violence accrues social, cultural, and symbolic meaning through the contextual prism of shared experiences, the construction of common understandings of normalcy and acceptability and even legal standards of obscenity are dependent upon wide-ranging public and democratic discourse. A potentially illuminating aspect of that discourse could be attention to the narratives importantly prevailing and shaping both media content and accounts of cyberspace development and new media regulation.

On a certain pragmatic level, the foregoing proposals betray the studious distance afforded observers of cultural and historical change but denied hands-on makers of law and public policy. They also defy precedents from throughout the past century: that is, they contrast the reactive anxieties about new technology, the unwillingness to question commercialization of new media, the regulatory preoccupation with prohibitions on specific content, and the reductive treatment of violence as clearly defined aberration. They also call for a legal narratology of cyberspace that has historically been omitted from public policy making and debates over the introduction of novel media technologies or the communities, commerce, and freedom of expression or access they supposedly engender.

At the same time, however, implicit throughout this essay is hope that this time, despite the culture of specialization underlying much of today's theorization and legislation of cyberspace regulation, things will be different. Indeed, the interdisciplinary reach and historical basis of many studies and even some legal approaches to cyberspace justify some optimism. The challenge is to maintain an expansive and historically mindful stance in the midst of developing focused and concrete new media regulation. Violence is an exemplary topic that both merits thoughtful review across media today and deserves special consideration in discussions of cyberspace. More generally, it is a topic that illustrates the value of integrating scrutiny of the *cultural* regulation of media content and consumption in broader regulatory formulations—especially if a priority is to move beyond traditionally narrow, superficial, and ineffectual efforts to suppress content.

The changes wrought by new technologies hold promise to accomplish nothing less than the cultivation of a global civic imagination. I have tried to suggest here that the negotiation of even one component of the cyberspace regulatory debate—namely, of violent expression—can be wide-ranging and potentially transformative of public discussion about the medium and its regulation. That requires, however, a willingness to coordinate critical and regulatory efforts and to expand understanding of media as dynamic components of contemporary social, cultural, legal, and commercial worlds. It also requires, finally, a commitment to reconceiving regulation, expanding our vision of media, and reinvigorating public discourse.

The goal here has been to suggest that that expansion should include critical attention to narrativizing tendencies and narrative evolution in cyberspace. Murray discusses narrative in relation to media content and individual interactions in cyberspace. But narrative form is not only operative *within* media productions; it is a form that continues to hold sway in models of cyberspaces and communities as well as in contemporary legal, economic, moral, and cultural regulations. Indeed, if it is, as Peter Brooks claims, "one of our large, all-pervasive ways of organizing and speaking the world—the way we make sense of meanings that unfold in and through time"—we must take care to recognize the implications of narrative at this moment in which the world appears to be changing.[65] Narrative is not merely a mode of storytelling; it is a powerful mode of interaction and of organization that persists in giving meaning and shape to cyberspace and the presence and regulation of violence in it.

NOTES

I am indebted to Martin Roberts for his insightful comments on many of the issues discussed in this essay. My thanks also to Thomas Hensley and to my two respondents at the Kent State symposium, Juliet Dee and Tim Smith.

1. Book-length examples include Peter Brooks and Paul Gewirtz, eds., *Law's Stories: Narrative and Rhetoric in the Law* (New Haven, Conn.: Yale Univ. Press, 1996); Gary Bellow and Martha Minow, eds., *Law Stories* (Ann Arbor: Univ. of Michigan Press, 1996); and Carol Weisbrod, *Butterfly, the Bride: Essays on Law, Narrative, and Family* (Ann Arbor: Univ. of Michigan Press, 1998).

2. See Richard Maltby, "The Genesis of the Production Code," in *Prima dei codici 2: Alle Porte di hays* [Before the Codes 2: The Gateway to Hays] (Venice: La Biennale di Venezia, 1991), 60–80. The bases for what Maltby terms "the official accounts of the genesis of the Production Code" are Will H. Hays, *The Memoirs of Will H. Hays* (Garden City, N.Y.: Doubleday, 1955), and Raymond Moley, *The Hays Office* (Indianapolis: Bobbs-Merrill, 1945).

3. Robert McChesney, *Telecommunications, Mass Media, and Democracy: The Battle for Control of U.S. Broadcasting, 1928–1935* (New York: Oxford Univ. Press, 1995).

4. Susan Smulyan, *Selling Radio: The Commercialization of American Broadcasting, 1920–1934* (Washington, D.C.: Smithsonian Institution Press, 1996).

5. Gaye Tuchman, "Objectivity as Strategic Ritual: An Examination of Newsmen's Notions of Objectivity," *American Journal of Sociology* 77 (1972): 660–79; Michael Schudson, *Discovering the News: A Social History of American Newspapers* (New York: Basic Books 1978); and Daniel Schiller, *Objectivity and the News* (Philadelphia: Univ. of Pennsylvania Press, 1981).

6. James Carey, "The Problem of Journalism History," *Journalism History* 1.1 (Spring 1974): 3–5, 27; reprinted in *James Carey: A Critical Reader*, ed. Eve Stryker Munson and Catherine A. Warren (Minneapolis: Univ. of Minnesota Press, 1997), 86–94.

7. For his seminal essay on this topic, see Antonio Gramsci, "Americanism and Fordism," in *Selections from the Prison Notebooks* (London: Lawrence and Wishart, 1971). The basic works by Aglieta are Michel Aglietta, *A Theory of Capitalist Regulation*, trans. David Fernbach (London: New Left Books, 1979), and Michel Aglietta, *A Theory of Capitalist Regulation: The U.S. Experience*, trans. David Fernbach (London: Verso, 1987). Examples of the theoretical attempts to integrate state formation and moral regulation in economic regimes of production and consumption include Philip Corrigan and Derek Sayer, *The Great Arch: English State Formation as Cultural Revolution* (Oxford: Blackwell, 1985), and Larry Ray and Andrew Sayer, *Culture and Economy after the Cultural Turn* (London: Sage, 2000).

8. For a helpful overview, see Jeffrey Alexander, "Introduction: Civil Society I, II, III: Constructing an Empirical Concept from Normative Controversies and Historical Transformations," in *Real Civil Societies: Dilemmas of Institutionalization*, ed. Jeffrey Alexander (Thousand Oaks, Calif.: Sage, 1998), 1–19; and, John Keane, "Introduction," in *Civil Society and the State: New European Perspectives*, ed. John Keane (London: Verso, 1988), 1–31.

9. See, for example, Norberto Bobbio, "Gramsci and the Concept of Civil Society," in *Civil Society and the State: New European Perspectives*, ed. John Keane (London: Verso, 1988), 73–100.

10. Jeffrey Alexander, "Bifurcating Discourses: Citizen and Enemy as Symbolic Classification: On the Polarizing Discourse of Civil Society," in *Real Civil Societies: Dilemmas of Institutionalization*, ed. Jeffrey Alexander (Thousand Oaks, Calif.: Sage, 1998), 99.

11. Alexander identifies democratic/nondemocratic codes across three discursive structures: social motives (activism/passivity, autonomy/dependence, rationality/irrationality, reasonableness/hysteria, calm/excitable, self-control/passionate, realistic/unrealistic, and sane/mad), social relationships (open/secret, trusting/suspicious, critical/deferential, honorable/self-interested, conscience/greed, truthful/deceitful, straightforward/calculating, deliberative/conspiratorial, friend/enemy), and social institutions (rule regulated/arbitrary, law/power, equality/hierarchy, inclusive/exclusive, impersonal/personal, contractual/ascriptive loyalty, social groups/factions, office/personality). See Alexander, "Bifurcating Discourses," 100–101, tables 6.1–3.

12. John Fiske, *Understanding Popular Culture* (Boston: Unwin Hyman, 1989), 134–37.

13. Foucault's pioneering work has been enormously influential in this regard; see, for example, Michel Foucault, *Power/Knowledge: Selected Interviews and Other Writings, 1972–1977*, ed. Colin Gordon (New York: Pantheon, 1980), esp. "Two Lectures" (1977), trans. Alessandro Fontana and Pasquale Pasquino, 78–108. For a provocative collection of essays on the implications of this reformulation, see

Robert C. Post, ed., *Censorship and Silencing: Practices of Cultural Regulation* (Los Angeles: Getty Research Institute for the History of Art and the Humanities, 1998).

14. Pierre Bourdieu, "Censorship and the Imposition of Form," in *Language and Symbolic Power*, intro. John Thompson, trans. Gino Raymond and Matthew Adamson (Cambridge, Mass.: Harvard Univ. Press, 1991), 137.

15. Furthermore, traditional efforts to regulate or censor have tended to engage traditional subjects. In terms of violence, most regulatory attention has focused on sexual violence, extending a long-standing and warranted concern that tends to exclude other consideration of much other violent content. See Edward Donnerstein and Daniel Linz, "Sexual Violence in the Mass Media," in *Violence and the Law*, ed. Mark Costanzo and Stuart Oskamp (Thousand Oaks, Calif.: Sage, 1994), 9–36.

16. See, relatedly, Pierre Bourdieu, "Description and Prescription: The Conditions of Possibility and the Limits of Political Effectiveness," in *Language and Symbolic Power*, intro. John Thompson, trans. Gino Raymond and Matthew Adamson (Cambridge, Mass.: Harvard Univ. Press, 1991), 127–36.

17. Ronald N. Jacobs, "The Racial Discourse of Civil Society: The Rodney King Affair and the City of Los Angeles," in *Real Civil Societies: Dilemmas of Institutionalization*, ed. Jeffrey Alexander (Thousand Oaks, Calif.: Sage, 1998), 140.

18. Jacobs, "The Racial Discourse of Civil Society," 140. See, also, Jean Cohen and Andrew Arato, *Civil Society and Political Theory* (Cambridge, Mass.: MIT Press, 1992), 415–20, 440–63.

19. See Sissela Bok, *Mayhem: Violence as Public Entertainment* (Reading, Mass.: Addison-Wesley, 1998), esp. introduction.

20. For a thoughtful explication of this shortcoming, see the essays by Michael Schudson and Nicholas Garnham in *Habermas and the Public Sphere*, ed. Craig Calhoun (Cambridge, Mass.: MIT Press, 1992), 143–63, 359–76.

21. Some recent legal scholarship has sought to develop the relationships between law, economics, and social norms. See, for example, Lawrence Lessig, "The Regulation of Social Meaning," *University of Chicago Law Review* 62 (1995): 943–1045; Cass R. Sunstein, "Social Norms and Social Rules," *Columbia Law Review* 96 (1996): 903–68; and the special issue on "Social Norms, Social Meaning, and the Economic Analysis of Law," *The Journal of Legal Studies* 27.2.pt.2 (June 1998).

22. Lev Manovich, "Database as a Symbolic Form" (1998), available on the World Wide Web at http://www.apparition.ucsd.edu/~manovich/docs/database.rtf; this essay will also appear in Lev Manovich, *The Language of New Media* (Cambridge, Mass.: MIT Press, 2000).

23. Janet H. Murray, *Hamlet on the Holodeck: The Future of Narrative in Cyberspace* (New York: Free Press, 1997).

24. Leo Bersani and Ulysse Dutoit, *The Forms of Violence: Narrative in Assyrian Art and Modern Culture* (New York: Schocken Books, 1985).

25. See, for example, Richard Coyne, *Technoromanticism: Digital Narrative, Holism, and the Romance of the Real* (Cambridge, Mass.: MIT Press, 1999).

26. See David Nye, *Narratives and Spaces: Technology and the Construction of American Culture* (New York: Columbia Univ. Press, 1998); and, Ruth Schwartz Cohan, *A Social History of American Technology* (New York: Oxford Univ. Press, 1997), esp. 201–23 and 273–300.

27. Manuel Castells, *The Information Age: Economy, Society and Culture*, vol. 2, *The Power of Identity* (Oxford: Blackwell, 1997), 312.

28. Lawrence Lessig, *Code, and Other Laws of Cyberspace* (New York: Basic Books, 1999), esp. 85–99, 235–39.

29. For a provocative essay on approaches to contemporary violence, see Joel Best, *Random Violence: How We Talk about New Crimes and New Victims* (Berkeley: Univ. of California Press, 1999).

30. For a helpful description of how this anxiety bears on attitudes toward regulating new media,

see Henry Jenkins, "Congressional Testimony on Media Violence," presented before the U.S. Senate Commerce Committee, May 4, 1999, available on the World Wide Web at http://media-in-transition.mit.edu/articles/dc.html (accessed May 15, 2000).

31. Ithiel de la Sola Pool, *Technologies of Freedom: On Free Speech in an Electronic Age* (Cambridge, Mass.: Belknap Press/Harvard Univ. Press, 1983).

32. See Brooks and Gewirtz, eds., *Law's Stories*; and, Robin West, *Narrative, Authority, and Law* (Ann Arbor: Univ. of Michigan Press, 1993).

33. Some even argue, in the realm of cyberspace, that they are constitutive of evolving communal structures. See Philip Giordano, "Invoking Law as a Basis for Identity in Cyberspace," *Stanford Technological Law Review* 1 (1998), available on the World Wide Web at http://stlr.stanford.edu/STLR/Articles/98_STLR_1/ (accessed May 15, 2000).

34. *Turner Broadcasting System, Inc. v. FCC*, 129 L.Ed. 2d 497 (1994).

35. Jonathan Weinberg, "The Internet and 'Telecommunications Services,' Universal Service Mechanisms, Access Charges, and Other Flotsam of the Regulatory System," *Yale Journal of Regulation* 16.2 (Summer 1999): 211–44.

36. The text of the Communications Decency Act (1996) can be viewed at http://www.epic.org/free_speech/cda/cda.html.

37. Two excellent overviews of the V-chip and Internet filter debates are, respectively, Monroe E. Price, ed., *The V-Chip Debate: Labeling and Rating Content from Television to the Internet* (Mahwah, N.J.: Lawrence Erlbaum, 1998); and, David Sobel, *Filters and Freedom: Free Speech Perspectives on Internet Content Controls* (Washington, D.C.: Electronic Privacy Information Center, 1999). The survey from which this latter report was produced is summarized at http://www2.epic.org/reports/filter-report.html.

38. Jonathan Weinberg, "Rating the Net," *Hastings Communications and Entertainment Law Journal* 19 (1997): 453–82.

39. The distinction assumed here sets aside the claim, made most familiarly by Catherine MacKinnon and Andrea Dworkin, that sexually explicit pornography is inherently violent against women. See, for example, Catharine A. MacKinnon, *Only Words* (Cambridge, Mass.: Harvard Univ. Press, 1993); and Andrea Dworkin, *Pornography: Men Possessing Women* (New York: Dutton, 1991).

40. Cyberstalking may also be prosecuted under 47 U.S.C. § 223, which makes it a federal crime, punishable by up to two years in prison, to use a telephone or telecommunications device to annoy, abuse, harass, or threaten any person at the called number. It nevertheless still applies only to direct communications between the perpetrator and the victim and therefore would not cover harassment by posting messages on a bulletin board or in a chat room encouraging others to harass or annoy another person. Compiled from the "1999 Report on Cyberstalking: A New Challenge for Law Enforcement and Industry," a report from the attorney general to the vice president, August 1999; available on the World Wide Web at http://www.usdoj.gov/criminal/cybercrime/cyberstalking.htm (accessed May 28, 2000).

41. For background, see Adam S. Miller, "The Jake Baker Scandal: A Perversion in Logic," available on the World Wide Web at: http://www.trincoll.edu/zines/tj/tj4.6.95/articles baker.html#Baker,%20 the%20Foreigner (accessed May 14, 2000).

42. Julian Dibbell, *My Tiny Life: Crime and Passion in a Virtual World* (New York: Owl Books, 1999).

43. Among many provocative pieces on this topic, see Tamir Maltz, "Customary Law and Process in Internet Communities," *Journal of Computer-Mediated Communication* 2.1.pt.1 (June 1996), available on the World Wide Web at http://www.ascusc.org/jcmc/vol2/issue1/custom.html (accessed May 15, 2000); William S. Byassee, "Jurisdiction of Cyberspace: Applying Real World Precedent to the Virtual Community," *Wake Forest Law Review* 30 (1995): 197–208; and, D. G. Post, "Anarchy, State, and the Internet: An Essay on Law-making in Cyberspace," *Journal of Online Law* (1995), available on the World Wide Web at http://warthog.cc.wm.edu/law/publications/jol/post.html (accessed May 15, 2000).

44. Sherry Turkle, *Life on the Screen: Identity in the Age of the Internet* (New York: Simon and Schuster, 1995). Relatedly, in legal scholarship, see Chris Gosnell, "Hate Speech on the Internet: A Question of Context," *Queens Law Journal* 23 (1998): 369–439.

45. For an illustrative study that critiques the "information superhighway" metaphor, see Clay Calvert, "Regulating Cyberspace: Metaphor, Rhetoric, Reality, and the Framing of Legal Options," *Hastings Communications and Entertainment Law Journal* 20 (1998): 541.

46. Among the first attempts to theorize community in cyberspace was Howard Rheingold, *The Virtual Community: Homesteading on the Electronic Frontier* (Reading, Mass.: Addison-Wesley, 1993); for an excellent and more recent overview of many of these issues, see Richard Holeton, *Composing Cyberspace: Identity, Community, and Knowledge in the Electronic Age* (Boston: McGraw-Hill, 1998).

47. Mike Godwin, *Cyber Rights: Defending Free Speech in the Digital Age* (New York: Time Books, 1998), 15.

48. Patrick T. Egan, "Note—Virtual Community Standards: Should Obscenity Law Recognize the Contemporary Community Standard of Cyberspace?" *Suffolk University Law Review* 30 (1996): 117–31; Llewellyn Joseph Gibbons, "No Regulation, Government Regulation, Self-Regulation: Social Enforcement or Social Contracting for Governance in Cyberspace," *Cornell Journal of Law and Public Policy* 6 (1997): 475.

49. See Lessig, *Code*, esp. 3–60.

50. Robert McChesney, "The Internet and U.S. Communication Policy-Making in Historical and Critical Perspective," *Journal of Communication* 46.1 (Winter 1996): 105.

51. "Developments in the Law: The Law of Cyberspace—Communities, Virtual and Real: Social and Political Dynamics of Law in Cyberspace" (student authored), *Harvard Law Review* 112 (1999): 1609.

52. Brian Kahn and Charles Neeson, eds., *Borders in Cyberspace: Information Policy and the Global Information Infrastructure* (Cambridge, Mass.: MIT Press, 1996).

53. See Cass R. Sunstein, "The First Amendment in Cyberspace," *Yale Law Journal* 104 (1995): 1757–804.

54. Such revision may not only be desirable but necessary for the continued authority of law as we know it. Although deserving more discussion than can be given here, consider Ethan Katsh's caution: "Writing and print are the structural supports for the modern ideal of dispute resolution and have contributed to law's growth over time, to our reliance on law, and to the authority of law. This is important today because as societies become increasingly reliant on electronic forms of communication, some of these structural supports are being eroded." M. Ethan Katsh, *The Electronic Media and the Transformation of the Law* (New York: Oxford Univ. Press, 1989), 51.

55. See Tom Gunning, *D. W. Griffith and the Origins of American Narrative Film: The Early Years at Biograph* (Urbana: Univ. of Illinois Press, 1994).

56. The best study of constitutive regulation in cinema, addressing sexuality in British film a decade later, is in Annette Kuhn, *Cinema, Censorship, and Sexuality, 1909–1925* (New York: Routledge, 1988).

57. For a summary of these effects, see Saskia Sassen, "Electronic Space and Power" (1997), in *Globalization and Its Discontents* (New York: New Press, 1998), 177–94.

58. McChesney, "The Internet and U.S. Communication Policy-Making in Historical and Critical Perspective," 107.

59. Lawrence Lessig has posited a similar notion, calling for what he terms a "new Chicago School" for the electronic age. See Lessig, "The New Chicago School," *Journal of Legal Studies* 27 (1998): 661–92. Lacking in Lessig's proposal, however, is explicit attention to the pervasive role of media across other realms.

60. For an incisive summary of these rationales, see Sissela Bok, "TV Violence, Children, and the Press: Eight Rationales Inhibiting Public Policy Debates" (Discussion Paper D-16; Joan Shorenstein Barone Center, Harvard University, April 1994).

61. Kevin W. Saunders, *Violence as Obscenity: Limiting the First Amendment's Protection* (Durham, N.C.: Duke Univ. Press, 1996), esp. 179–200.

62. Dov Cohen and Joe Vandello, "Meanings of Violence," *Journal of Legal Studies* 27 (June 1998): 567–83. See, also, Dov Cohen, Joe Vandello, and Adrian Rantilla, "The Sacred and the Social: Honor and Violence in Cultural Context," in *Shame: Interpersonal Behavior, Psychopathology, and Culture*, ed. Paul Gilbert and Bernice Andrews (New York: Oxford University Press, 1998); and Richard E. Nisbett and Dov Cohen, *Culture of Honor: The Psychology of Violence in the South* (Boulder, Colo.: Westview Press, 1996).

63. Yochai Benkler, "Communications Infrastructure Regulation and the Distribution of Control over Content," *Telecommunications Policy* 22.3 (1998): 183.

64. Cass Sunstein, "Freedom of Expression: The Future," *The Boundaries of Freedom of Expression and Order in a Democratic Society*, ed. Thomas Hensley (Kent, Ohio: Kent State Univ. Press, forthcoming 2001).

65. Peter Brooks, "The Law as Narrative and Rhetoric," in *Law's Stories*, 14.

It's Showtime

Response to Slocum

TIMOTHY D. SMITH

Journalism, Kent State University

It is a given that the law plays catch-up with technology. Radio was around for years before Congress adopted first the Wireless Ship Act of 1910 and later the Federal Communications Act of 1934. It is equally telling that regulators, casting about for a model to serve as a pattern for this new technology, settled on the one used for railroads. In hindsight, the connection seems tenuous, though maybe it made sense at the time.

In the last decade, the World Wide Web has moved from a curiosity to a phenomenon of such power and breadth that investors will plunge millions of dollars into its companies with no idea whether they will ever see any return on their investment.

Meanwhile, our legal system is still trying to sort out cable and satellite television. We still are not sure whether cable is a more like the phone company, subject to regulation as a monopoly, or more like a newspaper, with full First Amendment protection. With the dust far from settled on that subject, along comes the Net with countless new issues. Once again, the search for a model for regulation is under way.

David Slocum suggests that we need new models to think about the process through which the regulation is negotiated. Considering how previous "new media" have been handled using inappropriate models, I would agree; he raises a good point. I am not clear, though, exactly what his new model would look like. There are hints in his paper that we should be more expansive in our regulatory approach, but they are only hints. Slocum seems to fear that we will fall back on traditional models that do not really fit the new landscape. His fears have historical support. What is less clear, however, is what approach he proposes as an alternative, other than an inchoate plan to "expand understanding of media as dynamic components of contemporary social, cultural, legal, and commercial worlds."

It is apparent, again with the benefit of hindsight, that Americans were willing to trade freedom for order when the regulation of broadcasting was in its infancy. Order was essential to combat the chaotic situation that was developing—broadcasters were changing power levels and frequencies with abandon as they experimented with the new technology. Order was feasible without content regulation, but the government was simply unwilling to allow this technology the same freedom afforded the print medium. Only now, nearly a hundred years later, are we approaching a level playing field between broadcast and print, and there remains a distinct tilt against broadcast when it comes to content control.

Thus, there is merit in Slocum's concerns about the models for new regulation. He just needs to step up and make a concrete proposal. His "narrative" approach seems more to confuse the issue than clarify it. Adopting a "narrative" form does not appear to be something that amounts to a conscious choice. It is the way we explain ourselves and give meaning to our world. Now that I have agreed to that, where does it leave us? It would appear that having said this, Slocum would retire from the field, apparently in the belief that the problem has been solved.

I do not think it has.

I keep returning to the title of his paper: "Violent Expressions of Freedom." I do not see that issue addressed beyond the superficial criticism of the news media's coverage of the Columbine tragedy. What I saw in the aftermath of that event was a heart-rending attempt by school officials, police, parents, scholars, and commentators to make some sense of an event that defied analysis. Much of that effort struck me as being about as useful as trying to find meaning in the wake of a hurricane. But I am not critical of those who tried to find a reason why their lives had been changed forever by forces beyond their control and understanding.

In truth, in discussing new media, I can see some similarities between acts of random, senseless violence and the growth of the Internet. We feel the need to understand—as well as control—both because of their potential impact on our lives and our fear that simply ignoring them will not suffice. With the growth of violent content on the Net (not to mention sexual content), the desire for control seems to be growing exponentially.

It is easy to grasp for straws of certainty in such a situation. In unfamiliar territory, there are few staunch defenders of the middle ground. Some call for a no-limits, no-taxes, keep-your-hands-off-my-Napster approach to the Web, while others are ready to put a V-chip snugger than a chastity belt on your bandwidth in a nanosecond. The same Justice Department that looks like Goliath when dealing with Elian Gonzalez comes across as David when confronting Bill Gates. Wouldn't George Orwell have been delighted to learn that the corporation with so much control over our lives is called "Microsoft"? What a case of narratives paralleling reality paralleling narratives! That goes to the heart of my criticism of Slocum's paper. I am more anxious to join in the debate, and he is more concerned with finding a metaphor for it. Slocum seems concerned that commercial ventures, in league with government regulators, will turn the Net into another version of commercial television, with all its faults. But there he stops. I concur with the concern. What is the solution?

I do not know how it will all shake out. Following Slocum's approach and adopting current narrative forms, my guess is that the options range from *The Matrix* to *Home Alone Three*. I will freely confess that I cannot sort out what Slocum would recommend. Whatever the outcome, getting there promises to be a fascinating journey.

Do Narratives of Violence Come with a Price?
Response to Slocum

JULIET DEE

Communication, University of Delaware

David Slocum begins by urging us to look at the narratives by which we structure our world: he says that we need to look at narratives in both the media and the actual world that give violent incidents meaning and even legitimation, and he explains that in civil society we need to distinguish "between legitimate and illegitimate violence." So let's consider some real-world narratives about violence first:

Adolf Hitler: We need to exterminate six million Jews, because Aryans are superior to Jews.

Slobodan Milosevic: We need to massacre all the Bosnians and ethnic Albanians in order to accomplish "ethnic cleansing."

Eric Harris and Dylan Klebold: We need to kill all the teachers and students at Columbine High School, because a few classmates made some verbal taunts at us.

National Rifle Association (NRA): The Second Amendment should be interpreted to mean that everyone in the United States has the right to own assault weapons, because "Guns don't kill people; people do."

Someone in the Ohio National Guard at Kent State, May 4, 1970: We need to open fire, because these students are waving the flag of North Vietnam and taunting us.

Lyndon Johnson: We need to send American soldiers to Vietnam to stop the spread of communism.

Franklin Roosevelt, December 7, 1941: Congress needs to declare war in order to stop Japan, Germany, and Italy from committing further atrocities.

The statements above are real-world narratives attempting to justify violence, and at some point in history, millions of citizens of Germany, Yugoslavia, or the United States clearly agreed with the arguments stated above. Though we no doubt recoil in horror at the first five statements above and squirm uncomfortably with Lyndon Johnson's arguments regarding Vietnam, the vast majority of us would probably agree with Roosevelt's decision to enter World War II. Thus most of us would agree that there are times when the use of violence *is* legitimate.

Slocum also observes that the moral regulation of society demands that certain behaviors be established as "normal" and that others, such as violence, be marked as "unnatural or deviant." A number of sociologists, such as Emile Durkheim, have theorized that deviants serve to define society's norms by personifying behavior that is socially unacceptable.[1] Sociologist Kai Erikson has elaborated on this concept: "Each time a community censures some act of deviance, it sharpens the authority of the violated norm and re-establishes the boundaries of the group."[2] Social and legal confrontation of deviants and the ensuing publicity about their "correction" or stigmatization "constitute our main source of information about the normative outlines of society."[3] Erikson has likened these community standards to articles of common law—decisions made by the community over long periods that retain their validity through regular use as sources of values. Slocum comments, "Violence is an aberration in actual behavior and cultural practice alike, a break against which legitimate standards might be clarified."

As a society, we should profoundly hope that violence is indeed an aberration in real life, but is violence an aberration in our media narratives? I don't think so.

Our media narratives, often as not, *depend* on graphic violence as a simple formula for drama. Our popular culture occasionally reflects heightened awareness of formulaic violence: for example, although we once cheered when the "good guys" in a Western annihilated the "bad guys," Slocum explains, critics of Westerns finally brought the "intolerance, destructiveness, brutality and even genocide" integral to Hollywood Westerns to our attention. In response, Hollywood made Westerns such as *Little Big Man* and *Dances with Wolves*, which were more honest in portraying the white man's brutality toward native Americans.

Slocum continues: "The narrative forms featured in films, television and even journalism . . . have been shown to rely on violent action and incidents for their very structure." Indeed, Gene Roddenberry, creator of the original *Star Trek*, has said:

> Conflict is the source of drama. If television writers aren't allowed to do shows about ideological conflict, they'll do shows about physical conflict. If you can't show moral struggles over controversial issues, you'll show life and death struggles over non-controversial issues. The excessive reliance on physical violence is caused by censorship [by the networks' Standards and Practices departments]. The violence on TV results from the refusal of the networks to deal with political or social issues. . . . It is censorship that created this unwanted violence everyone is talking about. . . . We [writers] are capable of fashioning an exciting drama out of the thousands of real issues of life and the rights and wrongs of conflicts which exist in everything else. The structure of television, however, does not allow our people . . . to write on these things, and when you take all the meaningful subjects away from a writer, all you have left is sex and violence with which to provide the conflict that is necessary to draw the mass audience.[4]

Whether it is true or not, television network programming executives clearly *believe* that violent content (or "heavy action," as they say) wins higher ratings than nonviolent content. Because of the networks' abject reliance on the Nielsen ratings, network programmers' decisions to air graphic violence during prime time is unconstrained by concerns about copycat violence on the part of television viewers. Network programmers are guided by ratings and by the profit motive—the bottom line—above all else. Television networks have been taken over by conglomerates answerable to their shareholders (hence, the need for high ratings); these conglomerates do not consider themselves answerable to the general public that ostensibly "owns the airwaves," a fact that the Federal Communications Commission (FCC) and the broadcast licensees have all conveniently forgotten.

Slocum comments that "public discourse on media violence" is "avoiding close scrutiny of, or interference in, media institutional practice." Thus, congressmen hold hearings, garner publicity for themselves, and politely ask Hollywood to tone down violent content. Congress even passed legislation requiring V-chips and ratings for television programs so that parents could block violent programs if they had cable television; for Congress, this was a brave move. We must not forget that congresspersons are utterly dependent on press coverage, especially when they face re-election campaigns, so the pressure to regulate in favor of Hollywood and the television networks is enormous.

But television and films are now older technologies. Should we have different rules for violent content in the new media, such as computer games and the Internet? The graphic violence in movies such as *The Basketball Diaries* and *Natural Born Killers* is terrifying enough, and it is alleged that both movies have instigated copycat murders in real life. But viewers watching graphic violence on television or in movies are thought to be passive; researchers find that our brains quickly relax into an alpha-wave state when we watch films or TV.[5] Psychologists are far more concerned with the violence in video games, which require a child to be active rather than passive. Here, a child shoots at images of humans and "kills" them in a context that the child perceives as pleasurable and rewarding, totally disconnected from any real consequences of violence. Michael Carneal shot and killed three classmates at Heath High School in West Paducah, Kentucky, in 1997. Witnesses said that Carneal methodically pointed his gun at a new target after each shot as if he were playing a video game such as "Doom" or "Mortal Kombat."

Discussing a later school shooting, Slocum comments that "media coverage of the tragedy at Columbine High School demonstrated again the tendency to scapegoat individual media productions and . . . to avoid serious debate about contemporary media . . . practices. Even more, despite the recurrence of such tragedies, there seems little willingness to challenge traditional notions of a 'morally coherent civil society.'" Slocum is dead right. There have been four school shootings since

Columbine.[6] One of these was committed by a six-year-old boy, who shot and killed his classmate Kayla Rolland in Michigan. But in the wake of Columbine, after the Senate attempted to close the gun-show loophole by requiring background checks for all purchases at gun shows, Congressman (and NRA board member) Bob Barr of Georgia prevented any meaningful gun control legislation from passing in the House of Representatives.

Just as the NRA points to the Second Amendment to maintain a status quo that results in over thirteen thousand deaths from handguns each year, corporate America adopts the First Amendment to maintain a status quo in which it makes huge profits from such video games as "Doom" and "Mortal Kombat" and such Hollywood movies as *Natural Born Killers*. As Slocum says, the First Amendment provides corporate America with "a constitutional shield from justified public criticism" and from justified fears about school shootings and copycat violence.

If, as a society, we permit ourselves to remain awash in a sea of narratives glorifying gratuitous violence—if, as a society, we accept being inundated with violent video games, television programs, and Hollywood movies—we must also accept the fact that these pervasive and violent narratives will result in legitimation of violence in the minds of our children, so that the unthinkable massacre at Columbine High School becomes not only conceivable but easily accomplished. By now it is nearly a cliche to say that freedom of speech comes with a price. But if, as a society, we continue to blindly assert First Amendment freedoms without looking critically at the narratives that glorify and legitimize violence ad nauseum, we should not be surprised if we pay for this "freedom of expression" with the lives of our schoolchildren. It's time to stop kidding ourselves.

NOTES

1. Emile Durkheim, *The Division of Labor in Society* (Glencoe, N.Y.: Free Press of Glencoe, 1933).

2. Kai T. Erikson, "Notes on the Sociology of Deviance," in *Deviance, the Interactionist Perspective: Texts and Readings in the Sociology of Deviance*, ed. Earl Rubington and Martin S. Weinberg (New York: Macmillan, 1987), 26–39. See also Howard Saul Becker, *The Other Side: Perspectives on Deviance* (Glencoe, N.Y.: Free Press of Glencoe, 1964).

3. Erikson, 26–39.

4. Yvonne Fern, *Gene Roddenberry: The Last Conversation* (Berkeley: Univ. of California Press, 1994), 184.

5. James Mann, "What Is TV Doing to America?" in *Impact of Mass Media*, ed. Ray Eldon Hiebert and Carol Reuss (New York: Longman, 1985), 27.

6. On the World Wide Web at http://more.abcnews.go.com/sections/us/DailyNews/school shootings990420.html.

In the Ivory Tower and Beyond

Expanding Public Discourse about Cyberspace

Response to the Discussants

J. David Slocum

Juliet Dee and Tim Smith have provided responses that refract many of the central issues of my essay and, in the process, have rearticulated several concerns more pointedly than I had originally conceived. I am grateful to both for their thoughtfulness and insights.

Professor Smith is right to observe that my essay, for all its range, does not formulate or propose many concrete solutions. Instead, the essay surveys some of the extraordinarily broad context of contemporary media and begins to introduce areas that merit either fuller analysis or fuller inclusion in public policy making. The aim is to contribute to the public discourse in which concrete proposals are developed, assessed, deliberated, agreed upon, and implemented. So by looking closely at a handful of terms—narrative, regulation, community, violence—the essay attempts to enrich that discourse. Indeed, my chief assertion, that a narratological approach to media content and regulation would deepen our understanding of where we are vis-à-vis cyberspace, relies on a greater appreciation of how narratives accord meaning to violence and even shape our visions of and engagement with media and the world.

Juliet Dee, as I read her remarks, accepts that assertion and looks closely at specific terms—namely, narrative and violence. In fact, her embrace of the distinction drawn between the aberrant and normative status of violence in the social world and media illustrates how far reaching can be many of the assumptions typically excluded from public, legal, and scholarly debates. The embrace and interrogation of assumptions leads her to a closing question that begs for wide-ranging public discussion: do narratives of violence in the media come with a social price? Professor Dee does raise it as a question, and it is a troubling, difficult one that requires more than the continued rehearsal of debates over the purported "effects" of media content. It is a question that, with illuminated context, might be better informed and integrated into public, regulatory, and industry debates.

Calling for expanded public discourse or further discussion is itself, of course, a common scholarly tack that arguably keeps ideas distant from the actual concerns of citizens and regulators. As Tim Smith might reply, with some justification, Ivory Tower commentators who seek, however artfully or incisively, to alter the terms of public debate often fail in the process to propose concrete measures and solutions. I maintain, though, that some moments tolerate such seeming high-mindedness better than others, and even profit by them. These moments of technological innovation and social transformation, in which even popular understanding can be influenced significantly by new models and paradigms, benefit from the varied critical approaches employed by academicians. We are living in such a moment.

My essay focuses on terms like narrative, regulation, and violence. Yet the priority in its pages is not to extend given scholarly categories into the public realm or even to lay the groundwork for a more sensible and layered approach to the regulation of cyberspace (though I hope these aims, too, might be realized). The essay's overriding emphasis, rather, is on the public discourse that surrounds new media technologies and accords meaning to them and to our interactions with them. The emphasis is on the development of specific ways to expand public awareness of, debate over, and involvement with the proliferation of new media. It calls for a greater willingness to challenge existing attitudes and beliefs about media and society, especially as they are applied to or incorporated into our understanding of cyberspace.

In other words, the emphasis is on the forms of community that exist in and around cyberspace and through which cyberspace can be deliberated and comprehended. From popular commentators and psychoanalysts to legal experts and media and cultural-studies scholars, multiple approaches to "community" pervade contemporary discussions of cyberspace. The fundamental question is: What are communities in cyberspace? Yet how we go about answering that question, how we make sense of both of the key terms, and how we engage the difficult ancillary questions need also to be explicitly addressed. For example, what is the relevance or utility of conventional critical and popular approaches to individual or group identities in cyberspace? How do categories like race or gender or class or sexual orientation or nation of origin matter? What are the structures of social order in cyberrealms or the normative dynamics of cybercommunities? More specifically, how do conflicts arise and find mediation or resolution in cyberspace? Can these conflicts be construed as violence? Are they by nature narrativized, or would narrative form help in their resolution? Better coordinating the engagement of these questions would enrich how we understand, value, and participate in cybercommunities.

Such coordinated engagement would also contribute to the appreciation of how the cyberworld and actual world interrelate. This relationship is not important simply for law or policy makers wanting greater clarity in their applications of existing statutes to cyberspace. Whatever greater comprehension of new technologies emerges, regulators and the public alike need to remain mindful of the integrated places of those technologies in our lives. A great deal of theorizing about how the emergent dynamics of the virtual world will transform human relations in the actual world fails to acknowledge that most individuals hold attitudes, viewpoints, and values that bridge these realms. A challenge for regulators is to appreciate that while no straightforward transposition of "real-world" norms of community or standards for violence can be made to cyberspace, we bring to both identifiable values that beg to be more closely examined.

Because of the defining connections between violence and norms of social behavior and interaction, an enhanced understanding of community would further efforts to conceptualize and regulate violent media content. For example, the pressing question of whether norms for social interaction in cyberspaces are fundamentally or even substantially different from those in the actual world would presumably enable more sensitive application or adaptation of laws, regulations, and policies about violence in the actual world to cyberrealms. In particular, more fully understood norms of interaction in these realms would facilitate well-suited regulatory responses to violent content; instead of continuing to appropriate existing strategies initially developed for earlier media technologies, cyber-specific discussions and policies could be developed. Perhaps most ambitiously, such efforts to explore the forms of community in cyberspace and to comprehend the nature of violence there would require wide-ranging public debate about issues of violence central to contemporary life and social interaction in the "real world."

Put simply, the contemporary moment is pregnant with possibility. However, we do have to commit to making an effort to comprehend cyberspace more fully, to learning from past precedents, and to having the courage to assert that these new technologies belong to all of us and should be shaped and institutionalized accordingly. My synoptic essay touches on a great range of possibilities for expanding our understanding of this new realm and its relationship to the actual world. Underpinning many of those possibilities is a conviction that greater attention to the role of narratives in and about media would contribute to that understanding; in particular, the critical and popular tendency to develop contrasting narratives of order and disorder, of democracy and nondemocracy, continues to hold sway in our cultural imaginings of cyberspace. The recognition and comprehension of such tendencies can only aid our efforts to invigorate public debate and to enliven participation in communities in both cyberspace and the actual world.

5

A Right to Kill Bears or Bear Quills?
A Critical Commentary on the Linkage of the First and
Second Amendments in Recent Constitutional Theory

SAUL CORNELL

History, Ohio State University

THE RISE OF THE STANDARD MODEL

One of the most remarkable developments in recent constitutional theory is the rise of the so-called "Standard Model" of the Second Amendment. Supporters of this new approach to the Second Amendment claim that this provision of the Bill of Rights protects both an individual and a collective right. For Standard Modelers this right was expansive both in scope and coverage, including all citizens. Finally, the Standard Model asserts that the founders understood the right to bear arms as the final check on government tyranny. In effect, they argue that the Second Amendment incorporates a right of revolution into the Constitution.[1] By describing their interpretation as a Standard Model, advocates of this view have attempted to create an illusion of scholarly consensus.[2]

In reality, however, there is considerable division within the legal academy and among historians about how to understand the Second Amendment.[3] The stakes in the current debate over the meaning of the Second Amendment are hardly academic. The recent decision in *United States v. Emerson,* a case that relied on the Standard Model to overturn a federal gun law, is a sobering reminder of the potential for legal scholarship to influence the course of public policy and jurisprudence.[4]

Standard Modelers see a close connection between the rights embedded in the First and Second Amendments. In both instances Standard Modelers see an expansive individual right that was intended by the founders to serve as a checking function. While conceding that no right is absolute, even speech, Standard Modelers insist that the Second Amendment bars prior restraints on gun ownership by law-abiding citizens. Building on this body of scholarship, the First Amendment scholar L. A. Scott Powe declares that "the Second Amendment can best be understood to incorporate a common law rule against prior restraints." Following the logic of this claim, Powe notes that "the rule against prior restraints offers a sound meaning. The Second Amendment should be interpreted to guarantee an individual right to keep and bear appropriate arms, but no right to use them unlawfully and no right to join with others in an armed band not controlled by the state."[5]

It seems particularly appropriate at a forum honoring the memory of those Kent State students who lost their lives exercising their First Amendment rights to consider the relationship between the First and Second Amendments. It was the modern incarnation of the well-regulated militia, the National Guard, that opened fire on these students. At Kent State the difference between guns and words was obvious. It is remarkable that this distinction has been obscured in recent constitutional theory. The very real distinction between guns and words was not lost on the founders.

CONSTITUTIONAL SCHOLARSHIP AS HISTORICAL THIN DESCRIPTION

A critical examination of the shortcomings of the Standard Model not only sheds light on the Second Amendment but also provides an occasion to analyze a deeper problem in the methodology of contemporary constitutional scholarship as it is practiced by legal scholars and constitutional historians. The approach to constitutional history embodied in the Standard Model represents a form of historical "thin description," a style of historical analysis that stands in marked contrast to the ideal of "thick description" that has become so central to early American history. As historian Joyce Appleby has noted, the turn to cultural anthropology among historians interested in the founding era helped scholars recover lost languages and analyze how "structured consciousness influences social action."[6] The project of recovering the lost world of early American political and constitutional discourse inevitably led scholars to investigate the thoughts of nonelites, effectively restoring a voice to groups once deemed to be inarticulate.[7] Most historians would now concede that Americans of the revolutionary generation could draw on a variety of different political idioms and constitutional discourses.[8] The language of rights proved to be far more flexible than earlier accounts had suggested.[9] When one takes account of the ideological diversity of the founding period and the range of voices that contributed to the original debate over the Constitution, the idea of discerning a single, monolithic original understanding for something as complex as the right to bear arms now appears historically naive.

Standard Model scholarship is perhaps the most egregious example of the way in which constitutional history has failed to keep pace with the changes that have transformed American historiography. Traditional constitutional scholarship has not only failed to take account of recent developments in early American historiography but has failed to grapple with the profound transformation in American intellectual and cultural history that has taken place in the last few decades.[10] While constitutional history was once closely tethered to intellectual history, the two fields have grown increasingly estranged over the last two decades.[11] The contrast with recent writing in intellectual and cultural history is particularly instructive. Rather than treat texts as fixed and essentially univocal, intellectual and cultural historians have recognized that most texts are polyvalent.[12] Rather than assume that the same words meant the same things to different historical actors, it seems far more plausible to recognize the possibility that the right to bear arms meant distinctively different things to members of the planter elite, back-country farmers, and middling sorts.[13]

Although the Standard Model rests on a variant of the constitutional philosophy of originalism, its practitioners have presented a one-dimensional account of the founding era. Even if one acknowledges that originalism is a variant of "law office" or "forensic history" and therefore not subject to the same rules that govern professional historians, any theory of originalism must ultimately rest on some notion of fidelity to the past. Yet, even when evaluated by originalist standards, the Standard Model must be judged a failure.[14] Standard Modelers have not relied on the most recent and up-to-date historical scholarship but have drawn on an outdated model of consensus history. Nor have Standard Modelers grappled with the question of how one ought to choose from among the myriad intents articulated during ratification by Federalists and Anti-Federalists. Rather than deal directly with this problem, Standard Modelers have fallen back on the most simplistic style of law office history, selectively culling quotes from published primary sources with little regard for authorial intent or interest in establishing the relative influence of particular texts. The impressionistic, cut-and-paste methodology employed by Second Amendment originalists pays little attention to context and has produced a profoundly anachronistic reading of the sources.[15]

STANDARD MODEL, STANDARD ERRORS

Although largely championed by legal scholars, the Standard Model has attracted the support of a few historians. Sadly, the historians most closely identified with the Standard Model have reproduced many of the anachronisms that have marred legal scholarship on this topic. The most outspoken champion of the Standard Model is English historian Joyce Lee Malcolm, who has become a prominent spokesperson for The Second Amendment Foundation, Academics for the Second Amendment, and the NRA.[16] According to Malcolm, "The position of this amendment, second among the ten amendments added to the Constitution as a Bill of Rights, underscored its importance to contemporaries." Additional support for the Standard Model has been provided by historian Leonard Levy, whose *Origins of the Bill of Rights* categorically asserts that "the right to bear arms is an individual right" and that the "reference to the people's right did not mean the people collectively or society at large."[17] Proof for this claim, Levy argues, may be found in the Pennsylvania State Constitution of 1776, which placed the right to keep and bear arms "cheek-by-jowl with the rights to free speech and press, also personal rights." Levy also asserts that the right to bear arms had to be a personal right, because Pennsylvania did not even have a state militia in 1776. The Pennsylvania constitution has been widely cited by other writers associated with the Standard Model. Indeed, gun-rights advocate David Hardy declares emphatically that Pennsylvanians "sought an unquestionably individual right."[18] The example of Pennsylvania is therefore crucial to the individual-rights thesis.

All of the claims listed above are demonstrably false. Consider Malcolm's argument that the right to bear arms was deliberately and self-consciously positioned as the Second Amendment. The provision of the Bill of Rights that we now call the Second Amendment was actually the fourth amendment submitted to the states by the First Congress. Only after the first two amendments dealing with congressional salaries and apportionment were defeated did "the Right to Bear Arms" become the Second Amendment. A glance at the individual state constitutions drafted during the Revolutionary era reveals no consistent placement for the right to bear arms. Virginia listed the right to bear arms as the fifteenth provision, while Pennsylvania placed the right to bear arms as the thirteenth provision in its Declaration of Rights. Nor do the various amendments proposed by the state ratification conventions support Malcolm's contention that the placement of the right to bear arms in the federal Bill of Rights reflected a conscious decision on the part of the founders. New Hampshire's proposed amendments to the Constitution included two provisions dealing with the right to bear arms, which were ranked as tenth and twelfth, and Virginia's amendment was number seventeen.[19]

Leonard Levy's claims about the Pennsylvania state constitution also rest on an erroneous reading of the evidence. The right to keep and bear arms does appear directly after the right of freedom of the press in the Pennsylvania Declaration of Rights. Levy, however, provides no evidence to substantiate his claim that this decision was purposeful. The order in the Pennsylvania Declaration of Rights might just as easily be seen as mimetic of the Virginia Declaration of Rights, which Pennsylvanians simply copied. Given the limits of the historical record, there is simply no basis for Levy's claim that the positioning of these two amendments demonstrates a conscious linkage in the minds of Pennsylvanians.[20]

Levy's interpretation of the meaning of the phrase "rights of the people" also merits further scrutiny. There is no question that this phrase has evolved into a synonym for individual rights in modern jurisprudence, but it is less clear that it would have been understood in these terms by most eighteenth-century Pennsylvanians. To contextualize that term one must look at the entire Pennsylvania Declaration of Rights. Levy neglects to cite the third provision of the Pennsylvania Declaration of Rights, which affirms "that the people of this state have the sole, exclusive, and inherent right of governing and regulating the internal police of the same."[21] Used in this sense, a "right of the people" clearly does not translate into an individual right.[22] As historian Jack Rakove observes, "Nearly all the activities that constituted the realms of life, liberty, property, and religion were subject to regulation by the state; no obvious landmarks marked the boundaries beyond which its authority could not intrude, if its actions met the requirement of law." As far as the term rights of the people was concerned, Rakove makes this observation: "in the eighteenth century, however, many authorities would still have held that the primary holders of rights were not individuals but rather the collective body of the people."[23] In contrast to Levy's anachronistic reading of the sources, Rakove's approach to the problem of rights shows how Pennsylvanians could use the same language to discuss the police powers of the state, the rights of free speech, and the right to keep and bear arms. Additional support for this reading is provided by political scientist Donald Lutz, who notes that the first state constitutions generally treated most rights as alienable. Legislatures enjoyed broad powers to modify or limit rights when popularly elected legislatures thought such abridgements served the public interest.[24]

Finally, Levy's claim that Pennsylvania lacked a militia is also inaccurate. Section 6 of the "Plan or Frame of Government" provides that "the freeman of the commonwealth and their sons shall be trained and armed for its defense, under such regulations, restrictions, and exceptions as the general assembly shall by law direct." The Frame of Government bars plural office holding but explicitly exempts officers of the militia from this prohibition. The radical forces that helped transform the voluntary private militia into a state militia were also the driving forces behind the radical state constitution of 1776. It is also worth noting that Pennsylvania not only asserted that all men should be trained for military service but explicitly empowered the legislature to exclude individuals or groups when the public good required such actions. The notion that the militia was universal, that it included all citizens, also turns out to rest on a dubious historical foundation.[25]

THE PERILS OF FALSE ANALOGY

The example of Pennsylvania also provides compelling evidence that contradicts the Standard Model's equation of free speech with the right to bear arms. Guns and words were not identical to the founders. Shortly after adopting their state constitution, which affirmed that "the people have a right to bear arms for the defense of themselves and the state," Pennsylvanians passed a series of Test Acts, which imposed severe penalties on citizens who refused to take an oath of allegiance to the state. Individuals who refused to take the oath were disarmed. The right of bearing arms in Pennsylvania rested on the willingness of citizens to renounce any intention to take up arms against the state.[26] There was a broad consensus that prior restraint of the press was unacceptable; there was no consensus on the issue of prior restraints when it came to arms. The Constitutionalist Party, which framed the Pennsylvania constitution and passed the Test Acts, accepted that state could disarm peaceful citizens when the good of the community required such action.[27] Contrary to the claims of Powe and other Standard Modelers, Pennsylvania's Constitutionalists recognized a fundamental difference between guns and words. Prior restraints on gun ownership were not unconstitutional. Historian Michael Bellesiles has documented dozens of examples of legislatures regulating gun ownership in colonial and revolutionary America.[28] The notion that guns could not be extensively regulated turns out to be a modern myth, one that has been aggressively spread by supporters of the Standard Model. Thus, Robert Cottrol, a leading gun-rights advocate, could declare that "for much of American History there were few regulations concerning firearms ownership."[29] Cottrol's failure to examine systematically the kinds of laws that the founders thought would be compatible with the right to bear arms is typical of the Standard Model's method of historical thin description. Bellesiles's evidence about the regulation of firearms in early America makes clear the fatuousness of the Standard Model's effort to link the right to bear arms and freedom of the press. The laws enacted by individual state governments regulating gun ownership have no functional analog to restrictions on the press in Revolutionary America. Indeed, the records of militia musters and periodic gun censuses make the analogy even more problematic. Government not only regulated guns and ammunition; it kept close tabs on who had guns and the condition of those weapons. The state also retained the rights to compel citizens to submit to formal arms training and to exclude individuals and groups from service in the militia.[30]

TO BEAR ARMS AGAINST BEARS?

Standard Modelers have often invoked Pennsylvania's Anti-Federalist Minority's proposal for amendments as proof that the right to bear arms was intended to be an individual right. In a foundational text for the Standard Model, gun-rights proponent Don Kates declares that "the individual right nature of the Pennsylvania right to arms proposal is unmistakable."[31] The relevant amendment proposed by

Pennsylvanians reads as follows: "That the people have a right to bear arms for the defense of themselves and their own state, or the United States, or for the purposes of killing game; and no law should be passed for disarming the people or any of them, unless for crimes committed, or real danger of public injury from individuals; and as standing armies in the time of peace are dangerous to liberty, they ought not to be kept up; and that the military shall be kept under strict subordination to and be governed by the civil powers."[32]

This provision has also been used to prove that the phrase bear arms did not have an exclusively military connotation. In the view of the Second Amendment Foundation's Nelson Lund, "Contrary to a popular misconception, the military connotations frequently associated with the term 'bear arms' do not mean that the term invariably implies a military context. This was made perfectly clear in one of the earliest proposals for a bill of rights, which was drafted by the Anti-Federalist minority at the Pennsylvania ratifying convention." The "popular misconception" Professor Lund alludes to is Garry Wills's discussion of the military connotation of the term "bear arms." While the example from Pennsylvania might plausibly challenge the notion of a consensus on the meaning of this term, it falls far short of discrediting the argument that the most common understanding of this term was linked to a military context. A substantive rebuttal to Wills's contention would require that Lund demonstrate that the term was routinely used to refer to gun ownership outside of a military context. Rather than undertake the historical research necessary to document such a claim, Standard Modelers fall back on the lone example of Pennsylvania. While it is possible that the Pennsylvania usage was not exceptional, such a claim would require an exhaustive survey of contemporary usage, something Standard Modelers have studiously avoided. Thus, the Standard Model's claim about the nonmilitary meaning of bearing arms rests on a single counterexample.

Supporters of the Standard Model are probably correct to challenge Wills's dismissal of "The Dissent of the Minority." This Anti-Federalist text was both widely distributed and acknowledged by a number of contemporaries to be an influential statement of Anti-Federalist ideas.[33] Although often invoked by Standard Modelers, few individual-rights theorists have read this Anti-Federalist text carefully, and none has taken the time to situate it properly within the context of Anti-Federalist thought in Pennsylvania. "The Dissent" was written by the same individuals who supported the Pennsylvania State Constitution of 1776 and defended the constitutionality of the Test Acts. The provision of the Test Act that allowed individuals to be disarmed was still in effect when the "Dissent of the Minority" was published. The provision of the Dissent that allowed persons to be disarmed for "crimes committed, or real danger of public injury" was read in broad terms by Pennsylvanians.[34] Nelson Lund's contention that there is not "a shred of evidence to support the proposition that a single American, let alone any significant body of opinion, held that the federal government should have the power to disarm individual American citizens" ignores the very text that he himself cites as conclusive proof about the attitudes of Americans toward the meaning of the term "to bear arms." If Standard Modelers wish to use the authority of the Dissent to counter the claim that the right to bear arms might have had an exclusively military meaning, they must grapple with the fact that this amendment clearly would have allowed the federal government to disarm individuals deemed to be dangerous to public safety.[35]

Standard Modelers invariably read the term defense of "themselves" as a statement of an individual right. While such a reading is plausible, it is by no means the only possible reading of this text. It is important to recall that there were no organized police forces in eighteenth-century America and that the militia was often called on to serve as an agent of law enforcement.[36] The Test Act empowered the militia to disarm citizens who refused to take the loyalty oath. Thus, in addition to serving as a military force, the militia in Pennsylvania also functioned as a police force. Given this fact, it is far from obvious that the meaning of the phrase "defense of themselves" should be interpreted as a statement of individual rights.

The affirmation of the right to hunt, a provision not emulated by any other state ratification convention, does suggest a nonmilitary context for the right to keep arms. Here it seems that the traditional variant of the collective-rights thesis must be amended. At least in Pennsylvania, there appears to have been a recognition of a right to use weapons to hunt. Recognizing this type of individual right does not mean, however, that the right was understood to be somehow comparable to the right of free speech. The provision affirming a right to hunt proposed in the Dissent acknowledged that this right might be limited as to time and place. Hunting was obviously subject to extensive regulation, including some types of prior restraints, restrictions that would never have been permissible for speech.

Anti-Federalists were not shy when it came to predicting the horrors that would befall America if the Constitution were ratified without amendment. Given the lengthy and detailed list of horrors that Anti-Federalists prophesied, it is surprising how little concern there was during ratification that the federal government might violate the right of individuals to possess arms for personal use.[37] Positive assertions of an individual right to bear arms are also rare in the large body of literature generated by the ratification debates.[38] If the myth of the gun-toting frontiersmen dependent on his musket for survival were true, one would have expected to see this theme play a much more prominent role in the rhetoric of ratification.[39] Even the right to hunt championed by the "Dissent of the Minority"—one of the rare instances when the right to bear arms was discussed in a nonmilitary context— was not emulated by any other state ratification convention.[40]

Although the Standard Model draws heavily on the writings of Anti-Federalists, its supporters also quote liberally from Federalists, including James Madison. L. A. Powe's argument is typical of the way in which the Standard Model has read Madison's early drafts of what became the Second Amendment. Originally, Madison believed that the right to bear arms ought to be "placed in the grab bag of Article I, Section 9, after the prohibition against bills of attainder and ex post facto laws and before the limitation on direct taxation."[41] For Powe, this decision is clear proof that Madison understood this provision to be an individual right. "If the collective rights theory were correct," Powe asserts, "then Madison should have placed his 'Second Amendment' either in Article I Section 8, with the militia clauses, or in Article IV, Section 4, the Guarantee Clause."[42]

Once again supporters of the Standard Model fail to contextualize adequately the text they quote. Madison's decision to place the right to bear arms in Article I, Section 9, followed the practice common to virtually all of the individual state constitutions. The statement of a militia right was always separated from discussions about the specific form of the militia's organization and the scope of the militia's powers. The original placement of the right to bear arms in Madison's draft of the Bill of Rights does little to clarify whether he thought this was an individual or a collective right. Nor does it provide much insight into how Madison understood the relationship between this right and freedom of speech.[43] Supporters of the Standard Model have ignored a much more important piece of evidence about how Madison understood the connection between the right to bear arms and other fundamental rights. Madison originally proposed an amendment that read: "No State shall infringe the right of trial by Jury in criminal cases, nor the rights of conscience, nor the freedom of speech, or of the press."[44] It is important to recall that in 1788–89 Madison viewed the individual states, not the federal government, as the greatest threat to liberty. In a letter to Jefferson describing his views about the efficacy of a written bill of rights, Madison reminded Jefferson that "repeated violations of these parchment barriers have been committed by overbearing majorities in every State."[45] "There is," Madison warned, "more danger for those powers being abused by the State Governments than by the Government of the United States."[46] Although Madison's amendment was rejected by Congress, it provides clear evidence that he did not believe it necessary to protect individual citizens from efforts of their states to limit the right to bear arms. The right to bear arms was not a functional analog to the right of freedom of speech.

Additional evidence that the question of individual rights was not central to the debate over the Second Amendment in Congress is provided by the remarks of

Elbridge Gerry, the only Anti-Federalist author who participated in the congressional debate over the amendment. Gerry's comments in the First Congress are
vital to understanding the original debate over the right to bear arms. Gerry also
provides a useful reminder that not all Anti-Federalists were populist democrats, a
simplification and misconception that has been central to the argument of several
works associated with the Standard Model.[47] One of the original nonsigners of the
Constitution, Gerry was a key player in ratification, and his "Objections to the Constitution" was the most widely reprinted Anti-Federalist essay.[48]

Gerry objected to the way in which the clause about conscientious objection
status might allow the new government to disarm the militia of the states. "I am
apprehensive, sir, that this clause would give an opportunity to the people in power
to destroy the constitution itself. They can declare who are those religiously scrupulous, and prevent them from bearing arms."[49] Although Gerry might have used
this occasion to express concern that an individual right to own guns was in danger, he showed no interest in this issue. His concern was focused squarely on the
threat to the militia: "Whenever government means to invade the rights and liberties of the people, they always attempt to destroy the militia." If the Standard Model
were correct, one would expect Gerry to make at least passing mention of the potential for the conscientious-objector exclusion to provide a pretext to deprive individuals of a right to own weapons for personal use. Gerry apparently showed little
interest in this question, focusing on the danger that this power might pose to the
ability of the states to maintain their militias.[50]

THE STANDARD MODEL AND THE PROBLEM OF ANACHRONISM:
A CLOSER LOOK AT THE EVIDENCE

There are serious problems with the way Standard Modelers have interpreted eighteenth-century texts. Interpreting the phrase "rights of the people" to mean something akin to what modern jurists mean by the phrase "individual right" is the most
serious anachronism. Assuming that the invocation of "the people" meant a broadly
inclusive vision of the people is an equally problematic assumption, one that appears time and again in the Standard Model. The flaws in the model's use of evidence can be seen in libertarian constitutional scholar William Van Alstyne's use of
gun-rights advocate Stephen Halbrook's work. In another foundational text for the
Standard Model, Halbrook sets up a sharp dichotomy between a collective/states'-
rights interpretation and the individual-rights view. "In recent years it has been suggested that the Second Amendment protects the 'collective' right of states to maintain militias, while it does not protect the right of 'the people' to keep and bear arms.
If anyone entertained this notion in the period during which the Constitution and

Bill of Rights were debated and ratified, it remains one of the most closely guarded secrets of the eighteenth century, for no known writing surviving from the period between 1787 and 1791 states such a thesis."[51] It is difficult to reconcile this claim with the assertion of early American military historian Don Higginbotham that "if people believed passionately in gun ownership as an individual right, they rarely said so." Higginbotham concludes that such claims amount to little more than a handful of references.

How can these two contradictory claims be reconciled? It is important to look closely at Halbrook's claim, which sets modern legal terminology, "collective rights," against the eighteenth-century terminology, "rights of the people." Halbrook has set up a false dichotomy. The vast majority of references to the right to bear arms invoked a right of the people. The key question for historians is how that term should be translated into modern parlance. Was such a right an individual right, a collective right, or something in between? When the anachronism at the heart of the Standard Model is exposed, it is possible to see the truth of Higginbotham's statement. If one surveys the vast literature of ratification and the debates in Congress during the framing of the Bill of Rights, one finds surprisingly few instances in which an individual right to bear arms was explicitly defended. Most references to the right to bear arms were linked to the militia. A smaller, but certainly not insignificant, number of references invoked the right to bear arms as a right of the people. If one scans the entire corpus of literature associated with the Standard Model, paying close attention to the sources used to support its claims, it is readily apparent that the same pieces of evidence are endlessly recycled by one author after another. An exceedingly small number of texts from ratification espoused anything that might remotely resemble an individual right to bear arms.

The often-cited examples from Pennsylvania, including the Declaration of Rights and the Dissent of the Minority, illustrate the problems with the Standard Model's use of evidence. Even the right of the people to hunt, the most unambiguously non-military statement of a right to keep and use arms for personal use, was subject to extensive regulation by the state. One must also question how to weight a proposed amendment that was not emulated by any other state convention. While it would be a mistake to dismiss the "Dissent of the Minority," there is no reason to treat it as normative.

The original draft of Madison's version of the Second Amendment, another favorite example of Standard Modelers, has also been poorly contextualized. The placement of this right in the body of the Constitution does not, as Standard Modelers suggest, help us determine that Madison believed this right to be an individual one. Even more telling, however, is Madison's decision not to include the right to bear arms in his list of basic rights to be applied against the states, a fact generally ignored by Standard Modelers.[52]

Another favorite text of Standard Modelers is a hastily assembled newspaper essay defending the Bill of Rights prepared by Federalist Tench Coxe. In a letter to Madison, Coxe admitted that "I have therefore taken an hour from my present engagement" and "thrown together a few remarks upon the first part of the Resolutions."[53] Given Coxe's own description of his remarks, it is difficult to understand the importance that has been assigned to them by Standard Modelers.[54] In his essay Coxe does affirm "the right of the people to keep and bear their private arms." While it is possible to read this statement as an expression of an individual-rights point of view, Coxe's invocation of the right of the people within the context of resisting tyranny is more plausibly read as a reiteration of the necessity of a citizen militia composed of the sturdy yeomanry than it is of some sort of expansive individual right comparable to freedom of speech. Coxe's earlier writings in defense of the Constitution praised the militia but did not discuss an individual right of gun ownership. Coxe was an ardent opponent of Pennsylvania's Anti-Federalists, and it seems unlikely that his invocation of the phrase "bear arms" was meant to echo the nonstandard usage of the Anti-Federalist signers of the Dissent of the Minority. The reference to private arms that Coxe invoked most likely meant those arms that citizens owned to meet their obligations as members of the militia.[55]

Both the tone and argument of Coxe's essay seem far more republican than liberal in spirit. Indeed, Coxe explicitly invokes "the republican spirit" of Madison's draft of the Bill of Rights. While defending "the creed of liberty," Coxe underscored that government existed to pursue the public good. Interestingly, in discussing the core freedoms that would eventually constitute the First Amendment, Coxe chose to describe them as "political rights" not individual or personal rights. Although Coxe's republican language is not incompatible with liberal ideas about individual rights, it certainly does not bear the weight placed upon it by supporters of the Standard Model.[56]

When all of the evidence is carefully weighed and evaluated, Higginbotham's assessment appears much closer to the mark than do the claims of the Standard Model. There are relatively few examples from ratification and the early congressional debates that provide unambiguous evidence of an individual right to bear arms. Nor do the few examples that might plausibly be read to protect such a right support the contention that this right was understood in terms comparable to the right of freedom of speech or the press.

CONCLUSION

Rather than provide a "Standard Model," the new individual-rights model of the Second Amendment more closely resembles an elaborate check-kiting scheme. The historical claims made by the Standard Model are doubtful at best and in other instances demonstrably false. Unfortunately, the structure of law review publication, particularly the absence of blind peer review, has allowed historical errors to spread rapidly. Rather than contain mistakes and weed out dubious historical claims, anachronisms and mistakes have been instantly canonized. Mere publication in a law review creates its own form of scholarly legitimacy.[57] By endlessly recycling the same evidence and quoting each others' work, scholars associated with the Standard Model have created a reality effect, manufacturing an image of scholarly consensus where none exists.[58]

At the core of the Standard Model is a false analogy between the First and Second Amendments. In contrast to supporters of the Standard Model, the founders of our constitutional tradition understood the difference between words and guns. For anyone with even the most superficial acquaintance with the tragic events at Kent State, the importance of this distinction is obvious. If this symposium can help historians and legal scholars appreciate the difference between guns and words, it will have accomplished an important public service.

NOTES

1. On the term Standard Model, see Glenn Harlan Reynolds, "A Critical Guide to the Second Amendment," *Tennessee Law Review* 62 (Spring 1995): 461–512.

2. For an example of an effort to create an image of scholarly consensus, see Randy E. Barnett and Don B. Kates, "Under Fire: The New Consensus on the Second Amendment," *Emory Law Journal* 45 (1996): 1139–259. While supporters of the Standard Model claim that the collective-rights interpretation is a modern invention, political scientist Robert Spitzer argues the opposite case in "Lost and Found: Researching the Second Amendment," *Chicago-Kent Law Review* (forthcoming).

3. A useful guide to the scholarly controversy arising from the Standard Model may be found in Chris Moone, "Showdown," *Lingua Franca* (Feb. 2000).

4. *United States v. Emerson*, 46 F.Supp.2d 598 (N.D. Tex. 1999). The relationship between recent scholarship and the Emerson decision is discussed in Moone, "Showdown."

5. The notion of the First Amendment's checking function was framed by Vincent Blasi, "The Checking Value in First Amendment Theory," *American Bar Foundation Research Journal* (1977). Sanford Levinson, "The Embarrassing Second Amendment," *Yale Law Journal* 99 (Dec. 1989): 637–59. The most elaborate effort to draw out the connection between the First and Second Amendment is L. A. Powe, "Guns, Words, and Constitutional Interpretation," *William and Mary Law Review* 38 (May 1997): 1311–403.

6. On the ideal of thick description, see Clifford Geertz, *The Interpretation of Cultures* (New York: Basic Books, 1973). Geertz's influence on American history is discussed by Gordon S. Wood, "Intellectual History and the Social Sciences," in *New Directions in American Intellectual History*, ed. John Higham and Paul Conkin (Baltimore: Johns Hopkins Univ. Press, 1979), and Joyce Appleby, *Liberalism and Republicanism in the Historical Imagination* (Cambridge, Mass.: Harvard Univ. Press, 1992), 217.

7. For a useful overview of recent historical scholarship on the Revolutionary era that stressed ideological diversity, see Linda K. Kerber, "The Revolutionary Generation: Ideology, Politics, and Culture in the Early Republic," in *The New American History*, ed. Eric Foner, rev. ed. (Philadelphia: Temple Univ. Press, 1997).

8. Isaac Kramnick, "The 'Great National Discussion': The Discourse of Politics in 1787," *William and Mary Quarterly* 45 (1988): 3–32.

9. Hendrik Hartog, "The Constitution of Aspiration and the Rights That Belong to Us All," *Journal of American History* 74 (1987): 1013–34, and "Pigs and Positivism," *Wisconsin Law Review* (1985): 899–935.

10. For a concise overview of these trends, see Thomas Bender, "Intellectual and Cultural History," in *The New American History*. For a brief overview of the implications of postmodern theory to intellectual and cultural history, see Saul Cornell, "Splitting the Difference: Textualism, Contextualism and Post-Modern History," *American Studies* (Spring 1995): 57–80.

11. John Higham's list of the leading figures of postwar historiography is revealing in this regard. Richard Hofstadter, Edmund Morgan, Daniel Boorstin, and David Potter were all intellectual historians, and each showed considerable interest in constitutional issues broadly defined. John Higham and Paul K. Conkin, eds., "Introduction," *New Directions in American Intellectual History* (Baltimore: Johns Hopkins Univ. Press, 1979). For a discussion of the way in which the new social history displaced intellectual history, see Robert Darnton, "Intellectual and Cultural History," in *The Past before Us: Contemporary Historical Writing in the United States*, ed. Michael Kammen (Ithaca, N.Y.: Cornell Univ. Press, 1980), 327–54.

12. For an effort to pull together the methods of the new social history and recent intellectual and cultural history informed by poststructuralist insights, see Saul Cornell, *The Other Founders: Anti-Federalism and the Dissenting Tradition in America, 1788–1828* (Chapel Hill: Univ. of North Carolina Press, 1999).

13. For a discussion of the way the Standard Model has incorporated the assumptions of consensus history and been blind to the existence of profound tensions between elite and popular constitutional thought, see Saul Cornell, "Commonplace or Anachronism: The Standard Model, the Second Amendment, and the Problem of History in Contemporary Constitutional Theory," *Constitutional Commentary* 16 (1999): 221–46.

14. A detailed philosophical discussion of originalism may be found in Keith E. Whittington, *Constitutional Interpretation: Textual Meaning, Original Intent, and Judicial Review* (Lawrence: Univ. Press of Kansas, 1999), which provides little historical guidance on this issue of how one should weight different intents. For a useful sampling of other writings on this topic, see Jack N. Rakove, *Interpreting the Constitution: The Debate over Original Intent* (Boston: Northeastern Univ. Press, 1990). On the notion of standards for originalists, see H. Jefferson Powell, "Rules for Originalists," *Virginia Law Review* 73 (1987): 659. For a critique of law office history, see Alfred H. Kelly, "Clio and the Court: An Illicit Love Affair," *Supreme Court Review* (1965). On originalism as a form of "forensic history," see John P. Reid, "Law and History," *Loyola Los Angeles Law Review* 27 (1993). On the need for legal scholarship to remain current with historical scholarship, see Martin S. Flaherty, "History 'Lite' in Modern American Constitutionalism," *Columbia Law Review* 95 (1995).

15. The flawed version of originalism at the root of the Standard Model is discussed by Jack N. Rakove, "The Second Amendment: The Highest State of Originalism," *Chicago-Kent Law Review* (forthcoming). For other critiques of the Standard Model by historians, see Garry Wills, "To Keep and Bear Arms," *New York Review of Books*, Sept. 21, 1995; Saul Cornell, "Commonplace or Anachronism," *Constitutional Commentary* 16 (1999); Michael A. Bellesiles, "Suicide Pact: New Readings of the Second Amendment," ibid.; Don Higginbotham, "The Second Amendment in Historical Context," ibid.; and Robert E. Shalhope, "To Keep and Bear Arms in the Early Republic," ibid. The historian most closely identified with the Standard Model, is Joyce Lee Malcolm. For a discussion of the controversy between historians and legal scholars, see Chris Moone, "Showdown."

16. Malcolm signed the Academics for the Second Amendment brief in *United States v. Emerson* and is listed as a historical source on the Second Amendment Foundation's Web site, http://www.saf.org.

In an NRA press release Malcolm was listed along with Glenn Harlan Reynolds as "available for interviews with the news media to discuss the history and the 'Standard Model' interpretation of the Second Amendment by calling NRA Public Affairs"; available on the World Wide Web at http://www.nraila.org/news/20000215-AntiGunGroups-001.shtml.

17. Leonard W. Levy, *Origins of the Bill of Rights* (New Haven, Conn.: Yale Univ. Press, 1999), 134, 142. Levy's support for an individual right seems more qualified than that of many Standard Modelers.

18. Joyce Lee Malcolm, *To Keep and Bear Arms: The Origins of an Anglo-American Right* (Cambridge, Mass.: Harvard Univ. Press, 1994), 164; Levy, *Origins of the Bill of Rights*, 135, 142; David T. Hardy, "The Second Amendment and the Historiography of the Bill of the Rights," *Journal of Law and Politics* 4 (Summer 87): 1–62. For other examples of scholars who use the example of Pennsylvania to support the Standard Model, see Reynolds, "Critical Guide to the Second Amendment," 63; Thomas Macafee and Michael J. Quinlan, "Bringing Forward the Right to Keep and Bear Arms: Do Text, History, or Precedent Stand in the Way?" *North Carolina Law Review* 75 (1997): 781–899; Nelson Lund, "The Past and Future of the Individual's Right to Bear Arms," *Georgia Law Review* 31 (1996): 1–76; and Stephen P. Halbrook, "The Right of the People or the Power of the State: Bearing Arms, Arming Militias, and the Second Amendment," *Valparaiso Law Review* 26 (1991): 131–207. The evidence from Pennsylvania is central to the ruling in *United States v. Emerson,* the first example of a federal court endorsing the Standard Model. For additional evidence demonstrating the importance of Pennsylvania to the Standard Model and the Emerson decision, see "Academics for the Second Amendment," amicus brief in *United States v. Emerson* and the "Second Amendment Foundation," amicus brief, *United States v. Emerson.* All of these briefs are available on the Second Amendment Foundation's Web site, http://www.saf.org.

19. Jack N. Rakove, *Declaring Rights: A Brief History with Documents* (Boston: Bedford Books, 1998), 69–94. For the New Hampshire and Virginia–proposed amendments to the Constitution, see Helen E. Veit, Kenneth R. Bowling, and Charlene Bangs Bickford, eds., *Creating the Bill of Rights* (Baltimore: Johns Hopkins Univ. Press, 1991), 14–28, 182 (hereafter *CBR*).

20. The Virginia Declaration of Rights was used as a model by Pennsylvania, which makes it difficult to know if this juxtaposition was deliberate or simply mimetic. On state constitutions, see Willi Paul Adams, *The First American Constitutions: Republican Ideology and the Making of the State Constitutions in the Revolutionary Era*, trans. Rita and Robert Kimber (Chapel Hill: Univ. of North Carolina Press, 1973); and Donald S. Lutz, *Popular Consent and Popular Control: Whig Political Theory in the Early State Constitutions* (Baton Rouge: Louisiana State Univ. Press, 1980).

21. *Constitutions of the Several Independent States of America* (Philadelphia: 1781), 87.

22. Sanford Levinson, in his influential essay, "The Embarrassing Second Amendment," *Yale Law Journal* 99 (1989): 637–59, invokes the contemporary legal philosopher Ronald Dworkin for his notion of rights. While an excellent starting point for modern discussions of rights, Dworkin's theory of rights does not seem to be a good choice for understanding the founders' conception of rights.

23. Jack N. Rakove, *Original Meanings: Politics and Ideas in the Making of the Constitution* (New York: Knopf, 1996), 291; see also, Rakove, *Declaring Rights*, 22.

24. Donald Lutz, *Popular Consent and Popular Control*, 50. A similar view informs the work of Robert C. Palmer, "Liberties as Constitutional Provisions, 1776–1791," in *Liberty and Community: Constitution and Rights in the Early American Republic*, ed. William E. Nelson and Robert C. Palmer (New York: Oceana Publications, 1987).

25. *Constitutions of the Several Independent States of America* (Philadelphia: 1781), 90. The complex process by which Pennsylvania's private militias became the state militia is discussed in Steven Rosswurm, *Arms, Country, and Class: The Philadelphia Militia and "Lower Sort" during the American Revolution, 1775–1783* (New Brunswick, N.J.: Rutgers Univ. Press, 1987).

26. "A Further Supplement to the Act . . .; and for Disarming Persons. . . ," March 31, 1779.

27. Akhil Reed Amar, *The Bill of Rights: Creation and Reconstruction* (New Haven, Conn.: Yale Univ. Press, 1999), 52, cites the example of the Pennsylvania state constitution to support his claim that states did not have broad authority to disarm the general militia. Amar clearly did not consult the relevant primary sources or the standard secondary sources on Pennsylvania history; the Test Acts were opposed by the state's Republican "party." For more on the political struggle over the Test Acts, see Douglas M. Arnold, *A Republican Revolution: Ideology and Politics in Pennsylvania, 1776–1790* (New

York: Garland, 1989); and Robert L. Brunhouse, *The Counter-Revolution in Pennsylvania, 1776–1790* (Harrisburg: Commonwealth of Pennsylvania, 1942).

28. Michael Bellesiles, "Gun Laws in Early America: The Regulation of Firearms Ownership, 1607–1794," *Law and History Review* 16 (1998): 567–89.

29. Robert Cottrol, "Second Amendment," in *Oxford Companion to the Supreme Court*, ed. Kermit Hall (New York: Oxford Univ. Press, 1992), 763.

30. Bellesiles, "Gun Laws in Early America."

31. Don Kates, "Handgun Prohibition and the Original Meaning of the Second Amendment," *Michigan Law Review* (Nov. 1983): 222.

32. [Samuel Bryan,] "The Address and Reasons of Dissent of the Minority. . . ," in *The Documentary History of the Ratification of the Constitution*, vol. 2, ed. Merrill Jensen et al. (Madison: State Historical Society of Wisconsin, 1976–), 623–24.

33. Garry Wills, "To Keep and Bear Arms," 62–73. For a more specific discussion of how various Anti-Federalist texts might be weighted to reflect their distribution and influence, see *The Other Founders*, chap 1. Interestingly, as far as the question of original intent goes, Wills's dismissal of the relevance of the Dissent echoes the stance of William Findley, one of the Dissent's most influential signers. During the debate over the Jay Treaty in Congress several years later, Findley argued against using this document as a guide to interpreting the Constitution; on this point see ibid., 225.

34. On this point, see Cornell, "Commonplace or Anachronism," 233.

35. Nelson Lund, "The Ends of Second Amendment Jurisprudence: Firearms, Disabilities, and Domestic Violence Restraining Orders," *Texas Review of Law & Politics* (1999): n. 69. For the contrary view, see Garry Wills, "To Keep and Bear Arms."

36. Lawrence M. Friedman, *Crime and Punishment in American History* (New York: Basic Books, 1993), 67–68.

37. Consider some of the more hysterical fears voiced by opponents of the Constitution: the absence of religious tests would allow the pope to become president, the power to tax would allow the federal government to cripple the press, the new nation's capitol would become a refuge for all sorts of outrages, elections might be held in China to frustrate the popular will, the methods of the Spanish Inquisition applied to those accused of crimes. Examples such as these were central to Cecelia Kenyon's notion of the Anti-Federalists as "Men of Little Faith." On the exaggerated and sometimes hysterical character of Anti-Federalist rhetoric, see Cecelia Kenyon, "Introduction," *The Anti-Federalists* (Indianapolis: Bobbs-Merrill, 1966), lxii–lxxiv. More typical of Anti-Federalist fears, however, were the sober predictions that new government lacked a declaration of rights and that the state governments and their militias might easily be rendered ineffective by the consolidating tendencies of the new government; see Cornell, *Other Founders*.

38. Robert Shalhope suggests that historians must consider the possibility that silence on this point indicated a deeply rooted belief that did not require explicit affirmation, Shalhope, "To Keep and Bear Arms in the Early Republic," 280–81. Given that Anti-Federalists were capable of conjuring up almost every other nightmare scenario, it does seem strange that they would have missed the possibility to use this issue to their advantage.

39. For a critique of this myth, see Bellesiles, "Origins of Gun Culture in the United States, 1760–1865," *Journal of American History* 83 (1996): 425–55.

40. A sentiment similar to the Dissent was expressed by a Maine Anti-Federalist in a private letter expressing his hope that the amendments before Congress would affirm a right to hunt; Samuel Nasson to George Thatcher, 9 July 1789, *CBR*, 260–61. Standard Modelers also invoke Samuel Adams's proposed amendment to the Constitution that would have barred Congress from infringing on the right of the people "to keep their own arms"; quoted in Malcolm, *To Keep and Bear Arms*, 158. Even if one conceded that these texts provide evidence of a limited personal right to keep and bear arms, that right was subject to extensive regulation. Indeed, Massachusetts enacted a law that made possession of a

loaded firearm in the city of Boston a crime punishable by a fine and forfeiture; "An Act in addition to the several Acts already made for the prudent Storage of Gun-Powder within the City of Boston" (1786), in *The Perpetual Laws of the Commonwealth of Massachusetts. . . .* (Boston: 1789).

41. Powe, "Guns, Words, and Constitutional Interpretation," 1339.

42. Ibid. The notion that Madison's original intent might trump that of the final form of the amendment that emerged out of the give-and-take of the debate in the First Congress is one of the strangest elements of the Standard Model's variant of originalism.

43. For two different views of Madison's thinking about the Bill of Rights, see Donald Lutz, *A Preface to American Political Theory* (Lawrence: Univ. Presses of Kansas, 1992), 49–86; and Rakove, *Declaring Rights.*

44. Charles F. Hobson, "The Negative on State Laws: James Madison, the Constitution, and the Crisis of Republican Government," *William and Mary Quarterly*, 3d ser., 36 (1979): 215–35.

45. James Madison to Thomas Jefferson, Oct. 17, 1788, in *The Mind of the Founder: Sources of the Political Thought of James Madison,* ed. Marvin Meyers, rev. ed. (Hanover, N.H.: Univ. Press of New England, 1981), 157.

46. Ibid., 173.

47. David C. Williams, "Civic Republicanism and the Citizen Militia: The Terrifying Second Amendment," *Yale Law Journal* 101 (Dec. 1991): 551–615, and "The Militia Movement and Second Amendment Revolution: Conjuring with the People," *Cornell Law Review* 81 (May 1996): 879–952. Williams draws on Akhil Amar's "The Bill of Rights as a Constitution," *Yale Law Journal* 100 (1991): 1131–210, as the basis for this claim. For critiques of Amar's populist thesis, see Daniel J. Hulsebosch, "Tales of Popular Sovereignty: Civics 2000: Process Constitutionalism at Yale," *Michigan Law Review* 97 (1999): 1520–59; and G. Edward White, "Reading the Guarantee Clause," *University of Colorado Law Review* 65 (1994): 787–806.

48. For a discussion of Gerry's Anti-Federalism, see Cornell, *Other Founders*, chap. 2.

49. *CBR*,182.

50. Ibid.

51. Stephen P. Halbrook, *That Every Man Be Armed: The Evolution of a Constitutional Right* (1984): 83, quoted in William Van Alstyne, "The Second Amendment and the Personal Right to Arms," *Duke Law Journal* 43 (1994): 1236–55 n. 13, at 1243 n. 19. A similar claim has been repeated by Halbrook in an essay coauthored with David B. Kopel, "Tench Coxe and the Right to Keep and Bear Arms, 1787–1823," *William and Mary Bill of Rights Journal* 7 (Feb. 1999): 347–99.

52. It is certainly possible that Madison understood the right to be an individual one, different in character than the right of freedom of speech. This possibility has generally been ignored by the Standard Model. Robert Shalhope, the historian who has framed the most sophisticated version of an individual-rights argument, has recently recast his stance to acknowledge that the individual right protected by the Second Amendment was much less inclusive and expansive than his earlier work had suggested. Compare the arguments of Robert E. Shalhope, "The Ideological Origins of the Second Amendment," *Journal of American History* 69 (1982): 599–614, with Robert E. Shalhope, "To Keep and Bear Arms in the Early Republic."

53. Tench Coxe to James Madison, June 18, 1789; and *CBR*, 252–53.

54. Coxe's essay is central to the arguments of Stephen Halbrook, and to David B. Kopel, "Tench Coxe and the Right to Keep and Bear Arms, 1787–1823," *William and Mary Bill of Rights Journal* 7 (Feb. 1999): 347–99; Don Kates, "Handgun Prohibition and the Original Meaning of the Second Amendment," *Michigan Law Review* (Nov. 1983): 224.

55. For a critique of the Standard Model's reading of Coxe's statement, see Garry Wills, *A Necessary Evil: A History of American Distrust of Government* (New York: Simon and Schuster, 1999): 214–15, 257. Halbrook and Kopel provide a slightly more convincing case that at the end of his life Coxe articulated

a more fully developed individual-rights conception of the right to bear arms; "Tench Coxe and the Right to Keep and Bear Arms." Yet even this evidence seems questionable, given their tendency to treat any mention of the people and the right to bear arms as an unambiguous defense of an individual right. Much of their evidence comes from Coxe's attack on John Quincy Adams's defense of England's game laws.

56. [Tench Coxe] "A Pennsylvanian," "Remarks on the First Part of the Amendments...," *New York Packet*, June 23, 1789. Robert Shalhope, "To Keep and Bear Arms," wisely cautions against the dangers of overstating the corporate nature of republicanism. By contrast, the Standard Model's reading of Coxe overemphasizes the liberal individualist character of this text. Given Coxe's own admission to Madison that his effort was hastily assembled, it is probably a mistake to make this particular text a key to understanding the meaning of the Second Amendment.

57. For a discussion of the way the debate over the Standard Model has played itself out in the academy and the popular press, see Moone, "Showdown."

58. The rise of the Standard Model is another example of the profound problems with student-edited law reviews. For a discussion of the problems with the law review system, see James Lindgren, "An Author's Manifesto," *University of Chicago Law Review* 61 (1994): 527, 531. For a useful overview of the growing body of literature attacking legal scholarship generated by student-edited law reviews, see Bernard J. Hibbitts, "Last Writes? Reassessing the Law Review in the Age of Cyberspace," *New York University Law Review* 71 (1996): 615–88. The issue has spilled over into the press; Christopher Shea, "Students v. Professors: Law-Review Debate Heats Up as Student Editors Clash with Faculty Authors," *Chronicle of Higher Education*, June 2, 1995, A33; see also Rosa Ehrenreich, "Look Who's Editing," *Lingua Franca*, Jan./Feb.1996. There is some evidence that some pro-gun advocates have deliberately seeded law reviews with revisionist accounts to influence the courts on this issue; on this point see Carl T. Bogus, "The Hidden History of the Second Amendment," *University of California Davis Law Review* 31 (Winter 1998): 309–408.

The Right to Bear (and the Regulation of) Arms and Quills

Response to Cornell

PAUL HARIDAKIS

Communication Studies, Kent State University

In his essay, Professor Cornell provides a compelling critique of the "Standard Model." In so doing, he highlights some major issues and arguments that have permeated recent scholarly debate about the true intent and extent of Second Amendment rights. Two weaknesses of the Standard Model gleaned from Professor Cornell's essay on which I wish to comment are the seeming equation of First and Second Amendment rights by Standard Model proponents, and the lack of evidence supporting the Standard Model conclusion that the rights guaranteed by the Second Amendment are or were intended to be individual or personal.

A premise Dr. Cornell establishes early is the fallacy of arguing that there is a close connection between First and Second Amendment rights. He is critical, for example, of Standard Modelers' insistence that prior restraints on the regulation of arms are barred by the Second Amendment in the same way the First Amendment proscribes prior restraint of free speech and press. He argues convincingly, "There was no consensus on the issue of prior restraints when it came to arms." He points to Bellesiles's review of gun regulation in early U.S. history to highlight the fact that guns always have been subject to extensive regulation.[1] This latter position is well supported by case law as well. Although there are some cases over the years in which courts have struck down particular attempts to regulate guns, in general the right of states to regulate guns has been upheld by the courts.[2]

Professor Cornell provides a compelling refutation of the Standard Model equating of the right of speech with the right to bear arms by pointing to the early Pennsylvania experience, particularly the passage by that state of the Test Acts, which required that citizens pledge allegiance to the state or risk being disarmed. However, although the history of gun regulation in the United States supports the proposition that guns and words have been treated differently, our history includes similar restrictions on speech as arbitrary boundaries on expression have been established. For example, in 1798, less than a decade after adoption of the Bill of Rights, the federal government passed the Sedition Act. This act was aimed at punishing the publication of "any false, scandalous and malicious writing or writings against the government of the United States."[3] In addition to its chilling effect, numerous newspaper editors and private citizens were prosecuted for violating the act.

Space does not permit a listing of the numerous instances in which courts have affirmed the constitutionality of the regulation of speech. Representative examples include loyalty oaths requiring affirmation of loyalty to the federal or state constitutions,[4] prior restraint of movies by film licensing boards prior to the 1950s,[5] and the restriction of commercial speech.[6] Various categories of speech such as obscenity,[7] indecency,[8] and fighting words or inciteful speech[9] have been deemed to have reduced or no First Amendment protection. In addition, reasonable time, place, and manner restrictions have long been supported as not violating rights of expression guaranteed by the First Amendment.[10] Thus, while anti–gun-control advocates may argue that the Second Amendment bars attempts to require a permit to buy a gun, the Supreme Court has affirmed that speakers, at times, may be required to obtain a permit to speak.

The fact that restrictions on speech, at times, have been as severe as (and arguably more prevalent than) restrictions on the right to bear arms does not negate Professor Cornell's argument that the founders never intended a close connection between First and Second Amendment rights. It is offered simply to suggest that any fundamental difference between the right to bear arms and the right to bear quills has not always been as wide as some of us might expect.

Restrictions on speech and the press may support another point Professor Cornell makes—that perhaps few eighteenth-century authorities deemed rights guaranteed in state and the federal constitutions to be inalienable. This latter point brings me to another major theme in Professor Cornell's essay: Are the rights embodied in the Second Amendment collective or personal? Although I am not convinced that rights guaranteed by the Second Amendment are closely connected to those protected by the First Amendment, I am equally unconvinced that they were conceived solely as a collective right, inexplicably tied to militia regulation or activity. There are similarities in the spirit of rights guaranteed by the Bill of Rights that must continue to be explored.

Perhaps the most fruitful approach to take is, as Professor Cornell argues, to explore more deliberately the discourse and documents of the revolutionary period to understand better the extent to which there was consensus on meaning and where important differences existed. Too much literature to date picks and chooses texts that support the authors' positions and ignores contradictory texts that lend insight on the richness of the debates. This could be because much of the current debate revolves around the issue of gun control and therefore attracts gun-control and anti–gun-control advocates, who take diametrically opposed positions on the issue rather than considering that the true meaning of the Second Amendment may lie somewhere between their polarized positions.

With the above said, finding the true meaning of Second Amendment rights may prove difficult. Although the spirit of that inquiry is laudable, Cornell notes, historical texts are often ambiguous. There is a plethora of writings from which to draw to support either an individual-rights or a collective-rights view.

Some scholars have turned to state constitutions to support their interpretations of the original intent of the right to bear arms. Cornell effectively rebuts one conclusion, that the proximity of free speech guarantees and the right to bear arms in the early Pennsylvania constitution and U.S. Bill of Rights somehow evidence that each is an individual right. But even if such an argument has merit, state histories are just illustrative, and they are conflicting. State constitutions and statutes provide widely disparate notions about the right to bear arms. Some states have taken a collective-rights view, others have embodied the right as individual.[11]

Even more problematic for resolution of the individual-/collective-rights debate is the lack of agreement on use of the phrase "right of the people" in the Bill of Rights and other writings of that era. Cornell discusses how the phrase may have been understood in the eighteenth century. He cites arguments suggesting that eighteenth-century authorities seemed to view rights as held by a collective body of people, not individuals. He also suggests that the paucity of reference to the right to bear or possess arms as an individual right in the ratification era belies the argument that eighteenth-century thinkers felt passionate about the individual nature of the right. He also points out that many (if not most) references to the right in such writings are linked with discussions of the militia.

In this regard, he makes a strong case that eighteenth-century thinkers may not have interpreted rights guaranteed in the Bill of Rights as specifically individual or collective. Thus, Cornell argues, "Interpreting the phrase 'right of the people' to mean something akin to what modern jurists mean by the phrase 'individual right' is the most serious anachronism" of the Standard Model.

However, if the Standard Model is fundamentally flawed (Cornell makes a strong argument that it is), where does discrediting it leave us? It is not satisfactory to conclude that the phrase "the right of the people" and amendments in which it is used (including the Second Amendment) had different meanings for different people. Once the Bill of Rights was ratified, each amendment had a meaning and a purpose. Ultimately, it is up to the Supreme Court to provide a definitive interpretation for us. It has not done that. But the Court has hinted at how "the right of the people" should be viewed for purposes of constitutional analysis. For example, in *United States v. Verdugo-Urquidez* (1990), a Fourth Amendment case, Chief Justice William Rehnquist indicated that the Fourth Amendment protects the same "class of persons" as the First and Second Amendments.[12] Justice Rehnquist's observation that the "right of the people" appears to have been a "term of art" in the Bill of Rights is logical. The First Amendment guarantees "the right of the people peaceably to assemble, and to petition the Government for a redress of grievances." The Second guarantees "the right of the people to keep and bear Arms." The Fourth guarantees "the right of the people to be secure . . . against unreasonable searches and seizures." The Tenth provides that "any powers not delegated to the United States by the Constitution are reserved to the States, respectively, or to the people."

Thus, although the meaning of the Second Amendment "right of the people" may not be resolved, the Court has referenced some similarity among the rights guaranteed by the Bill of Rights. Because the Supreme Court has treated First and Fourth Amendment rights of the people as personal, flaws in a single perspective, such as that of the Standard Model, should not cloud the merit of the possibility that other rights reserved in the Bill of Rights are similarly personal.

Although some texts rebut that notion and support the position that the "right of the people" may be a collective right or that eighteenth-century thinkers viewed it as neither individual or collective, the argument that the Second Amendment gives the states power to confer or deny that right in the interest of militia activity is less convincing. We must be wary of interpreting the right as controllable by the states at their arbitrary discretion. As the tragedy that occurred at Kent State on May 4, 1970, demonstrated, we can never permit ourselves to assume carte blanche that the actions of a militia leader (e.g., a state governor) will be exercised on behalf of or in the interest of "the right of the people."

Finally, as the regulation of speech and arms over the years has demonstrated, various branches of government have set boundaries on the exercise of those rights. Thus, the debate over whether a constitutional right is viewed as collective or individual should not cloud the overarching concern: What boundaries on constitutional rights are acceptable to "the people"?

NOTES

1. Michael Bellesiles, "Gun Laws in Early America: The Regulation of Firearms Ownership, 1607–1794," *Law and History Review* 16 (1998): 567–89.

2. *Hickman v. Block*, 81 F.3d 98 (9th Cir. 1996); *Masters v. State*, 685 S.W.2d 654 (Tex. Crim., 1985).

3. Quoted in Thomas L. Tedford, *Freedom of Speech in the United States*, 3d ed. (State College, Penn.: Strata, 1997), 31.

4. *Cole v. Richardson*, 405 U.S. 676 (1972); *Knight v. Board of Regents*, 390 U.S. 36 (1968).

5. *Mutual Film Corp. v. Industrial Commission of Ohio*, 236 U.S. 230 (1915); *Freedman v. Maryland*, 380 U.S. 51 (1965).

6. *Valentine v. Chrestensen*, 316 U.S. 52 (1942).

7. *Miller v. California*, 413 U.S. 15 (1973).

8. *Sable Communications of California, Inc. v. FCC*, 492 U.S. 115 (1989).

9. *Brandenburg v. Ohio*, 395 U.S. 444 (1969); *Chaplinsky v. New Hampshire*, 315 U.S. 568 (1942).

10. *Hague v. CIO*, 307 U.S. 496 (1939).

11. For a review, see Steven H. Gunn, "A Lawyer's Guide to the Second Amendment," *Brigham Young University Law Review* 1998 (1998): 35–54.

12. *United States v. Verdugo-Urquidez*, 494 U.S. 259, 265 (1990).

Pulling the Trigger
Contextualizing the Second Amendment
Response to Cornell

DAVID E. KYVIG

History, Northern Illinois University

Professor Cornell's paper is the latest salvo in a vigorous scholarly debate having important consequences for American public policy regarding what regulations, if any, society may impose on citizen possession of firearms. The Cornell paper adds strength to calls that he and others have been making for reconsideration of the current conventional wisdom and judicial understanding of the Second Amendment to the U.S. Constitution. Cornell disputes modern readings that characterize the Second Amendment as a blanket protection of an individual right of gun ownership, akin to the First Amendment's protection of free speech. The core of his argument, that such claims are grounded on a misreading of these provisions' creation, has much merit.

Those legal scholars who developed what they call the "Standard Model" of the Second Amendment have looked closely at documents generated in the official debates over late-eighteenth-century state and federal constitutions. Such research is necessary and important, but it is insufficient, because unfortunately it examines only formal legislative history. This approach, which its critics jokingly or derisively call "law office history," is a common way of reaching into the past to find concrete evidence to buttress or refute conclusions; its flawed assumption is that uncontextualized official statements can be taken at face value and in such truncated form can provide a full picture of a past reality. It is hard to imagine today's political discourse being regarded so simplistically; why should past discourse be so treated? In footnotes to his paper that could themselves form the basis for a worthwhile discussion of the tension between free expression and social responsibility, Professor Cornell calls attention to broader problems of "law office history" and the undeserved stature it gains through frequent repetition in law journals that are run by student editors and lack sophisticated historical standards.

The Standard Modelers have sought to make a strong case for a libertarian Second Amendment. They find support for an individual right to bear arms in the language of early state constitutions, particularly the 1776 Pennsylvania constitution. They also claim corroboration in state ratification convention petitions of 1788 for a federal constitutional declaration of rights, and in the First Congress's construction of the Bill of Rights.

In contrast, Cornell and his allies place the evolution of the Second Amendment in a somewhat fuller context. They appropriately consider circumstances outside those well-documented legislative proceedings. Michael Bellesiles, for instance, casts important light on the issue with evidence that only about 14 percent of the population in revolutionary America owned guns. Talk about disarming evidence! By comparison, modern public schools seem like military garrisons. Cornell and his fellow critics of the Standard Model theory call for a return to a view of the Second Amendment that joins the amendment's two operative phrases, "a well-regulated militia being necessary to the security of a free state," and "the right to bear arms shall not be abridged," a linkage that emphasizes ordered community defense rather than an unrestricted individual right as the basis for bearing arms.

From the perspective of constitutional amendment history, it makes much greater sense to link the elements internal to the Second Amendment rather than to tie the right to bear arms to the individual protections of free speech in the adjacent First Amendment. Indeed, if amendment "adjacency" is to be taken seriously, the equally proximate Third Amendment, specifying restrictions on the quartering of troops, ought to be given as much weight as the First as a clarification of the Second Amendment. The Third Amendment indicates that restraint of potential military power was as much on the minds of the Bill of Rights drafters as was individual freedom.

Both sides in the current Second Amendment debate need to place the issue in richer historical context. This is very evident in the case of the Standard Modelers, but doing so would further strengthen the case for Cornell and his allies. The latter are moving in the right direction, but they need to travel considerably farther. I have a few modest suggestions about matters that need to be addressed.

The 1776 constitution of Pennsylvania is a problematic foundation for Standard Model claims about the eventual federal Bill of Rights. Pennsylvania's was the most radically democratic of any of the early state constitutions, and it was not at the time admired, much less emulated, in most other states. Indeed, Pennsylvania overhauled and substantially changed its constitution within two decades. Among the 1776 Pennsylvania constitution's many unusual and seldom-copied features, most striking was its council of censors, an independent body elected every seven years to review the constitution's operation, report on whether the government was adhering to it, and propose changes deemed worthwhile. Given the failure of states other than Vermont to follow Pennsylvania's lead on constitutional innovation, any claim that the Pennsylvania constitution heralded a national consensus on the individual right to firearms seems dubious; if such a claim is to be either sustained or refuted, a careful look at the deliberations of the council of censors would be helpful.

Likewise, the construction of constitutional amendments deserves fuller attention than it has been accorded, certainly more than it can be given here. Close consideration of the fashioning and adoption of the Bill of Rights may give pause to advocates of any particular original intent. Space permits only one specific observation.

It can be instructive to compare the construction of the Bill of Rights to the design of the later Fourteenth Amendment. In 1867 the Thirty-ninth Congress, in drafting the Fourteenth Amendment, deliberately put several distinct propositions into one amendment so that it would be impossible for the states to act on anything other than an all-or-nothing basis of ratification. In contrast, the First Congress put forth the Bill of Rights as a dozen separate proposals, choosing in only a few instances to join multiple elements in a single amendment. States considered the Bill of Rights amendments individually and ratified only ten. Claims of deliberate linkage of constitutional values seem most plausible when limited to separate elements of a single amendment. The values of conscience, worship, and speech contained in the First Amendment, the trial rights of the Fifth and Sixth Amendments, and the various equality protections of the Fourteenth Amendment were assuredly linked to a much greater degree than rights expressed in the separate amendments of the Bill of Rights.

Given the history of the amending process, it is as sensible to connect the Second Amendment to the free exercise of religion clause of the First Amendment as to the free speech clause. Does anyone seriously propose that bearing arms is an unquestionable extension of religious rights into which society cannot intrude? Little more of a stretch is required to tie Amendment Two to Eight, uniting the militia and gun provisions of Two with the ban on cruel and unusual punishment in Eight. One could then plausibly argue that if society wishes a death penalty, it ought to be carried out by militia firing squads chosen by lot. A case could be made that such a system falls within the bounds of original intent. Would such linkage of amendments start a rethinking of capital punishment? I suspect that at least more attention would be gained for Professor Cornell's sober reconsideration of whether separate amendments within the Bill of Rights are necessarily linked.

However far scholars of different persuasions choose to pursue arguments of original constitutional intent, they ultimately must recognize the limits of the originalist approach. The reality is that one of the clearest original intentions of the founders was that any amendment to the Constitution ratified by the Article V process was to carry as much constitutional weight as any other provision. While this may not resolve the First and Second Amendment dilemma of freedom versus social order, it at least reminds us that Article V can be used to deal with judicial interpretations of either amendment that do not satisfy modern sensibilities. A narrow construction could be adopted if the American polity concludes that Standard Model individualism has become intolerable. Does this seem implausible? It is no more so that the restriction on the First Amendment and free speech that would be the result of a flag-desecration amendment, a proposal that has already come within a few votes of achieving the congressional two-thirds support necessary to put it before the states for ratification.

Professor Cornell's paper reminds us of the vital role that historical scholarship, whether sound or questionable, plays in efforts to deal with current disputes over complex and important civic matters. Just as we inevitably and for the most part unconsciously draw on our memories, accurate or flawed, to deal with decisions large and small that we make in our personal lives, so do societies draw on history, likewise accurate or flawed, to deal with decisions confronting them. As Professor Cornell makes clear, there are consequences to our use—or misuse—of history.

That message seems to me particularly important here in the Buckeye State, where in recent years the Ohio Board of Regents has taken the unfortunate view that the state does not need research-oriented historians and therefore should not invest public money in their doctoral-level training. This benighted view has undermined once-robust graduate history programs on campuses around the state. The study of history will not provide simple or absolute answers to difficult issues such as the proper role of guns in our culture, but without the clearest possible understanding of the relevant past, wise policy choices on current public conundrums become vastly more problematic.

Ohio and the United States in general need well-trained historians because making sense of the past is not nearly as simple as it may seem at first glance, as the controversy over the Second Amendment bears testimony. It is time that citizens as well as scholars seek to understand the shaping of the Bill of Rights in historical context rather than settle for the narrow-gauged law office history of the Standard Modelers, or even the broader and better assessment of the Second Amendment that Saul Cornell offers us. Perhaps if Ohio invested more in historical research training, students here at Kent State or Professor Cornell's students at Ohio State could take the lead in providing the richer context and greater understanding that would help society come to terms with one of Ohio's and the nation's vexing problems, appropriate constitutional limits on guns.

Words Don't Kill People, Guns Do
Response to the Discussants

SAUL CORNELL

In his thoughtful comments on my paper, Professor Kyvig calls attention to the limits of "law office history" as a mode of historical analysis. As one might expect from a distinguished historian, Kyvig laments the all too typical tendency of this type of history to wrench texts from their historical contexts. When one takes the time to read systematically through the body of scholarship associated with the Standard Model, it is remarkable how time and again the same texts are used to buttress the same argument. Scholarship in this model is little more than recycling. Like any good historian, Kyvig reminds us of the need to move beyond published sources and consider the rich body of materials ignored by Standard Modelers. By focusing on the published documentary sources, particularly the essays of Federalist and Anti-Federalist authors but also, to a lesser extent, the state ratification debates, legal scholars have neglected important parts of the historical record. Perhaps the most egregious omission on the part of legal scholarship is its failure to examine the laws passed by the various states to implement their constitutional protections for the right to bear arms. When the laws governing the militia and firearms are read alongside the various state constitutions and declarations of rights, a very different understanding of the Second Amendment emerges. Eighteenth-century Americans accepted that state governments would keep track of who had firearms. The notion of a well-regulated militia presupposed the right of states to maintain records about who had guns and what types of guns were available to its citizens. Nor was the right to bear arms something all Americans enjoyed; states retained the right to limit access to guns. Even among those white men who enjoyed the full rights of citizenship, the right to bear arms could be limited by loyalty oaths and other types of legislation. Professor Kyvig also reminds us of the important work of Michael Bellesiles, who has provided striking evidence that Americans were not as well armed as had been previously thought. Indeed, the great irony of the current debate about the role of government in regulating weapons is that it has turned history on its head. In eighteenth-century America, citizens relied on the government to help them procure weapons. In modern America, citizens fear that the government will limit their unfettered access to the most deadly weapons.

This historical inversion reflects the fact that guns were relatively scarce in the eighteenth century and have become easily available in modern America.

Kyvig points out another oddity of the Standard Modeler's use of evidence. The heavy reliance on evidence from Pennsylvania is apt to strike any historian familiar with early American history as strange. Pennsylvania's radical 1776 constitution, arguably the most democratic in revolutionary America, was ridiculed and attacked by leading constitutional theorists and not widely emulated. To take the Pennsylvania example as normative seems odd, given its anomalous character.

Professor Haridakis's thought-provoking comments raise a number of important legal issues about the regulation of speech and arms. It is hard to accept the Standard Model's reading of the Second Amendment if one recalls that many of the supporters of the First Amendment also endorsed the Sedition Act of 1798. Standard Modelers are fond of quoting Virginia's St. George Tucker, the great Jeffersonian jurist and author one of the most important constitutional treatises of the early republic. Tucker's vigorous defense of the meaning of the right to bear arms may well come closer to articulating an individual right than does almost any other text cited by the Standard Modelers. Once again, however, the Standard Model has failed to dig deeply enough into the context. Tucker's treatise was not an expression of an American legal view to which all Americans adhered. In this sense the Standard Modelers have merely reasserted an outdated variant of consensus history that few historians would accept as an accurate reflection of post-Revolutionary society.

Tucker's point of view, it is important to recall, was distinctly Jeffersonian. While Tucker opposed the use of seditious libel prosecutions by the federal government, he accepted that individual state courts might continue to use libel to guard the reputations of public persons. In contrast to modern libertarians, Tucker did not believe that questions of individual liberty could be disentangled from issues of federalism. Culling a few quotes from Tucker falls far short of demonstrating a broad individual-rights consensus in the decade after the adoption of the Bill of Rights. Nor does this simplistic and highly impressionistic sampling of extracts from Tucker's voluminous writings help us understand his complex views about liberty. The Standard Model's caricature of Tucker would have us believe that Tucker afforded greater protection to the right to bear arms than he did to the right of freedom of speech. While such a claim might aptly characterize Charlton Heston, the president of the NRA, it does not ring true for Tucker, who was a product of an eighteenth-century world.

Professor Haridakis raises another important point when he calls our attention to the legitimate limits placed on speech. Americans have tolerated a wide range of restrictions on speech over the course of their history. Nor have Americans approached the individual provisions of the First Amendment uniformly. Speech in print has always enjoyed greater protection than other types of speech. The notion that the First Amendment bars prior restraint, a crucial part of the Standard Model's equation of the First and Second Amendments, ignores the other aspects of the First Amendment, such as the right of assembly. This right has always been subject to a much wider range of restrictions. As Professor Haridakis notes, if one needs a permit to have a parade or a demonstration, why does having to obtain a permit for a gun seem unreasonable?

If the Standard Model is wrong, does that mean that the collective-rights position is correct? Professor Haridakis raises a fascinating question about how we are to move beyond the current scholarly impasse, which has usually been cast in terms of monolithic individual-rights or collective-rights positions. He notes that Chief Justice Rehnquist has acknowledged the problem with treating some aspects of the Bill of Rights as though the phrase "right of the people" pertains to individuals and of treating other provisions as though they pertain to the people in their collective capacity.

One solution to this problem has been suggested by Yale law professor Akhil Amar, who argues that the eighteenth-century Bill of Rights was essentially populist and democratic in spirit. For Amar, even the First Amendment is part of a collective-rights ideology. In Amar's view it was not until the adoption of the Fourteenth Amendment that these original provisions were transformed into genuinely individual rights. I find Rehnquist's and Amar's interpretations equally unpersuasive. The discomfort felt by modern legal scholars and judges about the slippery and imprecise language of the Bill of Rights is a reflection of our own cultural and intellectual assumptions, not those of the founders of our constitutional tradition. Historians must grapple with such ambiguities if they are to avoid imposing a false intellectual coherence on the past. Although not very helpful to lawyers or judges, it seems quite plausible to argue that there was no consensus in eighteenth-century America on what exactly the "right of the people" meant. All too often it seems that our own desire for simple answers to hard legal questions leads us to project our own concerns and desires back into history, canvassing the ranks of the founders for witnesses to testify on behalf of our cause. This is precisely the kind of law-office history that Professor Kyvig attacks as simplistic and a distortion of the past. It may well be that there was no consensus among the founders about what the right to bear arms meant.

The absence of consensus among the founders brings me back to another of Kyvig's points and to the purpose of this symposium. The debate over the Second Amendment differs from other aspects of the Bill of Rights in several ways. While many elements of the Bill of Rights have sparked controversy, only the Second Amendment seems to have prompted serious commentators to call for its repeal. One of the most interesting features of public debate over the meaning of the Second Amendment, at least if letters to the editor in newspapers are taken to be a useful sampling, is the degree to which opponents of gun control have attempted to invoke the authority of the past to justify their opposition to contemporary policy. If opponents of gun control were better acquainted with our history, they might be less quick to quote the founders. Rather than oppose government regulation of firearms, the founders were apt to accept a range of restrictions on individual liberty that go well beyond anything the most zealous contemporary advocates of gun control have suggested. Freeing the current public debate over what to do about guns in contemporary America from historical mythology will not provide us with much practical guidance. It will, however, make us better historians and force us to be more active citizens.

6

Hate Speech, Viewpoint Neutrality, and the American Concept of Democracy

JAMES WEINSTEIN

Law, Arizona State University

INTRODUCTION

Are laws banning racist speech inconsistent with democracy? Most American legal scholars and, more importantly, the U.S. Supreme Court believe that they are. On this view, each person has a fundamental right to try to persuade others about any matter of public concern, including race relations. Accordingly, if government silences certain perspectives about race, it violates a basic precept of democracy. In the insular world in which most American legal academics work, it is easy to become smug about this position. But if we lift our eyes for a moment from the official reports of the United States Supreme Court, we will notice that most other democracies in the world today have some sort of ban on racist speech. Not only do courts and commentators in these countries generally see no inconsistency between hate-speech bans and democratic self-governance but they often assert that such prohibitions affirmatively promote democracy.

Of course, the mere fact that the United States is an outlier does not prove that the other democracies are correct and we are wrong about the compatibility of bans on racist speech with democratic self-governance. One possibility is that the difference stems from different social conditions. For instance, exigent circumstances, such as the religious and ethnic violence in Northern Ireland, the West Bank, and certain regions of India, might justify speech restrictions not ordinarily consistent with democratic ideals. But this would not explain the differences between the United States and democracies where pitched ethnic warfare is neither rampant nor imminent. A more speculative but also more interesting possibility is that the different positions on hate speech regulation reflect different visions of democracy.

To explore this possibility, I shall first discuss the relationship between free speech and democracy. I shall then review the basic structure of American free speech doctrine, including the values that underlie it, and show how a ban on racist propaganda would run afoul of the First Amendment. We will then be in a position to inquire whether various types of hate-speech laws comport with the commitment to democratic self-governance. I conclude that the answer is both more complex and more equivocal than most American commentators suppose.

FREE SPEECH AND DEMOCRACY

A basic right to free speech is an essential requirement of democracy. If the people are to be the ultimate source of political authority, they must be able to talk freely to each other about all matters within the scope of this authority—which is to say, all matters of public concern. If government could punish speech with which it disagrees, public opinion—which influences public policy and ultimately determines whether elected officials continue to govern—would reflect the will of the governing officials rather than the will of the people. Thus the U.S. Supreme Court has explained that the core purpose of the right to free speech is "to assure unfettered interchange of ideas for the bringing about of political and social changes desired by the people."[1]

It is sometimes alleged that a constitutional right to free speech *inhibits* democracy to the extent that it permits courts to void speech-restrictive laws duly enacted by the democratic process. For instance, Frederick Schauer argues that "any distinct restraint on majority power, such as a principle of freedom of speech, is by its nature anti-democratic, anti-majoritarian."[2] But democracy is something more than static majoritarianism. At minimum, the concept of democratic self-governance must include a right of the minority to try to persuade the majority to change its mind. Preventing a current majority from suppressing the discourse that allows for the creation of new majorities thus promotes rather than inhibits democracy.

What I have just described is a core free speech right necessary to any system of democratic self-governance. Various democracies could, consistently with this basic free speech principle, develop quite different free speech jurisprudence. One source of divergence arises from the disparate ways in which each democracy deals with speech that relates to but is not itself within the core free speech right just described. An example of such expression is political speech advocating violation of existing law. As Judge Learned Hand long ago observed, "Words . . . which have no purport but to counsel the violation of law cannot by any latitude of interpretation be a part of that public opinion which is the final source of government in a democratic state."[3] However, such words rarely appear in pure form, but rather are most often part of some impassioned critique of the status quo. To provide "breathing space" for such social commentary, a democracy may choose to afford some protection to speech that in principle need not be permitted in a democracy.

Another reason that the free speech jurisprudence of democracies might vary yet still respect the core democratic underpinning of free speech is that democracy is not the only possible free speech value. For instance, free speech has often been defended as serving the search for truth in the "marketplace of ideas," or as flowing from the right to self-expression. Under the former rationale, a democracy might choose to afford rigorous protection to scientific expression, while under the latter it might choose to protect even hard-core pornography. To discover what values underlie a particular democracy's free speech principle, it is necessary to examine the pattern of decisions that constitute that country's free speech jurisprudence. Examination of American free speech doctrine reveals that it is animated by a highly individualistic, equality-based vision of democracy.

AMERICAN FREE SPEECH DOCTRINE

The Basic Structure

The leitmotif of contemporary free speech jurisprudence is its intense hostility to laws that discriminate on the basis of the content of speech. Such laws, the Supreme Court has declared, "cannot be tolerated under the First Amendment."[4] Content-based laws are those by which the government seeks to regulate expression because of the message it conveys. A law prohibiting criticism of the government's antidrug policy is an example of a content-based regulation. Content-neutral laws, in contrast, regulate speech without reference to or concern with the message conveyed by the speech or the impact that the message has on the listener. Such laws typically regulate the "time, place, or manner" of speech—for instance, a law prohibiting the use of loudspeakers in residential neighborhoods after 10:00 P.M.

Content-based regulations come in different varieties, some worse than others from a First Amendment standpoint. As the Court explained in a recent decision, "viewpoint discrimination" is a particularly "egregious" form of content regulation.[5] Viewpoint discrimination occurs when the regulation is based on the "specific motivating ideology or the opinion or perspective of the speaker." A law prohibiting anyone from stating that abortion is the unjustified taking of human life would be considered viewpoint discriminatory, as would a law forbidding one from expressing the view that blacks are inherently inferior to whites.

Viewpoint discrimination does not, however, exhaust the universe of content-based restrictions. For instance, a law that prohibited any discussion of abortion (whether pro or con), although not viewpoint discriminatory, would nonetheless be content based. Such a regulation is said to discriminate on the basis of subject matter or topic. But the most peculiar feature of American free speech jurisprudence is that the rule against content-based restrictions of speech extends not just to laws that target particular ideas or subject matter but to laws that forbid the use of offensive words or symbols. For example, the Court held a law prohibiting flag desecration to be an unconstitutionally content-based speech regulation.[6] Similarly, it found that an antiwar protestor had a First Amendment right to wear a jacket in public bearing the message "Fuck the Draft."[7]

This rule against content discrimination is truly a cornerstone of contemporary American free speech jurisprudence. But as important as this rule may be, it does not apply across the entire expanse of human utterances. Speech is far too ubiquitous an activity and has too many real-world ramifications to permit any such general proscription of content-based regulations. To begin with, American free speech doctrine has always recognized that certain types of speech are categorically excluded from the protection of the First Amendment. Thus "fighting words" (i.e., face-to-face insults), obscenity (i.e., hard-core pornography), perjury, bribery, and solicitation of a crime may be banned because of their content.

It is often mistakenly believed that aside from the power to ban these categories of unprotected speech, government is generally forbidden by the First Amendment from regulating the content of speech. This is demonstrably not the case. Rather, the prohibition against content regulation is primarily limited to public discourse—that is, expression on matters of public concern occurring in settings dedicated or essential to public communication, such as books, magazines, films, the Internet, or in "public forums," such as the speaker's corner of a park. Where, however, the primary purpose of a particular setting is something other than public discourse, such as the effectuation of government programs in the government workplace, instruction in the public school classroom, or the administration of justice in the courtroom, government has considerable leeway to regulate speech.

For instance, government employees may be fired for speech disloyal to their superiors; students and teachers at state universities can be told to stick to the subject matter of the class and to "keep a civil tongue"; and lawyers can be fined or even imprisoned for using profanity in the courtroom. Nor are the settings in which government may regulate the content of speech confined to what is in some sense government property. The Constitution allows regulation of sexually and racially harassing speech in the private workplace, not to mention numerous content-based regulations of marketplace speech (such as laws against false or misleading advertising, regulations that sharply limit information that competitors may share or agreements that they can enter into, or prohibitions on what may be said about the value of stock or included in a proxy statement). Similarly, the First Amendment does not inhibit civil recovery for damage caused by negligent instructions on the use of commercial products.[8]

Values Underlying the American Free Speech Principle

What values give American free speech doctrine its particular shape, including its intense hostility against viewpoint discrimination and the suspension of civility norms within public discourse? It is something richer, I believe, than the core democracy-based right described above. That value could be respected merely by assuring that all views are heard, so that the electorate is fully informed about all matters of public concern. But although some have argued for this audience-centered concept of free speech, it is impossible to square with the actual case law assuring individual speakers the right to express their views in public discourse, regardless of how many times the view may already have been stated, and to do so in an offensive, inflammatory manner.

To explain this intensely individualistic, speaker-based right we need to look deeper, to the very foundation underlying the American concept of democracy. What we find is a moral view about the proper relationship between the state and the individual, a precept reflected in the Declaration of Independence and the Enlightenment philosophy that influenced that document. On this view, government must treat each individual as an equal, autonomous, and rational agent.[9] It follows from this precept that each person has a right to try to persuade others about any matter of public concern; if government prevents a speaker from participating in public discourse because it dislikes or disagrees with the speaker's worldview, it is not treating the speaker equally with other citizens. Similarly, if the state stops speech because it believes that the people may be persuaded to implement some unwise social policy, it insults its citizens by denying their rational capacities. This precept of democracy is thus at the same time deeply individualistic and radically egalitarian in the formal sense of the term.[10]

Some have argued that democratic self-governance is the only value underlying the American free speech principle, but this view is also impossible to square with American free speech decisions. For instance, the expression of scientific or mathematical ideas generally has no direct connection with democratic self-governance, yet this expression is rigorously protected against government regulation. The Supreme Court has explained that another value that free speech serves is the search for truth in the "marketplace of ideas." Unlike the democratic self-governance rationale, this purpose "carries beyond the political realm" to "the building of the whole culture [, including] all of the areas of human learning and knowledge."[11]

The rule against viewpoint discrimination is thus overdetermined, reflecting the twin commitments to democratic self-governance and truth seeking in the marketplace of ideas. In the words of the Supreme Court, it assures that the government does not "manipulate the public debate through coercion" or "drive certain ideas or viewpoints from the marketplace."[12] Although the scope of protection flowing from these rationales overlaps considerably, there is a crucial difference between the marketplace of ideas and democratic self-governance justifications for speech protection. The marketplace of ideas theory justifies free speech instrumentally— that is, in terms of the good that it produces for society as a whole. As such, it cannot explain why American free speech doctrine values free speech as an individual right. In contrast, the democratic self-governance rationale anchors free speech firmly as an individual right.

It is often claimed that in addition to democratic self-governance and truth seeking in the marketplace of ideas, autonomy and the individual interest in self-expression are basic free speech values. As just discussed, the very concept of democracy underlying the American free speech principle presupposes autonomous, rational actors. When combined with the basic mandate for equal treatment, this vision of autonomy generates a fairly broad right to self-expression. Similarly, the commitment to an unregulated, robust, and wide-open marketplace of ideas provides considerable protection to self-expression. Nevertheless, it is a mistake, though a common one, to view the American free speech principle as flowing from a freestanding, boundless fundamental autonomy right or some similar right to self-expression. One need look no farther than the cases finding no constitutional right to engage in homosexual conduct or for terminally ill people to hasten their death to see that no such autonomy right exists in American constitutional jurisprudence. More importantly for our purposes, the view that the Constitution generally prohibits government from infringing individuals' right of self-expression is belied by such commonplace regulations as those prohibiting nudity or sexual activity in public, the distribution of obscene material, or the use of "fighting words."[13]

Hate-Speech Bans and the First Amendment

Section 319(2) of the Canadian Criminal Code provides that "every one, who, by communicating statements, other than in private conversation, wilfully promotes hatred against any identifiable group" characterized by color, race, religion or ethnic origin, is guilty of an offense punishable by up to two years' imprisonment. Many European countries have similar laws.[14] The Canadian Supreme Court has upheld the constitutionality of Canadian hate-speech laws,[15] and the European hate-speech laws have similarly been found to accord with both national constitutions and the European Convention on Human Rights.[16] If enacted in the United States today, however, there can be no doubt that Canada's hate-speech law, or any other broad ban on racist expression, would be held unconstitutional.

A hate speech ban like Canada's would be patently unconstitutional under the First Amendment as a viewpoint-based restriction on highly protected speech. It is viewpoint discriminatory because anyone who wants to praise racial equality and ethnic diversity is free to do so, but those who want to convey opposing points of view may not. In addition, much of the speech proscribed by Canada's law would be considered core political speech. Consider, for example, the expression at issue in two Canadian prosecutions: "The allegation that 6 million Jews died during the second world war is utterly unfounded. [It is a] brazen fantasy . . . marking with eternal shame a great European nation, as well as wringing fraudulent monetary compensation from them; America is being swamped by coloureds who do not believe in democracy and harbour a hatred for white people; because Zionists dominate financial life and resources, the nation cannot remain in good health because the alien community's interests are not those of the majority; Hitler was right. Communism is Jewish."[17]

Racist speech such as this, although expressing an ugly, twisted view of the world, does nonetheless express a worldview. Thus, under American free speech doctrine, it would be considered core political speech entitled to rigorous protection. Further, to the extent that such speech occurs in a medium dedicated to or essential to public discourse or the marketplace of ideas (such as books, pamphlets, cable television, or the Internet, or in a public forum), the expression is even more certain to be afforded strong First Amendment protection.

A Supreme Court decision invalidating a narrow hate-speech restriction proves that a broad prohibition on racist speech such as Canada's would readily be found unconstitutional. In *R.A.V. v. City of St. Paul*, the Court held that although the city might proscribe the use of all face-to-face insults (so-called fighting words, expression long held to be without First Amendment protection), it was unconstitutional to single out for prohibition fighting words with a racist message.[18] If the state is not allowed to prohibit even unprotected speech because of its racist content, it follows that it may not ban what would otherwise be highly protected public discourse because of such content. *R.A.V.* thus shows that under the First Amendment racism is not some pariah perspective but rather a worldview that the government must treat neutrally in regulating speech.

ARE HATE-SPEECH BANS CONSISTENT WITH DEMOCRACY?

This section examines the compatibility of hate-speech bans with the commitment to democratic self-governance. The main purpose of this inquiry is to shed some light on the marked difference between the American position on hate-speech regulation, which does not allow even narrow restrictions on hate speech, and the approach of most other democracies, which permit quite broad bans. Is one approach more faithful to democracy than the other, or do the different positions reflect somewhat different concepts of democracy? Or are both approaches consistent with the same basic concept of democracy, diverging due to different pragmatic judgments about how best to accomplish this vision?

Banning Hate Speech Indirectly through Content-Neutral Regulations

Every democracy, including the United States, recognizes that certain categories of speech are not a legitimate part of public discourse or the search for truth and thus, in theory, may be banned consistent with free speech values. In the United States these categories include threats and "fighting words." Similarly, although incitement to criminal activity is afforded some First Amendment protection, it may be punished consistently with the First Amendment if likely to produce imminent lawless action.[19]

Through laws banning threats, fighting words, and incitement to criminal activity, governments, including state and local jurisdictions in the United States, can forbid some of the most harmful types of racist speech. In the United Kingdom, Section 5 of the Public Order Act, which bans "threatening, abusive or insulting speech" likely to cause a breach of the peace, has been used to prohibit racist speech directed to particular individuals. In *R.A.V.*, the Supreme Court was at pains to point out that the expression involved in that case—the burning of a cross on a black family's lawn—could constitutionally have been punished under any number of laws, including a prohibition against terroristic threats. By the same token, a racist advocating violence against minority groups may be punished under a general law against criminal incitement if the speech is likely to result in such lawless conduct. Putting aside problems of selective enforcement against racists, it is hard to see how such prohibitions are inconsistent with the core free speech principle essential to democracy.[20]

A particularly objectionable feature of much racist propaganda is its use of racist epithets or display of offensive symbols. Thus, one way to put a large crimp in racist rhetoric is to outlaw the use of all insulting epithets—not just in face-to-face encounters but in public discourse as well, including in books, pamphlets, and street-corner speeches. Other democracies do, in fact, impose civility norms even within public discourse (although these limitations tend to be selective rather than across the board, a problem addressed in the next section). As we have seen, however, the U.S. government may not constitutionally prohibit the use of even the most offensive words or symbols used in public discourse. In this country, antiwar protestors have a constitutional right to refer to the draft in vulgar terms or even to burn the American flag.

One consequence of extending such powerful protection to public discourse is that, like antiwar protestors, racists have a First Amendment right to pepper their speech with offensive epithets or to march through the streets displaying inflammatory symbols. If, like other democracies, government in the United States could impose even minimal civility norms on public discourse, it could, pursuant to a general ban on highly offensive words and symbols, dull some of the sharper edges of racist rhetoric. For decades some conservative justices have bemoaned this suspension of civility norms, reasoning that speakers can adequately express their ideas without resort to vulgar epithets or inflammatory symbols. On this view, it is not necessary that demonstrators be able to say "Fuck the draft" or to burn the American flag in order to express their opposition to the war or convey their disdain for the U.S. government; similarly, racist epithets are not necessary to express a racist worldview. The question therefore arises whether this suspension of civility norms within public discourse truly serves the democratic self-governance rationale or any other value underlying the free speech principle.

In upholding the right of an antiwar protestor to wear a jacket bearing the message "Fuck the Draft," Justice John Harlan wrote in *Cohen v. California* that "we can not indulge the facile assumption that one can forbid particular words without also running a substantial risk of suppressing ideas in the process." There are several reasons why this might be so. First, as Justice Harlan noted, "Governments might soon seize upon the censorship of certain words as a convenient guise for banning the expression of unpopular ideas." This fear has a particular bearing on the fundamental precept of equal treatment. As John Stuart Mill long ago recognized and American case law documents, uncivil language used to express ideas challenging the status quo will likely be seen as more egregious than the same coarse expression used to support positions approved of by those in power.[21] Thus it was no coincidence that the prosecution involved in *Cohen* was for a jacket that read "Fuck the Draft" rather than "Fuck the Vietcong." The claim that civility norms will not be fairly or equally applied is, however, a pragmatic objection rather than an objection that enforcement of such norms within public discourse is in principle contrary to free speech values.

A somewhat different objection is this: There is an essential connection between the form and content of speech, and thus any restriction on the words and symbols used to express an idea will limit a speaker's ability to express the precise idea she wants to convey. There is, for instance, no other way to express the full and exact meaning conveyed by the utterance "Fuck the draft." Moreover, as Justice Harlan noted, "Much linguistic expression serves a dual communicative function: it conveys not only ideas capable of relatively precise, detached expression, but otherwise inexplicable emotions as well."

Does the vision of democracy underlying the American free speech principle entail a right to express one's ideas within public discourse in exactly the way one chooses? It is difficult to see how an across-the-board imposition of civility norms violates the command for equal treatment.[22] Nor would norms imposed to make public discourse less vituperative seem to insult our rationality. But even if the

American vision of democracy in principle requires the suspension of civility norms within public discourse, the imposition of such norms would not seem to infringe the minimal free speech necessary to any democratic society.

Selective Bans on Unprotected Speech with a Racist Viewpoint

So far we have considered laws that do not single out racist speech as such but generally prohibit certain forms of speech that, in principle at least, can be banned consistently with the core free speech right essential to democratic self-governance. But what about laws that selectively target racist speech within such categories of unprotected speech? An example is the ordinance at issue in *R.A.V. v. City of St. Paul*, which banned only face-to-face expression "including but not limited to, a burning cross or Nazi swastika, which . . . arouses anger, alarm or resentment in others on the basis of race, color, creed, religion or gender." Writing for a bare majority of the Court, Justice Antonin Scalia held that although the city could ban unprotected speech such as "fighting words," it may not do so "based on hostility— or favoritism—towards the underlying message expressed."

If the state may legitimately ban certain types of expression consistently with democratic ideals, it is not immediately apparent how doing so, even in a viewpoint-discriminatory way, violates anyone's right to speak or, more importantly for purposes of this discussion, infringes the core free speech right necessary to democracy. On reflection, however, it becomes clear that viewpoint-discriminatory restrictions on unprotected speech can violate the basic precepts of democracy by skewing the debate on matters of public concern.

Within certain bounds, a democracy may legitimately define the boundaries of public discourse. It might, for instance, decide that face-to-face insults are not a proper way of advancing one's ideas and present too great a threat to public order. Alternatively, government could decide not to prohibit such expression, believing that heated personal exchanges, including the use of epithets, can play a legitimate role in public debate. (The Supreme Court's "fighting words" doctrine permits but does not require the suppression of fighting words.) But there is something troubling with government imposing a restrictive view of public discourse on those expressing views with which it disagrees, while allowing those with whom it agrees to engage in more freewheeling and abusive discourse.

Suppose, for instance, the government prohibited the use of fighting words during a labor strike, but only if the epithets expressed an antimanagement perspective (e.g., "scab") but not an antiunion sentiment; or forbade liberals from using epithets such as "fascist" in debates with conservatives but allowed conservatives to use terms such as "pinko" to refer to liberals; or selectively prohibited use of the term "baby killer" in face-to-face exchanges between pro-life and pro-choice demonstrators. Such laws might bias the debate on matters of public concern. Fear of prosecution might prevent those on one side of the debate from engaging in robust discourse that some may find offensive but that in fact does not contain fighting words but rather protected political speech. Even if such laws did not chill protected speech in this way, it is still likely that they would advantage one side in the debate. The unilateral ability of one side to use fighting words might allow that side to intimidate and thus silence the opposition. This would be particularly true if one side were allowed to use threatening speech (another category of unprotected speech) while its opponents could not. In addition, the selective application of a fighting-words prohibition might, through fines and legal defense costs, drain resources from one side on a highly contentious social issue. Because there is no clear, natural division between public discourse essential to a democracy and forms of communication that can legitimately be banned, this distinction must be conventionally drawn. If, however, the line is drawn is such a way as to advantage or disadvantage certain perspectives, the political process could be skewed in a way inconsistent with the core precept of democratic self-governance.

But what if a selective ban would not actually bias the political process? For instance, unlike selective banning of antiabortion or anti-employer speech, selective banning of the cross burning at issue in *R.A.V.* is not likely to deter protected speech or otherwise skew public discourse.[23] Unlike fighting words in an abortion or labor protest, the expression at issue in *R.A.V.* was more akin to a terrorist threat than to an attempt to persuade others to adopt the speaker's worldview. Arguably, viewpoint-discriminatory bans on certain types of patently harmful speech would have no real potential to warp the debate on matters of public concern. As such, these bans might not violate the core democratic precept underlying free speech, or for that matter, any free speech principle that is instrumental rather than constitutive of democracy. Still, it is possible that the vision of democracy underlying the American free speech principle limits viewpoint-discriminatory regulation of even such plainly undemocratic means of political expression as violence and terror.

Suppose that Congress selectively imposes harsh penalties on only those who use terrorism as a means of protesting the mistreatment of animals. It is one thing for government to single out all terroristic acts for severe punishment on the grounds that such acts may disrupt society more than does garden-variety crime. But it is difficult to imagine what legitimate interest it has in singling out terroristic acts of animal-rights protestors for increased punishment. If the only justification it can offer is that it opposes the view of animal-rights activists, or that their ideology is dangerous or offensive, then the law would seem to violate the basic command of equal treatment underlying the First Amendment. It bears emphasis that this conclusion holds whether or not it could be shown that such a viewpoint-discriminatory law would actually disadvantage the animal-rights movement or warp the marketplace of ideas. The equality principle underlying American free speech, as well as the American vision of democracy itself, is not an instrumental concern but a basic precept about the proper relationship between government and the individual. In this view, it is *in principle* wrong for government to use its coercive powers against anyone just because it disagrees with that person's worldview, regardless of the political impact of such coercion, and even if the government might otherwise prohibit the activity under a properly justified law.

The conclusion that selectively punishing unprotected speech because of its racist perspective impairs the fundamental equality principle of American democracy assumes that the racist perspective is a legitimate part of the debate on public issues, analogous to the perspectives of animal-rights protesters, pro-life demonstrators, or anti-employer picketers. I will consider below arguments for and against this assumption. But for now it is important to note that American free speech jurisprudence in general, and *R.A.V.* in particular, assumes that racist views are entitled to the same protection as any other perspective on matters of public concern.

I also want to emphasize that while I agree with the Court's premise in *R.A.V.* that restrictions on even unprotected speech motivated by hostility to particular political perspectives violate the American free speech principle, it is not clear that the purpose of the prohibition was disagreement with a particular ideology rather than the targeting of a particularly harmful type of fighting words. Racist fighting words arguably cause more harm, both in terms of the emotional injury they inflict and the greater likelihood that they will cause a fight, than do typical personal insults. The problem with this argument, however, is that racist fighting words are particularly hurtful and prone to cause fights because they convey a racist perspective. Whether selectively targeting racist fighting words on this harm-based rationale is consistent the basic equality precept underlying the American free speech principle is an extremely difficult question, one that divided the U.S. Supreme Court. I cannot fully explore this question here, but will merely observe that a key consideration is whether racist insults are in fact an especially harmful species of fighting words, and if so, to what extent a general ban on fighting words would be a less effective remedy than a selective one. The same analysis holds for selective prohibition of other types of unprotected speech, such as laws banning racist threats or advocacy of racist violence.

Let us now consider a more far-reaching restriction on racist speech: bans on racist epithets and symbols, not just in face-to-face confrontations but in all public discourse, including political pamphlets, parades, and street-corner orations. An example of such a law is Part III of Britain's Public Order Act of 1986; it outlaws "threatening, abusive, or insulting speech" likely to stir up racial hatred. In the United States, as we have seen, even a general ban on offensive words and symbols as part of public discourse is unconstitutional; a viewpoint-based one is all the more so.

However, as I suggested above, American free speech doctrine prohibits the enforcement of civility norms in public discourse, not because their enforcement is in principle inconsistent with the basic values underlying the First Amendment but for pragmatic, prophylactic reasons. No other democracy constitutionally prohibits the imposition of civility norms on public discourse. Thus, a ban on racist epithets and symbols in other democracies might be conceptualized as a selective regulation of unprotected (or perhaps less-protected) speech. Are such selective, viewpoint-discriminatory prohibitions consistent with the commitment to democratic self-governance?

As we have seen, an argument can be made that the use of racial epithets in face-to-face confrontations is in a class by itself with respect to its tendency to provoke violence. The same may be true of racist threats and advocacy of racist violence. It is, however, more difficult to make the case that use of racist language and symbols as part of public discourse is uniquely harmful. By what criteria are we to conclude that the Klan's burning of a cross at a political rally is more harmful than antiwar protestors burning an American flag? One obvious distinction is that flag burning is directed toward government, while cross burning insults individuals on the basis of their group membership. This difference might justify the application of civility norms to political speech that insults people, either individually or collectively, while exempting speech that insults government or even government officials. However, this rationale would still not justify singling out the use of insulting racist words and symbols within public discourse.

It has been argued that historically oppressed minorities are particularly vulnerable to hateful epithets or symbols, even when used in public discourse, and that such inflammatory expression is particularly likely to dissuade members of these groups from participating in democratic self-governance. The validity of this claim will vary over time and from culture to culture. One can imagine a situation where a group is so subordinated and racist speech so prevalent that vicious epithets in public discourse will likely impede their participation in democratic self-governance. Despite our continuing racial problems, this thankfully is not the situation in the United States today, and I doubt it is the case in Britain. It may well be that the use of racist words and symbols in public discourse might be particularly upsetting to blacks and other minorities in the United States. However, there is no evidence of which I am aware that such expression actually deters minorities from participating in public discourse or any other part of the democratic process. Indeed, if anything, racist propaganda in this country tends to mobilize minority groups and their allies to condemn this expression and otherwise express their own views.

In the absence of a persuasive justification for banning racist words and symbols in public discourse, the suspicion arises that the true motivation for such a law is abhorrence of racist ideology. As we have seen, it is a vexed question whether a law motivated by hostility to a particular worldview is consistent with core democratic principles, even if it does not skew the debate on matters of public concern. But it is particularly difficult to square such a law with the commitment to democratic self-governance if it actually warps the political debate, as any viewpoint regulation of the words and symbols that can be used in public discourse is likely to do.

Group Libel Laws

A common type of hate-speech restriction punishes libelous statements against racial, ethnic, or religious groups. It would not seem contrary to any precept underlying the commitment to democratic self-government to prohibit false statements of fact likely to damage individual reputation. Nor would the prohibition of false factual statements seem likely to impair the search for truth in the marketplace of ideas. Thus, every democracy, including the United States, has laws against defamation. But if defamatory statements about individuals may be prohibited consistently with democracy and the search for truth, why cannot scurrilous statements about racial, ethnic, and religious groups be similarly banned? At first glance, this question may seem to pose merely the problem of viewpoint-discriminatory bans on unprotected speech discussed in the previous section. But for several reasons, group libel laws are even more difficult to square with core free speech values than are the selective bans previously considered.

To begin with, unlike libelous statements about individuals (which often have no bearing on matters of public concern), defamatory statements about racial, ethnic, and religious groups are almost always inextricably bound up with some larger social critique, bigoted though it may be. It is true, of course, that group libel laws do not prevent racist social critique as such, only the dissemination of untrue factual statements about these groups. Arguably, therefore, group libel can be prohibited without significantly impeding dissidents' ability to argue for the social change they desire. Experience in the United States has shown, however, that it is difficult to excise libelous statements on matters of public concern from public discourse without significantly damaging democratic self-governance.[24] It is particularly difficult to pluck group libel from this debate without impeding a wide area of social critique.

Especially in multicultural democracies, where ethnic and religious groups often vie not just for recognition and material benefits but to define the national identity according to their own norms, the public debate will inevitably involve claims about the characteristics of the various groups.[25] Any significant restriction on factual claims about these groups will inevitably cramp the ability of speakers to express their ideas more than do most other attempts to rid public discourse of seemingly worthless yet harmful expression. Note, for instance, how much easier it would be for a speaker to denounce his nation's involvement in a war without expressly calling for draft resistance than it would be for him to urge racial segregation or the expulsion of immigrants without making assertions about group characteristics.

A more basic problem with group libel laws is that the typical racist libel is not what would ordinarily be considered a statement of fact. Rather, such statements are usually judgments about how to interpret data. Consider, for instance, the infamous claim of American racists that blacks are inherently predisposed to criminal activity, as "proved" by statistics showing that blacks are disproportionately represented in the prison population. Most right-thinking people, of course, reject this claim, and with good reason. It may be true that groups ghettoized in large American cities disproportionately engage in crime. But with all the obvious explanations for this phenomenon, such as centuries of discrimination and grinding poverty with little hope of escape, only someone viewing the world through a lens warped by bigotry would believe that inherent racial characteristics are the cause. This shows, however, that group libel laws punish speakers not so much for making false factual claims as for having a distorted, hateful perspective from which they view facts.[26]

A related problem is that racist statements about the inherent characteristics of certain groups are not falsifiable in the way that statements at issue in the typical libel suit are. No doubt science can tell us that racist claims about the genetic abilities and tendencies of minority groups are not very plausible explanations of the data. Still, given the insuperable difficulties of sorting out the causes of human behavior, particularly the relative contributions of nature and nurture, these claims will usually not be susceptible to the same definitive disproof as statements typically at issue in an individual libel suit (for instance, the statement that Jones is a criminal). As a result, it is likely that the judgment of prosecutors, judges, and juries in group libel cases will turn more on ideological disagreement with the defendant's statements than on some objective, empirical assessment of their truth.

Although calumny about inherent characteristics of minority groups is the stock in trade of racists, some bigots make claims more susceptible to conclusive disproof. For instance, anti-Semites often claim that the Holocaust is a myth invented by Jews to gain sympathy, reparations, and a homeland in Israel. (Again, note the close connection between the false factual statement and the broader social criticism.) From the standpoint of definitive, empirical disproof, this kind of statement is closer to the claim at issue in the typical libel suit than a claim about inherent group characteristics. Still, outlawing such statements might entail costs, perhaps not so much to democratic self-governance as to the marketplace of ideas. Radical historical revisionism has been an important part of the dialectic by which we gain a better understanding of the past. Criminal sanctions against Holocaust denial might deter publications by serious historians who in good faith believe that the accepted estimate of the number of victims is too high or who otherwise might want to challenge some received wisdom on the subject.

It could be argued, and with considerable force, that no serious historian would ever be prosecuted under Holocaust-denial prohibitions, even for a radically mistaken publication. The target of such laws are rabid anti-Semites who use Holocaust denial as a way of insulting the Jewish people. But if this is true, it goes to show that as with group defamation laws, the gravamen of the offense of Holocaust denial is the expression of a hateful worldview, not the making of false factual statements. On this view, Holocaust-denial laws too touch the nerve of democratic self-governance.

Excluding Racist Ideas from Public Discourse

In evaluating the various types of hate-speech bans in the preceding discussion, I have assumed that a hate-speech regulation is most vulnerable to the charge of being undemocratic when government bans this speech because of disagreement or antipathy to racist ideology.

In particular, I have assumed that the fundamental equality precept underlying American free speech means that a racist has the same right within public discourse to try to persuade others to accept his worldview as would someone advocating a higher minimum wage or protesting a war. I have also suggested that laws motivated by hostility to a racist worldview infringe even the core free speech necessary to any democracy, especially if applied not just to categories of speech that may legitimately be prohibited consistently with democratic ideals but to public discourse as well.

Although some of the hate-speech regulations in effect in other democracies can be regarded as selective bans on unprotected speech and thus arguably consistent with core democratic ideals, others are not so limited. For example, some laws bar not just incitement to racial violence or illegal acts of discrimination but also incitement to "racial hatred";[27] others ban statements that "insult" or "degrade" a group on the grounds of race, ethnicity, or religion.[28] Even more problematic are laws that ban the distribution of material "containing the expression of racism or xenophobia" or that disseminate "ideas based on racial superiority or hatred."[29] Under the assumption that it is in principle undemocratic for government to exclude any idea from public discourse because of disagreement with or hostility to a particular worldview, such laws are difficult to square with the commitment to democratic self-governance. I shall now carefully examine this assumption.

Does democracy really demand that advocacy of a constitutional amendment to reinstitute black slavery or to mandate the deportation of Jews be treated the same as speech urging campaign finance reform? It is not immediately apparent that it does. Why should a free speech principle in service to democracy protect speech inimical to the most basic precepts of democracy? Even if such highly antidemocratic speech must be afforded *some* protection, either for democratic reasons or to promote some other free speech value, such as truth seeking in the marketplace of ideas, does it follow that denying racist expression the same rigorous protection afforded other ideas expressed in public discourse is inconsistent with democracy?

Of course, not all racist speech advocates policies inconsistent with democracy. For instance, a tract supporting arguments against affirmative action with theories about the inherent intellectual inferiority of minority groups does not, though it is plainly racist, expressly advocate a policy inimical to the very foundations of democracy. But some of the most virulent forms of racist speech, such as advocating that minorities be stripped of their basic human rights or deported from the country, do call for political change arguably antithetical to any concept of democracy and thus seemingly could be prohibited consistently with democracy.

To take an actual case: Under the Dutch hate-speech law, leaders of a racist political party were convicted for possessing, with intent to distribute, leaflets addressed to "white fellow citizens," declaring that as soon as their political party came to power, it would remove "all Surinamers, Turks, and other so-called guest workers from the Netherlands." The defendants appealed to the European Commission on Human Rights, invoking the right to freedom of expression guaranteed by Article 10 of the European Convention on Human Rights. In holding that the conviction came within Article 10's exception for restrictions "necessary in a democratic society," the Commission relied on Article 17, which denies any person or group the right "to engage in any activity . . . aimed at the destruction of any rights" guaranteed by the Convention. The Commission stated that the purpose of this provision was to "prevent totalitarian groups from exploiting [the Convention] in their own interests."[30]

Underlying the argument that radically antidemocratic speech may be forbidden consistently with the commitment to democratic self-governance is the controversial premise that a democracy can, consistently with its own precepts, prevent the majority from abandoning democracy, or even from instituting some policy radically inconsistent with democracy. If, however, this view is incorrect—if failure to recognize antidemocratic outcomes chosen by the people is itself undemocratic—then forbidding people from even urging these outcomes is inconsistent with democracy.

Whether forbidding the majority to abandon democracy is itself inconsistent with democracy depends, of course, on one's view of democracy. Under Germany's "militant democracy," for instance, it is clear that the majority can be restrained from reinstituting Nazism. Indeed, the view that there are certain limits on majority power seems inherent in any version of liberal democracy, including the one practiced in the United States. All such democracies share the precept that majority rule is not an end in itself but rather the usual best means for protecting fundamental individual rights and liberties. Still, the question remains whether such restraint on popular sovereignty is consistent with the core concept of democracy.

Political theorists might differ about how much protection of minority rights is inherent in the very concept of democracy. But I take it that most would agree that an incumbent democratic government would not be violating the core precept of democracy if it refused to acknowledge a new constitutional order that abandoned democracy in toto, including majority rule, even if this new regime was established by impeccably democratic procedures and supported by a super-majority. More controversial is whether it would also be consistent with the core precept of democracy for a democratic government to refuse to recognize some constitutional change radically inconsistent with democracy, such as stripping a minority of their basic civil rights, but that otherwise kept intact the basic structure of democracy, including the possibility of popular repeal of this antidemocratic measure by the remaining electorate. If rule by the people means that no group may be excluded from governing authority because of color, ancestry, or religion; if Abraham Lincoln was right that a society that permitted slavery is to that extent "no democracy";[31] then it may well be consistent with the core vision of democracy for a democratic government to refuse to implement constitutional changes that only partially obliterate this core.

But even if certain substantive outcomes can be taken off the table in a democracy consistently with democratic values, it does not follow that *advocacy* of such outcomes can similarly be excluded. For instance, Robert Post argues that "the normative essence" of democracy is located "in the opportunity to participate in the formation of the will of the community through a running discussion between majority and minority." This process, Post argues, is crucial to instilling in citizens "a sense of participation, legitimacy, and self-determination."[32] On this view, prohibiting racist speech excludes those wishing to express this perspective from the democratic legitimization that occurs through participation in public discourse. To Post, the prohibition of racist speech is consistent with democracy only to the extent that such censorship is necessary to prevent racist speech from actually undermining democratic legitimation—as would be the case, for instance, if the expression of racist ideas in public discourse coercively silenced minorities from participating in this discourse. Excluding a racist (or anyone else) from participation in public discourse for any less compelling reason is inconsistent with this view of participatory democracy.

I agree with Post that "the case has not yet been made" that racist speech in American public discourse results in actual silencing of would-be speakers so as to justify suppressing this expression.[33] But the same may not be true in other democracies, particularly those in which the legal status of historically oppressed minorities is still precarious or in which widescale ethnic or religious violence is commonplace. Thus, even if instilling a sense of self-determination is thought to be the normative essence of democracy, it is not clear that banning advocacy of blatant oppression of minority groups is inconsistent with the minimal free speech essential to any democracy. In addition, as Post candidly recognizes, his account of the essence of democracy is not the only conceivable core normative vision of democracy. Although the sense of identification with law produced through participation in public discourse open to all is doubtless an important component of any democracy, one could still reasonably hold that it is not democracy's "normative essence."

I have suggested in this paper that a somewhat different normative vision of democracy underlies the American free speech principle. Like Post's description, this view is fundamentally egalitarian, but unlike his view, it requires no empirical psychological assumptions. Rather, the right of each person to participate in deciding all matters within the people's sovereign authority, and thus to voice his or her views on all matters of public concern, derives solely from the basic moral principle that government must treat each citizen as an equal, autonomous, and rational agent. This basic precept yields an extremely strong free speech right within public discourse. For instance, because the people in a democracy are the ultimate decision makers about whether the nation should go to war, the government may not stop someone from protesting the nation's involvement in a war, even though the government has reasonable grounds for fearing that such protests will lead to the formation of popular opinion that will induce elective representatives to commit a grievous foreign-policy error. Indeed, this vision of democracy may well require that such speech be protected literally unto death. Suppose, for instance, that it could have been shown to a moral certainly that the protests against the Vietnam War in this country caused the North Vietnamese to persevere, thus increasing deaths of American troops. Even under such circumstances, the American vision of democratic self-government would require that the speech be protected from government suppression.

But if enslaving one group of people because of color, or deporting another because of its religion or ethnic heritage, is not within the people's (or anybody's) authority to accomplish in a democracy even thinly conceived, much less in one premised on equal treatment, then it is difficult to see why, in principle at least, advocacy of such changes should be afforded the virtually absolute protection afforded advocacy of social change within the people's authority. In particular, it is far from obvious that with respect to such radically antidemocratic speech, society must endure the costs that the commitment to democratic self-governance sometimes requires it to bear. It is even less obvious when these costs are not evenly distributed but fall on particular groups within a society.

To cast this point more in doctrinal terms, just as speech that breaches certain democratic procedures—for instance, advocacy of law violation—may in principle be considered no legitimate part of public discourse, speech advocating certain substantive agendas that no democracy could permit—such as genocide or the deportation or enslavement of various groups—might similarly in principle be excluded from the protection ordinarily afforded public discourse. It still does not follow, however, that government may, consistently with core democratic principles, suppress speech just because it advocates radically antidemocratic measures. Even if the sense of self-determination as described by Post is not the normative essence of democracy, it is nonetheless an important feature of this and any conceivable vision of democracy. Accordingly, even people proposing measures impossible in a democracy should not, without good reason, be prevented from expressing their views. What constitutes "good reason," however, will vary with both the harm likely to be caused by such speech, as well as with the importance that a particular democracy places on instilling a sense of self-determination even within those who reject democracy's basic precepts.

Assume for instance that in a particular democracy, speech urging that people be deported because of their religion or ethnicity might substantially increase the chance that government will actually adopt such a policy—or that conditions in this country are such that the prevalence of such expression makes members of some historically oppressed group insecure in their basic civil rights. It is not obvious that suppressing such speech for either of these reason is inconsistent with the minimal free speech principle essential to the core of democracy.

Still, even where hate speech advocating radically antidemocratic policies has these ill effects, a somewhat richer vision of democracy underlying a society's free speech might prohibit suppression of this speech for these reasons. Depending on the precise vision of democracy in question, the participatory rights of both racists and minorities might be better accommodated if the standard for suppression for even radically antidemocratic speech were set considerably higher—requiring, for instance, a distinct likelihood that such expression will actually lead to repressive policies before it can be suppressed. Similarly, if, like the basic American democratic precept, a vision of democracy presupposes that government must treat people as rational agents, government might be required to trust its citizens to reject policies radically opposed to the very essence of democracy and thus resort to speech suppression only if adoption of these measures is imminent. My goal here, however, is not to discover the exact point at which a democracy might consistently with democratic ideals suppress speech advocating that minorities be stripped of their basic human rights. Rather, it is to suggest that it may in principle be consistent with the core vision of democracy, as well as the equality precept underlying American democracy, to fail to afford such speech the virtually absolute protection currently extended to advocacy of social change within American public discourse.

There are, however, strong practical reasons for not excluding even radically antidemocratic speech from this protection. The line between radically antidemocratic speech and speech that otherwise radically challenges the status quo, although perhaps identifiable in academic discourse, is too indefinite for real-world administration.[34] I am not sure about other democracies, but I have no doubt that in the United States an "antidemocratic speech exception" would seriously impair public discourse, especially dissident speech.[35] In addition, even if suppression of speech advocating radically antidemocratic programs is not in principle inconsistent with democracy, it may still impede the search for truth in the marketplace of ideas. Can we really be sure that democracy is for all times and all places the best form of government? Even if it is, our understanding of democracy may, as Mill suggests, be enhanced if alternative types of political ordering can be freely advocated. But surely, it might be objected, there is no truth to be found, or greater understanding gained, by permitting people to advocate such regressive, time-dishonored policies as slavery and deportation of minority religious and ethnic groups. Perhaps so, but it must be borne in mind that the theory of speech suppression that I have been discussing here embraces not just racist speech but advocacy of all radically antidemocratic speech, including many forms of Marxist speech. It is not surprising, therefore, that most radical critics of American free speech doctrine sedulously avoid invoking this principle as a rationale for suppressing hate speech.

CONCLUSION

A possible explanation of why American free speech doctrine is unique among democracies in forbidding even a narrow ban on racist speech is that the American vision of democracy is unique. I have suggested that it is a highly individualistic, formally egalitarian vision of democracy that best explains the free speech doctrine's intense hostility to viewpoint discrimination. Ironically, however, the precept that government must treat each individual as an equal and autonomous agent generates a free speech principle that allows citizens offensively to attack basic principles of racial equality or even to challenge the fundamental democratic precept itself, by advocating that the government strip some groups of their basic civil rights. A natural response is to deny such radically antidemocratic speech the rigorous protection generally afforded public discourse. However, for both pragmatic reasons and to avoid the threat of conceptual incoherence, the preferable course for this country at this time is to protect equally all advocacy of political or social change through democratic means, no matter how undemocratic the ends.

In suggesting that different visions of democracy may explain the suppression of hate speech in other democracies, I do not mean to discount other, more obvious explanations. Cultural, historical, and legal conditions not directly tied to a nation's vision of democracy might well have more to do with this divergence. An obvious example is found in the United Kingdom, where judges do not have the power to void hate-speech bans or any other act of Parliament. Nor do I mean to suggest that different visions of democracy ineluctably dictate different conclusions as to the validity of hate-speech restrictions. Much more than philosophers and law professors care to admit, legal doctrine is driven primarily by pragmatic judgment, not abstract theory. I have suggested, for instance, that the American vision of democracy does not in principle forbid the imposition of civility norms in public discourse, including the banning of racist epithets, or even, perhaps, the exclusion of certain racist ideas from public discourse. Rather, this speech is protected primarily to create adequate breathing space for expression that is truly constitutive of American democracy. But, even pragmatic limitations such as these are in service to some deeper normative vision. Thus, to an extent that cannot be precisely measured, the American constitutional prohibition against hate-speech regulation reflects the American concept of democracy.

NOTES

I thank Richard Dagger, Peter DeMarneffe, Ivan Hare, David Kader, David Kaye, James Nickel, and Robert Post for their helpful comments and suggestions.

1. *Connick v. Myers,* 461 U.S. 138 (1983).

2. Frederick Schauer, *Free Speech: A Philosophical Enquiry* (Cambridge: Cambridge Univ. Press, 1982), 40.

3. *Masses Publishing Co. v. Patten,* 244 Fed. 535 (S.D.N.Y. 1917).

4. *Regan v. Time, Inc.* 468 U.S. 641 (1984).

5. *Rosenberger v. Rector and Visitors of the Univ. of Va.,* 515 U.S. 819 (1995).

6. *Texas v. Johnson,* 491 U.S. 397 (1989).

7. *Cohen v. California,* 403 U.S. 15 (1971).

8. For a more detailed discussion of the distinction between highly protected public discourse and speech that the government has far more leeway to regulate, see James Weinstein *Hate Speech, Pornography and the Radical Attack on Free Speech Doctrine* (Boulder, Colo.: Westview Press, 1999), 40–49. In conceptualizing doctrinal rules as constructing a realm of public discourse in which content regulation is forbidden and other spheres in which such regulation is routinely permitted, I generally follow Robert Post's insightful description in his *Constitutional Domains: Democracy, Community and Management* (Cambridge, Mass.: Harvard Univ. Press, 1995).

9. See, e.g., Thomas Scanlon, "A Theory of Free Expression," *Philosophy & Public Affairs* 1 (1972): 215–16; Ronald Dworkin, *Freedom's Law* (Cambridge, Mass.: Harvard Univ. Press, 1996), 200.

10. The American free speech principle is formal, not substantive, in that it neither guarantees each citizen the resources to make one's view heard on an equal basis with all other citizens, nor privileges the current conception of racial equality within the realm of public discourse.

11. Thomas Emerson, *The System of Freedom of Expression* (New York: Random House, 1970), 6–7. See also *Police Dept. of Chicago v. Mosley,* 408 U.S. 92 (1972) (First Amendment permits "continued building of our politics and culture").

12. *Turner Broadcasting System, Inc. v. FCC,* 512 U.S. 622 (1994).

13. To be consistent with the Supreme Court's substantive due-process jurisprudence, as well as with the free speech cases allowing many types of expression to be readily regulated, any freestanding interest in autonomy or self-expression must be seen as a "liberty interest" rather than a fundamental right.

14. For an excellent discussion of the hate-speech laws in Britain, India, Israel, Canada, Denmark, France, Germany, and other democracies, see Sandra Coliver, ed., *Striking a Balance: Hate Speech, Freedom of Expression, and Non-Discrimination* (London: Article 19, 1992).

15. See *Regina v. Keegstra*, [1990] 3 SCR 697; *Regina v. Andrews*, [1990] 3 SCR 970; *Canada (Human Rights Commission) v. Taylor* 3 SCR 892.

16. See, e.g., Judgment of January 14, 1981, BGHSt, 1981 Neue Zeitschrift Für Strafrecht (Federal Supreme Court of West Germany); Supreme Court of the Netherlands, 18 Oct. 1988, NJ 1989, 476; 1981 NRt 1305 (Supreme Court of Norway); *J. Glimmerveen and J. Hagenbeek v. Netherlands*, App. Nos. 8348/78 and 8406/78, [1980] 23 *Yearbook of the European Convention on Human Rights* (Eur. Ct. H.R.); *X v. Federal Republic of Germany*, App. No. 9235/81, 29 *European Convention on Human Rights Decisions and Reports* 194 (1982).

17. *Regina v. Zundel*, [1987] 35 D.L.R. (4th) 338; *Regina v. Andrews*, [1990] 3 SCR 970.

18. 505 U.S. 377 (1992).

19. See *Brandenburg v. Ohio*, 395 U.S. 444 (1969).

20. Indeed, as I have argued elsewhere, even the limited protection that American doctrine affords incitement to criminal conduct is best understood as protecting the social criticism that often accompanies advocacy of law violation, not the incitement itself. See Weinstein, *Hate Speech and Pornography*, 169–70. Thus, other countries that ban advocacy of criminal activity outright, or do so on some lesser showing of potential harm than is required under the First Amendment, are not in principle acting inconsistently with democracy. To the extent, however, that such restrictions chill legitimate social criticism without some weighty justification, they do in practice interfere with democratic self-governance.

21. John Stuart Mill, *On Liberty and Other Essays*, ed. John Gray (Oxford: Oxford Univ. Press, 1991), 60–61.

22. Robert Post argues that there can be no such thing as the neutral imposition of civility norms, because these norms necessarily instantiate some particular community's vision of national identity. See Post, *Constitutional Domains*, 139. Unfortunately, space limitations do not allow me to address this interesting argument here.

23. It should be recalled, however, that the ordinance at issue in *R.A.V.* did not apply just to terroristic acts, such as cross burning, but rather to a large class of racist "fighting words."

24. It is for this reason that the Supreme Court extended substantial protection to false factual statements about public officials in *New York Times Co. v. Sullivan*, 376 U.S. 254 (1964) and has afforded lesser but still considerable protection to false statements about private individuals on matters of public concern. See *Gertz v. Robert Welch Co., Inc.* 418 U.S. 323 (1974).

25. For instance, in *Beauharnais v. Illinois*, 343 U.S. 250 (1952), the defendant was convicted under a group libel law for making scurrilous remarks about African Americans in a petition to the mayor of Chicago to institute racial segregation. Relying on the proposition that libel was categorically without First Amendment protection, the Court upheld the conviction in a 5–4 decision. (*Beauharnais* has effectively been overruled by subsequent developments in free speech law, particularly the extension of substantial First Amendment protection to libelous statements of public concern in *New York Times v. Sullivan* and its progeny.)

26. That the harm addressed by group libel laws is something other than injury flowing from falsity of the statements is shown by the *Beauharnais* prosecution, in which the defendant was not allowed to offer truth as a defense.

27. See, e.g., Section 131 of the German Penal Code, which prohibits distribution of materials that "incite racial hatred."

28. See, e.g., Article 266(b) of the Danish Penal Code, which outlaws statements "threatening, insulting or degrading a group of persons on account of their race, color, national or ethnic origin or belief"); Section 130 of the German Penal Code, prohibiting "attacks on the human dignity of others by insulting, maliciously degrading, or defaming part of the population"; and Section 137(c) of the Dutch Criminal Code, which forbids "deliberately giv[ing] public expression to views insulting to a group of persons on account of their race, religion or conviction or sexual preference."

29. See Joint Action of the European Community pursuant to Article K3 of the Treaty of European Union (1996), which requires each member state to prohibit "public incitement to discrimination, violence or racial hatred" and the "public dissemination or distribution of tracts, pictures or other material containing expressions of racism and xenophobia"; and Article 4 of the International Convention on the Elimination of All Forms of Racial Discrimination, which requires signatories to "declare as an offense punishable by law all dissemination of ideas based on racial superiority or hatred."

30. See *J. Glimmerveen and J. Hagenbeek v. Netherlands*, App. Nos. 8348/78 and 8406/78, [1979], 23 *Year Book of the European Convention on Human Rights* 366 (Eur. Ct. H.R.).

31. "As I would not be a slave, so I would not be a master. This expresses my idea of democracy. Whatever differs from this, to the extent of the difference, is no democracy." Mario Cuomo, ed., *Lincoln on Democracy* (New York: HarperCollins, 1991), 122.

32. Post, *Constitutional Domains*, 273 (internal quotation marks omitted).

33. Ibid., 319.

34. Thus, in the Dutch case discussed above, it is not clear that the defendants' advocacy that all "guest workers" be expelled from the country proposed a political change inconsistent with democracy. In this regard it is noteworthy that the European Commission interpreted the leaflets as proposing that "all non-white people" be removed from the Netherlands, regardless of their nationality.

35. In Canada and most European countries, criminal law is the responsibility of the national rather than provincial authorities. This structure allows the national legislature to impose tight constraints on the enforcement of speech regulations, such as the provision found in the United Kingdom's hate-speech law requiring the approval of the attorney general before a prosecution can be commenced. In contrast, the peculiar federalistic structure of the United States vests the primary responsibility for making and enforcing the criminal law in state and local government. If the U.S. Supreme Court were ever to uphold a hate-speech law under the "antidemocratic speech" exception, it would not only empower fifty states and countless local governments to enact and enforce such laws but more significantly would authorize each jurisdiction to enact any other speech regulation consistently with the "antidemocratic speech" exception. Applied in a principled way, this exception would permit a wide range of restrictions.

Democratic Morality
Needs First Amendment Morality
Response to Weinstein

NORMAN FISCHER

Philosophy, Kent State University

James Weinstein contrasts (a) prohibition under U.S. constitutional democracy of restrictions on hate speech with (b) permission of restrictions on hate speech in countries with different interpretations of the requirements of democracy.

Prohibition of hate-speech restrictions in the United States follows First Amendment law. In June 1992, *R.A.V.* struck down a hate-speech ordinance in the city of St. Paul, Minnesota, which had prohibited certain words and symbols that were commonly held to stigmatize individuals on the basis of their membership in groups, characterizing these words and symbols as "fighting words." The St. Paul ordinance went back to the famous *Chaplinsky* Supreme Court case, which had held that there were some words that were unprotected by the First Amendment, because their sole purpose was to make people fight. Edward Cleary, who successfully argued *R.A.V.* in front of the Supreme Court, has stated clearly the anti-hate-speech-code defense of *R.A.V.:* that it brings to fruition the line of legal thought that limits "fighting words" to a purely contextual definition. In contrast, Cass Sunstein and Tom Grey, the architect of the Stanford hate-speech code, which was struck down under *R.A.V.* in 1995, have both defended hate-speech restrictions against *R.A.V.*, which for them represents a constitutional aberration that blocks the full development of U.S. anti-discrimination law. Weinstein does not go this far, but he comes close to it.[1]

The debate is partly over the meaning of *R.A.V.* The majority opinion in *R.A.V.*, written by Antonin Scalia, struck the ordinance down for violation of content and viewpoint neutrality. To highlight Scalia's achievement it must be understood that not only did he strike down the alleged right to censor based on the group-membership aspect of the St. Paul ordinance, but he also identified this aspect as the core of the ordinance, hidden under the shell of the concept "fighting words." Beneath that shell, the core of the St. Paul ordinance, Scalia made clear, is the unjustified extension of Fourteenth Amendment equality rights to the idea that a class of words that are held to stigmatize groups can be censored. Hence, after *R.A.V.*, hate-speech restrictions in the United States can more easily be seen to censor a certain content or a certain viewpoint, even when hidden under the shell of a "fighting words" concept bloated far beyond a contextual definition of them.[2]

Although the minority in *R.A.V.* declined to strike the ordinance down for content and viewpoint discrimination, it did use the bloated nature of the fighting-words ordinance to strike it down for overbreadth and chill.[3] Grey's and Sunstein's answer to this is that overbreadth can be gotten around by a precise appeal to the constitutional concept of equality and nondiscrimination. Weinstein does not take up the challenge raised by the minority opinion, and by referring to the unprotected status of fighting words as a settled doctrine, he risks begging the question of whether a general ban on fighting words as broad as the one he considers as a possible answer to the majority opinion can really overcome the chill and overbreadth problems raised by the minority (and in all probability accepted by the majority) in *R.A.V.*[4] Nevertheless, he seems to agree with Sunstein and Grey that words of racial hatred could be constitutionally stopped in the United States by appealing to the equality clause of the Fourteenth Amendment, the foundation of U.S. antidiscrimination law.[5] But Scalia's majority opinion stops this tactic as an answer to the minority opinion. Scalia's ban on selective governmental restrictions against certain fighting words logically implies that the more the proponents of anti-hate ordinances and codes attempt to define the hate they want to get at in terms of a pure animus leading to group stigmatization, and thus to alleged violation of guarantees of nondiscrimination and equality of groups such as are implied by the Fourteenth Amendment, then the more the U.S. judiciary will want to throw out the hate-speech restriction because it is censoring the content of the speech, or the viewpoint that it represents.

The most obvious constitutional problem of hate-speech restrictions, key to the minority opinion against them, is overbreadth and chill, which is hard to get around. But the most insuperable constitutional barrier to hate-speech restrictions, the key to the majority opinion against them, is that the more critics of *R.A.V.* try to get around overbreadth and chill by appealing to equality and nondiscrimination—and by defining "fighting words," as in the St. Paul ordinance, in terms of group stigmatization that allegedly violates rights to equality and nondiscrimination under the Fourteenth Amendment—then the less these predefined fighting words can be censored, because they have become viewpoints, theories, and political statements that are actually defined by the political theory that opposes pure acts of hatred against fixed characteristics of race or gender. Hence the more defenders of hate-speech restrictions theorize about hate and make ordinances and codes against it, the more they elevate this speech (such as refusal to pledge allegiance, or the burning of a flag) to the status of the protected viewpoints, which have been the unique hallmarks of U.S. constitutional democracy.[6] In contrast to this political theorizing about hate and fighting words found in the St. Paul ordinance, the original "fighting words" case of *Chaplinsky* was arguably a case of pure insult, precisely because fighting words were defined entirely by the context.

It is no accident that "fighting words" has become the legal battle cry for hate-speech restrictions. The essence of the idea is that there are words, the primary intent of which is to make the people they are directed at react in as abusive and unreflective a mode as the people who uttered them. Hence, the idea of a politics based on them might seem absurd, since any philosophically elaborated politics involves persuasion. But this is not what results from Scalia's opinion, which logically implies that it is the hate-speech restrictions themselves that elaborate the "fighting words" into political stigmatization of groups, thus showing that the words that they want to censor must be protected by the First Amendment. The moral paradox is that the higher the theoretical, moral, and political ground on which the censorship occurs, the more the censorship itself elevates what it censors to a viewpoint, one that is then opposed by the viewpoint of the censor. Scalia was able to use the very elaborate theorizing by then making hate-speech ordinances and codes emblems of Fourteenth Amendment morality, precisely to bring about the constitutional downfall of hate-speech restrictions. Scalia had to deflate the range of the fighting-words *Chaplinsky* doctrine, so that theorizing about moral principles of which fighting words would be censored would be seen as implying viewpoint censorship, therefore leaving fighting words to be defined only contextually. Sunstein, Grey, and Weinstein never state in its true strength Scalia's opinion, which really shows that the more critics such as Grey and Sunstein write against *R.A.V.,* the more they prove it.

The pro-hate-speech-restriction position of Sunstein and Grey goes farther, to hold that one can accept the Supreme Court animus against even well-meaning viewpoint discrimination and argue that the cross burning dealt with in *R.A.V.,* along with many other acts of hate, is not a viewpoint. Weinstein is apparently willing to go along with this too.[7] But in doing so, he, like pro-hate-speech-restriction theorists Sunstein and Grey, no longer has a basis for defending such other landmark extensions of the concept of viewpoint as *Texas v. Johnson*, which saw flag burning as a viewpoint, and *West Virginia Bd. of Education v. Barnette*, which saw refusal to recite the Pledge of Allegiance as a viewpoint.[8] The bold message of *R.A.V.,* when added to those earlier cases, is that the Left and Right cannot censor each other in the United States.[9] Hence (a) U.S. restrictions on hate-speech codes are democratic. But how does U.S. constitutional democracy fare in relation to (b) alternate traditions of democracy and hate-speech restrictions?

Pro-hate-speech-restriction democratic theorists such as Sunstein and Michael Sandel anchor their censorship to an alternate theory of democracy that stresses three key ideas. The first idea is that defense of public reasoning is necessary for U.S. First Amendment law and for democracy.[10] Weinstein agrees with this, but this is no problem, since so do anti-hate-speech-restriction theorists.[11] The second idea is that two other key concepts in free speech theory, namely free speech as enabling a marketplace of ideas, and free speech as self-expression, are not necessary for First Amendment law and not necessary for democracy.[12] Weinstein agrees with this, and anti-hate-speech-restriction theorists do not.[13] The third idea is that civility in the form of restrictions on hate speech is necessary for public reasoning.[14] Weinstein does not agree with this, but neither does he agree with such anti-hate-speech-restriction theorists as Ronald Dworkin that imposition of civility-based restriction of hate speech is contradictory to democracy.[15] It is from their denial of the centrality of the marketplace of ideas and self-expression that civility democrats launch restrictions on hate speech. Since Weinstein accepts the premise that they start from, logically he cannot argue strongly against what they do, except in his refusal to accept that civility is necessary for democracy. Yet civility democratic theorists have cited little or no evidence that an emphasis on active democratic participation based on public spiritedness and public reasoning should envisage passive, fearful citizens for whom the paternalistic state must censor what might offend their sense of civility.

NOTES

1. *R.A.V. v. City of St. Paul* 505 U.S. 377 (1992); Edward Cleary, *Beyond the Burning Cross* (New York: Random House, 1994), 172–90; Thomas C. Grey, "How to Write a Speech Code Without Really Trying: Reflections on the Stanford Experience," 29 *University of California Davis Law Review* (1996) 917–23; Cass R. Sunstein, *Democracy and the Problem of Free Speech* (New York: Free Press, 1993), 189–93; *Chaplinsky v. New Hampshire* 315 U.S. (1942); *Corry v. Stanford*, no. 740309, California Superior Court, Santa Clara County, unpublished, but available on the World Wide Web at http://www-Leland.Stanford.edu/group/law/library/welcome.htm; James Weinstein, in this volume.

2. *R.A.V.*, 323.

3. Ibid., 327.

4. Weinstein.

5. Ibid., 19.

6. *West Virginia Board of Education v. Barnette* 63 S.Ct. 1178, 318 U.S. 624 (1943); *Texas v. Johnson* 491 U.S. 397 (1989).

7. Sunstein, *Democracy and the Problem of Free Speech*, 189; Grey, "How to Write a Speech Code Without Really Trying," 817–23; Weinstein, 17–18.

8. *Texas v. Johnson; West Virginia Board of Education v. Barnette.*

9. For Left and Right censorship see Nat Hentoff, *Free Speech for Me but Not for Thee* (New York: HarperCollins, 1992).

10. Sunstein, *Democracy and the Problem of Free Speech*, 120–24; Michael Sandel, *Democracy's Discontent* (Cambridge, Mass.: Harvard Univ. Press, 1996), 80.

11. Weinstein; Ronald Dworkin, *Freedom's Law* (Cambridge, Mass.: Harvard Univ. Press, 1996) 202–8.

12. Sunstein, *Democracy and the Problem of Free Speech*, 190; Sandel, *Democracy's Discontent*, 74–80.

13. Weinstein; Dworkin, *Freedom's Law*, 202–8.

14. Sunstein, *Democracy and the Problem of Free Speech*, 190; Sandel, *Democracy's Discontent*, 202–8.

15. *West Virginia Board of Education v. Barnette*; Weinstein; Dworkin, *Freedom's Law*, 222–24.

Equality and Expression
Response to Weinstein

JONATHAN L. ENTIN

Law and Political Science, Case Western Reserve University

Professor Weinstein has provided us with a concise and stimulating analysis of the values underlying the profound skepticism of American law toward content- and viewpoint-based restrictions on hate speech. He has focused on First Amendment jurisprudence without inundating us with a sea of jurisprudential arcana, emphasizing instead the core values that animate the case law and some of the commentary on that subject. He has also usefully afforded us a comparative perspective, suggesting that other conceptions of democracy tolerate restrictions on hate speech that American law rejects.

At bottom, Professor Weinstein suggests that our skepticism about expansive hate-speech rules reflects the American commitment to egalitarianism. I want to focus on this aspect of his analysis, because many of the arguments in favor of restrictions on hate speech proceed from an egalitarian premise: that hate speech reinforces the subordination of oppressed groups such as African Americans and women and therefore should be stripped of legal protection.[1] This premise strikes me as dubious, so I will devote my brief comments to explaining why.[2]

Those who see a conflict between equality and expression believe that the First Amendment protects the privileged. This view is reminiscent of A. J. Liebling's famous quip that "freedom of the press is guaranteed only to those who own one."[3] In fact, however, some of the most significant advances in First Amendment doctrine resulted from the civil rights movement. I want to touch briefly on some highlights and consider how we might respond to hate speech in ways that promote our concern for equality without unnecessarily weakening our commitment to freedom of expression.

Perhaps the greatest of all First Amendment cases, *New York Times Co. v. Sullivan*,[4] arose directly from civil rights protests. The case resulted from an advertisement seeking public financial and moral support for Dr. Martin Luther King, Jr., and other activists in the struggle for black freedom. The police commissioner of Montgomery, Alabama, who was never identified in the ad, obtained a jury verdict for $500,000 in damages over several comparatively minor factual mistakes concerning events that had occurred before he took office. The Supreme Court overturned

175

the verdict, explaining that the First Amendment embodied a commitment to "unin-hibited, robust, and wide open" debate on public issues and that the Constitution therefore protected even caustic criticism of public officials. The Court clearly under-stood that Sullivan's lawsuit, the first of a series of enormous claims against the *Times* and CBS, was meant to drive the national press out of the South and thereby diminish substantially press coverage of the civil rights movement. This ruling was a victory not only for the elite media: in it the Court announced a general rule that protects all critics of government. Moreover, it is often forgotten that the *Times* was not the only defendant in the case. Commissioner Sullivan had also sued four black Alabama min-isters who had taken leading roles in civil rights protests in the state (including Ralph Abernathy, Fred Shuttlesworth, and Joseph Lowery); those ministers faced bankruptcy and perhaps exile from the state and from the movement had Sullivan succeeded in levying against their homes and property to satisfy the judgment.[5]

Another line of cases generated by the civil rights movement deals with free-dom of association. The southern response to *Brown v. Board of Education*[6] included measures targeting the NAACP. Several states sought to outlaw the organization, others tried to exclude NAACP members from teaching in the public schools (a real threat to the black middle class, because teaching was one of the few professions open to African Americans under segregation), and at least one attempted to pre-vent the NAACP from litigating civil rights cases. The Supreme Court rejected all of these efforts, holding that they violated the First Amendment. So, for example, states could not compel the NAACP to turn over its membership lists where members faced a strong possibility of harassment simply for belonging to the organization.[7] Nor could authorities bar NAACP members from public employment simply for joining an entirely lawful group.[8] The ban on litigation was also rejected, as an infringe-ment on political advocacy rights.[9]

A third group of decisions makes clear that government may not suppress speech simply because it provokes a hostile audience reaction. The notion that a speaker could be silenced for her own protection would have allowed authorities to arrest civil rights advocates because segregationists objected to their message. That posi-tion had seemed to gain approval in earlier cases, but the Supreme Court ruled that this would allow a heckler's veto of otherwise protected speech.[10]

The last area that I will mention here concerns speech on public property. Al-though earlier decisions had suggested that the government could prohibit speech on land that it owned, just as a private owner could, the Court began its modern expansion of so-called public-forum doctrine in cases involving civil rights demon-strations.[11] The basic concept of the public forum idea is that some public property has traditionally been used for expressive purposes and is so appropriately used for speech that the government may not close off that property to demonstrations and protests.[12]

This brief discussion illustrates the possibility for close connections between expansive protection for speech and political action to enhance the status of African Americans. To be sure, not every First Amendment claim asserted by civil rights advocates prevailed, and the movement did not succeed in eliminating bigotry, as our continuing debate about hate speech demonstrates. At the same time, the speech-protective rules announced in those cases had wider doctrinal implications, providing protections against official attempts to silence criticism (through ruinous libel suits, harassment of unpopular groups by intrusive legislative investigations, suppression of controversial speakers at the behest of hostile bystanders), and guaranteeing that speech could occur in some public places. In these areas, there was no real conflict between equality and expression.

Perhaps the country has changed over the past generation. Today the problem comes from those who resent civil-rights progress, so we now face a conflict between equality and expression that did not exist thirty and more years ago. Hate speech silences traditionally disfavored groups and reinforces racist and sexist stereotypes. Because prejudice is largely subconscious, advocates urge that such speech be outlawed. Professor Weinstein is skeptical of the silencing argument, so he opposes hate-speech legislation.

Let us take proponents of speech regulation seriously, however. Blatantly racist or sexist speech can convey powerfully hostile messages that might affect behavior and aspiration. Even if the quantity of hate speech is limited, its mere existence can reinforce fears that the silent majority are also bigots. This poses a dilemma for a society that is rightly skeptical of viewpoint-based restrictions on speech. Legal suppression of obnoxious speakers conflicts with American norms of democracy, but tolerance seems an inappropriate response to hatred.

We might treat an incident of hate speech as an opportunity rather than a problem. Consider the response of the residents of Pulaski, Tennessee, when the Ku Klux Klan announced its intention to return to the town where it had been founded over a century earlier. Local officials knew they could not prevent the Klan from holding a parade, but the community responded by placing signs in the windows of businesses and hanging orange ribbons along the parade route to make clear their revulsion for the group's ideas.[13] Similarly, colleges and universities have reacted to instances of hate speech by holding open meetings to address the underlying issues in a way that engages more people than would ever be involved in a formal legal proceeding.

Professor Weinstein has thoughtfully explained the legal principles that militate against the kind of strong hate-speech laws in America that other democratic nations have adopted. There is a larger implication to his analysis. The spirit of liberty, as Learned Hand long ago reminded us, ultimately resides in the hearts of men and women.[14] Hate speech is incompatible with our values, but in the end we must rely more on each other than on the law to address the problem.

1. Prominent proponents of this view include Richard Delgado, Catharine MacKinnon, and Mari Matsuda.

2. Professor Weinstein develops a similar theme in his thoughtful book, *Hate Speech, Pornography, and the Radical Attack on Free Speech Doctrine* (Boulder, Colo.: Westview Press, 1999). Anyone who writes on this subject must also acknowledge an enormous debt to Harry Kalven's *The Negro and the First Amendment* (Chicago: Univ. of Chicago Press, 1966).

3. A. J. Liebling, *The Press*, rev. ed. (New York: Ballantine Books, 1964), 30.

4. 376 U.S. 254 (1964). For a detailed account, see Anthony Lewis, *Make No Law: The Sullivan Case and the First Amendment* (New York: Random House, 1991).

5. See Fred D. Gray, *Bus Ride to Justice* (Montgomery, Ala.: Black Belt Press, 1995), 161–72.

6. 347 U.S. 483 (1954).

7. The leading case in this area was *NAACP v. Alabama ex rel. Patterson*, 357 U.S. 449 (1958); see also *Gibson v. Florida Legislative Investigation Committee*, 372 U.S. 539 (1963); *Louisiana ex rel. Gremillion v. NAACP*, 366 U.S. 293 (1961); and *Bates v. City of Little Rock*, 361 U.S. 516 (1960).

8. See *Shelton v. Tucker*, 364 U.S. 480 (1960).

9. See *NAACP v. Button*, 371 U.S. 415 (1963).

10. See *Edward v. South Carolina*, 372 U.S. 229 (1963); *Cox v. Louisiana*, 379 U.S. 536 (1965). See also *Gregory v. City of Chicago*, 394 U.S. 111 (1969). These cases represent a substantial expansion of speech rights in the face of a hostile audience. Compare *Feiner v. New York*, 340 U.S. 315 (1951).

11. See *Cox v. Louisiana*, 379 U.S. 536 (1965).

12. The Supreme Court rejected public-forum defenses in some cases involving civil rights protests. See, e.g., *Adderley v. Florida*, 385 U.S. 39 (1966).

13. See "Town Closes Shops to Protest Neo-Nazi March," *Los Angeles Times*, Oct. 8, 1989, pt. 1, 28.

14. See Learned Hand, *The Spirit of Liberty* (New York: Alfred A. Knopf, 1959), 144.

Some Further Thoughts on Hate Speech and Democracy

Response to the Discussants

JAMES WEINSTEIN

I thank both Professors Entin and Fischer for their comments. Because these comments differ so markedly in tone, style, and substance, I shall reply to them separately.

Jonathan Entin concisely and accurately summarizes some key points of my paper and then extends the discussion by developing an important theme. Entin correctly grasps that "at bottom," I suggest that the American skepticism to expansive hate-speech restriction "reflects the American commitment to egalitarianism" and that contrary to those who see such laws as presenting a conflict between liberty and equality, I posit equality on both sides of the equation.[1] However, I drew a distinction between formal equality, which I suggested is at the core of democratic self-governance value underlying American free speech doctrine, and the substantive equality that hate-speech restrictions are supposed to advance. Entin makes an important contribution to this discussion by emphasizing that American free speech doctrine can also promote substantive equality.[2]

Professor Entin persuasively argues that contrary to the claims of certain radical critics, *New York Times v. Sullivan* was "not a victory only for the elite media" but for all critics of government. He properly reminds us that four black ministers were also defendants in that case and that libel suits such as this were meant "to drive the national press out of the South and thereby to diminish substantially press coverage of the civil rights movement." Entin also documents how the Supreme Court expanded the right to association to protect the NAACP from crippling legislation directed against it by hostile southern legislators in the wake of *Brown v. Board of Education*, and how it protected civil rights demonstrators by confining the heckler's-veto rationale for speech suppression as well as by strengthening the public-forum doctrine.

Professor Entin is certainly right that "some of the most significant advances in First Amendment doctrine resulted from the civil rights movement" and that this development "illustrates *the possibility* for close connections between expansive protection for speech and political action to enhance the status of African Americans" (my emphasis). But notice that Entin does not claim that this development in free speech doctrine was a crucial factor in the success of the civil rights movement. It is quite likely that even if the Court had not strengthened free speech doctrine in the way it did, American apartheid still would have been broken, the watershed civil rights acts would still been passed, and most Americans still would have come to reject at least the more blatant forms of racism. My own guess is that with the possible exception of the right-to-association decisions protecting the NAACP, the civil rights movement would have borne the same fruits in the same season without the protective shelter of a strengthened free speech doctrine. To be sure, the struggle may have been more expensive and more painful without these decisions. But is it really plausible that the result would have been different or even long-delayed if a dozen or so civil rights protestors' trespass or breach-of-the-peace convictions had been affirmed instead of reversed? Or if the *New York Times* and the black ministers had had to pay the libel judgment? Even if the Court had allowed the southern authorities to cripple the NAACP, the important legal principles that this organization's litigation produced would probably been delayed rather than never established.

This is not to deny that some basic right of free speech was not crucial to the success of the civil rights movement. But such a right existed before that movement, and by the time the Warren Court began deciding civil rights protest cases, civil rights was an idea whose time had come. The real importance of these cases from the standpoint of substantive equality is the protection it will afford future progressive movements in their infancy, when they are most vulnerable. More generally, the Warren Court may well be right that wide-open and robust public discourse is essential to political, social, and material progress. But as important as these instrumental concerns may be, they are not the whole story, or even the most important theme, of American free speech doctrine. Rather, at its deepest level, American free speech doctrine protects expression not because doing so makes for a better society but because of a vision of democracy that demands that government treat each of us as equal, autonomous, and rational agents.

Indeed, when it comes to restrictions on hate speech, it is not at all clear that such prohibitions would impede rather than advance the vision of racial, ethnic, and religious equality to which this nation is now dedicated. My own view, explained in detail elsewhere, is at this time in our nation's history broad hate-speech bans are likely to do little good and might even be counterproductive from a standpoint of substantive equality.[3] But this is a debatable assessment, with which others could reasonably disagree. If free speech were valued merely as an instrument of social good, it would be difficult to reject a plea to emulate European democracies and at least try hate-speech laws for a while to see if they might not lead to a more tolerant and racially just society. But precisely because free speech is an individual right, rooted in a basic moral precept of the relationship between government and citizen, such a viewpoint-discriminatory law cannot be imposed in this country on such speculative grounds.

Norm Fischer has some telling points to make against Professors Cass Sunstein, Tom Grey, and Michael Sandel. But in taking on these "pro–hate-speech-restriction theorists"[4] (as he calls them), Fischer inaccurately assimilates my views to theirs. Indeed, he attributes to me views that are the opposite of the ones I hold.[5] My position on hate-speech regulation in general, and *R.A.V. v. City of St. Paul* in particular, is much closer to Fischer's than to the theorists he criticizes. Fischer not only seriously misapprehends my position on hate-speech regulation but fails to grasp the major purpose of my paper. As Professor Entin correctly recognizes, my project was not to take a position on the perennial question of hate-speech regulation but to explore "the values underlying the profound skepticism of American law toward content- and viewpoint-based restrictions on hate speech."

Professor Fischer does not respond to the essence of my paper but instead uses this occasion to add his voice to the "anti-hate-speech-code" position and defend the majority opinion in *R.A.V.* For more than a decade, legal academics have staked out their positions on campus codes.[6] But this debate, quite useful in its time, has now grown stale, as has the closely related discussion of *R.A.V.* In an attempt to transcend entrenched positions (including my own) and to advance and enliven the debate on hate-speech regulation, I thought it useful to ask what accounts for the uniquely American position disallowing hate-speech regulation.

I have very little to say in reply to Professor Fischer's commentary, for despite the profound difference he imagines, I basically agree with him. As I explained at some length in my opening paper, I agree with the majority in *R.A.V.* that viewpoint-discriminatory regulation of even unprotected speech can violate the First Amendment as well as the commitment to democratic self-governance. Further, I agree with Fischer that "overbreadth and chill" are fundamental problems plaguing hate-speech regulation in general and the St. Paul ordinance in particular. As best I can tell, our only significant disagreement is whether the St. Paul ordinance is viewpoint discriminatory. Professor Fischer is certain that it is; I am not so sure. To explore this disagreement fully we would have to discuss in detail the ordinance and its legislative history, the city's justification for the ordinance, and the state court decision upholding it. Since such an exercise is both too technical and too lengthy for this occasion, the following cursory remarks will have to suffice.

First, contrary to Professor Fischer's assertion, the ordinance did not proscribe fighting words that "stigmatize" individuals on the basis of group membership. Rather, it prohibited words or symbols that arouse "anger, alarm or resentment in others on the basis of race, color, creed, religion or gender."[7] More significantly, it is unclear what "on the basis of race, etc." modifies. Thus the ordinance could have been interpreted as proscribing not words with a racist or even racial content but rather as forbidding speakers from directing even racially neutral fighting words to a person because of his race. Under this interpretation, a racist calling his new black neighbor a "dirty bastard" in order to alarm him would be proscribed despite the lack of any racial content to these fighting words. Even if the ordinance were interpreted as proscribing fighting words with a *racial* content, this does not necessarily mean that the words must express a *racist* worldview. In this regard it is interesting to note that Justice Scalia did not find the ordinance to be viewpoint discriminatory on its face; rather, he concluded that the ordinance was facially content based, and viewpoint discriminatory in its "practical operation."[8]

On the other hand, in defending the ordinance the city conceded that it applied only to fighting words with a racial content. Making matters worse, the city argued that only a specific prohibition of racial fighting words could communicate to minorities that "group hatred" is "not condoned by the majority."[9] Worse still, the Minnesota Supreme Court emphasized in its opinion that the ordinance was aimed at messages of "bias motivated" hatred and, in the cross-burning case at issue, to messages "based on virulent notions of racial supremacy."[10] Given the city's justification and the state court's rationale, the U.S. Supreme Court was warranted in deeming the ordinance viewpoint discriminatory.[11] It might have been wiser, however, if the Court had explicitly rested its holding on these narrow grounds.

NOTES

1. Jonathan Entin, "Comment: Equality and Expression," in *The Boundaries of Freedom of Expression and Order in a Democratic Society,* ed. Thomas Hensley (Kent, Ohio: Kent State Univ. Press, 2001).

2. I am puzzled, however, by Entin's assertion that "hate speech silences traditionally disfavored groups." (ibid.) This claim is at odds with his rejection of the premise that "hate speech reinforces the subordination of oppressed groups" and in tension with his observation that campus hate speech has led to "open meetings to address the underlying issue that engages more people than would be involved in a formal legal proceeding" (both ibid.).

3. See James Weinstein, *Hate Speech, Pornography and the Radical Attack on Free Speech Doctrine* (Boulder, Colo.: Westview Press, 1999), 125–90.

4. Norman Fischer, "Comment on James Weinstein, 'Hate Speech, Viewpoint Neutrality and the American Concept of Democracy,'" in Hensley, ed., *The Boundaries of Freedom of Expression.*

5. For instance, Fischer claims that I seem "to agree with Sunstein and Grey that words of racial hatred could be constitutionally stopped in the United States by appealing to the equality clause of the Fourteenth Amendment" (ibid.). Nothing could be farther from the truth. As I have written elsewhere, restricting speech rights by reference to the Equal Protection Clause "would likely have serious negative consequences for free speech doctrine," is a "formula for a conservative society," establishes an orthodoxy in a way that "betrays one of the fundamental purposes of the First Amendment," and is "little more than an attempt artificially to constrain a rationale for the suppression of hate speech." See Weinstein, *Hate Speech and Pornography,* 89, 165 (internal quotation marks omitted). Similarly, Fischer says I support a "bloated" or "expansive" version of fighting words (Fischer, "Comment"). In fact, I support an emaciated or narrow version of that doctrine. See James Weinstein, "A Constitutional Roadmap to the Regulation of Hate Speech on Campus," *Wayne Law Review* 38 (1991): 163, 186 n. 87. (Professor Fischer does, however, properly criticize me for not making clear that in light of several

Supreme Court decisions reversing fighting-words convictions on overbreadth and vagueness grounds and the absence of any affirming such a conviction since the doctrine was announced nearly fifty years ago, the unprotected status of fighting words is not "settled doctrine" [Fischer, "Comment"].)

I could go on pointing out examples of Fischer's mischaracterization of my views, but it suffices to say that in virtually every instance in which Fischer attributes a position to me, he gets it wrong.

6. For a review of some of the early literature as well as my views on the subject, see Weinstein, "A Constitutional Roadmap."

7. *St. Paul Bias-Motivated Crime Ordinance*, Legis. Code, § 292.02 (1990), quoted in *R.A.V. v. City of St. Paul*, 505 U.S. 377, 380 (1992). Fischer's misdescription of the ordinance proves the wisdom of Karl Llewellyn's admonition, "Never paraphrase a statute." See William Twining, *Karl Llewllyn and the Realist Movement* (London: Weidenfeld and Nicolson, 1973), 240.

8. 505 U.S. at 391.

9. Ibid. at 392.

10. Ibid., quoting from *In re Welfare of R.A.V.*, 464 N.W.2d 507, 508, 511 (Minn. 1991).

11. As I explained in my opening paper, however, whether an ordinance singling out racial fighting words should be deemed viewpoint discriminatory also depends heavily on whether such words are in fact more likely to provoke fights or inflict emotional injury than are other types of fighting words, and, if so, whether a general ban on fighting words would be less effective than a selective one.

7

Challenging Boundaries for a Boundless Medium

Information Access, Libraries, and Freedom of Expression in a Democratic Society

Susan B. Kretchmer

Area Studies, The Johns Hopkins University

Rod Carveth

Communication, Southern Connecticut State University

[Citizens] must always remain free to inquire, to study and evaluate, to gain new maturity and understanding . . . [to] explore the unknown, and discover areas of interest and thought . . . [for] access to ideas makes it possible for citizens generally to exercise their rights of free speech and press in a meaningful manner. . . . [The] library is the principal locus of such freedom.
—*Board of Education v. Pico* (1982, pp. 869–70; internal quotation marks omitted)

It is no exaggeration to conclude that the content of the Internet is as diverse as human thought . . . [a] new marketplace of ideas . . . . The Web is thus comparable, from the readers' viewpoint, to . . . a vast library including millions of readily available and indexed publications . . . . The interest in encouraging freedom of expression in a democratic society outweighs any theoretical but unproven benefit of censorship.
—*Reno v. American Civil Liberties Union* (1997, pp. 2335, 2351; internal quotation marks omitted)

The analogy the Supreme Court draws between the library and the Internet, as important repositories of information and gateways to knowledge in a democracy, is even more profound in a historical context. Originally, libraries were privately owned, and access was restricted to special classes of society—the wealthy and elite, scholars, and university students. In the last century, the role of libraries shifted as they became free, open-access facilities, serving people of all ages, all classes, and from all walks of life, performing a vital service to the community. Similarly, the initial use of information technology has historically been confined to privileged groups. Despite the growth of the Internet, as of June 2000 many people do not own or cannot afford a personal computer or connection to computer networks. As a result, the best hope for universal access to the information superhighway is in public libraries, which are already uniquely positioned to connect all Americans to information resources, electronic or otherwise.

Yet, public libraries today face a daunting dilemma, as well as new and challenging legal problems. Libraries across the country are besieged by a myriad of critics—from community groups to national organizations to the "Dr. Laura" radio talk show with eighteen million listeners a week—concerned about the availability of sexually explicit, "harmful," and otherwise "adult" or objectionable content on the Internet that they feel endangers the order and scholarly environment of libraries. Boston (Massachusetts), Austin (Texas), and Gilroy (California) are just a few of the focal points in a nationwide controversy over how or whether to limit or supervise Internet access by children and adults in public libraries. This debate is fueled by a political climate filled with new federal, state, and municipal legislation seeking to regulate Internet content and/or tie government telecommunications funding for libraries and schools to the mandatory use of Internet filters, the White House's high-profile initiative to create a "Family Friendly" Internet, and the industry's enthusiasm for developing content rating and blocking systems. In this charged atmosphere, libraries from coast to coast are installing stand-alone blocking software designed for the home market, such as CyberPatrol, X-Stop, and Net Nanny, on computers for public use connected to the Internet. Serious flaws in the software have raised complex free speech issues. Seen by some as a powerful tool for protecting children from online pornography and by others as "censorware," the problems related to Internet content filtering and blocking are magnified when mandated in publicly supported libraries, which are governmental institutions subject to the First Amendment.

Consequently, despite the decisive rejection of the Communications Decency Act by the Supreme Court, a second round in the fight over freedom of expression and the Internet is now shaping up, and public libraries are the battleground. Paralleling the conflict that created the May 4, 1970, tragedy at Kent State University, the current dispute over library Internet access brings to light the powerful kinetic tensions sparked when constitutional freedoms, the rule of law and order, and an emotionally charged public debate collide over government control at a public institution. Just as Kent State stands as a pivotal challenge in the nation's history, the outcome of the library Internet access controversy, as well as the entire national debate, will have a tremendous impact on the future of the First Amendment in the information age and, as a result, on the nature of our democratic society.

This essay explores the current status and proper limits of the relationship between the Internet and freedom of expression as exemplified by the controversy over library Internet access and the question of the constitutionality of the use of filtering/blocking software in public libraries. Specifically, we examine the nature of library Internet access, policies and filters, and the associated problems; review the current dispute, the concerns and issues raised, and the specific cases and legislation under contention; consider the legal arguments and applicable First Amendment precedents, both for and against blocking software in libraries, that speak to the proper limits of freedom of expression in contemporary American society; analyze the public debate and arguments, both for and against blocking software in libraries, that seek to define the proper limits of freedom of expression in contemporary American society; and discuss the confluence and disconnect at the volatile intersection of legal argument and public debate in the library Internet access controversy and the implications for the complex relationship between the Internet and the First Amendment.

LIBRARY INTERNET ACCESS

Libraries and the Internet

In America, the library has a long history as a revered and cherished community institution. Whether expressed as broadly as Andrew Carnegie's declaration that "there is not such a cradle of democracy upon the earth as the Free Public Library, this republic of letters, where neither rank, office, nor wealth receives the slightest consideration," or as personally as Oprah Winfrey's observation that "getting my library card was like citizenship; it was like American citizenship,"[1] we learn at an early age that the library holds a special and important place in civil society. Indeed, there are more public libraries in the United States than McDonald's—a total of 15,994, including branches. Americans visit school, public, and academic libraries three times more often than they go to movies and borrow an average of six books a year. Public libraries are supported by tax dollars at a cost of approximately twenty-one dollars per capita a year. As a testament to the degree to which libraries are perceived as an essential component of democratic culture, despite the advent of the digital revolution, the apparent rise of bytes over books, and the increased availability of information via computer, a 1998 Gallup poll found that nearly all respondents expected libraries to remain a necessity in the future.[2]

Appropriately, the public library and the Internet have developed a symbiotic function within American society. The number of the nation's public libraries offering Internet access to patrons has increased exponentially in the past four years, as has the number of people using this new service. According to American Library

Association data, as of 1998, more than 73 percent of the nation's public libraries offer Internet access to patrons, jumping from only 28 percent in 1996, and that number is growing daily. Of the public libraries that serve populations of a hundred thousand or more (serving over 57 percent of the U.S. population), more than 85 percent offer Internet access to patrons.[3] MCI's second annual LibraryLINK study recently showed that among those who access the Internet from places other than home, work, or school, public libraries are the top location—cited by 45 percent of users—up 86 percent from 1997 and up 500 percent from 1996.[4] Further, in the past, public Internet access had meant text-based, hard-to-maneuver browsers, or single station sign-ups for graphical access. Now, library patrons are a few mouse clicks away from the World Wide Web with Netscape or Microsoft Internet Explorer as a choice on computer catalogs throughout the building, featuring stunning visuals at high speed.

Library Information Technology Management Policies and Tools

As an integral part of the practice of librarianship, trained experts determine the principles and guidelines under which libraries operate. For example, every library or library system develops and employs policies that govern everything from collection development to the confidentiality of user services. In the age of electronic information, there are three primary issues about which libraries must make decisions in the process of implementing patron Internet access: the physical provisions of computer terminals, acceptable use policies (AUPs), and filtering/blocking software.

Although AUPs and software require further discussion, the most straightforward tool for library Internet use regulation is the physical manipulation of computer terminal availability. For instance, the library may impose time limits on Internet usage and must decide whether to place terminals in locations that serve to minimize or maximize public view and/or librarian oversight. Moreover, libraries can elect to purchase and attach to the face of computer monitors privacy screens that allow only the person sitting in front of the computer terminal to see the material displayed on the monitor; to anyone else who might see the monitor from an angle or distance, the image is obscured.

Acceptable Use Policies

While information technology represents a new medium, the framework for defining use and access policies is grounded in the library's traditional mission statement, other policies (such as codes of conduct), and the needs of the community served. The management of public library AUP development is usually handled by library staff and the local library governing board, frequently with input from the library Friends group and local elected officials. As with rules and procedures for the use of all library materials, a written, well-understood, broadly circulated, and effective acceptable use policy regarding Internet access is crucial to foster the opportunities, benefits, and productivity the technology affords library patrons. Given the nature of the medium with ready access to vast quantities but varying quality of information from throughout the world, AUPs also, of necessity, function as an institutional determination of the limitations placed on the patron in exchange for the privilege of using the library's computer and Internet services and may speak to the age-appropriate interests of young children, adolescents, and adults as do the materials selected for the age-appropriate sections of the physical library. As such, to preclude the risk of controversy and litigation, AUPs must be carefully crafted to respect the purposes of the library, community values, and legal and constitutional considerations.

Filtering/Blocking Software

While AUPs are generally acknowledged to be the least restrictive method of library Internet use regulation, filtering/blocking software is the most restrictive and often considered the least desirable. However, installing the software has become a viable option for public libraries confronted with the need, for example, to find a compromise between providing full Internet access to children and parental and community concerns about Internet material that may not be suitable for minors. When a library does decide to implement a filtered Internet access policy, it must purchase and install software that "blocks" or "filters" Internet content in some combination of the following three methods: (1) list-based blocking prevents users from viewing sites that are deemed inappropriate (according to a list compiled and maintained by the software manufacturer) but allows access to all other sites; (2) keyword-based blocking searches Web sites for objectionable words and phrases (again, as determined by the software vendor) and blocks access to sites that contain them; and (3) inclusion software allows access to only a limited number of predesignated sites.

Proponents of the software contend that it provides invaluable assistance in preventing access (intentional or accidental) to "inappropriate" or "harmful" content. Opponents argue that its use is tantamount to censorship. Serious flaws in the software have raised complex free speech issues, ranging from overbreadth to underinclusiveness. For example, sites, such as "breast cancer" and the city of "Middlesex," can be blocked inappropriately by filtering software and ratings insufficiently fine-tuned to label particular sites. Similarly, in addition to the inaccuracies that can also inadvertently allow "adult" sites to pass through unblocked, the rapidly expanding size and changing content of the Internet prevent the creation of any definitive list of sites featuring objectionable material. Consequently, the software can never fully eliminate access to everything from hardcore pornography to hate speech as long as it exists on the Internet.

The dispute between filtering and freedom of expression has generated some intriguing situations. For instance, in 1998, the American Family Association, an organization that advocates for public library filtering, found that its Web site was blocked by the filter CyberPatrol as an "intolerant" site because it adamantly opposes homosexuality. Further, ironically, the *Mein Kampf, The Catcher in the Rye,* Michelangelo's *David*, and *Playboy* available on a library's bookshelves could be banned from view on the filtered version of the Internet accessed at the very same library. Although many studies and reports on filtering/blocking have been released,[5] no undisputed systematic measurement and assessment of the effectiveness of the software are available.

THE CONTROVERSY

Since the Supreme Court overturned the Communications Decency Act (CDA) in June 1997, there has been widespread publicity, both on the Internet and in the traditional mass broadcast and print media, about obscenity and violence on the Internet. A classic example is the anecdote about the elementary schoolchild who wanted to see the NASA Web site with the extraordinary pictures of Mars being sent back to Earth from the Rover and Carl Sagan Lander that explored the Martian surface. Using an unfiltered computer, the child typed in http://www.nasa.com, not realizing that the domain should have been .gov, not .com, and went to that Web site. There he certainly found extraordinary images, but they were of nude women, because what he accessed was an adult entertainment Web site called Naked Eyes.com.

The defeat of the CDA coupled with the contemporary cultural climate have propelled national lawmakers to seek new ways in which to regulate questionable online content. The latest attempt, the Child Online Protection Act, a "CDA II" enacted through the Omnibus Appropriations Act for fiscal year 1999, was immediately challenged on constitutional grounds by the American Civil Liberties Union and others, who filed a lawsuit in U.S. District Court in Philadelphia on October 22, 1998. Likewise, the failure of the federal government to regulate indecency in cyberspace has convinced local governments to promulgate their own legislation. On the state level, since 1995, at least twenty-five states have considered or passed Internet censorship laws—with eleven of those bills in 1998 alone.

In this context, a passionate nationwide controversy has erupted as growing concerns about "inappropriate" material available in cyberspace have collided with the proliferation of Internet access at libraries, which are publicly funded governmental institutions subject to the First Amendment. Moreover, from the 1997 White

House summit to the 2000 presidential primaries, the library Internet access controversy has had powerful political currency. The paradox of the Internet in public libraries is that while the Internet epitomizes the most basic hallmark of libraries, the free flow of information, and the ideal of a collection unlimited by budgets and shelf space, it also, in many ways, diminishes the role of libraries as information arbiters. Caught in the middle of the turmoil, public libraries must, on a practical basis, balance the legal mandate to protect intellectual freedom and First Amendment rights with the need to manage public access to Internet content that is potentially harmful to juveniles and/or disruptive in a public facility.

Generally, it is conceded on all sides that there are problems. The debate centers on the proper method of solution. No clear consensus has emerged thus far—professional, technological, legal, political, or social—and each constituency seems to be pursuing its own agenda. As a result, polarization has plagued many communities, and the nationwide controversy continues to escalate. There have been disputes resolved without legal action, actual court cases, federal and state legislation, and, most recently, a ballot initiative. Consequently, this raging battle has been waged in two arenas simultaneously—the legal system and the court of public opinion.

Local Disputes across the Nation

Many of the battles over libraries and filtering that have occurred in cities and states across the United States have been resolved without legal action. Two of the most prominent conflicts involved the communities of Austin, Texas, and Boston, Massachusetts.

Austin, Texas

In 1995, the Austin library entered a partnership with the Austin Freenet to obtain funding from the Texas State Library to help underwrite the costs of providing patron Internet access, a project completed by the summer of 1996. Austin Public Library Director Brenda Branch initially supported unrestricted access, and none of the computers at either the central Austin library or its branches had filters, though each had a privacy screen.[6] To protect children, the library posted warnings that materials inappropriate for minors could be accessed via the Internet and distributed to parents printed materials, such as a pamphlet entitled *Child Safety on the Information Superhighway.*

Controversy arose in February 1997 when a patron was caught printing images of child pornography on the library printer and a library staff person witnessed another instructing a group of children on how to access pornographic sites on the Internet. The staff member subsequently wrote letters about the incident to the mayor, the city council, and the two city newspapers. Some library staff felt sexually harassed, but did not know if they had a right to interfere in the patrons' activities. Others were concerned that the library and staff might be vulnerable to prosecution if the patrons' actions violated Section 43.24 of the Texas Penal Code, which makes the display of harmful material to a minor a criminal offense.

Confronting this explosive issue, Brenda Branch decided to install CyberPatrol filtering software on every library computer connected to the Internet. Although many expressed support for Branch's decision to filter, others charged that the library was "censoring" sites and vigorously opposed the decision. In addition, the Austin chapters of the Electronic Freedom Frontier (EFF) and the American Civil Liberties Union (ACLU) threatened to file a class action lawsuit to eliminate the software.

In response, Branch invited representatives from a number of community groups—the EFF, ACLU, PTA, Austin Freenet, city council, and Austin Public Library Commission—to formulate a compromise policy on filters. After much sometimes-acrimonious negotiation, the stakeholders, except for the EFF and ACLU, unanimously agreed to keep CyberPatrol on the computers but to restrict the keyword blocks to just four categories: full nudity, partial nudity, gross depictions, and sexual activity. Further, library staff worked with CyberPatrol representatives to restore access to incorrectly blocked sites. Despite the revised policy, patrons still complained about the restrictions and voiced concern about blocked sites. Nevertheless, the situation at the Austin libraries finally moderated.[7]

Boston, Massachusetts

A similar situation occurred in Boston. In February 1997, parents expressed outrage that sexually explicit material was being downloaded in the children's section of the Boston Public Library, and the *Boston Herald* proclaimed that "Kids Cruise On-Line Porn in Library." As a result, Mayor Thomas Menino ordered the city's chief of computer technology, Michael Hernon, to restrict Internet access on the city's two hundred computers designated for use by children.

Hernon first instructed all Boston public schools, libraries, and the Boston Community Center to post an adult supervisor near all computer terminals in use by children. The city's second step was to install CyberPatrol blocking software on all computers. Copies of Netscape Navigator software were ordered replaced by Microsoft's Internet Explorer 3.0, because the Microsoft browser supports the Platform for Internet Content Selection (PICS) standard, which provides greater control over the kinds of material deemed appropriate for children.

Public reaction was heated and press coverage divided, with the *Boston Globe* supporting filters while the *Boston Phoenix* accused Mayor Menino of political grandstanding. The Massachusetts Civil Liberties Union (MCLU) threatened to file a lawsuit if the mayor did not change his position, asserting that it is the public libraries' duty to provide uncensored information. The MCLU abandoned the promise of litigation when it reached a compromise with the mayor and the Boston Public Library known as the "Boston Solution"—the library left computer terminals unfiltered for adults but filtered children's access.

Court Cases

The first two cases to test the constitutionality of mandatory library Internet blocking were argued in federal district court in 1998 and 1999. One is on appeal and will be decided in 2001. Widely regarded as one of the most important developments in the evolution of cyberspace, these cases will have far-reaching impact on the ability of libraries, schools, universities (both public and private), and government offices to install filtering/blocking software on their computers.

Mainstream Loudoun, et al. v. Board of Trustees of the Loudoun County Library, et al.[8]

The first case was filed in federal district court in late December 1997 against one of the strictest Internet use policies in the country. On October 20, 1997, the Board of Trustees of the Loudoun County Library in Loudoun County, Virginia, adopted a "Policy on Internet Sexual Harassment" that mandated the installation of blocking software on library computers to prevent access to pornographic material on the Internet that they contended would create a hostile work environment in violation of anti-discrimination laws. To implement the policy, the Library Edition of X-Stop blocking software was installed on all ten Internet-connected computers.

On December 22, 1997, with the assistance of the national organization People for the American Way, Mainstream Loudoun, a group of local residents, filed suit alleging that the use of the software on public library Internet access computers constituted a violation of their First Amendment rights of freedom of speech. About six weeks later, the American Civil Liberties Union moved to intervene on behalf of several publishers and authors of Web pages that X-Stop blocked from view in the Loudoun libraries and who sought to have the software removed as well. Thus, this case of first impression presented the district court with the novel issue of whether public libraries violate the constitutionally guaranteed free speech rights of speakers and receivers by employing blocking software on Internet access terminals.

Utilizing the standard of "strict scrutiny," Judge Leonie Brinkema, on November 23, 1998, ruled in favor of the plaintiffs and barred the Loudoun library from enforcing its blocking software policy. As such, the *Loudoun* case became the first decision in the United States to apply the First Amendment to the Internet in public libraries. The library elected not to appeal the decision and adopted a new policy that allows adult patrons to select filtered or unfiltered access, requires parents or legal guardians to specify the type of access for their minor children, and calls for the use of privacy screens on Internet-connected computers. Throughout this legal battle, the Loudoun community was wracked by the emotionally charged hostility of sharply divided local ideological constituencies, the powerful impact of polarizing external forces, and the pressure of the national spotlight.

Kathleen R. v. City of Livermore, et al.[9]

In contrast to *Loudoun*, the case involving the library system in Livermore, California, comes at the issues from the opposite direction. Kathleen R. is the parent of a twelve-year-old boy, Brandon, who, without permission, went to the public library on ten separate occasions, used the library's unfiltered computers to access online full-color photos of nude women in sexually explicit poses, and downloaded those images to a floppy disk. He then printed out the images on a computer at a relative's house and showed them to other children. Whereas the *Loudoun* case sought to stop the use of filtering software, this suit was filed to compel the Livermore public library to install filtering software on presently unfiltered Internet computer terminals with no restrictions on children's access.

With legal assistance from the Pacific Justice Institute, the original complaint against the City of Livermore was filed by the mother on May 28, 1998, asserting three legal claims that attempted to cast this case as a child safety, rather than free speech, issue. First, the plaintiff contended that the use of government money to pay for children's access to pornography constitutes a "waste of public funds" under Section 526 of the California Code of Civil Procedure. Second, the plaintiff argued that the library's policy constitutes a "nuisance." Third, the plaintiff alleged "premises liability." Declining to address these underlying claims, on October 21, 1998, Judge George Hernandez dismissed the case, ruling that Section 230 of the Telecommunications Act of 1996 bars suits against libraries for not filtering. However, the court allowed Kathleen R. the opportunity to try to plead her case in a way that would not invoke the Section 230 immunity provision.

An amended complaint filed on November 3, 1998, raised a fourth legal theory, substantive due process. Arguing that the library was violating her son's constitutional rights under the Fourteenth Amendment and 42 U.S.C. 1983, the plaintiff maintained that the library was knowingly causing her son, and all minors, direct harm. Since the abridgement of a constitutional right was now at issue, unlike in the original complaint, Section 230 would not provide a valid defense. Thus, the novel claim advanced in this case was that children have a basic constitutional right to be free from pain, that viewing obscenity induces pain, that the government must show a compelling interest to contravene constitutional rights, and that, since the government has no compelling interest in supplying Internet access, the library was unconstitutionally violating Brandon's rights. The city and its amicus curiae disputed these assertions, noting particularly that, as opposed to Brandon's affirmative action, the library was a passive provider of Internet access and took no specific action that caused the alleged harm; rather, Brandon, if he was harmed, had harmed himself. On January 13, 1999, the court dismissed the revised complaint as well, ruling that the plaintiff had not stated a claim on which any legal relief could be granted.

Subsequently, on March 11, 1999, Kathleen R. filed an appeal in the California First District Court of Appeal. Working with a very extended schedule, the appeals court will likely not rule on this case until 2001. Again, as with *Loudoun*, this case garnered widespread media attention and sparked a passionate, divisive local struggle with national import.

Federal Legislation

Throughout the controversy, the U.S. Congress has attempted to legislate the use of filtering software in schools and libraries. Every year, after much discussion and debate, the bills have failed to come to a vote on the floor of both houses, be ratified, and be signed into law. The proposed legislation usually involves government intervention through the $2.25 billion-per-year Schools and Libraries Program of the Federal Communications Commission (FCC). This program is based on Section 254 of the Telecommunications Act of 1996, which codified the FCC's long-standing policy of supporting universal telephone service in high-cost rural and low-income areas, and expanded it to include any school, library, and rural health clinic. In 1997, the FCC issued a report extending the "universal service" subsidies to assist schools and libraries in the acquisition of Internet access and various types of computer networking equipment, including network servers and server software, and internal connections, in addition to traditional telecommunications services. The report also established a sliding scale discount rate, or "e-rate," that takes into account the percentage of students on the school lunch program and whether the school or library is urban or rural.

Besides the basic issue of deciding the wisdom and legality of compelling schools and libraries that receive public funds to filter Internet access, a major point of contention in the discussion of the bills before the 105th Congress was language creating a loophole that would have allowed recipients to comply with the legislation by obtaining filtering software, even if it was never used. In the 106th Congress, four bills were under consideration. The Children's Internet Protection Act, HR 896 (appearing as HR 368 IH and HR 543 IH in earlier drafts), was sponsored by Representative Bob Franks (R-N.J.) and would have required schools and libraries receiving e-rate subsidies to certify to the FCC that they have and use filtering software to protect minors from

Internet pornography. Thus, this bill was stronger than similar bills sponsored by Representative Franks and Senator John McCain (R-Ariz.) in the 105th Congress, because it added the use requirement. An amended version of HR 896 was adopted as part of the House juvenile justice bill, but it went no further. The companion Senate bill, S 97, the Children's Internet Protection Act, was sponsored by Senator McCain. Although originally the same as HR 896, the version ultimately approved by the Senate Commerce Committee contained different language but included the same provisions.

HR 2560, the Child Protection Act, sponsored by Representative Ernest Istook (R-Okla.), required schools and libraries receiving federal funds to employ operational filtering software to protect children from Internet pornography. In contrast to the Children's Internet Protection Act, which affected institutions utilizing e-rate funds, this bill targeted schools and libraries receiving funds to acquire or operate the actual computers used for the networking and Internet access services. Finally, the Neighborhood Children's Internet Protection Act, S 1545, sponsored by Senator Rick Santorum (R-Penn.), was an attenuated alternative to the three other filtering bills. It required schools and libraries receiving e-rate subsidies to certify that they either installed filtering software or implemented an Internet use policy for minors. If an institution selected filtering, the software merely had to be installed, not necessarily operational or in use. If the institution chose the policy option, there were no specific requirements as to its content; therefore, an institution's policy could allow unrestricted access for minors.

By the end of the legislative session, much high-profile discussion, debate, and lobbying had occurred. In December 2000, Congress passed, and President Clinton signed into law, a Labor, Health and Human Services, and Education Appropriations Bill (HR 4577) with the Children's Internet Protection Act (S 97) as a rider, requiring libraries that receive federal funds to adopt mandatory AUPs and Internet filtering software. At the time of this writing, the ACLU plans to challenge the constitutionality of the legislation.

State Legislation

By 2000, three states (Kentucky in 1998, South Dakota and Arizona in 1999) had passed library and school filtering legislation. However, at the time of this writing, several states were considering legislation to require or encourage libraries and schools to adopt filtering software for Internet use by minors.

The legislatures in Hawaii (HB 2041), Indiana (HB 1310), and South Carolina (HB 1314) have proposed bills that would mandate filters on library computers. Bills in Colorado (SB 00-085) and Missouri (SB 758) tie funding for Internet access to preventing minors from viewing pornographic materials. The bill in Colorado also requires libraries to purchase Internet connectivity from an Internet service provider that supplies filtering, while the Missouri bill prohibits libraries from spending funds for computer equipment or services until they are in compliance with the law.[10]

Ballot Initiatives

The focus of the controversy recently shifted to the local voting booth. On February 22, 2000, voters in Holland, Michigan rejected, by a 54 to 46 percent margin, a measure that would have required the city to stop funding its share of the county library unless filters were installed on computer terminals. Thus, Holland became the first city to put the issue of library Internet access on the ballot.[11]

Supporters of the ordinance, claiming filters would shield children from pornographic, violent, and hate sites on the Internet, received more than $35,000 in financial backing from the Tupelo, Mississippi–based American Family Association (AFA), which has a thousand members in the Holland area. Opponents argued filters are flawed, unnecessary, too expensive, and often prevent library patrons from accessing legitimate information. The five-member board of the Herrick District Library opposed filters, declaring that its acceptable use policies adequately protect children. The board even threatened to shut down the computers rather than install filters on them.

Three additional issues influenced the vote. First, opponents of the filtering measure contended that an outside organization, the AFA, was using Holland to promote a national conservative agenda. Second, opponents said it was unfair for Holland residents, who represent less than a third of the taxpayers who fund Herrick District Library services, to make policy. Finally, opponents maintained that those who supported the ordinance had bypassed the library board and the Holland City Council in trying to force filters into the library.[12]

In the weeks leading up to the vote, both sides spent thousands of dollars on newspaper and radio ads. Pro-filtering forces hired pollsters and sent direct mailings to prospective voters. They also posted bright yellow signs that read "Internet Filters Protect Children YES!" across the city of 30,745. Opponents campaigned door to door and stood on street corners, waving to honking cars and holding magic-marker posters with slogans like "Support our Library."[13] Although the current ballot initiative was defeated, the head of the local AFA chapter announced on March 23, 2000, that they would continue the fight.[14]

THE LEGAL DEBATE

As a medium of communication, the Internet is like no other. The medium allows individuals to participate in a global forum that transcends age, social status, gender, ethnicity, and geography. Yet, the universal access promised by Internet technology comes bundled with complications. With the click of a mouse, users can access a space of words and images where truth and lies and the moral and the profane coexist.

The privacy accorded U.S. citizens allows them unfettered Internet access in their homes. The situation is more complex for the taxpayer-funded institution of the public library. Handling the volume and wide diversity of content on the Internet has become an unavoidable challenge for public libraries nationwide. The promise of universal access has become weakened as librarians struggle to promote freedom of information while simultaneously conforming to the state and federal laws governing pornography and the rights of minors.

The general question that must be resolved regarding Internet filtering in public libraries involves the determination of the proper boundaries for freedom of expression. The problem with finding an answer to this question is that the First Amendment is actually somewhat vague in its application. Even when the First Amendment was enacted, it was not clear whether the emphasis was on the protection of freedom of speech or freedom of speech combined with freedom from sedition laws. (Ironically, the Courts have generally held sedition laws to be constitutional. Although the Jefferson administration and Congress subsequently freed those convicted under President John Adams's heinous Alien and Sedition Acts and helped repay their fines, the Courts had upheld those laws.)

The result is that the First Amendment is something of a continuum—absolute free speech at one end, speech only if it does not harm society at the other. With the exception of a few Justices, such as William O. Douglas, the Supreme Court has generally held that there is a balancing act between freedom of speech and societal interest, but that freedom of speech gets preferential treatment; it is necessary to show a compelling state interest (such as a "clear and present danger") to limit it, and the restraint must be narrowly drawn to achieve that end. As a result, speech often gets protection that many in society find to be objectionable. These critics would prefer that the protection of society, rather than freedom of speech, get the preferred position. Consequently, in the courts, the legal arguments center around those wanting limits on speech (1) having to argue a compelling state interest to do so and (2) having to document the deleterious impact of not doing anything. There are some secondary issues, such as how speech is defined and what are public/private forums.

Complicating the matter of the proper boundaries for freedom of expression in library Internet access, the law has generally treated children as "special" and regarded them as different from adults. In addition to the creation of a juvenile justice system that parallels the adult justice system, Congress and federal agencies such as the Federal Trade Commission and the Federal Communications Commission have set up special protections for children in terms of advertising, educational programming, and most recently, televised violence. The legal intersection of children and free speech laws has generated even greater complexity, with the Congress,

FCC, and the Courts consistently articulating two compelling interests for speech restrictions: (1) protecting children from harm and (2) aiding the parental supervision of children. The difficulty has been that the Supreme Court has not been very specific in defining what harms children must be protected from and has unquestioningly promulgated the association between protecting children from harm and protecting them from exposure to obscenity and indecency. Also, there is the question of how to define the age limit at which a child ceases to require this protection and gains full free speech rights.

Therefore, the Court has adopted the concept of "variable obscenity"—that some content that is not "obscene" for adults is "obscene" for minors. This concept was most clearly articulated in *Ginsberg v. State of New York* (1968).[15] In that case, the Supreme Court upheld the constitutionality of a New York statute prohibiting the sale of "girlie" magazines to anyone under the age of seventeen. The statute specifically prohibited the sale to a minor of anything that contained nudity—even if that same content would not be a problem if sold to adults. The case also affirmed that the court gives particular weight to the government's claims to regulate in the interests of children in the area of obscenity. The notion of variable obscenity has been applied in subsequent cases involving children as well. For example, in *FCC v. Pacifica Foundation* (1978),[16] the Supreme Court upheld an FCC decision to fine WBAI-FM for airing indecent language at a time of the day when there was a reasonable risk children would be in the audience. In *New York v. Ferber* (1982),[17] the Supreme Court upheld a New York statute limiting the distribution of child pornography, even if the material in question might not be considered to be obscene under the definition of obscenity laid out in *Miller v. California* (1973).[18] Employing similar reasoning, the Telecommunications Act of 1996 requires television manufacturers to install a V-chip on every new television set so that parents can block out violent television programming. In all three cases, the Courts and Congress have drawn a distinction between what is appropriate content for children and what is appropriate content for adults.

Thus, the legal issues implicated by Internet access in public libraries are twofold. First, librarians must devise a way to prevent access to material available on the Internet, such as child pornography, that is illegal according to many state and federal statutes. Second, librarians must find a way to protect the First Amendment rights of adults to access adult content, while at the same time protecting minors from exposure to material inappropriate for them.

The debate over Internet access at public libraries comes at a time when legal opinion and technology have combined to create as many legal questions as answers. Specifically, the decision by the Supreme Court in *Reno v. ACLU* and the invention of filtering software have had a substantial impact on the course of the library Internet legal dispute.

On June 26, 1997, the U.S. Supreme Court held that the Communications Decency Act (CDA) violated the freedom of speech guaranteed by the First Amendment.[19] The CDA, part of the Telecommunications Act passed by Congress on February 1, 1996, had legislated that persons who distributed "indecent" content on the Internet could be subject to prosecution. The Supreme Court found that much of what the CDA deemed "indecent" was constitutionally protected and thus upheld the First Amendment rights of people involved in the exchange of information on the Internet. Essentially, the Supreme Court's decision extended the rights of print media to the electronic medium of the Internet.

The Court did hint, however, that filters might be a solution for regulating material on the Internet, citing them as a less restrictive means than the CDA for protecting children from illicit material. So, while the decision in *Reno v. ACLU* declared that no "decency standard" may be applied to material published on the Internet, the Supreme Court made no ruling regarding the use of filtering devices that block Web sites from Internet terminals. In addition to suggesting that filters might be a possible least restrictive means of controlling inappropriate speech on the Internet, the Supreme Court left intact the part of the CDA that exempted "interactive computer services" from prosecution for allowing its users to access and distribute obscene and indecent materials on the Internet. The library was identified as equivalent to an interactive computer service and, thereby, exempt from prosecution because of the actions of individual patrons. In effect, this decision left it up to individual libraries to determine what their policies would be regarding Internet access. In doing so, the Supreme Court ensured that the debate over Internet filters would become as much a political one (such as in Holland, Michigan) as a legal one.

Further, with the advent(ure) of new technology comes the need not only to learn to use it, but to understand it. As Marshall McLuhan suggests,[20] the cultural metaphors employed to define new media shape this understanding and, therefore, represent sites of struggle. Indeed, legal precedent functions in this fashion as the courts search for the proper analogy between the present situation and those of the past. The determinations of the Supreme Court, the ultimate arbiter of constitutional interpretation and public issues, have a profound impact on the nexus of the populace and technology in a democracy. As such, a key component of the library Internet access controversy is the legal definition of the boundaries of freedom of expression through the consideration of competing constructions of the nature of the new technology in the traditional library setting.

Perhaps the most important metaphor to be determined involves the definition of the interrelationship of the Internet, filters, and the library. In the *Loudoun* case, the library board contended that blocking Internet content was comparable to a library decision not to purchase a book, as opposed to the plaintiffs' assertion that blocking was equivalent to a decision to remove a book from library shelves. This characterization was crucial to the arguments on both sides as they each attempted to differentiate or invoke the precedent of *Board of Education v. Pico* (1982),[21] a case in which the Supreme Court ruled that the removal of books from library shelves by a school board violated the First Amendment. According to the defendants' analysis, the Internet is similar to a vast interlibrary loan system and, therefore, restricting access to selected Web sites was merely a standard library decision to selectively acquire certain materials. Antithetically, the plaintiffs suggested that since everything available on the Internet is connected by World Wide Web protocols, the Internet is in fact a "single, integrated system" analogous to a set of encyclopedias. Consequently, blocking software served as a means for the library board to expunge particular content deemed inappropriate for patrons.

Judge Brinkema concluded from the arguments that the defendants had misconstrued the nature of the Internet and filtering. She ruled that by purchasing Internet access, like it would an encyclopedia, the Loudoun libraries had instantly made all Internet publications immediately available within the library. Moreover, in contrast to an interlibrary loan or book purchase, no additional library resources or time were necessary to make any specific Internet publication accessible to a patron, whereas restricting that access through the purchase and implementation of blocking software did require such an expenditure.

Other important metaphorical considerations arose as the opposing sides debated the level of review that should be applied for the determination of the cases. For example, in *Loudoun*, each party differed in its definition of the nature of the library environment in comparison to the three categories of fora established in *Perry Education Ass'n v. Perry Local Ass'n* (1983).[22] The defendants attempted to equate the library with a non-public forum to invoke the intermediate scrutiny standard, while the plaintiffs contended that the library was a limited public forum subject to strict scrutiny. Further, in *Loudoun*, disparate conceptions of the nature of filters led to dispute over whether their use was a "time, place and manner" restriction, similar to a zoning ordinance intended to prevent a "sexually hostile environment" in the library, or a regulation of content.

In many ways, in *Kathleen R*, the construction of the necessary definitions required reverse analogies. For instance, rather than concentrating on the parallels between the Internet and traditional conceptions of books and libraries, the arguments centered on the comparison of the Internet to a pornography machine. Kathleen R. claimed that the Internet had deliberately been placed in the library to easily and effortlessly supply children with obscenity. Thus, the library was comparable to a source and distributor of pornography. Indeed, the basic premise of the plaintiff's case was the assertion of a correspondence between a library without filters and the denial of substantive due process through the invocation of harm arguments.

Thus, the convergence of free speech, children, and revolutionary technology in the library Internet access controversy has created a complex debate that at once mirrors the past and portends the future of the legal limits of freedom of expression in contemporary American society. The specific legal arguments presented in support of filtering are:

1. Filtering must be used for libraries to conform to federal and state laws that impose penalties for those who engage in the distribution of obscene speech.
2. Libraries receive public funding, and such funding should not be used to allow access to materials that are obscene or harmful to children.
3. Allowing minors access to materials that are obscene constitutes a public nuisance. The recent Supreme Court decision in *City of Erie v. Pap's A.M.* allowing communities to ban nude dancing because of the "secondary problems" associated with such activities may give this argument more force in the future.
4. Allowing minors access to materials that are harmful to them makes library premises unsafe.

The legal arguments advanced against filtering are:

1. 47 U.S.C., Section 230, states that interactive computer services are not to be considered the publisher or speaker of any information provided by another information content provider, and libraries are considered to be equivalent to "interactive computer services." Hence, federal and state laws prohibiting the distribution of obscene materials over the Internet would not apply to libraries.
2. While it is true that libraries receive public funding, they also serve the needs of both adults and children. Some material that is not legal for minors is perfectly fine for adult patrons. The Supreme Court has long held that the government may not "reduc[e] the adult population . . . to . . . only what is fit for children."[23] Or, in a more colorful analogy, the Court has declared: "'[R]egardless of the strength of the government's interest' in protecting children, '[t]he level of discourse reaching a mailbox simply cannot be limited to that which would be suitable for a sandbox.'"[24]
 3. The dangers of the dissemination of "inappropriate" material on the Internet are less than the danger of censoring constitutionally protected speech. As District Court Judge Stewart Dalzell declared in *ACLU v. Reno:* "Any content-based regulation of the Internet, no matter how benign the purpose, could burn the global village to roast the pig."[25]

The public debate over the use of filters in the library has often been a loud and bitter one, a dispute frequently shedding more heat than light on the issue. On the pro-filtering side, organizations such as the Family Research Council, the American Family Association, and Enough Is Enough; filtering companies such as CyberPatrol; and radio talk show host Dr. Laura Schlessinger have issued press releases, held news conferences, and written reports outlining the dangers to children if filters are not adopted, while vigorously attacking the anti-filter groups. Meanwhile, filtering opponents have fought back—the American Library Association (ALA) tries to educate parents about acceptable use policies and the First Amendment in their *Libraries and the Internet Toolkit;* the American Civil Liberties Union (ACLU) issues reports on the flaws and societal dangers associated with filtering; and groups such as Peacefire provide Web site visitors with instructions on how to break the code of filters such as CyberPatrol. Also, the controversy has forged some unusual alliances, as traditionally more liberal groups, such as the Anti-Defamation League, have joined the pro-filtering camp, and industry groups, such as Computer Professionals for Social Responsibility, have allied with traditionally liberal legal groups.

The furor over Internet filtering is an extension of the increased efforts over the past ten years to ban books from the library. Book censors have tried to ban books largely because of vulgarity or descriptions of sexual behavior but have also sought to eliminate books that describe nontraditional family relationships (such as gay couples with children), negative portraits of American authority, attacks against American business, and radical political philosophy. In addition to several books by best-selling children's author Judy Blume, other books that have drawn censors' ire include *The Diary of Anne Frank, Catch-22, The Catcher in the Rye, Manchild in the Promised Land,* and even *Stuart Little.*[26] Like the calls for filters on library computer terminals, the attempts to ban books have been locally mounted, but they have often been coordinated with national organizations, such as the National Citizens for Excellence in Education, the Association of Christian Educators, the Eagle Forum, or the Concerned Women for America. The conflict over filters on computer terminals is an extension of the debate over book banning. The key difference, however, is that book banning happens on a case-by-case basis. There is only one Internet.

Complicating matters is that the Supreme Court provided little guidance in the debate over book banning that could be applied to the issue of filtering Internet sites. For example, in *Board of Education v. Pico,* the Supreme Court agreed with a lower court's finding that a trial must be held on the merits of the argument as to why to remove books, but the Court refused to articulate standards for removing books. Generally, the lower courts have not permitted school and library boards to ban books because of ideas those boards did not agree with, but that has not always been the case. Thus, the murky public understanding of the definition of the proper legal limits of freedom of expression in the library has now been extended to the Internet. This clouded vision of what is authoritatively deemed right and wrong in American civil society has served to ignite and fuel the public debate on library Internet access as all sides struggle to gain standing for their interpretation of the proper limits.

The arguments put forth in the public arena differ significantly from those in the legal sphere, in terms of both content and style. The groups supporting filtering argue that filters are necessary because:

1. Cyberspace is a dangerous and perverse place. Using a combination of anecdotal and selective social science evidence (such as the controversial Martin Rimm study of the pervasiveness of online pornography), filtering supporters argue that children likely face harm if they explore cyberspace without proper protection. Online pornography can wreak severe harm: "Pornography is an overwhelming public health and safety issue. The link between the use of pornography and child molestation, rape, addiction, sexually transmitted diseases (STDs) and degrading attitudes and values has been demonstrated in every way possible by law enforcers, clinical experiments, social scientists and real-life experience."[27]

2. Mere short-term unintended exposure to online pornography can have a long-term deleterious effect on children. Filtering supporters use anecdotes and "common sense" to claim that children who happen to wander upon a site with pornographic images will suffer psychological damage.

3. Filters are needed because parents cannot always be present to supervise their children in libraries, and library staff are unable or unwilling to help. Pro-filtering forces observe how busy contemporary parents are and how they cannot always be at the library when their children are accessing the Internet. They then cite numerous anecdotes about how staff at various libraries "allowed their children" to access online pornography.

4. Parents, and not "liberal" organizations such as the ACLU or the ALA, ought to determine what is appropriate for their children to see. A quote from a post to the "Dr. Laura" Web site "Forum" succinctly describes this position: "The American Library Association (a group of left-wing, anti-American thugs) considers it everyone's right to view hardcore pornography (including child pornography) in our libraries."[28]

5. Filters are a reliable means of keeping children from being harmed in cyberspace. The filtering software industry has been very effective in communicating how filters function as an "extension" of parental supervision.

6. Some limits on First Amendment protections are necessary to insure children's welfare. Pro-filter advocates often accuse filter opponents of "hiding behind the First Amendment" while putting their children at risk. For filtering supporters, losing access to some sites that are mistakenly blocked is a small price to pay in exchange for the protection of children from harm.

By contrast, anti-filtering forces present the following arguments:

1. While there are sites in cyberspace that are not appropriate for children, the value of the plethora of useful sites clearly outweighs any limited risk children may face.
2. Parents should supervise their children at the library. Groups and individuals arguing against filtering note that despite all the pressures of daily life, it is still the parents' responsibility to know what is happening with their children, and they should not expect library staff to act as parents. In fact, they contend, libraries cannot assume the role of determining what is appropriate because that would be a violation of parental rights.
3. Filters are unreliable. Those against having filters mandated on library computers cite studies (such as those by Christopher Hunter or Censorware.org) that demonstrate how often filters block sites that are not potential dangers to minors. Thus, from this view, filters should not be depended upon to "protect" children when parents are not at the library.
4. "Conservative" organizations, such as the American Family Association or the Family Research Council, should not be setting the standards for what is appropriate for everyone to access in the library. In particular, anti-filtering forces see such organizations as promoting a larger national moral agenda at the local level. In contrast, they suggest, library patrons should be taught the skills necessary to be discerning information users—in essence, their own filters—because software filters devalue the power and dignity of the human mind.
5. Limiting speech puts a society on a slippery slope. Critics against filtering warn that small steps toward censorship can lead to more and more censorship. A few even cite what happened in Nazi Germany, when the government slowly chipped away at free speech rights in the name of the support and maintenance of the public good.
6. The percentage of children accessing pornography on the Internet is relatively small. According to a recent National Public Radio/Kaiser Foundation/Kennedy School of Government poll, only 15 percent of children aged ten to thirteen have ever accessed a pornographic Web site. By contrast, 84 percent of the adults in the sample worry about pornography and their children.[29]

Not only do the pro-filtering and anti-filtering advocates differ in the content of their arguments, each differs in its argumentation style. Pro-filtering groups tend to adopt *pathos* as a primary rhetorical strategy, evoking images of unsuspecting children menaced by the perversity of cyberspace. Consider this example, found at the Enough Is Enough Web site: "The institution of the family is one of the central pillars in our society. Both families and children (except in child pornography) are nonexistent in the world of pornography. Marriage is continually attacked, with the assumption of unfaithfulness with multiple partners. Families are ridiculed, except as objects for sex."[30] Consequently, in many ways, in the arena of public opinion, the pro-filtering groups have a persuasive advantage.

Anti-filtering groups, on the other hand, use *logos* as their principal rhetorical device, attempting to point out logically the pitfalls of adopting a flawed technological solution (i.e., filters) that may result in the curtailment of free speech. It is very difficult, however, to argue against the health and safety of children. Social Security has often been termed the "third rail of American politics"—propose cutting benefits, and your career as a politician is dead. In terms of the filtering debate, child welfare is the metaphorical third rail. As such, there are practical limits to which the anti-filtering side can take its argument. It is not clear, for instance, what, if any, harmful effects befall children who accidentally run across pornography while browsing on the Internet. Yet, to question the harmful effects asserted by pro-filtering groups risks appearing to be anti-children.

Another problem for those against filters in libraries is that the legal profession is not held in high esteem in contemporary society. Lawyers are often seen as getting guilty criminals "off" because of legal technicalities, or getting millions for their clients in undeserved civil judgments. So when opponents of filtering utilize a logical rhetorical approach that stresses the legalities of the issue, their public arguments become inseparable from the growing antipathy toward the legal profession.

Finally, the media have framed the legal and public issues in a fairly simplistic way. Those in the advocacy media, such as Dr. Laura Schlessinger, have generally taken a hard-line position for filters in libraries, dismissing the First Amendment arguments against filtering as silly and suggesting that groups such as the American Library Association are wrongheaded at best and dangerous at worst. For example, during the spring of 1999, "Dr. Laura" decried the ALA's inclusion of a link to "Go Ask Alice," a Web site produced by Columbia University's Health Education Program that discusses health issues, including those related to teenage sexuality and homosexuality. "Dr. Laura" then featured the same link on her own home page so that her listeners—some eighteen million per week—could check out the offensive Web site themselves and be equally appalled. Ironically, while the ALA did provide a link to the "Go Ask Alice" site, locating it required navigation through nine different pages on the ALA Web site. Within days after "Dr. Laura" posted a very prominent link to "Go Ask Alice" on her Web site, Columbia University reported that the number of "hits" on their site increased substantially.[31] By selectively focusing on a controversial Web site and distorting the ALA's role in connecting its visitors to "Go Ask Alice," "Dr. Laura" was able to establish an "us" (hardworking, moral parents) versus "them" (leftist, morally bankrupt organization) simplification of a complex issue.

The news media are not much better at framing the public debate. A paradigmatic illustration is provided by the two-part report on the filtering debate that was presented on the February 4, 1999, edition of ABC's *World News Tonight*. Peter Jennings opens the segment by saying, "We're taking another look tonight at the struggle to keep pornography at bay."[32] Immediately the issue becomes protecting children from pornography, not the more complicated issue of what is the most effective way of balancing access to information on the Internet versus ensuring that children are discouraged from accessing inappropriate material.

Jennings continues, "There are more than 30,000 sites on the Web now where the message is sex, and more than 30 percent of the people who go online check them out, including, according to one study, more than a million kids a year."[33] Nowhere is the actual study cited, nor are "kids" defined (e.g., are "kids" twelve and under, or eighteen and under?).

Reporter Peggy Wehmeyer, who, interestingly, is the ABC News religion correspondent, continues the report: "Elementary school children here [Plano, Texas] use the public libraries for class research. But, with very little effort, they can get to something else."[34] What is missing here is an explanation of how children can access pornographic sites so easily. Although it is technically easy to get to a pornographic site if you know the URL (and children often like to share information about "forbidden" topics), the chances of accidentally accessing a pornographic Web site while conducting research on, for instance, brittanica.com are fairly remote. Yet, the report implies that it is a common occurrence.

Later, Wehmeyer interviews Plano resident Jane Nedenfeuhr, who complains, "I said, 'There's two boys over there using that terminal over there, and they are accessing pornography.' And she said, 'Ma'am, there's really nothing I can do about it.'" Wehmeyer goes on, "Nothing she can do about it because the American Library Association believes that restricting full access to the Internet is tantamount to censorship, and the ACLU has successfully sued a county in Virginia that tried to do it."[35]

There are a couple of problems with the above report. First, whether or not a library staff person can do anything about children accessing pornography depends on the library's acceptable use policy, not the position of the American Library Association. In fact, the American Library Association supports AUPs that prevent minors from accessing pornography. Second, while the ACLU was involved in the *Loudoun* case mentioned by Wehmeyer, the organization intervened in an already-existing lawsuit on behalf of eight plaintiffs. Why single out the ACLU? Perhaps because the invocation of its name telegraphs a message, since the ACLU has been a lightning rod for controversy in supporting the free speech rights of clients who are not always popular, such as defending the rights of Nazis to march in Skokie, Illinois, in 1978.

The difficulty with this ABC News report is not the factual inaccuracies, though they are numerous. The problem is that the complex issue of filtering is reduced to a simplistic dichotomous confrontation. Implicit in the piece (though not explicitly stated) is that the battle is a political one, between the "moral majority" conservatives and the "free speech at any cost" liberals. What gets lost in the din of both advocacy media and news media, as well as in the general public debate, is the myriad of other issues and nuances of issues related to filters on computers in public libraries.

CONCLUSION

> In a borderless frontier, who sets the rules? When cultures collide via computer, who picks up the pieces?
>   —Anonymous Internet correspondent[36]

In summary, the library Internet access controversy is a wide-ranging battle raging not only in libraries across the nation but in the legal system and the court of public opinion as well. The law turns on precedent, while the heart of public opinion in the United States is shaped largely through a moral and ethical lens. Yet, although the nature of the debate varies from the legal to public arenas, both realms of civic discourse focus on the disparate visions, conceptions, and constructions of the library, the Internet, and filtering technology in American culture. Both speak to and attempt to define the proper limits of freedom of expression and order in contemporary American society. Both draw their strength of argument and power of appeal from their historical connections and familiarity.

Perhaps the most important lesson of this controversy is that the key to understanding the concept of democracy is the recognition that the law and public opinion are inextricably intertwined. Indeed, as the library Internet access controversy demonstrates, in American society, the proper limits of freedom of expression and order are negotiated and defined at the nexus of legal precedent and contemporary public opinion. Certainly, in part, the vagueness of the First Amendment itself necessitates this approach, but so too does the nature of American culture and the character of the citizenry; in a democracy, laws and courts do not exist in a vacuum, and public pressure can command a major impact on public as well as industry policy. The basis and rationale for determining what is "proper" varies, not just from person to person and nation to nation, for instance, but in a democracy, from forum to forum. Thus, legal argumentation defines the "proper" limits in an entirely different way than public opinion. Of course, values are integrally bound to both the law and the public voice in America. Nevertheless, discussions in each forum necessitate and produce a vastly different rhetoric and climate.

Sometimes public opinion and legal determinations are consistent. In fact, in a representative democracy, they should be. The truly interesting aspect, though, arises when public opinion begins to change (as with abortion recently) and/or technological innovation leaps beyond society's ability to keep up—intellectually, emotionally, morally, ethically, legally (as with the Internet). At that juncture, there is a disconnect between public opinion and legal precedent that must be resolved. In the library Internet access controversy, at present, legal precedent appears to be working at odds with public opinion, but that is precisely what makes this struggle and the volatile intersection of legal precedent and public opinion so important and crucial.

This exchange about the Internet in public libraries—and the more general discussion of the relationship between the Internet and the First Amendment—illustrates some of the central issues that must be addressed in the course of public discursive practices in a pluralistic democracy. For example, the historical antagonism between popular mediated culture and moral values frequently displaces complex social issues on to legal and cultural terrain and requires reconciliation through vastly divergent discourse. Framing the language of confrontation and accusation in terms of moral authority and national leadership in civic life, critics have claimed that our culture and way of life is being undermined by moral decay and that radical solutions are necessary to protect the most vulnerable of our society, particularly our children, from harm, most especially the harm that many kinds of speech (e.g., obscenity, violence, commercials, the Internet) can cause. Thus, it has been suggested that some speech rights must be restricted. Animating the public around a discussion of fundamental values, this debate begins in the powerful domain of the invocation of emotion, fear, ad hominem, and relative fallacy and fact, and then must progress to legal doctrine. And, there lies the challenge—in a democracy, moral condemnation is a decision for another court, not a court of law. Consequently, to conduct a robust deliberation, faithful to democratic principles, about the nature and definition of the proper limits of freedom of expression and order and reach true consensus, civil society must be mindful of and vigilant to pursue the exigencies of fostering the appropriate type of public debate.

Further, as demonstrated by the legal and public arguments in the library Internet access controversy, civic discourse, while embroiled in concern for specific harms, can fail to consider the broader harms overall to freedom of expression and democracy. The Internet has been heralded as the first truly democratic medium; because of the low barriers to entry, everyone can engage in worldwide public communication as both a speaker and receiver, and fully participate in society as a local, national, and global citizen. As such, the Internet has added significance as the embodiment of a genuine marketplace of ideas, representing the diversity of human thought, a boundless storehouse of knowledge and energy, and a space in which truth and falsehood can grapple and produce enlightenment. The Internet is also the locus of individual success and the resource that supports our shared destiny in the Information Age. The only impediment to access is a computer and an Internet connection, which for some can be a major hurdle to overcome. Consequently, policy makers have determined that Internet access provided through public institutions, especially public libraries, is pivotal to conquering the digital divide.

Absent from the library Internet access controversy, however, has been discussion of the impact of filtering/blocking on these sorts of issues. If those who have Internet access without the use of public facilities can choose whether or not to employ the software, but those who must depend on government-funded access have no choice, the democratic nature of the medium could be distorted or destroyed. For example, the marketplace of ideas can be compromised by the introduction of intrusive controls, as much random as organized, that function as screens on, rather than windows to, thought. Similarly, filtering software may socialize and condition unquestioning acceptance of restrictions on expression in public forums, which are the basis of democratic deliberation. A recent instance of great national import emphasizes additional difficulties; in 1998, those who did not have private Internet access and lived in areas where the public libraries have implemented Internet filtering found that Kenneth Starr's report on President Clinton and the Lewinsky affair was blocked by the software—the very report that our elected representatives in Congress posted on the Internet and declared the civic duty of every American to read.

Yet, the specific harm allegations cannot, and will not, be ignored. The technological problematics and economics suggest that libraries are too small a market to warrant the capital investment necessary for software companies to develop a filtering system that could pass constitutional muster. Thus, we are presented with an impasse between the calm, rational, authority of the law and the tension, tumult, and turbulence of public opinion over where to place boundaries in a boundless medium. Neither the legal system nor the public, operating alone, can resolve this civic dilemma.

As in the past, legal precedent and public opinion will likely merge to reach a compromise. Will that compromise be a "proper limit"? That will depend on who you talk to. But, it will be something everyone can live with. In a democracy, the majority does rule, and everyone may not agree that the de facto limits are "proper" (compare, for example, Kent State 1970). Nevertheless, the proper limits are negotiated and defined at the nexus of contemporary public opinion and legal precedent; as Americans, we all have a say in the future of our shared lives, but as part of a democracy, in exchange for the benefits of citizenship and the protections of the law, we agree to give up some of our own personal freedom to decide what is proper (both for ourselves and for others), delegate that authority instead to elected representatives and the legal system, and accept the resulting common determinations of the "proper limits" of all our freedoms.

Kent State University in 1970 may seem long ago and far away, certainly before most current undergraduates were even born. Still, that same struggle, that same potential for tragedy, that same painful confusion is at the heart of democracy at all times. That fateful day in 1970 is unique and special in many ways alone, but in many more, it is being played out continually around the world and in our own backyard, in strangers' lives and in our own lives, every day. Rather than a physical war, at present a fight is being waged in an institution that we have known, relied on, and probably even loved our whole lives—the public library. There are powerful passions fueling tension and strife there. And, caught up in the middle of it all is the beauty and the challenge of living in a democracy. As citizens in a democracy, it is our right and our responsibility to be informed of contentious issues, to stand up for what we believe, and to show mutual respect and concern for those who oppose us. For that, as Kent State 1970 has taught us, is perhaps the most difficult and greatest beauty and challenge of living in a democracy.

NOTES

1. American Library Association, "Quotable Quotes About Libraries," March 16, 2000, available on the World Wide Web at http://www.ala.org/advocacy/libraryquotes.html.

2. American Library Association, "Quotable Facts About America's Libraries," Nov. 10, 1998, available on the World Wide Web at http://www.ala.org/pio/quotablefacts.html.

3. American Library Association, "Public Libraries Today," April 26, 1999, available on the World Wide Web at http://www.ala.org/pio/factsheets/publiclibraries.html.

4. American Library Association, "American Library Association Washington Office Newsline," April 15, 1998, available on the World Wide Web at http://www.ala.org/washoff/alawon/alwn7041.html.

5. See, for example, American Civil Liberties Union, "Fahrenheit 451.2: Is Cyberspace Burning? How Rating and Blocking Proposals May Torch Free Speech on the Internet," *ACLU White Paper*, 1997,

available on the World Wide Web at http://www.aclu.org/issues/cyber/burning.html; American Civil Liberties Union, "Censorship in a Box: Why Blocking Software Is Wrong for Public Libraries," ACLU White Paper, 1998, http://www.aclu.org/issues/cyber/box.html; David Burt, "Survey of 24 Public Libraries Finds That Filtering Generates Few Complaints, Takes Up Little Staff Time," Filtering Facts, January 28, 1998, http://www.filteringfacts.org/survey.htm; Censorware.org, "Censorware: Reports," 2000, http://www.censorware.org/reports/; Electronic Privacy Information Center, "Faulty Filters: How Content Filters Block Access to Kid-Friendly Information on the Internet," December 1997, http://www.epic.org/reports/filter_report.html; Harry Hochheiser, "CPSR Filtering FAQ Version 1.1.1," Computer Professionals for Social Responsibility, October 24, 1998, http://www.cpsr.org/filters/faq.html; Christopher D. Hunter, *Filtering the Future? Software Filters, Porn, PICS, and the Internet Content Conundrum*, master's thesis, University of Pennsylvania, 1999; and Karen G. Schneider, "Learning from the Internet Filter Assessment Project," Internet Filter Assessment Project, 1997, http://www.bluehighways.com/tifap/learn.html.

6. Mark Smith, "Meeting the Pressure to Filter," *Texas Library Journal* (Feb. 1997).

7. Ibid.

8. *Mainstream Loudoun, et al. v. Board of Trustees of the Loudoun County Library, et al.*, United States District Court for the Eastern District of Virginia, at Alexandria, Va., case no. CV 97-2049 (1997).

9. *Kathleen R. v. City of Livermore, et al.*, Superior Court of California, County of Alameda, case no. V-015266-4 (1998); *Kathleen R., et al., v. City of Livermore*, Court of Appeal of the State of California, First Appellate District, Division 4, appeal no. A086349 (1999).

10. Filtering Facts, "Legislative Initiatives," March 25, 2000, available on the World Wide Web at http://www.filteringfacts.org/legal.htm.

11. Miguel Llanos, "Michigan Town Rejects Internet Filters," MSNBC, Feb. 23, 2000, available on the World Wide Web at http://www.msnbc.com/news/362856.asp.

12. Ibid.

13. Ibid.

14. Brian Bowe, "High-Profile Crusade," *The Holland Sentinel* Online Edition, Feb. 17, 2000, available on the World Wide Web at http://www.thehollandsentinel.net/stories/021700new_crusade.html.

15. *Ginsberg v. New York*, 390 U.S. 51 (1968).

16. *FCC v. Pacifica Foundation*, 438 U.S. 726 (1978).

17. *New York v. Ferber*, 458 U.S. 747 (1982).

18. *Miller v. California*, 413 U.S. 15 (1973).

19. *Reno v. American Civil Liberties Union*, 117 S. Ct. 2329 (1997).

20. Marshall McLuhan, *Culture Is Our Business* (New York: McGraw-Hill, 1970).

21. *Board of Education v. Pico*, 457 U.S. 853 (1982).

22. *Perry Education Ass'n v. Perry Local Ass'n.*, 460 U.S. 37, 45–46 (1983).

23. *Denver Area Telecomm. Consortium v. FCC*, 116 S. Ct. 2374, 2393 (1996) (citations omitted).

24. *Bolger v. Youngs Drug Products Corp.*, 463 U.S. 60 (1983).

25. *American Civil Liberties Union v. Reno*, 929 F.Supp. 824, 882 (E.D. Pa 1996).

26. Donald Pember, *Mass Media Law* (New York: Brown & Benchmark, 1997).

27. Enough Is Enough, "Myths," March 26, 2000, available on the World Wide Web at http://www.enough.org.

28. "Dr. Laura's Forum," "Stealth Pornography Aimed at Our Kids," post from "Alarmed Parent," March 17, 2000, available on the World Wide Web at http://www.drlaura.com/forum/index.html?action=view&id=78814&offset=0&limit=25.

29. National Public Radio, "Study: 31% of Internet Teens Have Porn Surfed," March 26, 2000, available on the World Wide Web at http://npr.org/programs/specials/poll/technology/index.html.

30. Enough Is Enough, "Myths."

31. Patrizia Dilucchio, "Dr. Laura Targets the New Sodom: Libraries," *Salon*, May 27, 1999, available on the World Wide Web at http://www.salon.com/tech/feature/1999/05/27/dr_laura/.

32. American Broadcasting Company, "Protecting Our Kids from Internet Porn," *World News Tonight with Peter Jennings*, Feb. 4, 1999, available from Federal Document Clearinghouse.

33. Ibid.

34. Ibid.

35. Ibid.

36. Quoted in C. Cobb, "Policing Internet, Freedom of Speech and Censorship Collide on the Information Highway," *Ottawa Citizen*, March 6, 1994, B2.

Fog at the Border
Response to Kretchmer and Carveth

DON A. WICKS

Library and Information Science, Kent State University

Within the field of library and information science, the issue of freedom of expression has been a longtime concern. The American Library Association issued a *Library Bill of Rights* in 1948, a *Freedom to Read Statement* and an *Intellectual Freedom Statement* in 1953, and a *Freedom to View Statement* in 1979. Since 1967 it has also maintained an Office of Intellectual Freedom. In the position statements just mentioned—and in a dozen additional statements that interpret them—this professional body advocates a very open policy for libraries and information centers and their patrons. The ALA states that materials and public facilities should be made freely available to all users, that materials should not be proscribed, and that libraries should challenge censorship and resist any abridgment of free expression and free access to ideas.

While the position of the ALA is quite clear, the application of intellectual freedom policies to specific situations is not always easy. As Kretchmer and Carveth rightly observe in their paper, "Challenging Boundaries for a Boundless Medium," public libraries are "caught in the middle." They face the practical reality of protecting both intellectual freedom (a legal *and a professional* obligation) and the juveniles who face potential harm posed by some aspects of the Internet. Accordingly, the library community has struggled with whether there are legitimate limits to free expression in a democratic society, and if so, what limits are appropriate. Recent contributors to the professional and academic literature of library and information science reiterate and expand on several of the issues raised by the authors—and some others besides. Beyond the debate over filtering the Internet, which is the main focus of the Kretchmer and Carveth paper, the literature has reported on the pressure experienced by school libraries and media centers from parents with regard to the availability in whatever format of certain materials.[1] Professional library associations have found it difficult to rationalize their belief in free expression with the allowance of space to extremist groups at their conferences.[2] Librarians have influenced the way Holocaust-denial literature is accessed by classifying it outside of history—for example, as anti-Semitism or prejudice literature.[3] Reference librarians have admitted to facing a dilemma when asked to provide information on how to commit suicide or how to make a bomb.[4] Alternate library associations, such as Family Friendly Libraries, have emerged to advocate some limits on free expression.[5] Researchers have investigated how well alternate views are represented in both academic and public libraries.[6] These examples show that the current discussion of Internet use in the public library is part of a larger debate in which the issues so ably addressed by Kretchmer and Carveth must be placed.

A number of issues raised by the authors warrant specific attention. The first relates to the discussion of AUPs. An important manifestation of thinking on Internet access is found in the formulation of acceptable-use policies (AUPs). Kretchmer and Carveth explain that AUPs are employed as ways to protect the library from legal action, especially if such policies relate their standards to the mission of the organization. Here again, the diversity of approach taken by public libraries is clearly seen. Hagloch found that 84 percent of the ninety-one Ohio public libraries she surveyed placed Internet stations in high-traffic areas, presumably to deter inappropriate use.[7] Seventy-three percent used the "tap on the shoulder" method, whereby a staff member asks a patron to desist from inappropriate use. Another 57 percent require parental permission before allowing minors to use Internet workstations, 26 percent require that the patron sign an "acceptable-use" policy statement, and 10 percent have installed privacy screens in order to reduce the possibility that passers-by will see something they consider offensive. Furthermore, only 17 percent use a filter on some or all of their Internet workstations.

In a random (though casual and unscientific) survey of the Internet access policies of ten public libraries in April 2000, this variety of approach among public libraries was again shown (see Table 1).[8]

It is easily seen that the libraries represented in this sample are concerned about how best to protect children. Even the two libraries that report no controls over Internet access require respect for existing laws against child pornography; they call on parents to exercise their responsibility to supervise their own children. Kretchmer and Carveth address this issue in their discussion of *Kathleen R. v. City of Livermore*, and in their summary of the legal arguments for and against filtering they show the central role children have in the "complex debate" on legal limits of freedom of expression.

A similar concern over the safety of adult library staff receives only brief mention in the paper. The authors draw our attention to the situation in Austin, Texas (where staff reported feeling sexually harassed by some users' choices of Web sites), and to the Loudoun County case (where the library board based its strict Internet-access policy on a stated desire to protect staff from having to work in a hostile environment). It is possible that the matter of staff safety will be raised in future cases as well. In Canada, a librarian and spokesperson for the union that represents Toronto library workers has drawn attention to the stressful, confrontational situations

Table 1

Casual Survey of Internet Policies

Number	Policy
2	Place no limitation on Internet use other than referring to legal & parental responsibility
4	Require an Internet use agreement be read and signed by all users
6	Require the Internet workstation to be signed out before use
3	Require written permission of parent for children under 14 or under 18
1	Requires parental accompaniment for children in Grades 1–3
2	Specific policies for children and young adults but not for adults
2–3	Use filters (one of these refers to implementation of "some software security measures")
2	Specify what is meant by objectionable material
4	Request patrons respect sensibilities of others
3	Indicate staff will monitor Internet use
2	Indicate staff will judge the appropriateness of Internet content accessed by the patron
2	Mention their mission statement as the basis for placing boundaries on Internet use

wherein library workers (who are often female) ask Internet users (who are often male) to stop viewing Web sites that are deemed to be disrupting the enjoyment of others using the library. "When the library develops an Internet policy," says this spokesperson, "the worker's rights and safety should be part of that policy."[9] The issue is not likely to go away, seeing that the "tap on the shoulder" approach to Internet regulation is so commonly used in public libraries.

A fourth issue raised in the Kretchmer and Carveth paper concerns the relationship of Internet provision to the normal collection practices of a library. In their Internet policy statements, none of the ten libraries in my sample used the argument that blocking Internet access is akin to the normal process of selecting books and other resources for a collection. That argument has some advocates, who contend that to block an Internet site is no different than to not purchase a given book that falls outside the library's collection policy, and who may add that both book selection and Internet selection must be governed by considerations related to the use of finite library resources.[10] Kretchmer and Carveth show that in the case of *Mainstream Loudoun et al. v. Board of Trustees of the Loudoun County Public Libraries et al.*, using normal selection practices as a defense for filtering was refused by the judge. Furthermore, the courts have not allowed libraries to remove books for content reasons alone and are not likely to allow Internet sites (for adults, at least) to be removed because certain "stop words" are found by a filtering system.[11] Similarly, using the argument that the library is a limited public forum that can block access consistent with its purpose may be difficult, inasmuch as public libraries traditionally exist for reference, research, *and* recreational or leisure purposes.[12]

The idea of adopting a clear, no-compromise approach to the filtering issue is appealing. This could mean unconditionally supporting the principles of intellectual freedom and the First Amendment in a way that rules out any filtering or other control of access to the Internet in public libraries; or it could mean the placing of filters on all library computers, coupled with various structural barriers to uncensored Internet use for all patrons. In reality, neither the law nor public sentiment is likely to allow either extreme to prevail. Indeed, the law already recognizes the need to prohibit the dissemination or receipt of child pornographic materials. Spokespersons on both sides of the debate agree to the principle of parental supervision of their own children and accept, within limits, the existence of AUPs. People on both sides of the issue can sometimes accept the presence of different rules for children and adults. It may be that a philosophical or rational choice leads to a willingness to alter one's view, though the February 2000 campaign for and against filters that was waged in Holland, Michigan (and reported by Kretchmer and Carveth as the first Internet access question to be placed on the ballot), showed that seriously held positions may be played out in a public political arena[13] as well as in a courtroom.

NOTES

1. See Robert Doyle, *Banned Books: 1998 Resource Book* (Chicago: American Library Association, 1998). In this seventeenth annual edition, Doyle assembles cases of challenges to books in various kinds of libraries, most often school libraries.

2. The California Library Association equivocated on whether to allow a publisher of Holocaust-denial literature to set up a booth at the association's 1984 conference in Los Angeles. See John C. Swan, "Untruth or Consequences," *Library Journal* 111 (July 1986): 45–52.

3. John Drobnicki, "Holocaust Denial and Libraries: Should Libraries Acquire Revisionist Materials?" *College & Research Libraries News* 60 (June 1999): 463–64.

4. Carolyn Havens, "Teen Suicide and the Library," *Public Library Quarterly* 10, no. 2 (1990): 33–42.

5. Charles Harmon and Ann Symons, "'But We're Family Friendly Already': How to Respond to the Challenge," *American Libraries* 27 (Aug. 1996): 60, 62–64.

6. Stephen Hupp, "Collecting Extremist Political Materials: The Example of Holocaust Denial Publications," *Collection Management* 14, nos. 3/4 (1991): 163–73; and "The Left and the Right: A Follow-Up Survey of the Collection of Journals of Popular Opinion in Ohio Libraries," *Collection Management* 18, nos. 1/2 (1993): 135–52.

7. Susan Hagloch, "To Filter or Not: Internet Access in Ohio," *Library Journal* 124 (1 Feb. 1999): 50–51.

8. The policies examined were from public libraries in the following locations: Alhambra, California (on the World Wide Web at http://www.alhambralibrary.org/); Beverley Hills, California (http://www.infopeople.org/bhpl/); Douglas County, Colorado (http://douglas.lib.co.us/); Elkhart, Indiana (http://www.elkhart.lib.in.us/); Elmhurst, Illinois (http://www.elmhurst.lib.il.us/); Fayette County, Ohio (http://www.washington-ch.lib.oh.us/); Fox Lake, Illinois (http://www.fllib.org/); Massillon, Ohio (http://www.massillon.lib.oh.us/); Mill Valley, California (http://www.millvalleylibrary.org/); Reedsburg, Wisconsin (http://elink.scls.lib.wi.us/reedsburg/).

9. Louise Surette, "Libraries and Net Porn: Safety versus Censorship," *Toronto Star*, April 14, 2000, available on the World Wide Web: http://www.thestar.com.

10. Julie Grafstein, "The Public Library and the Internet: Who Has a Right to What?" *Internet Reference Services Quarterly* 42, no. 2 (1999): 7–19.

11. Ibid.

12. Rinda Allison and Scott F. Uhler, "Libraries and the Internet, Part III: Library Authority to Filter/Block Internet Sites," *Illinois Libraries* 80 (Spring 1998): 43–45.

13. Brian Bowe, Nate Reens, and Dave Yonkman, "Filters Rejected," *Holland Sentinel*, Feb. 23, 2000, on the World Wide Web: http://www.thehollandsentinel.net.

Indistinct Boundaries of the First Amendment

Response to Kretchmer and Carveth

SUSAN NEWHART ELLIOTT

Law, University of Dayton

The Kretchmer and Carveth paper nicely sketches the increasing conflict between public concern about the provision of unregulated Internet access in public libraries and the obligations of those libraries, as public institutions, under the First Amendment to the Constitution. This conflict rests on interrelated questions about the boundaries of First Amendment—including the right of free expression, the right to receive information, and the right of access to information—both theoretically and as applied to Internet access within the public library, given the peculiar nature of the institution.

The complexity of defining the boundaries of First Amendment rights of expression is demonstrated by the Supreme Court case that gave rise to the quotation that begins the paper: "[Citizens] must always remain free to inquire, to study and evaluate, to gain new maturity and understanding . . . [to] explore the unknown, and discover areas of interest and thought . . . [for] access to ideas makes it possible for citizens generally to exercise their rights of free speech and press in a meaningful manner. . . . [The] library is the principal locus of such freedom" (as quoted by Kretchmer and Carveth).[1]

The *Pico* case, which involved a school board's removal of disfavored books from a school library, did indeed address far-reaching issues about the right of access to information and the place of the library in the development of intellectual freedom necessary for the effective exercise of democratic rights. The only issue on which a majority of the justices was able to agree was that the board did not possess *absolute* discretion to remove books on the basis of their content.[2] Even of the four justices who joined in the plurality opinion (from which the quotation is taken), one felt compelled to write separately to caution against an overly expansive view of First Amendment rights "somehow associated with the peculiar nature of the school library."[3]

Kretchmer and Carveth describe the indistinct boundaries of First Amendment rights as "a balancing act between freedom of speech and societal interest." Competing societal interests and obligations have resulted in reduced First Amendment protection, and thus various degrees of government regulation, for defamatory speech, "fighting words," commercial speech, and radio and television broadcasts. Although it has been argued that Internet communications should be subject to regulation as are radio and television broadcasts, the Supreme Court has determined that Internet communications do not bear critical features of radio and television broadcasts (including the likelihood of accidental receipt of offensive material) that justify reduced protection and increased governmental regulation.[4]

Obscene speech is not protected under the First Amendment. Although the Supreme Court determined in *Reno v. American Civil Liberties Union* (discussed in Kretchmer and Carveth) that provisions of the Communications Decency Act of 1996 (the "CDA"),[5] which prohibited Internet transmission of "indecent" and "patently offensive" communications, were overbroad, in violation of the First Amendment, the Court specifically upheld the CDA provision that prohibited Internet transmission of obscene material.[6] The Court reiterated earlier holdings (including the 1973 case *Miller v. California*) that the determination of what is obscene rests, at least in part, on local community values.[7] Furthermore, as Kretchmer and Carveth have noted, the Supreme Court emphasized its recognition of the "compelling interest in protecting the physical and psychological well-being of minors, which extend[s] to shielding them from indecent messages that are not obscene by adult standards."[8]

Thus, a library may block Internet transmission of obscene communications to all patrons, and may, in determining what constitutes obscenity, discriminate on the basis of the age of the recipient of the communication—provided that the blocking of obscene materials does not result in the suppression of materials that are protected under the First Amendment (including materials that may be "indecent" or "patently offensive"). Where speech is being suppressed, even pursuant to a "compelling interest," there is little tolerance for overbreadth.

Much of the Supreme Court's opinion in *Reno* focuses on the lack of precision and overbreadth of CDA provisions and remedies. The opinion may be read as a directive that the debate over the appropriate boundaries of freedom of expression in Internet communications must be framed through *logos*, not *pathos*. The Court emphatically distinguishes the CDA from the other portions of the Telecommunications Act of 1996 (of which the CDA was set forth under Title V) by the lack of extensive committee hearings, reports, and testimony underlying CDA provisions. Similarly, the Court noted not only the narrower scope of Federal Communications Communication regulation at issue in the *Pacifica* case but also the fact that the regulation had been the result of an expert evaluation.[9]

Most of the plaintiffs in the *Reno* case represented Internet services and potential originators of Internet communications, which is consistent with the traditional conception of the First Amendment as guaranteeing freedom of speech or expression. The Supreme Court also mentioned in *Reno* the "constitutional right to receive [speech],"[10] which was more specifically addressed in the Virginia federal district court case, *Mainstream Loudoun v. Board of Trustees*[11] (also discussed in Kretchmer and Carveth), where plaintiffs who were Internet service users were found to have standing to challenge the filtering of Internet communications by a public library.

The Supreme Court has long held that the right to receive speech is a necessary component of the right to freedom of speech (see *Martin v. City of Struthers*),[12] but the contours of that component are unclear. The dividing issue among the plurality in the *Pico* school library case was whether or not there was a right to receive information that might imply an affirmative obligation on the part of the state to provide information—a right of access to information.[13] The plurality opinion could be read to suggest an obligation on the part of the school library to provide a variety of materials on various viewpoints, consistent with the position of the American Library Association.[14] The dissents and Justice Harry Blackmun's concurrence challenged the implications of any affirmative obligation to satisfy a student's right of access, emphasizing the school's role in the transmission of local community values and the role of the school library in supporting that mission.

Perhaps even more significant are the implications of a *Pico*-type right of access in public libraries that offer Internet services. Reference services, which involve the library personnel in the patron's exploration of materials, are limited in traditional book collections by the volumes that the library has selected and purchased, through its own acquisitions policies. There is no such limit for what Kretchmer and Carveth appropriately call the "boundless medium," and the existence and scope of a right of access may become issues in future disputes.

Although courts, thus far, have generally upheld challenges to both legislation and library policies imposing Internet filtering, the dispute regarding appropriate boundaries is far from over. While libraries may be exempt from tort-based liability under legislation such as the CDA, courts have indicated that libraries may be subject to claims for prospective injunctive relief—that is, the library may not be subject to damages or fines for past behavior, but it may be hauled into court and compelled to conform to whatever order a court might issue for future operations.[15] As Kretchmer and Carveth have pointed out, additional legislation seeking to impose boundaries on Internet communications in libraries is being developed at both the federal and state levels. There will be more lawsuits, as those who favor boundaries adjust their approaches to court directives.

Libraries may find themselves in positions where the imposition of boundaries becomes desirable from the library's standpoint. Those who oppose filtering Internet communications object to the public library's *interference* in a patron's intellectual activity, regardless of the object of that activity. It is possible that library personnel may be asked to *participate* in assisting a patron, possibly a minor, to obtain access to indecent or offensive materials through the Internet. It may be unlikely that anyone would challenge a librarian's refusal to help a child obtain access to indecent materials on the Internet, but it is surely preferable for the library to adopt acceptable-use policies with carefully considered boundaries on library Internet services and patrons' rights of access than to have individual librarians imposing boundaries on an ad hoc basis, reflecting only a librarian's personal evaluation of the patron and the material being sought.

The essential problem, as the Supreme Court pointed out in *Reno v. ACLU*, is that the debate has not yet successfully identified the extent or nature of the risks of "unbounded" Internet services in the public library. The arguments of those who favor imposing boundaries have lacked empirical findings, objective expert evaluations, and the necessary precision—given that First Amendment rights are at stake—in proposed solutions. Those who oppose the imposition of boundaries, however, must not fail to recognize the genuine concerns that are being raised, or that courts have indicated some agreement in substance with the arguments of those who would impose boundaries. The Supreme Court has reiterated boundaries on obscene speech and child pornography, has recognized the significance of community values, and has acknowledged a compelling interest in protecting children in a manner different from adults.

In each of the cases described by Kretchmer and Carveth in their paper, the resolution has included the imposition of some limits on Internet services in the public library. All sides must accept that the dispute will continue and that the debate will be reframed in the process. The sides can meet and work together to negotiate acceptable boundaries, or they can wait, and boundaries will be imposed by legislation or court order—but for public libraries with Internet access, boundaries on the boundless medium will come.

NOTES

1. *Board of Education v. Pico*, 475 U.S. 853, 869–70 (1982).

2. Ibid., 862, 883.

3. Ibid., 878 (Blackmun, J., concurring).

4. *Reno v. American Civil Liberties Union*, 521 U.S. 844, 867 (1997).

5. *Telecommunications Act of 1996*, Title V (Community Decency Act of 1996). Pub. L. 104-104, 110 Stat. 56.

6. Ibid., 883.

7. Ibid., 872 (citing *Miller v. California*, 413 U.S. 15 [1973]).

8. *Reno v. ACLU*, 869.

9. Ibid., 867 (citing *FCC v. Pacifica Foundation*, 438 U.S. 726 [1978]).

10. *Reno v. ACLU*, 874.

11. *Mainstream Loudoun v. Board of Trustees*, 2 F.Supp.2d 783 (1998) (I), 24 F. Supp. 2d 552 (1998) (II).

12. *Martin v. City of Struthers*, 319 U.S. 141 (1943).

13. *Board of Education v. Pico*, 880 (Blackmun, J., concurring).

14. American Library Association, 1996, *The Library Bill of Rights* (originally adopted 18 June 1948) 1996.

15. *Mainstream Loudoun* (I), 789–90.

Meeting the Challenge
Response to the Discussants

SUSAN B. KRETCHMER & ROD CARVETH

We very much appreciate Professor Elliott's and Professor Wicks's thoughtful responses to our paper. In reply, we will engage the primary issues raised in their responses and then progress to a broader discussion of the import and suggested resolutions of the library Internet access controversy.

Professor Elliott astutely identifies the significance of the *Pico* case as it relates to the library filtering debate. As Elliott explains, "The *Pico* case, which involved a school board's removal of disfavored books from a school library, did indeed address far-reaching issues about the right of access to information and the place of the library in the development of intellectual freedom necessary for the effective exercise of democratic rights. The only issue on which a majority of the justices was able to agree was that the board did not possess *absolute* discretion to remove books on the basis of their content." We agree that *Pico* is pivotal, not only for the issues raised in the case but also because of the narrowness of the decision. While the ruling holds that school boards do not possess absolute discretion to remove books due to content considerations, it allows wide latitude for school boards—and, perhaps, by extension, library boards—to formulate policies on information source selection and use based on other criteria and circumstances and leaves considerable vagueness, as Professor Elliott later observes, regarding a library patron's right of access to information.

Professor Wicks notes that in our paper the issue of library staff safety "receives only brief mention." Wicks comments that in Canada "a librarian and spokesperson for the union which represents Toronto library workers has drawn attention to the stressful, confrontational situations wherein library workers (who are often female) ask Internet users (who are often male) to stop viewing Web sites that are deemed to be disrupting the enjoyment of others using the library." The brevity of the consideration of staff harassment in our paper does not reflect a judgment of the importance of the topic. Rather, to date, although staff harassment was advanced as a major impetus for the imposition of filtering/blocking software in the Loudoun County libraries, the issue received little attention in the ultimate judicial determination of the *Loudoun* case as well as in the most visible public arguments related to the entire controversy, which are the areas of direct concern in our paper. Further, staff harassment is not a new issue introduced into the library environment as the product of the recent addition of public Internet access; libraries have long managed these issues through traditional use and access policies, which are now being extended to the Internet.

Both Professor Elliott and Professor Wicks share our view that the current debate is likely to result in a compromise, instead of zero-sum, solution. As Elliott asserts: "The essential problem, as the Supreme Court explained in *Reno v. ACLU* (1997), is that the debate has not yet successfully identified the extent or nature of the risks of 'unbounded' Internet service in the public library. The arguments of those who favor imposing boundaries have lacked empirical findings, objective expert evaluations, and the necessary precision—given that First Amendment rights are at stake—in proposed solutions. Those who oppose the imposition of boundaries, however, must not fail to recognize the genuine concerns that are being raised, or that courts have indicated some agreement in substance with the arguments of those who would impose boundaries. The Supreme Court has reiterated boundaries on obscene speech and child pornography, has recognized the significance of community values, and has acknowledged a compelling interest in protecting children in a manner different from adults." Similarly, Wicks affirms, "Indeed, the law already recognizes the need to prohibit the dissemination or receipt of child pornographic materials. Spokespersons on both sides of the debate agree to the principle of parental supervision of their own children and accept, within limits, the existence of AUPS. People on both sides of the issue can sometimes accept the presence of different rules for children and adults."

We agree with Professors Elliott and Wicks that a compromise will be reached because (1) the courts do treat children and adults differently in relation to freedom of expression; (2) the courts have given local communities an increasing amount of authority by which to define their own standards of acceptable and unacceptable behavior; (3) each side in the filtering debate has valid positions; and (4) there is a continuum of possible resolutions that could be reached regarding filters in libraries. In fact, these issues point to perhaps the most important threshold for the library filtering debate—that the dispute can be reconciled in a variety of ways. At one extreme, no filters on library computers or restrictions on use would be allowed; at the other extreme, all computers would have filters. But, there are a number of possibilities between those divergent positions. For example, the physical provisions of the computer terminals can be manipulated to serve library objectives, acceptable use policies (AUPS) can control patron access and behavior, or some computers could have filters, some not. Or, there could be some combination of these efforts with, for instance, unfiltered computers designated for use only by adults and children who have obtained the permission of their parents.

How are these decisions made in a democracy? When viewed in an historical context, it becomes apparent that the library Internet access controversy, and the general confusion and distress about the nature, impact, and future of the Internet, mirror the legal turmoil and societal upheaval generated by every previous major innovation in communication technology. The advent of writing, the printing press, the telegraph, the telephone, radio, and television all aroused debates analogous to the present dispute.

The pace of technological change, whether in communication or other fields such as medicine, continues to raise unanticipated questions and consequences that tend to confound our ability to deal with them in both the legal and public arenas. Thus, for example, as we have learned, one of the key concerns fueling the library Internet access controversy is the fear of the sexual exploitation of children. Yet, while there is a grand total of almost eight hundred cases, confirmed or under investigation, of child sexual victimization related to the Internet,[1] there are 103,845 confirmed cases of sexual abuse of children by parents and caretakers per year in the United States.[2] Similarly, the combined budgets of all state Children's Trust Funds, government entities that work with the legislature and solicit private funds to prevent child abuse, does not even approach the more than seventy-five million dollars per year that will be spent to purchase Internet filtering/blocking software by 2001.[3]

Coupled with the disproportionate alarm that causes this type of disconnect, there is, in America, always a basic tension between free speech and censorship, between democratic values and human nature. As Carey McWilliams observes, "The paradox about censorship is that everyone is opposed to it—literally everyone. If proof be needed, just try to censure a censor. . . . The idea of censorship is inherently repugnant to most Americans. Asked if they approve of censorship, most of them, as a quick reaction, would say no. But then as they thought about it a bit, some of them would add, 'except, of course, in certain situations.'"[4]

Consequently, the way in which we resolve issues such as the library Internet access controversy is a test of our democracy and democratic values. This suggests that not only will there be compromise, but the jointly crafted boundaries will reflect the spirit of a robust civil society. Perhaps there might be a voluntary effort to transform the heart of the conflict by mobilizing one of the most fundamental tenets of free speech—a multiplicity of good speech drowns out the bad. Likewise, the civic participation and empowerment inspired by the passion of the dispute serves to further democratic ideals. There may be consensus that each local community is best able to decide for itself which policies it feels comfortable with adopting for library Internet access. In addition, policy determination at the local level encourages community members to become involved in such decision making, whether serving on a library board or attending town meetings. Moreover, of the possible remedies raised in the course of the debate, AUPs would seem to most closely parallel the democratic system of laws and justice. Our laws clearly delineate prohibited behaviors and the punishment to be prescribed for transgression. By adhering to those laws, we choose to limit some of our own freedom, but the state does not intervene until after an offense is committed. Comparably functioning in the same manner as laws, AUPS aspire to the dignity and fairness central to a democracy. Thus, as American society meets the challenge of deciding the "proper" boundaries of freedom of expression and order in public library Internet access, the democratic paradigm stands as the simple yet profound beacon that illuminates the rocky path to an equitable resolution.

NOTES

1. David Finkelhor, Kimberly J. Mitchell, and Janis Wolak, *Online Victimization: A Report on the Nation's Youth* (National Center for Missing and Exploited Children, June 2000), available on the World Wide Web: http://www.missingkids.org/download/InternetSurvey.pdf.

2. U.S. Department of Health and Human Services, *Child Maltreatment 1998: Reports from the States to the National Child Abuse and Neglect Data System* (Washington, D.C.: Government Printing Office, 2000).

3. P. J. Huffstutter, "Censors and Sensibility," *Los Angeles Times*, March 30, 1998, D1, D8.

4. Carey McWilliams, "Carey McWilliams," in *Censorship For and Against*, ed. Harold H. Hart (New York: Hart Publishing, 1971).

8

Free Speech on Campus
Academic Freedom and the Corporations

ELLEN W. SCHRECKER
History, Yeshiva University

In 1996, Nancy Olivieri, a pediatrician at the University of Toronto Medical School, discovered that the drug she was using in her clinical research on a genetic blood disease was having life-threatening side effects on her young patients. Though the contract she had signed with Apotex, the drug manufacturer that was sponsoring her research, contained a no-publication clause, Olivieri believed she had a moral obligation to disseminate her findings. When she published a report on them in the influential *New England Journal of Medicine* two years later, Apotex threatened legal action and then tried to get her fired. It almost succeeded. Had her colleagues and a bevy of eminent medical experts not intervened, the university, which was seeking a major grant from Apotex, would almost certainly have let her go.[1]

Such is the state of academic freedom as we enter the new millennium. In many ways it harks back to the situation at the beginning of the last century, when businessmen were also trying to silence the professors who criticized their operations, and a group of the nation's leading intellectuals responded by conceptualizing the modern notion of academic freedom and founding the American Association of University Professors (AAUP). What is happening within higher education today that could make it possible for a drug company to threaten the job of an academic scientist? The problems that I will explore are primarily systemic, and they reflect—both directly and indirectly—the growing power of the corporate sector within the nation's colleges and universities.

THE CRISIS OF AMERICAN HIGHER EDUCATION

It has become something of a cliché to expound upon the dire condition of the modern university and to announce, in the words of one of its most trenchant critics, that "the present model [of the university] is in its twilight."[2] Such doomsday language knows no political boundaries; from Martin Anderson to Stanley Aronowitz, conservatives, moderates, and radicals of all persuasions agree that something is grievously wrong with the present system of higher education and that it cannot, as the former president of Stanford put it, "continue business as usual."[3] Though each critic offers his or her own diagnosis and remedy, they all recognize the same symptoms—declining public support, declining academic performance, declining morale. True, a few voices do question the existence of such a crisis; they note that such jeremiads are standard rhetoric within academe, and they point to the international stature of American universities as an indication of their underlying strength.[4]

Still, the concern of many people both inside and outside academe that the university has lost its mission is not a trivial one, for it is hard to defend an institution that is floundering. But perhaps that has always been the case. Change invariably provokes confusion; since knowledge is constantly evolving, change may well be intrinsic to the very nature of higher education. But despite a disquieting tendency in certain (mainly administrative) circles to advocate change in and of itself as a goal for academe, such a mission based on change cannot justify the existence of an institution.[5] At the same time, it is equally clear that earlier formulations about the value of the university to the rest of society no longer draw widespread support.

Such was not the case during most of the twentieth century, when higher education seemed central to the American way of life. From designing Wisconsin's public-utilities law to building the atomic bomb, the academy derived its mission directly from its close relationship with the public sector—a relationship that gave it considerable legitimacy as well as material support. Today that public sector is shrinking and with it much of the universities' funding, as well as its raison d'être.

The late Bill Readings provides the most useful formulation for understanding how the global expansion of capitalism and the concomitant decline of the nation-state are undermining the university's basic mission. Traditional universities, Readings observes, inculcated a sense of national identity by transmitting a nation's culture. Today, however, both the nation-state and its distinctive identity are under attack. Globalization erodes national boundaries and homogenizes national cultures into a single Americanized "McWorld"—to use Benjamin Barber's apposite phrase. Thus, for Readings, "Since the nation-state is no longer the primary instance of the reproduction of global capitals, 'culture'—as the symbolic and political counterpart to the project of integration pursued by the nation-state—has lost its purchase. The nation-state and the modern notion of culture arose together, and they are . . . ceasing to be essential to an increasingly transnational global economy."[6]

Not only has the state surrendered many of its functions to the market, but the very notion of a unified national culture for universities to develop and transmit has come into question. To some extent the academy is itself responsible for the loss of its cultural mission. The culprit here is the postmodern form of multi-culturalism, a way of thinking that, as Frederic Jameson and David Harvey have argued, also reflects the fluidity of international capitalism.[7] Sensitized by the developing awareness that earlier scholarship tended to universalize all human experience as that of the proverbial "dead white men," many serious scholars now insist that there can no longer be a common identity that exists apart from a particular racialized, gendered subject. For that reason, Readings argues, "the grand narrative of the University, centered on the production of a liberal, reasoning subject, is no longer readily available to us."[8] Unfortunately, as we shall see, the nearly incomprehensible prose within which many contemporary cultural critics conceal their often valuable insights has given conservative opponents of the academic community a handy weapon with which to attack the entire academic world.

Without its civic mission, and without the unifying focus on Western civilization that seems so anachronistic in our multicultural world, what is a university to do? Is there any way to reconstruct the justification of higher education as a social good? The literature on "the crisis of the academy" contains dozens of answers, but in the real world, there seems to be only one: to enter the marketplace—and that is exactly what is happening. In the name of enhancing economic competitiveness, the university's mission has taken an entrepreneurial turn. Academic administrators now speak the language of business. They specialize in "human resource development."[9] In the corporate lingo of the associate vice chancellor at the University of California–San Diego, they contribute to "economic development by developing knowledge-linking activities that enhance technology commercialization, support organizational and community change, and enhance the competencies of workers and professionals."[10] If such a perspective is to be taken seriously—and I think it must—higher education now aims to become an engine of regional economic growth. But, so too, does the tourist industry. There's something a little depressing about appealing to Congress or the state legislature to save a local college because, like a defense plant rendered obsolete by the end of the Cold War, it provides jobs.

There is, it is true, another economic justification for higher education that carries, superficially at least, more appeal—its role as the primary agency for social mobility. Such a mission accords with both our individualistic and our egalitarian traditions. The university, the public university in particular, has become the twentieth- and possibly twenty-first-century version of the frontier, taking on that earlier institution's symbolic function as a social safety valve by offering poor, but talented, strivers the promise of the American dream of middle-class respectability, if not great wealth. It did fulfill that purpose, especially in the twenty-five years after World War II—at least for many working-class white men. Today, however, higher education is losing its value as an engine of social mobility. Not only do basketball prodigies and computer "geeks" eschew college for the big bucks they can earn in the real world, but the transformation of the American economy over the past twenty-five years has turned education from a mechanism of opportunity into a strand of the social safety net. Unless it comes from a top-tier university or college, a B.A. no longer carries the cachet it once did, even though, paradoxically, it has become increasingly necessary for economic survival. Deindustrialization has destroyed the well-paid, unionized, blue-collar jobs that provided economic security to previous generations of workers; the only alternative to immiseration is some kind of postsecondary education.

For most students, however, a sojourn within the academy has little if any intrinsic value. Its function is to provide the credential. As a result, higher education has become credentialing, an essentially vocational training process devoid of most cultural or intellectual content, and one that, as we shall see, encourages its increasing commodification.[11] Students are now customers—and increasingly grumpy ones at that.

It is hard to blame them. Whether or not the quality of the education that they receive has declined, the perception that it has is widespread. The nation's public institutions of higher education, which serve 80 percent of the students, are the main targets. Everybody, it seems, has some kind of gripe against these schools. Much of that griping comes from so-called "stakeholders," an indeterminate category of (usually influential) groups and individuals who claim to have some kind of interest in higher education. That interest, it turns out, is usually political or financial. As they have for years, politicians flay the university as a way to pander to the electorate's current discontents without having to spend money, while businessmen do so in the hope that they can reap bonanzas by privatizing the system. Their criticisms, and those of the academy's other detractors, have seriously eroded public support for higher education.

There is considerable irony here, for just as the university is losing its credibility with the public, the demand for its products is rising. This situation forces higher education into a vicious cycle. Because of its unpopularity, it has trouble coming up with the resources necessary for carrying out its functions, but the less well it fulfills those functions, the more criticism it attracts, further lowering its public standing. Moreover, as I hope to show, the measures that it takes to make up for its lost income not only further damage its credibility but also, and ultimately more seriously, distort its educational mission.

Because the decline of the university's reputation feeds into its other problems, I will explore that decline in some detail. In a sense, what we are dealing with here is the erosion of the intellectual and cultural authority of the academy. Most of the trouble comes from the wholesale transformation of public values caused by the growing corporatization of American life: if something does not make a lot of money, it gets shunted aside. Aggravating the damage, however, has been a carefully orchestrated conservative campaign to destroy the credibility of the academic community.

In a recent paper, Berkeley historian David Hollinger drew attention to a 1971 memorandum that Richmond attorney Lewis Powell had written at the request of a friend who was about to head the Education Committee of the National Chamber of Commerce. In it, the future Supreme Court justice recommended a multipronged campaign to offset what he believed was a massive attack on the American free enterprise system by left-wing academics.[12] Powell was not advocating a scatter-shot offensive but rather a program that required "careful long-range planning and implementation . . . over an indefinite period of years, in the scale of financing available only through joint action, and in the political power available only through united action and national organizations."[13] Powell urged the business community to establish centers of scholarship outside the universities and to reward the amenable professors inside them. He also outlined a wide-ranging media campaign to counter the Left's alleged hegemony over the world of ideas. The profound shift to the right in the nation's intellectual discourse that has occurred in the years since Powell wrote his memorandum attests to the efficacy of the program he outlined.

Powell was hardly alone. Whether or not there was an actual conspiracy in the legal sense of the term, it is clear that there has been a self-conscious attempt to disseminate a conservative challenge to the mainstream of academic scholarship within the social sciences and humanities. Funded by a group of right-wing foundations—John H. Olin, Lynde and Harry Bradley, Smith Richardson, and Sara Scaife among them—conservatives established a network of think tanks, scholarly associations, and publications that together have created a plush alternative to the traditional academic community. On campus, endowed chairs and research centers offer additional rewards to right-thinking intellectuals. At the same time, generous publicity budgets help these alternative institutions and individuals promote their often highly politicized output as if it were real scholarly work. According to Ellen Messer-Davidow, who has investigated these right-wing networks, "Cultural conservatives have used think tanks to produce the 'expert' knowledge they could not generate from within the academy. They have done so by conflating 'expertise' as pertains to knowledge produced by scholarly methods and 'expertise' as pertains to the aura of authority surrounding those who produce this knowledge. In this way, the think tanks have constituted an 'academized' aura of authority upon which conservatives have capitalized to advance their political agenda."[14]

The establishment of this parallel universe has serious consequences for the university. The political content of its operations aside, the mere existence of the right-wing cultural apparatus puts into question the authority of academic scholarship. If an equally credible institution can offer alternative explanations of the world, the traditional university can claim no monopoly over any methodology or body of knowledge. This is especially the case when academic scholarship is itself under attack, as it often is, from the very same conservative think tanks and writers who challenge its institutional hegemony.

Thus developed the "political correctness" furor of the early nineties. Operating on the same assumption as Powell—that radical social critics dominated the nation's leading universities—conservative journalists and academics systematically tore into mainstream scholarship. The deep pockets of Olin, Bradley, and the like enabled these people to popularize the notion that American higher education had been taken over by the forces of political correctness and multiculturalism. Besides recycling the same horror stories of liberal white males terrorized by racist students of color and feminists bent on castration, they also offered exaggerated caricatures of the abstruse and trivial scholarship that, they claimed, was flooding the nation's campuses. By the early 1990s, the campaign against the academy had taken its toll. As far as much of the public was concerned, professors were jargon-spouting deconstructionists (if not cross-dressers or worse) who wrote incomprehensible prose and mocked Western civilization.[15] English departments attracted most of the flak, but even in other fields, as the well-publicized controversy over the Smithsonian Institution's 1995 *Enola Gay* exhibit on the dropping of the atomic bomb revealed, outside critics were challenging the legitimacy of academic scholarship—and winning political support.[16]

At the same time, politicians and educational reformers began pecking away at other areas of vulnerability within the academy. Here, the main targets were the tenure that supposedly protected deadwood and the scandalously short work-weeks that college teachers allegedly enjoyed. With downsizing the norm throughout the private sector, the employment security that tenured professors enjoyed seemed an anomaly or worse, as did the twelve to fifteen hours a week that college teachers spent in the classroom. It was hard to condense into a sound bite an explanation of why academic freedom requires tenure or what professors did during the 53.6 hours they really work every week. It did not help that many academic administrators, eager to inject business expertise into their campuses, as well as a number of foundations and education-oriented organizations, not only called for more attention to teaching but began to experiment with alternatives to tenure.

To make matters worse, there was also some real cheating. Under pressure to publish and obtain grants, a few scientists were falsifying their research results. These transgressions occurred most frequently within the biological sciences, which is perhaps the area of academic inquiry most deeply affected by the incursions of the corporate sector. Because competition, always intense if not always acknowledged, has increased as federal support for research has declined, the environments in high-pressure laboratories have become overheated, and it should come as no surprise that fraud and other forms of unethical behavior have been spawned.[17] Fold in the profit motive, and one gets such travesties as the development by researchers at the University of California Medical School of an anticancer substance from the spleen cells of a leukemia patient who had never been told that his routine "checkups" were being used to harvest his cells for marketing.[18] When such scams reach the press, the understandable outrage fuels further disillusionment with the academy.

Perhaps all these problems could have been shrugged off, had it seemed that the institutions of higher learning were doing their job. But such was not the case; the nation's college classrooms were not happy places. It was hard for students—most of whom, after all, were only on campus to get themselves credentialed—to muster much enthusiasm for their academic work, especially when it came in the form of large lecture classes or courses taught by overworked, underpaid adjunct professors and teaching assistants. In such a situation, passivity, withdrawal, and cheating seemed rational responses. External critics looked at the numbers: retention rates were down, while the students who stayed were taking longer to graduate. In 1976 a bachelor of arts took 4.6 years; in 1992, the figure was up to 5.5.[19] Though financial problems caused most of these dropouts and delays, politicians and the public blamed the students and the schools.[20] They called for more accountability, higher standards, better management—remedies that would do little to solve the real problems of higher education.

THE FINANCIAL CRISIS OF THE UNIVERSITY

Those problems, like those of the students, were primarily financial, the result of cutbacks in public funding at both the state and national levels. We should not, it is true, attribute these cutbacks primarily to the conservatives' ideological assault on American higher education; much broader political and economic forces were at work. Still, the academy's dwindling credibility certainly did not help. In many states, these cuts were quite drastic. The University of Michigan, which had relied on the state legislature for 70 percent of its budget in the 1970s, saw that percentage drop to 30 percent by the mid-1990s. In 1992, the legislature reduced the University of California's appropriations by 10 percent; in the Empire State, the City University of New York lost 20 percent of its state funding in the early 1990s.[21] As we shall see, academic administrators were generally able to make up for the missing revenues, but they did so in ways that profoundly transformed the structure and culture of their schools and undermined their educational functions.

Before we can generalize about the impact of these cutbacks on the nation's colleges and universities, we must recognize the diversity of the institutions that constitute the system of higher education in this country. Obviously, a top-tier private research university like Stanford or the Massachusetts Institute of Technology operates in a completely different economic universe than a community college or small church-related school. In 1996, Yale University, to take one example, got 29 percent of its income from grants and contracts, 22 percent from investments, and only 13 percent from tuition and fees.[22] Administrators at smaller public and private colleges can rarely squeeze much income out of their endowments (if indeed they have them), nor can they tap into the largesse of drug companies or the National Institutes of Health. They must rely much more heavily on tuition or, if they are public schools, whatever support state and local governments decide to allocate. But whatever their situation, all types of institutions had to adjust to the decline in public spending that began in the 1970s.

Perhaps that adjustment would not have seemed so painful had the academic community not expanded so vibrantly during the previous twenty-five years—the golden age of American higher education. In the 1960s alone, the number of students enrolled in some form or another of postsecondary education had increased by 120 percent. New campuses sprang up everywhere. Of the 3,638 colleges and universities that now comprise the American system of higher education, more than half came into being after 1945.[23]

Much of that growth occurred as the result of the federal government's decision to use the universities as a way to underwrite the private sector. As Harvard biologist Richard Lewontin has pointed out, politics and ideology made it impossible for the United States to adopt the kind of official industrial policy that other nations used to promote economic growth. Instead, it accomplished the same ends by pouring money into the academic community. In the guise of furthering national defense, the government paid for the creation of a scientific and technological infrastructure that supplied the nation's businesses with the technical innovations and trained workers they needed. That federal money trickled down all over the campus. Not only did it cover most basic research in the physical and biological sciences as well as some work in the social sciences, but it also allowed the university to skim off enough overhead to support many of its other activities.[24] Though such funding carried relatively few strings (at least in comparison to the present), its availability did encourage ambitious administrators to redirect their universities' intellectual activities toward those departments and faculty members whose work conformed with the government's agenda.[25] Private foundations were also pouring money into higher education, supporting graduate students and programs in a wide variety of fields, including the humanities.[26]

But the good days came to an end in the seventies. Though the business campaign against the academic left that Lewis Powell had outlined did not really bear fruit until the Ronald Reagan years, other factors, including the economic crisis precipitated by the Vietnam-era deficits and the 1973 oil shock, began to eat away at the fiscal underpinnings of higher education. At the same time, the rightward drift of the American polity was reducing the willingness of lawmakers to support the public sector. Republican politicians attacked the welfare state, reduced spending for most social services, and called for privatizing the rest. For universities, the most important change, at least according to Sheila Slaughter and Larry L. Leslie, was the decision of the Richard Nixon administration in 1971 to shift the federal government's support for higher education away from general grants to institutions, in favor of individual students. Colleges would still get federal money, but they would have to earn it through the tuition payments made with the financial aid their students received from Washington.[27] Combined with the cutbacks in funding for research that we shall examine later, this development was to precipitate major changes in the ways that the nation's colleges and universities carried out their basic functions.

Though the implications of channeling money to students rather than to schools were not immediately apparent, by the 1980s most institutions of higher learning had transformed their operations to deal with the new reality. Ironically, for all the attention that demands for "student power" got in the 1960s, it is possible that these later changes empowered students in ways that shaped their colleges and universities far more profoundly. They had become consumers, courted by institutions whose very survival depended on their tuition dollars. Since the world of higher education was a highly imperfect market, schools could not compete for students by lowering their prices. In fact, as public funding declined, almost every institution, from Stanford to Slippery Rock, raised its tuition—a move that obviously did not endear these schools to the general public or to their potential customers and their parents. At the same time, they had to sell themselves to those potential customers. The problem here was that—especially in the years before the *U.S. News & World Report* rankings appeared—a future undergraduate and her parents had very little idea of what comprised a quality education. Just like the makers of such other high-priced consumer goods as luxury cars, colleges and universities had to advertise the ineffable quality of their product by relying on symbolic representations of its value. A high tuition was one such symbol; so too were elaborate athletic facilities and state-of-the-art computer centers. Enrolling gifted students was another sign of quality, and many schools put considerable resources into merit rather than need-based scholarships. Though high-prestige, "name brand" institutions had no trouble attracting applicants, even these schools scrambled to maintain the facade of educational quality.[28]

With their dorms and classrooms full of customers to be satisfied, the nation's colleges and universities pumped money into student services. They also made intellectual compromises to placate those customers, primarily by adding more vocationally oriented courses and programs to the curriculum. The liberal arts lost out, while the number of business majors soared—as did students' grade-point averages. Almost every institution sacrificed some measure of educational rigor in order to appease students who felt their tuition payments entitled them to good grades and short reading lists. Neither private schools whose revenues depended on keeping enrollments high nor professors whose raises and reappointments required positive student evaluations could afford to challenge their customers.[29]

On the financial side, the damage was inflicted on the university's physical and intellectual infrastructure. While institutions were putting their money into new facilities and student services, they were slighting other expenditures. Library budgets and plant maintenance took the biggest hits, but spending on classroom instruction also went down.[30] Faculty salaries declined, losing 4.4 percent of their real purchasing power after 1972.[31] In addition, many schools, especially community colleges and lower-tier public universities, began replacing full-time teachers with part-time ones. In the late 1970s, 60 percent of CUNY's faculty members had been full time; by the end of the 1990s, 40 percent of them were. There were similar reductions throughout the country. As of 1998, according to AAUP estimates, adjuncts were teaching nearly half the nation's college classes. Some were professionals in other fields, recruited specifically for their expertise outside the classroom. Many others, however, held Ph.D.s and were struggling to make their careers in academe. Though they were well-qualified and experienced college teachers, the conditions under which they worked—low pay, heavy teaching loads, no security, no benefits, no office space or secretarial help—militated against the quality of the education they could offer. Rarely did they have the time or energy to give their students the attention they deserved. Faculty cutbacks hurt students in other ways: they increased class size and limited educational options. Moreover, because some required courses were oversubscribed or not offered on a regular basis, students could not always graduate on time. No wonder they became dissatisfied or dropped out.[32]

Academic administrators, eager to keep instructional costs down, are now eyeing the Internet and other new technologies. After all, students who take their courses in cyberspace need neither classrooms nor dormitories. Nor will they need many teachers. Distance education promises real economies of scale. Already it lets small institutions pool their resources and offer upper-level courses in subjects like foreign languages that would draw too few students to be offered at a single campus. A single instructor can handle any number of students from a central location and does not necessarily need to do it in "real time." Moreover, once the initial capital investments are made, such a system should begin to turn a profit. Such, at least, is the scenario that is luring many schools to experiment with this new form of instruction, even to the extent of undertaking joint entrepreneurial projects with corporate partners. Whether these digital ventures will actually pay off and how they will affect the shape and function of higher education remain very much open questions. Though it is possible that distance education may in fact make inroads into certain kinds of technical or vocational training, there is no indication that students who have the choice will want to give up the traditional on-campus form of higher education. When the highly touted Internet-based Western Governors' University finally opened for business in 1998, it attracted many fewer students than anticipated.[33]

While support for instruction declines, there is one traditional area of academic endeavor that remains a high priority on most campuses—research. It is, after all, a prestige item for both faculty members and their schools.[34] It is also—or at least is believed to be—an important source of revenue. But that revenue has become much harder to come by. Though the federal government still provides most of the money for academic research, it has become increasingly stingy in many fields. Funding for the physical sciences dropped sharply with the end of the Cold War. Similar cutbacks affected the humanities. Grants from the National Endowment for the Humanities to higher education have declined by 25 percent over the past twenty years. Foundations have also reduced their giving. In the early 1980s, the Guggenheim Foundation offered over 250 fellowships in the humanities; in 1994 it gave about 150. In the social sciences, foundations shifted their attention from academic research to policy planning and pilot programs. Even in fields where cutbacks did not occur, the competition has increased. In palmier days, the National Institutes of Health funded one-third of all grant applications, now it funds one out of ten.[35] Part of the problem, former Stanford president Donald Kennedy explains, stems from the fact that the cost of research has gone up. Most of the easy problems in science have been solved; the remaining ones take time and complicated equipment.[36]

Scientists face additional problems that stem from changes in the way Washington funds their research. Not only is the federal government putting money into different fields—the biological rather than the physical sciences—but it has also changed the way in which it awards grants. In the face of congressional pressure, the National Science Foundation began to abandon the system of peer review. Instead, it now sponsors large projects on specific campuses or in specific localities, a process that not only erodes the ability of the scientific community to set its own research agenda but diminishes the quality of that research.[37] A further threat to the quality of academic science comes from the government's growing demand for accountability and from the requirement that recipients of its aid submit increasing quantities of paperwork. Theoretically justifiable, these demands, coupled with the already large amounts of time that investigators spend on grant applications, actually reduce the productivity of many academic researchers.[38]

The institutions that house those researchers face equally stringent demands for accountability, demands that may have even more serious repercussions, for they are contributing to the growth of academic administrations. By the late 1980s, while the number of students had increased by 10 percent since 1975 and the number of faculty members by 6 percent, the number of administrators had risen 45 percent.[39] There are several explanations for this growth—the expansion of student services, the increasing amount of litigation, the need for new resources. Many administrators, for example, claim that the complicated federal regulations governing everything from the use of human subjects to sexual harassment has forced their institutions to hire specialized personnel just to handle the paperwork.[40] These new administrators differ from their predecessors in more than number. Many of them have had little if any faculty experience. Full-time managers with their own career ladders, networks, and professional associations, they often have little patience with or understanding of the peculiar culture of academe.[41]

Besides growing bigger, academic administrations are also growing meaner. Here the influence of the increasing commercialization of higher education is most obvious. Like most other institutions within American society, colleges and universities are adapting to the growing power and prestige of the corporate sector by absorbing its values and methods of operation and paying more attention to the bottom line. "Can a university be run more like a business?" a UCLA administrator asks. "You bet it can. . . . Most universities can do a significant job of cutting costs through the same re-engineering of processes and work that have characterized the best for-profit corporations."[42] Along with that "re-engineering" comes a more corporate, top-down style of operations, downgrading the collegial governance structures that had once distinguished the academic world. The standard justification is that the university's traditional decision-making procedures are too unwieldy for the dog-eat-dog world out there.[43]

The keyword here is "flexibility," a concept whose corporate provenance is readily apparent. Even administrators savvy enough to avoid head-on collisions with their faculties are transforming their campuses in its name and in the process are reducing those faculties' autonomy and ability to set their schools' intellectual agendas.[44] Thus, for example, the demand for flexibility lets administrators chip away at the procedures of shared governance and the faculty's responsibility for portions of the academic enterprise—like personnel and curriculum—that relate directly to their own teaching and research. A similar demand for flexibility has become a justification for doing away with tenure, with all the ominous implications for academic freedom that such a proposition entails. A more subtle, but perhaps more far-reaching, change is the erosion of the intellectual structure of the academy that occurs when, again invoking the "F word," the university establishes interdisciplinary centers and programs. From the administration's point of view, creating new units that are not under the control of the traditional academic departments is a useful way to circumvent the turf-protective rigidities of older faculty members and to inject the necessary flexibility into the institution's intellectual life.[45]

Interdisciplinary work has, of course, produced many of the most exciting breakthroughs in fields like women's studies and ethnic studies, and it is true that traditional departments and disciplines can sometimes shelter outdated types of knowledge and even impede innovation. What makes the current movement to create interdisciplinary units problematic is that the impetus for it comes from above. These centers and programs are not developing as havens for faculty members who are exploring new lines of inquiry; they have a more entrepreneurial cast. Many have come into existence at the behest of outside funders with a corporate or ideological agenda. Typical of such centers is Lehigh University's Iacocca Institute for Economic Competitiveness, named after and bankrolled by the Chrysler Corporation's then-president. An early mission statement from its advisory board, which contained not a single academic figure, explained that the "Institute, rather than being just a think tank, would act as a catalyst to begin action-oriented programs to strengthen U.S. manufacturing." The growth of such centers has been explosive. In 1982 there were 5,422 of them; in 1993 there were more than thirteen thousand. Some, like George Mason University's Institute of Humane Studies, which gets millions of dollars from tobacco companies, also rake in support from right-wing foundations like Olin and Scaife.[46]

Beside their obvious potential for conflicts of interest, these enterprises further erode the credibility of higher education by giving an academic cachet to what are clearly self-serving ventures. In a more profound sense, however, they also undermine the university's cultural and intellectual authority by weakening the disciplines and departments that form its institutional core. If we consider the creation and transmission of knowledge—once viewed as the university's primary function—to be a communal, rather than an individual, undertaking, the communities of scholarship that have crystallized into the disciplines are its necessary infrastructure. By disrupting or dismantling the departments that house those disciplines, the establishment of independent research centers not only fosters dissension on campus but eats away at the faculty's sense of intellectual community. In addition, whether intentional or not, such actions play into the conservative agenda of destroying the academy's traditional authority.

They also threaten academic freedom—for the disciplines are, as Louis Menand notes, "the linchpins of academic freedom."[47] According to Joan Scott, the "disciplinary community" creates the institutional structure that protects academic freedom. The discipline offers "support for the individual, verifying his or her technical expertise and qualifications," and it allows that individual to speak out. "Academic freedom," she explains, "protects those whose thinking challenges orthodoxy; at the same time the legitimacy of the challenge—the proof that the critic is not a madman or a crank—is secured by membership in a disciplinary community based upon shared commitment to certain methods, standards, and beliefs."[48] Thus, when university administrators respond to market influences and set up interdisciplinary research centers outside the departments for reasons that are extraneous to the scholarly concerns of the faculty, they are directly undermining the intellectual independence of that faculty.

THE UNIVERSITY AS ENTREPRENEUR

But they may not care. After all, their mission is the preservation and perhaps even aggrandizement of their institutions. If, in an age where corporate values predominate, fulfilling that mission seems to require shedding many of the university's traditional functions, so be it. If it requires adopting an authoritarian managerial style, so be it. There is no alternative; such, at least, is the standard wisdom these days. Money is the name of the game. It has always been, of course; academic administrators have always kept their eyes on the bottom line. What has changed is that now, besides adopting corporate modes of operation, they have also entered the market. They still raise money by courting donors and lobbying state legislatures, but they also engage directly in business. So, to be fair, do many of their professors.

After all, quite a few academics are prospering under the new economic regime. In many ways, the corporate restructuring of the university imitates the simultaneous restructuring of American society that is turning it into a three-tiered system, with an overcompensated elite at the top, a shrinking and struggling middle class, and an increasingly impoverished underclass at the bottom. Similar inequalities not only exist between institutions but are becoming increasingly common within them as well. Because universities adjust their salaries to the market, some professors, especially those whose fields are most in demand, often make tens of thousands of dollars more than equally eminent colleagues in less remunerative areas like education or the humanities.[49] This is aside from the money that these academics make when they go into business for themselves, as many in the biological and information sciences have done. Millionaire entrepreneurs on one hand, underpaid adjuncts on the other—such may be the future of academe.

It is a future in which academic institutions become venture capitalists. At many schools, this has already happened. When university administrators began to cast around for new sources of revenue in the 1980s, they began to look more closely at their own faculties. While professors had always been able to make money on the side from consulting or writing textbooks, their schools had never been able to get a "piece of the action." In 1980, however, Congress passed what came to be known as the Bayh-Dole Amendment, a measure that allowed universities to patent the discoveries their scientists made while supported by federal grants. Suddenly, there was money to be made on campus; many schools rushed to cash in on the intellectual property their academic employees had created. Though universities had always claimed ownership of the fruits of their faculty's labors, they had rarely tried to enforce those claims. But now that real income was at stake, many schools became quite assiduous about marketing their faculties' research. Over the course of the 1990s, for example, Columbia University's income from its professors' patents and royalties rose from four million dollars to more than $100 million.[50]

Universities soon found other ways to turn a profit. Schools with winning basketball teams could license their logos to clothing manufacturers. They could also market themselves on the Internet, selling distance education courses directly or, more commonly, finding private companies to do it for them. Some institutions went into partnership with entrepreneurial professors, providing seed money for those professors' spin-off biotech or software ventures. Other schools took advantage of unused land on their campuses to build research parks to house those new enterprises. Other schools all but leased their departments to private companies.[51]

These deals, though questionable in many ways, could bring in real money. To a certain extent, they resembled the earlier connections that had developed between engineers and the so-called military-industrial complex or between plant biologists and agribusinesses. But these ventures were different, not only in their scale but in their focus on broad programs rather than the projects of specific scientists. Most, but not all, of these programs involve pharmaceutical companies creating long-term strategic alliances with individual universities, medical schools, and research institutions. In 1989, the Japanese cosmetics company Shisheido contracted with the dermatology department of the Massachusetts General Hospital for eighty-five million dollars. In 1997, the European drug company Sandoz paid $300 million for a sixteen-year contract with the Scripps Institute. Just recently, the University of California-Berkeley negotiated a deal with the Novartis Agricultural Discovery Institute in which that corporation would fund most of the research of the Plant Biology Department in the School of Natural Resources in return for the first rights to the products of that research.[52]

While these and other corporate-university collaborations do bring considerable advantages to the schools and scientists who participate in them, they have some obvious disadvantages as well. To begin with, because most of the money from private industry goes to the elite research universities, these arrangements tend to reinforce the already great discrepancies between top-tier and lower-tier institutions.[53] A more serious danger is the damage that the commodification of academic research may do to the scientific enterprise itself. Business values are not scholarly ones. Corporations generally operate on shorter time spans than academics; they encourage risk taking, quick decisions, and marketable results. If something does not pay, it is not worth doing.[54] As academics take on that corporate mentality, the way in which they think about their work changes. According to Henry Etzkowitz and Andrew Webster, "the intellectual transformation of the research role of the professor that ensues from the capitalization of knowledge" means "that instead of thinking only in basic research terms they also think in terms of applied research funding and commercializable re-sults." The distinctions between applied and basic research blur. At the same time, scientists, who used to conceive of their work as benefiting society, now talk of paying their own way or providing useful products.[55]

Moreover, as the capitalist mindset entrenches itself, there is a real possibility that universities will allow the market to reorient their priorities, leading them to hire people in fields with commercial applications and sloughing off those in less rewarding ar-eas. They may also decide not to undertake research that, although scientifically valu-able, will not make money. Already, some younger academics find themselves under a double pressure to do work that is not only publishable but profitable.[56] There are other problems as well. Corporate funding is far from secure; if a particular project does not bear fruit or does not do so quickly enough, the company can cancel its contract. Similarly, a corporation can go bankrupt, merge, or simply abandon the line of business in which it had contracted the university to do research.[57]

But the most serious problems come from the private sector's proprietary atti-tude toward intellectual property. That attitude has so transformed the conditions governing the conduct of research that one can imagine a situation in which a sci-entist who has just made a major breakthrough will have to choose between turn-ing that discovery into a Nobel Prize or a $200 million drug company deal. This dilemma stems from the conflict between the corporate world's need to protect its trade secrets and the scientific community's traditional practice of publishing the results of its research. The restrictions that their corporate sponsors impose on the dissemination of their research are causing professional damage to academics at all stages of their careers. Some young scientists have lost chances for tenure or pro-motion because they could not publish the results of their work. Similarly, gradu-ate students who do commercial research are publishing less, and what they do publish is often considerably delayed. Professors find that they cannot discuss their own research with their students or colleagues.[58] At every level, the corporate world's insistence on secrecy undermines the open communication that has been such a crucial component of scientific progress.

The threat that these "gag rules" pose to academic freedom is even more obvious. Researchers whose results undermine their corporate sponsors' business interests are particularly at risk. When a group of scientists at the University of California medical school discovered that the drug they were working on had no advantages over its competitors, the company that was funding their research refused to let them publish their results.[59] The experiences of Nancy Olivieri noted above offer an even more chilling example of the dangers of such corporate censorship. But such crude incursions against academic freedom, while obviously to be regretted, are much less dangerous than the indirect threat posed by the growing commodification of our nation's campuses.

The decline of academic freedom concerns us all. At a time when corporate mergers are rapidly diminishing the available outlets in the media and the publishing world, and the demand for profits dictates a focus on sound bites, celebrities, and best-sellers, it has become increasingly more difficult for serious ideas in any area to reach the public. It has become even harder for serious ideas that challenge the status quo to do so. As what one writer has called our "conceptual commons" shrinks, so too does our ability to envision alternatives to what we already have and understand where we have been.[60] Universities, as among the few—if not perhaps the only—remaining enclaves of serious intellectual activity in our society, have thus become absolutely central to the preservation of free speech in the United States. Because of their traditions of academic freedom and their comparative insulation from the pressures of the marketplace, they offer a protected space where we can still speak, write, and raise uncomfortable, unprofitable, and unorthodox questions. They are also the only institutions that foster the development of critical thought, something that may well be essential for the survival of a free society. "If there is no fundamental criticism," Joan Scott asks, "and no place where it is practiced, taught and perfected, what will be the sources of renewal and change? Without critical thinking, and the conflicts and controversies it articulates, will there be democracy at all?"[61]

As corporate values and business practices suffuse the nation's campuses, we find Scott's question increasingly troubling. In the face of the academy's increasing obsession with the bottom line, will it be possible to preserve the protected space that it still provides to ideas and voices outside the marketplace? Will it be possible to preserve the intellectual diversity that an informed and responsible citizenry requires? I am not sure. I do know, however, that we cannot close our eyes to what is happening. Otherwise, the university is going to be sold right out from under us—and we will not be able to buy it back.

1. "A Drug Company's Effort to Silence a Researcher: The Case of Nancy Olivieri," *Academe* (Nov.–Dec. 1999): 25.

2. Bill Readings, "The University without Culture?" *New Literary History* 26 (Summer 1995): 479.

3. Donald Kennedy, "Making Choices in the Research University," in *The Research University in a Time of Discontent*, ed. Jonathan R. Cole, Elinor G. Barger, and Stephen R. Graubard (Baltimore: Johns Hopkins Univ. Press, 1994), 113.

4. Wesley Shumar, *College for Sale: A Critique of the Commodification of Higher Education* (London: Falmer Press, 1997), 81–82; Francis X. Sutton, "The Distinction and Durability of American Research Universities," in Cole et al., eds., *Research University*, 311–15.

5. David L. Kirp, "The New U," *The Nation*, April 17, 2000, 28.

6. Bill Readings, *The University in Ruins* (Cambridge, Mass.: Harvard Univ. Press, 1996), 12.

7. Frederic Jameson, *Postmodernism, or the Cultural Logic of Late Capitalism* (Durham, N.C.: Duke Univ. Press), 1991; David Harvey, *The Condition of Postmodernity* (Oxford: Blackwell, 1989).

8. Readings, *University in Ruins*, 9.

9. Ibid., 12.

10. Mary Lindenstein Walshok, "Expanding Roles for Research Universities in Regional Economic Development," in *The University's Role in Economic Development: From Research to Outreach*, ed. James P. Pappas (San Francisco: Jossey-Bass, 1997), 17.

11. David F. Labaree, *How to Succeed in School without Really Learning: The Credentials Race in American Education* (New Haven, Conn.: Yale Univ. Press, 1997), 2; Stanley Aronowitz, *The Knowledge Factory: Dismantling the Corporate University and Creating True Higher Learning* (Boston: Beacon Press, 2000), 9–10.

12. David A. Hollinger, "Money and Academic Freedom Fifty Years after the Loyalty Oath: Berkeley and Its Peers amid the Force Fields of Capital," unpublished paper in the possession of the author; Lewis F. Powell, "The Powell Memorandum," Aug. 23, 1971, reprinted in National Chamber of Commerce, *Washington Report Supplement* (n.d.), author's copy, courtesy of David Hollinger.

13. Powell, "The Powell Memorandum," 181.

14. Ellen Messer-Davidow, "Manufacturing the Attack on Liberalized Higher Education," *Social Text* 36 (Fall 1993): 54.

15. Michael Berubé, "Bite Size Theory: Popularizing Academic Criticism," *Social Text* 36 (Fall 1993): 84–97; Joan W. Scott, "Academic Freedom as an Ethical Practice," in *The Future of Academic Freedom*, ed. Louis Menand (Chicago: Univ. of Chicago Press, 1996), 163–80.

16. Mike Wallace, "The Battle of the Enola Gay," in *Hiroshima's Shadow*, ed. Kai Bird and Lawrence Lifschultz (Stony Creek, Conn.: Pamphleteer's Press, 1998), 317–37.

17. Rodney W. Nichols, "Federal Science Policy and the Universities: Consequences of Success," in Cole et al., eds., *Research University*, 285; Donald Kennedy, *Academic Duty* (Cambridge, Mass.: Harvard Univ. Press, 1997), 17, 222–24.

18. Karen Seashore Louis and Melissa S. Anderson, "The Changing Context of Science and University-Industry Relations," in *Capitalizing Knowledge: New Intersections of Industry and Academia*, ed. Henry Etzkowitz, Andrew Webster, and Peter Healey (Albany: State Univ. of New York Press, 1998), 80–81.

19. Paul Lauter, "'Political Correctness' and the Attack on American Colleges," in *Higher Education under Fire*, ed. Michael Berubé and Cary Nelson (New York: Routledge, 1995), 77.

20. Christopher J. Lucas, *Crisis in the Academy: Rethinking Higher Education in America* (New York: St. Martin's Press, 1996), 7; Ernst Benjamin, "A Faculty Response to the Fiscal Crisis: From Defense to Offense," in Berubé and Nelson, eds., *Higher Education under Fire*, 62.

21. Earl Lewis, paper delivered to the Organization of American Historians, April 1998; Stanley

Aronowitz and William DiFazio, *The Jobless Future: Sci-Tech and the Dogma of Work* (Minneapolis: Univ. of Minnesota Press, 1994), 350.

22. Rick Wolff, "Universities and Economic Interest," paper delivered at conference, "Challenging Corporate Control," Yale University, April 17, 1999.

23. Lucas, *Crisis in the Academy*, 12.

24. R. C. Lewontin, "The Cold War and the Transformation of the Academy," in *The Cold War & the University: Toward an Intellectual History of the Postwar Years*, ed. Noam Chomsky et al. (New York: New Press, 1997), 1–34.

25. For an insightful study of the way in which one university restructured itself in response to the challenges and opportunities of the Cold War, see Rebecca S. Lowen, *Creating the Cold War University: The Transformation of Stanford* (Berkeley and Los Angeles: Univ. of California Press, 1997).

26. John H. D'Arms, "Funding Trends in the Academic Humanities, 1970–1995: Reflections on the Stability of the System," in *What's Happened to the Humanities?* ed. Alvin Kernan (Princeton, N.J.: Princeton Univ. Press, 1997).

27. Sheila Slaughter and Larry L. Leslie, *Academic Capitalism: Politics, Policies, and the Entrepreneurial University* (Baltimore and London: Johns Hopkins Univ. Press, 1998), 72–73.

28. For an incisive discussion of the way in which universities marketed themselves during the 1980s, see Michael S. McPherson, Morton Owen Schapiro, and Gordon C. Winston, *Paying the Piper: Productivity, Incentives, and Financing in U.S. Higher Education* (Ann Arbor: Univ. of Michigan Press, 1993).

29. Readings, *University in Ruins*, 11; Zachary Karabell, *What's College For? The Struggle to Define American Higher Education* (New York: Basic Books, 1998), 11–12.

30. McPherson et al., *Paying the Piper*, 105–6; Steven Muller, "Presidential Leadership," in Cole et al., eds., *Research University*, 123–24; Slaughter and Leslie, *Academic Capitalism*, 86.

31. *Academe*, March/April 1999, 14.

32. Slaughter and Leslie, *Academic Capitalism*, 15–16.

33. Dan Carnevale, "Two Models for Collaboration in Distance Education," *Chronicle of Higher Education*, May 19, 2000, A53–55. A recent discussion of the impact of instructional technology on higher education can be found in the September–October 1999 issue of *Academe*.

34. Slaughter and Leslie, *Academic Capitalism*, 17.

35. D'Arms, "Finding Trends," 35–40; Aronowitz and DiFazio, *The Jobless Future*, 340; Francis X. Sutton, "The Distinction and Durability of American Research Universities," in Cole et al., eds., *Research University*, 326.

36. Kennedy, *Academic Duty*, 11.

37. Stephen M. Stigler, "Competition and the Research Universities," in Cole et al., eds., *Research University*, 145–47; Rodney W. Nichols, "Federal Science Policy and the Universities: Consequences of Success," in ibid., 276; Donald Kennedy, *Academic Duty* (Cambridge, Mass.: Harvard Univ. Press, 1997), 154; Slaughter and Leslie, *Academic Capitalism*, 59–60.

38. Walter E. Massey, "Can the Research University Adapt to a Changing Future?" in Cole et al., eds., *Research University*, 196.

39. Ernst Benjamin, "A Faculty Response to the Fiscal Crisis: From Defense to Offense," in Berube and Nelson, eds., *Higher Education under Fire*, 60.

40. Donald Kennedy, "Making Choices in the Research University," in Cole et al., eds., *Research University*, 92–96; Robert M. Rosenzweig, "Governing the Modern University," in ibid., 299–308.

41. Muller, "Presidential Leadership," 123–24.

42. Jan Currie and Lesley Vidovich, "Micro-Economic Reform through Managerialism in American and Australian Universities," in *Universities and Globalization, Critical Perspectives*, ed. Currie and Janice Newson (Thousand Oaks, London, New Delhi: Sage, 1998), 154.

43. Currie and Vidovich, "Micro-Economic Reform through Managerialism," 154–55.

44. Kennedy, *Academic Duty*, 144–46.

45. Readings, *University in Ruins*, 39; Kennedy, "Making Choices," 92–96; Frank H. T. Rhodes, "The Place of Teaching in the Research University," in Cole et al., eds., *Research University*, 188.

46. Lawrence C. Soley, *Leasing the Ivory Tower: The Corporate Takeover of Academia* (Boston: South End Press, 1995), 91–121; Slaughter and Leslie, *Academic Capitalism*, 152–59.

47. Louis Menand, "The Demise of Disciplinary Authority," in Kernan, ed. *What's Happened to the Humanities?* 214.

48. Scott, "Academic Freedom as an Ethical Practice," 166–68.

49. Hollinger, "Money and Academic Freedom"; Slaughter and Leslie, *Academic Capitalism*, 57.

50. Jonathan R. Cole, "Balancing Acts: Dilemmas of Choice Facing Research Universities," in Cole et al., eds., *Research University*, 31; Karen W. Arenson, "Columbia to Put Learning Online for Profit," *New York Times*, April 3, 2000, B3.

51. Henry Etzkowitz and Andrew Webster, "Entrepreneurial Science: The Second Academic Revolution," in *Capitalizing Knowledge: New Intersections of Industry and Academia*, ed. Henry Etzkowitz, Andrew Webster, and Peter Healey (Albany: State Univ. of New York Press, 1998), 28–33.

52. Hollinger, "Money and Academic Freedom"; Etzkowitz and Webster, "Entrepreneurial Science," 30; Andrew Webster, "Strategic Research Alliances: Testing the Collaborative Limits?" in Etzkowitz et al., eds., *Capitalizing Knowledge*, 95–97.

53. Etzkowitz and Webster, "Entrepreneurial Science," 29.

54. Slaughter and Leslie, *Academic Capitalism*, 145, 148.

55. Etzkowitz and Webster, "Entrepreneurial Science," 46; Slaughter and Leslie, *Academic Capitalism*, 21, 179; Cole, "Balancing Acts," 32.

56. Slaughter and Leslie, *Academic Capitalism*, 20

57. Etzkowitz and Webster, "Entrepreneurial Science," 46; Cole, "Balancing Acts," 31; Slaughter and Leslie, *Academic Capitalism*, 194–95.

58. Louis and Anderson, "The Changing Context of Science and University-Industry Relations," 81–84; Slaughter and Leslie, *Academic Capitalism*, 166–67; Etzkowitz and Webster, "Entrepreneurial Science," 14.

59. Kennedy, *Academic Duty*, 177.

60. Seth Shulman, "Education, the Free Market, and Academic Freedom," paper delivered at conference, "Challenging Corporate Control," Yale University, April 17, 1999.

61. Joan W. Scott, "The Rhetoric of Crisis in Higher Education," in Berube and Nelson, eds., *Higher Education under Fire*, 303; Benjamin R. Barber, *Jihad vs. McWorld* (New York: Ballantine, 1996; orig. ed., Times Books, 1995), 276.

What about the First Amendment?
Response to Schrecker

FLORENCE W. DORE

English, Kent State University

Ellen Schrecker argues that the "growing power of the corporate sector within the nation's colleges and universities" currently poses a threat to academic freedom in the United States. The interference of big business in university business has, of course, been an important issue in the history of academic freedom,[1] and Professor Schrecker is quite right to emphasize that it persists today. Indeed, Nike billionaire Phil Knight recently announced that he would not make an intended thirty-million-dollar contribution to the University of Oregon, because the university had decided to join an antisweatshop group, the Worker's Rights Consortium.[2] Professor Schrecker offers a broad critique of the "corporatization" of universities today. She argues that this trend will end in a future where, in her words, "academic institutions *become* venture capitalists" (emphasis supplied).

Professor Schrecker is justifiably concerned that corporate interests and free speech on campus are at odds. Moreover, her impressively wide-ranging economic analysis is primarily an argument about "free speech on campus," as her opening discussion of the Nancy Olivieri case suggests. Indeed, she argues that universities, "as one of the few—if not perhaps the only—remaining enclaves of serious intellectual activity in our society, have . . . become absolutely central to the preservation of free speech in the United States." She worries—rightly, I think—that "corporatization" of the university will quash the "uncomfortable, unprofitable, and unorthodox questions" that mark free speech and vigorous debate in a university setting.

I want to return to the example of Nike, because I think it usefully complicates the picture of free speech on campus that the Olivieri case, considered in isolation, implies. On March 8, 1997, which was International Women's Day, fifty-six women working at a Nike plant in Vietnam were punished for wearing the wrong shoes to work. An interested banker, Thuyen Nguyen, investigated allegations of labor abuses in Nike factories, reporting to *The New York Times* that the women were ordered to run around the factory in the hot sun; many fainted, and twelve collapsed and spent the rest of the day in the emergency room.[3] Nike had reportedly established operations in Vietnam because labor there was "even cheaper than in Indonesia." In November of 1997, Steven Greenhouse of *New York Times* reported that in addition to corporal punishment, Nike's workers in Vietnam are exposed to 177 times more than the local standard of carcinogens, and that 77 percent of them suffer from respiratory problems. Greenhouse also wrote that Nike forces employees to work sixty-hour weeks and that it pays less than the Vietnamese minimum wage.[4]

What does all of this have to do with free speech on U.S. campuses? For the past ten years or so, students on college campuses in the United States have been loudly protesting university business relations with Nike. In 1997, Marion Traub-Werner, for example, then a junior at the University of North Carolina, refused to stop her campaign against Nike's labor abuses when asked by a famous basketball coach to do so. Her group, the "Nike Awareness Committee," dedicated itself to pressing the university, with whom Nike then was doing an eleven-million-dollar business, to start challenging Nike's labor practices abroad.[5] In the spring of 1997, Traub-Werner wrote a paper in a world markets class at UNC on shoe manufacturers in Southeast Asia, with a concentration in Indonesia. She told *New York Times* reporter Harvey Araton that the paper was "scathing."[6] In response to the demands for more accountability by similar student groups at Harvard, Yale, Princeton, Duke, Georgetown, the University of Michigan, and the University of Arizona—in coordination with a broader movement—Nike in October 1999 disclosed the names and sites of its factories.[7]

The Nike story suggests that today, free speech on U.S. campuses is not easily trumped by big business interests. This is in part because U.S. law seeks to prevent this kind of abuse; indeed, it seems to me that any picture of "free speech on campus" today would be somewhat incomplete without a look at the current state of First Amendment on campuses. Professor Schrecker laments the "current movement to create interdisciplinary units"; she argues that interdisciplinary centers mark the "erosion of the intellectual structure of the academy." Professor Schrecker further worries that because of this erosion, far-right think tanks are passing off "politicized" dogma for "real scholarly work." She is surely right to observe this. But I wonder if an interdisciplinary study of academic freedom—interdisciplinary in particular—might not in fact embody the kind of scholarship Professor Schrecker worries is being sacrificed in the name of good business. Legal scholar Robert Post argues that the law tells us something particular about culture: "As the uniquely authorized discourse of the state," occidental law attempts to legitimize its coercive bite through distinctive aspirations toward such values as objectivity, neutrality, and rationality. . . . A fascinating dialectic is thus set in motion, in which our law uses the resources of the larger culture precisely in order to establish its own particular kind of cultural discourse."[8] First Amendment law provides us with a unique opportunity to examine academic freedom as it is taken up in the aim of "objectivity, neutrality, and rationality." It seems to me that this would add something crucial to an understanding of free speech on campus. Indeed, I wonder whether the absence of law from Professor Schrecker's analysis might be an unfortunate omission.

On March 22, 2000, just about a month ago, the Supreme Court ruled—in a unanimous decision—that the University of Wisconsin at Madison could charge all students a fee for "registered student organizations," even if a portion of those fees would go to organizations that individual students opposed ideologically. In the case, *Regents v. Southworth*, the Court argued this: "The First Amendment permits a public university to charge its students an activity fee used to fund a program to facilitate extracurricular student speech, provided that the program is viewpoint neutral."[9] Sponsored by a right-wing organization in Arizona, a group of conservative students at Madison filed a suit arguing that they should not be forced to pay student fees that would go to fund an abortion-rights program, a gay film festival, and a conference sponsored by gay-rights groups. The decision to affirm the university's right to charge the fee is thus an endorsement of what the Court calls "vibrant campus debate" (5), an important aspect, according to the Court, of the university's mission. The Court argued that the requirement hinged on "viewpoint neutrality," the crux of which it defines in *Southworth* thus: "When a university requires its students to pay fees to support the extracurricular speech of other students, all in the interest of open discussion, it may not prefer some viewpoints to others" (5). Thus, the university can charge fees as long as the process by which student groups are allocated funding refuses to discriminate on the basis of "viewpoint." Constitutionally, then, "viewpoint neutrality" makes it legally impermissible to suppress protected speech in a public university setting. The reason for maintaining viewpoint neutrality, according to the Court, is precisely what Professor Schrecker argues: that is, that Universities are special enclaves of free speech. The Court in fact affirms Wisconsin's sense that the "important and substantial purposes of the University" include the requirement "to facilitate a wide range of speech" (5). In a public university setting, indeed, the "state undertakes to stimulate the whole universe of speech and ideas" (1), and the fees are permissible because they are exacted "for the sole purpose of facilitating the free and open exchange of ideas by, and among, its students" (1).

I do not wish to argue that big business does not have the potential to be coercive in an academic context. In fact, I appreciate Ellen Schrecker's drawing our attention to the influence of companies like Nike. Like the students at University of North Carolina, she is implicitly asking us to put pressure on our universities to maintain a value that we cherish. But I do wish to ask Professor Schrecker how the prevailing legal trends that bear on First Amendment protections in public universities square with her claim that "the global expansion of capitalism" is destroying the university. It is not quite accurate to claim that the Olivieri case demonstrates the erosion of free speech on campuses. Rather, as with the hate speech cases of the eighties, it demonstrates the uneasy and sometimes incommensurable relationship between the First Amendment and other discourses of law, in this case contract and intellectual property laws.

I believe that it is important to understand the issue of free speech on campuses—especially in the context of the May 4 shootings—in terms of law. The unconscionable shooting of four unarmed students protesting the war was an egregious violation of not only their right to speak out on campus but of the rule of law itself. There are certainly economic motivations for this kind of violation, but I think Professor Schrecker's analysis—as an analysis of free speech on campus—is too narrow. To imagine that the Olivieri case is an easy one—that is, that her contract should have been simply dismissed, or that intellectual property is irrelevant—is to suggest that law can or should be easily circumvented. In the context of the May 4 tragedy, it is perhaps a truism to point out that the question of legality is often deeply complicated, but I wonder if we might understand the shootings as a blindness to law.

NOTES

1. Walter P. Metzger argues that the "Jacksonian transformation of American society—the decline of aristocratic standards, the liberation of entrepreneurial energies, the conquest of the open continent, the growth of a new business class—made profits and efficiency, the foes of intellectual curiosity, predominant social values." See *Academic Freedom in the Age of the University* (New York: Columbia Univ. Press, 1955), 11. He also points to the end of the nineteenth century as the age of the philanthropist: "In the final decades of the last century, the leaders of American business began to support our universities on a completely unprecedented scale" (139). He observes that "the largest single gift to an American college before the Civil War was Abbott Lawrence's $50,000 to Harvard" (139), and that in these decades, by contrast, Johns Hopkins received $3,300,000, and the University of Chicago received $34,000,000 (from the founder of the Standard Oil Company) (138).

2. Steven Greenhouse, "Nike's Chief Cancels a Gift Over Monitor of Sweatshop," *New York Times*, April 25, 2000. In fact, Knight's contribution had been intended to help pay for the renovation of an athletic stadium, and so we might note that even in this particular case the decision had no real effect on free speech in the academy.

3. Bob Herbert, "Brutality in Vietnam," editorial, *New York Times*, March 28, 1997.

4. Steven Greenhouse, "Nike Shoe Plant in Vietnam Is Called Unsafe for Workers," *New York Times*, Nov. 8, 1997.

5. Harvey Araton, "Athletes Toe the Nike Line, but Students Apply Pressure," *New York Times*, Nov. 22, 1997.

6. Ibid.

7. See Steven Greenhouse, "Nike Identifies Plants Abroad Making Goods for Universities," *New York Times*, Oct. 8, 1999.

8. See Robert C. Post, ed., *Law and the Order of Culture* (Berkeley: Univ. of California Press, 1991), vii–viii.

9. See *Board of Regents of the University of Wisconsin System v. Scott Harold Southworth, et al.* 120 S. Ct. 1346; 2000 LEXIS 2196; 146 L. Ed. 193 (2000), 1. Page numbers in the text refer to Lexis version.

Academic Freedom and the Academic Enterprise
Response to Schrecker

Mark A. Graber

Political Science, University of Maryland

Professor Ellen Schrecker documents two threats to academic freedom in her wonderful essay. The narrower threat is that professors may be sued and fired for publishing research findings in violation of contractual agreements not to publish those findings. The more serious threat is that professors are making contractual agreements not to publish. The first threat may or may not raise questions concerning academic freedom and free speech; the second clearly raises questions concerning academic integrity and the academic enterprise. These threats should be distinguished. Intellectual tools fashioned to combat political attacks on academic freedom may prove too blunt when fighting corporate attacks on academic integrity. Professor Schrecker's paper suggests that universities are rapidly becoming places where persons engaged in traditional academic enterprises are no longer valued, not just places where persons engaged in traditional academic enterprises risk sanctions. Her observations suggest the need to revisit and renew scholarly commitments to the distinctive academic purposes that provide the best foundations for academic freedom and free speech.

That courts or universities might enforce contracts not to publish is not, standing alone, a serious threat to academic freedom or free speech. A central element of freedom has always been the right to make contracts. Abraham Lincoln and fellow antebellum Republicans championed a free-labor ideology that regarded the right to make contracts as the central right of free persons.[1] The Civil Rights Act of 1866 declared that all persons "shall have the same right . . . to make and enforce contracts . . . as is enjoyed by white persons."[2] Scholars have the same right to make contracts as other persons. Persons who make contracts with scholars presumably have the same right as other persons to have those contracts enforced.

Contracts not to publish seem judicially enforceable. Persons who obtain lucrative grants in return for agreements not to publish certain findings can hardly complain of the "gross disparity in the values exchanged" that typically characterize unconscionable contracts (but which are not sufficient to make them unconscionable).[3]

A promise not to publish research findings adverse to the organization sponsoring the research is not an agreement "unreasonably in restraint of trade."[4] Certainly, governmental restraints on publication as a condition of public employment or federal largess are problematic under a free speech analysis.[5] Still, business agreements not to publish ought to be analyzed as other business agreements, not as matters relevant to the First Amendment, the freedom of speech, or academic freedom.

The problem with contracts not to publish is that they are business arrangements, not academic arrangements. Academics are expected to pursue truth, not the interests of outside organizations. As Professor Schrecker meticulously details elsewhere, the central claim for barring communists from the academy was that "academics 'have special obligations' that 'involve questions of intellectual honesty and integrity.'" "Communism," university administrators insisted, "because of its demand for uncritical acceptance of the Party's line," interferes with that quest for truth "'which is the first obligation and duty of the teacher.'"[6] Whether the academics dismissed during the 1950s lacked such academic integrity is very, very doubtful. Academics who sign contracts not to publish findings adverse to their business sponsors openly confess an "uncritical acceptance of [a p]arty line" that "interferes with th[e] quest for truth." Conventional academic norms suggest that such persons should be fired, not protected. Yet, in sharp contrast to university behavior during the McCarthy years, academic administrators now encourage faculty to reach the very same understandings with corporations that faculty were fired for when allegedly established with left-wing organizations.

That many university administrators encourage faculty agreements not to publish suggests fundamental changes in the academic universe since the McCarthy era. During the 1940s and 1950s, academic freedom was denied in the name of academic integrity and the academic enterprise. Such anticommunists as Sidney Hook maintained that communists should not be allowed to teach high school or college students, because communists lacked the commitment to the open engagé of ideas that was the essence of democratic education.[7] Contemporary academic controversies over the corporate presence on campus cannot be similarly characterized as disputes over the implementation of a common notion of the academic enterprise. University administrators who encourage the existence of departments and programs that are extensions of private businesses, pressure faculty and graduate students to seek funding that may limit their capacity to publish research findings, and agree for a price to place corporate logos on the most visible places on campus make no pretension that these activities will directly promote intellectual diversity or any other goal traditionally associated with academic freedom or free speech. Rather, the mantra of the MBAS and MBA "wannabees" that play an increasingly dominant role on many campuses is that "'a university [can] be run more like a business.'" "Higher education," Professor Schrecker notes, "now aims to become an engine of regional economic growth."

Professor Schrecker details the numerous ways the traditional academic enterprise is subverted when the university enters the marketplace and understands its mission as fostering "economic development." The quality of teaching and intellectual exchange in the classroom is diminished, as tenured or tenure-track professors are replaced by adjuncts and by classes over the Internet. Humanistic concerns once central to a liberal education are shortchanged as university priorities shift to subjects where more lucrative outside funding is available. Corporations willing to fund particular academic enterprises gain more influence over university direction than faculty. Traditional publication norms are replaced by a business need for secrecy in the development of new product lines.

These developments suggest that "the university has lost its mission," but they do not "threaten academic freedom" in a traditional sense. An institution in which alleged communists are not permitted to chair departments[8] is very different from an institution that might give carte blanche to a scholar who obtained a seven-figure grant from the Communist Party. Tenured faculty and students at the dawn of the twenty-first century are freer to speak their minds in and out of the classroom than they were during the 1950s. The fundamental threat to the freedom of expression inside and outside of the academy is not that purveyors of unorthodox ideas will not have the right to speak but they will not have the resources necessary to make themselves heard.[9] Academic freedom was threatened during the McCarthy era because faculty risked serious harm when they advocated certain ideas. Academic integrity is at stake at present because faculty are increasingly being rewarded for reasons having little to do with the quest for truth. An important analytic difference exists between threats and offers,[10] even when the line between the two is fuzzy and when the academic reward system has a substantial impact on intellectual life.

The claim that the academy must be more like a business threatens academic freedom more subtly, by weakening the special status of intellectual life and exchange in our political regime. The freedom of speech, the First Amendment, and academic freedom in their contemporary guises are rooted in beliefs that certain expressive activities are so intrinsically valuable to human beings that they should not be regulated in the same manner or for the same reasons as for-profit behavior. The Constitution of the United States recognizes the preferred position of speech in public life. Congress may not abridge the freedom of speech, but it has the power to regulate interstate commerce, a category that now includes all commerce.[11] Citizens in the present constitutional order may choose to discourage more production of butter in order to produce more guns; they may not choose to discourage more production of ideas or any particular idea in order to get more guns or butter.

Government may affirmatively encourage certain ideas, though not certain religious ideas. Speech, however, is a distinctively good constitutional activity that may not be regulated, unless perhaps a particular urgent need exists. Implicit in this ordering of values is the constitutional judgment that human beings flourish more when they engage in public discourse than when they pursue commercial enterprises.

The corporatization of the academy dilutes this rationale for academic freedom by extending protection for uninhibited searches for truth to essentially commercial behavior. This trend is already taking place in much constitutional law. Prof. Mark Tushnet notes that over the past twenty years the Supreme Court has interpreted the First Amendment as providing far more protection to corporate activities than to political dissenters.[12] American businesses able to co-opt university facilities are likely to be able to use these decisions to provide constitutional protection for many of their for-profit activities. Ideas and public discourse will become indistinguishable from other goods markets made available according to supply and demand.

The reconceptualization of the university as a commercial venture also undermines the foundations for academic freedom. The traditional academy was unregulated, because its purposes were thought different and constitutionally higher than ordinary businesses. When the point of the academic enterprise becomes to produce more guns and butter, and the means for achieving those ends are increasingly the means preferred by private businesses, then no good reason exists why the academic enterprise should be less subject to government regulation than any other business enterprise aimed at producing more guns and butter. If government officials believe a highly regulated academy will better foster regional economic growth, constitutional values suggest that the academy ought to be heavily regulated. This is not to say that academic life *should* be heavily regulated, or regulated at all. Good reasons exist for not regulating business enterprises. Society may be better off when Du Pont forms alliances with college chemistry departments. When analyzing such alliances, however, we should think in terms of the conditions under which it is business, not speech, that is regulated.

Such developments may be cheered by faculty whose interests are not *immediately* threatened,[13] and they may be promoted by the demise of traditional academic norms. The MBAS and MBA "wannabees" in academic administration did not conduct a stealth march or overwhelm a united faculty. Professors are as attracted by the lure of the market as administrators are. Celebrity academics want to drive the same cars, live in the same houses, send their children to the same private schools, and generally enjoy the same lifestyles as do more affluent doctors, lawyers, and business entrepreneurs (and do so without sacrificing the distinctive benefits of academic life). Oblivious to the gross disparities in pay between academics and secretaries at most universities, faculty claiming to be impoverished frequently support endeavors that promise to make the university more like a business. When professors are willing to sacrifice some traditional academic under-standings for the market, should we expect the general public to be more resistant? We have met the enemy, Pogo points out, and they are us.

NOTES

1. Eric Foner, *Free Soil, Free Labor, Free Men: The Ideology of the Republican Party before the Civil War* (New York: Oxford Univ. Press, 1970).

2. *Restatement of the Law: Second: Contracts 2d*, vol. 1 (St. Paul, Minn.: American Law Institute, 1981), 108.

3. Ibid.

4. *Restatement of the Law: Second: Contracts 2d*, vol. 2 (St. Paul, Minn.: American Law Institute, 1981), 37.

5. See *Snepp v. United States*, 444 U.S. 507, 516–23 (1980) (Stevens, J., dissenting).

6. Ellen W. Schrecker, *No Ivory Tower: McCarthyism and the Universities* (New York: Oxford Univ. Press, 1986), 103 (quoting Pres. Raymond B. Allen of the University of Washington).

7. Ibid., 105–12. See Mark A. Graber, "Old Wine in New Bottles: The Constitutional Status of Un-constitutional Speech," *Vanderbilt Law Review* 48 (1995): 369–71 (noting that during the Cold War the leading opponents of free speech rights for communists relied on the same democratic premises as the leading *proponents* of free speech rights for communists).

8. See *Ollman v. Evans*, 750 F.2d 970 (D.C. 1984).

9. See Mark A. Graber, *Transforming Free Speech: The Ambiguous Legacy of Civil Libertarianism* (Berkeley: Univ. of California Press, 1991), 184–233.

10. See, e.g., Robert Nozick, "Coercion," in *Philosophy, Science, and Method*, ed. Sidney Morgenbesser, Patrick Suppes, and Morton White (New York: St. Martin's Press, 1969).

11. See, e.g., *Wickard v. Filburn*, 317 U.S. 111 (1942).

12. Mark Tushnet, *Taking the Constitution Away from the Courts* (Princeton, N.J.: Princeton Univ. Press, 1999), 129–33. See, e.g., *First National Bank of Boston v. Bellotti*, 435 U.S. 765 (1978); *Central Hudson Gas v. Public Service Comm'n*, 447 U.S. 557 (1980).

13. In the long run, the corporatization of the academy is likely to threaten academics who are doing well under the present regime. If adjuncts can be used to teach some courses, why bother having expensive professors teach *any* courses?

Siblings Not Twins
Academic Freedom and Free Expression
Response to the Discussants

Ellen Schrecker

The value of getting comments from such perceptive and thoughtful critics as Florence Dore and Mark Graber is that it forces me to confront my underlying assumptions and to refine some of my fuzzier conceptualizations. In particular, it forces me to make a clearer distinction between academic freedom and free speech. The two are related, but they are by no means the same.

As Dore correctly points out, I am using academic freedom in a "narrow" sense (though whether it may be "too narrow" I leave up to my readers). Academic freedom, at least as I understand it, ensures the ability of professors to carry out their research and to express themselves in the classroom or in a public forum without fearing retaliation from the institutions that employ them.[1] This protection, enshrined in the key American Association of University Professors (AAUP) "1940 Statement of Principles on Academic Freedom and Tenure," is both broader and narrower than that provided by the First Amendment, which guarantees an individual's freedom of speech against reprisals by the state but not against those by private employers. Moreover, because the First Amendment, as the courts have interpreted it, privileges political speech, it does not necessarily extend to such things as the ability of a professor to criticize his or her university's administration without getting fired—as Bennington College philosopher Carlin Romano was right in the middle of the spring semester of 2000.[2]

Nonetheless, academic freedom certainly falls within the same universe of discourse as classic freedom of speech, in the sense that academic freedom is protecting an important space for the exercise of free speech. It is, I would argue, a subset of the rights that constitute freedom of expression and has been recognized as such for many years. In a 1967 decision invalidating New York State's McCarthy-era loyalty program for teachers, the Supreme Court explained that academic freedom "is of transcendent value to all of us and not merely to the teachers concerned" and "is therefore a special concern of the First Amendment."[3] In that decision, the Court was simply acknowledging the significant benefits that the unfettered pursuit of scholarship and learning provides to the rest of society. For that reason, campuses, the Court seemed to be saying, must serve as sanctuaries for free expression.

Few people disagree with that finding. To the extent that the traditional form of academic freedom does partake of the protections guaranteed under the First Amendment for political speech, it seems clear, as both Dore and Graber point out, it is not currently under attack. There is a lot of free speech on American campuses. A professor will not lose his or her job these days for advocating unpopular or even repugnant political ideas. Though uniformly banned during the early Cold War, communists, if there are any left at the moment, could probably teach without interference at most American colleges and universities. The courts today are pretty good about maintaining such protections.

But, unlike Florence Dore, I would be hesitant to rely on the U.S. legal system as the sole protector of academic freedom. This is not to say that I would want to scrap the existing legal and constitutional barriers against interfering with the professoriate's right to speak out and pursue its research. Nor am I anything but pleased about the Supreme Court's invocation of the university's educational mission and its endorsement of intellectual diversity in its recent *Southworth* decision, with regard to the University of Wisconsin's student fees.[4] Nonetheless, a primarily legalistic appraisal of the nature of academic freedom seems somewhat out of touch with realities of American political culture.

In his contribution elsewhere in this volume, Gerald N. Rosenberg argues that "the current legalistic understandings of freedom of speech in the United States make democratic deliberation about the appropriate limits of freedom of expression difficult to sustain. They may also fail to serve underlying democratic interests." Having spent the past twenty years studying the anticommunist political repression of the early Cold War and its impact on the academic community, I can only agree with Rosenberg's pessimism about the rule of law. Throughout the McCarthy era, the American judiciary up to and including the Supreme Court condoned the most serious violations of the First Amendment. In the name of national security, the courts looked the other way as thousands of people were imprisoned, deported, and dismissed for their political views and associations. The nation's colleges and universities collaborated with that political repression, firing over a hundred professors and creating an atmosphere that severely circumscribed the political freedom of the rest of the academic community. Not until McCarthyism petered out for other reasons did American judges begin to resuscitate the First Amendment.[5] Though a repeat of that grim era's violations of civil liberties is not in the works at the moment (unless, of course, you are a young black man), the history of the past half-century makes it hard to share Dore's belief that the system works.

Mark Graber's analysis of the prospects for academic freedom accords more closely with my own. I can, in fact, only echo his assessment: "The fundamental threat to the freedom of expression inside and outside of the academy is not that purveyors of unorthodoxy will not have the right to speak but they will not have the resources necessary to make themselves heard." Protecting academic freedom, as I think he envisions it, is not therefore a legal problem but a political and ideological one. It is not a question of whether someone's utterances are or are not limited by the state, or even whether the right to free expression can be abridged by enforcement of a contract. Rather, the issue becomes one of whether, given the recent structural and cultural changes within American society, and within the university, that have granted such an increasingly powerful voice to the market, the traditional academic practices that encourage intellectual diversity and critical thought can survive.

Litigation will not protect those traditional ways of thinking, for the challenges to them are systemic, the product of the reallocation of political and cultural power that the global expansion of capitalism has encouraged. While necessary for the maintenance of an informed citizenry in a democratic society, they are not necessary for participation in an increasingly privatized world of consumption and technical expertise. As Cass Sunstein argues in another venue, the system of freedom of expression requires that people have enough information and opportunity to make reasoned choices.[6] The academy is a crucial part of that system, for it has been, along with the media, the nation's main source of the information and opportunity that responsible citizens require. But, as the pursuit of profit replaces the pursuit of truth within American higher education, the academic community's ability to supply the prerequisites for an enlightened public debate is seriously endangered. The nation's legal system is not going to restore the traditional values of academe. As Mark Graber so wisely notes, we must do so ourselves.

NOTES

1. American Association of University Professors, "1940 Statement of Principles on Academic Freedom and Tenure," in *Policy Documents & Reports* (Washington: American Association of University Professors, 1995), 3.

2. Robin Wilson, "Bennington President Fires a Professor Who Criticized Her Fiercely and Openly," *Chronicle of Higher Education*, April 28, 2000, A20.

3. *Keyishian v. Board of Regents* 385 U.S. 589 (1967).

4. *Board of Regents of the University of Wisconsin System v. Scott Harold Southworth, et al.* 120 S. Ct. 1346 (2000).

5. For a more detailed discussion of the violations of free speech and academic freedom during the McCarthy era, see Ellen Schrecker, *No Ivory Tower: McCarthyism and the Universities* (New York: Oxford Univ. Press, 1986), and *Many Are the Crimes: McCarthyism in America* (Boston: Little, Brown, 1998).

6. Cass R. Sunstein, "Academic Freedom and Law: Liberalism, Speech Codes, and Related Problems," in *The Future of Academic Freedom*, ed. Louis Menand (Chicago: Univ. of Chicago Press, 1996), 114.

9

Student Academic Freedom
An Oxymoron?

KATHERYN KATZ

Albany Law School, Union University

Colleges no more exist for students than armies exist for soldiers.

—James R. Kreutzer (1967)

Academic institutions exist for the transmission of knowledge, the pursuit
of truth, the development of students and the general well-being of society.

—Joint Statement on Rights and Freedoms of Students (1990)

INTRODUCTION

I recently chatted with a judge who had graduated from law school some thirty-five
years ago. "I'll tell you," he said, "what students' academic freedom was in my day:
'Sit here. Learn this.'" Has the law moved beyond what was a common stance thirty-
five or forty years ago to a recognition that students, too, are entitled to some measure of academic freedom? If so, of what does that freedom consist, and what are
its limits? How do we balance students' rights against faculty and institutional needs
or even those of other students?

Academic freedom as a concept originated (and now has an existence) apart
from the First Amendment's protection of expression and association.[1] Nevertheless, the Supreme Court has identified academic freedom as a particular concern of
the First Amendment and has incorporated it (to an unclear degree) within that
amendment.[2] Even though there is continued disagreement over whether academic
freedom is a separate constitutional right or merely a restatement of a general expressive norm in a particular setting, the academic freedom of educators and institutions is firmly embedded in First Amendment jurisprudence.[3] The expressive

rights of faculty members have been extensively litigated and studied. By the same token, the academic freedom of colleges and universities—more particularly, their interests in institutional autonomy—has received a great deal of deferential attention.[4] Notions of student academic freedom have had a more limited development. Perhaps because many of those writing and thinking about the subject are themselves faculty members, because faculty members have personal stakes in the outcome of controversies regarding their roles as professor, and because educational institutions have an important interest in self-governance, free from political pressure, the majority of the scholarly commentary and litigation regarding academic freedom does not directly involve students. In what little litigation there is concerning students' rights, the landmark cases involve high school rather than college students and address more general First Amendment protections of expressive rights, albeit in an educational setting.

Despite the paucity of precedent, let us explore the dimensions of academic freedom for students as it has been recognized by the courts. Many of the controversies involving students may be resolved by First Amendment principles, independent of claims of encroachment on the students' academic freedom. Faculty and students are on the same side in some controversies, but I am particularly interested in instances in which student expression of ideas clashes with both faculty and institutional interests. Although there is the occasional case in which university students object to curricular content,[5] contemporary conflicts most often center on censorship of the student press and the imposition of mandatory student fees that are used to support viewpoints and activities that are anathema to particular students.

THE MEANING OF ACADEMIC FREEDOM

The meaning of "academic freedom" depends to some extent on its source. One definition is derived from scholars' notions of the necessary conditions for the acquisition of knowledge, particularly the need for unfettered inquiry in research, publication, and teaching. The other definition exists as a special subset, or at least concern, of First Amendment jurisprudence.

The Scholar's Concept of Academic Freedom

The scholar's concept of academic freedom predates the Constitution.[6] Today, educational institutions and members of the academic community rely on the American Association of College and University Professors (AAUP) "Statement of Principles on Academic Freedom and Tenure" (1940).[7] This statement is prefaced by a declaration that "academic freedom in its teaching aspect is fundamental for the protection of the rights of the teacher in teaching and of the student to freedom in learning."[8] Nevertheless, the statement itself does not mention students. Instead, it recognizes a teacher's freedoms in research, the publication of results, and in the classroom, and the teacher's freedom from institutional censorship or discipline based on extramural speech.[9] The AAUP also mentions students in the foreword to its *Recommended Institutional Regulations on Academic Freedom and Tenure,* quoting the Supreme Court: "Teachers and students must always remain free to inquire, to study and to evaluate, to gain new maturity and understanding; otherwise our civilization will stagnate and die."[10] Despite this language, the *Recommended Regulations* do not specifically address the meaning of students' freedom in learning.

Arguably, students' "freedom of learning" is entirely derived from the teacher's freedom in teaching. In 1967, however, the AAUP issued a *Joint Statement on Rights and Freedoms of Students.*[11] The new statement was intended to set forth "essential provisions for student freedom to learn."[12] Classroom protections included freedom of discussion, expression, and inquiry. In student affairs, the enumerated freedoms included freedom of association, freedom of expression and inquiry, and student participation in institutional governance. Student press and student publications, it declared, "should be free of censorship and advance approval of copy,"[13] and student editors and managers "should be protected from arbitrary suspension or removal because of student, faculty, administrative or public disapproval of editorial policy or content."[14] The statement also addresses students' off-campus rights. Students' rights as citizens "include the same rights of freedom of speech, petition and assembly as are enjoyed by other citizens,"[15] but as "members of the academic community they are subject to the obligations which accrue to them as members of this community." The statement also sets forth procedural safeguards in disciplinary proceedings.[16] The statement is quite detailed; nevertheless, it might as well not exist, for all the attention it has received in scholarly and judicial inquiries into the scope of students' rights.

Academic Freedom and the First Amendment

The extent to which academic freedom enjoys constitutional status is found in the Supreme Court's First Amendment jurisprudence. Although the modern concept of academic freedom arose from threats from university trustees and administrators to professors' scholarly independence,[17] Supreme Court protection of academic freedom grew out of threats from the state.[18] Supreme Court opinions reveal a history of eloquent rhetoric in support of academic freedom in the relatively rare instances in which the government has sought to punish a professor's unorthodox views.[19] This much is clear. The Supreme Court recognizes academic freedom as a special concern of the First Amendment's guarantee of free speech even if academic freedom is not a constitutionally protected right.[20] Academic freedom, however, is both broader and narrower than the First Amendment's protection of free expression. Academic freedom is broader because it is protected by doctrines and sanctions in addition to those available for constitutional violations.[21] At the same time, academic freedom is narrower in scope because academic freedom is limited to educational settings.[22]

When considering the interplay between the First Amendment and principles of academic freedom, several caveats are in order. The first is that the acts of officials at private colleges and universities are not limited by the First Amendment, which forbids only government censorship.[23] Private institutions' dedication to academic freedom, contract law governing student enrollment,[24] and the sanctions of the AAUP offer the only protections against their censorship of student and faculty speech and association, unless state law imposes constitutional norms on private colleges and universities.[25] Fortunately, most private schools, if only for competitive reasons, do recognize and respect academic freedom. In fact, private institutions do not usually suffer the attentions of politicians who, on occasion, seek to intervene in academic matters at public institutions. A recent example of such politicians includes Wyoming legislators who have sought to close a law school because Professor Deborah Donahue published a book suggesting that the federal Bureau of Land Management terminate grazing on much of the land on which it is now permitted;[26] another is the Arizona legislature's effort to limit sites that public university students and faculty may visit on the Internet.[27]

In turn, the fact that academic freedom necessarily involves educational institutions means that powerful countervailing interests are present. Institutional (and societal) concerns often outweigh students' or faculty members' interest in a particular expressive activity. This reality is exemplified by Justice Felix Frankfurter's identification of "four essential freedoms" of a university: "to determine for itself on academic grounds who may teach, what may be taught, how it shall be taught, and who may be admitted to study."[28] It is evident that these "essential freedoms" are institutional and not individual concerns.[29] By the same token, Justice William Brennan spoke of our nation's deep commitment to protecting academic freedom, "which is of transcendent value to all of us and not just to the teachers concerned."[30] Justice Brennan further stated: "The nation's future depends upon leaders trained through wide exposure to that robust exchange of ideas which discovers truth 'out of a multitude of tongues,' [rather] than any kind of authoritative selection."[31]

Furthermore, the fact that education is at the heart of academic freedom means that the educational setting may at times limit students' freedom in learning. As we will see, the Supreme Court's First Amendment jurisprudence allows the educational institution to limit students' liberties in ways and to a degree that would be unconstitutional in other settings. The Supreme Court has consistently reaffirmed the right of the public universities to "make academic judgments as to how best to allocate scarce resources"[32] and to "exclude even First Amendment activities that violate reasonable campus rules or substantially interfere with the opportunity of other students to obtain an education."[33] Nevertheless, the academic freedom of educators and institutions does not bar students from challenging the policies, activities, or curriculum as violative of constitutional guarantees, although academic freedom may provide or at least strengthen the defense to these claims.[34]

The final caveat is that this discussion of Supreme Court decisions regarding student academic freedom is highly selective. I focus only on the decisions in which students' expressive rights are explicitly at issue. Even as to these cases, I do not discuss other constitutional principles and theories that may have played a part in the result. I believe the brief review that follows demonstrates that the Court employs, as it does in its decisions involving faculty speech,[35] sweeping rhetoric that when applied to concrete cases may turn out to be just that—rhetoric. Nevertheless, recent decisions establish that there is a special realm of freedom of learning on university campuses—that is, the sphere of extracurricular activities. There, students' educational experiences are enhanced by opportunities for advocacy and debate on many and diverse issues chosen by the students, for participation in the governance of the university and for developing administrative and social skills.

THE SUPREME COURT AND STUDENT ACADEMIC FREEDOM, 1942–1988

In 1943, in *West Va. State Board of Education v. Barnette*,[36] the Supreme Court first established that even local boards of education are not beyond the reach of the First Amendment. In that case, Jehovah's Witnesses sought an exemption from the duty of teachers and students to salute the flag and recite the Pledge of Allegiance.[37] Although the protestors grounded their argument in their rights to free exercise of religion and to freedom of expression, Justice Jackson, writing for the majority, questioned whether such a duty may be imposed on any individual and stated that the issue did not depend on the individual's particular religious beliefs or the sincerity with which they are held.[38] Justice Jackson concluded that the mandate transcended constitutional limitations on the board's power and invaded the "sphere of intellect and spirit which the First Amendment reserve[s] from official control."[39] Boards of education have "important, delicate, and highly discretionary functions,"[40] but "that they are educating the young for citizenship is reason for scrupulous protection of Constitutional freedom for the individual if we are not to strangle the free mind at its source and teach youth to discount important principles of government as mere platitudes."[41]

Although not thought of as an academic freedom case at the time, *Barnette* made clear that the First Amendment sets limits upon the power of school officials, at least where education is compulsory, and that even young students do not have to conform to every school mandate. The more generalized effect of the *Barnette* decision has been to establish a right of conscience and belief that limits the government's power to compel uniformity of sentiment from any citizen.

The issue of students' constitutional rights is usually considered to have first arisen with *Tinker v. Des Moines*, a decision involving the expressive rights of junior high and high school students. Stating that students do not "shed their constitutional rights to freedom of speech or expression at the schoolhouse gate,"[42] the Supreme Court held that students in junior high and high school could not be suspended for wearing black armbands to show their objections to the hostilities in Vietnam, since there was no actual or potential disruption of the "requirement of appropriate discipline in the operation of the school."[43] The only mention of academic freedom, however, is in a footnote reference to a law review note entitled "Academic Freedom."[44]

Ironically, the Supreme Court first explicitly recognized university student academic freedom against a backdrop of "the widespread civil disobedience on some campuses, accompanied by the seizure of buildings, vandalism, and arson."[45] In fact, students had shut down some colleges altogether, "while at others files were looted and manuscripts destroyed."[46] The Court itself noted, "Although the causes of campus disruption were many and complex, one of the prime consequences of such activities was the denial of the lawful exercise of First Amendment rights to the majority of students by the few."[47]

Nevertheless, building on *Tinker*, a later case, *Healy v. James*, held that the president of Central Connecticut State College could not deny campus recognition to a local organization of Students for a Democratic Society (SDS) based on his view, in part, that approval should be withheld from "any group that 'openly repudiate[d]' the College's dedication to academic freedom," as he believed SDS did.[48] In affirming the students' right to associate to further their personal beliefs, Justice Lewis Powell restated language from *Tinker*: "State colleges and universities are not enclaves immune from the sweep of the First Amendment."[49] Further, Justice Powell anchored the application of the First Amendment in campus settings to academic freedom, stating that "the college classroom with its surrounding environs is peculiarly the 'marketplace of ideas' and we break no new constitutional ground in reaffirming this Nation's dedication to safeguarding academic freedom."[50] Nevertheless, the *Healy* Court reiterated *Tinker*'s recognition of the right of campus authorities to prohibit actions "which materially and substantially disrupt the work and discipline of the school."[51] Accordingly, the case was remanded for further proceedings to determine whether SDS would agree to abide by university regulations regarding campus conduct.

In *Papish v. Board of Curators of the University of Missouri*,[52] the Supreme Court expanded *Tinker* and *Healy*. The university had expelled a graduate student for distributing an underground newspaper containing "indecent speech" consisting of a political cartoon depicting policemen raping the Statute of Liberty and the Goddess of Justice, in addition to an article entitled "M—— F—— Acquitted."[53] The lower court held that "on a university campus 'freedom of expression' could properly be subordinated to other interests such as conventions of decency in the use and display of language and pictures."[54] The Supreme Court, however, held that neither the political cartoon nor the headline story could be deemed as constitutionally obscene or otherwise unprotected.[55] Furthermore, the Court stated that "*Healy* makes clear that mere dissemination of ideas—no matter how offensive to good taste—on a state University campus may not be shut in the name of conventions of decency."[56]

Read together *Tinker*, *Healy*, and *Papish* fashion a right to some measure of academic (and political) freedom for students, at least outside the classroom.[57] The Supreme Court, however, has made manifest that the academic judgments of the faculty and the educational institution are not to be second-guessed by the courts. In *Board of Curators of the University of Missouri v. Horowitz*[58] and *Regents of University of Michigan v. Ewing*,[59] two decisions involving dismissal from medical school for academic failings, the Court used notions of comparative institutional competence in denying the students a remedy: "Adding to our concern for lack of standards (there are none obviously provided by the Constitution or elsewhere according to which judges or juries can say what norms of academic competence are suitable or unsuitable for any university as such) is a reluctance to trench on the prerogatives of educational institutions and our responsibility to safeguard their academic freedom."[60]

Unfortunately for university students (and college professors), the Supreme Court also decided two cases restricting the expressive rights of high school students that have since been extended to postsecondary students and faculty members by the lower courts. *Bethel v. Fraser*[61] held that a student could be punished for giving speech containing sexual innuendo at a school assembly, even though the evidence at trial did not "show that the speech had materially disruptive effect on the educational process."[62] The Court relied on the school's authority to prohibit "unanticipated conduct disruptive of the educational process,"[63] a reliance that is misplaced, given that it is entirely speculative under the facts of the case. The Court distinguished the speech from the wearing of armbands in *Tinker* by characterizing it as "unrelated to any political viewpoint," a characterization that is fraught with peril for the expressive rights of students and teachers.

Certainly, given that high school students are compelled to attend school, are presumed to be immature, and that the *Bethel* Court recognized that First Amendment rights of students in the public schools "are not automatically coextensive with the rights of adults in other settings,"[64] the Court's ruling is explicable. Its language that the "school need not tolerate student speech that is inconsistent with its basic educational mission," however, been transposed to litigation involving professors' classroom speech. Lower courts have also read *Bethel* as announcing a general rule that "indecent language and profanity" may be regulated in colleges as well as high schools and that the rule applies to teachers as well as students. Accordingly, the Court of Appeals for the Fifth Circuit upheld the discharge of a college teacher for swearing at his class in an effort to motivate them.[65] The court found it unnecessary to reach his academic freedom claim, since it viewed his speech as not germane to the subject matter of his class and as having no educational function.[66]

The 1988 decision *Hazelwood v. Kuhlmeier*[67] held that school officials may exercise prior restraint in their editorial control over the contents of a high school newspaper produced as part of the school's journalism curriculum. Again, there was no evidence that the principal could have reasonably predicted that the censored articles "would have materially disrupted classwork or given rise to substantial disorder in the school."[68] Nevertheless, the Court gave great deference to educational institutions' control of the curriculum and their right to decide what speech is considered not suitable for immature audiences. Although the Court stated that it was not addressing what deference is appropriate with respect to school-sponsored activities in a postsecondary educational setting,[69] like *Bethel*, this ruling has since been extended to the activities of university students. Some courts have held that to be protected, student speech must be nondisruptive, nonobscene, and not school sponsored.

The student press is a chronic source of tension between university control and student intellectual freedom. If *Hazelwood* is extended to the university student press, it will have wide repercussions for students' expressive rights. Censorship of the student press takes a variety of forms. Cutting funds for student presses, or eliminating them entirely, is a common tactic. Confiscation of offending articles is another. The student editors may be required to submit articles for approval before theirs papers are printed or distributed—a classic example of prior restraint.[70] The administration may seek to control the content of advertisement in the campus newspaper.[71] On occasion, administration or faculty members may strike directly at the editor by such means as firing, refusing to renew work-study funds, or in some cases, by suspension or expulsion.[72]

Moreover, administrators are not the only ones who seek to control, or at least limit, student newspapers or yearbooks. There have been instances in which members of student governments have been displeased with student newspapers' coverage of their activities and have sought to exclude student reporters altogether from their meetings, or to cut off money for the paper.[73] Furthermore, dissenting students have mounted legal challenges to mandatory student fees used to fund student newspapers or student organizations with which they disagree. The students contend that their expressive and associational rights are violated by mandated fees, inasmuch as the fees require the students' support of political views and doctrine that in fact they oppose.[74]

On the authority of *Tinker, Bethel*, and *Hazelwood*, the U.S. Court of Appeals for the Eleventh Circuit held that content-based regulations governing student government elections did not unconstitutionally limit the free expression of students interested in running for office.[75] The court accepted the university's position that the student government was a "learning laboratory," similar to the student newspaper or yearbook, a supervised experience for students interested in politics and government.[76] The court explicitly stated that in this case the university's academic freedom—that is, its autonomous decision making—was owed deference. Bowing to the school officials' need to regulate expressive activities in furtherance of the university's educational mission,[77] the court ruled that the restrictions were "reasonably related to the university's legitimate interest in minimizing the disruptive effect of campus electioneering."[78]

STUDENT ACADEMIC FREEDOM: ITS HOUR COME ROUND AT LAST

Despite the Supreme Court's deference to educational institutions' control of the classroom—a deference that clearly trumps students' free speech claims—recent decisions dealing with student organizations on university campuses offer strong support for the concept of student intellectual freedom. The Supreme Court has recognized that when a public university uses mandatory student fees to create a fund for financing channels of communication for student organizations, the university has created a limited public forum for private speakers "who convey their own messages."[79] Since student speech is involved, the university may not refuse the use of university facilities to a student religious group, even on Establishment Clause grounds.

In *Widmar v. Vincent*, an official rule forbade the use of campus buildings and grounds for "religious worship or religious teaching."[80] A group of evangelical Christian students from various denominational backgrounds found themselves unable to use university facilities for the purposes of the group: to share their religious enthusiasm and hold prayer services. The students prevailed in their suit against the university on First Amendment free speech grounds. The Court relied on *Tinker* and *Healy* in holding that the university could not make content-censoring decisions about which student groups to accommodate. Justice Stevens, however, wrote a concurrence to express his concern that the decision not be read as allowing the courts to supersede the institution's academic value judgments in allocating space.[81]

In *Rosenberger v. Rectors and Visitors of the University of Virginia*, a student university organization that published a newspaper with a Christian perspective sued the school, challenging the school's denial of funds for its printing costs solely on the basis of its religious editorial viewpoint.[82] The university contended that it was entitled to "substantial discretion in determining how to allocate scarce resources to accomplish its educational mission."[83] The Court, however, ruled that "the University may not discriminate based on the viewpoint of private persons whose speech it facilitates does not restrict the University's own speech, which is controlled by different principles."[84] In fact, the majority turned the university's academic freedom claims against it, recognizing the peril "in granting the State the power to examine publications to determine whether or not they are based on some ultimate idea and, if so, for the State to classify them."[85] The second danger to speech was a corollary of the first: "the chilling of individual thought and expression."[86] Moreover, "that danger is especially real in the University setting, where the State acts against a background and tradition of thought and experiment that is at the center of our intellectual and philosophic tradition."[87]

Justice Anthony Kennedy, writing for the majority, noted that in ancient Athens and during the Renaissance "universities began as voluntary and spontaneous assemblages or concourse for students to write and to learn."[88] In what is surely a high-water mark for student intellectual freedom, Justice Kennedy stated, "The quality and creative power of student intellectual life remains a vital measure of a school's influence and attainment."[89] He continued: "For the University, by regulation, to cast disapproval on particular viewpoints of its students risks the suppression of free speech and creative inquiry in one of the vital centers for the Nation's intellectual life, its college and university campuses."[90] Determining that the university's denial of funding had violated the students' right of free speech, the Court concluded that the violation was not necessitated by the prohibition against state establishment of religion.[91] Justice Sandra Day O'Connor's concurring opinion in *Rosenberger*, however, invited legal challenges to mandatory fees to fund student organizations on the ground that an objecting student should not be compelled to pay for speech with which he or she disagrees.

Mandatory student fees are generally used to fund student government, student associations, speakers bureaus, campus newspapers, and student organizations formed for social, academic, political, athletic, recreational, cultural, or artistic purposes. A large university may have between 150 to 200 of these diverse associations,[92] aside from the many student groups that do not receive funding.[93] The use to which mandatory student activity fees are put has been one of the most ideologically charged issues of the past decade. On occasion, student associations to which all students belong as a result of their fees may engage in lobbying efforts off campus. The student association at the University of Nebraska has been embroiled in a heated dispute resulting from the association's decision to lobby in the Nebraska legislature against a bill that would cut off funding for research on cells from aborted fetuses.[94] A related controversy involved a state university student's challenge to the University of California's mandatory registration fee as violative of free exercise of religion, because the fee was used, in part, to subsidize the university's health insurance program, a program that covered abortion services.[95]

University officials may seek to deny recognition to groups whose purposes they oppose or to regulate the content of expression at student demonstrations, rallies, or parades. For example, at Jackson State University, regulations provided that all events sponsored by student organizations had to be registered with the director of student activities, who "approves activities of a wholesome nature."[96] Two Iranian students who had been subjected to disciplinary action by the university for their participation in two on-campus demonstrations without complying with the regulations were victorious in their suit against the Mississippi State Board of Trustees.[97] Relying on *Papish*, the Fifth Circuit held that demonstrations are a form of protected speech and that disciplinary action against university students must not be based on the content of their speech.

State legislatures may also try to limit the type of groups that can be recognized as campus organizations. Lawmakers and university officials have targeted gay and lesbian student groups in particular over the past twenty-five years.[98] Legislature efforts include statutes that prohibit the expenditure of public funds in sanctioning, recognizing, or supporting any group that advocates for homosexual rights. Whether imposed by the legislature or the university, prohibitions on recognizing gay and lesbian student groups operates as a prior restraint on the associational and expressive rights of the students seeking to organize. Challenges to restrictive edicts have resulted in numerous federal court decisions striking down such measures as violating the students' rights of free speech and assembly as well as the unenumerated right of freedom of association.[99]

Dissenting students first brought legal challenges to the constitutionality of mandatory student activity fees during the tumult of the late 1960s and early 1970s.[100] Legal challenges to mandatory fees fall into two groups. One is an attack on the ground that the university lacks the power to impose the fees *ab initio*. So far, this has proved to be a dead end. The courts have uniformly held that imposition of the fees is within the power of the governing board of a school.[101] The other line of attack—that the compelled support of organizations violates the objecting students' rights of speech, association, and free exercise of religion—has proved more problematic. A number of Supreme Court decisions regarding compelled support of labor unions during the 1980s and 1990s provided hope to the dissenters that they could enjoin certain uses of their fees.

Students who oppose the imposition of fees to support student activities rely on two strands of the Supreme Court's First Amendment jurisprudence. One is that strand protecting the freedom not to speak, believe, or associate—a corollary to the freedoms of speech, belief, and association. "A system which secures the right to proselytize religious, political, and ideological causes must also guarantee the concomitant right to decline to foster such beliefs."[102] Thus, the Constitution denounces compelled speech, whether the speech consists of the Pledge of Allegiance[103] or the requirement that one's automobile license plate bear the state motto.[104]

A related strand of First Amendment jurisprudence concerns compulsory fees that are used for political or ideological purposes by the association charging the fees. One of the foundational decisions, *Abood v. Detroit Board of Education*, involved a labor union whose compulsory fees were charged under a closed-shop agreement permitted under state law.[105] Another, *Keller v. State Bar of California*, involved an "integrated" state bar, meaning that the right to practice law in the state was conditioned upon membership in the organization and payment of dues to the state bar.[106] In neither case did the Supreme Court hold that the organization could not compel membership or the payment of fees, even though there was a significant burden on associational rights, since in both cases a sufficiently strong government interest was present. In *Abood*, the justification was the promotion of labor peace and avoidance of a "free rider" problem; in *Keller*, the overriding interest was the regulation of the legal profession. However, since there was a notable burden on associational rights, the Court held that the association could not expend a dissenting individual's dues for ideological activities not germane to the purpose for which association had been compelled. In other words, the groups could work to advance a political or ideological agenda beyond that purpose, but these expenditures could not be financed from assessments or dues from dissenting members.[107]

As a result of *Abood* and *Keller*, a number of federal and state courts declared certain mandatory fee expenditures unconstitutional. Because lower courts addressing First Amendment challenges to similar fee programs had reached conflicting results, the Supreme Court agreed to hear *Board of Regents of the University of Wisconsin System v. Southworth*, a case challenging the University of Wisconsin's use of mandatory student fees to support on-campus student organizations "that engage in political and ideological advocacy, activities and speech" to which some students are opposed.[108] The lawsuit had been brought by Scott Southworth and other Christian students at the Madison campus, who sued when the school refused to waive the $331 annual activity for the 1995–96 school year. They alleged that the school's use of their mandatory fees to fund private organizations that engaged in political and ideological advocacy, activities, and speech violated their rights of free speech and association, the Free Exercise Clause of the First Amendment, the Religious Freedom Restoration Act (since ruled unconstitutional), and various state laws.[109] Arguing that their "deeply held religious and personal beliefs" had been offended, the students presented evidence involving eighteen organizations they found objectionable, including a Lesbian, Gay and Bisexual Campus Center, the Women's Center, an environmental center, an AIDS support network, a socialist organization, Amnesty International, Community Action on Latin America, and the Student Labor Coalition. All of the targeted groups may fairly be said to have fallen on the left side of the political and ideological spectrum. The regents did not contest the fact that these groups engaged in political and ideological speech; it had been stipulated, moreover, that the distribution of funds to student groups was viewpoint neutral.

The federal district court entered a declaratory judgment to the effect that the students' First Amendment rights had been violated.[110] The Seventh Circuit Court of Appeals affirmed it, in part.[111] Since the students had not argued that the regents lacked a legitimate interest in compelling funding, the only question the Court of Appeals considered was whether the challenged activity was germane to the government's asserted interests. The university's asserted interests in education and allowing for diverse expression were rejected as not germane, since the Supreme Court had stated that germaneness should not be read so broadly (in the context of a private-sector labor union) as to embrace "political and ideological activities."[112] Moreover, even if political and ideological speech was germane, neither the university's broad interest in education nor its interest in shared governance were strong enough to justify compelled support of such speech. The regents could not prove that mandated funding did not "add significantly to the burdening of free speech inherent in achieving those interests."[113] Finally, the Seventh Circuit read *Rosenberger*'s mandate of viewpoint neutrality to mean that it was imperative that students not be forced to support organizations that engaged in political or ideological activities.

In March 2000, a unanimous U.S. Supreme Court ruled that Wisconsin's program was consistent with the First Amendment, provided that the program was viewpoint neutral.[114] The Court acknowledged that First Amendment rights are implicated when a university conditions the opportunity to receive a college education on supporting objectionable expression; therefore, objecting students may insist on certain safeguards. Although Justice Kennedy, writing for the majority, used an *Abood/Keller* analysis to identify the objecting students' interests, he found the "germane speech" standard of *Abood/Keller* unworkable in the new context. Since speech the university seeks to encourage through its activities program is "distinguished by . . . its vast, unexplored bounds," to require the courts to determine what speech is germane "would be contrary to the very goal the university seeks to pursue."[115] By the same token, the "vast extent of permitted expression" increases the risk of encroaching on the rights of objecting students. One way to protect those interests would be to permit a refund arrangement or an optional system, but the Court refused to mandate that the university put the entire program at risk, stating that while a university is free to implement alternative systems, such arrangements are not constitutional requirements, due to the expense and disruption that they would cause.[116]

The objecting students had also unsuccessfully contended that the off-campus activities of the student groups often bore "no relationship to the university's reason for imposing the segregated fee in the first instance, to foster vibrant campus debate among students."[117] Justice Kennedy stressed the university's interest in "encouraging students to take advantage of the social, civic, cultural, and religious opportunities in surrounding communities and throughout the country."[118] He cautioned against making distinctions between campus and off-campus activities, noting that "in an age marked by revolutionary changes in communications, information transfer and the means of discourse,"[119] it is difficult to impose the traditional conceptions of territorial boundaries.[120]

Although the Court reversed the Seventh Circuit in the main, it remanded for further resolution the constitutionality of one aspect of the Wisconsin program: the referendum feature, under which by a majority vote of the student body a given activity may be funded or defunded.[121] Since the record on that point was very brief, it was not clear whether there was any protection for viewpoint neutrality. If majority rule were substituted for viewpoint neutrality, the constitutional underpinning for the entire program would be undermined, since minority speech is entitled to the same respect given to majority speech.[122]

Justice Souter, joined by Justices Stevens and Breyer, concurred but contended that the majority had framed the issue incorrectly, since the parties had stipulated that the scheme was viewpoint neutral.[123] The question was whether Southworth had a claim to relief from the operation of this particular viewpoint-neutral grant scheme; the answer was that he did not. In seeking the resolution of the issue, Justice Souter discussed academic freedom, but solely in regard to the university's autonomy: "Our understanding of academic freedom has included not merely liberty from restraints on thought, expression, and association in the academy, but also the idea that universities and schools should have the freedom to make decisions about how and what to teach."[124] Stating that the Court had spoken in the past of "wide protection for the academic freedom and autonomy that bars legislatures (and courts) from imposing conditions on the spectrum of subjects taught and viewpoints expressed in college teaching," Justice Souter conceded that the Court has "never held that universities lie entirely beyond the reach of students' First Amendment rights." Still, he noted that "protecting a University's discretion to shape its educational mission may prove to be an important consideration in First Amendment analysis of objections to student fees."[125]

The concurring opinion ultimately based its support of the Wisconsin student activity fee on the basis that the case bore little resemblance to the cases involving compelled or controlled speech, that is, requiring the individual to hear an offensive statement or affirm a moral or political commitment. Since the Wisconsin funding scheme lacked the clear connection between the fee payer and offensive speech that played a role in the *Abood/Keller* decisions, those cases did not control the remedy. In this case the government's collection of a fee that indirectly funded "a jumble of messages" did not restrict or modify the objecting student's message.[126] Moreover, the program at issue sought "to broaden public discourse."

Justice Souter also distinguished the prior compelled speech and funding cases because the university's interest was indisputably legitimate and the students' fees supported activities that had educational value. Finally, Justice Souter was clearly aware of the danger to the university's freedom to control its curriculum that upholding the students' challenge would pose. Had the Court ruled for the objecting student, the way would have been cleared for lawsuits in which students at a public institution sought tuition refunds based on their objections to particular courses or faculty speech to which the students had ideological or political opposition. Justice Souter noted that the university setting is one in which students are "inevitably required to support offensive viewpoints in ways that cannot be thought constitutionally objectionable unless one is prepared to deny the University its choice over what to teach."[127] The requirement of viewpoint neutrality, however, does not mean the university is required to offer a spectrum of courses to satisfy that standard.[128]

The plaintiffs in *Southworth* have vowed to press on and hope to prove on remand that the allocation of the student activity fee at the University of Wisconsin is not viewpoint neutral but is tilted leftward. Although the plaintiffs in *Southworth* would not agree, the decision is a great victory for student academic freedom, including their own. The Court has often remarked that the university is particularly the "marketplace of ideas." When this abstract notion meets the concrete reality of university autonomy, however, it has little consequential meaning except in the noncurricular aspects of the university. There is nothing that requires a university to offer a broad spectrum of courses or to be viewpoint neutral as to their content. The unofficial student "curriculum" is the true bazaar, rich with offerings of every stripe and color.

I regard the trilogy comprising the *Widmar, Rosenberger,* and *Southworth* decisions as monumentally important for student intellectual freedom. They recognize that student groups have the ability to enrich the learning experience by bringing to the campus many and varied issues, ideologies and perspectives that are not included within the curriculum. Thus, students contribute to the "spectrum of available knowledge."[129] As Justice Kennedy has noted for the Court, "The student activity fee [is] designed to reflect the reality that student life in its many dimensions includes the necessity of wide-ranging speech and inquiry and that student expression is an integral part of the university's educational mission."[130]

1. See generally, William W. Van Alstyne, "Academic Freedom and the First Amendment in the Supreme Court of the United States: An Unhurried Historical Overview," *Law and Contemporary Problems* 53 (Summer 1990): 79.

2. *Regents of University of California v. Baake,* 438 U.S. 265, 312 (1978); *Regents of the University of Michigan v. Ewing,* 474 U.S. 214, 226, n.12 (1985).

3. See generally, Van Alstyne, "Academic Freedom and the First Amendment in the Supreme Court of the United States."

4. See, for example, Peter J. Byrne, "Academic Freedom: A 'Special Concern' of the First Amendment," *Yale Law Journal* 99 (1989): 251, suggesting that constitutional academic freedom should insulate the university from extramural political pressure.

5. See, for example, *Kissinger v. Board of Trustees of Ohio State University, College of Veterinary Medicine,* 5 F.3d 177 (6th Cir. 1993), in which a required course in surgery that involved operations on live animals did not violate a student's right fully to exercise her religion.

6. Matthew W. Finkin, "Intramural Speech and Academic Freedom," *Texas Law Review* 66 (1988): 1323, 1324, noting academic freedom's roots in the Middle Ages. See also Walter P. Metzger, "Profession and Constitution: Two Definitions of Academic Freedom in America," *Texas Law Review* 66 (1988): 1265, 1265–1284, describing pivotal definitions of academic freedom from the past; and Thomas L. Haskell, "Justifying the Rights of Academic Freedom in the Era of Power/Knowledge," in *The Future of Academic Freedom,* no. 3, ed. Louis Menand (Chicago: Univ. of Chicago Press, 1996).

7. *AAUP Policy Documents and Reports* 3 (1990). The statement is reproduced each year in *Academe: The Bulletin of the American Association of University Professors.* The principles of the 1940 statement have undergone refinement in a number of ways: "Customary acceptance, understandings mutually arrived at between institutions and professors or their representatives, investigations and reports by the American Association of University Professors and formulations of statements by that association either alone or in conjunction with the Association of American Colleges." Ibid., 5.

8. Ibid.

9. Ibid. All of these freedoms are qualified. For example, teachers are admonished that freedom to teach carries with a responsibility "not to introduce into their teaching controversial subject matter which has no relation to their subject."

10. Ibid., 21.

11. Ibid., 153.

12. Ibid.

13. Ibid., 156.

14. Ibid.

15. Ibid.

16. Ibid., 157. The AAUP has also issued a report discussing its opposition to harassment in any form and its inconsistency with academic freedom. American Association of College and University Professors, *American Association of College and University Professors Policy Documents and Reports* (1995): 171–72.

17. David M. Rabban, review of *The Future of Academic Freedom,* ed. Louis Menand, *California Law Review* 86 (1998): 1377.

18. See, for example, *Sweezy v. New Hampshire,* 354 U.S. 234 (1957); *Keyishian v. Board of Regents,* 385 U.S. 589 (1967).

19. See, for example, *Sweezy:* "The essentiality of freedom in the community of American universities is almost self-evident. No one should underestimate the vital role in a democracy that is played by those who guide and train our youth. To impose any strait upon the intellectual in our colleges and universities would imperil the future of our Nation.... Teachers and students must always remain free

to inquire, to study and to evaluate, to gain new maturity and understanding, otherwise our civilization will stagnate and die."

20. *Keyishian*, 603.

21. Faculty members, even at private schools, may have contractual protection of their academic freedom, a property interest, an institution of higher education's commitment to academic freedom, and the protection offered by the AAUP's imposition of sanctions against offending schools. See Michael A. Olivas, "Reflections on Professorial Academic Freedom: Second Thoughts on the Third 'Essential Freedom,'" *Stanford Law Review* 45 (1993): 1835.

22. For example, the concept of academic freedom does not offer protection for extra-institutional activities.

23. Courts have consistently rejected First Amendments challenges to the policies and practices of private institutions of higher education as being beyond the scope of the amendment. See, for example, *Hack v. President & Fellows of Yale College*, 16 F.Supp.2d 183 (1995), in which Jewish students at Yale University who objected to coed dormitories on religious grounds had no constitutional claim, as a school is not a state actor; *Becker v. Gallaudet*, 66 F.Supp.16 (1999), dismissing former nontenured faculty members' claims asserting violations of due process, free speech, and equal protection; the university was not subject to federal constitutional restraints. See generally Julian N. Eule, "Transporting First Amendment Norms to the Private Section: With Every Wish There Comes a Curse," *UCLA Law Review* 45 (1998): 1537, exploring routes to expand the reach of the First Amendment to private actors, with particular attention to private universities, and suggesting that imposition of First Amendment obligations on private parties presumptively conflicts with the First Amendment's core protection against government-compelled orthodoxy.

24. See, for example, John Gray and Andrew Ciofalo, "Student Press Protected by Faculty Academic Freedom under Contract Law at Private Colleges," *Education Law Report* 52 (1989): 43.

25. See, for example, *State v. Schmid*, 84 N.J. 535 (1980); *Corry v. The Leland Stanford Junior University*, Case No. 740309, Supr. Ct. State of California, County of Santa Clara, Order on Preliminary Injunction, Feb. 27, 1995.

26. Tom Kenworthy, "A Discouraging Word in Tome on the Range," *USA Today*, 3 March 2000, A3. In Rhode Island, the state senate has recently and unanimously passed a resolution calling on the board of governors to adopt a policy that would allow clergy to lead "nonsectarian" invocations and benedictions at the University of Rhode Island's graduation, a move that led the faculty senate to adopt its own resolution in the name of academic freedom.

27. David J. Cieslak, "Bid to Put Filters on UA Computers Fails," *Tucson Citizen*, Jan. 15, 2000, C1, describing a legislative effort to limit student access to World Wide Web by requiring content filters on university computers.

28. *Sweezy*, 263 (citations omitted).

29. See also *Baakke*, 438 U.S. 265, 312 (1978) reaffirming the "freedom of a university to make its own judgments as to education" including the selection of the student body (Powell, J., announcing the judgment of the Court).

30. *Keyishian*, 385 U.S. 589, 603 (1967).

31. 385 U.S., 603 (citations omitted).

32. *Widmar v. Vincent*, 454 U.S. 263, 276 (1981).

33. Ibid., 277.

34. *Mincone v. Nassau Community College*, 923 F.Supp. 398, 402 (1996), in which students' claims that contents of a course on human sexuality violated their rights, inter alia, under free exercise of religion would not be dismissed on academic freedom grounds; but see *Gheta v. Nassau Community College*, 33 F. Supp. 2d 179 (E.D.N.Y. 1999), which granted defendants' motion for summary judgment on grounds that a course did not have primary effect of endorsing or disparaging religion.

35. Katheryn D. Katz, "The First Amendment's Protection of Expressive Activity in the University Classroom: A Constitutional Myth," *University of California at Davis Law Review* 16 (1983): 857.

36. 319 U.S. 624 (1943).

37. In order to promote national unity, the state board of education had mandated that all students and teachers in the public schools salute the flag with a stiff-arm salute and recite the Pledge of Allegiance to the flag. Students who refused to conform committed an act of insubordination, punishable by expulsion from school followed by delinquency proceedings for unlawful absence. Their parents could be fined and jailed. Ibid., 626.

38. Ibid., 624.

39. Ibid., 642.

40. Ibid., 637.

41. Ibid.

42. *Tinker v. Des Moines Independent Community School District,* 393 U.S. 503, 506 (1969).

43. Ibid., 505, quoting *Burnside v. Byars,* 363 F. 2d 744, 749 (5th Cir. 1966).

44. 393 U.S., 506, n.2, citing, among others, Note, "Academic Freedom," *Harvard Law Review* 81 (1968): 1045.

45. *Healey v. James,* 408 U.S. 169, 171 (1972).

46. Ibid.

47. Ibid., 172.

48. Ibid., 176. The students had sought campus recognition in order to qualify for the use of bulletin boards, the right to place notices in the student press and to use campus facilities in order to hold meetings.

49. Ibid., 180.

50. Ibid., citing *Keyishian* and *Sweezy* (plurality opinion of Warren, C. J., at 262).

51. Ibid., 189.

52. 410 U.S. 667 (1973).

53. Ibid.

54. 464 F.2d 136, 145 (8th Cir. 1972).

55. One of many examples of expansive protection for the rights of the student press is the Fifth Circuit's holding that a university president has no right to control the free speech embodied in the publication of a student newspaper, absent special circumstances. Any regulations infringing free speech must be "shown to be necessarily related to the maintenance of discipline and order within the educational process." *Bazaar v. Fortune,* 476 F.2d 570, 574–75, rehearing *en banc* 489 F.2d 225 (5th Cir. 1973). Alleged grammatical and spelling mistakes and the use of "embarrassing language" that might bring disrepute to the school were not special circumstances. Ibid., 260–61.

56. 410 U.S., 670. The Court also held that expulsion could not be justified as a nondiscriminatory application of reasonable rules governing student conduct.

57. Van Alstyne, "Academic Freedom," 125.

58. 435 U.S. 78 (1978).

59. 474 U.S. 214 (1985).

60. Ibid., 225–26.

61. *Bethel School District No. 403 v. Fraser,* 478 U.S. 675 (1986).

62. 755 F.2d 1356, 1359 (9th Cir. 1985).

63. 478 U.S., 675, 686.

64. Ibid., 675, 682.

65. *Martin v. Parrish,* 805 F.2d 583 (5th Cir. 1996).

66. Ibid., 584, n.1.

67. 484 U.S. 260 (1988).

68. 795 F.2d 1368, 1375 (8th Cir. 198), rev'd 484 U.S. 260 (1988).

69. 484 U.S., 260, 273, n. 7.

70. Greg C. Tenhoff, "Censoring the Public University Student Press: A Constitutional Challenge," *Southern California Law Review* 64 (1990): 511, 515. Any system of prior restraint bears a "heavy burden against its constitutional validity." *Bantam Books v. Sullivan,* 372 U.S. 58, 70 (1963).

71. Ibid., 512.

72. See, for example, *Schiff v. Williams,* 519 F.2d 257 (5th Cir. 1978), in which the court held that a university president's dismissal of students from positions as editors for alleged poor spelling, grammar, and use of language that could embarrass and bring disrepute to the school were not circumstances leading to the kind of significant disruption of educational processes that entitled the president to control the right of free speech embodied in publication of the newspaper.

73. For example, in 1992, the student government at Russell Sage College was responsible for stopping publication of *The Quill,* in retaliation for an article that brought to light the student government's overspending of its budget. *Albany Times Union,* Nov. 21, 1999.

74. See, e.g., *Larson v. Board of Regents of the University of Nebraska,* 189 Neb. 688, 691, 204 N.W. 568, 571 (1973), in which imposition of mandatory fees on university students to support a newspaper, student association, and a speakers program did not violate students' rights so long as the uses reflected "a broad spectrum of university life and reasonable representation of the various aspects of student thought and actions;" *Lace v. University of Vermont,* 131 Vt. 170, 303 A.D.2d 475 (1973), in which students objected to expenditure of mandatory student funds for the speakers bureau, campus newspaper, expenses of student association for attending a conference, and the purchase of certain films. The court held that mandatory student fees do not violate the students' First Amendment freedom of association, as the students had failed to demonstrate that they had been denied "equal and proportional access" to the funds.

75. *Alabama Student Party v. Student Government Association of University of Alabama,* 867 F.2d 1344 (11th Cir. 1989). The regulations restricted distribution of campaign literature to the students three days prior to the election and permitted its distribution only at residences or the outside of classrooms; they also limited debate on campaign issues.

76. Ibid., 1347.

77. Ibid.

78. Ibid.

79. *Rosenberger v. Rectors and Visitors of the University of Virginia,* 515 U.S. 819, 835 (1995).

80. 454 U.S. 263 (1981).

81. Ibid., 277 (Stevens, J., concurring).

82. 515 U.S. 819, 827 (1995).

83. Ibid., 832.

84. Ibid., 834 (citations omitted).

85. Ibid., 836.

86. Ibid.

87. Ibid., 835 (citations omitted).

88. Ibid., 836.

89. Ibid.

90. Ibid.

91. Ibid., 846.

92. See *Smith v. Regents of the University of California,* 4 Cal.4th 843, 849, 844 P.2d 500, 504, 16 Cal. Rptr.2d 181, 185 (1993), in which a mandatory student activities fee collected by the University of California at Berkeley subsidized activities of 150 student organizations in addition to activities of student government.

93. The University of Wisconsin-Madison had during the 1995–96 academic year 623 registered student groups, of which 183 received student fee money. *Respondent's Brief, Board of Regents of University of Wisconsin v. Southworth,* 1999 WL 618376.

94. Sara Salkeld, "U. Nebraska Approves Fetal Research Bill," *Daily Nebraskan,* Feb. 3, 2000.

95. *Goehring v. Brophy,* 94 F.3d 1294 (9th Cir. 1996); *cert. denied* 520 U.S. 1156 (1997).

96. *Shambloo v. Mississippi State Board of Trustees of Institutions of Higher Learning,* 620 F. 2d 516 (5th Cir. 1980).

97. Ibid.

98. See, for example, *Gay Lesbian Bisexual Alliance v. Sessions,* 917 F.Supp. 1548 (N.D. Ala 1996), *aff'd sub. nom. Gay Lesbian Bisexual Alliance v. Pryor,* 110 F.3d 1543 (11th Cir. 1997), in which a statute prohibiting colleges or universities spending public funds or using public facilities to sanction, recognize, or support any group that promotes lifestyle or action prohibited by sodomy and sexual-misconduct laws violates students' First Amendment rights.

99. See, for example, *Gay Lesbian Bisexual Alliance v. Sessions,* 917 F.Supp. 1548 (N.D. Ala 1996); *Student Coalition for Gay Rights v. Austin Peay State University,* 477 F.Supp. 1267 (M.D.Tenn. 1979); *Gay Lib v. University of Missouri,* 558 F.2d 848 (8th Cir. 1997), *cert. denied, Ratchford v. Gay Lib,* 434 U.S. 1080; *Gay Alliance of Students v. Matthews,* 544 F.2d (4th Cir. 1976); *Gay Student Organization of the University of New Hampshire v. Bonner,* 509 F.2d 652 (1st Cir. 1974).

100. See, for example, *Larson v. Board of Regents of the University of Nebraska,* 189 Neb. 688, 692, 204 N.W. 568, 571 (1973), in which students objected to imposition of mandatory fees on university students where fees funded activities such as a student strike against foreign policy of the United States in 1970, a conference on human sexuality, and purchase of a handbook on birth control; *Lace,* in which students objected to expenditure of mandatory student funds for "radical causes."

101. Ibid. See also *Smith v. Regents of the University of California,* 4 Cal.4th 843, 844 P.2d 500 (1993).

102. *West Virginia State Board of Education v. Barnette,* 319 U.S. 624, 633–34 (1943).

103. Ibid. The Court also stated: "If there is any fixed star in our constitutional horizon, it is that no official, high or petty, can proscribe what shall be orthodox in politics, nationalism, religion or other matters of opinion." Ibid.

104. *Wooley v. Maynard,* 430 U.S. 705, 714 (1977), in which the Court stated that "freedom of thought protected by the First Amendment against state action includes both the right to speak freely and the right to refrain from speaking at all."

105. *Abood v. Detroit Board of Education,* 431 U.S. 209 (1977).

106. *Keller v. State Bar of California,* 496 U.S. 1 (1990); see also *Lehnert v. Ferris Faculty Association,* 500 U.S. 507 (1990), holding, inter alia, that college faculty bargaining representatives and their parent union could not charge objecting employees for the expenses of lobbying; the government's interest in promoting labor peace and avoiding the "free rider" problem is not served by charging objecting employees for lobbying, electoral, and other political activities not related to their collective bargaining agreement.

107. Ibid., 519. See also *Lehnert,* which offered a three-part test to determine which activities a union may constitutionally charge to dissenting employees: the chargeable activities "must be 'germane' to collective bargaining activity, be justified by the government's vital interest in labor peace and avoiding 'free riders,' and 'not significantly add to the burden' on free speech inherent in permitting an agency or union shop."

108. *Board of Regents of the University of Wisconsin System v. Southworth,* 526 U.S. 1038 (1999), 120 S.Ct.1346 (2000), reversing and remanding *Southworth v. Grebe,* 151 F.3d 717, 718–19 (7th Cir. 1998).

109. 151 F.3d 717, 718–19. Southworth has stated that "as a conservative and a Christian, it was frustrating to see the money going to organizations [he] personally disagrees with." *Washington (D.C.) Times,* Feb. 23, 2000, A1.

110. 120 S.Ct. 1346, 1352.

111. *Southworth v. Grebe*, 151 F.3d 717 (7th Cir. 1998).

112. Ibid., 725, quoting 500 U.S., 516.

113. Ibid., 729.

114. *Board of Regents of the University of Wisconsin System v. Southworth*, 120 S.Ct. 1346 (2000), reversing and remanding *Southworth v. Grebe*, 151 F.3d 717 (7th Cir. 1998).

115. Ibid., 1348.

116. Ibid., 1355.

117. Ibid., 1356.

118. Ibid., 1356–57.

119. Ibid., 1357.

120. Ibid. The majority opinion noted that an entirely different First Amendment analysis is needed in the case of the speech of the university or its agents and employees: the speech of faculty, administrators, or regents. The Court left open the suggestion that such speech, including faculty speech, is government speech, subject to the analysis of *Rust v. Sullivan*, 500 U.S. 173 (1991) (when the government funds an activity, the government may impose restrictions on the speech of the funded agency).

121. Ibid., 1357.

122. Ibid.

123. Ibid., 1358 (Souter, J. concurring).

124. Ibid.

125. Ibid., 1359.

126. Ibid., 1359.

127. Ibid., 1361.

128. Ibid.

129. *Griswold v. Connecticut*, 381 U.S. 479, 482 (1965).

130. *Rosenberger v. Rector*, 515 U.S., 830, 840; *Widmar v. Vincent*, 454 U.S. 263, 267, n. 5 (1981).

Oxymoron on the Commons

Response to Katz

DONALD M. HASSLER

English, Kent State University

Darkness visible.—John Milton, *Paradise Lost,* Book 1, l.63

I hate violence, and I am haunted by terrible memories if I have to confront violence. Recently I had to have one of our old cats put to sleep, and as I held him for
the vet to administer the shot I felt like a Nazi prison-camp guard. Except when I
was very young, I never wanted to be a soldier and never had to go to war. I do not
even enjoy the heated arguments in the English department where I work, although
I know that English teachers, like cats, grow skillful by tussling with one another.
There lies the oxymoron, an apparent contradiction that is true in a pithy way. My
cat had to die, and it was better for him to die in my arms. Soldiers and warfare,
such as George Washington and his men on the Delaware, can produce progressive
forward steps—and argument is always helpful.

Such pointed paradoxes, or oxymorons, are messy and ugly in their stark reality. I was teaching here at Kent in May 1970, and I am certain that the awful events
of that balmy weekend should not have played out as they did. Now we scholars
discuss constitutional issues and the fertile freedoms that are embodied in our students—and in ourselves, when we are at our student best. Thus we are haunted by
paradox, even by oxymoron, and at times we see, as John Milton puts it, by means
of "darkness visible."

Professor Katz has written a case for student freedom of expression and freedom of assembly. I am impressed by how well appointed her paper is. The argument that Katz puts forward is an argument for the carnival openness (she calls it a
"bazaar") and messy fertility of student work in the academy. I suggest that the
paper itself is an oxymoron. It is heavy and well loaded with legal reference. The
Katz message is one of bursting, open freedom of expression and freedom of movement. Everyone wants to speak. Everyone may speak. And out of the chorus, even
the cacophony, emerges the university.

The problem is that the university, or the academy, also carries a very heavy
load of tradition and of precedent. I suspect that no discipline in the university

depends more on precedent than does the law school. We must remember that an oxymoron is always a bit like a fulcrum, or a balance; Milton's expression "darkness visible" means both that one can see in the dark and that when one sees, it is often darkly. Thus the equilibrium, or balance, in a good oxymoron is always more or less in a state of dynamic flux. Thus we can be nervous about student freedoms, indeed about our own freedoms, at the same time that we cherish the potential for new growth in such freedoms. Perhaps this nervousness would make us all lawyers in order to construct the careful law that protects the freedom. I know that the Russian Marxists a century ago did not believe in freedom at all but rather in the inevitable, scientific certitude of the changes they were working to produce. Also, of course, there is always the rough beast of the student body—and I think this means the body of all of us—pushing against the law, the science, even the law that protects such pushing. I like such oxymoronic thinking, and I like the heavy paper the Professor Katz has written in order to help us make such ideas fly high, to set them free.

Finally, I think the May 4 tragedy here at Kent is a symbol of exactly why these discussions of freedom become so complex. The tragedy is a symbol of our fallenness. Were we not fallen, freedom would surely be easier to conceive. Milton's oxymoron, in fact, refers to fallen angels; the "darkness visible" is for Milton the condition in Hell. Satan never has the wit or the grace to make his way out of Hell. But our students, our lawyers, our English teachers may do better, if we can master oxymoron. Or it may be that we are simply given the grace to wrestle with it. The discussion at Kent and at Jackson State did not end with the shootings thirty years ago. We, the survivors, have been given the grace to continue the discussion. So I would ask Professor Katz to speak one more time to exactly that puzzle: whether student freedoms and rights are destined to challenge the law, to expand the law, to break the law in the Marxist, revolutionary manner that will lead to a utopian and "scientific" certitude—or whether a continual give-and-take, a continual wrestling, is the best we can expect. I think that our dead students would like to hear that answer, and the oxymoron is that should they be able to hear it, we will not.

Until the Justices Hold Court
in My Classroom

An Interdisciplinary Approach to Student Academic Freedom
Response to Katz

NANCY C. CORNWELL

Communication, Western Michigan University

I am particularly pleased to have the opportunity to comment on the topic of student academic freedom. My favorite class at Western Michigan University is a course in the Department of Communication devoted to freedom of expression. Central to this course is a semester-long project where students exercise their First Amendment rights on issues important to them. They spend a good deal of time learning the extent of their rights as students to hold rallies, distribute pamphlets, write op-ed pieces, and the like. I often receive feedback indicating that students had had no idea they could express their views in certain ways or that the university could restrict their ability to do so in other ways.

The legal parameters they learn are similar to those described by Professor Katz. These students quickly catch onto the subtleties of their particular university's application of these judicial decisions in light of the courts' deference to the school's educational mission.

But as Professor Katz pointed out, there is more to student academic freedom than the relationship between students' expressive rights and the university's educational mission, even though this relationship is still being fleshed out by the courts, as noted in the most recent Supreme Court decision regarding student activity fees.[1] Professor Katz has pointed to a less clear area of free expression/academic freedom—that is, student expressive rights and limitations in the classroom environment.

A host of issues can merge in such a discussion: student-to-student sexual harassment, hate speech, respect and tolerance for ideas, equality between students, civility, individual rights versus social responsibility. I say "merge," because we encounter them at different points as both areas of intellectual inquiry and as potential sources of consternation. Judicial insight is not there to guide the kinds of discussions that occur in the "sanctity" of the classroom.

The classic liberal response to the most problematic forms of speech—that is, to respond with more speech—reinforces the marketplace-of-ideas model that is coming to be the definitive metaphor for an inadequate philosophical rationale for a system of free expression. Those who have attempted unsuccessfully to exercise their First Amendment rights know well that though they ultimately might be vindicated through the judicial process, it is of little consequence or comfort in the heat of the moment. The courts thrash around bits and pieces of academic freedom judicial precedent while there are glaring inadequacies in their abilities to navigate issues like hate speech or the corporatization of the university in a sophisticated manner.

With those contradictions in mind, my own thinking has moved in a more philosophical, nonlegal, pedagogical direction. I have returned to the underlying values that shape the current application of free expression doctrine in American liberal society, and I question their ability to account for contemporary challenges to free speech. In particular, I want to comment on hate speech, and hateful speech in the classroom.

My approach reflects my particular intellectual background. That background is influenced by philosophy, feminist political theory, critical legal studies, critical race theory, and theories of communication. Given what I see are the oversimplified explanations that liberalism provides for the protection of some forms of speech, I have drawn somewhat freely upon my interdisciplinary background to critique and rethink the nature, meaning, and scope of a system of free expression.

The system we currently and formally embrace is rooted in a political/social/economic system that privileges individual autonomy and justifies a system of free expression within that framework, as a fundamental individual right, if not a human *need*. We make numerous claims to value speech as part of the democratic process, but when push comes to shove and the arguments are distilled, the core value that emerges is the *individual right of expression.*

Perhaps I would not dispute the importance of expressing oneself as a means, as Thomas Emerson puts it, of self-fulfillment.[2] But I would argue that it is an incomplete rationale, ill equipped to account fully for a system of free expression. Free expression as articulated through the language of rights (and the language of the judiciary, as reflected in Professor Katz's paper) is not descriptive of the way communication occurs. Furthermore, the marketplace of ideas—the prevailing liberal ideology for free expression—has built in an assumption of a level playing field. Yet we know this is not the case, at multiple levels, ranging from access to the means of mass communication to interpersonal communication between individuals. Critical race theorists make this point well when attempting to make explicit the harm of hate speech. Mari Matsuda's proposal for remedies for hate speech include the requirement, among others, that the target be a historically oppressed group.[3] Charles Lawrence has argued that the purpose of hate speech is not to engage ideas but rather to silence, to shut down, communication and reaffirm the victim's second-class status.[4]

He remarks that the response to hate speech is more likely to be silence, not the marketplace-of-ideas remedy of more speech.

These same issues of power, race, and culture infuse the classroom with complicated dynamics that undermine the hypothetical marketplace. In the case of hate speech, in particular, the marketplace approach to free expression in the classroom is at times a perpetuation of the inequities and injustices that most feminist or critical pedagogical practices, for example, attempt to overcome.

A key factor in these dynamics involves the "role and authority of the teacher."[5] I suspect that many of us in the classroom who hold dear the ideal of academic freedom and (maybe too easily) allow it to be translated into an absolutist position on freedom of expression in the academy, may want to consider the potentially oppressive qualities of that position. If the role of a teacher is, at least in part, to facilitate dialogue, careful analyses of the assumptions about the teacher need to be made. One has to recognize the presence of institutional power in an educational setting and its influence on the relationship between teacher and student. A teacher, endorsing an abstract idea of free discourse in response to claims of hateful speech, may in effect, even when well intentioned and trying to turn an encounter into a learning experience, reinforce a set of relationships and a particular educational environment that ultimately have the opposite effect for victims of hate speech (an extension of the argument made by the critical race theorists mentioned earlier).

The reality is that students enter the classroom at different levels of power, and these differences in power exist between students as well as between students and the teacher. Even within the spirit of free and open discourse—considered essential to learning—how can one facilitate a community of mutual respect and understanding within a sphere of openness? Ultimately, the learning environment needs to be transformed into a setting that recognizes and adapts to these differences so that a "caring" form of communication or "dialogue," instead of rights of "expression," can guide the classroom experience.

Let me elaborate. The idea of "care" comes out of the feminist literature on the ethic of care.[6] To oversimplify, it marks a shift toward a social life that is constituted by the relationship between individuals. Thus, it may lay the groundwork for reorienting speech rights so they are not simply extensions of individual rights. Instead, free expression would be viewed as part of the social relation between individuals; consequently, attention could be paid to the social implications of that relationship.

Communication, speech, conversation, and dialogue are all, from the perspective of the ethic of care, essential to establishing, maintaining, and nurturing relationships. Communication is the key connection that forms the foundation of human identity and meaning.[7] Speech and the practice of free speech are a social activity and inextricable from the system of social, racial, ethnic, and cultural relationships that shape individuals. It is part of the "collective activity of social life."[8] Free speech, therefore, is valued by this ethic but with a different conceptual framework, one based not on abstract rules but on visions of connections, normative senses of value, and foundations of respect for the humanity of others.

The ethic of care is particularly useful for understanding hate speech, in that it is formulated around the same contextual, situated, interpreted, and interconnected descriptions of reality that define hate speech. The very aspects of hate speech that frustrate liberal attempts to seize it and make sense of it fall precisely within the sphere of values that make up the ethic of care. Caring about hate speech means squarely facing the contextual, situated reality of such communication. Caring about hate speech means recognizing the particular and discrete nature of hate speech's harm, the reality of which is, at best, indeterminate from a liberal perspective. A caring approach to hate speech recognizes that hate speech is a form of communication that creates meaning through a context of racism and bigotry. That context is what provides hate speech with its force and its ability to harm. The ethic of care recognizes that the harm of hate speech may not be easily quantified, empirically measured, visually observed, or even causally linked to a specific hate-speech act.

Finally, let me add that the ethic of care takes a social constructionist approach to the problem of hate speech. From this perspective, external factors in human life participate in the formation of the internal factors that define individual identity. Therefore, the external, implicit, societal endorsement of hate speech (even if only through a lack of explicit condemnation) is part and parcel of the internal construction of racism, sexism, and other expressions of hate and bigotry. If individuals are who they are through their social relations with others, the language of hate speech constructs a "truth" about the victims of hate speech that invariably impacts on *their* liberty.[9]

I realize that these ideas, offered in response to Professor Katz's description of the academic freedom of students, are only lightly sketched. I also realize that these ideas are decidedly nonlegal. But as such they are perhaps especially helpful for thinking about ways to navigate a diverse classroom and construct an intellectually diverse classroom environment conducive to "communication," "dialogue," and academic freedom for a diverse student body.

NOTES

1. *Board of Regents of the Univ. of Wisconsin Sys. v. Southworth, et al.* 120 S. Ct. 1346 (2000).

2. Thomas Emerson, *The System of Free Expression* (New York: Random House, 1970).

3. Mari Matsuda, "Public Response to Racist Speech: Considering the Victim's Story," *Michigan Law Review* 87 (1989): 2320–81.

4. Charles Lawrence III, "If He Hollers, Let Him Go: Regulating Racist Speech on Campus," *Duke Law Journal* (1990): 431–83.

5. Kathleen Weiler, "Freire and a Feminist Pedagogy of Difference," in *Debates and Issues in Feminist Research and Pedagogy,* ed. Janet Holland, Maud Blair, and Sue Sheldon (Philadelphia: Multilingual Matters, 1995), 31.

6. Carol Gilligan, *In a Different Voice: Women's Conceptions of Self and Morality* (Cambridge, Mass.: Harvard Univ. Press, 1982).

7. James Carey, *Communication as Culture: Essays on Media and Society* (Boston: Unwin Hyman, 1989).

8. Martha Minow, *Making All the Difference: Inclusion, Exclusion and American Law* (Ithaca, N.Y.: Cornell Univ. Press, 1990), 217.

9. Robin West, "Toward a Jurisprudence of Respect: A Comment on George Fletcher's Constitutional Identity," *Cardozo Law Review* 14 (1993): 764.

Student Academic Freedom Redux
Response to the Discussants

Katheryn Katz

Although Professors Cornwell and Hassler's responses to my paper on student academic freedom raise different issues, they are similar in one aspect: both responses bring to bear scholarly analyses that are grounded in disciplines other than law. Their nonlegal explications contribute thought-provoking insights to the question of how much freedom within the academic sphere is consistent with the other interests and values of the educational institution.

Professor Cornwell's response raises the compelling issue of hate speech in the classroom—an issue I omitted from my paper for fear that I could not do justice to such an important concern without its consuming the entire discourse on student academic freedom. There is no question that as university campuses have become more diverse, there has been an increase in displays of racism, sexism, homophobia, and anti-Semitism in all areas of campus life.[1] Professor Cornwell has limited her discussion of hate speech to the classroom—the educational setting in which student academic freedom is subject to the greatest institutional control.

In general, even public academic institutions make content-based speech distinctions that would be unconstitutional in other settings.[2] As an institution with an educational mission, the university, through its faculty, has control over the subject matter discussed in the classroom and the grades assigned to student work. Faculty judgments about the quality of ideas expressed by students are not only permitted but necessary.[3]

I share Professor Cornwell's concern about the very real harms caused by racist, sexist, and other disrespectful and hateful speech, not just in the classroom but in the entire university environment. If freedom to learn is to be a concrete reality as well an abstract right, there must be a classroom atmosphere that is conducive not just to discussion and debate but also to understanding of, and receptiveness to, new ideas and insights. There is no sound pedagogical reason to allow students to harass and intimidate one another in the classroom. The reality is, however, that the most egregious instances of hate speech occurring on university campuses have taken place not in classrooms but in dormitories, campus grounds, and other extracurricular settings in which university control of student speech is more limited.

Unfortunately, Professor Cornwell's nonlegal approach to hate speech does not obviate the difficulty posed by First Amendment jurisprudence regarding expressive rights in a university setting. Hate speech is an issue that presents us with a very real dilemma. Professor Linda E. Fisher has summarized the dilemma well: Encouraging the free expression of ideas and constant debate enhances creativity and diminishes misdirected suppression of dissidents; however, giving free rein to bigots and bullies ultimately undermines the very academic atmosphere necessary to sustain creative debate. Restraining group-based harassment also can foster multiculturalism. Permitting the suppression of disapproved speech, however, creates almost insurmountable problems of line drawing and enforcement. Further, imposing sanctions on certain speech can make martyrs of bigots.[4]

I am in complete agreement with Professor Cornwell that students should be respectful of and civil to one another. I also share her belief that an ethic of caring should permeate the classroom. The fact remains, however, that the courts are the controlling arbiters in disputes regarding academic institutions' efforts to stifle abhorrent expression, even if the censorship in question is believed to serve worthy causes. There may be informal negotiations of these issues, but legal rules will guide and limit the negotiation. Adjudication remains a compelling presence even when it does not occur.[5]

To date, conflicts that have reached the litigation stage have resulted in judicial opinions that cast doubt on a university's ability effectively to limit hate speech, except in vary narrowly defined circumstances. A general requirement of civility and respect may pass constitutional muster if it does not single out any particular speech but restricts a general class of speech that is incompatible with the educational mission.[6]

Finally, whatever the weaknesses of classic liberal theory for protection of the interests of those who are relatively powerless, we should bear in mind that it is the First Amendment that licensed the protests, rallies, organizing, and agitation that so galvanized the nation in a bygone era[7] and led to landmark civil rights victories.

Professor Hassler, as well, casts doubt on the notion that unfettered expressive rights for students are an unalloyed boon. Professor Hassler has written a moving and elegiac reflection on the dark side of freedom as symbolized by the terrible events that unfolded at Kent State University on May 4, 1970. He begins with the epigraph, "darkness visible," a phrase from John Milton's *Paradise Lost* evoking Hell. Professor Hassler urges us to be mindful of the complexity inherent in discussions of freedom, noting that "were we not fallen, freedom would surely be easier to conceive." He challenges me to go beyond my advocacy of student academic freedom, to speak to the "puzzle" of "whether student freedoms and rights are destined to challenge the law, to expand the law, to break the law in the Marxist, revolutionary manner that will lead to a utopian and 'scientific' certitude—or whether a continual give-and-take, a continual wrestling, is the best we can expect."

I cannot give a poet's answer. I can, however, appreciate that there are many dimensions other than legal ones to questions of freedom and restraint and that events challenge theory at every turn. My response to the challenge posed by Professor Hassler is a lawyer's answer. My remarks on student academic freedom are intended to determine the allocation of decision-making power over permitted expression in the university setting. I have confined my search for doctrinal guidance to the Supreme Court's constitutional jurisprudence. So limiting the search necessarily ignores the multiple variables that come into play when doctrine meets reality. The culture of the institution, the personalities of those in authority, and the political realities all factor into any analysis of events. What I have tried to do is far more prosaic than determining the possible or even probable consequences of enhanced student freedom. Instead, I have hoped to show that there is one sphere of student freedom that the desires of politicians, administrators, and even faculty must respect: namely, that of student control of an informal curriculum that finds expression in their extracurricular pursuits—student presses, speakers' forums, student-led organizations, and even student protests. I found it worth noting that the Supreme Court has recognized that students are not just empty vessels into which the faculty pours in wisdom, experience, and knowledge—that students also have a contribution to make to the intellectual life of the campus.

I have no gift of prescience to foretell the shape of future events or what the consequences of student academic freedoms may be. It is my devout hope, however, that we will continue to believe that academic freedom, grounded as it is in an understanding that no one has a monopoly on the truth, is a value worth protecting even at the risk of turbulence. Accordingly, the academic enterprise must encourage "that continual and fearless sifting and winnowing by which alone the truth may be found."[8]

NOTES

1. Fletcher N. Baldwin, Jr., "The Academies, Hate Speech and the Concept of Academic Intellectual Freedom," *University of Florida Journal of Law and Public Policy* 7 (1995): 41, 44.

2. Cass R. Sunstein, "Academic Freedom and Law: Liberalism, Speech Codes, and Related Problems," in *The Future of Academic Freedom*, ed. Louis Menand (Chicago: Univ. of Chicago Press, 1996), 93, 105–6.

3. Ibid.

4. Linda E. Fisher, "A Communitarian Compromise on Speech Codes: Restraining the Hostile Environment Concept," *Catholic University Law Review* 44 (1994): 97, 100.

5. Marc Galanter, "Worlds of Deals: Using Negotiations to Teach about Legal Process," *Journal of Legal Education* 34 (1984): 268.

6. Sunstein, "Academic Freedom and Law," 108.

7. Henry Louis Gates, Jr., "Critical Race Theory and Free Speech," in *The Future of Academic Freedom*, Menand, ed., 93, 119–20.

8. David Ward, foreword to *Academic Freedom on Trial: 100 Years of Sifting and Winnowing at the University of Wisconsin-Madison*, ed. W. Lee Hansen (Madison: Univ. of Wisconsin Press, 1998), xi.

10

Unspoken Dangers
The Curtailment of Free Expression and
the Endangerment of Youth

DANIEL PERLSTEIN
Education, University of California at Berkeley

Just as the 1970 killings at Kent State epitomized American cultural and political conflicts thirty years ago, high-profile school shootings have become a focal point of recent American anxieties and debates. Neither the 1970 killings at Kent State nor currently popular responses to school violence reflect a conflict between free expression and the order necessary to sustain that freedom. Rather, in the same way that the Kent State killings suggested then that United States aggression abroad was leading to violent government assaults and repression of free speech in America, punitive responses to school violence today not only impede free expression but also undermine the very safety of students. Still, now as in 1970, calls for compassion challenge demands for repression, and just as punitive school policies are deeply rooted in American institutions and history, so too is the impulse to challenge them.

School killings have become a seemingly regular feature of mainstream American life, and calls for educators to reach out to alienated and troubled youth have echoed through public discussions of school violence. Commentators have charged that schools such as Colorado's Jefferson County Columbine High School ignored or encouraged "casual cruelty . . . small slights and public humiliations" by which favored students harassed classmates and "reinforced the rigid high school caste system."[1] Press accounts have sympathetically portrayed violent students as youths who had been tormented and excluded from the mainstream of school life. The lesson of Columbine, Jefferson County school superintendent Jane Hammond told concerned educators, is that empathy and the strengthening of human relationships are more crucial to school safety than the purchase of metal detectors or the deployment of security guards.[2]

Still, pleas for compassion have not displaced calls for repression and retribution. Rather, recent shootings have led American legislators and school administrators to intensify efforts to police youth.[3] The 1998 Jonesboro shooting revived efforts to lower to twelve the age at which Arkansas youth could be tried as adults.[4] When a Richmond, Virginia, student was wounded by gunfire, Governor James Gilmore proposed eliminating after-school programs and nighttime athletic events, despite the success such activities have demonstrated in deterring crime. Senator Orrin Hatch declared that unless his colleagues passed legislation that would send youths guilty of running away from home to jail with adult offenders, "the country's going to see more and more of these [school shootings]."[5] President William Clinton marked the first anniversary of the killings at Columbine by offering sixty million dollars in federal funds to station police officers in schools, adding to the 2,200 school police already funded by the federal government.[6]

In the wake of recent shootings, school districts across the United States have earmarked hundreds of millions of dollars to upgrade security. Schools have hired armed guards, purchased metal detectors, redesigned entryways, and installed motion-sensitive cameras.[7] Administrators have mandated that students' backpacks be made of clear plastic, prohibited dark clothes and darkly dyed hair, and banned students from posing with cannons in their yearbook pictures. Hundreds of students have been suspended or expelled for actions that would not raise an eyebrow in other settings—drawing pictures and writing stories in which teachers or students are killed, or using penknives to open school computers.[8] Police are routinely called to intervene in school fights that would once have been handled by educators or clinicians.[9] Following the shooting at Columbine High School, administrators there announced a policy of zero tolerance for "cruelty, harassment, excessive teasing, discrimination, violence, intimidation."[10] In Sayreville, New Jersey, four five-year-old boys were suspended from school because they pretended to "shoot" classmates with their fingers during recess. "This is a no-tolerance policy," said superintendent William Bauer. "We're very firm on weapons and threats."[11]

The imposition of increasingly harsh punishments on young offenders comes despite the fact that weapons possession and violence by youth is declining,[12] despite the fact that school shootings remain exceedingly rare—far less common than gun violence in children's own homes,[13] and despite the fact that police methods failed to protect children in the very schools where attacks generated national concern. A police officer was on duty at Columbine High School, for instance, but had no impact on the crisis there. Video surveillance cameras, police dogs, and an armed sheriff's deputy could not protect students from a young man who shot a half-dozen classmates at Georgia's Heritage High School. It was assistant principal Cecil Brinkley who convinced T. J. Solomon to put down his gun and then embraced the youth.[14]

Police approaches geared to spectacular school disturbances are ineffective, because they ignore, divert attention from, or even reinforce the mundane, widely accepted behaviors that set the stage for extreme—and extremely rare—forms of student violence. Right before opening fire on his fellow students, T. J. Solomon remarked to a friend that he was "real mad" about having broken up with his girlfriend. Echoing once-popular rationales for treating domestic violence as a private matter and a crime of passion, Solomon's explanation for the transformation of affection into deadly possessiveness was so unexceptional that authorities were unable to "suggest a motive" for his actions. Rather, in Georgia and in many of the high-profile school shootings of recent years, sentimental invocations by students, reporters, and authorities of failed romance have served to obscure and trivialize the fraught, asymmetrical gender relations of youth.[15]

Gendered patterns of bullying, sexual harassment, and homophobic taunting set the stage for Solomon's actions and for other recent school shootings. By expressing revulsion against degraded females and males identified with them, such behaviors, Margaret Smith Crocco argues, are integral to the "system of sexualized male supremacy" perpetuated in American schools. Moreover, the stigmatization of girls and imposition of narrow standards of behavior on boys serves as a means by which students maintain the school pecking order and as a model for other forms of bias and discrimination.[16]

Pervasive in schools, this normal, systematic student violence is frequently overlooked by teachers and administrators.[17] The failure to address accepted forms of stigmatization, violence, and inequality has pervaded many schools' responses to sexual harassment. Litigation has won important protections for students, but schools, as Nan Stein has argued, consistently confuse harassment that is "sexually targeted" with student expression that is "sexually charged." The result is that students are left unprotected, while free speech is repressed. For instance, following allegations that a star football player sexually assaulted eleven girls, the Millis, Massachusetts, school district banned hand-holding.[18]

Boys who have killed classmates replicate in their own extreme and twisted way the accepted school hierarchy. One does not condone their actions by noting that such boys were themselves the victims of taunting and harassment. What better way for stigmatized boys to prove their manhood than by shooting a young woman whose actions had seemed to confirm classmates' ridicule?[19]

The hierarchies maintained by students mirror those imposed by school authorities through formal and informal pedagogical and disciplinary practices. By means of yearbooks, proms, student councils, "gifted" programs, the celebration of athletics, and a myriad of other enshrined elements of school life, authorities confirm and exacerbate status differences among youth. In short, school authorities and youth join in reproducing a culture that fosters violence. Punitive approaches to discipline leave this culture unquestioned and untouched.[20]

Punitive approaches to discipline reinforce school hierarchies in part because they are inevitably inequitable. A 1994 Office of Civil Rights survey concluded that blacks youths were 2.5 times more likely than whites to be among the 470,000 students paddled that year.[21] Blacks are suspended substantially more often (perhaps twice as often) and for longer periods than whites.[22] Policies that criminalize student behavior exacerbate inequalities. Minority youths are more likely to be arrested for a violent felony than whites, and even when charged with the same crime, researchers Mike Males and Dan Macallair conclude, "the discriminatory treatment of minority youth arrestees accumulates within the justice system and accelerates measurably if the youth is transferred to adult court."[23]

Whereas affluent white youths can often call upon a nexus of supportive institutions if they get into trouble, poor and minority students are more likely to face punishment. They often turn to violence precisely because they have come to believe that schools and other institutions will not offer them protection. Inequity inevitably undermines the effectiveness of punishment.[24]

Punitive approaches are not merely unproductive, they are counterproductive. Uncompromising zero-tolerance attempts to divide children into faultless victims and graceless brutes misrepresent actual patterns of violence, in which people frequently alternate between being perpetrators and victims. Research on bullying confirms the frequency with which school children pass back and forth between being perpetrators and victims of violence. Indeed, as teen suicide rates have risen, youth increasingly occupy both categories simultaneously. Of the thirty-four youths who were killed at school in the 1997–98 school year, nine were suicides. By the 1998–99 school year, twenty-six students died violently at school, but 2,700 youths aged ten to nineteen took their own lives. A 1997 study concluded that one in every thirteen high school students attempts suicide.[25]

Punitive approaches to school violence mirror typical school disciplinary practices. By imposing punishment on individuals believed by school authorities to have committed a prohibited act, disciplinary codes presuppose a shared understanding of school standards. This presumed consensus is undermined, however, by the considerable autonomy of individual teachers in the management of their classrooms. As Henry Lufler has demonstrated, even where schoolwide rules exist, discipline codes vary "from teacher to teacher, with some tolerating or encouraging behavior—such as speaking out in class—which other teachers found offensive."[26] The potential of such discrepancies to demoralize school life is exacerbated by the frequency with which petty infractions lead to disciplinary action in schools. If, moreover, students are overpoliced, they are also underdirected.[27] Interventions styled on criminal procedures are too cumbersome to deal consistently with petty misbehavior and are ill suited to inculcating democratic values or addressing the real needs of troubled students.[28]

Finally, because the sources of student violence often lie in complicated, ambiguous, and poorly understood but widely accepted patterns of social life, youth are necessarily conflicted and confused. Students need opportunities to analyze and discuss conditions that foster such violence. Schools therefore need to develop pedagogical interventions that integrate study of the nature of normal violence into the academic curriculum. Incorporating study of the violence youth confront in their own lives into science, history, literature, and other classes requires tact on the part of educators. Still, students' efforts to make sense of their own lives will necessarily illuminate fundamental aspects of the wider society. Ineffective, punitive disciplinary practices that curtail rather than expand freedom of inquiry and expression abandon the educational mission of the schools. They have added to the dangers youth face.

THE POPULARITY OF PUNISHMENT

If punishment deflects attention from pervasive forms of violence; if punitive policies, which suppose that rules are clear, are incapable of addressing the ambiguities of social relations; if punishment is poorly suited to the myriad of children who are both victims and victimizers; and if punishment is inevitably inequitable—why does it persist?

Although authorities frequently trace the recent adoption of zero-tolerance codes to high-profile school shootings, the move toward punitive practices in school and in other youth policies has been building for many years. For a decade, more and more states have enacted laws leading to the trial of more and more juveniles as adults. Thousands are jailed in adult prisons, many for nonviolent offenses. Hundreds are serving life terms for crimes committed when under eighteen.[29]

The epidemic of punishment did not develop as a response to schoolhouse misbehaviors. Rather, zero-tolerance policies, which punish severely all offenses, no matter how minor, originated in the drug enforcement policies of the early 1980s. Within a decade, the targets of zero tolerance had grown to include trespassing, homelessness, sexual harassment, skateboarding, racism, and boom boxes. By the early 1990s, schools began adopting their own zero-tolerance policies, often broadened to include not only drugs and weapons but also tobacco use, tardiness, and other nonviolent behaviors. With the 1994 Gun-Free Schools Act, which mandated that students bringing weapons to school be expelled and referred to the criminal justice system, the federal government lent its imprimatur to zero tolerance.[30]

Even this decade-old campaign to criminalize youth is but the current manifestation of a long-standing reliance on punishment in schools. American schooling first took hold in colonial New England. Children had few legal rights, and parental authority was largely unquestioned. Seen as instruments of children's salvation, strict discipline and corporal punishment were readily available to Puritan teachers and parents. "Better Whipped," Puritan prelate Cotton Mather advised, "than Damned."[31] This notion—that in sparing the rod one spoils the child—continues to provide religious sanction for corporal punishment today. Best-selling authors Gary and Anne Marie Ezzo stress spanking as a critical element in their book "Growing Kids God's Way."[32]

Yet as historian Barbara Finkelstein has argued, "If traditions of violence against children are time honored in the United States, so too are an array of dialectically linked counter-traditions that successive generations of social reformers have organized in an attempt to elevate the status of children, shroud them in blankets of legal, moral, social, cultural, and ideological protection, and root out violence from the arsenal of permissible disciplinary actions taken against them."[33] Across the entire history of American schooling, threads of violence have been interwoven with threads of compassion.

There was more to Puritan theory than the rod. If original sin marked children with a depravity that needed to be broken, each youth also possessed the capacity for spiritual knowledge. Cotton Mather preached that parents' authority should not be "harsh, fierce, and crabbed" but "sweet" and "tempered with kindness, and meekness and loving tenderness." Because he believed that education should promote reason and honor, Mather never "dispence[d] a Blow; except it be for an atrocious Crime," preferring instead to punish his children by banning them from his presence. According to his son Samuel, Mather always treated his children with "the familiarity of an acquaintance; and thus he would instruct and edify, thus allure and charm us, thus make us love his society . . . and never leave it but with sorrow." Such a gentle approach, Samuel believed, was more likely to "incline [children] to be good and virtuous than any crabbed looks, austere orders, or sour demands." For his part, Cotton Mather considered "the slavish way of education, carried on with raving and kicking and scourging" to be "abominable; and a dreadful judgment of God upon the world." Thus, the Puritans' legacy laid a groundwork for compassionate schools as well as for punitive practices.[34]

Just as compassion competed with repression in Puritan ideals of moral instruction, American revolutionaries wrestled with their own disciplinary dilemmas in the molding of citizens. They added political rationales for punishment to Puritan religious ones. Having been created as a nation through violent dissent, the United States, in the famous phrase of Benjamin Rush, needed to convert its young into "republican machines."[35] Rush proposed that American schools be modeled on those of ancient Sparta. "In the education of youth," he suggested, "let the authority of our masters be as *absolute* as possible. The government of schools like the government of private families should be *arbitrary*."[36] Thomas Jefferson considered the "deportment between father and son" as the best model for the tutor-pupil relationship, and with his approval the University of Virginia included such punishments as "a seat of degradation," "removal to a lower class," and "imposition of a task" as punishments for minor infractions.[37]

Like calls for education to break children's depraved wills, calls for schools to constrain the anarchic impulses of youth have persisted. "Uncontrolled and uncontrollable liberty," Supreme Court justice Hugo Black wrote in 1969, "is an enemy to domestic peace." Extending First Amendment protection to students wearing black armbands in protest against the Vietnam War, Black luridly warned, would inaugurate an age "when pupils of state-supported . . . kindergartens, grammar schools, or high schools . . . will be ready, able, and willing to defy their teachers on practically all orders. . . . It is the beginning of a new revolutionary era of permissiveness in this country."[38]

Still, efforts to educate future citizens have led to calls for cultivating reason and honoring individual freedom as well as for inculcating obedience. "Children are seldom sent to school before they are capable of feeling the force of rational or moral obligation," Benjamin Rush reasoned. "They may therefore be deterred from committing offenses, by motives less disgraceful than the fear of corporeal punishments."[39] The education of citizens, Jefferson argued, required "avoiding too much government[,] . . . not multiplying occasions for coercion," and leaving "enough room [to] the student for habitually exercising his own discretion." For revolutionaries committed to freedom and order, to liberty and republicanism, some discipline other than force was needed in the country and the young. "Hardening [students] to disgrace, to corporal punishment, and servile humiliations," Jefferson warned, "cannot be the best process for producing erect character." Rather, Jefferson called for "affectionate" relations between teacher and student, by means of which "the combined spirit of order and self-respect" would be "woven into the American character."[40]

The notion that blind obedience is poor training for democratic life did not disappear with Jefferson's generation. In 1969, a narrow Supreme Court majority rejected Hugo Black's apocalyptic fears of armband-wearing students. Arguing that armbands presented no threat to schoolhouse order, Justice Abe Fortas cited a 1943 Supreme Court decision holding that the role of schools in "educating the young for citizenship is reason for scrupulous protection of Constitutional freedoms of the individual, if we are not to strangle the free mind at its source and teach youth to discount important principles of our government as mere platitudes."[41]

Unable to reconcile its contradictory goals in the governing of democracy's young,

Jefferson's generation failed to create a system of schooling. Beginning in the early nineteenth century, however, other developments set the stage for the emergence of the common school. Layered on religious and political ideals, new concerns again transformed the terms in which punishment of the young was considered and lent new legitimacy to nonpunitive forms of discipline. The growing force of market relations and changing roles for American women, together with the still-living legacy of the American Revolution, suggested to many reformers that American society was becoming unglued and that common schools governed by maternal forms of discipline could restore social bonds.

As increasing numbers of American fathers left home for work, women gained primary responsibility for shaping children's characters. In 1833, *Mother's Magazine* contrasted the old, patriarchal approach to child rearing with the new maternal one. The magazine condemned an old-fashioned mother who "undertook to conquer her little son. A whip was placed on the chimney in the sitting room; and this, with the dark closet where he was told ugly creatures would catch him, frightened William into decent behavior while in the presence of his mother." In her absence however, the boy was willful and disobedient. In contrast, a successful mother responded to her son's misbehavior with the warning that if it continued, "I would not smile upon you, I should not receive your flowers, but should have to separate you from my company." "Mother," the boy responded, "I should rather have your sweet kisses, and your pleasant smiles than ten rolls of gingerbread. I could not be happy if you did not love me."[42]

Ironically, authority over children in the isolated domestic sphere led to the entry of women into public school life. "Mother," a young girl implores in an 1829 evangelical pamphlet, "there are so many societies! . . . I longed for you this afternoon when I came home from school, and they told me you were gone to the Maternal Society."[43] As the dialogue suggests, women's domestic role propelled their entry into the world of voluntary associations. Meanwhile, at the same time as much of the moral work of motherhood was being appropriated by the school, teaching expanded the domestic sphere of countless American women, who brought to education new maternal forms of discipline. "The only perfect guardian and cherisher of free self-activity," wrote kindergarten reformer Elizabeth Peabody, "is the mother's love, who respects it in her own child by an instinct deeper than all thought, restraining her own self-will, and calling out a voluntary obedience (the only obedience worthy of the name)."[44]

The complex, conflicting impulses that transformed approaches to student discipline were embodied in the life and work of Peabody's brother-in-law, the preeminent Common School Movement leader Horace Mann. As historians David Tyack and Elisabeth Hansot have observed, Mann epitomized the social and political tensions of his age. "A lawyer who glorified railroads and economic development," he sought, in his own words, to be "a fluid sort of man." At the same time, Mann saw growing class conflict and inequality as threats to the social order, and he fretted over the fragmentation of American society.[45]

Mann drew on the popular view that the moral influence of women could do more to maintain order than could coercion by schoolmen. His commitment to students' internalization of discipline rather than fearful obedience to external authority led to one of the most celebrated battles of his career. In 1844, thirty-one Boston schoolmasters attacked Mann's *Seventh Annual Report*. The schoolmen belittled the preparation of female teachers in normal schools, defended recitation and the "abcderian approach" against the "oral method" and the "word method," scorned the idea that interest could provide sufficient motivation to inspire student learning, and denounced Mann's desire to eliminate "all fear, emulation, and punishments" from classrooms. "Duty," they claimed, "should come first, and pleasure should grow out of the discharge of it." Extolling the use of corporal punishment in subduing young sinners, the men argued that "all authority is of God and must be obeyed."[46]

Horace Mann and his allies were able to chase a number of the schoolmen out of Boston's schools, and the number of floggings declined dramatically. Still, punitive approaches persisted in American schools.[47] In 1865, Dorchester, Massachusetts, instructed every teacher to "take notice of any misdemeanor or outrage that any of his students have committed . . . [so that] admonition and correction shall be administered. . . . The rod of correction is a rule of God. . . . The Schoolmaster shall have full power to punish all or any of his scholars."[48] Some of America's most popular nineteenth-century children's books portrayed similar practices. "Mr. Dobbin's lashings were very vigorous ones," Mark Twain wrote in *The Adventures of Tom Sawyer*. "He seemed to take a vindictive pleasure in punishing the least shortcomings. The consequence was, small boys spent their days in terror and sufferings and their nights plotting revenge."[49] Small girls suffered as well. Anyone who fidgeted or whispered in school, Laura Ingalls learned in *On the Banks of Plum Creek*, "had to walk up to Teacher's desk and hold out her hand while Teacher slapped it many times, hard, with a ruler."[50]

Schools, as Madeleine Grumet has argued, could not possibly keep the sentimental promise that a compassionate maternal disciplinary order could restore social cohesion. In the first half of the nineteenth century, industrialization, urbanization, and immigration threatened patriarchal authority, intensified class conflict, and accentuated cultural differences in American society. "The intimacy, spirituality, and innocence that teachers and students were to inherit from the mother/child bond," Grumet argues, "collapsed into strategies for social control."[51]

At the end of the nineteenth century, social conflicts once again shook American society and again reshaped the terms in which Americans wrestled with the relationship of discipline and punishment in schools. According to progressive reformers, the specialization of labor required in new, large-scale industrial centers deprived those involved of complete knowledge of the nature of production. Dispossessed of such transcendent awareness, people in related occupations developed group identities and class consciousness, threatening the moral and political virtues of American society. Reformers invested new hopes in the power of the state to promote the common good—at least as they understood it—in the face of threats to American life. In addition to promoting compulsory schooling and creating the juvenile court, they sought to regulate children's lives with new, bureaucratized forms of discipline that challenged the disciplinary order of the common school.[52]

Bureaucratic forms of schooling, as historian Ronald Butchart argues, "embedded new and elaborated disciplinary technologies in structures, procedures, rituals, and processes . . . rather than in the teacher, his pedagogy, or student interests." Such systems as tracking and the graded school facilitated the imposition of "impersonal bureaucratic surveillance." Moreover, the use of retention and other educational procedures as punishments was entirely consistent with the bureaucratic organization of schooling.[53]

Bureaucratic reforms, however, capture only half of the disciplinary regime of progressive education. Noting "connections between therapeutic conceptions of society, the rise of social pathology as a profession, and the appropriation of familial functions by agencies of socialized reproduction," Christopher Lasch has argued that in progressive institutions "the juvenile delinquent was treated not as a criminal but as a victim of circumstances." Progressive educators combined maternal compassion with science and professionalism in their rejection of punitive approaches to discipline.[54]

Wiltwyck School for delinquent New York City boys epitomized the progressive commitment to internalized discipline grounded in child-centered pedagogy and compassionate, therapeutic relationships. The school employed many of the familiar elements of progressive education in addressing what it understood as the psychological pathologies and academic deficits of its troubled students. Teachers tailored instruction to each boy's interests and needs. Exploring the woods and streams surrounding Wiltwyck, future boxer Floyd Patterson caught a snake. When Wiltwyck director Ernst Papanek told him he could study the animal in class, Patterson, for the first time in his life, began to take interest in his studies. Wiltwyck's pedagogy was epitomized by art teacher/therapist Edith Kramer. Born in Austria, Kramer had studied painting in Vienna and Freudian child psychology at the Psychoanalytic Institute of Prague. Kramer saw art as a way for students to bring order to conflicting emotions and impulses. Like psychological well-being, Kramer believed, artistic creation was "always menaced from two sides: primeval chaos and stereotyped order." Like the artist, the troubled student created a healthy order through purposeful activity.[55]

In addition to guiding students' activity, teachers befriended the boys and became their confidants. Student Butch Bosket often escaped to the attic, where one of the women on the staff mended the boys' clothes. "The only real sense of family I ever had," Bosket would write counselor Bill Ballard three decades after his stay at the school, "I had at Wiltwyck."[56]

Reliance on purposeful activity and intrinsic motivation rather than on artificial rewards and punishments infused Wiltwyck's approach to discipline. In order "to keep a sense of democracy alive in the school and alive in the boys," a student council was organized; through it, boys were encouraged to work out problems with each other. There was, Floyd Patterson would recall, "no punishment in the sense a kid off the streets expects. Nobody gets whipped or locked up." "Punishment," Wiltwyck director Ernst Papanek explained to Patterson, "teaches the child only how to punish. Scolding teaches him how to scold. By showing him that we understand, we teach him to understand. By helping him, we teach him to help. He learns cooperation by cooperating."[57]

In 1943, reformers attempted to bring Wiltwyck's approach to New York's public schools. The Harlem Project sought to convince educators that every academic failure served only to heighten students' insecurity, and that "law-enforcing" techniques served only to discourage a student's sense of inner direction and self-worth. If schools were less committed to mindless enforcement of rules, thus generating resistance and aggravating behavior problems, reformers argued, antisocial behavior would decline and learning would increase. Rather than molding the child to the school, the project demanded that educators incorporate "knowledge of children's problems" into their classroom practices and demonstrate "flexibility in shaping the school to meet the child's needs."[58]

Unfortunately, reformers concluded, urban schools were inhospitable to humane approaches. Bias in law enforcement, inadequate social services, economic deprivation, "the walls of race prejudice," and "emotional emptiness at home" circumscribed the potential of school-based interventions. Moreover, instead of fighting against the brutalization experienced by their students, Harlem's schools were themselves obstacles to mental hygiene: classrooms were barren, humiliations and violent punishment pervaded students' days, racism was widespread among teachers, and few adults challenged the abusive norms of the school. Reformers objected to the policy of denying promotion as a punishment for excessive absence. Teachers and administrators saw truancy as a violation of school rules; clinicians saw it as a reaction to "frustration," a symptom of a deeper problem.[59]

For a brief time in the 1950s and 1960s, amid the hopes of civil rights activists that the integration of schools would herald the establishment of racial justice in America, attempts to apply progressive forms of discipline to troubled urban youth expanded.[60] Over the course of the 1960s, however, these efforts to embed discipline in the educational processes of established institutions and in relationships between professional educators and disadvantaged youth lost much of their luster.

With the displacement of integrationism by nationalism among blacks and the flowering of the New Left among white dissidents, activists became increasingly convinced that the interventions of professional educators in bureaucratic urban schools oppressed the youthful inmates assigned to them. Sonny Carson had served time in prison before becoming a leader in the struggle to win "community control" of New York's ghetto schools. For his first nineteen years, Carson would recall, "the school houses were the prisons, and the prisons were the prisons posing as schoolhouses, and the many sides of genocide continued to perpetuate itself, in whatever form."[61] Similarly, referring to the number of secondary school students and to the political trials of the late 1960s, a white underground newspaper urged, "Free the New York City 275,000."[62] The oppressive pathology of school bureaucracy was the central theme of such popular authors as Jonathan Kozol, Herb Kohl, and John Holt. With the very legitimacy of schooling under attack, the disciplinary strategies that had been employed at Wiltwyck smacked increasingly of paternalism and colonialism.

The changing fate of liberal discipline mirrored wider political changes in America. "There is a time when the operation of the machine becomes so odious, makes you so sick at heart," Mario Savio had argued in his famous 1964 injunction to Free Speech Movement protesters, "that you can't take part; and you've got to put your bodies upon the gears and upon the wheels, upon the levers, upon all the apparatus and you've got to make it stop."[63] The 1970 protests at Kent State and the wider antiwar movement drew on widespread discontent with the bureaucratic state, as did calls for school decentralization and the deinstitutionalization of mental hospitals,[64] together with a series of Supreme Court decisions that extended civil rights and liberties to youth and students.[65] Whereas in 1960 virtually no states banned corporal punishment in schools, today a majority do so.[66]

The expansion of their rights proved to be a mixed bag for troubled youth, however. As leading liberal juvenile court judge Justine Wise Polier argued, the winning of due process had reduced the injustices faced by children and youth, but they had "paid an unanticipated price for its benefits. Higher benches were raised between judges and youths brought before the Juvenile Courts. Hands-on efforts to help youth by probation were restricted. Antiseptic distancing between court personnel and youth obscured their pain. Counsel bent on preventing intervention overlooked suffering that called for help."[67]

Moreover, if youthful movements promoting the New Left, Black Power, and the youth culture catalyzed the critique of liberal institutions and of the progressive disciplinary nexus of compassion, self-directed activity, and bureaucratic surveillance, it was the political Right, in the decades following the 1960s, that brought the attack on liberalism to ironic life. The declining fortunes of liberal approaches to discipline mirrored the declining fortunes of New Deal politics in American life and of the industrial economy that had sustained it.[68]

With the eclipse of compassionate notions of social control, the decades following the 1960s witnessed both escalating attacks on government social welfare programs and the growth of intensely punitive approaches to social control. The spread of school security forces in the face of black protest eroded school administrators' authority to deal informally with troubled students and encouraged the criminalization of misbehaving youth.[69] Teachers rationalized a growing reluctance to discipline students by the mistaken belief that students' new rights exposed teachers to a likelihood of being sued.[70]

At the same time, the movement to expand students' rights proved short-lived. The 1975 Goss decision was the high-water mark of legal restrictions on punitive disciplinary practices; thereafter, the Supreme Court steadily cut back on students' rights. By 1985, the Supreme Court claimed that "the primary duty of school officials and teachers . . . is the education and training of young people. . . . Without first establishing discipline and maintaining order, teachers cannot begin to educate their students."[71]

In recent years, the trend toward criminalization of youth has accelerated. As Chicago schools began expelling students for nonviolent misbehavior, authorities imposed twenty times more expulsions in the 1998–99 school year than five years earlier.[72] Meanwhile, New York City placed its 3,300 school security officers under police department control. Playground fistfights, which used to result in some sort of school-based discipline, now lead to arrests. Although teachers initially worried about police in the schools, they led the successful campaign to add nine hundred more school safety officers.[73]

Over time, the means and ends of school discipline have shifted, but patterns of classroom order have always mirrored the values of the wider society. Today, the force of punishment dominates compassionate methods of discouraging violence in schools. This punitive approach to classroom order does not reflect a reasoned response to actual behavior of youth but rather biases deeply embedded in the culture and structure of American schooling.

Still, today as in the past, the mix of compassion and punishment in schools is not predetermined. The culture and structure of schooling present educators and citizens with possibilities, however incomplete, to model a more compassionate disciplinary order.

Americans cannot create safe schools by ignoring the tensions that characterize contemporary life. Given the pervasive, oppressive institutionalized social inequalities of the schools and the inevitable confusion of children and adults about proper standards of conduct in contemporary American life, educators face the contradictory tasks of simultaneously inculcating democratic predispositions while encouraging free-wheeling inquiry, of using their authority to foster compassion and to protect the disenfranchised while also fostering the intellectual and moral agency of each child.

The same dilemmas that pervade the task of creating safe schools pervade the task of creating a good society. Punitive measures threaten students, and freedom of expression is vital to their well-being. On the other hand, the history of discipline calls attention to beneficent elements of compassionate social control for troubled youths.

We are ill equipped, in both our legal and our pedagogical thinking, to encourage freedom of students' expression without abandoning youth. Yet as philosopher John Dewey argued, "there is no such thing as liberty in general. One has to examine what persons *can* do and what they *cannot* do."[74] Freedom, then, is not a generic condition but rather the possibility of doing particular things; one might say the same of order. If order is defined as the conditions that foster purposeful activity, free-wheeling inquiry—by means of which students learn to think critically and compassionately about the society in which they live and about their individual and collective places in it—is vital to orderly schools. The promotion of such inquiry does far more to protect school children than do ill-conceived, counterproductive campaigns to police youth.

NOTES

An earlier version of portions of this chapter appeared in Daniel Perlstein, "Failing at Kindness: How the Fear of School Violence Has Endangered Children," *Educational Leadership* 57 (Mar. 2000): 76–79.

1. Frank Kogan, "School's Been Blown to Pieces," *Village Voice*, Apr. 28, 1999.

2. "A Year after Columbine Tragedy, Hard Lessons for Administrators," *Education Week*, Mar. 15, 2000, 14.

3. "Clinton Wants More Police Assigned to School Beats," *Washington Post*, June 17, 1998.

4. John Pennington, "Jonesboro Boys Can't Be Tried as Adults under State Law," *Hot Springs (Ark.) Sentinel-Record*, March 27, 1998; "Legislation Offered for Juvenile Murder," *Commercial Appeal*, Apr. 16, 1998. See, however, "Don't Lower Adult Crime Age, Huckabee Says," *Commercial Appeal*, Apr. 23, 1998.

5. Elizabeth Donohue, Vincent Schiraldi, and Jason Ziedenberg, *School House Hype: The School*

Shootings, and the Real Risks Kids Face in America (San Francisco: Justice Policy Institute, 1998).

6. William Clinton, "Radio Address by the President to the Nation" (Atlanta: White House Office of the Press Secretary, Apr. 15, 2000); available on the World Wide Web at http://www.pub.whitehouse.gov/uri-res/I2R?urn:pdi://oma.eop.gov.us/2000/4/18/1.text.1). By contrast, the administration offered only twenty million dollars for counseling programs.

7. Jessica Portner, "Girl's Slaying Elicits Calls for Metal Detectors," *Education Week*, 15 March 2000, 3.

8. Donohue, Schiraldi, and Ziedenberg, "School House Hype."

9. Irwin Hyman and Pamela Snook, *Dangerous Schools: What We Can Do about the Physical and Emotional Abuse of Our Children* (San Francisco: Jossy-Bass, 1999), 5, 87. Succumbing to widespread ridicule and protests that had resulted in fifty students being suspended, Nevis (Minn.) High School amended its zero-tolerance policy and allowed Samantha Jones to pose with the cannon at the local VFW post for the yearbook as long as the cannon was draped in an American flag ("Flag-Covered Cannon Ends Yearbook Dispute," *New York Times*, Nov. 26, 1999).

10. Tom Kenworthy, "Eager Return to Columbine," *Washington Post*, Aug. 17, 1999.

11. Maria Newman, "Parents Find That the Rules for Play Have Changed," *New York Times*, Apr. 7, 2000; Jennifer Harper, "'Robbers' Suspended from N.J. School; 'Cops' Too," *Washington Times*, Apr. 7, 2000.

12. Paul Kingery, Mark Coggeshall, and Aaron Alford, "Weapon Carrying by Youth," *Education and Urban Society* 31 (May 1999): 309.

13. Donohue, Schiraldi, and Zeidenberg, "School House Hype." Whereas approximately forty people (including adults) have been killed in schools in recent years, some 1,700 children have died at the hands of family members. Three thousand children have been killed by gunfire away from school.

14. Daniel Perlstein, "Failing at Kindness: How the Fear of School Violence Endangers Children," *Educational Leadership* 57 (March 2000): 76–79. The FBI recommended that schools pay students from five to a hundred dollars for tips that proved instrumental in stopping crimes. It also distributed a school killer profile that advised authorities to be on the lookout for students who had troubles with their parents, disliked popular students or bullies, had recently broken up, wore sloppy clothing, or had an interest in Nietzsche. The bureau was forced to admit that the profile had no demonstrated predictive value. Stephen Band and Joseph Harpold, "School Violence: Lessons Learned," *FBI Law Enforcement Bulletin*, Sept. 1999, 12–15; "Educators Wary of Misuse of FBI 'Profiling' for Schools," *Education Week*, Oct. 6, 1999, 15.

15. Daniel Perlstein, "Saying the Unsaid: Girl Killing and the Curriculum," *Journal of Curriculum and Supervision* 14 (Fall 1998): 88–104.

16. Margaret Smith Crocco, "The Missing Discourse about Gender and Sexuality in the Social Studies," *Theory and Research in Social Education*, forthcoming.

17. Nan Stein, *Classrooms and Courtrooms* (New York: Teachers College Press, 1999); Tracy Harachi, Richard Catalano, and J. David Hawkins, "United States," in *The Nature of School Bullying*, ed. Peter Smith, Yohji Morita, Josine Junger-Tas, Dan Olweus, Richard Catalano, and Phillip Slee (London: Routledge, 1999), 279–95.

18. Stein, *Classrooms and Courtrooms*, 79, 84, 92. Schools create zero-tolerance policies in part out of fear that they will be sued for applying rules unevenly. This has contributed substantially to a vast increase in expulsions and suspensions over the past decade. Dirk Johnson, "Schools Are Cracking Down on Misconduct," *New York Times*, Dec. 1, 1999; Mark Walsh, "Shootings Raise Host of Legal Questions," *Education Week*, 5 May 1999, 1, 14–15; Harper, "'Robbers' Suspended."

19. See Daniel Perlstein, "Saying the Unsaid."

20. Barrie Thorne, *Gender Play: Girls and Boys in School* (New Brunswick, N.J.: Rutgers Univ. Press, 1993); Penelope Eckert, *Jocks and Burnouts: Social Categories and Identity in the High School* (New York: Teachers College Press, 1989).

21. Hyman and Snook, *Dangerous Schools*, 45. Eighty percent of corporal punishments involved

nonviolent acts. As the authors point out, authorities do not respond to a knifing with a paddle (39).

22. Susan Kaeser, "Suspensions in School Discipline," *Education and Urban Society* 11 (Aug. 1979): 465–84.

23. Mike Males and Dan Macallair, *The Color of Justice: An Analysis of Juvenile Adult Court Transfers in California* (San Francisco: Justice Policy Institute, 2000).

24. Deborah Prothrow-Stith, *Deadly Consequences* (New York: HarperCollins, 1991), 24; Pedro Noguera, "Listen First: How Student Perspectives on Violence Can Be Used to Create Safer Schools," in *Violence in Children's Lives*, ed. Valerie Polakow (New York: Teachers College Press, forthcoming).

25. Hawkins, "United States," 281; Robert Sampson, "The Community Context of Violent Crime," in *Sociology and the Public Agenda*, ed. William Julius Wilson (Newbury Park, Calif.: Sage, 1993), 260; Jessica Portner, "Complex Set of Ills Spurs Rising Teen Suicide Rate," *Education Week*, Apr. 12, 2000, 1, 22–31.

26. Henry Lufler, Jr., "Debating with Untested Assumptions," *Education and Urban Society* 11 (Aug. 1979): 453.

27. John Devine, *Maximum Security: The Culture of Violence in Inner-City Schools* (Chicago: Univ. of Chicago Press, 1996), 98.

28. Kay Hymowitz, *Ready or Not: Why Treating Children as Small Adults Endangers Their Future and Ours* (New York: Free Press, 2000); William Clune III, "Evaluating School Discipline through Empirical Research," *Education and Urban Society* 11 (Aug. 1979): 441.

29. Franklin Zimring, *American Youth Violence* (New York: Oxford Univ. Press, 1998); Keith Bradsher, "Fear of Crime Trumps Fear of Lost Youth," *New York Times*, Nov. 21, 1999.

30. Russ Skiba and Reece Peterson, "The Dark Side of Zero Tolerance: Can Punishment Lead to Safe Schools?" *Phi Delta Kappan* 80 (Jan. 1999): 372–76, 381–82.

31. Rodger Bybee and E. Gordon Gee, *Violence, Values, and Justice in the Schools* (Boston: Allyn and Bacon, 1982), 28. See also Philip Greven, *Spare the Rod: The Religious Roots of Punishment and the Psychological Impact of Physical Abuse* (New York: Vintage, 1992); Robert Lane, *Beyond the Schoolhouse Gate: Free Speech and the Inculcation of Values* (Philadelphia: Temple Univ. Press, 1995), 17.

32. Gary and Anne Marie Ezzo, *Growing Kids God's Way* (Simi Valley, Calif.: Growing Families International, 1990), 74. See also Den Trumbull and S. DuBose Ravenel, "Spare the Rod? New Research Challenges Spanking Critics" (Washington, D.C.: Family Research Council, Oct. 1996); Lee Shearer, "Spanking Hits at Core of Debate," *Athens (Ga.) Daily News*, March 22, 1998.

33. Barbara Finkelstein, "A Crucible of Contradictions: Historical Roots of Violence against Children in the United States," *History of Education Quarterly* 40 (Spring 2000): 2.

34. Cotton Mather, *Bonifacius* (1701), in *Social History of American Education*, ed. Rena Vassar, vol. 1 (Chicago: Rand McNally, 1965), 17; N. Ray Hiner, "Cotton Mather and His Children: The Evolution of a Parent Educator, 1686–1728," in *Regulated Children, Liberated Children: Education in Psychohistorical Perspective*, ed. Barbara Finkelstein (New York: Psychohistory Press, 1979), 33, 35–36, 39.

35. Benjamin Rush, "A Plan for the Establishment of Schools and the Diffusion of Knowledge. . . ," quoted in Carl Kaestle, *Pillars of the Republic* (New York: Hill and Wang, 1983), 7. See David Tyack, "Forming the National Character: Paradox in the Educational Thought of the Revolutionary Generation," *Harvard Educational Review* 36 (Winter 1966): 29–41; and Daniel Perlstein, "'There is No Escape . . . from the Ogre of Indoctrination': George Counts and the Civic Dilemmas of Democratic Educators," in *Reconstructing the Common Good in Education: Coping with Intractable American Dilemmas*, ed. Larry Cuban and Dorothy Shipps (Stanford, Calif.: Stanford Univ. Press, 2000), 51–67.

36. Lorraine Smith Pangle and Thomas Pangle, *The Learning of Liberty: The Educational Ideas of the American Founders* (Lawrence: Univ. of Kansas Press, 1993), 33.

37. Jefferson quoted in R. J. Honeywell, *The Educational Works of Thomas Jefferson* (New York: Russell & Russell, 1964), 134; Pangle and Pangle, *The Learning of Liberty*, 165.

38. *Tinker v. Des Moines Independent Community School District*, 393 U.S. 503 (1969).

39. Benjamin Rush, "Thoughts on the Amusements and Punishments which are proper for Schools" (1790), in *Children and Youth in America: A Documentary History*, ed. Robert Bremner, vol. 1 (Cambridge, Mass.: Harvard Univ. Press, 1970), 221.

40. Jefferson quoted in Honeywell, *Educational Works*, 134.

41. *West Virginia v. Barnette*, 319 U.S. 637, quoted in *Tinker v. Des Moines Independent Community School District*.

42. Mary Ryan, *Cradle of the Middle Class* (Cambridge: Cambridge Univ. Press, 1981), 158–59.

43. Ryan, *Cradle of the Middle Class*, 105.

44. Elizabeth Peabody, foreword to Friedrich Froebel, *Mother-Play and Nursery Songs*, trans. Fannie Dwight and Josephine Jarvis (Boston: Lothrop, Lee & Shepard, 1906), 7.

45. David Tyack and Elisabeth Hansot, *Managers of Virtue: Public School Leadership in America, 1820–1980* (New York: Basic Books, 1982), 56–57.

46. Jonathan Masserli, *Horace Mann: A Biography* (New York: Knopf, 1972), 414, 417, 420; David Tyack and Elisabeth Hansot, *Learning Together: A History of Coeducation in American Public Schools* (New Haven, Conn.: Yale Univ. Press, 1990), 67.

47. Barbara Finkelstein, *Governing the Young: Teacher Behavior in Popular Primary Schools in 19th Century United States* (New York: Falmer 1989), 155–265.

48. Henry Van Dyke, "Corporal Punishment in Our Schools," *The Clearing House* 57 (March 1984): 296.

59. Mark Twain, *The Adventures of Tom Sawyer*, quoted in Van Dyke, "Corporal Punishment," 299.

50. Laura Ingalls Wilder, *On the Banks of Plum Creek* (New York: HarperCollins, 1953), 151.

51. Madeleine Grumet, *Bitter Milk: Women and Teaching* (Amherst: Univ. of Massachusetts Press, 1988), 43.

52. See Daniel Perlstein, "Community and Democracy in American Schools: Arthurdale and the Fate of Progressive Education," *Teachers College Record* 97 (Summer 1996): 625–50.

53. Ronald Butchart, "Punishments, Penalties, Prizes, and Procedures: A History of Discipline in U.S. Schools," in *Classroom Discipline in American Schools: Problems and Possibilities for Democratic Education*, ed. Ronald Butchart (Albany: State Univ. of New York Press, 1998), 25.

54. Christopher Lasch, *Haven in a Heartless World: The Family Besieged* (New York: Free Press, 1977), 15.

55. Edith Kramer, "Art and Emptiness: New Problems in Art Education and Art Therapy," *Bulletin of Art Therapy* 1 (Fall 1961): 7.

56. Fox Butterfield, *All God's Children: The Bosket Family and the American Tradition of Violence* (New York: Avon, 1996), 95–98.

57. Floyd Patterson (with Milton Gross), *Victory over Myself* (New York: Bernard Geis, 1962), 24–28, 31–32.

58. Joint Advisory Committee on the Harlem Project, Research Committee, *The Role of the School in Preventing and Correcting Maladjustment and Delinquency: A Study in Three Schools, September 1943–June 1945* (New York: privately published, 1947) 16–17, 58, 180–81.

59. Joint Advisory Committee, *The Role of the School*, 16–17, 34, 154, 156.

60. Lois Weiner, *Preparing Teachers for Urban Schools: Lessons from Thirty Years of School Reform* (New York: Teachers College Press, 1993), 14. On the impact of civil rights activism in challenging current zero-tolerance policies, see Robert Johnson, "Decatur Furor Sparks Wider Policy Debate," *Education Week*, Nov. 24, 1999, 1.

61. Mwlina Imiri Abubadika (Sonny Carson), *The Education of Sonny Carson* (New York: Norton, 1972), 57.

62. "Free the New York City 275,000," *New York Herald Tribune*, March 1970.

63. Mario Savio, Dec. 3, 1964, quoted in Charles Burress, "Symbolic Steps: UC Berkeley Names Legendary Protest Spot after Mario Savio," *San Francisco Chronicle*, Dec. 3, 1997.

64. Dan A. Lewis, *Worlds of the Mentally Ill: How Deinstitutionalization Works in the City* (Carbondale:

Southern Illinois Univ. Press, 1991); Dan A. Lewis, *Race and Educational Reform in the American Metropolis: A Study of School Decentralization* (Albany: State Univ. of New York Press, 1995).

65. *In re Gault*, 387 U.S. 1 (1967); *Tinker v. Des Moines Independent Community School District*, 393 U.S. 503 (1969); *Goss v. Lopez*, 419 U.S. 565 (1975).

66. Hyman and Snook, *Dangerous Schools*, 3.

67. Justine Wise Polier, *Juvenile Justice in Double Jeopardy: The Distanced Community and Vengeful Retribution* (Hillsdale, N.J.: Erlbaum, 1989), 11.

68. Butchart, *Classroom Discipline*, 25; Ruth Gilmore, "Globalisation and U.S. Prison Growth: From Military Keynesianism to Post Keynesian Militarism," *Race & Class* 40 (Fall 1998/Winter 1999): 171–88. On the relationship of Right and Left ideologies in the 1960s, see Rebecca Klatch, *A Generation Divided: The New Left, the New Right, and the 1960s* (Berkeley: Univ. of California Press, 1999).

69. Larry Burgan and Robert Rubel, "Public School Security: Yesterday, Today, and Tomorrow," *Contemporary Education* 11 (Fall 1980): 13–15.

70. Lufler, "Debating with Untested Assumptions," 460.

71. *New Jersey v. T.L.O.*, 469 U.S. 325 (1985).

72. Johnson, "Schools Are Cracking Down"; Natalie Pardo, "Expulsions Rise, But Safety Issues Persist," *Chicago Reporter*, Sept. 1998; Kimberly Fornek, "Program Loses Seats as Expulsions Soar," *Catalyst*, Feb. 1999.

73. Adrienne Coles, "Crime Drops since NYPD Takeover of School Security," *Education Week*, March 15, 2000, 6.

74. John Dewey, "Liberty and Social Control," *Social Frontier* (Nov. 1935): 41.

Competing and Compelling Interests
Response to Perlstein

MARY ANNE HIGGINS

Communication Studies, Kent State University

Daniel Perlstein argues against punitive approaches to discipline. As he notes, in the wake of recent school shootings, many educators and legislators have promoted and adopted policies that punish students and police schools. Among the examples Perlstein cites are a statewide campaign to lower to twelve the age at which a child can be tried as an adult, a governor's plan to ban after-school activities and evening sports events, and a school district's decision to ban hand-holding in response to claims that a star athlete had sexually assaulted eleven girls. He describes efforts to fortify school security that involve metal detectors, motion-sensitive cameras, and armed security guards.

According to Perlstein, lawmakers and administrators who support the punitive approach to discipline have wrongly concluded that it will strengthen the security of schools and ensure the safety of students. Instead, Perlstein claims that such repressive measures jeopardize student welfare because they fail to address the root causes of school violence: inequality, bullying, sexual harassment, and homophobic teasing.

The points that Perlstein makes about punitive approaches to discipline are well taken and well supported. As he suggests, such approaches cannot restore an orderliness that has never existed; they can only reinforce an established order that supports male supremacy, stigmatizes girls, and imposes narrow behavioral standards on boys. The real threat to students is represented by the status quo that maintains the social hierarchy in schools, situates students in "out groups" and "in groups," and confers the status of "outsider" or "insider" upon each student. All of the students who went on shooting sprees in Georgia, Colorado, Kentucky, and Oregon were outsiders.[1] Before they became victimizers, they were victims.

As Perlstein keenly observes, a punitive model of discipline would reject that duality, but a compassionate model would embrace the concept that a student can be both victim and victimizer. Teachers, counselors, and other individuals who support compassionate approaches to discipline recognize that either/or statements and zero-tolerance policies cannot account for dualities, ambiguities, and other bewildering elements that characterize contemporary life. They also recognize the importance of maintaining an atmosphere of trust and an environment conducive

309

to communication. They, like Perlstein, believe that disciplinary approaches encouraging free expression and thoughtful reflection help students develop the courage and confidence needed to share their concerns with each other. Perhaps then the conditions that foster school violence would be replaced with those that foster a sense of community.

Perlstein and those who echo his concerns should be commended for their commitment to a cause that is often ignored or misunderstood by the media. Unlike punitive disciplinary approaches, which emphasize conflict and other "news values," compassionate approaches to discipline do not attract much media coverage. Both approaches, though, will continue to attract controversy.

From a historical perspective, Perlstein notes that debates about punitive and compassionate approaches date back to Puritan New England and Cotton Mather's seemingly paradoxical sermons on moral instruction. Mather urged parents to employ strict rules and corporal punishment to restrain the sinful influences of their children; he also urged parents to employ gentle guidance to cultivate their children's spirituality. As Perlstein points out, the debate about disciplinary approaches also reflects the difficulty encountered by revolutionaries who have sought to strike a balance between order and freedom in a democratic society. The competing interests that have characterized the history of our society and the history of our schools will continue to stir debate about legislation and education.

From a utopian perspective, compassionate approaches would hold sway over punitive approaches. Every student in school and every member of society would be self-motivated and self-disciplined. Behavior would be guided by internal standards instead of external controls. Those standards would be based on a set of assumptions that are consistent with the ideals of a democratic society and assure a balance between freedom and order. One of those assumptions holds that disputes are best settled and policies are best established through a process of communication, not coercion.

But that assumption, however noble, is flawed. "Fighting words" and "hate speech" blur the distinction between communication and coercion. Our society does not always function democratically. When it does, the majority rules, and history demonstrates that the minority voice has often sounded the more reasoned opinion. The balance between freedom and order is far from perfect.

So it is with the tension between punitive and compassionate methods of discipline in our schools. Like the right to a fair trial and the right to a public trial, the need to impose order and the right to free expression sometimes clash. When that occurs, the resolution, whether it is determined in the schools or by the courts, must favor the interest that is more compelling. In the wake of the recent school shootings, the more compelling interest is order. When acts of violence or threats of violence perpetrated by an individual or a group of students threaten the rights and the lives of other students, the perpetrators must be punished.

That decision, though, is far from perfect. It is a decision forced by expedience. In that regard, it is similar to the choice fifteen-year-old Kip Kinkel made three years ago. Shortly after he killed his parents, he drove to Thurston High School and killed four of his classmates and wounded several others. Before the day was over, he had surrendered to police, who questioned him about the shooting spree. "I had to do it," Kip replied. In a more desperate tone, he added that "the voices in his head" would not go away until he committed the murders.[2]

The month of May 2000 marks not only the thirtieth anniversary of the tragedy at Kent State. It also marks the third anniversary of the tragedy in Springfield, Oregon. Both events serve to remind us of the delicate balance between freedom and order and the tragic consequences that result when expedience dictates choice.

NOTES

1. Stephen King, "The Bogeyboys" (speech presented at the meeting of the Vermont Library Conference, VEMA Annual Meeting, May 26, 1999).

2. PBS, *Killer at Thurston High*, Jan. 18, 2000.

The Work of the School

Response to Perlstein

LESLIE FRIEDMAN GOLDSTEIN

Political Science, University of Delaware

> This case does not concern speech or action that intrudes upon the work of
> the school or the rights of other students.
>
> —Justice Abe Fortas, *Tinker v. Des Moines* (1969)

The title of my remarks is drawn from a statement in Justice Abe Fortas's opinion
upholding the right of high school students to wear black armbands in silent protest against the same war that gave rise to the conflicts involved in the Kent State
killings of thirty years ago. What is, after all, the "work of the school," and how
exactly does that work relate to the freedom of expression that most scholars consider the hallmark of what is attractive about American society?

This theme, or this query, underlies the Dan Perlstein essay. His essay offers a
historic overview of the contrasting and yet always interwoven threads in the American tapestry of efforts to school children in preparation for democratic citizenship.
The thread of compassion has competed with the thread of sternness, freedom with
order, loving-kindness with corporal punishment. A Deweyan·emphasis on moti-
vation-driven learning has competed with prescriptive, fear-driven memorization.
So it has gone on, up to the present, in which a majority of states—in sharp contrast to the 1960s—now ban corporal punishment; on the other hand, however,
urban and even suburban schools employ metal detectors, uniformed police, video
cameras, and frequent expulsions.

In his admirable effort to provide a comprehensive picture of this complex reality,
Perlstein ends up on occasion appearing to argue against himself. Twice we are told
that fistfights at school, which used to be settled by teachers or other school staff, now
trigger the involvement of police. Misbehaving students receive expulsions or criminal penalties at much higher rates than in the past. The basic argument of the essay is
that "punitive disciplinary practices that curtail rather than expand freedom of inquiry and expression abandon the educational mission of the schools." Yet we also
learn that schools are unfortunately permeated with a violence-laden, sexualized hierarchy in which macho males (such as school sports heroes), and those who admire

them, bully and taunt and act violently toward girls and what they consider girlish boys. The author rightly complains that "systematic student violence is frequently overlooked by teachers and administrators," leaving certain students unprotected.

How then does he lament educational administrators' attempts to combat school violence, even if their policies of "zero tolerance" for "cruelty, harassment, excessive teasing, discrimination, violence, intimidation" do end up not accomplishing what the author wants but being both ineffective and repressive. I am not trying to score petty contradiction-counting points here; I am trying to get to the bottom of the real relation between discipline, on the one hand, and "the work of the school" on the other. While I agree with Perlstein that this "work" is to prepare students for engaging in free inquiry and for participating in the polity as citizens free to express their views on matters of public import, I wish to draw attention to the potential role of discipline as a handmaiden in this endeavor. His paper does not suggest more compassionate varieties of discipline as alternatives to jailing and expulsions. Rather, his paper offers only the suggestion that punitive approaches be supplanted by educational opportunities—by "pedagogical interventions that integrate study of . . . normal violence into the academic curriculum."

Let me offer, by contrast, at least one cheer for such things as expulsions and zero-tolerance policies. If students are to learn to enjoy the free inquiry that schools aim (or should aim) to foster, students, including girls and "girlish boys," need to feel safe and secure. Moreover, they need a certain peacefulness of atmosphere, a quiet in their surroundings, that will enable them to focus on the task at hand. If they have to function in fear of chronic intimidation or harassment, let alone fear of sexual assault by or fistfights with schoolyard bullies, then learning—"the work of the school"—is impaired. If creating such safe and secure conditions in public schools entails expelling students who beat up other students or sexually assault them, or imprisoning people who bring loaded guns to school, then regretfully, it becomes the work of the school to do those things too.

Perlstein points to the inevitable "inequity" that harsh school expulsion policies exact upon children of low-income and minority races. It would be foolish to deny that there are administrators prejudiced by both class and race, who implement these policies with an uneven hand. But it is also no news that low-income neighborhoods experience elevated rates of violent crime, and it is not praiseworthy to fail to protect low-income people against becoming victims of crime out of some misguided fear that evenhanded law enforcement would result in statistics that look biased.

Professor Perlstein singles out egregious examples of idiotic administrators who have punished five-year-olds for pointing their fingers and saying "bang, bang," or who ban all hand-holding in response to multiple sexual assaults. But the fact that one can find school officials who behave incompetently does not demonstrate that all punishments against in-school violence or bullying are misguided.

In blaming "punitive disciplinary practices" per se for curtailing freedom of inquiry, Professor Perlstein winds up, strangely enough, aligned with the very jurist whose point of view in the *Tinker* case he most criticizes, Justice Hugo Black. It is Justice Black, bewailing the "permissiveness" that would allow schoolchildren to express their own points of view on issues as controversial as the war in Vietnam, who links freedom for the expression of opinion to a total breakdown of school discipline. For Black (as for Perlstein), freedom of inquiry and freedom of expression in the schoolhouse are intrinsically *contrary* to and undermine classroom discipline. The Perlstein/Black position contrasts directly with that of Justice Abe Fortas, who carefully distinguished permissible school disciplinary policies—targeting "disruptive conduct" that materially interferes with class work or with the rights of other students—from constitutionally forbidden school policies that would punish the mere expression of nonconforming opinions. In drawing this distinction Justice Fortas is suggesting that protection of the rights of the nondisruptive students—including their rights to learn and exchange ideas in a safe and secure atmosphere—is a part of the work that schools have to do. It is Justice Black, by contrast, who lumps together *all* disobedience to any order from a school official, whether banning the silent wearing of a political armband or forbidding "crimes committed by youth . . . of school age[, such as] . . . break-ins, sit-ins, lie-ins, and smash-ins[,] . . . rioting, property seizures, and destruction."[1] It is an unfortunate implication of Professor Perlstein's paper that all punitive discipline in schools, whether aimed at protecting innocent students or directly at suppression of free inquiry, ends up in the same place, the repression of freedom of inquiry and expression. I would argue to the contrary, that a distinction between liberty and license lies at the core of the concept of a free society, and that Professor Perlstein's essay too often displays an unfortunate tendency to blur that distinction.

NOTE

1. *Tinker v. Des Moines* 393 U.S. 503 (1969), 525–26.

Discipline and Democracy
Response to the Discussants

DANIEL PERLSTEIN

My "Unspoken Dangers" argued that the drive to punish students is based on deeply held social, religious, and political beliefs, not on a dispassionate or compassionate analysis of the actual behavior of youth. This argument is confirmed in the two responses to the article. Professor Higgins laments the need to punish violent youth; Professor Goldstein seems more to relish it. Neither, however, offers evidence for the necessity or effectiveness of punishment. Both embrace punishment as an act of faith.

In fact, a substantial body of research has documented the ineffectiveness and bias of punitive youth policies. "As schools become more militarized," William Ayers and Bernadine Dohrn have argued, "they become less safe, in large part because the first casualty is the central, critical relationship between teacher and student, a relationship that is now being damaged or broken in favor of tough-sounding, impersonal, uniform procedures."[1]

On the other hand, educators have long promoted the creation of programs that ground discipline in compassionate relationships, democratic processes, and freedom of student-centered inquiry, rather than in punishment. "School discipline or order," John Dewey asserted over a century ago, is "relative to an end. If you have the end in view of forty or fifty children learning set lessons, to be recited to a teacher, your discipline must be devoted to securing that result." Such discipline, Dewey makes clear, is unworthy of democracy. Rather, he argued, discipline must "grow out of and be relative to . . . the development of a spirit of social cooperation and community life." It must be the active, noisy, messy order of the workshop, and not the "silent . . . arms folded . . . traditional school discipline," wherein "the social spirit" is "eminently wanting."[2]

Professor Goldstein charges that "Unspoken Dangers" focuses on extreme, exceptional cases of injustice and stupidity on the part of school authorities, but today extreme cases are far from exceptional. Schools across the United States have imposed hundreds of cruel punishments. In Centralia, California, a five-year-old who found a razor blade on his way to school and showed it to his teacher was expelled for violating the school district's zero-tolerance weapons policy. In Belle, West Virginia, and Colorado Springs, Colorado, children were suspended for giving cough drops to classmates. In Fairborn, Ohio, a thirteen-year-old was suspended for nine days and forced to attend drug-awareness classes for accepting a Midol tablet from a classmate. (The girl who shared the pill was deemed a drug trafficker and received an even harsher punishment, one that was upheld in federal court despite the girl's claim of racial bias in the disparate sentences.) In San Diego, a twelve-year-old was expelled for fighting with classmates who had taunted him for being fat. In Chicago, a high school junior who flicked a paper clip at a classmate, missed, and caused a small cut on a cafeteria worker was expelled from school, jailed for seven hours, charged with battery, and advised to drop out of school. In Ohio, a high school student was suspended, threatened with expulsion, and criminally charged for writing a satirical school newspaper horoscope column suggesting that students blow up their houses, assassinate the president, and wear hats to school. Another Ohio student saw his expectations of being valedictorian end when he was suspended for making a student council campaign poster threatening to blow up the boys' room—a poster that even school officials acknowledged to be satirical.[3]

Over the past decade, zero-tolerance policies have spread from violence and illegal drug to such misbehaviors as truancy, tardiness, disrespect, disobedience, and defiance. Surveying what it called "school officials' extreme and even bizarre reactions to student misbehavior," the *American Bar Association Journal* concluded that authorities meted out "punishments ranging from suspension to expulsion to referral to the juvenile court system for behaviors that even the schools agree do not actually compromise safety."[4]

Extreme, unfair punishment is inherent in punitive approaches to school discipline. As researchers Russ Skiba and Reece Peterson note, there are few incidents of serious violence in schools, but many incidents involving minor disruptions. It is inevitable therefore that "policies that set harsh consequences indiscriminately will capture a few incidents of serious violence and many incidents of minor disruption." Moreover, zero tolerance is merely the current and extreme manifestation of long-standing punitive approaches. Confusing, mean-spirited attempts to enforce order not only harm students who have shown poor judgement but also demoralize the education of innocent children whom they entrap in the absurdities of intolerance.[5]

By distancing troubled youth from school personnel, tough punishments actually increase the chances of explosive disorders. Keenly sensitive to issues of fairness, students inevitably respond to excessive punishment with cynicism and alienation, feelings that infect not only their relationship with school authorities but also their commitment to schoolwork. Because punitive approaches target speech as well as actions, they undermine the ability of students to grapple with difficult issues. In the past few years, punitive absolutism has been extended to academic work. California and a number of other states have outlawed "social promotion" and so threatened to punish thousands of children who fail to meet arbitrary standardized-test benchmarks with flunking.

The disproportionate impact of punishment on minority youth is not the result of a few bigoted, atypical individuals. Punitive policies that apply harsh penalties to all offenses do not overcome the racial and class bias of punishment; they merely add a layer of arbitrariness to it. Ironically, although the double burden of over-punishment and undereducation falls most heavily on poor and minority students, privileged youth gain no benefit from the misfortune of others. Deployed disproportionately against minorities and the poor, the cruelties of arbitrary punishment have increasingly spilled over to entrap privileged youth as well. For all students, the lessons of democracy, preached in sentimental civics lessons, are regularly contradicted in disciplinary procedures.

Unencumbered by any evidence that harsh punishment leads to better student behavior, school authorities often claim that they treat minor incidents as harshly as major ones in order to deter serious crime. When a Woonsocket, Rhode Island, twelve-year-old who brought a toy gun to class was suspended, his principal stated that suspension "sends an unambiguous message to students." Yet the principal's message is far from clear. As I argued, punishment has done little to clarify the rules for students' and educators' conduct in schools. The primary function of harsh punishment, as Pedro Noguera argues, is not to deter student misbehavior but to reinforce the power of school authorities.[6]

In "Unspoken Dangers," I critiqued both the inattention of administrators to violence and overreliance on punitive legalistic responses. Despite the important role the courts have played in addressing such matters as sexual harassment in school, the overall impact of efforts to win legal redress for students has been quite limited. In part, the influence of extreme right-wing political beliefs in the federal judiciary accounts for the limited rights students enjoy in school. In addition, a focus on rights abandons troubled youth and invites a focus on punishment. Thus, even where the courts have helped protect students, the threat of litigation has encouraged myopic, inflexible responses as often as compassionate ones.

Like punishment, compassion requires intervention in students' lives. Both approaches place limits on freedom, and both create dilemmas for educators wrestling with competing ideals. Still, by combining compassionate forms of discipline with critical, free-wheeling inquiry into the complexities of school and social life, teachers and students can overcome some of the limitations of punishment and better understand the difficult choices they face. Such a dual approach can promote both learning and safety.

Quoting Justice Abe Fortas, Professor Goldstein rightly asks, "What is the work of the school?" The question, however, contains more ambiguity than Goldstein allows. Modeling the kind of society we value is as much the work of schools as instruction in the three Rs. Moreover, Fortas's question suggests both the work schools actually do and the work schools would ideally do. Any discussion of school discipline cannot ignore the inequitable ways punishment actually functions. But even if schools could punish equitably, punishment—as Thomas Jefferson, Elizabeth Peabody, Horace Mann, John Dewey, and countless others have held—is an impoverished vision of schooling for democracy. We can do better.

NOTES

1. William Ayers and Bernadine Dohrn, "Resisting Zero Tolerance," *Rethinking Schools* (Spring 2000): 14.

2. John Dewey, *The School and Society* (Chicago: Univ. of Chicago Press, 1956), 15–17. See also William Ayers, Michael Klonsky, Gabrielle Lyon, eds., *A Simple Justice: The Challenge of Small Schools* (New York: Teachers College Press, 2000).

3. Russ Skiba and Reece Peterson, "The Dark Side of Zero Tolerance: Can Punishment Lead to Safe Schools?" *Phi Delta Kappan* 80 (Jan. 1999): 372–76, 381–82; Margaret Graham Tebo, "Zero Tolerance, Zero Sense," *ABA Journal* 86 (Apr. 2000): 40–46; "'Joke Horoscope' Leads to Student's Suspension," *Akron Beacon Journal*, May 20, 1999; Perry A. Zirkel, "Courtside, The Midol Case," *Phi Delta Kappan* 78 (June 1997): 803–4.

4. Tebo, "Zero Tolerance."

5. Skiba and Peterson, "Dark Side of Zero Tolerance."

6. Pedro Noguera, "Preventing and Producing Violence: A Critical Analysis of Responses to School Violence," *Harvard Educational Review* 65 (Summer 1995): 189–212.

11

Freedom of Expression in the United States
The Future

Cass R. Sunstein

Law, University of Chicago

What is the relationship between the killings at Kent State and the idea of free expression? Many people think that the killings carry lessons about government censorship of dissent. I do not believe that they are wrong. But the Kent State killings raise other questions as well, questions that point to some distinctive features of a system of free expression. The students at Kent State, like students in many other places, were engaged in a protest on a *commons*—a public space. Their activity was also emphatically communal; many people were there partly or largely because other people were there. At the same time, the student movement was greatly affected by the fact that like-minded students were talking mostly, and sometimes only, with one another—while those critical of the student movement were also speaking, all or most of the time, with like-minded skeptics of college students perceived as "radical," "unpatriotic," or "anti-American."

The two principal issues that I explore here are closely connected with these points: the value of common spaces in a democratic order, and the need to ensure that people of diverse views are speaking with one another rather than hearing countless echoes of their own voices. This value and this need, I suggest, will present central issues and problems for the next half-century—very possibly more important issues and problems than those raised by conventional government censorship.

THE DAILY ME

A Question and a Thesis

My purpose here is to cast some light on the relationship between democracy and new communications technologies. I do so by emphasizing the most striking power provided by emerging technologies: the growing power of consumers to "filter" what it is that they see. In the extreme case, people will be fully able to design their own communications universes. They will find it easy to exclude, in advance, topics and points of view that they wish to avoid. I will also provide some notes on the constitutional guarantee of freedom of speech.

An understanding of the dangers of filtering permits us to obtain a better sense of what makes for a well-functioning system of free expression. Above all, I urge that in a heterogeneous society, such a system requires something other than free, or publicly unrestricted, individual choices. On the contrary, it imposes two distinctive requirements. First, people should be exposed to materials that they would not have chosen in advance. Unanticipated encounters, involving topics and points of view that people have not sought out and perhaps find quite irritating, are central to democracy and even to freedom itself. Second, many or most citizens should have a range of common experiences. Without shared experiences, a heterogeneous society will have a much more difficult time addressing social problems; people may even find it hard to understand one another.

A Thought Experiment: Unlimited Filtering

The central puzzle is a thought experiment: an apparently utopian dream, that of complete individuation, in which consumers can entirely personalize (or "customize") their own communications universes.

Imagine, that is, a system of communications in which each person has unlimited power of individual design. If people want to watch news all the time, they would be entirely free to do exactly that. If they dislike news and want to watch football in the morning and situation comedies at night, that would be fine, too. If people care only about America and want to avoid international issues entirely, that would be very simple indeed; so too if they care only about New York, or Chicago, or California. If people want to restrict themselves to certain points of view, by limiting themselves to conservatives, moderates, liberals, vegetarians, or Nazis, that would be entirely feasible, through a simple "point and click."

In such a system, the market for information would be *perfected*—in the sense that consumers would be able to see exactly what they want, no more and no less. When filtering is unlimited, people can decide, in advance and with perfect accuracy, what they will and will not encounter. They can design something very much like a communications universe of their own choosing.

Our communications market is moving rapidly toward this apparently utopian picture. Any report on the details will quickly become dated, but as of this writing, a number of newspapers allow readers to create filtered versions, containing exactly what they want and excluding what they do not want. If you are interested in getting help with the design of an entirely individual paper, you can consult a number of sites, including Individual.com and Crayon.com. In reality, we are not so far from the thought experiment of complete personalization of the communications network. Thus MIT professor Nicholas Negroponte refers to the emergence of "the Daily Me"—a communications package that is personally designed, with components fully chosen in advance.

Precursors and Intermediaries

Of course, this is not entirely different from what has come before. People have always had a great deal of power to filter out unwanted materials. People who read newspapers do not read the same newspaper; some people do not read any newspaper at all. People make choices among magazines based on their tastes and their point of view. But in the emerging situation, there is a difference of degree, if not of kind. What is different is a dramatic increase in individual control over content and a corresponding decrease in the power of general-interest intermediaries. These include newspapers, magazines, and broadcasters.

People who rely on such intermediaries have a range of chance encounters, involving shared experience with diverse others and also exposure to material that they did not exactly choose. You might, for example, read the city newspaper and in the process come across a range of stories that you would not have selected if you had had the power to do so. Your eyes may come across a story about Germany, or crime in Los Angeles, or innovative business practices in Tokyo, and you may read those stories, although you would hardly have placed them in your "Daily Me." You might watch a particular television channel—perhaps you prefer Channel 4—and when your favorite program ends, you might see the beginning of another show, one that you would not have chosen in advance. Reading *Time* magazine, you might come across a discussion of endangered species in Madagascar, and this discussion might interest you, even affect your behavior, although you would not have sought it out in the first instance. A system in which individuals lack control over the particular content that they see has a great deal in common with a public street, where you might encounter not only friends but a heterogeneous variety of people engaged in a wide array of activities (including perhaps political protests and begging). I will return to this point below.

Politics, Freedom, and Filtering

One question, which I mean to answer in the affirmative, is whether individual choices, perfectly reasonable in themselves, might produce a large set of social difficulties. Another question, which I also mean to answer in the affirmative, is whether it is important to maintain the equivalent of "street corners," or "commons," where people are exposed to things quite involuntarily.

More particularly, I seek to defend a particular conception of democracy—a deliberative conception—and to evaluate in its terms the outcome of a system with perfect power of filtering. I also mean to defend a conception of freedom associated with the deliberative conception of democracy and to oppose it to a conception that sees consumption choices by individuals as the very embodiment of freedom.

AN ANALOGY AND AN IDEAL

The problems in individual filtering and the value of shared experiences and unchosen exposures are best approached through two routes. The first involves an unusual constitutional doctrine based on the idea of the "public forum." The second involves a general constitutional ideal, indeed the most general constitutional ideal of all: that of deliberative democracy. As we will see, a system of individualized filtering may violate that ideal. As a corrective, we might build on the understandings that lie behind the notion that a free society creates a set of public forums, providing access by speakers to a diverse population and ensuring in the process that each of us hears a wide range of speakers, spanning many topics and opinions.

The Idea of the Public Forum

In the popular understanding, the free speech principle forbids government from "censoring" speech of which it disapproves. In the standard cases, the government attempts to impose penalties, whether civil or criminal, on political dissent, and on speech that it considers dangerous, libelous, or sexually explicit. The question is whether the government has a legitimate and sufficiently weighty basis for restricting the speech that it seeks to control.

But an important part of free speech law takes a quite different form. The Supreme Court has also held that streets and parks must be kept open to the public for expressive activity.[1] Hence, governments are obliged to allow speech to occur freely on public streets and in public parks—even if many citizens would prefer to have peace and quiet, and even if it seems irritating to come across protesters and dissidents whom one would like to avoid. To be sure, the government is allowed to impose restrictions on the "time, place, and manner" of speech in public places. No one has a right to use fireworks and loudspeakers on the public streets at midnight to complain about the size of the defense budget. But time, place, and manner restrictions must be both reasonable and limited, and government is essentially obliged to allow speakers, whatever their views, to use public property to convey messages of their choosing.

A distinctive feature of this idea is that it creates a right of speakers' access, both to places and to people. Another distinctive feature is that the public forum doctrine creates a right, not to avoid governmentally imposed penalties on speech but to ensure government subsidies of speech. There is no question that taxpayers have to support expressive activity that, under the public forum doctrine, must be permitted on the streets and parks. Indeed, the costs that taxpayers devote to maintaining open streets and parks, including cleaning up each day, can be quite high. Thus the public forum represents one place in which the right to free speech creates a right of speaker access to certain areas and also demands public subsidy of speakers.

Just Streets and Parks? Of Airports and the Internet

There is now good reason to expand the public forum well beyond streets and parks. In the modern era, other places occupy their traditional role. The mass media, including the Internet, have become far more important than streets and parks as arenas in which expressive activity occurs.

Nonetheless, the Supreme Court has been wary of expanding the public forum doctrine beyond streets and parks, perhaps on the theory that once the historical touchstone is abandoned, lines will be extremely hard to draw. Thus the Court rejected the seemingly convincing argument that many other places should be seen as public forums too. In particular, it has been urged that airports, more than streets and parks, are crucial to reaching a heterogeneous public; airports are places where diverse people congregate and where it is important to have access if one wants to speak to large numbers of people. The Court rejected the argument, suggesting that the public forum idea should be understood by reference to historical practices—and airports certainly have not been treated as public forums from "ancient times."

At the same time, the Court has shown considerable uneasiness with a purely historical test. In the most vivid passage on the point, Justice Anthony Kennedy wrote, "Minds are not changed in streets and parks as they once were. To an increasing degree, the more significant interchanges of ideas and shaping of public consciousness occur in mass and electronic media. The extent of public entitlement to participate in those means of communication may be changed as technologies change."[2] What Justice Kennedy is recognizing here is the serious question of how to "translate" the public forum idea into the modern technological environment. If the Supreme Court is unwilling to do any such translating, it remains entirely open for Congress and state governments to do exactly that.

The Supreme Court has given little sense of why, exactly, it is important to ensure that the streets and parks are open to speakers. This is a question that must be answered if we are to know whether, and how, to extend the public forum doctrine to contemporary problems.

We can make some progress here by noticing that the public forum doctrine promotes three important functions. First, it ensures that speakers can have access to a wide array of people. If we want to claim that taxes are too high or that police brutality against African Americans is common, we can press this argument on many people who might otherwise fail to hear the message. Those who use the streets and parks are likely learn something about the substance of the argument urged by speakers; they might also learn the nature and intensity of views held by their fellow citizens. Perhaps their views will be changed; perhaps they will become curious, even enough to investigate the question on their own. It does not much matter if this happens a little or a great deal. What is important is that for some people, some of the time, speakers are authorized to press concerns that would otherwise go ignored.

On the speakers' side, the public forum doctrine thus creates a right of general access to heterogeneous citizens. On the listeners' side, the public forum creates not exactly a right but an opportunity, if perhaps an unwelcome one: shared exposure to diverse speakers with diverse views and complaints. It is important to emphasize that the exposure is shared, in the sense that many people will be simultaneously so exposed, and also that it involves viewing people and claims that these people might well have refused to seek out in the first instance. Indeed, the exposure might well be, much of the time, irritating or worse.

Second, the public forum doctrine allows speakers not only to have access to heterogeneous people generally but also to specific persons and specific institutions against whom they have complaints. Suppose, for example, that you believe that the state legislature has behaved irresponsibly with respect to crime or health care for children. The public forum ensures that you can make your views heard by legislators, simply by protesting in front of the state legislature itself.

The point applies to private as well as public institutions. If a clothing store is believed to have cheated customers or to have acted in a racist manner, protestors are allowed a form of access to the store itself. This is not by virtue of a right to trespass on private property—there is no such right—but because a public street is highly likely to be close by, and a strategic protest will undoubtedly catch the attention of the store and its customers. Here speakers are permitted, by the public forum doctrine, to have access to particular audiences, and particular listeners have a duty, undoubtedly unwelcome in many cases, to hear complaints that are directed against them. In other words, listeners have sharply limited power of self-insulation.

Third, the public forum doctrine increases the likelihood that people generally will be exposed to a wide variety of people and views. When we go to work or visit a park, it is possible that we will have a range of unexpected encounters, however fleeting or seemingly inconsequential. We cannot easily wall ourselves off from contentions or conditions that we would not have sought out in advance or that we would have chosen to avoid if we could have. Here too the public forum doctrine tends to ensure a range of experiences that are widely shared—streets and parks are public property—and also a set of exposures to diverse circumstances. A central idea here must be that these exposures help promote understanding and perhaps, in that sense, freedom. All of these points can be closely connected to democratic ideals, as we will soon see.

General-Interest Intermediaries

Of course, there is a limit to how much can be done on streets and in parks. Even in the largest cities, streets and parks are emphatically local. But many of the social functions of streets and parks, as public forums, are performed by other institutions too. In fact, society's general-interest intermediaries—newspapers, magazines, television broadcasters—can be understood as public forums of an especially important sort.

The reasons are straightforward. When you read a city newspaper or a national magazine, your eyes come across a number of articles that you might not have selected in advance, and if you are like most people, you read some of those articles. Perhaps you did not know that you had an interest in minimum-wage legislation, or Somalia, or the latest developments in the Middle East, but such a story might catch your attention. What is true for topics is also true for points of view. You might think that you have nothing to learn from someone whose view you abhor; once you come across the editorial pages, however, you might well read what they have to say, and you might well benefit from the experience. Perhaps you will be persuaded on one point or another. At the same time, the front-page headline, or the cover story in *Newsweek,* is likely to have a high degree of salience for a wide range of people.

Television broadcasters have similar functions, perhaps above all in what has become an international institution: the evening news. If we tune into the evening news, we learn about a number of topics that we would not have chosen in advance. Because of its speech and immediacy, television broadcasters perform this public forum–type function even more than do general-interest intermediaries in the print media. The "lead story" on the networks is likely to have a great deal of public salience, helping to define central issues and creating something of a shared focus of attention for many millions of people. What is presented after the lead story—a menu of topics both domestic and international—creates something like a speakers' corner, one beyond anything imagined in Hyde Park.

None of these claims depends on a judgment that general-interest intermediaries always do an excellent job, or even a good job. What matters for present purposes is that they expose people to a wide range of topics and views at the same time that they provide shared experiences for a heterogeneous public. Indeed, general-interest intermediaries of this sort have large advantages over streets and parks precisely in that most of them tend to be not local but national, even international. Typically, they expose people to questions and problems in other areas, even other nations. They even inculcate a kind of back-door cosmopolitanism, ensuring that many people will learn something about diverse areas of the world, regardless of whether they are much interested in doing so.

Of course, general-interest intermediaries are not public forums in the technical sense. Most important, members of the public do not have a legal right of access to them. These are emphatically not institutions with respect to which individual citizens are allowed to override the editorial and economic judgments and choices of private owners. A sharp constitutional debate on precisely this issue has resulted in a resounding defeat for those who claimed a constitutionally guaranteed access right. But the question of legal compulsion is really incidental. The general-interest intermediaries, even without legal compulsion, promote many of the functions of public forums. They promote shared experiences; they expose people to information and views that would not have been selected in advance.

Deliberative Democracy

The public forum doctrine is an odd and unusual one, especially inasmuch as it creates a kind of speaker-access right, subsidized by taxpayers, to people and places. But the doctrine is closely associated with a long-standing constitutional ideal, one that is far from odd: that of republican self-government. From the beginning, the American constitutional order was designed to be a republic, as distinguished from a monarchy or a direct democracy. We cannot understand the system of freedom of expression or the effects of new communications technologies and filtering without reference to this ideal.

In a republic, government is not managed by a king or queen; there is no sovereign operating independently of the people. The American Constitution represents a firm rejection of the monarchical heritage; the framers quite deliberately transferred sovereignty from any monarchy (explicitly banning "titles of nobility") to "We the People." At the same time, the founders were extremely fearful of popular passions and prejudices, and they did not want government to translate popular desires directly into law. They sought to create institutions that would "filter" those desires so as to ensure policies that would promote the public good. Further, the founders placed a high premium on the idea of "civic virtue," which required participants in politics to act as citizens, dedicated to something other than their self-interest, narrowly conceived.

The specifically American form of republicanism thus involved an effort to create a "deliberative democracy." In this system, representatives would be accountable to the public at large, but there was also supposed to be a large degree of reflection and debate, both within the citizenry and within government itself. The aspiration to deliberative democracy can be seen in many places in the constitutional design. The system of bicameralism, for example, was intended as a check on action without sufficient deliberation in either legislative chamber; the Senate in particular was supposed to have a "cooling" function on popular passions. The longer term of service for senators was designed to make deliberation more likely; so too were their large voting districts. The Electoral College was originally a deliberative body, ensuring that the choice of a new president would result from some combination of popular will and of reflection and exchange on the part of representatives. Most generally, the system of checks and balances had, as its central purpose, the promotion of deliberation within the government as a whole.

From these points it should be clear that the Constitution was not rooted in the assumption that direct democracy was the ideal, to be replaced by republican institutions only because direct democracy was not practical in light of what were, by our standards, extremely primitive technologies for communication. Today, it has been suggested that for the first time in the history of the world something like direct democracy has become feasible. It is now possible for citizens to tell their government, every week if not every day, what they would like it to do. Indeed, Web sites have been designed to enable citizens to do precisely that, and we should expect more experiments in this direction. But from the standpoint of constitutional ideals, this is nothing to celebrate; indeed it is a grotesque distortion of founding aspirations. The problem is that direct public communication, if accompanied by direct governmental response, would compromise the deliberative goals of the original design.

Two Conceptions of Sovereignty

We are now in a position to distinguish between two conceptions of sovereignty. The first involves *consumer* sovereignty; the second involves *political* sovereignty. The first ideal underlies enthusiasm for "the Daily Me." The second ideal underlies the democratic challenge to this vision, on the ground that it is likely to undermine both self-government and freedom, properly conceived.

Consumer sovereignty means that individual consumers are permitted to choose as they wish, subject to the constraints represented by the price system, and also by their current holdings and requirements. This is the idea that lies behind free markets, and it plays a significant role in thinking about both politics and communications as well. When we talk as if politicians are "selling" a message, even themselves, we are treating the political domain as a kind of market, subject to the forces of supply and demand. When we act as if the purpose of a system of communications is to ensure that people can see exactly what they "want," the notion of consumer sovereignty is very much at work. The notion of political sovereignty stands on different foundations. It does not take individual tastes as fixed or given. It prizes democratic self-government, understood as a requirement of "government by discussion," accompanied by the giving of reasons in the public domain. Political sovereignty comes with its own preconditions, and these are violated if government power is not backed by justifications but represents instead the product of force or simple majority will.

Of course, the two conceptions of sovereignty are in potential tension. A commitment to consumer sovereignty may well compromise political sovereignty if, for example, free consumer choices result in insufficient understanding of public problems, or if they make it difficult to have anything like a shared culture.

FRAGMENTATION

I now turn to my central concern. In a system with public forums and general-interest intermediaries, people will frequently come across materials that they would not have chosen in advance—and for diverse citizens, this provides something like a common framework for social experience. Let us suppose that the communications market had become far more fragmented, in exactly the sense prophesied by those who celebrate "the Daily Me." What problems would be created by this fragmentation?

E Pluribus Plures

It is obvious that if there is only one flavor of ice cream and only one kind of toaster, a wide range of people will make the same choices. (Some people will refuse ice cream and rely on something other than toasters, but that is another matter.) It is also obvious that as choice is increased, different individuals and different groups will make increasingly different choices. This has been the growing pattern over time with the proliferation of communications options.

Consider some details. If we take the ten most highly rated television programs for whites and then the ten most highly rated programs for African Americans, we find little overlap between them. Indeed, over half of the ten most highly rated programs for African Americans rank among the ten *least* popular programs for whites. Similar divisions can be found on the Internet. Not surprisingly, people tend to choose like-minded sites and like-minded discussion groups. With respect to politics, for example, those with committed views on some topic—gun control, abortion, affirmative action—speak mostly with each other. It is exceedingly rare for a site with an identifiable point of view to provide links to sites with opposing views; it is very common, however, for such a site to provide links to like-minded ones.

Of course, any system that allows for freedom of choice will create balkanization of this kind. Long before the advent of the Internet, in an era of a handful of television stations, people made choices among newspapers and radio stations. Since the early nineteenth century, African-American newspapers have been widely read by African Americans, and these newspapers offer significantly different coverage of common issues and also make dramatically different choices as to what issues are important.[3]

What is emerging is a change of degree, not one of kind, but it is no less significant for that. With an increase in options and a greater power to customize comes an increase in the range of actual choices, and those choices are likely in many cases to match demographic characteristics. Of course, this is not all bad; among other things, it will greatly increase variety, the aggregate amount of information, and the entertainment value of actual choices. But there are problems as well. If diverse groups are each seeing and hearing quite different points of view or focusing on quite different topics, mutual understanding might be difficult, and it might turn out to be hard for people to solve problems that society faces collectively.

We can sharpen our understanding of this problem if we attend to the phenomenon of *group polarization*. This phenomenon raises serious questions about any system in which individuals and groups choose extremely diverse communications universes.

Group Polarization in General

The term "group polarization" refers to something very simple: After deliberating with one another, people are likely to move toward a more extreme point in the direction to which they were previously inclined, as indicated by the median of their predeliberation judgments. With respect to the Internet, the implication is that groups of people, especially if they are like-minded, will end up thinking the same thing that they thought before—but in more extreme form.

Consider some examples of the basic phenomenon, which has been found in over a dozen nations.[4]

· A group of moderately profeminist women become more strongly profeminist after discussion.
· After discussion, citizens of France become more critical of the United States and its intentions with respect to economic aid.
· After discussion, whites predisposed to show racial prejudice offer more negative responses to the question of whether white racism is responsible for conditions faced by African Americans in American cities.
· After discussion, whites predisposed not to show racial prejudice offer more positive responses to the same question.

As a matter of statistical regularity, it should follow, for example, that people moderately critical of an ongoing war effort will, after discussion, sharply oppose the war; that people tending to believe in the inferiority of a certain racial group will be entrenched in this belief as a result of discussion; that after discussion, people who tentatively think that the Second Amendment protects the right to own guns and that government efforts at gun control are unconstitutional efforts to eliminate the public's power of self-defense, will end up thinking that these propositions are undoubtedly true and call for an immediate public response.

The phenomenon of group polarization has conspicuous importance for the communications market, where groups with distinctive identities increasingly engage in within-group discussion. If the public is balkanized and if different groups design their own preferred communications packages, the consequence will be further balkanization, as group members move one another toward more extreme points in line with their initial tendencies. At the same time, different deliberating groups, each consisting of like-minded people, will be driven increasingly far from the first group, simply because most of their members' discussions are with one another. Extremist groups will often become more extreme; as we will soon see, the largest group polarization typically occurs with individuals already inclined toward extremes.

Two Mechanisms and a Refinement

There have been two main explanations for group polarization, and both have been extensively investigated. Massive support has been found on behalf of both explanations.[5]

Persuasive Arguments

The first explanation emphasizes the role of persuasive arguments. It is based on a commonsense intuition: the position an individual takes on any issue is (fortunately!)

a function, at least in part, of which arguments seem convincing to him or her. If our position is going to move as a result of group discussion, it is likely to move in the direction of the most persuasive position defended within our group, taken as a collectivity. Of course—and this is the key point—a group whose members are already inclined in a certain direction will offer a disproportionately large number of arguments supporting that orientation, and a disproportionately small number of arguments the other way. The result of discussion will therefore be to move individuals farther in the direction of their initial inclinations.

On this account, the central factor behind group polarization is the existence of a *limited argument pool*, one that is skewed (speaking purely descriptively) in a particular direction. If a group of moderately feminist women becomes more feminist, a group moderately opposed to affirmative action more extremely so, and so forth, one reason is that the argument pool of any such group will contain a preponderance of arguments in the direction suggested. It is easy to see how this might happen with discussion groups on the Internet, and indeed with individuals not engaged in discussion but consulting only ideas to which they are antecedently inclined. The tendency of such discussion groups, and such consultations, will be to entrench pre-existing positions.

Social Comparison

The second mechanism, involving social comparison, begins with the claim that people want to be perceived favorably by other group members, and also to perceive themselves favorably. Once they hear what others believe, they adjust their positions in the direction of the dominant position. People may wish, for example, not to seem too enthusiastic, or too restrained in their enthusiasm for, affirmative action, feminism, or an increase in national defense; hence their views may shift when they see what other people, and in particular what other group members, think.

The dynamic behind the social-comparison explanation is that most people (of course, not all) want to take a position of certain socially preferred sorts. Within groups, no one can know what such a position will be until the positions of others are revealed. Thus individuals move their judgments in order to preserve their images to others and their images to themselves. A key claim here, supported by evidence, is that even information alone about the actual positions of others—without discussion—will produce a shift. The point has implications for exposure to ideas and claims in the absence of a chance for interaction. If group polarization occurs merely on the basis of exposure, it is likely to be a common phenomenon in a balkanized speech market.

A Refinement, with Special Reference to Shared Group Identity

Group polarization is a highly general phenomenon, but in certain circumstances it can be decreased, increased, or even eliminated. For present purposes, the most important refinement has to do with perceptions of identity and group membership. Group polarization significantly increases if people think of themselves, antecedently or otherwise, as part of a group having a shared identity and a degree of solidarity. If they think of themselves in this way, group polarization is both more likely and more extreme. If, for example, people in an Internet discussion group think of themselves as opponents of high taxes or advocates of animal rights, their discussions are likely to move them in quite extreme directions. Similar movements should be expected of those who listen to radio shows known to be conservative or a television program dedicated to traditional religious values or to exposing white racism.

This should not be surprising. If ordinary instances of group polarization are products of social influences and limited argument pools, it stands to reason that when group members think of one another as similar along a salient dimension, or if some external factor (politics, geography, race, sex) unites them, group polarization will be heightened.

Group Polarization and the Internet

Group polarization is highly likely to occur on the Internet. Indeed, it is clear that the Internet is serving for many as a breeding ground for extremism, precisely because on it like-minded people are deliberating with one another, without hearing contrary views.

Consider in this regard a revealing study of not extremism, but serious errors within working groups, face to face but also, and more importantly, online.[6] The purpose of the study was to see how groups might collaborate to make personnel decisions. Resumes for three candidates, applying for a marketing manager position, were placed before the groups; the attributes of the candidates were rigged by the experimenters so that one applicant was clearly best matched for the job described. Packets of information, each containing only a subset of information from the resumes, were given to subjects, so that each had only part of the relevant information. The groups consisted of three people, some operating face to face, some operating online. Two results were especially striking: group polarization was common, and almost none (!) of the deliberating groups made what was conspicuously the right choice. The reason is that they failed to share information in a way that would permit objective decisions.

In online groups, the level of error was especially high, for the simple reason that members tended to share positive information about the winning candidate and negative information about the losers, while suppressing negative information about the winner and positive information about the losers. These contributions served to "reinforce the march toward group consensus rather than add complications and fuel debate."[7] In fact, this tendency was twice as prominent within the online groups than for the face-to-face ones.

What has been said thus far should be sufficient to show that group polarization can be especially pronounced under conditions of discussion via computer, in a way that magnifies mistakes and biases. Though the study just described did not involve political or moral issues, the results show that one-sidedness, and consequently extremism, can be heightened in communication over the Internet. We have seen a great deal of real-world evidence in the same direction.

Fragmentation, Polarization, Radio, and Television

An understanding of group polarization casts light on radio and television more generally. Recall that mere exposure to the views of others creates group polarization; it follows that this effect will be at work for nondeliberating groups, collections of individuals whose communications choices go in particular directions and who do not expose themselves to alternative positions. Indeed, the same process is likely to occur for newspaper choices.

Group polarization also raises more general issues about communications policy. Consider the "fairness doctrine," now largely abandoned but once requiring radio and television broadcasters to (a) devote time to public issues and (b) allow opportunities for opposing views to speak. Prong (b) of the doctrine was designed to ensure that listeners would not be exposed to any single view. When the Federal Communications Commission abandoned the fairness doctrine, it did so on the ground that this second prong led broadcasters, much of the time, to avoid controversial issues entirely and to present views in a way that suggested a bland uniformity.[8] Subsequent research has suggested that the elimination of the fairness doctrine has indeed produced a flowering of controversial substantive programming, frequently with extreme views of one kind or another; consider talk radio.[9]

Typically, this is regarded as a story of wonderfully successful deregulation, because the effects of eliminating the fairness doctrine were precisely what had been intended. But from the standpoint of group polarization, the picture is far more complicated. The growth of issues-oriented programming, with strong, often extreme views, creates group polarization. All too many people are now exposed to louder echoes of their own voices, resulting on occasion in social fragmentation, misunderstanding, and sometimes even enmity. Perhaps it is better for people to hear fewer controversial views than for them to hear a single such view, stated over and over again.

Of course, we cannot say, from the mere fact of polarization in a given instance, that there has been a movement in the *wrong* direction. Perhaps the more extreme tendency is better; indeed, group polarization is likely to have fueled many movements of great value, including, for example, the movement for civil rights, the antislavery movement, the movement for sex equality. All of these movements were extreme in their time, and within-group discussion bred greater extremism; still, "extremism" need not be a word of opprobrium. If greater communications choices produce greater extremism, society may in many cases be better off as a result. Nonetheless, when group discussion tends to lead people to more strongly held versions of the views with which they began, and if social influences and limited argument pools are responsible, there is legitimate reason for concern. Consider discussions among hate groups on the Internet and elsewhere. If the underlying views are unreasonable, it makes sense to fear that these discussions may fuel increasing hatred and a socially corrosive form of extremism. This does not mean that the discussions can or should be regulated in a system dedicated to freedom of speech. But it does raise questions about the idea that "more speech" is necessarily an adequate remedy—especially if people are increasingly able to wall themselves off from competing views.

The basic issue here is whether something like a "public sphere," with a wide range of voices, might not have significant advantages over a system in which isolated consumer choices produce a highly fragmented speech market. The most reasonable conclusion is that it is extremely important to ensure that people are exposed to views other than those with which they currently agree, in order to protect against the harmful effects of group polarization on individual thinking and on social cohesion. This does not mean that the government should jail or fine people who refuse to listen to others. Nor is what I have said inconsistent with deliberative "enclaves," on the Internet or elsewhere, designed to ensure that positions that would otherwise be silenced or squelched have a chance to develop. But the benefit of such enclaves is that positions may emerge that otherwise would not, though they deserve to play large roles in the heterogeneous public. Properly understood, the case for "enclaves"—or more simply, discussion groups of like-minded people—is that they will improve social deliberation, democratic and otherwise. If these improvements are to occur, members must not insulate themselves from competing positions, or at least such attempts at insulation must not be prolonged.

The adverse effects of group polarization, then, show that with respect to communications, consumer sovereignty is likely to produce serious problems for individuals and society at large. Further, these problems will occur by a kind of iron logic of social interactions.

The phenomenon of group polarization is closely related to the widespread phenomenon of *social cascades*. No discussion of social fragmentation and emerging communications technologies would be complete without a discussion of it.

It is obvious that many social groups, both large and small, seem to move both rapidly and dramatically in the direction of the same set of beliefs or actions.[10] These sorts of "cascades" often involve the spread of information; in fact, they are driven by information. A key point here is that if we have little private information, we may well rely on information provided by the statements or actions of others. A stylized example: If Joan is unaware whether or not abandoned toxic waste dumps are hazardous, she may be moved in the direction of fear if Mary seems to think that fear is justified. If Joan and Mary both believe that fear is justified, Carl may end up thinking so too, at least if he lacks reliable independent information to the contrary. If Joan, Mary, and Carl believe that abandoned hazardous waste dumps are hazardous, Don will have to have a good deal of confidence to reject their shared conclusion.

The example shows how information travels, and how it often becomes quite entrenched even if it is entirely wrong. The view, widespread in many African-American communities, that white doctors are responsible for the spread of AIDS among African Americans is a recent illustration. Often cascades of this kind are quite local and take different forms in different communities. Hence, one group may end up believing something and another group the exact opposite, the reason being the rapid transmission of information within one group but not the other. In a balkanized speech market, this danger takes on a particular form: different groups may be led to quite different perspectives, as local cascades lead people in dramatically different directions.

I hope that I have demonstrated that for citizens of a heterogeneous democracy, a fragmented communications market creates considerable dangers. There are dangers for each of us as individuals; constant exposure to one set of views is likely to lead to error and confusion. To the extent that the process makes people less able to work cooperatively on shared problems, there are also dangers for society as a whole.

SOCIAL GLUE

Solidarity Goods

In a heterogeneous society, it is extremely important for diverse people to have common experiences. Most people understand this fact, and many of our practices reflect a judgment to this effect. National holidays, for example, help constitute a nation by encouraging citizens to think, all at once, about events of shared importance. In fact, they do much more than this: they enable people, in all their diversity, to share certain memories and attitudes. At least this is true in nations where national holidays have a vivid and concrete meaning. In the United States, many national holidays have become mere days off from work, and the precipitating occasions—President's Day, Memorial Day, Labor Day—have come to be nearly invisible. This is a serious loss. With the possible exception of July 4th, Martin Luther King Day is probably the closest thing to a genuinely substantive national holiday, largely because that celebration involves something that can be treated as concrete and meaningful. In other words, it is *about* something.

Communications and the media are, of course, exceptionally important here. Sometimes millions of people follow a presidential election, or a Superbowl, or the coronation of a new monarch; many of them do so because of the simultaneous actions of others. In this sense, some of the experiences made possible by modern technologies are *solidarity goods*, in the sense that their value goes up when, and because, many other people enjoy or consume them. The point very much bears on the historic role of both public forums and general-interest intermediaries. Public parks are places where diverse people can congregate and see one another; general-interest intermediaries, if they are operating properly, give a simultaneous sense of problems and tasks.

The Value of Shared Experiences

Why might these shared experiences be so desirable? There are three principal reasons. Simple enjoyment, the first reason, is probably the least of it, but it is far from irrelevant. People like many experiences more simply because they are being shared. Consider a popular movie, the Superbowl, or a presidential debate. For many of us, these are goods that are worth less, and possibly worthless, if many others are not enjoying or purchasing them too. Hence a presidential debate may be worthy of individual attention for many people simply because so many other people consider it worthy of individual attention.

Second, shared experiences sometimes ease social interactions, permitting people to speak with one another and to congregate around a common issue, task, or concern, whether or not they have much in common with one another. In this sense they provide a form of social glue. They help make it possible for diverse people to believe that they live in the same culture. Indeed, they help constitute that shared culture, simply by creating common memories and experiences, and a sense of common tasks.

Third, a fortunate consequence of shared experiences—many of them produced by the media—is that people who would otherwise see one another as quite unfamiliar, in the extreme case as belonging to a different species, can come instead to regard each other as fellow citizens, with shared hopes, goals, and concerns. This is a subjective good for those directly involved. But it can be an objective good as well, especially if it leads to cooperative projects of various kinds. When people learn about a disaster faced by fellow citizens, for example, they may respond with financial or other help. The point applies internationally as well as domestically; massive relief efforts are often made possible by virtue of the fact that millions of people learn all at once about the need.

Fewer Shared Experiences

Even in a nation of unlimited communications options, some events inevitably attract widespread attention. But an obvious risk of an increasingly fragmented communications universe is the reduction of shared experiences having salience to diverse people. This is a simple matter of numbers. When there were three television networks, much of what appeared would have the quality of a genuinely common experience. The lead story on the evening news, for example, would provide a common reference point for many millions of people. As choices proliferate, it is inevitable that diverse individuals, and diverse groups, have fewer shared experiences and fewer common reference points. For example, events that are highly salient to some people will barely register on others' "viewscreens"; some views and perspectives that seem obvious to many people will for others seem barely intelligible.

This is hardly a suggestion that everyone should be required to watch the same thing. We are not speaking of requirements at all. In any case, a degree of plurality, with respect to both topics and points of view, is highly desirable. My only claim is that a common set of frameworks and experiences is valuable for a heterogeneous society and that a system with limitless options, making for infinitely diverse choices, will compromise the underlying values.

FREEDOM OF SPEECH

The points made thus far raise questions about whether a democratic order is helped or hurt by a system of unlimited individual choice with respect to communications. It is not unreasonable to fear that such a system will produce excessive fragmentation, with group polarization as a frequent consequence. It is also possible to fear that such a system will produce too little in the way of solidarity goods or shared experiences. But does the free speech principle bar government from responding to the situation? If that principle is taken to forbid government from doing anything to improve the operation of the speech market, the answer must be a simple yes.

I believe, however, that this is a crude and unhelpful understanding of the free speech principle, one that is especially ill suited to the theoretical and practical challenges of the next decades and beyond. If we see the First Amendment through a democratic lens, we will be able to make a great deal more progress.

Emerging Wisdom?

On an emerging view, the First Amendment to the Constitution requires government to respect consumer sovereignty. Indeed, the First Amendment is often treated as if it incorporates the economic ideal. Although it is foreign to the original conception of the First Amendment, this view can be found in many places in current law.

For one thing, it helps to explain the constitutional protection given to commercial advertising. This protection is exceedingly recent. Until 1976,[11] the consensus within the Supreme Court and in the legal culture in general was that the First Amendment did not protect commercial speech at all. Since that time, commercial speech has come to be treated more and more like ordinary speech, to the point where Justice Clarence Thomas has even doubted whether the law should distinguish at all between commercial and political speech.[12] Justice Thomas has not prevailed on this count, but the Court's decisions are best seen as a way of connecting the idea of consumer sovereignty with the First Amendment itself.

Belonging in the same category is the continuing constitutional hostility to campaign-finance regulation. The Supreme Court has held that financial expenditures on behalf of political candidates are protected by the free speech principle—and also that it is illegitimate for government to attempt to promote political equality by imposing ceilings on permissible expenditures.[13] The inequality that comes from divergences in wealth is not, on the Court's view, a proper subject for political control. Here too an idea of consumer sovereignty seems to be at work. Indeed, the political process itself is being treated as a kind of market, in which citizens are being seen as consumers, expressing their will not only through votes and statements but also through expenditures.

Most relevant for present purposes is the widespread view, which finds support in current constitutional law, that the free speech principle forbids government from interfering with the communications market by, for example, attempting to draw people's attention to serious issues or regulating the content of what appears on broadcast networks. To be sure, everyone agrees that the government is permitted to control monopolistic behavior and thus to enforce antitrust law, designed to ensure genuinely free markets in communications. Structural regulation, not involving direct control of speech but intended to make sure that the market works well, is also unobjectionable. But if government attempts to require television broadcasters to cover public issues, provide free air time for candidates, or ensure a certain level of high-quality programming for children, many people will claim that the First

Amendment is being violated. The same is true for government efforts to improve the operation of the Internet by, for example, enlisting the public forum doctrine so as to promote exposure to materials that people would not have chosen in advance.

Free Speech Is Not an Absolute

We can identify some flaws in this emerging view of the First Amendment, by investigating the idea that the free speech guarantee is "an absolute," in the specific sense that government may not regulate speech at all. This view certainly plays a large role in public debate, and in some ways it is a salutary myth. Certainly the idea that the First Amendment is "an absolute" helps to discourage government from doing things that it ought not to do, and at the same time it gives greater rhetorical power to critics of illegitimate government censorship. But a myth, even if in some ways salutary, remains a myth, and any publicly influential myth is likely to create many problems.

There should be no ambiguity on the point: free speech is not an absolute. The government is allowed to regulate speech by imposing neutral rules of property law, telling would-be speakers that they may not have access to certain speech outlets. But this is only the beginning. Government is permitted to regulate unlicensed medical advice, attempted bribery, perjury, criminal conspiracies ("Let's fix prices!"), threats to assassinate the president, criminal solicitation ("Might you help me rob this bank?"), child pornography, false advertising, purely verbal fraud ("This stock is worth a hundred thousand dollars"), and much more. Many of these forms of speech are not especially harmful. A ridiculous and doomed attempt to entice someone to commit a crime, for example, is still criminal solicitation; a pitifully executed attempt at fraud is still fraud. It is possible for reasonable people to disagree with the view, settled as a matter of current American law (and that of most other nations as well), that these forms of speech are all unprotected by the free speech principle. But it is not possible for reasonable people to believe that each of these forms of speech should be protected by that principle. If one or more of these forms of speech is regulable, free speech absolutism is something of a fraud, masking the real issues that must be confronted in separating protected from unprotected speech.

This is not the place for a full account of the reach of the First Amendment of the Constitution.[14] But it is plain that some distinctions must be made between different kinds of speech. We might, for example, distinguish between speech that can be shown to be quite harmful and speech that seems relatively harmless. As a general rule, the government should not be able to regulate the latter. We might also distinguish between speech that bears on democratic self-government and speech that does not; certainly an especially severe burden should be placed on government efforts to regulate political speech. Less simply, we might want to distinguish among the kinds of lines that government is drawing, in terms of the likelihood that government is acting on the basis of illegitimate reasons.

These ideas could be combined in various ways, and indeed the fabric of modern free speech law in America reflects one such combination. Despite the increasing prominence of the idea that the free speech principle requires unrestricted choices by individual consumers, the Court continues to say that political speech receives the highest protection and that government may regulate (for example) commercial advertising, obscenity, and libel of ordinary people without meeting the especially stringent burden of justification required for political speech. But for present purposes, all that is necessary is to say that no serious scholar really believes that the free speech principle, or the First Amendment, is an absolute. We should be very thankful for that.

The First Amendment and Democratic Deliberation

There are profound differences between those who emphasize consumer sovereignty and those who stress the democratic roots of the free speech principle. For the latter, government efforts to regulate commercial advertising need not be objectionable; certainly, false and misleading commercial advertising is more readily subject to government control than false and misleading political speech. For those who believe that the free speech principle has democratic foundations and is not about consumer sovereignty, government regulation of television, radio, and the Internet need not be objectionable, at least so long as it takes the form of reasonable efforts to promote democratic goals.

Suppose, for example, that government proposes to require television broadcasters (as indeed it now does) to provide three hours per week of educational programming for children. Or suppose that government decides to require television broadcasters to provide a certain amount of free air time for candidates for public office, or a certain amount of time on coverage of elections. For those who believe in consumer sovereignty, these requirements are quite troublesome; indeed, they seem like core violations of the free speech guarantee. For those who associate the free speech principle with democratic goals, however, these requirements are fully consistent with its highest aspirations.

There is nothing novel or iconoclastic in the democratic conception of free speech. On the contrary, this conception lay at the heart of the original understanding of freedom of speech in America. In attacking the Alien and Sedition Acts, for example, James Madison claimed that they were inconsistent with the free speech principle, which he linked explicitly to the American transformation of the concept of political sovereignty. In England, Madison noted, sovereignty was vested in the king. But "in the United States, the case is altogether different. The People, not the Government, possess the absolute sovereignty." It was on this foundation that any "Sedition Act" must be judged illegitimate. "The right of electing the members of the Government constitutes . . . the essence of a free and responsible government," and "the value and efficacy of this right depends on the knowledge of the comparative merits and demerits of the candidates for the public trust."[15] It was for this reason that the power represented by the Sedition Act ought, "more than any other, to produce universal alarm; because it is leveled against that right of freely examining public characters and measures, and of free communication among the people thereon, which has ever been justly deemed the only effectual guardian of every other right."

In this way Madison saw "free communication among the people" not as an exercise in consumer sovereignty, in which speech was treated as a kind of commodity, but instead as a central part of self-government, the "only effectual guardian of every other right." A central part of the American constitutional tradition, then, places a high premium on speech that is critical to democratic processes and is hardly hostile to government efforts to promote such speech. If history is our guide, it follows that government efforts to promote a well-functioning system of free expression, as through extensions of the public forum idea, are entirely acceptable.

American history is not the only basis for seeing the First Amendment in light of the commitment to democratic deliberation. The argument can be justified by basic principle as well. Consider the question of whether the free speech principle should be taken to forbid efforts to make communications markets work better from the democratic point of view. Some standard examples include educational programming for children, free air time for candidates for public office, closed-captioning for the hearing impaired, and requirements that Web sites contain links to sites with different views. Perhaps some of these proposals would do little or no good, or even harm; but from what standpoint should they be judged inconsistent with the free speech guarantee?

If we believed that the Constitution gives all owners of speech outlets an unbridgeable right to decide what appears on "their" outlets, the answer would be clear: government can require none of these things. But why should we believe that? Broadcasters owe their licenses to a government grant, and owners of Web sites enjoy their rights of ownership in large part because of the law that creates and enforces property rights. None of this means that government can regulate television and the Internet as it chooses. But if government is not favoring any point of view, and if it is genuinely improving the operation of democratic processes, it is hard to find a legitimate basis for complaint. Indeed, the Supreme Court has expressly held that the owners of shopping centers—areas where a great deal of speech occurs—

may be required to keep their property open for expressive activity.[16] Shopping centers are not Web sites, but if a democratic government is attempting to build on the idea of a public forum, so as to increase the likelihood of exposure to diverse views, is there really a reasonable objection, from the standpoint of free speech itself?

In a similar vein, it is reasonable to say that speech that is political in character, in the sense that it relates to democratic self-government, cannot be regulated without a special showing of government justification—and that speech that is not political in that sense can be regulated on the basis of a somewhat weaker government justification. I will not attempt to offer a full defense of this idea here, which, of course, raises some hard line-drawing problems. But in light of the importance of the question to imaginable government regulation of new technologies, there are three points that deserve brief mention.

First, an insistence that government's burden is greatest when it is regulating political speech emerges from a sensible understanding of government's own incentives. It is here that government is most likely to be acting on the basis of illegitimate considerations, such as self-protection or protection of powerful private groups. Government is least trustworthy when it is attempting to control speech that might harm its own interests. When speech is political, its own interests are almost certainly at stake. This is not to deny that government is often untrustworthy when it is regulating commercial speech, art, or other speech that does not relate to democratic self-government. But we have the strongest reasons for distrust when political issues are involved.

Second, an emphasis on democratic deliberation protects speech not only when regulation is most likely to be biased but also when regulation is most likely to be harmful. If government regulates sexually explicit speech on the Internet or requires educational programming for children on television, it remains possible to invoke the normal democratic channels to protest these forms of regulation as ineffectual, intrusive, or worse. But when government forbids criticism of a war effort, the normal channels are foreclosed, in an important sense, by the very regulation at issue. Controls on public debate are distinctly damaging, because they impair the process of deliberation that is a precondition for political legitimacy.

Third, an emphasis on democratic deliberation is likely to fit, far better than any alternative, with our most reasonable views about particular free speech problems. However much people disagree about certain speech problems, they are likely to believe that at a minimum, the free speech principle protects political expression unless government has exceedingly strong grounds for regulation. On the other hand, such forms of speech as perjury, attempted bribery, threats, unlicensed medical advice, and criminal solicitation are not likely to seem to be at the heart of free speech protection.

An understanding of this kind does not answer all constitutional questions. It does not give a clear test for distinguishing between political and nonpolitical speech, a predictably vexing question. (To those who believe that the absence of a clear test is decisive evidence against the distinction itself, the best response is that any alternative test will lead to line-drawing problems of its own.) It does not say whether and when government may regulate art or literature, sexually explicit speech, or libelous speech. In all cases, government is required to have a strong justification for regulating speech, political or not. What I have suggested here, without fully defending the point, is that a conception of the First Amendment that is rooted in democratic deliberation is an exceedingly good place to start.

PROPOSALS

My goal here has been to understand what makes for a well-functioning system of free expression and to show how consumer sovereignty, in a world of limitless options, is likely to undermine that system. I have also attempted to show that the First Amendment should not be taken to ban reasonable efforts, on the part of government, to improve the situation. I do not intend to offer a set of policy reforms or any kind of blueprint for the future. But it will be useful to offer a few ideas, if only by way of introduction to questions that are likely to engage public attention in the first decades of the twenty-first century.

Identifying the Problem

In thinking about reforms, it is important to have some sense of the problems that we aim to address, and of some possible ways of addressing them. If the discussion thus far is correct, there are three fundamental concerns from the democratic point of view.

- The need to promote exposure to materials, topics, and positions that people would not have chosen in advance, or at least enough exposure to produce a degree of understanding and curiosity
- The value of a range of common experiences
- The need for exposure to substantive questions of policy and principle, combined with a range of positions on such questions

Of course, it would be ideal if citizens were demanding, and private information providers were creating, a range of initiatives designed to alleviate the underlying concerns. Perhaps they will; there is some evidence to this effect. In fact, new technology creates growing opportunities for exposure to diverse points of view, and indeed growing opportunities for shared experiences. It is certainly possible that private choices will lead to far more, not less, in the way of exposure to new topics and points of view, and also to more, not less, in the way of shared experiences. But to the extent that they fail to do so, it is worthwhile to consider government initiatives designed to pick up the slack.

A Catalog of Reforms

There are many reform possibilities. Each of them would require a lengthy discussion. But if we draw on recent developments in regulation generally, we can see the potential appeal of five simple alternatives. Of course, different proposals would work better for some communications outlets than others.

1. Producers of communications might be subject not to regulation, but to *disclosure requirements*. In the environmental area, this strategy has produced excellent results. The mere fact that polluters have been asked to disclose toxic releases has produced voluntary, low-cost reductions. Apparently fearful of public opprobrium, companies have been spurred to reduce toxic emissions on their own. The same strategy has been used in the context of both movies and television, with ratings systems designed partly to increase parental control over what children see. On the Internet, many sites disclose that they are inappropriate for children. The same idea could be used far more broadly. Television broadcasters might, for example, be asked to disclose their public-interest activities. On a quarterly basis, they might be asked to say whether and to what extent they have provided educational programming for children, free air time for candidates, and closed-captioning for the hearing impaired. They might also be asked whether they have covered issues of concern to the local community and allowed opposing views chances to speak. The Federal Communications Commission has already taken steps in this direction; it could do much more. Web sites might be asked to say if they have allowed competing views chances to speak. Of course, disclosure is unlikely to be a full solution to the problems that I have discussed here. But modest steps in this direction are likely to do little harm and at least some good.

2. Producers of communications might be asked to engage in *voluntary self-regulation*. Some of the difficulties in the current speech market stem from relentless competition for viewers and listeners, competition that leads to a situation that many journalists abhor, and from which society does not benefit. The competition might be reduced via a "code" of appropriate conduct, agreed upon by various companies and encouraged (but not imposed) by government. In fact, the National Association of Broadcasters maintained such a code for several decades, and there is growing interest in voluntary self-regulation

for both television and the Internet. The case for this approach is that it avoids government regulation while at the same time reducing some of the harmful effects of market pressures. Any such code could, for example, call for opportunities for opposing views to speak, for avoidance of unnecessary sensationalism, or for arguments rather than quick "sound bites" whenever feasible.

3. The government might *subsidize speech*, as, for example, through publicly subsidized programming or publicly subsidized Web sites. This is, of course, the idea that motivates the Public Broadcasting System, but it is reasonable to ask whether the PBS model is not outmoded in the current communications environment. Other approaches, similarly designed to promote educational, cultural, and democratic goals, might well be ventured. Perhaps government could subsidize a "Public.Net" designed to promote debate on public issues among diverse citizens—and to create a right of access to speakers of various sorts.[17]

4. If the problem lies in the failure to attend to public issues, the government might impose *"must carry" rules* on the most *popular* Web sites, rules designed to ensure more exposure to substantive questions.[18] Under such a program, viewers of especially popular sites would see icons for sites that deal with substantive issues in serious ways. They would not be required to click on them. But it is reasonable to expect that many viewers would do so, if only to satisfy their curiosity. The result would be to create a kind of Internet "sidewalk," promoting some of the purposes of the public forum doctrine. Ideally, those who create Web sites might move in this direction on their own. If they do not, government should explore imposing requirements of this kind, making sure that no program draws invidious lines in selecting the sites whose icons will be favored. Perhaps a lottery system of some kind could reduce this risk.

5. The government might impose "must carry" rules on *highly partisan Web sites,* so as to ensure that viewers learn about sites containing opposing views. This policy would be designed to make it less likely that people will simply hear echoes of their own voices. Of course, many people would not click on the icons of sites whose views seem objectionable; but some people would, and in that sense the system would not operate so differently from general-interest intermediaries and public forums. Here too the ideal situation would be voluntary action. But if this proves impossible, it is worth considering regulatory alternatives.

These are brief thoughts on some complex subjects. My goal has not been to evaluate any proposal in detail but to give a flavor of some of the possibilities for those concerned with promoting constitutional goals in a dramatically changed environment.[19]

My principal claim here has been that a well-functioning democracy depends on far more than restraints on official censorship of controversial ideas and opinions. It also depends on some kind of public domain, in which a wide range of speakers have access to a diverse public—and also to particular institutions and practices against which they seek to launch objections.

Emerging technologies are hardly enemies here. They hold out at least as much promise as risk. But to the extent that they weaken the power of general-interest intermediaries and increase people's ability to wall themselves off from topics and opinions that they would prefer to avoid, they create serious dangers. If we believe that a system of free expression calls for unrestricted choices by individual consumers, we will not even understand the dangers as such. Whether such dangers will materialize will ultimately depend on which aspirations, for freedom and democracy, we choose to evaluate our practices against. What I have sought to establish here is that in a free republic, citizens aspire to systems that provide a wide range of experiences—of people, topics, and ideas—that they would not have selected in advance.

NOTES

1. *Hague v. CIO*, 307 U.S. 496 (1939).

2. See *Denver Area Educational Telecommunications Consortium, Inc. v. FCC*, 518 U.S. 727, 803 (1996) (Kennedy, J., dissenting).

3. For a fascinating discussion, see Ronald Jacobs, *Race, Media, and the Crisis of Civil Society* (Cambridge: Cambridge Univ. Press 2000).

4. For citations and general discussion, see Cass R. Sunstein, "Deliberative Trouble? Why Groups Go to Extremes," *Yale Law Journal* (2000).

5. See ibid. for details.

6. See ibid.

7. See Patricia Wallace, *The Psychology of the Internet* (Cambridge: Cambridge Univ. Press, 1999), 82.

8. Ibid.

9. Thomas W. Hazlett and David W. Sosa, "Was the Fairness Doctrine a 'Chilling Effect'? Evidence from the Postderegulation Radio Market," *Journal of Legal Studies* 26 (1997): 279 (offering an affirmative answer to the question in the title).

10. See, e.g., Sushil Biikhchandani et al., "Learning from the Behavior of Others," *Journal of Economic Perspectives* (Summer 1998): 151.

11. *Virginia State Bd. of Pharmacy v. Virginia Citizens Consumer Council*, 425 U.S. 748 (1976).

12. *44 Liquormart, Inc. v. Rhode Island*, 517 U.S. 484 (1996).

13. See *Buckley v. Valeo*, 424 U.S. 1 (1979).

14. For an effort in this direction, see Cass R. Sunstein, *Democracy and the Problem of Free Speech* (New York: Free Press, 1993).

15. James Madison, "Report on the Virginia Resolution, January 1800," in *Writings of James Madison,* ed. Galliard Hunt, vol. 6 (New York: G. P. Putnam's Sons, 1906), 385–401.

16. *Pruneyard Shopping Center v. Robins,* 447 U.S. 74 (1980).

17. See Andrew Shapiro, *The Control Revolution* (New York: Basic Books, 1999).

18. See Andrew Chin, "Making the World Wide Web Safe for Democracy," *Hastings Communication and Entertainment Law Journal* 19 (1997): 309.

19. See Cass R. Sunstein, *Republic.com* (Princeton, N.J.: Princeton Univ. Press, 2001), for more detail.

Selected Bibliography

COMPILED BY NATALIE MARTIN
Law, Ohio State University

Abubadika, Mwlina Imiri [Sonny Carson]. *The Education of Sonny Carson*. New York: Norton, 1972.

Adams, Willi Paul. *The First American Constitutions: Republican Ideology and the Making of the State Constitutions in the Revolutionary Era*. Trans. Rita and Robert Kimber. Chapel Hill: Univ. of North Carolina Press, 1973.

Aglietta, Michel. *A Theory of Capitalist Regulation*. Trans. David Fernbach. London: New Left Books, 1979.

———. *A Theory of Capitalist Regulation: The U.S. Experience*. Trans. David Fernbach. Rev. ed. London: Verso, 1987.

Alexander, Jeffrey, ed. *Real Civil Societies: Dilemmas of Institutionalization*. Thousand Oaks, Calif.: Sage, 1998.

Allison, Rinda Y., and Scott F. Uhler. "Libraries and the Internet, Part 3: Library Authority to Filter/Block Internet Sites." *Illinois Libraries* 80 (Spring 1998): 43–45.

Amar, Akhil Reed. "The Bill of Rights as a Constitution." *Yale Law Journal* 100 (1991): 1131–210.

———. *The Bill of Rights: Creation and Reconstruction*. New Haven, Conn.: Yale Univ. Press, 1999.

Anon. *Constitutions of the Several Independent States of America*. Philadelphia, 1781.

Appleby, Joyce. *Liberalism and Republicanism in the Historical Imagination*. Cambridge, Mass.: Harvard Univ. Press, 1992.

Araton, Harvey. "Athletes Toe the Nike Line, but Students Apply Pressure." *New York Times*, Nov. 22, 1997.

Arenson, Karen W. "Columbia to Put Learning Online for Profit." *New York Times*, Apr. 3, 2000, B3.

Arnold, Douglas M. *A Republican Revolution: Ideology and Politics in Pennsylvania, 1776–1790*. New York: Garland, 1989.

Aronowitz, Stanley. *The Knowledge Factory: Dismantling the Corporate University and Creating True Higher Learning*. Boston: Beacon Press, 2000.

Aronowitz, Stanley, and William DiFazio. *The Jobless Future: Sci-Tech and the Dogma of Work*. Minneapolis: Univ. of Minnesota Press, 1994.

Auerbach, Jerold. *Unequal Justice*. New York: Oxford Univ. Press, 1976.

Ayers, William, and Bernadine Dohrn. "Resisting Zero Tolerance." *Rethinking Schools* (Spring 2000): 14.

Ayers, William, Michael Klonsky, and Gabrielle Lyon, eds. *A Simple Justice: The Challenge of Small Schools*. New York: Teachers College Press, 2000.

Baldwin, Fletcher N., Jr. "The Academies, Hate Speech and the Concept of Academic Intellectual Freedom." *University of Florida Journal of Law and Public Policy* 7 (1995): 41, 44.

Band, Stephen, and Joseph Harpold. "School Violence: Lessons Learned." *FBI Law Enforcement Bulletin* (Sept. 1999): 12–15.

Barber, Benjamin R. *Jihad v. McWorld*. New York: Ballantine, 1996.

Barber, Kathleen. "The Legal Status of the American Communist Party: 1965." *Journal of Public Law* 15 (1966): 94, 103n.92.

Barnett, Randy E., and Don B. Kates. "Under Fire: The New Consensus on the Second Amendment." *Emory Law Journal* 45 (1996): 1139–259.

Becker, Howard Saul. *The Other Side: Perspectives on Deviance*. Glencoe, N.Y.: Free Press, 1964.

Bedau, H., ed. *Civil Disobedience*. New York: Pegasus, 1969.

Bellesiles, Michael A. "Gun Laws in Early America: The Regulation of Firearms Ownership, 1607–1794." *Law and History Review* 16 (1998): 567–89.

———. "Origins of Gun Culture in the United States, 1760–1865." *Journal of American History* 83 (1996): 425–55.

———. "Suicide Pact: New Readings of the Second Amendment." *Constitutional Commentary* (1999).

Bellow, Gary, and Martha Minow, eds. *Law Stories*. Ann Arbor: Univ. of Michigan Press, 1996.

Bender, Thomas. "Intellectual and Cultural History." In Foner, *New American History*.

Benjamin, Ernst. "A Faculty Response to the Fiscal Crisis: From Defense to Offense." In Berube and Nelson.

Benkler, Yochai. "Communications Infrastructure Regulation and the Distribution of Control Over Content." *Telecommunications Policy* 22.3 (1998): 183.

Bersani, Leo, and Ulysse Dutoit. *The Forms of Violence: Narrative in Assyrian Art and Modern Culture*. New York: Schocken Books, 1985.

Berube, Michael. "Bitesize Theory: Popularizing Academic Criticism." *Social Text* 36 (Fall 1993): 84–97.

Berube, Michael, and Cary Nelson. *Higher Education Under Fire*. New York: Routledge, 1995.

Best, Joel. *Random Violence: How We Talk about New Crimes and New Victims*. Berkeley: Univ. of California Press, 1999.

Biikhchandani, Sushil, et al. "Learning from the Behavior of Others." *Journal of Economic Perspectives* (Summer 1998): 151.

Bird, Kai, and Lawrence Lifschultz. *Hiroshima's Shadow*. Stony Creek, Conn.: Pamphleteer's Press, 1998.

Blasi, Vincent. "The Checking Value in First Amendment Theory." *American Bar Foundation Research Journal* (1977).

————. "The Pathological Perspective and the First Amendment." *Columbia Law Review* 85 (1985): 449, 508.

Bobbio, Norberto. "Gramsci and the Concept of Civil Society." In *Civil Society and the State: New European Perspectives.* Ed. John Keane. London: Verso, 1988.

Bogus, Carl T. "The Hidden History of the Second Amendment." *University of California Davis Law Review* 31 (Winter 1998): 309–408.

Bok, Sissela. *Mayhem: Violence as Public Entertainment.* Reading, Mass.: Addison-Wesley, 1998.

————. "TV Violence, Children, and the Press: Eight Rationales Inhibiting Public Policy Debates." Discussion Paper D-16, April 1994, The Joan Shorenstein Barone Center, Harvard University.

Bollinger, Lee C. *The Tolerant Society.* New York: Oxford Univ. Press, 1986.

Bontecou, Eleanor. *The Federal Loyalty-Security Program.* Ithaca, N.Y.: Cornell Univ. Press, 1953.

Bourdieu, Pierre. "Censorship and the Imposition of Form." In *Language and Symbolic Power.* Trans. Gino Raymond and Matthew Adamson. Cambridge, Mass.: Harvard Univ. Press, 1991.

Bowe, Brian. "High-Profile Crusade." *The Holland Sentinel* Online Edition, Feb. 17, 2000, http://www.thehollandsentinel.net/stories/021700/new_crusade.html.

Bowe, Brian, Nate Reens, and Dave Yonkman. "Filters Rejected." *The Holland Sentinel* Online Edition, Feb. 23, 2000, http://www.thehollandsentinel.net/stories/022300/new_crusade.html.

Bowen, Barbara. "The Corporatization of Higher Education and the Labor-Based Response." Talk at Socialist Scholars Conference, New York City, April 10, 1999.

Bowen, William, and Neil Rudenstine. *In Pursuit of the Ph.D.* Princeton, N.J.: Princeton Univ. Press, 1992.

Bradsher, Keith. "Fear of Crime Trumps Fear of Lost Youth." *New York Times,* Nov. 21, 1999.

Branscomb, Anne Wells. "Anonymity, Autonomy, and Accountability: Challenges to the First Amendment in Cyberspaces." *Yale Law Journal* 104 (1995): 1639–80.

Brooks, Peter, and Paul Gewirtz, eds. *Law's Stories: Narrative and Rhetoric in the Law.* New Haven, Conn.: Yale Univ. Press, 1996.

Brown, R., and J. Kulik. "Flashbulb Memories." *Cognition* 5 (1977): 73–99.

Brown, Ralph S., Jr. *Loyalty & Security: Employment Tests in the United States.* New Haven, Conn.: Yale Univ. Press, 1958.

Brunhouse, Robert L. *The Counter-Revolution in Pennsylvania, 1776–1790.* N.p., 1942.

Bryan, Samuel. "The Address and Reasons of Dissent of the Minority . . ." In *The Documentary History of the Ratification of the Constitution,* vol. 2. Ed. Merrill Jensen et al. Madison: State Historical Society of Wisconsin, 1976.

Buckholtz, Alison. "Electronic Genesis, E-Journals in the Sciences." *Academe* (Sept.–Oct. 1999): 65–68.

Burgan, Larry, and Robert Rubel. "Public School Security: Yesterday, Today and Tomorrow." *Contemporary Education* 11 (Fall 1980): 13–15.

Burress, Charles. "Symbolic Steps: UC Berkeley Names Legendary Protest Spot After Mario Savio." *San Francisco Chronicle,* Dec. 3, 1997.

Burt, David. "Survey of 24 Public Libraries Finds that Filtering Generates Few Complaints, Takes Up Little Staff Time." *Filtering Facts,* Jan. 28, 1998, http://www.filteringfacts.org/survey.html.

Butchart, Ronald. "Punishments, Penalties, and Procedures: A History of Discipline in U.S. Schools." In *Classroom Discipline in American Schools: Problems and Possibilities for Democratic Education*. Ed. Ronald Butchart. Albany: SUNY Press, 1998.

Butterfield, Fox. *All God's Children: The Bosket Family and the American Tradition of Violence*. New York: Avon, 1996.

Byassee, William S. "Jurisdiction of Cyberspace: Applying Real World Precedent to the Virtual Community." *Wake Forest Law Review* 30 (1995): 197–208.

Bybee, Rodger, and E. Gordon Gee. *Violence, Values and Justice in the Schools*. Boston: Allyn and Bacon, 1982.

Byrne, Peter J. "Academic Freedom: A 'Special Concern' of the First Amendment." *Yale Law Journal* 99 (1989): 251

Calhoun, Craig, ed. *Habermas and the Public Sphere*. Cambridge, Mass.: MIT Press, 1992.

Calvert, Clay. "Regulating Cyberspace: Metaphor, Rhetoric, Reality and the Framing of Legal Options." *Hastings Communications and Entertainment Law Journal* 20 (1998): 541.

Carey, James. *Communication as Culture: Essays on Media and Society*. Boston: Unwin Hyman, 1989.

———. "The Problem of Journalism History." *Journalism History* 1 (Spring 1974): 3–5, 27.

Carnevale, Dan. "Two Models for Collaboration in Distance Education." *Chronicle of Higher Education* (May 19, 2000): A53–55.

Carli, L. L., and J. B. Leonard. "The Effect of Hindsight on Victim Derogation." *Journal of Social and Clinical Psychology* 8 (1989): 331–43.

Carroll, Jon. "Manufacturing Consensus." *San Francisco Chronicle*, Feb. 6, 1998.

Carter, Stephen L. *Civility: Manners, Morals and the Etiquette of Democracy*. New York: Basic Books, 1998.

Carvajal, Doreen. "Book Publishers Seek Global Reach and Grand Scale." *New York Times*, Oct. 19, 1998, C1.

Casper, Jonathan D. *The Politics of Civil Liberties*. New York: Harper and Row, 1972.

Castells, Manuel. *The Information Age: Economy, Society and Culture*. Vol. 2: *The Power of Identity*. Oxford: Blackwell, 1997.

Centra, John A. *Determining Faculty Effectiveness*. San Francisco: Jossey-Bass, 1979.

Chin, Andrew. "Making the World Wide Web Safe for Democracy." *Hastings Communications and Entertainment Law Journal* 19 (1997): 309.

Chomsky, Noam, et al. *The Cold War and the University: Toward an Intellectual History of the Postwar Years*. New York: New Press, 1997.

Cieslak, David J. "Bid to Put Filters on UA Computers Fails." *Tucson Citizen*, Jan. 15, 2000, 1C.

Cleary, Edward. *Beyond the Burning Cross*. New York: Random House, 1994.

Clinton, William. "Radio Address by the President of the Nation." The White House Office of the Press Secretary, Apr. 15, 2000.

Clune, William, III. "Evaluating School Discipline through Empirical Research." *Education and Urban Society* 11 (1979): 440–49.

Cobb, C. "Policing Internet, Freedom of Speech and Censorship Collide on the Information Highway." *Ottawa Citizen*, Mar. 6, 1994, B2.

Cockburn, Alexander. "CNN and PSYOPS." *Counterpunch*, Mar. 26, 2000.

Cohen, Carl. "Law, Speech, and Disobedience." *The Nation*, Mar. 28, 1966, 357–62.

Cohen, Dov, and Joe Vandello. "Meanings of Violence." *Journal of Legal Studies* 27 (June 1998): 567–83.

Cohen, Dov, Joe Vandello, and Adrian Rantilla. "The Sacred and the Social: Honor and Violence in Cultural Context." In *Shame: Interpersonal Behavior, Psychopathology, and Culture.* Ed. Paul Gilbert and Bernice Andrews. New York: Oxford Univ. Press, 1998

Cohen, Jean, and Andrew Arato. *Civil Society and Political Theory.* Cambridge, Mass.: MIT Press, 1992.

Cole, Jonathan R., Elinor G. Barger, and Stephen R. Graubard. "Balancing Acts: Dilemmas of Choice Facing Research Universities." In *The Research University in a Time of Discontent,* eds., Johnathan R. Cole, Elinor G. Barger, and Stephen R. Graubard. Baltimore: Johns Hopkins Univ. Press, 1994.

Cole, Jonathan R., Elinor G. Barger, and Stephen R. Graubard. *The Research University in a Time of Discontent.* Baltimore: Johns Hopkins Univ. Press, 1994.

Coles, Adrienne. "Crime Drops Since NYPD Takeover of School Security." *Education Week,* Mar. 15, 2000, 6.

Coliver, Sandra, ed. *Striking a Balance: Hate Speech, Freedom of Expression, and Non-Discrimination.* London: Article 19, 1992.

Contanzo, Mark, and Stuart Oskamp, ed. *Violence and the Law.* Thousand Oaks, Calif.: Sage, 1994.

Cornell, Saul. "Commonplace or Anachronism: The Standard Model, the Second Amendment, and the Problem of History in Contemporary Constitutional Theory." *Constitutional Commentary* 16 (1999): 221–46.

———. "Splitting the Difference: Textualism, Contextualism and Post-Modern History." *American Studies* (Spring 1995): 57–80.

———. *The Other Founders: Anti-Federalism and the Dissenting Tradition in America, 1788–1828.* Chapel Hill: Univ. of North Carolina Press, 1999.

Corrigan, Philip, and Derek Sayer. *The Great Arch: English State Formation as Cultural Revolution.* Oxford: Blackwell, 1985.

Cotta, Sergio. *Why Violence? A Philosophical Interpretation.* Gainesville: Univ. of Florida Press, 1985.

Cottrol, Robert. *Oxford Companion to the Supreme Court.* New York: Oxford Univ. Press, 1992.

Cowan, Ruth Schwartz. *A Social History of American Technology.* New York: Oxford Univ. Press, 1997.

Coxe, Tench. "A Pennsylvania." Remarks on the First Part of the Amendments (1789). *New York Packet,* June 23, 1789.

Coyne, Richard. *Technoromanticism: Digital Narrative, Holism, and the Romance of the Real.* Cambridge, Mass.: MIT Press, 1999.

Crocco, Margaret Smith. "The Missing Discourse about Gender and Sexuality in the Social Studies." *Theory and Research in Social Education,* forthcoming.

Cuomo, Mario, ed. *Lincoln on Democracy.* New York: HarperCollins, 1991.

Currie, Jan, and Janice Newson, eds. *Universities and Globalization, Critical Perspectives.* Thousand Oaks, Calif.: Sage, 1998.

Currie, Jan, and Lesley Vidovich. "Micro-Economic Reform through Managerialism in American and Australian Universities." In Currie and Newson.

Dahl, Robert A. "Epilogue." In *Political Oppositions in Western Democracies*. Ed. Robert A. Dahl. New Haven, Conn.: Yale Univ. Press, 1966.

D'Arms, John H. "Funding Trends in the Academic Humanities, 1970–1995: Reflections on the Stability of the System." In Kernan.

Darnton, Robert. "Intellectual and Cultural History." In Kammen.

Davies, Peter. *The Truth about Kent State*. New York: Farrar Straus Giroux, 1973.

Dawson, Richard E. *Public Opinion and Contemporary Disarray*. New York: Harper and Row, 1973.

Deans, Bob. "Showdown Over Iraq: Policy Pitch Meets Flak." *The Atlanta Journal and Constitution*, Feb. 19, 1998.

DeMott, Benjamin. "Seduced by Civility." *The Nation*, Dec. 9, 1996.

de Tocqueville, Alexis. *Democracy in America*. Ed. J. P. Mayer. Garden City, NY: Anchor, 1969.

Devine, John. *Maximum Security: The Culture of Violence in Inner-City Schools*. Chicago: Univ. of Chicago Press, 1996.

Dewey, John. "Liberty and Social Control." *Social Frontier* (Nov. 1935): 41.

———. *The School and Society*. Chicago: Univ. of Chicago Press, 1956.

Dibbell, Julian. *My Tiny Life: Crime and Passion in a Virtual World*. New York: Owl Books, 1999.

Diggins, John Patrick. "Class, Classical, and Consensus Views of the Constitution." *University of Chicago Law Review* 55 (1988): 570.

Dilucchio, Patrizia. "Dr. Laura Targets the New Sodom: Libraries." *Salon*, May 27, 1999, http://www.salon.com/tech/feature/1999/05/27/dr_laura/.

Donnerstein, Edward, and Daniel Linz. "Sexual Violence in the Mass Media." In *Violence and the Law*. Ed. Mark Costanzo and Stuart Oskamp. Thousand Oaks, Calif.: Sage, 1994.

Donohue, Elizabeth, Vincent Schiraldi, and Jason Ziedenberg. *School House Hype: The School Shootings, and the Real Risks Kids Face in America*. San Francisco: Justice Policy Institute, 1998.

Dorsen, Norman, Paul Bender, and Burt Neuborne. *Emerson, Haber and Dorsen's Political and Civil Rights in the United States*. 4th ed. Boston: Little, Brown, 1976.

Doyle, Robert P. *Banned Books: 1998 Resource Book*. Chicago: American Library Association, 1998.

Dreyfus, Hubert L., and Paul Rabinow. *Michel Foucault: Beyond Structuralism and Hermeneutics*. 2d ed. Chicago: Univ. of Chicago Press, 1983.

Drobnicki, John A. "Holocaust Denial and Libraries: Should Libraries Acquire Revisionist Materials?" *College and Research Libraries News* 60 (June 1999): 463–64.

Durkheim, Emile. *The Division of Labor in Society*. Glencoe, N.Y.: Free Press, 1933.

Dworkin, Andrea. *Pornography: Men Possessing Women*. New York: Dutton, 1991.

Dworkin, Ronald. *Freedom's Law*. Cambridge, Mass.: Harvard Univ. Press, 1996.

———. *Taking Rights Seriously*. Cambridge, Mass.: Harvard Univ. Press, 1977.

Eckert, Penelope. *Jocks and Burnouts: Social Categories and Identity in the High School*. New York: Teachers College Press, 1989.

Egan, Patrick T. "Note—Virtual Community Standards: Should Obscenity Law Recognize the Contemporary Community Standard of Cyberspace?" *Suffolk University Law Review* 30 (1996): 117–31.

Ehrenreich, Rosa. "Look Who's Editing." *Lingua Franca* (Jan.–Feb. 1996).

Emerson, Thomas. *The System of Freedom of Expression.* New York: Random House, 1970.

Erikson, Kai T. "Notes on the Sociology of Deviance." *Deviance, the Interactionist Perspective: Texts and Readings in the Sociology of Deviance.* Earl Rubington and Martin S. Weinberg, eds. New York: Macmillan, 1987.

Erskine, Hazel. "The Polls: Freedom of Speech." *Public Opinion Quarterly* 34 (1970): 483, 485–86.

Estlund, David. "Beyond Fairness and Deliberation: The Epistemic Dimension of Democratic Authority." In *Deliberative Democracy.* Ed. James Bohman and William Rehg. Cambridge, Mass.: MIT Press, 1997.

———. "Political Quality." *Social Philosophy and Policy* 17 (Winter 2000): 127–60.

Etzkowitz, Henry, and Andrew Webster. "Entrepreneurial Science: The Second Academic Revolution." In Etzkowitz, Webster, and Healey.

Etzkowitz, Henry, Andrew Webster, and Peter Healey, eds. *Capitalizing Knowledge: New Intersections of Industry and Academia.* Albany: SUNY Press, 1998.

Eule, Julian N. "Transporting First Amendment Norms to the Private Section: With Every Wish There Comes a Curse." *UCLA Law Review* 45 (1998): 1537.

Evans, David. "Heckled in Columbus." *Columbus Free Press,* Feb. 25, 1998.

Ezzo, Gary, and Anne Marie Ezzo. *Growing Kids God's Way.* Simi Valley, Calif.: Growing Families International, 1990.

Fern, Yvonne. *Gene Roddenberry: The Last Conversation.* Berkeley: Univ. of California Press, 1994.

Finkelhor, David, Kimberly J. Mitchell, and Janis Wolak. *Online Victimization: A Report on the Nation's Youth.* National Center for Missing and Exploited Children, June 2000, http://www.missingkids.org/download/InternetSurvey.pdf.

Finkelstein, Barbara. "A Crucible of Contradictions: Historical Roots of Violence Against Children in the United States." *History of Education Quarterly* 40 (Spring 2000): 2.

———. *Governing the Young: Teacher Behavior in Popular Primary Schools in 19th Century United States.* London: Falmer, 1989.

Finkin, Matthew W. "Intramural Speech and Academic Freedom." *Texas Law Review* 66 (1988): 1323–24.

Fisher, Linda E. "A Communitarian Compromise on Speech Codes: Restraining the Hostile Environment Concept." *Catholic University Law Review* 44 (1994): 97, 100.

Fiske, John. *Understanding Popular Culture.* Boston: Unwin Hyman, 1989.

Flaherty, Martin S. "History 'Lite' in Modern American Constitutionalism." *Columbia Law Review* 95 (1995).

Foner, Eric, ed. *Free Soil, Free Labor, Free Men: The Ideology of the Republican Party before the Civil War.* New York: Oxford Univ. Press, 1970.

———. *The New American History.* Rev. ed. Philadelphia: Temple Univ. Press, 1997.

Fornek, Kimberly. "Program Loses Seats as Expulsions Soar." *Catalyst* (Feb. 1999).

Foucault, Michel. *Power/Knowledge: Selected Interviews and Other Writings, 1972–1977.* Ed. Colin Gordon. New York: Pantheon, 1980.

Frankl, Viktor E. *Man's Search for Meaning.* New York: Washington Square, 1959.

Frazier, Clyde. "Between Obedience and Revolution." *Philosophy and Public Affairs* 1 (Spring 1972): 315–34.

Friedman, Lawrence M. *Crime and Punishment in American History*. New York: Basic Books, 1993.

Galanter, Marc. "Worlds of Deals: Using Negotiations to Teach about Legal Process." *Journal of Legal Education* 34 (1984): 268.

Gallup, George H. *The Gallup Poll: Public Opinion 1935–1971*. 3 vols. New York: Random House, 1972.

Garrow, David J. *The FBI and Martin Luther King, Jr.* New York: Penguin, 1981.

Gates, Henry Louis, Jr. "Critical Race Theory and Free Speech." In Menand.

Geertz, Clifford. *The Interpretation of Cultures*. New York: Basic Books, 1973.

Gibbons, Llewellyn Joseph. "No Regulation, Government Regulation, Self-Regulation: Social Enforcement or Social Contracting for Governance in Cyberspace." *Cornell Journal of Law and Public Policy* 6 (1997): 475.

Gilligan, Carol. *In a Different Voice: Women's Conceptions of Self and Morality.* Cambridge, Mass.: Harvard Univ. Press, 1982.

Gilmore, Ruth. "Globalisation and U.S. Prison Growth: From Military Keynesianism to Post Keynesian Militarism." *Race & Class* 40 (Fall 1998/Winter 1999): 171–88.

Giordano, Philip. "Invoking Law as a Basis for Identity in Cyberspace." *Stanford Technological Law Review* 1 (1998).

Glendon, Mary Ann. *Rights Talk: The Impoverishment of Political Discourse*. New York: Free Press, 1991.

Godwin, Mike. *Cyber Rights: Defending Free Speech in the Digital Age*. New York: Time Books, 1998.

Goldstein, Robert Justin. *Political Repression in Modern America from 1870 to the Present*. Cambridge, Mass.: Shenkman, 1978.

Goodell, Charles. *Political Prisoners in America*. New York: Random House, 1973.

Gordon, Dan. "Limits on Extremist Political Parties: A Comparison of Israeli Jurisprudence with That of the United States and West Germany." *Hastings International & Comparative Law Review* 10 (1987): 347, 366.

Gosnell, Chris. "Hate Speech on the Internet: A Question of Context." *Queens Law Journal* 23 (1998): 369–439.

Graber, Mark A. "Old Wine in New Bottles: The Constitutional Status of Unconstitutional Speech." *Vanderbilt Law Review* 48 (1995): 369–71.

———. *Transforming Free Speech: The Ambiguous Legacy of Civil Libertarianism*. Berkeley: Univ. of California Press, 1991.

Grafstein, Julie. "The Public Library and the Internet: Who Has a Right to What?" *Internet Reference Services Quarterly* 42 (Nov. 1999): 7–19.

Gramsci, Antonio. "Americanism and Fordism." In *Selections from the Prison Notebooks*. London: Lawrence and Wishart, 1971.

———. *Selections from the Prison Notebooks*. London: Lawrence and Wishart, 1971.

Gray, Fred D. *Bus Ride to Justice*. Montgomery, Ala.: Black Belt Press, 1995.

Gray, John, and Andrew Ciofalo. "Student Press Protected by Faculty Academic Freedom Under Contract Law at Private Colleges." *Educational Law Report* 52 (1989): 443.

Greenhouse, Steven. "Nike Identifies Plants Abroad Making Goods for Universities." *New York Times*, Oct. 8, 1999.

———. "Nike's Chief Cancels a Gift Over Monitor of Sweatshop." *New York Times*, Apr. 25, 2000.

———. "Nike Shoe Plant in Vietnam Is Called Unsafe for Workers." *New York Times*, Nov. 8, 1997.

Greenstone, J. David. "Against Simplicity: The Cultural Dimensions of the Constitution." *University of Chicago Law Review* 55 (1988): 413, 428.

Greven, Philip. *Spare the Rod: The Religious Roots of Punishment and the Psychological Impact of Physical Abuse*. New York: Vintage, 1992.

Grey, Thomas C. "How to Write a Speech Code without Really Trying: Reflections on the Stanford Experience." *University of California Davis Law Review* 29 (1996).

Grumet, Madeleine. *Bitter Milk: Women and Teaching*. Amherst: Univ. of Massachusetts Press, 1988.

Guchemo, Jean-Marie. "Legal and Constitutional Protections of Freedom of Speech in France." In *Liberty of Expression*. Ed. Philip S. Cooke. Washington, D.C.: Wilson Center, 1990. 65.

Gunn, Steven H. "A Lawyer's Guide to the Second Amendment." *Brigham Young University Law Review* (1998): 35–54.

Gunning, Tom. *D. W. Griffith and the Origins of American Narrative Film: The Early Years at Biograph*. Urbana: Univ. of Illinois Press, 1994.

———. "Now You See It, Now You Don't: The Temporality of the Cinema of Attractions." *Velvet Light Trap* 32 (Fall 1993).

Habermas, Jürgen. *Moral Consciousness and Communicative Action*. Cambridge, Mass.: MIT Press, 1990.

Hagloch, Susan B. "To Filter or Not: Internet Access in Ohio." *Library Journal* 124 (Feb. 1, 1999): 50–51.

Halbrook, Stephen P. *That Every Man Be Armed: The Evolution of a Constitutional Right*. Albuquerque: Univ. of New Mexico Press, 1984.

———. "The Right of the People or the Power of the State: Bearing Arms, Arming Militias, and the Second Amendment." *Valparaiso Law Review* 26 (1991): 131–207.

Halbrook, Stephen P., and David B. Kopel. "Tench Coxe and the Right to Keep and Bear Arms, 1787–1823." *William and Mary Bill of Rights Journal* 7 (Feb. 1999): 347–99.

Hand, Learned. *The Spirit of Liberty*. New York: Knopf, 1959.

Hansen, Marian. "Early Cinema, Late Cinema: Permutations of the Public Sphere." *Screen* 34 (Autumn 1993).

Harachi, Tracy, Richard Catalano, and J. David Hawkins. "United States." In *The Nature of Bullying*. Ed. Peter Smith, et al. London: Routledge, 1999.

Hardy, David T. "The Second Amendment and the Historigraphy of the Bill of Rights." *Journal of Law and Politics* 4 (Summer 1987): 1–62.

Harmon, Charles, and Ann K. Symons. "'But We're Family Friendly Already': How to Respond to the Challenge." *American Libraries* 27 (Aug. 1996): 60, 62–64.

Harper, Jennifer. "'Robbers' Suspended from New Jersey School; 'Cops' Too." *Washington Times*, Apr. 7, 2000.

Hartog, Hendrik. "Pigs and Positivism." *Wisconsin Law Review* (1985): 899–935.

———. "The Constitution of Aspiration and the Rights that Belong to Us All." *Journal of American History* 74 (1987): 1013–34.

Harvey, David. *The Condition of Postmodernity*. Oxford: Blackwell, 1989.

Harvey, John H. *Embracing Their Memory: Loss and the Social Psychology of Storytelling*. Needham Heights, Mass.: Allyn and Bacon, 1996.

Haskell, Thomas L. "Justifying the Rights of Academic Freedom in the Era of Power/Knowledge." In Menand.

Havens, Carolyn. "Teen Suicide and the Library." *Public Library Quarterly* 10 (1990): 33–42.

Hays, Will H. *The Memoirs of Will H. Hays*. Garden City, N.Y.: Doubleday, 1955.

Hazlett, Thomas W., and David W. Sosa. "Was the Fairness Doctrine a 'Chilling Effect'? Evidence from the Postderegulation Radio Market." *Journal of Legal Studies* 26 (1997): 279.

Heider, Fritz. *The Psychology of Interpersonal Relations*. New York: Wiley, 1958.

Hentoff, Nat. *Free Speech for Me but Not for Thee*. New York: HarperCollins, 1992.

Hibbitts, Bernard J. "Last Writes? Reassessing the Law Review in the Age of Cyberspace." *New York University Law Review* 71 (1996): 615–88.

Higginbotham, Don. "The Second Amendment in Historical Context." *Constitutional Commentary* (1999).

Higham, John, and Paul K. Conkin, ed. *New Directions in American Intellectual History*. Baltimore: Johns Hopkins Univ. Press, 1979.

Hiner, N. Ray. "Cotton Mather and His Children: The Evolution of a Parent Educator, 1686–1728." In *Regulated Children, Liberated Children: Education in Psychohistorical Perspective*. Ed. Barbara Finkelstein. New York: Psychohistory Press, 1979.

Hobson, Charles F. "The Negative on State Laws: James Madison, the Constitution, and the Crisis of Republican Government." *William and Mary Quarterly* 3d ser., 36 (1979): 215–35.

Hochheiser, Harry. "CPSR Filtering FAQ Version 1.1.1." Computer Professionals for Social Responsibility, Oct. 24, 1998, http://www.cpsr.org/filters/faq.html.

Hodges, Ann. "White House Sends Message to Iraq in CNN-Staged Town Meeting." *Houston Chronicle*, Feb. 20, 1998.

Holeton, Richard. *Composing Cyberspace: Identity, Community, and Knowledge in the Electronic Age*. Boston: McGraw-Hill, 1998.

Hollinger, David A. "Money and Academic Freedom Fifty Years after the Loyalty Oath: Berkeley and Its Peers Amid the Force Fields of Capital." Unpublished paper.

Honderich, Ted. "Democratic Violence." *Philosophy and Public Affairs* 2 (Winter 1973): 190–214.

Honeywell, R. J. *The Educational Works of Thomas Jefferson*. New York: Russell and Russell, 1964.

Hoyt, Olga G., and Edwin P. Hoyt. *Freedom of the News Media*. New York: Seabury Press, 1970.

Huffstutter, P. J. "Censors and Sensibility." *Los Angeles Times*, Mar. 30, 1998, D1, D8.

Hulsebosch, Daniel J. "Tales of Popular Sovereignty: Civics 2000: Process Constitutionalism at Yale." *Michigan Law Review* 97 (1999).

Hunter, Christopher D. *Filtering the Future? Software Filters, Porn, PICS, and the Internet Content Conundrum*. Master's thesis, University of Pennsylvania, 1999.

Hupp, Stephen L. "Collecting Extremist Political Materials: The Example of Holocaust Denial Publications." *Collection Management* 14 (1991): 163–73.

———. "The Left and the Right: A Follow-Up Survey of the Collection of Journals of Popular Opinion in Ohio Libraries." *Collection Management* 18 (1993): 135–52.

Hyman, Herbert H. "England and America: Climates of Tolerance and Intolerance." In *The Radical Right*. Ed. Daniel Bell. Garden City, N.Y.: Anchor, 1964.

Hyman, Irwin, and Pamela Snook. *Dangerous Schools: What We Can Do about the Physical and Emotional Abuse of Our Children*. San Francisco: Jossey-Bass, 1999.

Hymowitz, Kay. *Ready or Not: Why Treating Children as Small Adults Endangers Their Future and Ours*. New York: Free Press, 2000.

Jacobs, Ronald. *Race, Media, and the Crisis of Civil Society*. Cambridge: Cambridge Univ. Press, 2000.

Jacobs, Ronald N. "The Racial Discourse of Civil Society: The Rodney King Affair and the City of Los Angeles." In Alexander.

Jameson, Frederic. *Postmodernism, or the Cultural Logic of Late Capitalism*. Durham, N.C.: Duke Univ. Press, 1991.

Janoff-Bulman, Ronnie. *Shattered Assumptions: Towards a New Psychology of Trauma*. New York: Free Press, 1992.

Jay, Gregory S. *American Literature and the Culture Wars*. Ithaca, N.Y.: Cornell Univ. Press, 1997.

Jefferson, Thomas. "Letter to James Madison." In Meyers.

Jenkins, Henry. "Congressional Testimony on Media Violence." Presented before the U.S. Senate Commerce Committee, May 4, 1999.

Joelson, Mark R. "The Dismissal of Civil Servants in the Interests of National Security." 1963 *Public Law* (1963): 51, 54–56.

Johnson, Dirk. "Schools Are Cracking Down on Misconduct." *New York Times*, Dec. 1, 1999.

Johnson, John. *The Struggle for Student Rights: Tinker v. Des Moines and the 1960s*. Lawrence: Univ. of Kansas Press, 1997.

Johnson, Robert. "Decatur Furor Sparks Wider Policy Debate." *Education Week*, Nov. 24, 1999, 1.

Kaeser, Susan. "Suspensions in School Discipline." *Education and Urban Society* 11 (Aug. 1979): 465–84.

Kaestle, Carl. *Pillars of the Republic*. New York: Hill and Wang, 1983.

Kahn, Brian, and Charles Neeson, eds. *Borders in Cyberspace: Information Policy and the Global Information Infrastructure*. Cambridge, Mass.: MIT Press, 1996.

Kalven, Harry, Jr. *The Negro and the First Amendment*. Chicago: Univ. of Chicago Press, 1966.

Kammen, Michael, ed. *The Past Before Us: Contemporary Historical Writing in the United States*. Ithaca, N.Y.: Cornell Univ. Press, 1980.

Karabell, Zachary. *What's College For? The Struggle to Define American Higher Education*. New York: Basic Books, 1998.

Kates, Don. "Handgun Prohibition and the Original Meaning of the Second Amendment." *Michigan Law Review* (Nov. 1983): 222, 224.

Katsh, M. Ethan. *The Electronic Media and the Transformation of the Law*. New York: Oxford Univ. Press, 1989.

Katz, Katheryn D. "The First Amendment's Protection of Expressive Activity in the University Classroom: A Constitutional Myth." *University of California at Davis Law Review* 16 (1983): 857.

Keane, John, ed. *Civil Society and the State: New European Perspectives*. London: Verso, 1988.

Kelly, Alfred H. "Clio and the Court: An Illicit Love Affair." *Supreme Court Review* (1965).
———, ed. *Foundations of Freedom in the American Constitution.* New York: Harpers, 1958.
Kennedy, Donald. *Academic Duty.* Cambridge, Mass.: Harvard Univ. Press, 1997.
———. "Making Choices in the Research University." In Cole, Barger, and Graubard.
Kennedy, Randall. "State of the Debate: The Case against Civility?"*American Prospect* 41 (Nov.–Dec. 1998), 84.
Kenworthy, Tom. "A Discouraging Word in Tome on the Range." *USA Today*, Mar. 3, 2000, 3A.
———. "Eager Return to Columbine." *Washington Post,* Aug. 17, 1999.
Kenyon, Cecelia. *The Anti-Federalists.* Indianapolis: Bobbs-Merrill, 1966.
Kerber, Linda K. "The Revolutionary Generation: Ideology, Politics, and Culture in the Early Republic." In Foner, *New American History*.
Kernan, Alvin, ed. *What's Happened to the Humanities?* Princeton, N.J.: Princeton Univ. Press, 1997.
King, Stephen. "The Bogeyboys." Speech presented at the Vermont Library Conference, VEMA Annual Meeting, May 26, 1999.
Kingery, Paul, Mark Coggeshall, and Aaron Alford. "Weapon Carrying by Youth." *Education and Urban Society* 31 (May 1999): 309.
Kingwell, Mark. *A Civil Tongue: Justice, Dialogue and the Politics of Pluralism.* University Park: Pennsylvania State Univ. Press, 1995.
Kirp, David L. "The New U." *The Nation,* Apr. 17, 2000, 28.
Klatch, Rebecca. *A Generation Divided: The New Left, the New Right and the 1960s.* Berkeley: Univ. of California Press, 1999.
Kogan, Frank. "School's Been Blown to Pieces." *Village Voice* (Apr. 28, 1999).
Kramer, Daniel C. *Comparative Civil Rights and Liberties.* Lanham, Md.: Univ. Press of America, 1982.
Kramer, Edith. "Art and Emptiness: New Problems in Art Education and Art Therapy. *Bulletin of Art Therapy* 1 (Fall 1961): 7.
Kramnick, Isaac. "The 'Great National Discussion': The Discourse of Politics in 1787." *William and Mary Quarterly* 45 (1988): 3–32.
Kreuzer, James R. "A Student Right Examined." *AAUP Bulletin* (Summer 1967): 196–97.
Krupat, Kitty. "GSOC-UAW vs. NYU." *Workplace,* Mar. 10, 2000.
Kuhn, Annette. *Cinema, Censorship, and Sexuality, 1909–1925.* New York: Routledge, 1988.
Kurland, Philip B. "The Irrelevance of the Constitution: The First Amendment's Freedom of Speech and Freedom of Press Clauses." *Drake Law Review* 29 (1979): 1, 10.
Labaree, David F. *How to Succeed in School without Really Learning: The Credentials Race in American Education.* New Haven, Conn.: Yale Univ. Press, 1997.
Lane, Robert Wheeler. *Beyond the Schoolhouse Gate: Free Speech and the Inculcation of Values.* Philadelphia: Temple Univ. Press, 1995.
Langer, Ellen J., and L. Imber. "The Role of Mindlessness in the Perception of Deviance." *Journal of Personality and Social Psychology* 39 (1980): 360–67.
Lasch, Christopher. *Haven in a Heartless World: The Family Besieged.* New York: Free Press, 1977.
Latham, Earl. *The Communist Controversy in Washington.* Cambridge, Mass.: Harvard Univ. Press, 1966.
Lauter, Paul. "'Political Correctness' and the Attack on American Colleges." In Berubé and Nelson.

Lawrence, Charles III. "If He Hollers, Let Him Go: Regulating Racist Speech on Campus." *Duke Law Journal* (1990): 431–83.

Lerner, Melvin J. *The Belief in a Just World: A Fundamental Delusion.* New York: Plenum, 1980.

Lessig, Lawrence. *Code, and Other Laws of Cyberspace.* New York: Basic Books, 1999.

———. "The New Chicago School." *Journal of Legal Studies* 27 (1998): 661.

———. "The Regulation of Social Meaning." *University of Chicago Law Review* 62 (1995): 943–1045.

Levinson, Sanford. "The Embarrassing Second Amendment." *The Yale Law Journal* 99 (Dec. 1989): 637–59.

Levy, Leonard W. *Origins of the Bill of Rights.* New Haven, Conn.: Yale Univ. Press, 1999.

Lewis, Anthony. *Make No Law: The Sullivan Case and the First Amendment.* New York: Random House, 1991.

Lewis, Dan A. *Race and Educational Reform in the American Metropolis: A Study of School Decentralization.* Albany: State Univ. of New York Press, 1995.

———. *Worlds of the Mentally Ill: How Deinstitutionalization Works in the City.* Carbondale: Southern Illinois Univ. Press, 1991.

Lewontin, R. C. "The Cold War and the Transformation of the Academy." In *The Cold War and the University.* Ed. Noam Chomsky et al. New York: New Press, 1997.

Liebling, A. J. *The Press.* Rev. ed. New York: Ballantine Books, 1964.

Lindgren, James. "An Author's Manifesto." *University of Chicago Law Review* 61 (1994): 527, 531.

Llanos, Miguel. "Michigan Town Rejects Internet Filters." MSNBC, Feb. 23, 2000, http://www.msnbc.com/news/362856.asp

Locke, John. *An Essay Concerning Human Understanding.* London: Penquin Books, 1997.

Lofton, John. *The Press as Guardians of the First Amendment.* Columbia: Univ. of South Carolina Press, 1980.

Louis, Karen Seashore, and Melissa S. Anderson. "The Changing Context of Science and University-Industry Relations." In *Capitalizing Knowledge: New Intersections of Industry and Academia.* Eds., Henry Etzkowitz, Andrew Weber, and Peter Healey. Albany: SUNY Press, 1998.

Lowen, Rebecca S. *Creating the Cold War University: The Transformation of Stanford.* Berkeley: Univ. of California Press, 1997.

Lucas, Christopher J. *Crisis in the Academy: Rethinking Higher Education in America.* New York: St. Martin's Press, 1996.

Lufler, Henry, Jr. "Debating with Untested Assumptions." *Education and Urban Society* 11 (1979): 453, 460.

Lund, Nelson. "The Ends of Second Amendment Jurisprudence: Firearms, Disabilities, and Domestic Violence Restraining Orders." *Texas Review of Law and Politics* (1999).

———. "The Past and Future of the Individual's Right to Bear Arms." *Georgia Law Review* 31 (1997): 1–76.

Lutz, Donald. *Popular Consent and Popular Control: Whig Political Theory in the Early State Constitutions.* Baton Rouge: Louisiana State Univ. Press, 1980.

———. *A Preface to American Political Theory.* Lawrence: Univ. of Kansas Press, 1992.

Macafee, Thomas, and Michael J. Quinlan. "Bringing Forward the Right to Keep and Bear Arms." *North Carolina Law Review* 75 (1997): 791–899.

McChesney, Robert. "The Internet and U.S. Communication Policy-Making in Historical and Critical Perspective." *Journal of Communication* 46 (Winter 1996): 105.

————. *Telecommunications, Mass Media, and Democracy: The Battle for Control of U.S. Broadcasting, 1928–1935.* New York: Oxford Univ. Press, 1995.

McClosky, Herbert, and John Zaller. *The American Ethos: Public Attitudes toward Capitalism and Democracy.* Cambridge, Mass.: Harvard Univ. Press, 1984

MacKinnon, Catharine A. *Only Words.* Cambridge, Mass.: Harvard Univ. Press, 1993.

McGuire, John F. "When Speech Is Heard around the World: Internet Content Regulation in the United States and Germany." *New York University Law Review* 74 (1990): 750.

McLuhan, Marshall. *Culture Is Our Business.* New York: McGraw-Hill, 1970.

McPherson, Michael S., Morton Owen Schapiro, and Gordon C. Winston. *Paying the Piper: Productivity, Incentives and Financing in U.S. Higher Education.* Ann Arbor: Univ. of Michigan Press, 1993.

McWilliams, Carey. "Carey McWilliams." In *Censorship For and Against.* Ed. Harold H. Hart. New York: Hart Publishing, 1971.

Madison, James. "Report on the Virginia Resolution, January 1800." In *Writings of James Madison.* Vol. 6. Ed. Galliard Hunt. New York: G. P. Putnum's Sons, 1906.

Malcolm, Joyce Lee. *To Keep and Bear Arms: The Origins of an Anglo-American Right.* Cambridge, Mass.: Harvard Univ. Press, 1994.

Males, Mike, and Dan Macallair. *The Color of Justice: Analysis of Juvenile Adult Court Transfers in California.* San Francisco: Justice Policy Institute, 2000.

Maltby, Richard. *Prima dei codici 2: Alle Porte di hays.* Venice: La Biennale di Venezia, 1991.

Maltz, Tamir. "Customary Law and Process in Internet Communities." *Journal of Computer-Mediated Communication* 2.1 (June 1996) http://www.ascusc.org/jcmc/vol2/issue1/custom.html (accessed May 15, 2000).

Mann, James. "What Is TV Doing to America?" In *Impact of Mass Media.* Ed. Ray Eldon Hiebert and Carol Reuss. New York: Longman, 1985.

Manovich, Lev. *The Language of New Media.* Cambridge, Mass.: MIT Press, 2000.

Marcus, David L. "Many Doubts That Polls Don't Show." *Boston Globe,* Feb. 22, 1998.

Marcuse, Herbert. "Repressive Tolerance." In *A Critique of Pure Tolerance.* Ed. Robert Paul Wolff, Barrington Moore, Jr., and Herbert Marcuse. Boston: Beacon Press, 1969.

Masserli, Jonathan. *Horace Mann: A Biography.* New York: Knopf, 1972.

Massey, Walter E. "Can the Research University Adapt to a Changing Future?" In Cole, Barger, and Graubard.

Mather, Cotton. *Bonifacius.* 1701. In *Social History of American Education.* Vol. 1: Ed. Rena Vassar. Chicago: Rand McNally, 1965.

Matsuda, Mari. "Public Response to Racist Speech: Considering the Victim's Story." *Michigan Law Review* 87 (1989): 2320–2381.

Meiklejohn, Alexander. *Political Freedom.* New York: Harper, 1960.

Menand, Louis. "The Demise of Disciplinary Authority." In Kernan.

————, ed. *The Future of Academic Freedom No. 3.* Chicago: Univ. of Chicago Press, 1996.

Messer-Davidow, Ellen. "Manufacturing the Attack on Liberalized Higher Education." *Social Text* 36 (Fall 1993): 54.

Metzger, Walter P. *Academic Freedom in the Age of the University.* New York: Columbia Univ. Press, 1955.

———. "Profession and Constitution: Two Definitions of Academic Freedom in America." *Texas Law Review* 66 (1988): 1265.

Meyers, Marvin, ed. *The Mind of the Founder: Sources of the Political Thought of James Madison.* Rev. ed. Hanover, N.H.: Univ. Press of New England, 1981.

Mill, John Stuart. *On Liberty and Other Essays.* Ed. John Gray. Oxford: Oxford Univ. Press, 1991.

Miller, Adam S. "The Jake Baker Scandal: A Perversion in Logic." http://www.trincoll.edu/zines/tj/tj4.6.95/articles/baker.html Baker, %20the%20foreigner (accessed May 14, 2000).

Milton, John. *Paradise Lost.* London, 1667.

Minow, Martha. *Making All the Difference: Inclusion, Exclusion and American Law.* Ithaca, N.Y.: Cornell Univ. Press, 1990.

Minsky, Leonard. "Education, the Free Market, and Academic Freedom." Comments at conference on "Challenging Corporate Control," Yale University, Apr. 17, 1999.

Moley, Raymond. *The Hays Office.* Indianapolis: Bobbs-Merrill, 1945.

Mollan, Robert. "Smith Act Prosecutions: The Effect of the *Dennis* and *Yates* Decisions." *University of Pittsburgh Law Review* 26 (1965): 705, 708–10.

Moone, Chris. "Showdown." *Lingua Franca* (February 2000).

Moten, Fred, and Stefano Harney. "The Academic Speed-Up." *Workplace,* Mar. 10, 2000.

Mueller, John. "Trends in Political Tolerance." *Public Opinion Quarterly* 52 (1988): 1, 22.

Muller, Steven. "Presidential Leadership." In Cole, Barger, and Graubard.

Murphy, Paul L. *World War I and the Origins of Civil Liberties in the United States.* New York: W. W. Norton, 1979.

Murray, Janet H. *Hamlet on the Holodeck: The Future of Narrative in Cyberspace.* New York: Free Press, 1997.

Musser, Charles. *The Emergence of Cinema: The American Screen to 1907.* New York: Scribner's, 1990.

Myers, David G. *Social Psychology.* 5th ed. New York: McGraw-Hill, 1996.

Nagel, Robert E. "How Useful Is Judicial Review in Free Speech Cases?" *Cornell Law Review* 69 (1984): 302, 316.

Nelson, Cary. *Manifesto of a Tenured Radical.* New York: New York Univ. Press, 1997.

Nelson, William E., and Robert C. Palmer, eds. *Liberty and Community: Constitution and Rights in the Early American Republic.* New York: Oceana, 1987.

Newman, Maria. "Parents Find that the Rules for Play Have Changed." *New York Times,* Apr. 7, 2000, 22.

Nichols, Rodney W. "Federal Science Policy and the Universities: Consequences of Success." In Cole, Barger, and Graubard.

Nisbett, R., and L. Ross. *Human Inference: Strategies and Shortcomings of Social Judgment.* Englewood Cliffs, N.J.: Prentice Hall, 1980.

Nisbett, Richard E., and Dov Cohen. *Culture of Honor: The Psychology of Violence in the South.* Boulder, Colo.: Westview Press, 1996.

Noguera, Pedro. "Listen First: How Student Perspectives on Violence Can Be Used to Create Safer Schools." In *Violence in Children's Lives.* Ed. Valerie Polakow. New York: Teachers College Press, forthcoming.

———. "Preventing and Producing Violence: A Critical Analysis of Responses to School Violence." *Harvard Educational Review* 65 (Summer 1995): 189–212.

Nozick, Robert. "Coercion." In *Philosophy, Science, and Method*. Ed. Sidney Morgenbesser, Patrick Suppes, and Morton White. New York: St. Martin's Press, 1969.

Nunn, Clyde Z., Harry J. Crockett, Jr., and J. Allen Williams, Jr. *Tolerance for Nonconformity*. San Francisco: Jossey-Bass, 1978.

Nye, David. *Narratives and Spaces: Technology and the Construction of American Culture*. New York: Columbia Univ. Press, 1998.

Nye, Russel B. *Fettered Freedom*. East Lansing: Michigan State Univ. Press, 1963.

Olivas, Michael A. "Reflections on Professorial Academic Freedom: Second Thoughts on the Third 'Essential Freedom.'" *Stanford Law Review* 45 (1993): 1835.

Otten, Alan L. "Cambodia: Escalation on the Home Front." *Wall Street Journal*, May 7, 1970, 12.

Paletz, David, and William Harris. "Four Letter Challenges to Authority." *Journal of Politics* 37 (Nov. 1975): 955–79.

Pangle, Lorraine Smith, and Thomas Pangle. *The Learning of Liberty: The Educational Ideas of the American Founders*. Lawrence: Univ. of Kansas Press, 1993.

Pappas, James P., ed. *The University's Role in Economic Development: From Research to Outreach*. San Francisco: Jossey-Bass, 1997.

Pardo, Natalie. "Expulsions Rise, But Safety Issues Persist." *Chicago Reporter* (Sept. 1998).

Patterson, Floyd, with Milton Gross. *Victory Over Myself*. New York: Bernard Geis, 1962.

Peabody, Elizabeth. "Foreword." *Mother-Play and Nursery in America Songs*. Trans. F. E. Dwight and J. Jarvis. 1906. Reprint, Boston: Lothrop, Lee and Shephard, 1978.

Peltason, Jack W. "Constitutional Liberty and the Communist Problem." In Kelly.

Pember, Donald. *Mass Media Law*. New York: Brown and Benchmark, 1997.

Pennington, John V. "Jonesboro Boys Can't Be Tried as Adults Under State Law." *Hot Springs Sentinel-Record*, Mar. 27, 1998.

Perlstein, Daniel. "Community and Democracy in American Schools: Arthur Dale and the Fate of Progressive Education." *Teachers College Record* 97 (1996): 625–50.

———. "Failing at Kindness: How the Fear of School Violence Endangers Children." *Educational Leadership* 57 (March 2000): 76–79.

———. "Kent State 1970–1977." *Politics & Education* 1 (1977): 23.

———. "Saying the Unsaid: Girl Killing and the Curriculum." *Journal of Curriculum and Supervision* 14 (1998): 88–104.

———. "There Is No Escape . . . From the Ogre of Indoctrination: George Counts and the Civic Dilemmas of Democratic Educators." In *Reconstructing the Common Good in Education: Coping with Intractable American Dilemmas*. Ed. Larry Cuban and Dorothy Shipps. Stanford, Calif.: Stanford Univ. Press, 2000.

Polier, Justine Wise. *Juvenile Justice in Double Jeopardy: The Distanced Community and Vengeful Retribution*. Hillsdale, N.J.: Erlbaum, 1989.

Portner, Jessica. "Complex Set of Ills Spurs Rising Teen Suicide Rate." *Education Week*, Apr. 12, 2000, 22.

———. "Girl's Slaying Elicits Calls for Metal Detectors." *Education Week*, Mar. 15, 2000, 3.

Post, D. G. "Anarchy, State, and the Internet: An Essay on Law Making in Cyberspace." *Journal of Online Law* (1995) http://warthog.cc.wm.edu/law/publications/jol/post.html (accessed May 15, 2000).

Post, Robert C. *Constitutional Domains: Democracy, Community and Management*. Cambridge, Mass.: Harvard Univ. Press, 1995.

———. "Reconciling Theory and Doctrine in First Amendment Jurisprudence." *California Law Review* 89 (Jan. 2001).

———, ed. *Censorship and Silencing: Practices of Cultural Regulation*. Los Angeles: Getty Research Institute for the History of Art and the Humanities, 1998.

———, ed. *Law and the Order of Culture*. Berkeley: Univ. of California Press, 1991.

Powe, L. A. "Guns, Words and Constitutional Interpretation." *William and Mary Law Review* 38 (May 1997): 1311–403.

Powell, H. Jefferson. "Rules for Originalists." *Virginia Law Review* 73 (1987): 659.

Powell, Lewis F. "The Powell Memorandum" *Washington Report* Supplement, Aug. 23, 1971.

Preston, William, Jr. *Aliens and Dissenters.* New York: Harper and Row, 1963.

Prewitt, Kenneth. "America's Research Universities under Public Scrutiny." In Cole, Barger, and Graubard.

Price, Monroe E., ed. *The V-Chip Debate: Labeling and Rating Content from Television to the Internet*. Mahwah, N.J.: Lawrence Erlbaum, 1998.

Prothrow-Stith, Deborah. *Deadly Consequences*. New York: HarperCollins, 1991.

Rabban, David M. "Book Review: Can Academic Freedom Survive Postmodernism?" *California Law Review* 86 (1998): 1377.

———. "Distinguishing Excluded Managers from Covered Professionals under the NLRA." *Columbia Law Review* 89 (1989): 1775–860.

———. "The First Amendment in Its Forgotten Years." *Yale Law Journal* 90 (1981): 514–95, 541.

———. *Free Speech in its Forgotten Years.* New York: Cambridge Univ. Press, 1997.

Rakove, Jack N. *Declaring Rights: A Brief History with Documents*. Boston: Bedford Books, 1998.

———. *Interpreting the Constitution: The Debate Over Original Intent*. Boston: Northeastern Univ. Press, 1990.

———. *Original Meanings: Politics and Ideas in the Making of the Constitutions*. New York, 1996.

———. "The Second Amendment: The Highest State of Originalism." *Chicago-Kent Law Review* (forthcoming).

Rawls, John. *A Theory of Justice.* Cambridge, Mass.: Harvard Belknap Press, 1971.

———. *The Law of the Peoples.* Cambridge, Mass.: Harvard Univ. Press, 1999.

———. *Political Liberalism.* New York: Columbia Univ. Press, 1993.

Ray, Larry, and Andrew Sayer. *Culture and Economy after the Cultural Turn*. London: Sage, 2000.

Readings, Bill. *The University in Ruins*. Cambridge, Mass.: Harvard Univ. Press, 1996.

———. "The University without Culture?" *New Literary History* 26:3 (Summer 1995): 479.

Reid, John P. "Law and History." *Loyola Los Angeles Law Review* 27 (1993).

Reynolds, Glenn Harlan. "A Critical Guide to the Second Amendment." *Tennessee Law Review* 62 (Spring 1995): 461–512.

Rheingold, Howard. *The Virtual Community: Homesteading on the Electronic Frontier*. Reading, Mass.: Addison-Wesley, 1993.

Rhodes, Frank H. T. "The Place of Teaching in the Research University." In Cole, Barger, and Graubard.

Richardson, Elliot L. "Freedom of Expression and the Function of Courts." *Harvard Law Review* 65 (1951): 1, 54.

Rokeach, M. *The Open and Closed Mind.* New York: Basic Books, 1960.

Romer, Nancy. "The CUNY Struggle: Class and Race in Public Higher Education." *New Politics* 7 (Winter 1999).

Rosenzweig, Robert M. "Governing the Modern University." In Cole, Barger, and Graubard.

Rosswurm, Steven. *Arms, Country and Class: The Philadelphia Militia and "Lower Sort" during the American Revolution, 1775–1783.* New Brunswick, N.J.: Rutgers Univ. Press, 1987.

Rush, Benjamin. "Thoughts on the Amendments and Punishment which are Proper for Schools." In *Children and Youth in America: A Documentary History*, vol. 1. Ed. Robert Bremner. Cambridge, Mass.: Harvard Univ. Press, 1970.

Ryan, Mary. *Cradle of the Middle Class.* Cambridge: Cambridge Univ. Press, 1981.

Salkeld, Sara. "U. Nebraska Approves Fetal Research Bill." *Daily Nebraskan* (University of Nebraska), (Feb. 3, 2000) U-Wire, 2000 WL 12897370.

Sample, Robert B., Jr. "Nixon Says Violence Invites Tragedy." *New York Times,* May 5, 1970. 17.

Sampson, Robert. "The Community Context of Violent Crime." In *Sociology and the Public Agenda*. Ed. William Julius Wilson. Newburg Park, Calif.: Sage, 1993.

Sandel, Michael. *Democracy's Discontent.* Cambridge, Mass.: Harvard Univ. Press, 1996.

Sanders, Lynn. "Against Deliberation." *Political Theory* 25 (June 1, 1997): 347.

Sassen, Saskia. "Electronic Space and Power." In *Globalization and Its Discontents.* New York: New Press, 1998.

Saunders, Kevin W. *Violence as Obscenity: Limiting the First Amendment's Protection.* Durham, N.C.: Duke Univ. Press, 1996.

Scanlon, Thomas. "A Theory of Free Expression." *Philosophy & Public Affairs,* 1 (1972).

Schauer, Frederick. *Free Speech: A Philosophical Enquiry.* Cambridge: Cambridge Univ. Press, 1982.

Schiller, Daniel. *Objectivity and the News.* Philadelphia: Univ. of Pennsylvania Press, 1981.

Schneider, Karen G. "Learning from the Internet Filter Assessment Project." Internet Filter Assessment Project, 1997, http://www.bluehighways.com/tifap/learn.html.

Schrecker, Ellen W. *No Ivory Tower: McCarthyism and the Universities.* New York: Oxford Univ. Press, 1986.

———. *Many Are the Crimes: McCarthyism in America.* Boston: Little, Brown, 1998.

Schudson, Michael. *Discovering the News: A Social History of American Newspaper.* New York: Basic Books, 1978.

Scott, Joan W. "Academic Freedom as an Ethical Practice." In Menand.

———. "The Rhetoric of Crisis in Higher Education." In Berube and Nelson.

Semple, Robert B., Jr. "Nixon Says Violence Invites Tragedy." *New York Times,* May 5, 1970, 17.

Shalhope, Robert E. "The Ideological Origins of the Second Amendment." *Journal of American History* 69 (1982): 599–614.

———. "To Keep and Bear Arms in the Early Republic." *Constitutional Commentary* 16 (1999): 280–81.

Shapiro, Andrew. *The Control Revolution.* New York: Basic Books, 1999.

Shapiro, Martin. *Freedom of Speech: The Supreme Court and Judicial Review.* Englewood Cliffs, N.J.: Prentice Hall, 1966.

Sharrett, Christopher, ed. *Mythologies of Violence in Postmodern Media.* Detroit: Wayne State Univ. Press, 1999.

Shea, Christopher. "Students v. Professors: Law Review Debate Heats Up as Student Editors Clash with Faculty Authors." *Chronicle of Higher Education,* June 2, 1995.

Shearer, Lee. "Spanking Hits at Core of Debate." *Athens (Georgia) Daily News,* Mar. 22, 1998.

Shumar, Wesley. *College for Sale: A Critique of the Commodification of Higher Education.* London: Falmer Press, 1997.

Silber, Glenn, and Alexander Brown. *Vietnam: The War at Home.* 1979. Film distributed by MPI Home Video. 1986.

Skiba, Russ, and Reece Peterson. "The Dark Side of Zero Tolerance: Can Punishment Lead to Safe Schools?" *Phi Delta Kappan* 80 (Jan. 1999): 372–76, 381–82.

Slaughter, Sheila, and Larry L. Leslie. *Academic Capitalism: Politics, Policies and the Entrepreneurial University.* Baltimore: Johns Hopkins Univ. Press, 1998.

Smith, Craig R., ed. *Silencing the Opposition: Government Strategies of Suppression.* Albany: SUNY Press, 1996.

Smith, Mark. "Meeting the Pressure to Filter." *Texas Library Journal* (Feb. 1997).

Smulyan, Susan. *Selling Radio: The Commercialization of American Broadcasting, 1920–1934.* Washington, D.C.: Smithsonian Institution Press, 1996.

Sobel, David. *Filters and Freedom: Free Speech Perspectives on Internet Content Controls.* Washington, D.C.: Electronic Privacy Information Center, 1999.

Sola Pool, Ithiel de la. *Technologies of Freedom: On Free Speech in an Electronic Age.* Cambridge, Mass.: Belknap Press/Harvard Univ. Press, 1983.

Soley, Lawrence C. *Leasing the Ivory Tower: The Corporate Takeover of Academia.* Boston: South End Press, 1995.

Spitzer, Robert. "Lost and Found: Researching the Second Amendment." *Chicago-Kent Law Review* (forthcoming).

Stein, Nan. *Classrooms and Courtrooms.* New York: Teachers College Press, 1999.

Stewart, David P. "U.S. Ratification of the Covenant on Civil and Political Rights." *Human Rights Law Journal* 14 (1993): 77.

Stigler, Stephen M. "Competition and the Research Universities." In Cole, Barger, and Graubard.

Stouffer, Samuel A. *Communism, Conformity, and Civil Liberties: A Cross-Section of the Nation Speaks Its Mind.* Gloucester, Mass.: Peter Smith, 1963.

Sullivan, John L., James Pierson, and Gregory E. Marcus. "An Alternate Conceptualization of Political Tolerance: Illusory Increases 1950s-1970s." *American Political Science Review* 73 (1979): 781, 787.

Sunstein, Cass R. "Academic Freedom and Law: Liberalism, Speech Codes, and Related Problems." In Menand.

———."Deliberative Trouble? Why Groups Go to Extremes." *Yale Law Journal* (2000).

———. *Democracy and the Problem of Free Speech.* New York: Free Press, 1993.

———. "The First Amendment in Cyberspace." *Yale Law Journal* 104 (1995): 1757–804.

———. *Republic.com.* Princeton, N.J.: Princeton Univ. Press, 2001.

———. "Social Norms and Social Rules." *Columbia Law Review* 96 (1996): 903–68.

Surette, Louise. "Libraries and Net Porn: Safety Versus Censorship." *The Toronto Star* Online Edition, Apr. 14, 2000.

Sutton, Francis X. "The Distinction and Durability of American Research Universities." In Cole, Barger, and Graubard.

Swan, John C. "Untruth or Consequences." *Library Journal* 111 (July 1986): 45–52.

Tebo, Margaret Graham. "Zero Tolerance, Zero Sense." *ABA Journal* 86 (Apr. 2000): 40–46.

Tedford, Thomas L. *Freedom of Speech in the United States,* 3d ed. State College, Pa.: Strata, 1997.

Tenhoff, Greg C. "Censoring the Public University Student Press: A Constitutional Challenge." *Southern California Law Review* 64 (1990): 511–15.

Thorne, Barrie. *Gender Play: Girls and Boys in School.* New Brunswick, N.J.: Rutgers Univ. Press, 1993.

Trumbull, Den, and S. DeBose Ravenel. "Spare the Rod? New Research Challenges Spanking Critics." *Family Research Council* (Oct. 1996).

Tuchman, Gaye. "Objectivity as Strategic Ritual: An Examination of Newsmen's Notions of Objectivity." *American Journal of Sociology* 77 (1972): 660–79.

Turkle, Sherry. *Life on the Screen: Identity in the Age of the Internet.* New York: Simon and Schuster, 1995.

Tushnet, Mark. *Taking the Constitution Away from the Courts.* Princeton, N.J.: Princeton Univ. Press, 1999.

Twain, Mark. *The Adventures of Tom Sawyer.* New York: Grosset and Dunlap, 1965.

Twining, William. *Karl Llewllyn and the Realist Movement.* London: Weidenfeld and Nicolson, 1973.

Tyack, David. "Forming the National Character: Paradox in the Educational Thought of the Revolutionary Generation." *Harvard Educational Review* 36 (Winter 1966): 29–41.

Tyack, David, and Elisabeth Hansot. *Learning Together: A History of Coeducation in American Public Schools.* New Haven, Conn.: Yale Univ. Press, 1990.

——— . *Managers of Virtue: Public School Leadership in America, 1820–1980.* New York: Basic Books, 1982.

Van Alstyne, William W. "Academic Freedom and the First Amendment in the Supreme Court of the United States: An Unhurried Historical Overview." *Law and Contemporary Problems* 53 (Summer 1990): 79.

——— . "The Second Amendment and the Personal Right to Arms." *Duke Law Journal* 43 (1994): 1236–55.

Van Dyke, Henry. "Corporal Punishment in Our Schools." *The Clearing House* 57 (Mar. 1984): 296.

Veit, Helen E., Kenneth R. Bowling, and Charlene Bangs Bickford, eds. *Creating the Bill of Rights.* Baltimore: Johns Hopkins Univ. Press, 1991.

Wallace, Mike. "The Battle of the Enola Gay." In Bird and Lifschultz.

Wallace, Patricia. *The Psychology of the Internet.* Cambridge: Cambridge Univ. Press, 1999.

Walsh, Mark. "Shootings Raise Host of Legal Questions." *Education Week,* May 5, 1999, 1, 14–15.

Walshok, Mary Lindenstein. "Expanding Roles for Research Universities in Regional Economic Development." In Pappas.

Ward, David. "Foreword." In *Academic Freedom on Trial: 100 Years of Sifting and Winnowing at the University of Wisconsin-Madison.* Ed. W. Lee Hansen. Madison: Univ. of Wisconsin Press, 1998.

Webster, Andrew. "Strategic Research Alliances: Testing the Collaborative Limits?" In *Capitalizing Knowledge: New Intersections of Industry and Academia,* ed. Harry Etzkowitz, Andrew Webster, and Peter Healey. Albany: SUNY Press, 1998.

Weiler, Kathleen. "Freire and a Feminist Pedagogy of Difference." In *Debates and Issues in Feminist Research and Pedagogy*. Ed. Janet Holland, Maud Blair, and Sue Sheldon. Philadelphia: Multilingual Matters, 1995.

Weinberg, Jonathan. "The Internet and 'Telecommunications Services,' Universal Service Mechanisms, Access Charges, and Other Flotsam of the Regulatory System." *Yale Journal of Regulation* 16 (Summer 1999): 211–44.

———. "Rating the Net." *Hastings Communications and Entertainment Law Journal* 19 (1997): 453–82.

Weiner, Lois. *Preparing Teachers for Urban Schools: Lessons from Thirty Years of School Reform*. New York: Teachers College Press, 1993.

Weinstein, James. "A Constitutional Roadmap to the Regulation of Hate Speech on Campus." *Wayne Law Review* 38 (1991): 163.

———. *Hate Speech, Pornography, and the Radical Attack on Free Speech Doctrine*. Boulder, Colo.: Westview Press, 1999.

Weisbrod, Carol. *Butterfly, the Bride: Essays on Law, Narrative, and Family*. Ann Arbor: Univ. of Michigan Press, 1998.

West, Robin. *Narrative, Authority, and Law*. Ann Arbor: Univ. of Michigan Press, 1993.

———. "Toward a Jurisprudence of Respect: A Comment on George Fletcher's Constitutional Identity." *Cardozo Law Review* 14 (1993): 764.

Westin, Alan F. "Constitutional Liberty and Loyalty Programs." In Kelly, *Foundations*.

Whipple, Leon. *The Story of Civil Liberty in the United States*. New York: Vanguard, 1927.

White, Edward G. "Reading the Guarantee Clause." *University of Colorado Law Review* 65 (1994).

Whittington, Keith E. *Constitutional Interpretation: Textual Meaning, Original Intent and Judicial Review*. Lawrence: Univ. Press of Kansas, 1999.

Wilder, Laura Ingalls. *On the Banks of Plum Creek*. New York: Dell, 1945.

Williams, David C. "Civic Republicanism and the Citizen Militia: The Terrifying Second Amendment." *Yale Law Journal* 101 (Dec. 1991): 551–615.

———. "The Militia Movement and Second Amendment Revolution: Conjuring with the People." *Cornell Law Review* 81 (May 1996): 879–952.

Wills, Garry. *A Necessary Evil: A History of American Distrust of Government*. New York: Simon and Schuster, 1999.

———. "To Keep and Bear Arms." *New York Review of Books,* Sept. 21, 1995, 62–73.

Wilson, H. H., and Harvey Glickman. *The Problem of Internal Security in Great Britain 1948–1953*. Garden City, N.Y.: Doubleday, 1954.

Wilson, Robin. "Bennington President Fires a Professor Who Criticized Her Fiercely and Openly." *Chronicle of Higher Education,* April 28, 2000, A20.

Wolff, Rick. "Universities and Economic Interest." Paper delivered at the conference "Challenging Corporate Control," Yale University, Apr. 17, 1999.

Wood, Gordon S. "Intellectual History and the Social Sciences." In Higham and Conkin.

Young, Iris. "Activist Challenges to Deliberative Democracy." A paper presented at the "Deliberating about Deliberative Democracy," University of Texas, Austin, Feb. 3–4, 2000.

Zimring, Franklin. *American Youth Violence*. New York: Oxford Univ. Press, 1998.

Zirkel, Perry. "Courtside, the Midol Case." *Phi Delta Kappan* 78 (June 1997): 803–4

Case Citations

COMPILED BY SARAH NORTHCRAFT

Law, The University of Akron

44 Liquormart, Inc. v. Rhode Island, 517 U.S. 484 (1996).

Abood v. Detroit Board of Education, 431 U.S. 209 (1977).

Abrams v. United States, 250 U.S. 616 (1919).

Adderley v. Florida, 385 U.S. 39 (1966).

Alabama Student Party v. Student Government Association of University of Alabama, 867 F.2d 1344 (11th Cir. 1989).

American Booksellers Association v. Hudnut, 771 F.2d 323 (7th Cir. 1985), *aff'd* without opinion, 475 U.S. 1001 (1986).

American Civil Liberties Union v. Reno, 929 F. Supp. 824 (E.D. Pa 1996).

American Communications Association v. Douds, 339 U.S. 382 (1950).

Australian Communist Party v. Commonwealth (1950) 83 CRL 1.

Bantam Books v. Sullivan, 372 U.S. 58 (1963).

Barenblatt v. U.S., 360 U.S. 109 (1959).

Bates v. City of Little Rock, 361 U.S. 516 (1960).

Bazaar v. Fortune, 476 F. 2d 570, *rehearing en banc* 489 F.2d 225 (5th Cir. 1973).

Beauharnais v. Illinois, 343 U.S. 250 (1952).

Becker v. Gallaudet, 66 F. Supp.2d 16 (1999).

Bethel School District No. 403 v. Fraser, 478 U.S. 675 (1986).

Board of Curators of the University of Missouri v. Horowitz, 435 U.S. 78 (1978).

Board of Education v. Pico, 457 U.S. 853 (1982).

Board of Regents of the University of Wisconsin System v. Southworth, 526 U.S. 1038 (1999), 120 S. Ct. 1346 (2000).

Bolger v. Youngs Drug Products Corp., 463 U.S. 60 (1983).

Brandenburg v. Ohio, 395 U.S. 444 (1969).

Brown v. Board of Education, 347 U.S. 483 (1954).

Buckley v. Valeo, 424 U.S. 1 (1976).

Burnside v. Byars, 363 F. 2d 744 (5th Cir. 1966).

Canada (Human Rights Commission) *v. Taylor*, 3 SCR 892.

Chaplinsky v. New Hampshire, 315 U.S. 568 (1942).

City of Erie v. Pap's A. M. (2000).

Cohen v. California, 403 U.S. 15 (1971).

Cole v. Richardson, 405 U.S. 676 (1972).

Communist Party of Indiana v. Whitcomb, 414 U.S. 441 (1974).

Connick v. Myers, 461 U.S. 138 (1983).

Corry v. The Leland Stanford Junior University, Case No. 740309, Supr. Ct. State of California, County of Santa Clara, Order on Preliminary Injunction, 27 February 1995.

Cox v. Louisiana, 379 U.S. 536 (1965).

Dennis v. United States, 341 U.S. 494 (1951).

Denver Area Educational Telecommunications Consortium, Inc. v. FCC, 518 U.S. 727 (1996).

Edwards v. South Carolina, 372 U.S. 229 (1963).

FCC v. Pacifica Foundation, 438 U.S. 726 (1978).

Feiner v. New York, 340 U.S. 315 (1951).

Freedman v. Maryland, 380 U.S. 51 (1965).

Gay Alliance of Students v. Matthews, 544 F.2d 162 (4th Cir. 1976).

Gay Lesbian Bisexual Alliance v. Sessions, 917 F.Supp. 1548 (N.D. Ala. 1996).

Gay Lesbian Bisexual Alliance v. Prior, 110 F.3d 1543 (11th Cir. 1997).

Gay Lib v. University of Missouri, 558 F.2d 848 (8th Cir. 1997).

Gay Student Organization of the University of New Hampshire v. Bonner, 509 F. 2d 652 (1st Cir. 1974).

Gertz v. Robert Welch Co., Inc. 418 U.S. 323 (1974).

Gheta v. Nassau Community College, 33 F.Supp. 2d 179 (E.D. N.Y. 1999).

Gibson v. Florida Legislative Investigation Committee, 372 U.S. 539 (1963).

Ginsberg v. State of New York, 390 U.S. 51 (1968).

Gitlow v. New York, 268 U.S. 45 (1925).

Goehring v. Brophy, 94 F.3d 1294 (9th Cir. 1996), *cert. denied* 520 U.S. 1156 (1997).

Goss v. Lopez 419 U.S. 565 (1975).

Gregory v. City of Chicago, 394 U.S. 111 (1969).

Griswold v. Connecticut, 381 U.S. 479 (1965).

Hack v. President and Fellows of Yale College, 16 F. Supp. 2d 183 (1998).

Hague v. CIO, 307 U.S. 496 (1939).

Hazelwood School District v. Kuhlmeier, 484 U.S. 260 (1988).

Healey v. James, 408 U.S. 169 (1972).

Herndon v. Lowry, 301 U.S. 242 (1937).

Hickman v. Block, 81 F.3d 98 (9th Cir. 1996).

In re Anastaplo, 366 U.S. 82 (1961).

In re Gault, 387 U.S. 1 (1967).

In re Welfare of R.A.V., 464 N.W. 2d 507, 508, 511 (Minn. 1991).

J. Glimmerveen and J. Hagenbeek v. Netherlands, App. Nos. 8348/78 and 8406/78 [1979], 23 Y.B.Eur. Conv. on H.R. 366 (Eur. Ct. H.R.).

Kathleen R., et al. v. City of Livermore, Court of Appeal of the State of California, First Appellate District, Division 4, Appeal No. A086349 (1999).

Kathleen R. v. City of Livermore, et al., Superior Court of California, County of Alameda. Case
No. V-015266-4 (1998).

Keller v. State Bar of California, 496 U.S. 1 (1990).

Keyishian v. Board of Regents, 385 U.S. 589 (1967).

Kissinger v. Board of Trustees of Ohio State University, College of Veterinary Medicine, 5 F.3d 177
(6th Cir. 1993).

Knight v. Board of Regents, 390 U.S. 36 (1968).

Konigsberg v. California, 366 U.S. 36 (1961).

Lace v. University of Vermont, 131 Vt. 170, 303 A. 2d 475 (1973).

Laird v. Tatum, 408 U.S. 1 (1972).

Lamont v. Postmaster General, 381 U.S. 301 (1965).

Larson v. Board of Regents of the University of Nebraska, 189 Neb. 688, 204 N.W. 2d 568 (1973).

Law Students Civil Rights Research Council v. Wadmond, 401 U.S. 154 (1971).

Lehnert v. Ferris Faculty Association, 500 U.S. 507 (1991).

Lerner v. Casey, 357 U.S. 468 (1958).

Louisiana ex rel. Gremillion v. NAACP, 366 U.S. 293 (1961).

Mainstream Loudoun, et al. v. Board of Trustees of the Loudoun County Library, et al., United
States District Court for the Eastern District of Virginia, at Alexandria, Virginia. Case
Number CV 97-2049 (1997).

Mainstream Loudoun v. Board of Trustees, 2 F.Supp.2d 783 (1998) (1), 24 F.Supp.2d 552 (1998)
(II).

Martin v. City of Struthers, 319 U.S. 141 (1943).

Martin v. Parrish, 805 F.2d 583 (5th Cir. 1996).

Masses Publishing Co. v. Patten, 244 Fed. 535 (S.D.N.Y. 1917).

Masters v. State, 685 S.W.2d 654 (Tex. Crim., 1985).

Miller v. California, 413 U.S. 15 (1973).

Mincone v. Nassau Community College, 923 F.Supp. 398 (1996).

Mutual Film Corp. v. Industrial Commission of Ohio, 236 U.S. 230 (1915).

NAACP v. Alabama ex rel. Patterson, 357 U.S. 449 (1958).

NAACP v. Button, 371 U.S. 415 (1963).

National Bank of Boston v. Bellotti, 435 U.S. 765 (1978).

National Labor Relations Board v. Yeshiva University, 444 U.S. 672 (1980).

New York Times Co. v. Sullivan, 376 U.S. 254 (1964).

New York Times Co. v. United States, 403 U.S. 713 (1971).

New York v. Ferber, 458 U.S. 747 (1982).

Papish v. Board of Curators of the University of Missouri, 410 U.S. 667 (1973).

People v. Sinclair, 86 Misc. 426, 149 N.Y.S. 54 (Ct. Gen. Sess. 1914).

Perry Education Asociation v. Perry Local Association, 460 U.S. 37 (1983).

Police Dept. of Chicago v. Mosley, 408 U.S. 92 (1972).

Pruneyard Shopping Center v. Robins, 447 U.S. 74 (1980).

R.A.V. v. City of St. Paul, 505 U.S. 377 (1992).

Regan v. Time, Inc., 468 U.S. 641 (1984).

Regents of the University of Michigan v. Ewing, 474 U.S. 214 (1985).

Regents of University of California v. Baake, 438 U.S. 265 (1978).

Regina v. Andrews, 3 SCR 970 (1990).

Regina v. Keegstra, 3 SCR 697 (1990).

Regina v. Zundel, 35 D.L.R. (4th) 338 (1987).

Reno v. American Civil Liberties Union, 117 S. Ct. 2329 (1997).

Reno v. American Civil Liberties Union, 521 U.S. 844 (1997).

Robert J. Lorry et al. v. The Leland Stanford Junior University, et al., Case No. 740309, Supr. Ct. State of California, County of Santa Clara, Order on Preliminary Injunction, Feb. 27, 1995.

Rosenberger v. Rector and Visitors of the University of Virginia, 515 U.S. 819 (1995).

Rust v. Sullivan, 500 U.S. 173 (1991).

Sable Communications of California, Inc. v. FCC, 492 U.S. 115 (1989).

Scales v. United States, 367 U.S. 203 (1961).

Schiff v. Williams, 519 F. 2d 257 (5th Cir. 1978).

Shambloo v. Mississippi State Board of Trustees of Institutions of Higher Learning, 620 F.2d 516 (5th Cir. 1980).

Shelton v. Tucker, 364 U.S. 480 (1960).

Smith v. Regents of the University of California, 4 Cal. 4th 843, 844 P.2d 500, 16 Cal. Rptr.2d 181 (1993).

Southworth v. Grebe, 151 F.3d. 717 (7th Cir. 1998).

State v. Schmid, 84 N.J. 535, 423 A.2d 615 (1980).

Student Coalition for Gay Rights v. Austin Peay State University, 477 F. Supp. 1267 (M.D. Tenn. 1979).

Sweezy v. New Hampshire, 354 U.S. 234 (1957).

Texas v. Johnson, 491 U.S. 397 (1989).

Tinker v. Des Moines Independent Community School District, 393 U.S. 503 (1969).

Turner Broadcasting System, Inc. v. FCC, 512 U.S. 622 (1994).

United States v. Asociated Press, 53 F.Supp. 362 (D.C.S.D.N.Y. 1943).

United States v. Emerson, 46 F.Supp.2d 598 (N.D. Tex. 1999).

United States v. Spock, 416 F.2d 165 (1st Cir. 1969).

United States v. Verdugo-Urquidez, 494 U.S. 259 (1990).

Uphaus v. Wyman, 360 U.S. 72 (1959).

Valentine v. Chrestensen, 316 U.S. 52 (1942).

Virginia State Board of Pharmacy v. Virginia Citizens Consumer Council, 425 U.S. 748 (1976).

Whitney v. California, 274 U.S. 357 (1927).

Widmar v. Vincent, 454 U.S. 263 (1981).

Wooley v. Maynard, 430 U.S. 705 (1977).

X v. Federal Republic of Germany, App. No. 9235/81, 29 Eur. Comm'n H.R. Dec. & Rep. 194 (1982).

Yates v. United States, 354 U.S. 298 (1957).

Index

Macallair, Dan, 294
McCain, John, 195
McCarthyism. *See* Anticommunist repression
McChesney, Robert, 81–82, 96
McLuhan, Marshall, 199
McWilliams, Carey, 225
Madison, James, 123, 125–26, 340–41
Mainstream Loudon v. Board of Trustees of Loudon County Library, 192–93, 199–200, 214–15, 220, 223
Malcolm, Joyce Lee, 117–18
Males, Mike, 294
Maltby, Richard, 81
Mann, Horace, 298–99
Manovich, Lev, 87
Marcus, David, 56
Marcuse, Herbert, 54–57
Martin v. City of Struthers, 220
Mather, Cotton, 296, 310
Mather, Samuel, 296
Matsuda, Mari, 283
May 4 shootings, at Kent State, 2; analyzing threat by students', 6–8, 10–12; meaning of, 41; and relationship of First and Second Amendments, 116; responses to, 17–20, 38–39; and rules for civility of protests, 77; uniqueness of, 38, 40, 46
Media, 28; CNN and "International Town Meeting," 55–56; consumer sovereignty in, 328, 334, 338, 340; effects of *New York Times Co. v. Sullivan* on, 175–76; effects of violence and pornography in, 10–11; freedom of student presses, 265–68; as general-interest intermediaries, 325–26; government harassment of, 20–21; and group polarization, 329–35; influences on, 84–87, 96–97; narratives in, 90, 109–10; and need to have common experiences, 336–37; news coverage by, 8, 19, 247–48, 310; proposals for changes in, 344–45; public access to, 98, 333; on regulating the Internet, 206–7; regulation of, 80–83, 105–6, 199, 219, 340–41; scapegoating of, 89–90, 110; violence in, 80, 109–10. *See also* Cyberspace
Meiklejohn, Alexander, 51, 55
Menand, Louis, 239
Menino, Thomas, 191–92

Militias, 3, 116, 119; and right to bear arms, 123–26, 139; states regulating, 142
Mill, John Stuart, 54–55, 154
Miller v. California, 198, 219
Moffett, Anthony, 19
Multiculturalism, in universities, 228–29, 232, 288
Murray, Janet, 87–88, 95

Narratives, 80, 82, 90, 97, 99, 106, 108; in cyberspace, 94, 114; violence in, 85–86, 88–89, 98, 108–10; *vs.* database form, 87–88, 95
National Guard, against protestors, 4
National Rifle Association (NRA), 111
Nedenfeuhr, Jane, 206
Negroponte, Nicholas, 321
Netherlands, 162
New York Times Co. v. Sullivan, 175–76, 179–80
New York v. Farber, 198
Newspapers: customized coverage in, 320–22; regulation by judiciary *vs.* agency, 81–82. *See also* Media
Nixon, Richard, response to Kent State shootings, 7, 10, 18–19
Nunn, Clyde, 26
Nye, David, 88

Obscenity/pornography, 32, 60; effects of, 10–11; no First Amendment protection for, 149, 219, 339; online, 92–93, 190–91, 203–6; protection for children from, 190–91, 198
O'Connor, Sandra Day, 268
Ohio State, "International Town Meeting" at, 53, 55–56, 59–61
Olivieri, Nancy, 227, 243, 249–50
Order. *See* Social order
Originalism, in constitutional scholarship, 117, 140–41
Overbreadth, in hate-speech bans, 171

Papanek, Ernst, 300–301
Papish v. Board of Curators of the University of Missouri, 265, 269
Patterson, Floyd, 300–301
Peabody, Elizabeth, 298
Pentagon Papers, government attempt to censor, 20

Traub-Werner, Marion, 248
Truth, 82, 252, 289; as goal of deliberative democracy, 54–56, 68–69, 71, 73–75; as purpose of free speech, 148, 150
Tucker, St. George, 143
Turkle, Sherry, 93
Turner Broadcasting, 90–91
Tushnet, Mark, 254
Twain, Mark, 25
Tyack, David, 298–99

Underground press, harassment of, 20–21
United Nations, 9
United States v. Emerson, 115
United States v. Verdugo-Urquidez, 135–36
Universal Declaration of Human Rights, 9
Universities, 141; academic integrity at, 253–55; corporations' influence on, 251–55; declining credibility of, 231–35; financial crisis at, 233–37, 240–43; freedom of expression at, 282–85; hate speech at, 287–88; limitations of free speech at, 262–63, 265–66; mission of, 228–30, 239, 272–73, 282; problems with, 227–30, 251; protests at, 4, 29–30, 40–41, 264; students' resistance to supporting organizations, 249, 268–73. *See also* Academic freedom

Van Alstyne, William, 124
Vietnam War: public opinion of, 29–30. *See also* Antiwar activism
Viewpoint discrimination, 249, 341; and hate-speech bans, 170–71, 181–82; in speech restrictions, 148–49, 152, 155–59; in university students' speech, 267–68, 271
Violence, 97; arising from speech, 6–8, 10–12, 19; in cyberspace, 92–93, 97–99, 106; incitement to, 5, 157–58; justifications for political, 62–64; in media, 80, 85–86, 91–93, 114, 198; in narratives, 88–89, 108–10; in schools, 110–11, 291–304, 309–13

Warren, Earl, 20
Webster, Andrew, 242
Wehmeyer, Peggy, 206–7
West Virginia State Board of Education v. Barnette, 172, 263–64
Whitney v. California, 7
Widmar v. Vincent, 267, 273
Wills, Garry, 121
Wireless Ship Act of 1910, 105
World Trade Organization (wto) protests, 43, 46–47

Zero-tolerance policies, in schools, 292, 294–95, 313, 316

Contributors

MICHAEL BYRON is assistant professor of philosophy at Kent State University. After receiving his Ph.D. from the University of Notre Dame in 1996, he spent a year at the Ethics Center of the University of Florida, supported by a Frances Elvidge Postdoctoral Fellowship. His research interests include ethical theory, rational choice theory, and the history of ethics; he is the coauthor (with Deborah Barnbaum) of *Research Ethics: Text and Readings*.

ROD CARVETH is associate professor of communication at Southern Connecticut State University, where he teaches marketing communication courses. His research interests include media economics as well as the causes and consequences of unequal access to communication technologies.

SAUL CORNELL is associate professor of history at the Ohio State University, where he has been teaching since 1991. He received his Ph.D. from the University of Pennsylvania. His book *The Other Founders: Anti-Federalism and the American Political Tradition* is forthcoming from the Institute of Early American History and Culture, University of North Carolina Press. Professor Cornell is currently at work on a study of Jefferson, Monticello, and the Enlightenment.

NANCY C. CORNWELL is assistant professor of communication and women's studies at Western Michigan University. She received her Ph.D. from the University of Colorado in 1997. Her teaching and research focuses on First Amendment theory and communication law and policy, especially as they pertain to questions of race and gender.

JULIET DEE is associate professor in the Department of Communication at the University of Delaware and teaches courses in mass media law, broadcast programming, and mass communication effects. She is coauthor of *Mass Communication Law in a Nutshell* (2000) and has published articles in the area of media liability for copycat violence.

FLORENCE W. DORE, assistant professor of English at Kent State University is currently visiting faculty fellow at New York University's Draper Program in Humanities and Social Thought. She is writing a book entitled *The Novel and the Obscene: Free Speech and the Law of Unspeakability in the Modern U.S. Novel*.

SUSAN NEWHART ELLIOTT received her J.D. summa cum laude from the University of Dayton School of Law in 1987. That same year she received the Lawyer's Lawyer Award. She is currently working toward an M.A. in library science at Kent State University, which she expects to complete in 2001.

JONATHAN L. ENTIN is professor of law and political science at Case Western Reserve University. He received his J.D. from Northwestern University in 1981 and was a law clerk for Judge Ruth Bader Ginsburg. The author of many articles on constitutional law, civil rights, and free speech issues, he is writing a book on equal protection.

DAVID ESTLUND is associate professor of philosophy at Brown University. He received his Ph.D. from the University of Wisconsin in 1986. His teaching and research is in moral and political philosophy. His published articles concentrate especially in normative issues in democratic theory.

NORMAN FISCHER is professor of philosophy at Kent State University. He teaches and writes in the areas of social, political, and legal philosophy; philosophy of art; and environmentalism. His most recent law-related article is a 1999 article in the *Oklahoma City University Law Review* entitled, "Civic Republican Political/Legal Ethics and Echoes of the Classical Historical Novel in Thomas Pynchon's *Mason & Dixon*."

LESLIE FRIEDMAN GOLDSTEIN is Unidel Professor of Political Science and International Relations at the University of Delaware. She is author of *Constituting Federal Sovereignty: The European Union in Comparative Context, Contemporary Cases in Women's Rights, The Constitutional Rights of Women*, and *In Defense of the Text: The Politics of Constitutional Theory*.

MARK A. GRABER is professor of political science and associate chair of the Department of Government and Politics at the University of Maryland. He has a law degree from Columbia University and a Ph.D. in Political Science from Yale University. He is the author of two books, *Transforming Free Speech* and *Rethinking Abortion*, as well as many articles on American constitutional politics.

THOMAS R. HENSLEY is professor of political science and chair of the Department of Political Science at Kent State University. He received his Ph.D. from the University of Iowa in 1970. He has won several teaching awards, including Ohio Professor of the Year in 1991, and he is the author of *The Changing Supreme Court: Constitutional Rights and Liberties*.

PAUL HARIDAKIS is assistant professor of communication studies at Kent State University, where he received his Ph.D. He has also practiced law since 1984. His principal research interests include free speech, media policy, new media technologies, and media effects. His work has appeared in the *Journal of Mass Media Ethics* and *Communication Yearbook*.

DONALD M. HASSLER is professor of English at Kent State University. He received his Ph.D. from Columbia University in 1967. His writing and teaching range from Enlightenment literature to modern science fiction; he is the author of *Erasmus Darwin* and *Isaac Asimov*.

MARY ANNE HIGGINS is adjunct instructor of communication studies at Kent State University, where she received her Ph.D. in 1992. Her teaching interests are in rhetoric and media, while her major research interests are in rural and urban communication and disability studies. She is the author of several articles and book chapters.

KATHERYN KATZ is professor of law at Albany Law School of Union University. She received her A.B. from the University of California, Berkeley, and her J.D. from Albany Law School. Her teaching and research interests focus upon the allocation of power between the state and the individual in making choices that are essential to personal dignity and autonomy.

SUSAN B. KRETCHMER is a writer, magazine editor for a publishing company, and student at The Johns Hopkins University. Active in scholarly research, publishing, and professional organizations in communication since 1986, her interests are the historical, social, and cultural relationship between communication and technology, particularly in popular media, law and public policy, and social change.

DAVID E. KYVIG is Presidential Research Professor and professor of history at Northern Illinois University. A specialist in the history of constitutional amending, he is the author of *Repealing National Prohibition* and *Explicit and Authentic Acts: Amending the U.S. Consitution, 1776–1995.* Most recently, he edited *Unintended Consequences of Constitutional Amendment.*

ANTHONY LEWIS is a columnist for the *New York Times.* He received his B.A. from Harvard College in 1948 and has taught courses on the Constitution and the press at Harvard Law School and the Columbia Graduate School of Journalism. He is the author of *Gideon's Trumpet* and *Make No Law: The Sullivan Case and the First Amendment.*

LADELLE MCWHORTER is professor of philosophy and women's studies at the University of Richmond. She received her Ph.D. from Vanderbilt University in 1986. Her current research focuses on race, civil rights movements, and philosophical conceptions of power. She is the author of *Bodies and Pleasures: Foucault and the Politics of Sexual Normalization.*

ERIC D. MILLER is assistant professor of psychology at Kent State University, East Liverpool Campus. With a Ph.D. in psychology from the University of Iowa, he has research and teaching interests focusing on the study of how adults cope with major loss. He is also co-editor of *Loss and Trauma: General and Close Relationship Perspectives.*

ROBERT M. O'NEIL is professor of law at the University of Virginia and director of the Thomas Jefferson Center for the Protection of Free Expression. He teaches in the field of constitutional law and in 1970 chaired a special committee of the American Association of University Professors to explore the implications for university faculty of the tragic events at Kent State and Jackson State.

DANIEL PERLSTEIN is assistant professor in the Graduate School of Education at the University of California at Berkeley. His work focuses on the institutional and political influences on American education. He is particularly concerned with the ways schooling reflects both democratic aspirations in American life and diversity and inequality in American society. His interests include urban school reform, teacher organizing, and progressive education. His forthcoming book, *Justice, Justice: School Politics and the Eclipse of Liberalism,* explores the place of race and class conflicts in American schools.

GERALD N. ROSENBERG is associate professor of political science and lecturer in law at the University of Chicago. He earned an M.A. in Politics and Philosophy from Oxford University in 1979, a J.D. from the University of Michigan Law School in 1983, and a Ph.D. in Political Science from Yale University in 1985. He is the author of *The Hollow Hope: Can Courts Bring About Social Change?*

ELLEN SCHRECKER is professor of history at Yeshiva University and editor of *Academe*, the official publication of the American Association of University Professors. She has written extensively on academic freedom and political repression, including *Many Are the Crimes: McCarthyism in America* and *No Ivory Tower: McCarthyism and the Universities.*

J. DAVID SLOCUM is assistant dean in the Graduate School of Arts and Science at New York University, where he teaches cinema studies. His research and writing primarily address violence in film, media, and culture. He is the editor of the Routledge/American Film Institute reader on *Violence and American Cinema.*

TIMOTHY D. SMITH is professor in the School of Journalism and Mass Communication at Kent State University and director of the Center for Privacy and the First Amendment, located within the school. He received his J.D. from the University of Akron in 1977. He teaches media law and senior reporting courses. His research interests are access to government and commercial speech.

KATHLEEN SULLIVAN is dean of the Stanford University Law School. She began teaching law at Harvard at age twenty-nine; earned tenure at Harvard at age thirty-three; was first mentioned in national legal publications as a potential future Supreme Court nominee at age thirty-six; and was appointed the first Stanley Morrison Professor of Law at Stanford at age forty-one. She is the coauthor of the thirteenth and most recent edition of *Constitutional Law*, the leading casebook in the field for a generation.

CASS R. SUNSTEIN teaches at the University of Chicago Law School and the Department of Political Science. His books include *Republic.com* (2001), *Free Markets and Social Justice* (1997), *Legal Reasoning and Political Conflict* (1996), and *The Partial Constitution* (1993). He has assisted with constitution-making and law reform initiatives in many countries, including South Africa, Ukraine, China, Bosnia, and Russia.

JAMES WEINSTEIN is the Amelia D. Lewis Professor of Constitutional Law at Arizona State University College of Law. He received his B.A. in 1975 and J.D. in 1978 from the University of Pennsylvania. He has litigated several significant free speech cases and is the author of *Hate Speech, Pornography, and the Radical Attack on Free Speech Doctrine.*

DON A. WICKS received his Ph.D. from the University of Western Ontario in 1997 and now teaches at the School of Library and Information Science, Kent State University. His teaching, research, and conference presentations have focused on information sources and services (especially for older adults) and collection management. Journal publications have appeared in, among others, *Library & Information Science Research*.

The Boundaries of Freedom of Expression & Order in American Democracy
was designed by Will Underwood;
composed by Christine Brooks
in 10.5/14 Stone Print Roman
on an Apple G4 using PageMaker
at The Kent State University Press;
printed by sheet-fed offset lithography
on 60-pound Glatfelter Supple Opaque stock
(an acid-free paper with recycled content),
notch bound in signatures with paper
covers printed in four color process
by Thomson-Shore, Inc.,
of Dexter, Michigan;
and published by
The Kent State University Press
Kent, Ohio 44242